CRIMINAL INVESTIGATION

FIFTH EDITION

Aric W. Dutelle
Washington State University

Ronald F. Becker
Director of the Criminal Justice Program
Chaminade University of Honolulu

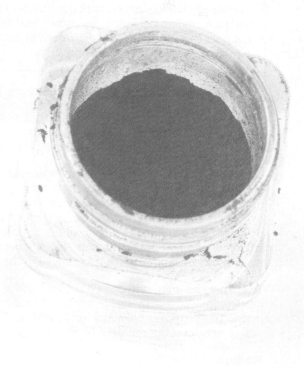

JONES & BARTLETT
LEARNING

World Headquarters
Jones & Bartlett Learning
5 Wall Street
Burlington, MA 01803
978-443-5000
info@jblearning.com
www.jblearning.com

Jones & Bartlett Learning books and products are available through most bookstores and online booksellers. To contact Jones & Bartlett Learning directly, call 800-832-0034, fax 978-443-8000, or visit our website, www.jblearning.com.

Substantial discounts on bulk quantities of Jones & Bartlett Learning publications are available to corporations, professional associations, and other qualified organizations. For details and specific discount information, contact the special sales department at Jones & Bartlett Learning via the above contact information or send an email to specialsales@jblearning.com.

Production Credits

VP, Product Management: David D. Cella
Director of Product Management: Matthew Kane
Product Specialist: Audrey Schwinn
Product Assistant: Loren-Marie Durr
Director of Vendor Management: Amy Rose
Vendor Manager: Molly Hogue
Marketing Manager: Lindsay White
Manufacturing and Inventory Control Supervisor: Amy Bacus
Composition: SourceHOV LLC

Project Management: SourceHOV LLC
Cover Design: Kristin E. Parker
Text Design: Scott Moden
Rights & Media Specialist: Thais Miller
Media Development Editor: Shannon Sheehan
Cover Image: © Comaniciu Dan/Shutterstock, Inc.
Printing and Binding: LSC Communications
Cover Printing: LSC Communications

ISBN: 978-1-284-08285-2

Library of Congress Cataloging-in-Publication Data Unavailable at Time of Printing

6048

Printed in the United States of America
22 21 20 19 18   10 9 8 7 6 5 4 3 2 1

Brief Table of Contents

Table of Contents

7 Interviewing and Interrogation   152

9   Death Investigation   201

11 Assault Investigation 251

© Shutterstock, Inc. / happykanppy

16 Underwater Investigation

348

PART 4 Preparing for Court

363

17 Defense Lawyers, Prosecutors, and Investigators   364

Preface

We so often watch police dramas that end with apprehension that we forget that much of the real work is yet to come. Surely, the most exciting part of the investigation is the chase and capture, but these are of little value if they do not support laboratory analysis and successful criminal prosecution. It is hard to make laboratory tests, reports, witness statements, and offense documentation exciting, and so there is little place for them in the television crime drama, but it is on the investigation's supporting documentation that success or failure depends.

This text attempts to include forensic and Constitutional considerations to help place criminal investigation in its proper context. It has always seemed strange that we compartmentalize criminal justice function and education. Police have little interaction with the forensic personnel who process crime scenes and test evidence. Police and forensic personnel have even less contact with prosecutors, who are dependent on their work at the time of trial. To exacerbate the situation, we separate criminal justice programs from forensic science programs, and both from law school, and then seem surprised when we work at cross purposes. The good news is that many universities are beginning to recognize the need for more cross-communication between disciplines and are creating "Justice and Forensic Institutes" to ensure mutual understanding. Unfortunately, these programs are all too rare, and forensic science and criminal justice continue to be taught separately more often than together. It is to this "compartmentalization" that this text is directed. Where applicable, we have included forensic and Constitutional considerations along with the investigative process.

In keeping with the comprehensive nature of the text, the reader will have a look at the history relating to criminal investigation. Hopefully, by understanding how we got to where we are today, the reader will gain an appreciation of, and an understanding for, the complexities and difficulties relating to the topics presented within the text. If one is to be educated on and understand what criminal investigation is and what it encompasses, it is necessary to go beyond the "how to's" relating to such matters. Therefore, in addition to the methods, motives, and motions necessary, the text also provides an in-depth look at the investigative process, as well as the ethical considerations applying to such matters. Discussions on investigative procedures, detailed figures, and real-life examples will enhance the reader's understanding and demonstrate how to apply the techniques and tools of the trade.

The Student Experience

This text is assembled with a pragmatic, critical, and multidisciplinary approach. It also recognizes that many of the concepts and methods relating to the field of criminal investigation are likely to be unfamiliar. It is for this reason that special instructional devices and learning strategies are utilized throughout the text.

Student Learning Outcomes

Student Learning Outcomes are listed at the beginning of each chapter. Emphasis is placed on active learning. The learning objectives concentrate on the acquisition of knowledge and the foundations needed to understand, compare, contrast, define, explain, predict, estimate, evaluate, plan, and apply.

STUDENT LEARNING OUTCOMES

Upon completion of this chapter, students will be able to:

- Recognize the responsibilities of all of the members of the crime scene team
- Describe how to process crime scenes, big and small
- Explain the use of templates and virtual photography in constructing crime-scene sketches
- Construct crime-scene notes
- Appreciate the importance of recording/documenting the crime scene

Key Terms

In the field of criminal investigation, it is necessary to become familiar with the associated terminology and vocabulary. Key Terms are highlighted in bold within each chapter to direct the reader to specific terms of particular importance with definitions provided in the margins for review.

Justifiable homicide is the killing of a person under authority of the law. This includes killing in self-defense or in the defense of another person if the victim's actions and capability present imminent danger of serious injury or death. It also includes killing an enemy during wartime, capital punishment, and deaths caused by police officers while attempting to prevent a dangerous felon's escape or to recapture a dangerous felon who has escaped or is resisting arrest.

justifiable homicide
The killing of a person under authority of the law

Investigator's Notebook

Many chapters include *Investigator's Notebook* boxes, which contain checklists, suggestions, and guidelines regarding best-practice methodology associated with the chapter content.

INVESTIGATOR'S NOTEBOOK

Guidelines for Handling DNA-Bearing Evidence

- Wear gloves; Change them between handling each item of evidence
- Use disposable instruments or clean the instruments thoroughly before and after handling each evidence sample
- Avoid touching the area where you believe DNA may exist
- Avoid touching your face, nose, and mouth when examining and packaging evidence
- Put dry evidence into new paper bags or envelopes; do not use plastic bags
- Do not use staples
- Handle all evidence as though a jury were watching
- Photograph or take video of the handling and packaging process

Real-World Examples

Case in Point, Ripped from the Headlines, and Exhibits

In an effort to apply the theory and guidelines addressed within the book, the reader is provided with examples of real-world incidents and cases involving the content discussed within the chapter. This application to real-world situations will enable the reader to better grasp the concepts presented.

CASE IN POINT

A Telling Drop

In one case involving an open-field death, the female victim was found face down with knife wounds to the front of her body. A cursory examination of the body revealed a single circular dried blood droplet on her buttocks. Investigators discussed various ways of retrieving the blood after having photographed it.

Determining that the blood would probably not survive handling and moving of the body, they decided to remove it prior to moving the body. The circumference of the blood drop indicated that it fell perpendicular to the vic...
to be t...
lift it w...
convic...

EXHIBIT 1.1

The Fifth and Sixth Amendments to the U.S. Constitution

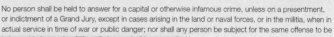

Fifth Amendment

No person shall be held to answer for a capital or otherwise infamous crime, unless on a presentment, or indictment of a Grand Jury, except in cases arising in the land or naval forces, or in the militia, when in actual service in time of war or public danger; nor shall any person be subject for the same offense to be twice put in jeopardy of life or limb; nor shall be compelled in any criminal case to be a witness against ...
due process of law; nor shall private property be ...

...ht to a speedy and public trial, by an impartial ...been committed, which district shall have been ...ature and cause of the accusation; to be con-...y process for obtaining witnesses in his favor,

— Ripped from the Headlines —

Blood Evidence Used to Convict Boston Marathon Bomber

On April 8, 2015, Dzhokhar Tsarnaev was convicted of the 2013 Boston Marathon bombing, which killed three and injured 260. Blood evidence and DNA analysis featured prominently within the case investigation and litigation. Prosecutors presented DNA evidence and blood to tie in the involvement of both Tsarnaev brothers in the event, although only Dzhokhar was prosecuted for the crime, since Tamerlan died during the course of subsequent events.

Questions for Review

Knowledge and skills must be reinforced. Questions for review are provided for student self-study or for instructors who are developing written assignments and examinations.

QUESTIONS FOR REVIEW

1. What is it about fingerprints that suggests individuality?
2. Why is it incorrect to refer to visible fingerprints at a crime scene as latent prints?
3. What are fingerprint patterns, and of what value are they to the criminal investigator?
4. How is a latent print visualized, developed, and lifted?
5. Why is it important to photograph a fingerprint that the investigator plans to lift anyway?
6. What is superglue fuming?
7. For what is ninhydrin spray used?
8. How would you develop fingerprints on the sticky side of duct tape?
9. What is small particle reagent used for?
10. What are iodine crystals used for?
11. What chemical is used to test for blood that luminesces under ultraviolet light?
12. What is a composite picture, and in what ways might an investigator obtain one?
13. What is a suggestive lineup?
14. What is CODIS? Describe the three-tiered identification system.
15. What does ACE-V stand for?
16. What was the cause of the Madrid, Spain, fingerprint misidentification?
17. Is it possible to develop fingerprints from a corpse? If yes, describe the process; if not, why not?
18. Explain how fingerprints corroded in a brass shell casing can be recovered.

References

At the conclusion of each chapter, the reader will find the scholarly references that were used to assemble the information contained within the chapters, which will include suggested readings pertaining to the key areas addressed within the chapter. In addition, many chapters include a list of *Key Legal Cases*, which the reader may consult for a more in-depth understanding relating to the subject matter.

REFERENCES

Ancestry. (n.d.). Ancestry Guide for Law Enforcement. Retrieved November 6, 2017, from http://www.ancestry.com/cs/legal/lawenforcement

Bond, J. W. (2009, July). Visualization of latent fingerprint corrosion of brass. *Journal of Forensic Sciences*, 1034–1041.

Coppock, C. A. (2007). *Contrast* (2nd ed.). Springfield, IL: Charles C. Thomas.

Futrell, I. R. (1996). Hidden evidence: Latent print on human skin. *FBI Law Enforcement Bulletin*, April.

Indovina, M., Dvorychenko, V., Tabassi, E., Quinn, G., Grother, P., et al., & National Institute of Standards and Technology (NISTIR). (2009). *An evaluation of automated latent fingerprint identification technologies* (NISTIR 7577). Retrieved August 1, 2009, from http://fingerprint.nist.gov/latent/NISTIR_7577_ELFT_PhaseII.pdf

Innocence Project. (n.d.). http:www.innocenceproject.org/. Retrieved September 1, 2017.

Joint POW/MIA Accounting Command (JPAC), United States Department of Defense. (2009). Mission overview. Retrieved October 2, 2012, from http://www.jpac.pacom.mil/index.php?page=mission_overview

Lerner, E. (2000). Biometric identification. *Industrial Physicist*, 6(1), 18–21.

Maldarelli, C. (2015, October 16). Could having your DNA tested land you in court? *Popular Science*. Retrieved November 7, 2017, from https://www.popsci.com/could-submitting-your-dna-to-private-genetics-companies-land-you-in-court

Saferstein, R. (2014). *Criminalistics: An introduction to forensic science* (11th ed.). Englewood Cliffs, NJ: Prentice Hall.

Wambaugh, J. (1985). *The Blooding*. New York, NY: Bantam.

Teaching Tools

Test Bank containing Multiple Choice, True/False, Short Answer, and Essay questions. These questions allow you to originate tailor-made classroom tests and quizzes quickly and easily by selecting, editing, organizing, and printing a test along with an answer key that includes page references to the text.

Lecture Outlines provide you with complete, ready-to-use lesson plans that outline all of the topics covered in the text. Lesson plans can be edited and modified to fit your course.

PPT Lecture Outlines in PowerPoint format provide you with a powerful way to make presentations that are both educational and engaging. Slides can be modified and edited to meet your needs.

Image Bank in PowerPoint format is an easy-to-use multimedia tool that provides all of the illustrations and photos from the text (to which Jones & Bartlett Learning holds the rights to reproduce electronically) for use in classroom presentation.

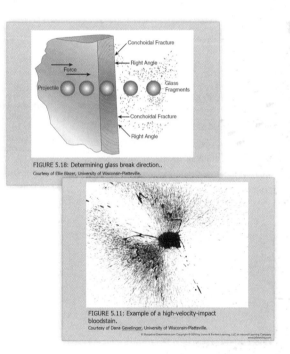

Acknowledgments

We would like to thank the following individuals for reviewing this text:

Carla R. Allen, Harris Stowe State University

B. Irene Britt, Ivy Tech Community College

J. W. Carter II, College of Mount St. Joseph

Janis Cavanaugh, East Los Angeles College

Thomas J. Chuda, Bunker Hill Community College

Todd Lough, Western Illinois University

John R. Schafer, Western Illinois University

James Smith, Troy University

Michael Smith, Glendale Community College

We would also like to thank the following reviewers of previous editions of this text:

Karen S. Boyd, Retired Sergeant

Jack Bozeman, Ivy Bridge College of Tiffin University

Ron Davis, Mayland Community College

Darrell Hawkins, University of Cincinnati-Clermont College

Michael Herbert, Bemidji State University

Jon Mandrell, Sauk Valley Community College

Douglas P. Smith, Bethany College

James Smith, Troy University

The authors would also like to thank Robert Roberts (University of Wisconsin Oshkosh) for his professional insight and suggestions during development, as well as his willingness to peruse the manuscript and offer his much appreciated feedback, prior to publication. Your breadth of experience within the criminal justice field and your willingness to discuss development ideas were much appreciated.

The authors would also like to thank the entire editorial, production, and marketing staff at Jones & Bartlett Learning for assisting us with the production and marketing of what we hope will be a work that will fill a much-needed void in professional education. You are all professionals, and it was a pleasure to work with you once again.

About the Authors

Aric W. Dutelle

Aric Dutelle has been involved in law enforcement since 1999. During this time, he has held positions as a police officer, deputy sheriff, crime scene technician, and reserve medico-legal investigator. He has a Master of Forensic Sciences (MFS) degree, with a specialty in impression evidence and is the author of over 20 articles, as well as author and co-author of four texts, including *An Introduction to Crime Scene Investigation (three editions)* and *Criminal Investigation (4th and 5th editions)* by Jones & Bartlett Learning; *Ethics for the Public Service Professional (two editions)* by Taylor & Francis Publishing, and *Basic Crime Scene Photography (two editions)*. He was previously a tenured professor with the University of Wisconsin System, teaching there for 11 years and having been responsible for developing and implementing a Bachelor's of Science program in Forensic Investigation. In addition to his university obligations, Dutelle served for 7 years as a forensic instructor for the U.S. Department of Justice's International Criminal Investigation Training Assistance Program (ICITAP), specializing in and providing training in crime scene processing methodologies and techniques around the globe. The author continues to be actively involved in training, consulting, and assisting law enforcement agencies with criminal investigations and crime scene processing around the United States and internationally.

Ronald F. Becker

Professor Becker completed his studies for a Bachelor of Science degree in Police Science at Sam Houston State University in 1969. He went on to finish his Master's Degree in Curriculum and Instruction at Texas Agricultural & Mechanical University in 1972. A short hiatus from higher education found him with the Mineral County, Montana, Sheriff's Office, culminating his work as a criminal investigator there and then leaving for St. Mary's Law School in 1981.

Upon completion of his law studies and passing the Texas Bar Examination in 1983, Professor Becker became a partner in the general litigation firm of Gish, Radtke and Becker in Boerne, Texas. The firm became a successful personal injury litigation practice. During that time, Professor Becker served as the Boerne Municipal Court Judge, County Judge, and Juvenile Court Judge.

In 1991, Professor Becker began a teaching career at Texas State University in the Criminal Justice Department. In 1994, he created a facility for training public safety divers in underwater investigation based on a forensic protocol. He has published four books and five editions of this text. During his tenure, he has published numerous articles and textbook chapters.

Professor Becker is currently a full professor at Chaminade University, serving as chair for the Criminal Justice and Criminology Program. Professor Becker is a member of the Hawaii Emergency Preparedness Executive Consortium and an advisory board member for the Hawaii Law Enforcement Memorial.

PART 1

CRIMINAL INVESTIGATION

chapter

1

Introduction to Criminal Investigation

> "*It is a capital mistake to theorize before one has data. Insensibly one begins to twist facts to suit theories, instead of theories to suit facts.*"
>
> **Sherlock Holmes**
> *"A Scandal in Bohemia"*

KEY TERMS

Alec Jeffreys

Alphonse Bertillon

American Academy of Forensic Sciences (AAFS)

analysis

arrest

August Vollmer

beyond a reasonable doubt

bobby

constable

copper

coroner

crime

deductive reasoning

Edward T. Blake

Edmond Locard

evidentiary foundation

forensic evidence

forensic investigation

forensic pathology

forensic science

genetic fingerprint

Henry Faulds

hue and cry

hypothesis

inductive reasoning

investigate

inquest

Jack the Ripper

medical examiner

Miranda v. Arizona

observation

pathology

Paul Leland Kirk

predicate

principle of parsimony

probative

protocol

recording

scientific method

Sir Francis Galton

specification

synthesize

taxonomy

theory

thief catcher

Tommie Lee Andrews

trier of fact

STUDENT LEARNING OUTCOMES

Upon completion of this chapter, students will be able to:

- Discuss how criminal investigation developed in England
- Describe how the English system was employed in the United States
- Employ the scientific method as it applies to criminal investigation
- Recognize the objectives of a criminal investigation

What Is Criminal Investigation?

We live in a world where the term "criminal investigation" is thrown around quite freely. Nightly news shows, Internet feeds, blogs, and, for those who still read them, magazines and newspapers, are all frequent users of the term. But what does it mean?

The word **investigate** means to make a systematic examination or to conduct an official inquiry. In law enforcement terms, this is used with reference to the investigation of a crime. But what then is a crime? **Crime** is defined as an act or the commission of an act that is forbidden by a public law and that makes the offender liable to punishment by that law. Therefore, when we take the definitions of the two separate and distinct words and combine them, we arrive at criminal investigation. This is the often-used term relating to the process associated with the investigation of a criminal event. As will be discussed throughout this text, a criminal investigation is not concerned with guilt or innocence. That determination is left to the **trier of fact**, such as a judge or a jury of one's peers. Instead, a criminal investigation is concerned with determination of the truth. Attempting to determine the truth behind what occurred and whether or not such events were criminal in nature has been occurring for thousands of years. Since humans first began to walk upon the earth, there have been cases of foul play. Although technology and education have improved the process of determining wrongdoing, the elementary concepts have remained nearly constant. To gain some appreciation for where criminal investigation is today, let us explore the historic development of the subject.

Early History

China, 12th Century

The Chinese death investigator Song Ci wrote a book titled, *Xi Yuan Ji Lu* (translated as *Collected Cases of Injustice Rectified*, in 1247) in which he discussed a number of murders. One such case took place in a village in which the victim had been slashed repeatedly. The local magistrate suspected that a sickle had been used, but repeated questioning of witnesses proved fruitless. Finally, the magistrate ordered all of the local men to assemble, each with his own sickle. It was a hot summer day and flies, attracted by the smell of blood, eventually gathered on a single sickle. Confronted with such evidence, the sickle's owner confessed to the murder. The book also offered advice on how to distinguish between a drowning (water in the lungs) and strangulation (broken neck cartilage), along with other evidence from examining corpses to determining if a death was caused by murder, suicide, or an accident.

England, 13th Century

In England at the end of the 13th century, the king established a system consisting of justices of the peace and parish constables, a system that served England and the United States until 1829. This system, though inefficient, did maintain a modicum of order in the class-based agrarian societies of this era, where conflict resolution was more often the result of a tradition of deference than of law enforcement; social and geographic mobility was restricted; and transience was virtually unknown. In agrarian societies, people typically were born and died within the confines of the same community, and values that were important to the community were maintained through community vigilance and a series of informal sanctions, from public rebuke to ostracism. Residents found that a vigilant community had little need for external sanctions.

In the United States and in Western Europe, the Industrial Revolution led to the urbanization of manufacturing centers. The formerly agrarian population began to evolve into a labor pool for industrial complexes. People began moving about the countryside, and community vigilance had little impact on those who were merely passing through. The industrial centers brought strangers together in a new environment in which a sense of community was replaced by exploitation of laborers, deplorable living conditions, ghettos, and poverty. In the United States, a growing tide of European immigrants generated population pressure in Northeastern and Midwestern cities. The flow of immigration created cultural and religious tensions between the new arrivals and the existing inhabitants that caused resentment, segregation, and discrimination.

These evolving industrial problems were not unique to the United States. England had earlier tasted the fruit, sweet and bitter, of industrialization and discovered that the system of social sanctions, justices, and constables that had been somewhat effective in rural areas was totally inadequate to bring order to its industrial centers. In 1829, the creation of a metropolitan police department altered the London system of law enforcement.

investigate
To make a systematic examination or to conduct an official inquiry

crime
An act or the commission of an act that is forbidden by a public law and that makes the offender liable to punishment by that law

trier of fact
A judge or magistrate in a trial by the court, or a jury of one's peers in a trial by jury, whose duty it is to weigh the evidence presented and determine guilt or innocence

constable
Law enforcement officers in London appointed by local justices, to whom they owed their allegiance and continued employment

hue and cry
Alarm sounded by constables to summon help from citizens to apprehend a criminal

thief catcher
A person hired to locate someone's stolen goods; this person was often a thief himself or a moonlighting constable

FIGURE 1.1: Sir Robert Peel (1788–1850).

© Georgios Kollidas/Shutterstock, Inc.

London, 1829

In 1829, Sir Robert Peel established and subsequently headed the Metropolitan Police Force for London, based at Scotland Yard (**FIGURE 1.1**). The 1,000-member force became known as "Bobbies." They proved to be very successful in reducing the crime rate. Peel also was responsible for defining ethical requirements of policing officers through what became known as "Peelian Principles." His most memorable principle is summarized by the concept that the police are themselves the public, and the public are themselves the police. This is the earliest recorded reference to the idea of community-oriented policing efforts.

London's police department served as a model for other British municipalities as well as for emerging American cities. The rural areas of England and the United States did not require such elaborate policing arrangements, and the simpler constabulary system continued to serve such communities and remains to this day throughout much of rural America. In U.S. cities, however, population increases, high rates of immigration, and economic development made it increasingly more difficult to control the violence and criminality inherent in large urban populations (Miller, 1977).

Law Enforcement Developments in England and in the United States

London

The constabulary system was organized around a group of constables appointed by local justices, to whom they owed their allegiance and

continued employment. The **constables** were responsible for patrolling their precincts and could raise an alarm should it become necessary to solicit assistance from citizens to arrest a fleeing wrongdoer. Some constables were held in low esteem, as demonstrated by the failure of the citizenry to come to their assistance and by the ridicule heaped upon them while in pursuit of criminals. This tradition was upheld in the United States, and most states still have a **hue and cry** statute in their penal codes that requires citizens to come to the aid of a police officer when requested to do so. When responding to a police officer request for assistance, a citizen is given the powers and shackled with the responsibilities of a police officer.

Thieves were the primary plague of industrial London. A burgeoning class of unemployed, displaced rural families turned to theft as a profession when they found the doors to industrial employment closed to them. Constables were ineffective in stopping the wave of crime washing over London. Merchants and others were left to their own devices in trying to protect themselves from robbery and assault. When goods were stolen, it was customary for the victim to use his or her own financial resources to hire a **thief catcher**. Many thief catchers were thieves themselves, or moonlighting constables. Although this was an effective method of recovering stolen goods, hiring thief catchers did nothing to deter theft and may even have encouraged it, for in many instances, the thief catcher was the very person who had stolen the goods in the first place.

In 1730, Sir Thomas De Veil was appointed magistrate for the Bow Street district of London. During the 17 years that he was in office, he established the most effective police operations in the London area. In 1748, Henry Fielding, best known as a novelist, replaced Sir Thomas and continued improving police service in the Bow Street district.

Henry Fielding and his brother John advocated a single, unified police organization. They hoped to establish a systematic criminal intelligence-gathering apparatus, create a coherent police administration, and develop a preventive strategy for crime management (Radzinowicz, 1986). One of Henry's plans was to promote a small force of these catchers, directing and deploying them in a coherent manner around the city of London and its suburbs. Equivalent to bounty hunters, his new paid police, called the Bow Street Runners, were to be under a central command with appropriate administrative supervision and controls (McMullan, 1996). Henry was also responsible for organizing the first police intelligence organization, which published its gathered criminal intelligence in the *Covent Garden Gazette*. By 1800, the Bow Street Police Office was hailed as the leading law enforcement agency in the metropolitan London area (Johnson, Wolfe, & Jones, 2008).

The rising crime rate in London taxed even the Bow Street district police. It was becoming apparent that the traditional methods of law enforcement were inadequate to combat crime in London. Effective enforcement in one precinct caused criminals to move to a less policed or less effectively policed district. Leaving each district to create its own law enforcement methodology meant that districts had no uniformity in enforcement and no common grounds for communication or for the exchange of information and policing techniques. Entire portions of London were left without any effective means of preventing or punishing crimes.

The first step toward standardizing law enforcement in London came in 1785 as the result of the efforts of William Pitt the Younger, who attempted to introduce a bill establishing a police force that would have jurisdiction throughout the city. Although soundly defeated, the bill served as the blueprint for legislation passed in 1829, creating the London Metropolitan Police (Radzinowicz, 1986). The new headquarters were established at 4 Whitehall Place, and the back entrance, used by visitors, was in Scotland Yard, which led to the headquarters being called Scotland Yard.

The continued high crime rate set the stage for Sir Robert Peel, who proffered a preventive approach to law enforcement. It was the association of the Metropolitan Police with Sir Robert that gave rise to the use of "**bobby**" as a colloquial term for a police officer. Peel established patrol areas and patrol functions, the collection of intelligence, and the centralization of all law enforcement activities. Police officers eventually accepted the notion of uniforms, although officers originally viewed them as livery, that is, the uniforms worn by servants. Peel's highly visible and mobile force was easily recognized, and it acted as a deterrent on metropolitan streets. The bobby came to know his beat and those who lived and worked on it. Assigning officers to areas other than those in which they lived avoided fraternization with residents. Sir Robert Peel set the structure and the salaries of the new Metropolitan Police force as:

- Eight superintendents (£200 per annum)
- Twenty inspectors (£100 per annum)
- Eighty-eight sergeants (3s 6d per day)
- Eight hundred and ninety-five constables (3 shillings per day; Tobias, 1979)

The formation of an investigative branch of the Metropolitan Police was inevitable. Patrol responsibilities precluded bobbies from devoting sufficient time to the investigation of crimes whose perpetrators were not apprehended immediately. To solve this problem, carefully selected police officers took on investigative duties. These officers were chosen from the foot patrol police, giving the latter an incentive to develop observational skills and intelligence networks. This method of selecting investigators, along with civil service testing, is still used by most contemporary police agencies (Johnson et al., 2008).

Chicago

In 1849, Chicago saw the appointment of its first detective. Allan Pinkerton, an immigrant from Scotland, was both the first detective in the Chicago area and the cofounder of the Northwestern police agency, a forerunner to the Pinkerton National Detective Agency. Pinkerton is credited with developing investigative techniques and surveillance methods that are still employed today. He was also responsible for developing the foundations of what is now the criminal database, maintained by the Federal Bureau of Investigation.

bobby
Colloquial term for a police officer, which arose due to the close association of Sir Robert Peel with the Metropolitan Police Department in London

CASE IN POINT

© Shutterstock, Inc./Vlastas.

Tenacity

Three men, Weskett, Bradley, and Cooper, burgled the residence of the Earl of Harrington. Fielding's network of thief takers spent two years pursuing and eventually apprehending the group. The pursuers were successful in tracing one of the stolen banknotes. They circulated information and descriptions of the thieves throughout the country, and by following leads, they penetrated the burglars' disguises, tricks, and aliases. They fostered the betrayal of a prostitute who knew Bradley, and they apprehended Bradley shortly thereafter. Bradley testified against Cooper, who received 14 years from the King's Bench (Linebaugh, 1991).

© Shutterstock, Inc./Nutink.

CASE IN POINT

Jack the Ripper

In the years 1888–1891, residents of London's East End regarded the name **Jack the Ripper** with terror, and his name was known the world over. Jack the Ripper is the popular name given to a serial killer who murdered a number of prostitutes in the East End of London in 1888. The name comes from a letter written and published at the time of the murders. The killings took place in the districts of Whitechapel, Spitalfields, Aldgate, and the City of London proper.

SUSPECTS

Of the many suspects whose names were bandied about at the time, only four were suspected based on any credible evidence:

- Aaron Kosminski, a Polish Jewish resident of Whitechapel
- Montague John Druitt, a 31-year-old lawyer and schoolteacher who committed suicide in December 1888
- Michael Ostrog, a Russian-born thief
- Dr. Francis J. Tumblety, an American who was arrested in November 1888 for indecency offenses and who fled the country

Of the many murders that had occurred in 1888 that were attributed to Jack, only five are generally accepted as his work:

- Mary Ann (Polly) Nichols, murdered Friday, August 31, 1888
- Annie Chapman, murdered Saturday, September 8, 1888
- Elizabeth Stride, murdered Sunday, September 30, 1888
- Catharine Eddowes, also murdered Sunday, September 30, 1888
- Mary Jane (Marie Jeanette) Kelly, murdered Friday, November 9, 1888

The killer cut the throats of Mary Ann Nichols, Annie Chapman, Elizabeth Stride, Catharine Eddowes, and Mary Kelly. There were abdominal mutilations in all of the cases except that of Elizabeth Stride. The killer took Annie Chapman's uterus, Catharine Eddowes's uterus and left kidney, and Mary Kelly's heart.

THE LETTER

Jack the Ripper's name was written at the end of a letter that was dated September 25, 1888, and sent to the Central News Agency, which turned the letter over to the police.

> *Dear Boss,*
> *I keep on hearing the police have caught me but they wont fix me just yet. I have laughed when they look so clever and talk about being on the right track. That joke about Leather Apron gave me real fits. I am down on whores and I shant quit ripping them till I do get buckled.*
> *Grand work the last job was. I gave the lady no time to squeal. How can they catch me now. I love my work and want to start again. You will soon hear of me with my funny little games. I saved some of the proper red stuff in a ginger beer bottle over the last job to write with but it went thick like glue and I cant use it. Red ink is fit enough I hope ha. ha. The next job I do I shall clip the ladys ears off and send to the police officers just for jolly wouldn't you. Keep this letter back till I do a bit more work, then give it out straight. My knife's so nice and sharp I want to get to work right away if I get a chance. Good Luck.*
>
> *Yours truly*
> *Jack the Ripper*
>
> *Dont mind me giving the trade name*
> *PS Wasnt good enough to post this before I got all the red ink off my hands curse it No luck yet. They say I'm a doctor now. ha ha. (Begg, 2004)*

New York City

New York City had adopted a system of law enforcement similar to the one that preceded the birth of the London Metropolitan Police. New York employed a system composed of locally elected constables and justices of the peace. Just as high crime rates relegated the constabulary system to the refuse heap in London, the same occurred in New York. The evolution of police operations in London prompted New York City to abandon the constabulary system in 1845 and institute instead a uniformed, centrally organized police force. Officers wore a badge made of copper and soon became known as "**coppers**" (Miller, 1977).

The constabulary system continued to work well in rural areas, where crime was deterred by community sanction and watchfulness. To this day, the only prerequisite for serving as a constable or justice of the peace is widespread recognition and public esteem.

The Birth of Forensic Investigation

Criminal investigation involves the application of the scientific method to the analysis of a crime scene. As policing evolved, so did the need for field practitioners to understand evidence and the information that can be obtained from evidence preserved for forensic evaluation. This led to the evolution of forensic investigation and forensic science.

Forensic science is the application of science to civil and criminal law. Coupled within the fields of policing and forensic science is the area of **forensic investigation**. The term essentially means the application of forensic science to the process of investigating a criminal event. Just as with law enforcement, the growth and evolution of the field of forensics has been occurring for thousands of years.

As early as 1248, the Chinese recognized that the body itself could contain information about the cause and method of death. *Hsi Yuan Lu*, a handbook published in 1250, gave guidelines for the postmortem examination of bodies. It included descriptions of various wounds caused by sharp versus blunt instruments and offered advice on how to determine whether an individual found in the water had died of drowning or had been killed beforehand and whether a burned individual was dead before the onset of the fire.

Doctors and other medical practitioners who, through observation, noted certain consistencies in natural deaths and uncharacteristic aspects of violent deaths took the first steps in the forensic journey. These practitioners were the first medical pathologists. The written records of the development of **forensic pathology** in Europe begin in 1507, when a volume known as the Bamberg Code appeared. Twenty-three years later, Emperor Charles V issued a more extensive penal code, known as the *Constitutio Criminalis Carolina*, for all the lands included in his empire. The two documents recognized the importance of medical testimony as an integral part of trials involving possible infanticide, homicide, abortion, or poisoning.

In the latter half of the 16th century, Ambrose Pare performed official medicolegal autopsies. He reported findings from the examination of the lungs of smothered children and studied the traces left by sexual assault (Thorwald, 1965). As a result of advances in knowledge about violent death, judicial authorities and the police in Europe soon began to call on physicians to help solve fatal crimes. Most of the larger jurisdictions developed centers, commonly known as institutes of forensic medicine, where experts carried out their investigations.

Forensic Investigation in the United States

The historic development of forensic investigation in the United States can be traced to the English **coroner** system. The justice courts authorized the coroner to attach or arrest witnesses or suspects and to appraise and safeguard any lands or goods that might later be forfeited by reason of guilt of the accused. William Blackstone wrote a succinct description of the coroner's duties at the time of King Edward I in 1272:

> *The office and power of a Coroner are also like those of a Sheriff, either judicial or ministerial, but principally judicial. ... And consists, first in inquiring, when a person is slain or dies suddenly, or in prison, concerning the manner of his death. And this must be upon sight of the body; for if the body be not found, the coroner cannot sit. He must also sit at the very place where death happened and the inquiry must be made by a jury of 4, 5, or 6 of the neighboring towns over which he is to preside. If any be found guilty by this inquest of murder or other homicide, the coroner is to commit them to prison for further trial and must certify the whole of his inquisition, together with the evidence thereon, to the Court of King's Bench, or the next assizes. (Latrobe, 1861, p. 6)*

forensic pathology
Area of medicine pertaining to studying the causes of human death

copper
Colloquial term for a police officer, coined because the members of the first uniformed police force in New York City wore badges made of copper

coroner
In the English coroner system, this person was authorized by the justice courts to attach or arrest witnesses or suspects and to appraise and safeguard any lands or goods that might later be forfeited by reason of guilt of the accused

forensic science
The application of science to civil and criminal law

forensic investigation
The application of forensic science to the process of investigating a criminal event

inquest
A formal inquiry

pathology
The branch of medicine associated with the study of structural changes caused by disease or injury

Alphonse Bertillon
Person who developed the first scientific system of identification for use in criminal investigation

Henry Faulds
Scottish physician working in Japan, noticed the practice of identifying pottery and sealing documents through the use of handprints and fingerprints

Sir Francis Galton
Published *Finger Prints*, a book-length monograph that contained a basic system of classification

medical examiner
A physician who works for a law enforcement agency to investigate the cause of any death that could have resulted from a crime or that occurred in a suspicious or unusual manner

In 1877, the English parliament enacted a law requiring an **inquest** to be conducted whenever the coroner had reasonable cause to suspect that a violent or unnatural death had occurred or when the cause of death was unknown. This had the effect of granting the coroner wide authority to investigate cases and was in sharp contrast to the practice on the European continent, where prosecutors and police began investigations. Thus, the coroner's office developed as a broad spectrum investigative agency concerned with a large proportion of all deaths. The United States ultimately adopted an act similar to the English law. It is reflected in current statutes that empower the medical examiner's office and lay the jurisdictional foundation for the performance of medical examinations.

In 1789, a professor of physiology at the University of Edinburgh began giving lectures in legal medicine and public health. In general, professors of legal medicine, by doing research and authoring textbooks, were most responsible for establishing legal medicine and pathology as an independent scientific pursuit.

American colonists brought the coroner system from England intact. An early definition of a coroner's duties in the colonies can be found in the governor of Maryland's 1640 appointment of John Robinson to be high constable and coroner for St. Mary's County. According to the definition, the coroner, among other duties, was required:

> upon notice or suspicion of any person that hath or shall come to his or her death entirely within the limits of that county to warn as many inhabitants of the said county as you conveniently may to view the dead body and to charge the person with an oath truly to inquire and true verdict to grant how the person viewed came upon his or her death according to the evidence. (Browne, 1885, p. 417)

The earliest mention of a physician in connection with the duties of a coroner was in 1860 in Maryland, where the Code of Public General Laws authorized the coroner or his jury to require the attendance of a physician in cases of violent death. Eight years later, the legislature authorized the governor to appoint a physician as sole coroner of Baltimore. In Boston in 1877, the Commonwealth of Massachusetts adopted a statewide system requiring that a physician known as a **medical examiner** supplant the coroner. In 1915, New York City adopted a law eliminating the coroner's office and creating a medical examiner system, authorizing the investigation of any death resulting from criminal violence, casualty, or suicide; occurring suddenly while the person was in apparent health, was unattended by a physician, or was imprisoned; or occurring in any suspicious or unusual manner (Spitz, Spitz, & Fisher, 2006).

The Growth of Forensic Science

The latter part of the 19th century witnessed the emergence of the science of **pathology** as a subspecialty of medicine. At the same time, the related fields of forensic science began to develop. During this period, **Alphonse Bertillon** devised the first scientific system of identification; his anthropometric system was accepted as the most accurate method of criminal identification until the early 1900s.

Bertillon came from a family dominated by medical doctors, naturalists, and mathematicians, but his unassuming air and lack of personal grace resulted in his being assigned to an assistant clerkship in the records room of the French Surete's archives in Paris. It was his task to file identifying data on all criminals apprehended and convicted throughout France, and this tedious task was rendered additionally distasteful by his realization that virtually all of the descriptions were so vague as to be useless. In 1879, he decided, on the basis of his observations and his knowledge of science, that no two people could have exactly the same physical characteristics. If enough measurements were taken, a high degree of individuality could be developed for each person in a police agency's files. By February 1883, his technique was shown to be successful, and it was referred to in the newspapers as *anthropometry* or *Bertillonage*. Bertillon's methods gained immediate attention. In the United States, they were widely adopted, and a central file of measurements was maintained at Sing Sing prison.

Bertillon's system was destined to be short-lived, because it often provided incorrect identification. **Henry Faulds**, a Scottish physician working in Japan, noticed the practice of identifying pottery and sealing documents through the use of handprints and fingerprints. In 1892, **Sir Francis Galton** published *Finger Prints*, a book-length monograph that contained a basic system of classification (Galton, 1892). Galton's system was expanded into a practical method of categorization which was widely adopted around the world by 1903.

American fingerprinting efficiency was increased in 1924 when federal prisoner identification files maintained at the federal prison at Leavenworth were combined with the files maintained by the International Chiefs of Police at Sing Sing. The consolidated fingerprint bureau, later to be relocated to the Federal Bureau of Investigation (FBI) in Washington, DC, proved invaluable not only for criminal investigation but also for the identification of the victims of accidents and natural disasters (Johnson et al., 2008).

In the 1870s, a Frenchman, Albert Florence, developed a definitive chemical test for the presence of human semen, and another Frenchman, Ambroise Tardieu, discovered that dot-like blood spots under the pleura (the membrane that lines the chest and covers the lungs) were characteristic of death by rapid suffocation. In 1882, an Austrian, Eduard von Hoffmann, discovered that persons burned alive had soot in their windpipes and lungs and carbon monoxide in their blood.

A German physician, Paul Uhlenhuth, developed a test in 1901 that permitted scientists to distinguish one species of animal blood from another, while his countryman, Karl Landsteiner, discovered that human blood cells could be grouped into what came to be known as A, B, and O types. In 1915, a simple procedure for determining the blood group of a dried bloodstain was developed by Leone Lattes in Italy.

Closely related to blood typing is deoxyribonucleic acid (DNA) matching, which is often used in criminal investigations. DNA is located in all human cells, and its precise configuration is determined by heredity. DNA is the architect, foreman, and bricklayer of life. In every creature, DNA carries the coded messages of heredity and governs everything from eye color to toe length. It is present in every one of the trillions of cells in the human body. Based on the work of **Alec Jeffreys** at the University of Leicester, a method was developed to extract DNA from a specimen of blood, semen, or other tissue, slice it into fragments, and tag the fragments with a radioactive probe so that they would expose x-ray film. The resulting pattern of stripes on the film is as distinctive as a fingerprint, and Jeffreys and his colleagues named the process of isolating and reading DNA markers *DNA fingerprinting*.

In one of the first experiments using **genetic fingerprinting**, Jeffreys tested a family group to see if the pattern of inheritance was as simple as he expected it to be. The experiment showed that half of the bands and stripes were from the mother and the rest from the father (Beeler & Wiebe, 1988). Determining whether these characteristics held true for tissues other than blood

was his next task. Jeffreys's team took both blood and semen and found that the genetic map was constant, regardless of the kind of cells from which the material had come. To determine test sensitivity, the team tested small quantities of blood and semen. A drop of blood or a tiny amount of semen was sufficient. Jeffreys clearly had developed a laboratory technique that provided seemingly irrefutable results. His concern, however, was to ensure proper identification of the forensic materials available at a crime scene. How effective would his procedure be in identifying degraded DNA? Additional testing on 3-year-old blood and semen stains turned out to be equally successful.

In March 1985, Jeffreys published his first scientific report, in which he estimated that the chance of two people having the same DNA fingerprint (absent identical twins) was zero:

> You would have to look for one part in a million million million million million before you would find one pair with the same genetic fingerprint and with a world population of only five billion it can be categorically said that a genetic fingerprint is individually specific and that any pattern does not belong to anyone on the face of this planet who ever has been or ever will be. (Wambaugh, 1985, p. 94)

Development of Crime Laboratories

Scientific fields, such as chemistry, physics, biology, and microscopy, have a long history of separate development. Although the noted German jurist Hans Gross published a textbook in 1893 detailing the application of information derived from these separate fields to criminal investigation, it was not until 1910, when **Edmond Locard** established the first crime laboratory in Lyon, France, that these specialties were brought together for the sole purpose of improving criminal investigation (**FIGURE 1.2**). The success of Locard's laboratory led to the formation of similar laboratories in different parts of Europe, and, in 1923, the first complete crime laboratory in the United States was established in the Los Angeles Police Department by August Vollmer. Locard's work gives us the foundation upon which forensic investigation is based; any time two objects come into contact with one another, there is a cross-transfer of evidence that occurs. Therefore, every suspect/victim/witness can be connected to a scene/object and every scene/object to a suspect/victim/witness (typically through

Alec Jeffreys Scientist who developed the method of DNA fingerprinting

Edmond Locard Established the first crime laboratory in Lyon, France. Locard's theory that any time two objects come into contact with one another, there is a cross-transfer of evidence became the foundation upon which trace evidence analysis is based

genetic fingerprinting The DNA fingerprint of an individual

FIGURE 1.2: Edmond Locard.

© Maurice Jarnoux/Paris Match/Getty Images.

FIGURE 1.3: August Vollmer.

© Bettman/Getty Images.

trace evidence analysis). This has since become known as "Locard's Exchange Principle."

Because of widespread corruption and brutality among police forces throughout the United States, **August Vollmer** advocated increased police professionalism through higher education. While chief of the Berkeley Police Department, he instituted police training and college requirements for police candidates at the University of California. Vollmer also taught police administration courses at the University of California and the University of Chicago (**FIGURE 1.3**). His department was the first in the country to use radio communications and automobile patrols while other departments were using street corner call boxes. During his tenure as president of the California Police Chiefs Association (CPCA) in 1907 and as president of the International Association of Chiefs of Police (IACP) in 1922, he promoted the hiring of women in law enforcement and the study of human behavior as an integral part of police training. His contributions to the improvement of police and their work have prompted many to refer to him as the Father of Police Professionalism. To some extent, the fact that you are most likely a criminal justice student as you read this is, in part, a continuing legacy of his many contributions to making law enforcement a profession.

Paul Leland Kirk was a leader in establishing criminology as an academic discipline. He worked as a professor at the University of California, Berkeley, where he wrote the groundbreaking textbook *Crime Investigation* (Kirk, 1953). The book provided a scientific protocol for processing crime scenes and included chapters on fingerprints, firearms, and blood spatter. He was a consultant on numerous criminal cases. During his time at the University of California, he

developed a scientific approach to the study of forensics and its application to criminal investigation. In 1937, he was appointed head of the criminology program at the university, and in 1950, along with August Vollmer, he established the first school of criminology at the University of California, Berkeley.

For more than 30 years, forensic scientist **Edward T. Blake** has been considered an expert in DNA analysis. He was the first to use polymerase chain reaction (PCR)-based DNA testing in the United States, during the civil court case *People v. Pestinikas* in 1986. Since that time, he has worked as a consultant to analyze biological evidence in many criminal cases.

Tommie Lee Andrews became the first person to be convicted of a crime in the United States based on DNA evidence. In 1987, Tommie Lee Andrews was sentenced to 22 years for committing rape. In Virginia the following year, a killer dubbed the "South Side Strangler" was convicted of murder after DNA linked him to several rapes and murders in the Richmond, Virginia, area (James, 2009).

A laboratory organized within the FBI that was established in 1932 was the first to make forensic science available nationwide. This

August Vollmer
The father of law enforcement professionalism

Edward T. Blake
Provided the DNA testimony and evidence for the first DNA trial in the United States

Tommie Lee Andrews
The first person to be convicted in the United States based on DNA evidence

Paul Leland Kirk
Established criminology as an academic discipline and wrote *Crime Investigation*

laboratory has served as the model for the formation and organization of forensic laboratories at local, state, and national levels throughout the world (Spitz et al., 2006). In modern, well-equipped forensic laboratories, experts from the fields of serology and immunology, ballistics, document analysis, fingerprinting, polygraphy, analytical chemistry, and geology work together to solve crimes and provide scientifically validated evidence. In the past decades, many of the sophisticated analytical techniques and scientific instruments developed primarily for medicine and industry have been incorporated into forensic laboratories. Technologies, such as gas-liquid chromatography, infrared spectroscopy, nuclear magnetic resonance, and mass spectroscopy, have found their fullest applications in criminal investigation.

Although much of the testing falls to the scientists, it is the responsibility of the criminal investigator to preserve physical evidence and to exercise good judgment in determining which scientific measurements and evaluations are appropriate. The rapid expansion of scientific methods of investigation has placed special demands on the training and financial resources of police agencies. Use of sophisticated techniques requires a high level of formal education, a comprehensive knowledge of modern science, and the ability to work with highly trained professionals in anatomy, physiology, chemistry, and physics. It was under these types of pressures that the old American system of elected coroners began to give way to trained medical examiners after 1935, and the work of police detectives soon came to involve coordinating the investigations of many professional scientists and applying their discoveries to the solution of criminal cases.

Advancing Forensic Science

The **American Academy of Forensic Sciences (AAFS)** was established in 1948 to promote education for and research in the forensic sciences. In an assessment of forensic sciences,

American Academy of Forensic Sciences (AAFS) A professional organization associated with the forensic sciences

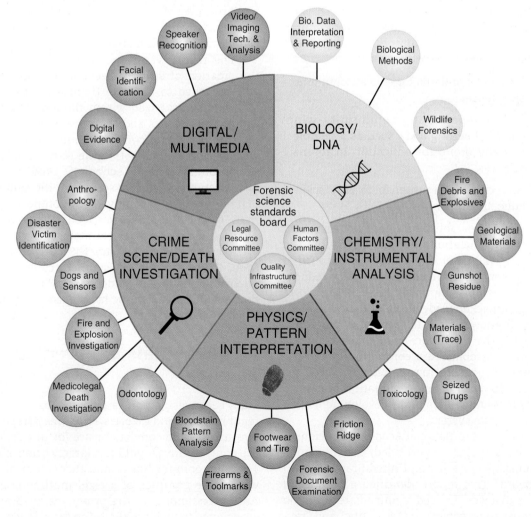

Courtesy of the National Institute of Standards and Technology.

— Ripped from the Headlines —

Defunding Forensic Science Improvement

On April 10, 2017, Attorney General Jeff Sessions announced that the U.S. Department of Justice would no longer be requiring the services of scientists and practitioners who had previously been partnering with the government to enhance national standards pertaining to forensic science. Sessions said that he would not be extending the term to fund the National Commission on Forensic Science (NCFS). The attorney general also gave notice of the suspension of an expanded review of FBI testimony on, and techniques for the use of, forensic evidence.

Initially founded under the Obama administration, the NCFS was respon-sible for developing a number of "far-reaching final recommendations" and policies for improving forensic standards. Many of these will remain hanging and unimplemented as a result of the attorney general's announcement.

Data from Burns, J. (2017). Sessions scraps Federal Commission on forensic accuracy, for some reason. Retrieved from https://www.forbes.com/sites/janetwburns/2017/04/11/sessions-scraps-federal-commission-on-forensic-accuracy-because-reasons/#8176a776c219

© Shutterstock, Inc./rzarek.

---

published in 1999 by the National Institute of Justice (NIJ), titled, *Forensic Sciences: Review of Status and Needs*, the forensic sciences were described as being in serious need of educa-tion and training. In addition, the assessment included a demand for:

- National standards for education in foren-sic sciences

- An independent, community-wide, standard-setting body, such as a technical working group for education in forensic sciences

- An accreditation system for forensic science education programs

The NIJ established a technical working group for education and training in forensic sciences (TWGED) in 2001 for the purpose of recommending curricular guidelines for educa-tional programs in forensic sciences. The work-ing group acknowledged the importance of an accreditation system for academic programs. In 2002, the American Academy of Forensic Sciences established a committee, called the Forensic Education Program Accreditation Com-mittee, to develop an accreditation system to explore issues related to the development of an accreditation system.

In 2009, the National Academy of Sciences (NAS) assembled a report titled, "Strengthening Forensic Science in the United States: A Path Forward." This report identified a number of areas that were in need of immediate attention in order to be considered "scientific" and "reli-able." Additionally, the report made suggestions for unification of several fields that encompass modern forensic science and for codifying and universally defining terms and testimony asso-ciated with forensic analysis.

The report was responsible for spurring the creation of several research committees, which rushed to dedicate themselves to the concepts summarized within the NAS report. Out of these efforts and committees, the Orga-nization of Scientific Area Committees (OSAC) was developed, from within the National Insti-tute of Standards and Technology. OSAC's aim is to strengthen forensic science in the United State. It was a collaborative body composed of more than 500 forensic science professionals, representing academia; local, state, and federal agencies; as well as industry. NIST established OSAC to support the development of forensic science standards and guidelines, and to ensure that a sufficient scientific basis exists for each subdiscipline.

Fundamentals of Forensic Science

Many see investigation as art or magic—a mat-ter of hunches and theories. From this perspec-tive, arrests and convictions are fortuitous. To the contrary, investigation is largely scientific. There is room for hunch and theory, but only within the confines of a rigid methodology. An understanding of the principles of foren-sic science (which are the same for science in

forensic evidence
Physical evidence that requires scien-tific validation

protocol
Set of steps followed to arrive at a con-clusion that can be replicated by others using the same set of steps

principle of parsimony
Principle that one should seek the simplest explanation for the phenomenon being examined

TABLE 1.1 Types of Evidence	
Physical evidence	Evidence that can be touched and evaluated tactually
Testimonial evidence	Words communicated by testifying witnesses
Circumstantial evidence	Everything that is not eyewitness testimony
Forensic evidence	Physical evidence that requires scientific validation

general) is essential to successful investigations. Many investigations are resolved within hours of the commission of the crime, primarily as a result of victim and witness statements testimonial evidence but these statements themselves may be bolstered at the time of the trial by corroborating **forensic evidence**. **TABLE 1.1** contains a short list of the various types of evidence, which can be admitted into court as supporting information associated with a criminal event.

Scientists utilize the scientific method to structure their investigations. The terminology varies, but the steps are generally the same. The objective is to arrive at a conclusion that others can replicate by applying the same **protocol**. Scientists have developed a vocabulary for discussing this protocol; many of the terms are defined in the following sections.

Parsimony

According to the **principle of parsimony**, one should seek the simplest explanation for the phenomenon being examined. For example, if an automobile refuses to start, a mechanic might list possible reasons, from the simplest to the most complex:

1. No gas
2. No spark
   a. Low water in battery
   b. Bad battery cables
   c. Bad battery connections
   d. Failed battery
   e. Failed starter

A skilled mechanic would check the battery and its connections before replacing the starter. In doing so, he or she would be applying the principle of parsimony.

Specification

In any scientific experiment, **specification** of exactly what is going to be done and how it is to be done is important. Researchers may evaluate the procedure employed to determine if anything in the setup might have affected the outcome in ways other than intended.

Scientific Method

Researchers must first decide which particular phenomenon they wish to observe. It is imperative that the working **hypothesis** formulated by the research group that is utilizing the **scientific method** include an anticipated outcome and a supposed cause (i.e., a variable being tested to see whether it is a cause of the outcome). Only one variable can be examined or changed at a time. Changing or testing more than one variable at a time would render any observed outcome useless, for it would be impossible to tell which of the variables caused the outcome.

Observation

Scientists conduct experiments under controlled conditions to determine what happens when certain variables change. In many instances, what happens cannot be observed with the naked eye. Therefore, scientists use an array of instruments to assist in the **observation** process, such as microscopes, spectrometers, chromatographs, audio recorders, and cameras, to mention just a few. Note that scientists occasionally observe with senses other than sight.

Recording

Most scientific experiments take place over time and involve complex designs. **Recording** each step of the experimental method ensures that other experimenters can replicate the results. It is replicability that moves a phenomenon from art or "magic" to science.

Taxonomy

After the experiment, it may be necessary to group specific characteristics of the observed phenomena to create a **taxonomy**. Firearm examiners use taxonomic characteristics in classifying cartridges, cases, and bullets. During examination, they focus on one characteristic at a time.

Analysis

Data can only be used if broken down into parts. As in the construction of a jigsaw puzzle, the placement of a piece requires a detailed examination of that piece as well as the adjoining

specification
Designation of what is going to be done and how it is to be done

hypothesis
Prediction of outcome made in advance of testing a particular phenomenon

scientific method
Formulation of a hypothesis and development of a protocol to test a hypothesis to identify factors causing a particular phenomenon

observation
Determination of what happens in an experiment when certain variables are changed

recording
Making note of each step of the experimental method employed so that the experiment can be repeated and the results replicated

taxonomy
Classification of observed phenomena into groups that share specific characteristics

CASE IN POINT

The Scientific Method at Work

A homicide investigator has been called to the scene of an apparent suicide. In the kitchen of a small rural home, a body lies next to an overturned chair and a shotgun. The right foot of the deceased is bare, and a string tied in a bow around the big toe is also tied around the trigger of the shotgun. There is a large wound in the victim's chest and considerable tissue and blood residue on the barrel of the shotgun. Behind the victim is a waist-high hole in the wall about the size of a little finger. These facts, considered in their totality, give some support to the hypothesis that this was a suicide. There appears to have been no struggle, and the weapon is in close proximity to the body. The hole in the wall is a bit troubling. The investigator's experience (inductive reasoning) tells him that shot shells do not leave such a hole unless they are chambered for a rifled round (shotguns have a cartridge that contains either numerous pellets or a single projectile). He examines the shotgun (analysis) and discovers that the two chambers of the double-barreled shotgun both contain a shell. One is spent. Upon removing it, he notes that the shell contains pellets. His hypothesis that a suicide occurred does not explain the hole in the wall (synthesis). If he is wedded to his hypothesis, he may choose to ignore this anomaly. Or he may begin to ask some additional questions:

- Who was present at the time of the shooting?

- Did the hole in the wall exist prior to the shooting?

- Are there other weapons on the premises?

Pursuing answers to these questions will provide information that can be used as a basis for further reasoning. The investigator learns that only the victim's wife was present at the time of the incident, and she does not seem to be aware of any structural flaws in the kitchen wall. She tells the investigator that there is also a 30-caliber hunting rifle in the gun cabinet in the living room. Another hypothesis begins to take shape. Could the wife have murdered her husband? There are only two possibilities if the wife is telling the truth: suicide or homicide (with the wife as the primary suspect).

The investigator notices that the victim is wearing his wristwatch on his left wrist, which suggests he was right-handed. The investigator begins to gather information that he sees as consistent with right-handedness (classification):

- The wristwatch is on the victim's left wrist.

- The victim's wallet is in his right rear pants pocket.

- The victim's right front pants pocket is worn.

- There is a pocketknife in the right front pants pocket.

- There is a ballpoint pen in the left shirt pocket.

The wife confirms that her husband was right-handed.

The investigator begins to gather information that he sees as inconsistent with right-handedness (classification):

- The right foot has been bared.

- The string is tied to the right big toe.

The investigator's assumption, based on experience and reason, is that a right-handed person would have bared his left foot and tied the string to his left big toe (induction). That the facts conflict with this assumption suggests that someone else tied the string (deduction). The investigator suspects homicide (synthesis, theory), and he has the crime scene handled in a manner appropriate for an investigation of a homicide.

The medical examiner confirms that a hole consistent with the passage of a 30-caliber bullet through the body was made prior to the shotgun blast. The laboratory discloses that the bow tied to the victim's big toe was tied not from the victim's position but rather from a reversed position, by someone facing the sole of the foot. The prosecution's theory of the case, which it will attempt to prove by presenting forensic evidence, is that the wife shot her husband with the hunting rifle while they were both sitting at the kitchen table. She then took the shotgun and placed the barrel at her husband's chest and fired, thereby obscuring the original and fatal wound. Stripping his foot bare and tying the string to his toe was her final attempt at making the homicide look like a suicide.

pieces. At the crime scene, the investigator gathers information from three separate sources: people, records, and physical evidence (Osterburg & Ward, 2010). Exceptional organizational skills are required to gather information from these sources and to render that information into a usable form. The organization of the information is the first step in the analytic process. It is difficult to analyze anything when overwhelmed by incoming data. Sorting, classifying, and organizing the information allows **analysis** to begin.

Once investigators have interviewed people, reviewed records, and examined evidence, they must **synthesize** the discrete data elements into a working hypothesis. What happened? When did it happen? Where did it happen? How did it happen? Who made it happen? These are the questions investigators seek to answer. In creating a hypothesis, investigators must try to suggest answers to as many of the posed questions as possible, based not on conjecture but on an examination of the gathered data.

Hypothesis

A working hypothesis is like an incomplete jigsaw puzzle that comes together a piece at a time. To carry on the analogy, the puzzle is old and in a container other than the original; you do not know what the puzzle picture is; and you do not know if all the pieces are provided or if there are pieces that do not belong to that puzzle. A picture will nonetheless begin to form as you put pieces together. At some point, what the puzzle depicts may suddenly seem apparent, and you will be able to form a hypothesis as to the full image. If subsequent pieces show the image to be different than first assumed, the hypothesis must be revised. Any criminal investigation faces the challenges of arriving at an apparent image without sufficient puzzle pieces and of disregarding the pieces that do not fit. As the investigation progresses, new corroborating facts will be added and the interpretation of some old facts changed. This is the process whereby the hypothesis advances toward becoming a theory.

Theory

As data are added, the hypothesis begins to take on a life of its own. It becomes more solidly based and evolves into a **theory** that begins to explain and predict.

Inductive Reasoning

We all come to answers in life based on experience. A series of similar or repeated experiences allows us to generalize to conclusions. If a person has had a bad experience with drinking water in another country and then suffers a repeat episode, he or she may jump to the conclusion that water in other countries is not safe to drink. This conclusion is incorrect. It may well be that water in the particular village, city, or establishment was tainted, but generalizing to the quality of water in all other countries is an unsupported leap.

Most of life's lessons (which we might place under the rubric "common sense") are brought to us by way of **inductive reasoning**, which is also an integral part of the scientific method. When applying inductive reasoning, you must keep in mind that you are usually dealing with probabilities, not certainties.

Deductive Reasoning

Conclusions can be reached through **deductive reasoning** as well. In a valid deductive argument, if the premises are true, the conclusion must be true. Consider this argument: All other countries have poor-quality water. Canada is a country. Therefore, Canada has poor water quality. The conclusion is certain on the condition that the premises are true. Note, however, that if even one of the premises of a deductive argument is not true, the conclusion remains uncertain. As pointed out earlier, many other countries have stringent sanitation regulations, which means that the first premise of the example deductive argument, far from being known to be true, is known to be false. Therefore, the argument does not help us determine whether Canada has poor-quality water—it may, or it may not.

Criminal Investigation and the Scientific Method

The scientific method is usually only employed partially in a criminal investigation. Two variables dictate the determination of which parts can be used: the type of crime being investigated and the type of information available. In a homicide, investigators use a variety of skills that derive from the scientific method. The following scenario identifies the various components of the scientific method and where they come into play.

It is apparent that an investigation goes through many stages in the attempt to reconstruct the past. What is not apparent is the scientific method employed in most investigations (**TABLE 1.2**). Investigators may lack the necessary vocabulary or be ignorant of scientific method and thus attribute many conclusions reached during investigations to "street savvy,"

analysis
Rendering information into a form that allows it to be used

inductive reasoning
Drawing conclusions based on probabilities rather than certainties

synthesize
Combining data to form a working hypothesis

deductive reasoning
Drawing conclusions based on premises that are certain (known to be true)

theory
A hypothesis that is supported by data

TABLE 1.2 Applying the Scientific Method	
Scientific Method	Criminal Investigation
Describe the phenomenon.	Identify what crime was committed.
Build a hypothesis.	Develop a working hypothesis based on information and evidence.
Collect data.	Gather records, evidence, and corroborative or uncorroborative information.
Test the hypothesis.	Constantly review all the facts, whether consistent or inconsistent with the working hypothesis; focus the case when the facts allow; interview or interrogate the suspect.
Continue to collect data.	As the finger of suspicion begins to point, gather any and all additional corroborative data.
Arrive at a theory.	Once probable cause has been attained, arrest the suspect. Provide all evidence to the prosecution, both inculpatory and exculpatory.

Osterburg and Ward (2010).

hunches, or intuition. Rather, what is really at work is the process of inductive reasoning progressing through to the use of deductive reasoning. Many of the steps may be unidentified or misidentified, but they are still there. If investigators applied the scientific method intentionally and systematically rather than unconsciously or haphazardly, they would be greatly assisted in their reconstruction of the past.

Importance of Forensic Evidence

Crime lab reports seem to have an aura of invincibility about them. Maybe we believe that the reported results are based on "science," which, in turn, can be empirically tested. Because report contents can be checked, we assume that no lab technician would falsify a report.

What happens to a piece of forensic evidence from the time of its discovery until it appears in the courtroom? First, we should realize that the discovery itself could affect the integrity of the evidence. After the evidence is discovered, it has to be collected; it is then packaged, labeled, and transported—four more chances for error. It is then stored, removed from storage, and again transported, this time to the laboratory. At the laboratory, the evidence is logged in, placed in storage, again removed from storage, kept from intermingling with other

evidence, and documented properly. All of this activity occurs before any tests are performed.

Next, the evidence is taken to a clean, contamination-free work area, where it must be unpack-aged properly. The item must be inspected visually and described properly in detail to document its condition before any work is performed on it. In most instances, it will be photographed, weighed, and sketched. Only then will the lab technician consider beginning any laboratory work.

The technician must figure out what test or tests are appropriate, determine if sufficient amounts of the evidence exist for those tests, and then properly dissect the portion to be tested and properly prepare the testing material, all while continuing to document each step. Only then does any testing begin. Some tests might include as many as five or six separate procedures, each of which must be performed properly and documented, with the evidence afterward being repackaged, relabeled, and once again transported to storage properly. Then the technician interprets what the experiments have disclosed.

The evidence must next be removed from the lab's storage area, logged out, transported to the police evidence area, logged in, and stored properly until the prosecuting attorney decides whether more testing should be performed, at which point the whole process begins anew. Once tested and recorded, the evidence has to make it to the courtroom for the preliminary examination,

EXHIBIT 1.1

The Fifth and Sixth Amendments to the U.S. Constitution

Fifth Amendment

No person shall be held to answer for a capital or otherwise infamous crime, unless on a presentment, or indictment of a Grand Jury, except in cases arising in the land or naval forces, or in the militia, when in actual service in time of war or public danger; nor shall any person be subject for the same offense to be twice put in jeopardy, of life or limb; nor shall be compelled in any criminal case to be a witness against himself, nor be deprived of life, liberty, or property, without due process of law; nor shall private property be taken for public use, without just compensation.

Sixth Amendment

In all criminal prosecutions, the accused shall enjoy the right to a speedy and public trial, by an impartial jury of the State and district wherein the crime shall have been committed, which district shall have been previously ascertained by law, and to be informed of the nature and cause of the accusation; to be confronted with the witnesses against him; to have compulsory process for obtaining witnesses in his favor, and to have the assistance of counsel for his defense.

U.S. Constitution. Art./Amend. V-VI.

© Shutterstock, Inc./Africa Studio.

back to storage, possibly back to the lab for more testing, back to the police, and so on.

It is clear that no other type of evidence is exposed to anywhere near as many opportunities for destruction, mishandling, contamination, or other conceivable catastrophes that can be brought on by human or natural error as forensic evidence. Forensic science in police work is becoming increasingly important, not only because of advances in science but also because of changes in the legal system. In *Miranda v. Arizona* (1966), the U.S. Supreme Court held that a suspect must be told of the Fifth Amendment protection against self-incrimination and the Sixth Amendment right to counsel during interrogations (**EXHIBIT 1.1**). This decision required police to rely less on confessions and more on forensic evidence in obtaining convictions.

Objectives of an Investigation

It is a common misconception that every crime is solvable and that the perpetrator always leaves traces at the crime scene that inevitably lead to his or her door. What is true is that a person cannot enter a crime scene without leaving something and taking something (perhaps only something microscopic). Finding the perpetrator's traces does not guarantee a resolution to the investigation, but it is a step in that direction.

Solving a crime means different things to the public than to a criminal investigator. The public believes a crime has been solved when the perpetrator has been identified and apprehended. However, identification and apprehension are but two of the seven objectives of a police investigation:

1. Crime detection

2. Locating and identifying suspects (Before a crime scene can be processed, individual perpetrators must be removed from the premises because they pose a danger to police, investigators, and others.)

3. Locating, recording, and processing evidence while observing all constitutional considerations

4. Arresting the perpetrator(s) while observing all constitutional considerations

5. Recovering property pursuant to Fourth Amendment requirements

6. Preparing for trial, including completing accurate documentation

7. Convicting the defendant by testifying and assisting in the presentation of legally obtained evidence and statements

Presuming a crime has been committed, the search for truth and the reconstruction of the crime scene are of little value if evidence necessary to the trial of the case is lost, destroyed, or contaminated. Recognizing that the evidence

> **Miranda v. Arizona**
> Supreme Court decision that requires that a suspect be told of the Fifth Amendment protection against self-incrimination and the Sixth Amendment right to counsel during interrogations

INVESTIGATOR'S NOTEBOOK

Definition of a Successful Investigation

For the purposes of this text, a successful investigation is one in which the following statements are true:

- All available physical evidence is handled competently.
- All witnesses are interviewed intelligently.
- All suspects are interrogated effectively.
- All leads are developed.
- All documentation is completed comprehensively, clearly, and accurately.

recovered and the steps in its recovery are the foundations upon which the prosecution must build its case allows for a wider view of the criminal investigation process.

Finding the perpetrator is often the simplest part of the job. Obtaining evidence in support of a conviction may be more difficult. Some "successful" investigations do not result in convictions, and some "failed" investigations do result in convictions. A less-than-elegant investigation may nonetheless result in a plea bargain, whereas the best-run investigation may run out of leads.

Investigator's Role

The expansion of science and technology raises the question of whether the forensic scientist has replaced the criminal investigator. The answer is clearly no. On the contrary, the investigator's role has been enhanced, because the evidence collected has increased value in the hands of a forensic specialist who knows how to extract its meaning but who depends on the investigator to put its meaning into context. The investigator and the forensic scientist work cooperatively (albeit frequently physically apart). The investigator recognizes what is important physical evidence, and the scientist processes it. Because of his or her experience, the investigator knows where to look for evidence and how to weigh its significance. The scientist knows how to handle, analyze, record, and interpret forensic evidence.

Many agencies, especially those with a large volume of cases and extensive resources, place an intermediary between the criminal investigator and laboratory scientists. In these agencies, forensic technicians actually recover,

tag, and bag all evidence discovered by on-scene investigators. A criminal investigator need only locate prospective evidence and then leave it to the trained technicians to process it. Note that this text will treat the criminal investigator as both the finder of evidence and the person responsible for photographing, tagging, handling, and maintaining all evidence gathered at the crime scene.

Selecting Investigators

A criminal investigator must possess a variety and range of skills not called for in any other profession (**TABLE 1.3**). In addition, the investigator must be emotionally stable, physically fit, and self-motivated. Where are such extraordinary people found? The story of criminal investigation is the story of men and women who developed an understanding of the criminal mind and criminal motivation while on the street.

Indeed, there has been a time-honored tradition of selecting prospective investigators from the ranks of patrol personnel, with little regard for education and training. It was presumed that any officer who had accrued time in the ranks possessed the basic qualifications needed by a criminal investigator, and few other departmental requirements existed. Whatever skills were required by the job could be readily picked up on the job, supplemented by a brief stint at a school for investigators.

Many agencies now have incorporated a civil service examination to standardize the requirements for criminal investigators. The future will see men and women selected as criminal investigators because of their background in science or the law. University criminal justice

TABLE 1.3 Skills and Competencies Crucial in Criminal Investigators

Rational thinking (deductive and inductive reasoning)	This includes the ability to relate a large number of seemingly unrelated facts. The investigator must let facts determine a hypothesis and theory, rather than fitting facts into a preexisting theory. The hypothesis and theory must be based on scientific (objective) observation and recall.
Critical thinking	The investigator must be able to "see" and not just look; to allow critical thinking to flow as facts are gathered and a hypothesis is synthesized.
Analytic thinking	The investigator must recognize evidence or potential loci of trace evidence and digest information from numerous sources. He or she must have the ability to see where pieces of the puzzle may fit based on the relationship of various bits of information to other bits of information.
Ethics and integrity	The investigator should possess a personal philosophy based on honor, integrity, and duty and should avoid confusion, ambiguity, and corruption.
Human anatomy	The investigator should be able to determine the nature and quality of wounds inflicted on a victim and to separate postmortem (after death) from antemortem (before death) injuries. He or she should be able to recognize defensive wounds and possible rape.
Human physiology	The investigator should know something about putrefaction (gas formation) and decomposition, as well as insect larvae cycles and marine depredation.
Psychology	All human discourse is based on concepts of worth and esteem. An ability to assess the mental state of victims, witnesses, and suspects is essential for successful interviewing and interrogation.
Sociology	Effective communication depends on the ability to recognize socioeconomic factors and their effect on the language, customs, and sensitivities of victims, witnesses, and suspects.
Archaeology	Like field and marine archaeologists, the criminal investigator must locate all evidence geographically (where) and temporally (when).
Pharmacology	In a death or drug investigation, the investigator may need to identify controlled substances, clandestine laboratories, or death as a result of poison.
Firearms	In a society that values self-defense and handguns, the investigator must be able to handle, identify, and process firearms safely.
Language and communication	Approximately 90% of what an investigator does involves language-based communication, from interviews to court testimony.
Constitutional law	Of what value is a superb investigation if, in the process, individual constitutional rights are violated, rendering evidence inadmissible?
Law of evidence and its admissibility	Although it is not necessary to be a lawyer to be a competent criminal investigator, it is necessary to know the evidentiary predicates (formal steps required of a lawyer attempting to admit particular types of evidence) for all evidence to be admitted at the time of trial.
Criminalistics (forensic science)	The more an investigator knows about forensic evidence, the less likely mishandling and contamination are to occur.

— Ripped from the Headlines —

What Does It Take to Become a Police Officer?

Tested both mentally and physically for over 28 weeks, the most important aspect of what it takes to become a police officer happens prior to the classroom. "First, you have to start with the passion to do the job. It's not just a job, it's a calling."

Recruits are trained in firearms, driving, defensive tactics, communication skills, problem-solving skills, crisis intervention, cultural competency, laws, investigations, policies and procedures, report writing, de-escalation, and mental and physical health. It is difficult and exhausting training. It is conducted in a stressful, burdensome manner for a reason. "Because sometimes, on a shift, you will be on a scene and you're mentally exhausted, but

you have to remember what you're taught and remember why you're there."

Police and investigative training doesn't end with academy graduation, however. The field is built upon continuing education. If a person is not the type who enjoys lifelong learning, police and investigative work is not for them.

Data from Pagan, G. (2017). What it takes to become a Knoxville police officer. Retrieved from http://wate.com/2017/07/06/what-it-takes-to -become-a-knoxville-police-officer/

© Shutterstock, Inc./rzarek.

curricula will require more science, computer, and law courses and will favor minors in science rather than sociology or psychology. Most agencies recognize that detective candidates need:

- An active imagination
- Patience
- An ability to be a team player
- An ability to communicate
- An ability to recognize his or her audience
- An understanding of search and seizure law and its application
- An understanding of *Miranda v. Arizona* and the line of cases flowing from it
- Tenacity
- Honesty and integrity
- Good physical condition
- Excellent writing skills
- An ability to recognize discrimination and remove it from the investigative process
- An ability to testify objectively and professionally
- An ability to be a leader

The Legal Team

Investigators and prosecutors are the most visible members of the criminal investigation team. Mutual respect fosters communication and assists in the trial and pretrial process, but the relationship between prosecutors and police

beyond a reasonable doubt
The standard of certainty necessary to convict someone of a crime

arrest
To place a person in the custody of a law enforcement agency

is often adversarial or nonexistent. Police think that prosecutors frequently dismiss good cases or plea-bargain cases that should be tried. In most instances, their attitude toward prosecutors is a product of a difference in the legal criteria police and prosecutors use in carrying out their duties. Whereas police need only probable cause to arrest a suspect, prosecutors must prove a case **beyond a reasonable doubt**—two different standards. When this fact is noted, it makes sense that conflict will sometimes arise between police, who may believe they have a good case and made a "righteous" arrest, and prosecutors, who may not see sufficient evidence to win a conviction. Police may have done everything correctly and their case may still not satisfy the legal requirements for a conviction.

Police are bound by Fourth Amendment considerations in the delivery of their services to the community (**EXHIBIT 1.2**). Police must have probable cause to search or to seize people or property. The seizure of people is called **arrest**, and it must be predicated upon information that would convince a reasonable person that a crime has been or is about to be committed. In trying to understand the standard of probable cause, it is often useful to view it as requiring a 51% probability that the individual has committed or is committing a crime (i.e., it is more likely than not).

Prosecutors, on the other hand, must evaluate evidence in its entirety, including that which justifies the arrest, and must determine whether they can convict the defendant on evidence beyond a reasonable doubt. For comparison purposes, we can consider reasonable

EXHIBIT 1.2

The Fourth Amendment to the U.S. Constitution

The right of the people to be secure in their persons, houses, papers and effects, against unreasonable searches and seizures, shall not be violated, and no warrants shall issue, but upon probable cause, supported by oath or affirmation, and particularly describing the place to be searched, and the persons or things to be seized.

© Shutterstock, Inc./Africa Studio.

U.S. Constitution. Art./Amend. IV.

doubt as approximately equivalent to requiring more than a 90% probability that the person has committed the crime for which he or she is charged. That 39% difference (between 51% and 90%) constitutes a considerable gap and partly explains why arrest rates are higher than conviction rates. Police and prosecutorial staff will find it easier to cultivate a good relationship if they understand and appreciate that difference.

Prosecutors prosecute those cases in which they have confidence. That confidence is based on the quantity and quality of evidence, the quality of documentation supporting an investigation, and the ability of investigative witnesses to communicate from the witness stand.

If the conditions are favorable to the prosecution, the case will be prosecuted or a severe plea bargain will be reached. Victories do no damage to a prosecutor's or to an investigator's career. Victory is self-perpetuating. If an investigator's cases consistently meet the conditions described above, they will be prosecuted consistently and conviction will result frequently. If, on the other hand, a case fails to meet one of these conditions, the probability of prosecution or conviction (if the case is prosecuted) diminishes. A prosecutor who has serious misgivings about a case or about an investigator is less likely to prosecute not only the case in question but also future cases handled by that investigator.

Admissibility of Evidence

It is the investigator's job to collect all of the available evidence, and it is the prosecutor's and the court's job to weigh the significance of the evidence. The first threshold that evidence must

pass is that of proof of admissibility in court, called the **predicate**. All investigators must not only have an understanding of the rules of evidence admissibility but also a working knowledge of the foundation upon which all types of evidence are ushered before the court. It also pays to have a working relationship with the prosecutor and an understanding of the prosecutor's style when he or she asks formal questions, allowing evidence to be admitted. New prosecutors may be less familiar with required evidentiary predicates than an experienced investigator. If the appropriate predicate is absent, evidence that would otherwise admissible will not be admitted. It is helpful if the testifying investigator can assist the prosecutor in establishing the necessary predicates and can anticipate the types of questions that will establish those predicates. For example, the predicate for admitting photographs is not complicated, but the standard could remain unmet if either the prosecutor or the testifying investigator is not familiar with the format.

All evidence has a specific predicate that must precede its submission to the court. In essence, all evidence comes to the jury through the mouth of a witness. A piece of evidence will have no bearing on the outcome of the case, despite having been appropriately handled, stored, and presented to the prosecution, if the **evidentiary foundation** (predicate) for its admissibility is lacking. Once evidence has passed the test of admissibility and is made a part of the court record, it has the potential to influence the outcome of the trial. Such evidence is said to be **probative** (more likely than not to prove a fact in issue). Evidence is not the same as a fact. Facts are derived from evidence. Evidence may tend to prove a fact, or may not, or it may be just strong enough to create a reasonable doubt.

The investigator must know what evidence is required to determine the issue of guilt; whether such evidence indicates or fails to indicate guilt; and, when guilt is apparent, whether such evidence is likely to prove guilt beyond a reasonable doubt. The success of an investigation, as already noted, depends on the evidence collected and its legal significance. It is important to remember that a verdict of acquittal does not mean the defendant is innocent, but rather that the defendant has not been proven guilty beyond a reasonable doubt. A not-guilty verdict is not always a vindication, contrary to what defendants usually claim, as evidenced by findings of negligence in a civil suit based on the same testimony and evidence.

predicate
Proof of admissibility in court

evidentiary foundation
Basis for a conclusion that was determined using collected evidence; predicate

probative
Likely to prove a fact

INVESTIGATOR'S NOTEBOOK

Proper In-Court Admission of Evidence

Q: Lieutenant, I hand you what has been marked as State's Exhibit No. 1 and ask you if you recognize it.
A: Yes.
Q: What is it?
A: A photograph of the bedroom at 337 Sisterdale Road.
Q: Does it fairly and accurately portray the scene as you remember it?
A: Yes.

    The prosecution would then offer the photo to the defense for any objections. Once those objections had been addressed, the prosecution would offer the photograph to the court as evidence.

CONCLUSION

In this chapter, we were introduced to the world of the criminal investigator, and we discovered some of the players and some of the contributors to the methodology employed in processing a crime scene. It must be noted that an entire academic life could be spent studying the history of criminal investigation in the United States and in England and that the purpose of this chapter is to provide only a historic perspective. The ultimate objective of all of the work done by criminal investigators, laboratory personnel, and prosecutors is to be able to present the discovered evidence in a court of law. Recent news reports tell us of serologists and DNA technicians who have fabricated evidence in an effort to save time and effort. Even in the trial of O.J. Simpson, where the suspect was accused of multiple homicides, forensic personnel handled evidence with their bare hands and a criminal investigator lied on the witness stand. To what end is the best investigation if what we discover cannot be presented at trial?

Everything brought to the crime laboratory came from a crime scene. As such, the next chapter deals with crime scenes and the information needed to understand the nature, breadth, and scope of what is left to be processed after a crime has been committed.

QUESTIONS FOR REVIEW

1. Are all crimes solvable?

2. What are the seven objectives of a police investigation?

3. What was the significance to investigators of the U.S. Supreme Court decision in *Miranda v. Arizona*?

4. What are the steps and characteristics of a successful criminal investigation?

5. What types of skills and competencies should a criminal investigator possess?

6. What is the purpose of using the scientific method?

7. What is meant by "all evidence comes to the jury through the mouth of a witness"?

8. What type of law enforcement system was established in early colonial America? Where did it come from and what were its shortcomings?

9. What were thief catchers, and what role did they play in the evolution of law enforcement in London?

10. Who were the Bow Street Runners, and what contribution did they make to the evolution of English law enforcement?

11. How did the office of coroner evolve, and what was its impact on the establishment of the office of medical examiner?

12. What is DNA?

13. What was Alec Jeffrey's contribution to the study of DNA?

14. What role does the AAFS play in the standardization of forensic processes?

15. What was Edward T. Blake's contribution to forensic science?

16. What crime did Tommie Lee Andrews commit?

17. Who was Paul Leland Kirk?

REFERENCES

Beeler, L., & Wiebe, W. R. (1988). DNA identification tests and the courts. *Washington Law Review, 63*, 903.

Begg, P. (2004). *Jack the Ripper: The facts*. London: Robson Books.

Browne, W. H. (Ed.). (1885). *Archives of Maryland. Vol. 3*. Baltimore, MD: Maryland Historical Society.

Burns, J. (2017, April 11). Sessions scraps Federal Commission on forensic accuracy, for some reason. *Forbes Magazine*. Retrieved July 7, 2017, from https://www.forbes.com/sites/janetwburns/2017/04/11/sessions-scraps-federal-commission-on-forensic-accuracy-because-reasons/#8176a776c219

Galton, F. (1892). *Finger prints*. London: MacMillan.

James, R. (2009, June 19). A brief history of DNA testing. *Time*. Retrieved August 14, 2011, from http://www.time.com/time/nation/article/0,8599,1905706,00.html

Johnson, H. A., Wolfe N. T., & Jones, M. (2008). *History of criminal justice* (4th ed.). Burlington, MA: Elsevier.

Kirk, P. L. (1953). *Crime investigation*. New York, NY: Interscience.

Latrobe, J. G. (1861). *Justices' practice under the laws of Maryland* (6th ed.). Baltimore, MD: Lucas.

Linebaugh, P. (1991). *The London hanged: Crime and civil society in the eighteenth century*. London: Veros.

McMullan, J. L. (1996). The new improved monied police: Reform, crime control, and the modification of policing in London. *British Journal of Criminology, 36*, 85–108.

Miller, W. R. (1977). *Cops and bobbies: Police authority in New York and London, 1830–1870*. Chicago, IL: University of Chicago Press.

National Institute of Justice. (1999). *Forensic sciences: Review of status and needs*. Retrieved August 13, 2011, from www.ncjrs.gov/pdffiles1/173412.pdf

Osterburg, J. W., & Ward, R. H. (2010). *Criminal investigation: A method of reconstructing the past* (6th ed.). New Providence, NJ: LexisNexis Group.

Pagan, G. (2017, July 6). What it takes to become a Knoxville police officer. *WATE.com*. Retrieved July 7, 2017, from http://wate.com/2017/07/06/what-it-takes-to-become-a-knoxville-police-officer/

Radzinowicz, L. (1986). *A history of English criminal law and its administration from 1750*. London: Stephens.

Spitz, W. U., Spitz, D. J., & Fisher, R. S. (2006). *Spitz and Fisher's medicolegal investigation of death: Guidelines for the application of pathology to crime scenes* (4th ed.). Springfield, IL: Charles Thomas.

Thorwald, J. (1965). *The century of the detective*. New York, NY: Harcourt World.

Tobias, J. J. (1979). *Crime and police in England 1700–1900*. London: St. Martin's Press.

Wambaugh, J. (1985). *The blooding*. New York, NY: Bantam.

chapter

2

The Laws of Search and Seizure

You see, Watson, no mystery; everything above-board! In some way the legal forms have undoubtedly been complied with, and they think that they have little to fear.

Sherlock Holmes
"A Reminiscence of Sherlock Holmes"

KEY TERMS

arm's-reach concept
consent search
curtilage
derivative evidence
due process
due process clause
emergency exception
exclusionary rule
exigent circumstances
frisk

fruit-of-the-poisonous-tree doctrine
good faith exception
immediately apparent
inadvertent discovery
inevitable discovery doctrine
inventory
legitimately on the premises

Miranda warnings
open field
probable cause
reasonableness
return
search incident to an arrest
stop
vehicle inventory
warrant affidavit
warrant procedure

STUDENT LEARNING OUTCOMES

Upon completion of this chapter, students will be able to:

- Explain due process of the law
- Discuss warrantless searches and seizures pursuant to the Fourth Amendment
- Recognize the guarantee against self-incrimination as defined in the Fifth Amendment
- Describe the implication of *Miranda v. Arizona* for criminal investigations

The U.S. Constitution and Due Process

The U.S. Constitution is a blueprint for the building of a democratic government. It outlines the structure of the U.S. government and the powers granted to the three branches. The authors of the Constitution realized that they had not included guarantees of individual freedom, despite the fact that violations of the colonists' individual rights laid the foundation for the American Revolution. The founders amended the Constitution to include guarantees that addressed the original grievances against the English crown. The first 10 amendments of the U.S. Constitution, known as the Bill of Rights, form the groundwork of **due process**, specifically, those rights considered to be criminal procedural rights, which are contained in the Fourth, Fifth, and Sixth Amendments to the U.S. Constitution. These three amendments and their case law interpretations have established the fundamentals of due process.

The Bill of Rights was not intended to apply to the states. It was the objective of the drafters of the Constitution to protect the citizens of the colonies from an oppressive central government, a government insensitive to the rights of its citizens, a government that levied abuses upon its citizenry; since that is what many feared within the 18th-century English government After passage of the Fourteenth Amendment (**EXHIBIT 2.1**), the U.S. Supreme Court began to interpret the due process guaranteed in this amendment as the same due process guaranteed in the Bill of Rights. Over time, the Bill of Rights was incorporated into what is now the Fourteenth Amendment until virtually all of it had been made part of this amendment's due process clause.

The Fourteenth Amendment contains three separate but equally important clauses:

1. The privileges and immunities clause
2. The due process clause
3. The equal protection clause

We will be most concerned with the **due process clause** as we study searches and seizures. The Supreme Court has embraced the Fourth, Fifth, and Sixth Amendments as the touchstones that limit the discretion available to police in conducting searches of people and places and in seizing people and things.

The Fourth Amendment

The Fourth Amendment provides two guarantees that ensure citizens due process when confronted by police seeking to conduct a search or to seize a person or thing. First, it proclaims, "the right of the people to be secure in their persons, houses, papers, and effects, against unreasonable searches and seizures, shall not be violated." The most important part of this procedural safeguard is that all searches and seizures must be reasonable. The Supreme Court has gone to significant lengths to define what kind of searches and seizures are reasonable. An understanding of **reasonableness** as promulgated by the Court can only be achieved by examining some of the salient cases that provide the definition of reasonableness.

Second, the amendment proclaims, "no warrants shall issue, but upon probable cause, supported by oath or affirmation, and particularly describing the place to be searched, and the persons or things to be seized." When we think of seizures, we generally think of things other than persons, but the Fourth Amendment provides for the restrictions on police conduct in effecting an arrest. Disputes pertaining to this clause generally arise in regard to the **probable cause** requirement for a warrant to search or arrest. Probable cause to arrest is information upon which a reasonable person would believe that a crime has been committed or is about to be committed. Probable cause to search is the minimum information a reasonable person would need to believe that an item is where it is purported to be. Not only must police have reasonable information that the item in question is contraband, the fruit of a crime, or otherwise illegal to possess, but they must also have reasonable information as to the location of the item.

EXHIBIT 2.1

The Fourteenth Amendment to the U.S. Constitution

Section 1. All persons born or naturalized in the United States, and subject to the jurisdiction thereof, are citizens of the United States and of the State wherein they reside. No state shall make or enforce any law that shall abridge the privileges or immunities of citizens of the United States: nor shall any State deprive any person of life, liberty, or property, without due process of law; nor deny to any person within its jurisdiction the equal protection of the law.

© Shutterstock, Inc./Africa Studio.

U.S. Constitution. Art./Amend. XIV.

due process clause
A constitutional provision that prohibits the government from unfairly or arbitrarily depriving a person of life, liberty, or property

due process
The conduct of legal proceedings according to established rules and principles

reasonableness
The quality of being fair, proper, or moderate under the given circumstances

probable cause
A reasonable ground to suspect that a person has committed or is committing a crime or that a place contains specific items connected with a crime

■ Expectation of Privacy

U.S. citizens believe in a right of privacy that is enforceable through the Fourth Amendment. An examination of the Fourth Amendment carries no mention of privacy; in fact, an examination of the Bill of Rights carries no mention of privacy. How is it that Americans have come to recognize a right of privacy, protected under the U.S. Constitution? The U.S. Supreme Court in *Griswold v. Connecticut* (1965) found a right of privacy in the Bill of Rights and lodged firmly in the Fourth Amendment. Griswold was the executive director of the Planned Parenthood League, and Dr. Buxton was a licensed physician who served as medical director of the league. The league provided information, instruction, and medical advice to a married couple on how to prevent conception. Provision of such information was a violation of a Connecticut statute. Griswold and Dr. Buxton were found guilty of having violated state statute and were fined $100. Their appeals were ineffective until they reached the U.S. Supreme Court. Justice Douglas, writing for a majority, found that information of the type provided in this case was a matter of personal privacy. Although the word "privacy" was found nowhere in the Constitution, Justice Douglas described the right of privacy as a penumbral right, emanating from the Third, Fourth, Fifth, and Eighth Amendments to the Constitution and enforceable through the Fourteenth Amendment's due process clause. In time, the right of privacy came to be lodged and included within the Fourth Amendment.

The question left unanswered by *Griswold* was about which types of privacy were protected. The Supreme Court gave the concept wide latitude for interpretation. In *California v. Greenwood* (1988), the Supreme Court had to deal with an unusual set of circumstances. The Greenwoods were using and selling drugs. Complaints by neighbors about the noise and traffic at the Greenwood residence put police on notice. Seeking probable cause for a warrant, the police placed the Greenwood residence under surveillance. They confirmed the noise and traffic but also noticed that the Greenwoods placed their garbage on the curb for pickup. The police contacted the garbage collectors and asked them to pick up the Greenwood's garbage, keep it separate, and give it to them. Upon examination of the contents of the garbage, police discovered evidence of use of narcotics. A warrant was issued, a search was conducted, and narcotics were found. The Greenwoods claimed that they had an "expectation of privacy" in their garbage, which was manifest in the fact that

the garbage bag was opaque, closed, and under the control of the Greenwoods. The Supreme Court held that the Greenwoods may have had an expectation of privacy in their garbage, but not all expectations of privacy were protected under the Fourth Amendment. Only those expectations that society accepts as reasonable are protected. Because garbage outside of the **curtilage** of the home is available to marauding pests, children, and adults, it is also available to the police. Garbage placed in the public domain outside of the curtilage of the home does not have an expectation of privacy recognized by the Court.

Since September 11, 2001, legislation has been passed providing what is seen as extraordinary power to federal law enforcement agencies. The Fourth Amendment protects the right of the people to be secure in their persons, houses, papers, and effects. The primary abuse that this amendment addressed was the colonial practice of law enforcement and military personnel entering a residence to seize a person or thing. The primary protection is to homes, people, and things associated directly with people and their homes. The right does not protect against:

- Books checked out of the library
- Videos checked out of video stores
- Hospital records
- Photographs taken in public
- Videos taken in public

It has become popular to complain about these things and invoke illusory rights within the Fourth Amendment as having been violated. There are state tort laws that protect privacy and property rights that have nothing to do with the Fourth Amendment.

An analysis of the Fourth Amendment is a four-part process. It goes something like this:

1. Is there government conduct?
2. Is there an expectation of privacy?

If both are present, a Fourth Amendment issue is present. The two fundamental elements are government conduct and an expectation of privacy. It should be noted that when we talk about the Fourth Amendment and the "government conduct" requirement, we usually refer to police in some context. However, that element can be met by a school principal, a hospital administrator, or a prison guard or warden. This element does not require a specific law enforcement quality, but only the force from a government

curtilage
The area surrounding a home that is used in the course of daily living

employee. The "expectation of privacy" element is comparatively straightforward. If the behavior involves a person, his or her home or possessions, or anything directly associated with him or her, an expectation of privacy probably exists. Keep in mind that in *California v. Greenwood*, the Supreme Court said that not all expectations of privacy are protected under the Fourth Amendment, but only those that society sees as reasonable and only if that expectation deals with a person or that person's home, possessions, or curtilage.

Once it has been determined that there is a Fourth Amendment issue, the next step is to determine if the conduct in question is reasonable. There are two elements to the reasonableness requirement:

1. A warrant was issued.
2. An exception to the warrant requirement applies.

The basic premise upon which the Fourth Amendment rests is this: All searches and seizures of persons and things are presumed unconstitutional without a warrant.

Even though there are numerous warrant exceptions based on probable cause, reasonable suspicion, or a reasonable government interest, it is easy to forget in light of all of the applicable exceptions that the idea is to obtain a warrant whenever practicable (reasonable). Once a warrant has been obtained, appropriate police conduct in searching and seizing by default is reasonable. The only question then is whether the warrant is valid—that is, it contains the correct address, person, property, and so on. However, a warrant takes time. Using an exception to the warrant requirement puts the burden of proof on the searching or seizing officer to explain what the exception is and how it applies to the pertinent situation. If it turns out that the warrant exception that police were relying on was inapplicable, all evidence seized and any statements made will be inadmissible. Get a warrant whenever possible. Find a magistrate who will not sign just anything. Find one who will apply a rigorous examination of the affidavit in support of the request for a warrant. That kind of judge can save you a lot of time in the long run.

It is important to have a word about the affidavit submitted in support of a warrant. The affidavit provides a narration of the probable cause that the officer has and a list of things the officer seeks. The courts recognize that not everything investigators expect to find pursuant to a warrant needs to be included. Some things may be so readily identifiable that they would be recognized as being illegal to possess without examining them. If a warrant provides for a particular pistol, and while searching for that pistol in places a pistol may be secreted, a firearms suppressor is spotted, it may be seized pursuant to the "plain view" rule. If police immediately recognize that what they see is illegal to possess, they can seize it. When drafting warrant affidavits, it makes sense to let the "plain view" rule work for you. You may not need to include everything that was stolen in an affidavit, but

— Ripped from the Headlines —

Police Chief Says Housing Authority Is to Blame for Search Confusion

A Longmont, Colorado, police chief insists that his officers did nothing wrong when they accompanied property management on mandatory landlord inspections and asked if they could search for drugs.

Property management sent residents a letter giving them the legally required "notice to enter." Included within the notification was the following: "Please note that we will occasionally have K-9 units with LPD accompany us for purposes of training and compliance. Apartments will be chosen at random."

Subsequently, a tenant refused entry to an officer and K-9, but the officer still made entry after building management told her they were allowed to look around, just not look inside any drawers.

At issue are the tenant's Fourth Amendment rights to privacy and voluntariness. Also, whether the terms "training," "compliance" and "random" used within the notice of entrance were entirely truthful.

Data from Clark, K. (2017). *Longmont police chief says housing authority is to blame for search confusion.* Retrieved July 7, 2017, from http://www.9news.com/news/local/next/longmont-police-chief-says-housing-authority-is-to-blame-for-search-confusion/446727711

you should always include the smallest thing taken. The size of the smallest object listed in the warrant dictates where the search can be conducted. A firearm can be hidden in a drawer but not a small box. Ammunition may be hidden in a small box. An affidavit to search for a pistol should include the ammunition for the pistol, thereby broadening the area where the search can be conducted.

The Fifth Amendment

Because of the colonists' experience at the hands of a government that denied them the right to remain silent and allowed coerced confessions to be used against them in colonial courts presided over by British jurists, the drafters of the Bill of Rights included a provision that specifically forbade the government from requiring that a person incriminate him- or herself. Through later Supreme Court decisions, the self-incrimination clause of the Fifth Amendment took on unprecedented significance in American jurisprudence.

The clause provides testimonial protection, with its focus being the spoken word (and, in some instances, the written word). It is important to understand the testimonial nature of the protection offered by the amendment when considering police conduct. A videotape of a person performing badly during a field sobriety test is as incriminating as an admission that he or she is, in fact, intoxicated. Yet, the videotape is admissible at the time of trial, whereas the confession is not, at least absent certain judicially required warnings explaining the right to remain silent. At first glance, there seems to be little difference in the potential effects upon the jury of the videotape and a confession. It is not the impact that is the determining difference but the nature of the self-incriminating evidence. One is an instance of verbal self-incrimination prohibited by the Fifth Amendment; the other is not.

The Supreme Court has laid down a further condition for the applicability of the Fifth Amendment: The admission or verbal statement must have resulted from an attempt on the part of the police to solicit such a statement or must have occurred during the gathering of criminal evidence.

The Sixth Amendment

The Sixth Amendment requires that a person caught up in the criminal justice system be provided legal representation. When dealing with the police, at what point is a citizen entitled to the assistance of counsel? The answer is: at the point at which he or she asks for such assistance. The Supreme Court, however, has determined that this fundamental right may not be known, may be forgotten, or may be unevoked because of intimidation or fear. In a far-reaching decision in *Miranda v. Arizona* (1966), the Supreme Court required that a series of warnings be provided whenever a citizen is subjected to an interrogation while in the custody of the police. These warnings, in recognition of the landmark nature of the case, are commonly known as **Miranda warnings**.

The Sixth Amendment contributed to the content of the Miranda warnings: "In all criminal prosecutions, the accused shall enjoy the right ... to have the assistance of counsel for his defense." Although the amendment speaks

Miranda warnings
Warnings read to a suspect in police custody that inform the suspect of his or her constitutional rights

---

CASE IN POINT

Pennsylvania v. Muniz, 1990

In the case of *Pennsylvania v. Muniz* (1990), an officer stopped Muniz's vehicle and directed him to undergo standard field sobriety tests, which, unbeknownst to him, were videotaped. He performed poorly and was taken into custody. At the station, he was booked, and as part of the booking process, he was asked for seven standard pieces of information, including his name, address, height, weight, eye color, date of birth, and age. He was also asked to give the year in which his 6th birthday occurred. The videotape and the answer to the question about his 6th birthday were admitted at the time of his trial over the objection of the defendant's lawyer. Muniz was convicted of driving under the influence.

The Supreme Court held that police may ask routine questions of a person suspected of driving while under the influence and may videotape their responses without violating the defendant's Fifth Amendment right prohibiting self-incrimination. The routine questions and the videotape do not elicit testimonial responses that are protected by the Fifth Amendment. The question about Muniz's 6th birthday, however, was not a routine question. It was designed to elicit an incriminating response during a criminal investigation (a response that was testimonial in nature) and was, therefore, in violation of the Fifth Amendment.

specifically of "criminal prosecutions," the Supreme Court has presumed that the investigation of a criminal offense begins the prosecutorial process and thus brings into play the right to the assistance of counsel.

The Exclusionary Rule

History

In *Weeks v. United States* (1914), the Supreme Court decided that evidence obtained (seized) as a result of an illegal search, arrest, or interrogation would not be admissible at the time of trial (i.e., it would be excluded). This case applied only to the federal government and its law enforcement agencies. It was not until 1961 that the states felt the brunt of the holding in the Weeks case.

In addition to imposing federal constitutional standards on police within the states, the Supreme Court, in *Mapp v. Ohio* (1961), indicated that both the Fourth and Fifth Amendments were the genesis of the exclusionary rule, which meant that the **exclusionary rule** would govern illegal searches and seizures and

also that illegally obtained confessions would be excluded at the time of trial.

The logical extension of the exclusionary rule as a deterrent to police misconduct in conducting searches, seizures, or interrogations is to exclude any evidence discovered as a result of an illegally conducted search, seizure, or interrogation. An illegally obtained confession is excluded, and any evidence discovered as the result of the confession is likewise excluded. Such evidence is referred to as **derivative evidence** and is subject to the exclusionary rule. The idea that evidence can be derivatively tainted is commonly called the **fruit-of-the-poisonous-tree doctrine**.

Exceptions

The easiest way to avoid the impact of the exclusionary rule is to obtain a search warrant and execute that warrant legally—that is, in a manner consistent with the authorization contained in the warrant. Remember that the presumption regarding searches and seizures is that, without a warrant, all searches and seizures of persons and things are presumed unconstitutional. However, Supreme Court justices

derivative evidence
Evidence found as the result of a confession or the seizure of other evidence; usually used to denote evidence that is tainted by being acquired as a result of illegally obtained original evidence

fruit-of-the-poisonous-tree doctrine
Common name for the idea that evidence can be tainted derivatively

exclusionary rule
Rule resulting from *Weeks v. United States* (1914) that excludes evidence at the time of trial that was obtained (seized) as a result of an illegal search, arrest, or interrogation

CASE IN POINT

Mapp v. Ohio, 1961

In 1961, three Cleveland police officers went to the residence of Dolree Mapp, looking for a person who was wanted for a recent bombing. The officers demanded entrance but were refused. After the arrival of other officers, the police broke down the door. Mapp demanded that she be shown the search warrant authorizing the intrusion into and the search of her home. When a paper was held up by one of the officers, Mapp grabbed the paper and placed it in the bodice of her blouse. The police forcibly removed the paper and handcuffed Mapp. A search of the house produced no bomber but did produce some drawings and books that the police believed to be obscene. The materials were admitted into evidence during the trial over Mapp's objection. Dolree Mapp was convicted of possession of obscene materials.

The Supreme Court held that the exclusionary rule promulgated in *Weeks* and applicable in federal cases was also applicable in state criminal proceedings. There were three questions that the Court had to address in *Mapp v. Ohio*:

1. Was there a warrant?

2. If not, was there an exception to the warrant requirement?

3. If the search was, in fact, illegal, what remedy should be applied?

There was no warrant produced at the time of the trial, although the probable cause that the police had could have been best used to obtain a warrant. There are few exceptions to the warrant requirement that override the privacy inherent in a person's home. A prior panel of Supreme Court justices, in *Wolf v. Colorado* (1949), had determined that the exclusionary rule born in *Weeks* did not apply to the states. That Court believed that there were sufficient state remedies available to a person who had been illegally arrested or searched and that it was unnecessary to extend federal protection against such police conduct. Yet, in this case, *Wolf v. Colorado* (1949) was overturned and the exclusionary rule was extended to the states.

inevitable discovery doctrine
Doctrine that allows derivative evidence that would generally be rendered inadmissible by the fruit-of-the-poisonous-tree doctrine to be admitted if the evidence would have been discovered anyway, without the assistance of the illegally seized evidence

good faith exception
Exception to the exclusionary rule that allows evidence obtained illegally to be used in trial when the officers obtaining the evidence had reason to believe that they were operating under a warrant that was issued properly

are not able to foresee all situations, and most rules have exceptions. The Court has defined the exclusionary rule further to assist police in determining what conduct is acceptable in conducting searches and seizures. The object of the exclusionary rule is to deter police misconduct. If important evidence is excluded, it may be impossible to obtain a conviction based on the remaining evidence.

■ The Inevitable Discovery Exception

In an effort to ameliorate the impact of the exclusionary rule, the Court proffered the **inevitable discovery doctrine** in the 1984 case of *Nix v. Williams*. Simply stated, the doctrine allows derivative evidence that would generally be rendered inadmissible by the fruit-of-the-poisonous-tree doctrine to be admitted if the evidence would have been discovered anyway, without the assistance of the illegally seized evidence.

The Supreme Court decided that although fruit-of-the-poisonous-tree evidence is usually inadmissible, it may be admissible if the state can prove that the evidence would have been discovered anyway by legal means. The state must prove, through police testimony, the inevitability of the discovery; simply saying that it would have been inevitable is not sufficient.

■ The Good Faith Exception

The most significant exception to the exclusionary rule, the **good faith exception**, results from the Supreme Court's decision in *United States v.*

Leon (1984). Acting on information provided by an informant, police began a drug investigation. Three deputy district attorneys prepared and reviewed an affidavit for a search warrant and, in response to the affidavit, a state court judge issued the requested warrant. A search of the premises disclosed large quantities of drugs. The defendant was indicted, but his motion to suppress evidence was granted based on the fact that the affidavit and warrant contained insufficient probable cause. The Court dismissed the case against the defendant.

The Fourth Amendment allows the use of evidence obtained by officers acting in reasonable reliance on a search warrant issued by a neutral and detached magistrate, even if the warrant is ultimately found to be invalid. Once the officer has complied with the prerequisites for obtaining a warrant, there is little more that the officer can do to comply with the law. Furthermore, there is little deterrent value in penalizing the officer for the magistrate's error. Any evidence seized in a search conducted pursuant to a warrant that was issued by a neutral and impartial magistrate, appearing valid on its face, and procured without fraud on the part of the police is immune to exclusion. It goes without saying that the prudent officer will obtain a search warrant whenever possible. The value of the warrant is not only that it ensures that probable cause in fact exists, but also that it avoids lengthy pretrial suppression motions because it affords immunity to police pursuant to the "good faith" holding of *United States v. Leon* (1984).

CASE IN POINT

Nix v. Williams, 1984

On December 24, 1984, a 10-year-old girl was kidnapped from a YMCA in Des Moines, Iowa. A man, later determined to be Robert Williams, was seen carrying a large bundle wrapped in a blanket with two skinny, white legs protruding. Williams's car was later found 160 miles east of Des Moines. Articles of clothing belonging to the missing child and a blanket were found at a rest stop between the YMCA in Des Moines and where the car was found. The car and the YMCA became the east and west boundaries for a massive search. Williams was arrested in Davenport, close to where the car had been found, and was arraigned. The attorney for the defendant was told that Williams was to be returned to Des Moines. The attorney told the transporting police that they were not to interrogate his client. During the return trip, one of the officers engaged Williams in conversation. Knowing Williams to be a lay preacher, the officer began what became known as the "Christian burial speech," in which he told Williams that the girl should be given a Christian burial before a snowstorm prevented the body from being found. Williams agreed to take the officers to the child's body. The body was found about 2 miles from where the search party was looking.

At the trial, a motion to suppress was denied, and Williams was convicted of first-degree murder. On appeal, it was determined that the evidence was wrongfully admitted as a product of an illegal interrogation (interrogation in the absence of the suspect's lawyer). At the second trial, the prosecutor did not offer Williams's statement into evidence and did not seek to show that Williams had led the police to the body, but rather that the body would have been discovered had the search continued. Williams was convicted of murder.

INVESTIGATOR'S NOTEBOOK

Warrant Procedures

The **warrant procedure** comprises three individual actions on the part of the police:

1. Drafting an affidavit that, on its face, establishes, to the satisfaction of a neutral and detached magistrate, sufficient probable cause

2. Serving the warrant

3. Preparing and rendering the search warrant return

Experience and preparation are the keys to preparing an adequate search **warrant affidavit**. It is better to provide too much information than not enough. A competent magistrate will not ask any questions pertaining to probable cause and the information contained in the affidavit. The language used should be free of jargon and abbreviations, because defense counsel will scrutinize it should the matter progress to trial or to a suppression motion. Real skill is required to be able to draft readable, legally sufficient search warrant affidavits.

It goes without saying that everything contained in an affidavit should be true or corroborated. Known falsities repeal the "good faith" defense against defective warrants. The affidavit is a legal road map that tells the magistrate what has been done in obtaining probable cause and what is going to be done with it. Each legally sufficient affidavit includes the following:

- A statement outlining the facts the officer believes constitute probable cause

- A description of what the probable cause allows to be sought

- Identification of the places the probable cause allows to be searched

Keep in mind that the search is not over until the things sought have been found or the possibilities for searching have been exhausted. When filling out the affidavit, the officer should include the smallest item sought that is supported by the probable cause. A warrant for a rifle allows only those places that can house a rifle to be searched legitimately. A warrant for a rifle and ammunition increases the scope of the search and allows a search of those places that could house a rifle or rifle ammunition. Exceptions to the warrant requirement are discussed later in the chapter, but during a search, anything found that is illegal to possess, even if it was not included in the warrant, is seizable if the place where it is discovered is a possible location for the items being sought.

Every search warrant (**EXHIBIT 2.2**) must contain certain essentials to pass constitutional and legal muster. All warrants contain the following:

1. Authorization by a magistrate in the name of and by the authority of the state

2. Authorization to seize specifically described items

3. Issuance based on probable cause

4. A specific location (to be confused with no other)

5. Authorization granted to a specifically named officer

6. A return that includes the following:
   a. Date of the search
   b. Items seized
   c. Name of the serving officer
   d. Signature of the serving officer
   e. Signature of the issuing magistrate

The **return** is an itemized inventory of all of the property seized by the executing officers. It is prepared in duplicate, and a copy is left with the defendant or, in his or her absence, at the residence. The original is returned to the issuing magistrate no later than 24 hours after service of the warrant.

---

warrant procedure Three individual actions on the part of the police: (1) drafting an affidavit that on its face establishes, to the satisfaction of a neutral and detached magistrate, sufficient probable cause; (2) serving the warrant; and (3) preparing and rendering the search warrant return

warrant affidavit Document that establishes, to the satisfaction of a neutral and detached magistrate, sufficient probable cause

return An itemized inventory of all the property seized by the officers executing a warrant

Search Warrants

The basic presumption inherent in the Fourth Amendment is that warrantless searches of and arrests in someone's home are illegal. Without **exigent circumstances**, police may not enter a private home to make a routine, warrantless arrest (*Payton v. New York*, 1980). Exigent circumstances occur when the suspect may destroy or secrete evidence or abscond. They never justify the warrantless entry of a residence for the purposes of effecting a search or an arrest for an offense other than a felony. The warrant is not only a law enforcement tool but also an absolute necessity when dealing with a person and his or her residence.

A warrant represents the authority of the state mediated by an impartial magistrate. It may be easy to find a "law-and-order" judge who will give the police anything they want. But remember, if the warrant is patently lacking in probable cause, the officer may still be held civilly liable for false arrest or criminal trespass; the judge has absolute immunity from suit for any action arising from his or her judicial duties. It is far better to find a judge who will require the officer to get the necessary probable cause. This type of judge is an asset and will assist in providing competent assessments of probable cause for good searches and arrests.

A good search also benefits the prosecutor, who now can demand that the defendant demonstrate a failure of probable cause before having to prove otherwise. The amount of time and effort required to defend probable cause pursuant to a warrant is less than without a warrant, and evidence obtained pursuant to a warrant is more readily accepted by the court than evidence obtained without the benefit of a warrant.

> **exigent circumstances** Circumstances that occur when the suspect may destroy or hide evidence or abscond

---

EXHIBIT 2.2

Search Warrant

STATE OF TEXAS

SEARCH WARRANT

THE STATE OF TEXAS

To the Sheriff or any Peace Officer of _____ County, Texas, or any Peace Officer of the State of Texas

Greetings:

Proof by affidavit being made this day, before me, by _____ (name of officer), a Peace Officer under the laws of Texas, that there is probable cause to believe that in the herein described (building, premises, or vehicle) is located the following property, possession of which is a violation of the laws of Texas or constitutes evidence of a violation of the laws of Texas, and is particularly described as follows:

Controlled substances to include:

Cocaine and associated paraphernalia

The described (building, premises, or vehicle) should be searched by reason of the following grounds:

Possession of the above-described controlled substances is evidence of violation of the Texas Health and Safety Code.

You are, therefore, commanded at any time, day or night, to make an immediate search of the residence at 337 Sisterdale Road, Sisterdale, Texas, more specifically described as:

A single-family dwelling located on the property of Filmore Duckworth and wife Dusty, attached outbuildings including a farm shop, barn, and garage.

Herein fail not, but have you then and there this Warrant within three days, exclusive of the day of its issuance and exclusive of the day of its execution, with your return thereon, showing you how you have executed the same, files in this court.

Issued this the _____ day of _____ 2017, at _____ o'clock am/pm _____ Judge

© Shutterstock, Inc./Africa Studio.

Warrantless Searches Based on Probable Cause

The Fourth Amendment protects persons and their houses, papers, and effects against unreasonable searches and seizures. There is only one method whereby that protection may be waived—the obtainment of a warrant based on probable cause. A careful examination of the Fourth Amendment will disclose no mention of any exceptions to the warrant requirement. The most important word in the evaluation of the Fourth Amendment is the word *warrant*; in context, its significance is paramount and should not be mitigated by any interpretation that suggests that exceptions to the warrant requirement are the norm. They are not. We concentrate on the exceptions because it is to these that police must often resort as a result of exigencies, not to avoid basic Fourth Amendment requirements, but to respond to rates of crime that did not exist at the time the amendment was drafted, when the low levels of mobility and transience and a sense of community often served to suppress misconduct.

The history of exceptions to the Fourth Amendment can be divided into two periods. In the first, probable cause provided the basis for most exceptions, thereby making probable cause the most important part of the Fourth Amendment. In the second, the issue of reasonableness came to play a more important role. Clearly, the focal point of the amendment has changed, depending on its application.

Search Incident to Arrest

The law of arrest, although governed by the Fourth Amendment, has long recognized probable cause as an exception to the warrant requirement outside of the home. One of the first issues that arose as a result of allowing arrests based on probable cause was the latitude granted to the police to search the arrestee. There is a definite safety concern in waiting to search a person until a warrant can be obtained. Police would be at substantial risk in placing suspects in their vehicles without first searching them, and the backseats of police cars would become repositories for undiscovered contraband and evidence. Once the suspect had been taken to the jail for booking, the danger would continue to increase if a warrant were not awaiting the suspect's arrival. The suspect might be placed in and among a jail population while in possession of a weapon or drugs. The Supreme Court addressed this potentially volatile situation in *Chimel v. California* (1967). The purpose of such a search is to protect the police and the public and to prevent the destruction of evidence. The Court was of the opinion in *Chimel v. California* (1967) that the probable cause of the arrest gave the probable cause to search required by the Fourth Amendment.

Chimel establishes the scope of a **search incident to an arrest** in an individual's home. The Supreme Court went on to say that the area under an arrestee's immediate control is that area into which he might reach (an arm's span). The Court presumed that the suspect was going to be removed immediately from the premises. In those instances where it is necessary to move the defendant about the premises, another arm's-span search might be authorized (e.g., if a semiclad suspect requests to clothe himself, the officers could subject the area where he intends to seek clothing to another search incident to arrest). In fact, if the suspect is transferred to another officer, that officer may perform another search of the suspect's person before placing him or her in the officer's vehicle, even

> **search incident to an arrest**
> Search that is allowed when an officer is carrying out an arrest authorized by an arrest warrant

CASE IN POINT

Chimel v. California, 1967

Chimel was suspected of having robbed a coin shop. The police, who had an arrest warrant but no search warrant, went to the suspect's home. Chimel was not there, but his wife admitted the police. Upon Chimel's arrival at his home, the police took him into custody. The police asked for consent to search the premises.

Consent was denied, but the police conducted a search nonetheless. A search of the entire house disclosed coins that had been stolen from the coin shop. The coins were introduced at trial over the defendant's objection. Chimel was convicted of robbery. The Court decided that, after making a legal arrest, the police may search the area within the suspect's immediate control to ensure that the suspect does not have access to a weapon or evidentiary items.

CASE IN POINT

United States v. Ross, 1982

Police stopped Ross based on a reliable informant's tip that Ross was dealing drugs out of the trunk of his car. After the stop and arrest, the police searched the interior of the vehicle and found a bullet. That bullet provided probable cause to believe that the vehicle could have contained a gun. The trunk was opened, and a paper bag was searched and found to contain heroin. A later search of the trunk at the station disclosed a bank bag of money. The Supreme Court held that the arrest of Ross was based on probable cause provided by an informant and that the search of the interior of the vehicle was justified incident to the arrest of Ross. The search of the trunk was justified upon finding the bullet; that provided probable cause to believe that the vehicle contained a firearm. The search of the containers in the trunk was "reasonable" in that they could have contained the weapon that was being sought.

though the suspect was previously searched by an officer at another location. It is a good rule of thumb, however, not to use the movement of the suspect about the house to justify further searches; for safety's sake, the suspect should be removed from the premises as soon as possible.

The **arm's-reach concept** promulgated in *Chimel* was elaborated upon in dealing with the high mobility and compactness of an automobile. The most straightforward way of applying *Chimel* to automobile searches is to recognize that everywhere within an automobile is within an arm's reach (except the trunk). The Supreme Court has determined that when a suspect is arrested in a vehicle, the immediate area is defined as the entire passenger compartment of the vehicle, including closed but not locked containers (*New York v. Belton*, 1981).

In 1982, the Supreme Court addressed the propriety of the police searching the trunk of a car whose driver had been lawfully arrested. The Court held that probable cause to stop and search a vehicle justifies the search of every part of the vehicle and its contents, including any containers in which the contraband sought might be secreted. In many instances, the search of the vehicle, as of the person, is focused not on any particular evidence but rather on any evidence that might be uncovered. When searches are performed on packages or luggage in the trunk, individual probable cause must be satisfied. That is, the police must be looking for something in particular when searching the trunk, and the thing they seek must be based on probable cause, although a warrant or exigent circumstances are not required.

This exception to the warrant requirement of the Fourth Amendment is based on the amendment's probable cause clause and reasonableness requirement. The probable cause for the arrest establishes the requisite probable cause for the search. A search incident to arrest

can never be legal if the arrest giving rise to the search is not legal.

Warrantless Searches Based on Reasonableness

Consent Searches

The most important tool in a police officer's arsenal against crime is the **consent search**. A consent search need not be supported by any quantity of cause or any individual suspicion. The notion of police requesting permission to search is at odds with the self-concept of many officers, according to which they demand, they do not ask. Getting police out of cars and onto the streets ameliorates this difficulty. An officer needs no probable cause to engage a citizen in a conversation, nor to request permission to search a citizen's person, automobile, or effects, as long as the officer remembers that the citizen is free to decline to give consent. A citizen's declination should not result in retaliation or threat. Consent must be voluntary—that is, free from psychological or physical coercion.

In *Bumper v. North Carolina* (1968), the U.S. Supreme Court determined that consent given based on the false assertion of the police that they were in possession of a valid search warrant was coerced. The term *consent search* itself is virtually an oxymoron, in that, because permission was given, the Fourth Amendment does not apply (as long as consent was voluntary, was given by a person legally able to give consent, and the scope of the search was within the given or inferred consent). A proper consent search for Fourth Amendment purposes is a search in which the Fourth Amendment plays no direct role. In a sense, a properly conducted consent search is not really a search. However, consent given by a person illegally in custody is

arm's-reach concept
Concept established in *Chimel v. California* (1967), in which it was ruled that a house search may be conducted in the area under the arrestee's immediate control, that is, the area into which he or she might reach; when applied to automobiles, the entire passenger compartment of the vehicle, including closed but not locked containers, can be searched

consent search
A warrantless search that is voluntarily permitted by a person who is legally able to give consent; the scope of the search must be within the given or inferred consent

not really consent and anything seized (derivative evidence) as a result of that consent would be excluded (*Florida v. Royer*, 1983).

Most departments provide consent forms for officers, realizing that written consent is more effective than oral consent at the time of a suppression motion. The question that invariably arises with respect to consent to search is whether the consent was given voluntarily and knowingly. The requirement for voluntariness is self-explanatory and predicated upon a coercion-free consent. A written consent goes a long way toward proving voluntariness if it also contains an admonition to the citizen that consent must be freely given and not as the product of coercion. The requirement for knowing is not self-evident; it too is more easily proven if a written consent form provides an additional caveat indicating that consent may be withheld, suspended, withdrawn, or limited in scope or duration (*Florida v. Enio Jimeno*, 1991).

In *Schneckloth v. Bustamonte* (1973), the U.S. Supreme Court relieved the police of the responsibility of having to provide consent warnings comparable to those required in the *Miranda* decision. At the same time, however, it indicated that the burden would be on the police and the state to prove that the consent was given knowingly. The Court went on to say that the touchstone of knowing consent was sufficient. In other words, to give consent, a citizen has to be of an age and possess the education, intelligence, cultural familiarity, and language skills to understand that he or she is free to

withhold, withdraw, or limit consent without fear of recrimination. The officer obtaining consent, therefore, has the responsibility of providing testimony that the consent giver had the sophistication necessary to presume that he or she had the right to withhold, withdraw, or limit consent—a heavy burden in light of the situations in which consent is generally sought. The prudent officer will use a consent form with warnings about coercion and the citizen's rights (**EXHIBIT 2.3**). Without a consent form, the next best approach is to utter an oral warning outlining the citizen's rights (which must be given in the same fashion in court as on the street).

Memory is not a reliable source for ensuring that a citizen's rights have not been violated nor his or her will overborne. Departments should provide consent warning cards for officers similar to those provided for *Miranda* situations. Although approved by the Supreme Court, the worst-case scenario for the officer is to obtain consent without providing some kind of warning. The end result will be that the officer will be confronted on the witness stand with the task of explaining the considerations employed in determining the age, intelligence, education, cultural familiarity, and language skills of the person from whom the consent was obtained.

The courts have long abhorred general searches (what one might call fishing expeditions). Remember, the Fourth Amendment requires that the particular thing sought and the place in which it is believed to be must be cited in a warrant. The scope of a valid consent

---

EXHIBIT 2.3

Example of a Consent Search Form

CONSENT TO SEARCH

I _____, having been informed of my constitutional right not to have a search made of the building, premises, and/or vehicle, consent to such search, and hereby authorize Officer _____, a police officer of the City of _____, _____ County, Texas, to conduct a search of the building, premises, and/or vehicle. This consent is given with full knowledge of my right to refuse to grant consent, withdraw consent, or to limit consent in scope or duration. This authorization is given to allow the search of the building, premises, and/or interior of my vehicle; containers, locked or unlocked; glove compartment; and the trunk of the automobile for anything that is illegal to possess. Upon discovery of contraband or evidence, I also consent to the seizure of those items by the searching officers. This consent has been granted voluntarily and without threats or promises of any kind. Signed this _____ day of _____, 2017

Signature of person granting consent _____

Signature of officer(s) requesting consent _____

Police Department

_____ County, Texas

CASE IN POINT

Florida v. Enio Jimeno, 1991

Enio Jimeno was overheard discussing the pickup of drugs by Dade County police. Police officers followed Jimeno and, when he failed to stop at a stop sign, pulled him over. The officer told Jimeno that he believed Jimeno was involved in a drug transaction and that he would like permission to search the vehicle. Jimeno gave consent, and officers found a bag of cocaine on the passenger-side floor of the automobile. Jimeno was arrested and charged, but the Florida courts granted a motion to suppress, which claimed the consent to search the vehicle was not consent to search individual containers found within the vehicle.

The U.S. Supreme Court held that the scope of a search is defined by the object being sought. Jimeno had been told by the officer that he believed Jimeno had been involved in a drug transaction and that the officer was looking for drugs. The Court was of the opinion that it was reasonable for the police to interpret the consent given to include consent to search containers within the vehicle that might bear drugs.

The Court went on to say that containers that could be opened easily and had no additional indices of an expectation of privacy could be opened but that locked containers would need specific consent or a warrant. The Court was very specific about the right of a citizen to limit the scope of the search to which he or she gave consent, but it held that if consent is given to search for a particular thing, the search may include unlocked containers that may contain the thing sought without requiring further or more explicit consent.

---

emergency exception
Exception to the warrant requirement; it states that if police are brought to the premises to deal with an emergency, then any evidence discovered in the course of handling that emergency is admissible despite the fact the police had no probable cause or warrant to enter the premises

search was addressed by the Supreme Court in *Florida v. Enio Jimeno* (1991), which established the basis for determining how far a search based on consent could go and what the responsibility of the officer was in requesting consent to search.

Emergency Searches

Police or firefighters may find themselves on premises to provide a service other than to arrest, interrogate, interview, or search. If police are brought to the premises to deal with an emergency, any evidence discovered in the course of handling the emergency is admissible despite the fact that the police had no probable cause or warrant to enter the premises. The entry would be reasonable under the Fourth Amendment and exempt from any warrant or probable cause requirement (*Mincey v. Arizona*, 1978). The discovery would fall within

the plain-view doctrine (discussed in a following section), repealing the need for particularized suspicion, probable cause, or a warrant. The item discovered would have to meet the requirements set forth later in the chapter.

The **emergency exception** to the warrant requirement only justifies entry to the premises without probable cause or a warrant. Another exception to the warrant requirement would be necessary to justify the **inadvertent discovery** of contraband or evidence (*Arizona v. Hicks*, 1987).

Exigent Circumstances Exception

Similar to the emergency exception, and sometimes considered to be part of that exception, is the exception for situations in which the police are concerned that a criminal may destroy evidence or abscond from the scene. If the police have probable cause to believe that a felony has

---

inadvertent discovery
One of the original elements of a plain-view discovery of evidence; meant to convey the accidental discovery of an item that is illegal to possess. It is no longer an element of the plain-view exception, based on *Arizona v. Hicks* (1987)

INVESTIGATOR'S NOTEBOOK

Requirements for Plain-View Searches

The Supreme Court has laid out the following specific requirements for the admissibility of evidence discovered in "plain view":

- The officer must be on the premises legitimately.
- The item viewed must have been found through inadvertent discovery (access was not gained through subterfuge for the purpose of examining the premises).
- It is immediately apparent that the item is evidence, contraband, or otherwise illegal to possess.

been committed and that the evidence may be destroyed in the time that it takes to procure a warrant, a warrantless entry may be made. A search of the premises based on the probable cause justifying the entry is permissible. Any entry based on exigent circumstances will be the subject of vigorous examination at the suppression hearing. Police will be required to prove the probable cause as well as the exigency that justified entry without a warrant.

Plain-View Searches

Often, evidence will come to the attention of an officer who is on a citizen's premises for a reason other than a search, an arrest, or exigent circumstances. The courts have unanimously recognized that when police are **legitimately on the premises** and recognize contraband or evidence in plain view, it is unreasonable to think that the same contraband or evidence will be there at the time the police return with a warrant.

The court does not treat a plain-view discovery as a search. Because a search was not anticipated and access to the premises was not gained for the purposes of conducting a search, the Fourth Amendment does not apply. If the item to be seized is immediately recognizable as illegal to possess, no search is necessary to reveal that to the police; thus, once again, the Fourth Amendment does not apply. If any manipulation of the item in question occurs, however, a search in fact has occurred and must be justified pursuant to the Fourth Amendment or one of its exceptions. The **immediately apparent** requirement establishes that no search was necessary to discover the items or to identify them as illegal to possess (*Coolidge v. New Hampshire*, 1971).

Open-Field Exception

The open-field exception is often confused with the plain-view exception, but when they are examined in light of the Fourth Amendment, it becomes easy to distinguish between the two. The Supreme Court has held that open fields are not protected by the Fourth Amendment. The only concern that the Court has is in defining an **open field**. The Fourth Amendment protects a citizen's home and, by extension, the area around the home that is used in the course of daily living, known as its curtilage. Any area outside of the curtilage of the home is an open field and is unprotected by the Fourth Amendment. Therefore, any examinations of such areas are, with regard to the Fourth Amendment, not searches.

The police need no excuse for treading on an open field. They need no justification for looking for whatever they choose once in that field. Their conduct is not subject to constitutional scrutiny if it has been determined that the area in question is not a house or its curtilage but rather an open field. There is no legally-on-the-premises requirement because there are no premises.

If the area of interest to the police is an open field that is fenced and posted to prohibit trespassing, they can enter without further justification, because the Fourth Amendment protects

open field
Any area outside of the curtilage of the home and is unprotected by the Fourth Amendment

legitimately on the premises
Legally allowed to be in a location despite not having a warrant; in such cases, officers are allowed to collect evidence that is in plain view and likely will not still be there when the officers return with a warrant

immediately apparent
Immediately recognizable as illegal to possess, with no search having been necessary to reveal that to the police

CASE IN POINT

Oliver v. United States, 1984

Police received a tip that Oliver was growing marijuana on a noncontiguous plot of land near his house. Police located the area in question, determined it was not contiguous to Oliver's home or farm, and, although it was fenced and posted, found a path leading through a locked gate to a field of marijuana surrounded by trees that kept the field from public view. Oliver was arrested and convicted of manufacturing a controlled substance. The question raised was whether the field searched was protected by the Fourth Amendment. Oliver's position was that the field was not in public view—in fact, it demonstrated an expectation of privacy by the signs, fencing, and locked entrance and, therefore, was not an "open field." The Supreme Court determined that since this land was not involved in the activities of daily living, it was not curtilage and, therefore, not protected under the Fourth Amendment. The fact that Oliver had demonstrated an expectation of privacy in the field and that it was not subject to cursory public view was not persuasive to the Court. The justices said that although the police officers' conduct may have been subject to criminal or civil sanction for trespass, it did not violate the Fourth Amendment, since the area was an open field.

The Supreme Court's interpretation of the open-field doctrine suggests that the area in question need not be a field, nor need it be open, to fall within the exception. Fenced yards have been considered open fields when viewed by the police from the air. Because the same view is available to any member of the public, it is also available to the police.

persons, homes, and effects—not open fields. They may have committed a criminal trespass, but they have not rendered their conduct subject to the exclusionary provisions of the Fourth Amendment. Unlike in the case of the plain-view exception, there is no "legitimately on the premises" requirement, nor any "inadvertent discovery" requirement. Once the trespass has been completed, the police may search wherever and for whatever they choose without fear of having their evidence suppressed. Once an item is found, it may be handled and examined to determine if it is, in fact, evidence or contraband without rendering it inadmissible.

Vehicle Inventories

From the outset, it is important to recognize that an inventory is not a search. An **inventory** is an administrative procedure that is governed by the Fourth Amendment as it applies to administrative procedures. Because it is not an effort to obtain evidence and is civil rather than criminal in nature, Fourth Amendment requirements are relaxed. The purpose of a **vehicle inventory** is to:

- Ensure that a citizen's property is accounted for properly
- Protect the police from spurious claims of theft
- Protect the public and the police from the possibility of explosive devices secreted in the vehicle

The inventory may be conducted at the scene or after a vehicle has been impounded.

inventory
An administrative procedure that accounts for a citizen's property

vehicle inventory
Accounting for the items contained in a vehicle

If an inventory is used as a method for conducting an otherwise illegal search, the inventory procedure has been violated and the evidence is suppressible. The attack on a vehicle inventory can be based on either of two claims: (1) no procedure for taking a vehicle inventory has been standardized in written form in a policy and procedures manual, or (2) the guidelines for an existing procedure were not followed correctly. Proof of either will establish that a search has been conducted and that an attempt has been made to describe it as an inventory. Many texts refer to an inventory procedure as an inventory search, but it cannot be both an inventory and a search. It is a bad habit to refer to the procedure as an inventory search, for it lays the semantic foundation for impeachment of the officer's credibility.

Stop and Frisk

Police encounter citizens in a variety of suspicious circumstances that do not give rise to probable cause. Society expects police officers to act on their suspicions in their efforts to "protect and serve." However, citizens are free from unnecessary restraint in our society, and the Fourth Amendment thus requires probable cause (**TABLE 2.1**). The U.S. Supreme Court has provided law enforcement the necessary tools to act on reasonable suspicion. A police officer may detain a citizen if the officer has reasonable suspicion that the citizen has committed or is about to commit a crime. The officer's suspicion must be based on articulable facts rather than mere speculation. The facts may be a product of an officer's training, education, and experience.

TABLE 2.1 Standards of Proof

Standard	Explanation
Criminal Law	
Beyond a reasonable doubt	Trial sufficiency of evidence (99%)
Clear and convincing	Some sanity determination
Probable cause	Legal sufficiency of evidence (more likely than not; 51%)
Reasonable suspicion	Foundation of investigatory detentions (less than 51%)
Significant government interest	No particularized suspicion
Civil Law	
Preponderance of the evidence	Comparable to probable cause

INVESTIGATOR'S NOTEBOOK

Frisk Criteria

Two separate thresholds of causation must be crossed before an officer is entitled to stop and frisk a suspect. The two quanta of cause must be satisfied independently of one another.

1. The officer must have a reasonable suspicion that the suspect has committed or is about to commit a crime (this is the quantity of cause necessary for detaining the suspect).

2. The officer must also have a reasonable suspicion that the individual is carrying a weapon and poses a threat to the officer or others (this is the quantity of cause necessary for frisking the suspect).

Such a **stop** is not a seizure as provided for in the Fourth Amendment but rather is a temporary detention similar to a traffic stop, where the motorist knows that, after a brief interruption, they will be allowed to continue driving (without certain infractions).

If, during the course of a temporary detention, a police officer becomes fearful that the person detained may possess a weapon, the officer may conduct a pat-down **frisk** of the outer clothing to ensure that the subject is not armed. This frisk is not a search, but is a reasonable intrusion upon a person's expectation of privacy based, again, on articulable facts that give rise to a fear or concern that the subject is armed (*Terry v. Ohio*, 1968).

Police Roadblocks and Sobriety Checkpoints

It might appear that police stopping motorists for the purpose of determining their sobriety would be a serious intrusion upon a citizen's freedom to come and go and would, therefore, constitute an unconstitutional seizure. The answer to that proposition depends on whether the detention was for the purpose of assessing sobriety or for some other law enforcement purpose.

The Michigan Department of State Police had been using sobriety checkpoints since 1986. State police stopped all vehicles passing through the checkpoint and briefly examined their drivers for signs of intoxication. If the field tests and the officer's observations suggested that the driver was intoxicated, the driver was arrested. A citizen group of motorists filed a request for an injunction and a declaratory judgment with the Michigan courts. The state courts ruled that the checkpoints were a violation of the Fourth Amendment requirement for probable cause, or, at least, reasonable suspicion. The Michigan Court of Appeals affirmed

the holding of the trial court, saying that sobriety checkpoints do not deter drunk driving.

The United States Supreme Court (*Michigan Department of State Police v. Sitz*, 1990) held that the roadblocks were a seizure under the Fourth Amendment. The court went on to say, however, that the seizures were a limited intrusion on motorists and, therefore, reasonable in light of the significant government interest in reducing highway deaths, injuries, and property damage caused by intoxicated drivers.

■ Drug Interdiction Checkpoints

The city of Indianapolis operated vehicle checkpoints on its roads in an effort to prohibit unlawful drugs. Motorists who were stopped at such a checkpoint filed suit, claiming that the roadblocks violated the Fourth Amendment. The District Court denied their request for a preliminary injunction, but the Seventh Circuit reversed, holding that the checkpoints violated the Fourth Amendment.

The Supreme Court, in its opinion, briefly addressed the exceptions to the Fourth Amendment requirement of individualized suspicion. The Court's position is that a search or seizure is unreasonable under the Fourth Amendment without individualized suspicion of wrongdoing, for which there are limited exceptions. For example, the Court has upheld brief, suspicion-free seizures at a fixed checkpoint designed to intercept illegal aliens (*United States v. Martinez-Fuerte*, 1976) and at a sobriety checkpoint aimed at removing drunk drivers from the road (*Michigan Department of State Police v. Sitz*, 1990). The Court has also suggested that a similar roadblock to verify drivers' licenses and registrations would be permissible to serve a highway safety interest (*Delaware v. Prouse*, 1979). However, the Court has never approved a checkpoint program whose primary purpose was to detect evidence of ordinary criminal wrongdoing.

stop
Detaining a citizen, which is allowed when an officer has reasonable suspicion, based on articulable facts rather than mere speculation, that the citizen has committed or is about to commit a crime

frisk
A pat-down search of the outer clothing of a person to ensure that the subject is not armed, conducted when the officer has a reasonable suspicion, based on articulable facts, that the subject is armed

The detection of ordinary criminal wrong-doing is what principally distinguishes drug interdiction checkpoints from those that the Supreme Court has previously approved, which were designed to serve purposes closely related to the problems of policing the border or the necessity of ensuring roadway safety. Attorneys for Indianapolis said that the *Sitz* and *Martinez-Fuerte* checkpoints had the same ultimate purpose of arresting those suspected of committing crimes. Securing the border and apprehending drunken drivers are law enforcement activities, and authorities employ arrests and criminal prosecutions to pursue these goals. The Court was not persuaded and expressed a concern that if this case were to be granted the same latitude as border searches, driver's license checks, and sobriety checkpoints, there would be little check on the authorities' ability to construct roadblocks for almost any conceivable law enforcement purpose. The Court went on

to say that the checkpoint program is also not justified by the severe and intractable nature of the drug problem. The gravity of the drug threat alone cannot be the deciding factor in questions concerning what means law enforcement may employ to pursue a given purpose.

The Supreme Court was not swayed by the argument that sobriety checkpoints, driver's license checkpoints, and drug interdiction checkpoints could all be conducted simultaneously. They held that if drug interdiction checkpoints could be justified by their lawful secondary purposes of keeping impaired motorists off the road and verifying licenses and registrations, authorities would be able to establish checkpoints for virtually any purpose, as long as they also included a license or sobriety check. The Court, therefore, left it to local tribunals to determine the primary purpose of the checkpoint program (*City of Indianapolis v. Edmond*, 2000).

CONCLUSION

Much of what police do must be considered in the context of the rights that each citizen enjoys. Police often see the U.S. Constitution as an impediment to law enforcement and criminal investigation. A broader understanding of the U.S. Supreme Court cases regarding the Fourth and Fifth Amendments serves as a tool that can be added to a toolbox used to ensure that all searches and seizures of persons and things are done constitutionally. It is this perspective that

we must consider when recognizing that we only get one chance to process a crime scene.

One of the most challenging forms of evidence awaiting the homicide investigator is blood evidence. It is the most common evidence found at a homicide crime scene and requires special attention to detail, handling, and packaging. The next chapter introduces us to blood evidence and the evidentiary considerations pertaining thereto.

QUESTIONS FOR REVIEW

1. What portion of the Fourth Amendment pertains to arrests?

2. What portion of the Fourth Amendment pertains to searches?

3. What are exigent circumstances, and how do they affect the warrant requirement of the Fourth Amendment?

4. In what amendment or amendments do we find the equal protection, privileges and immunities, and due process clauses? Of what importance is the due process clause to the rights of citizens of various states?

5. What area may police search when arresting a felon in his or her home pursuant to a lawful warrant? What case supports this type of search?

6. What is the fruit-of-the-poisonous-tree doctrine?

7. What is the exclusionary rule, and how did it come to be applied to the states?

8. What are the elements of a plain-view exception to the warrant requirement?

9. What exception to the exclusionary rule did *United States v. Leon* (1984) establish? How does this exception assist police in avoiding civil liability?

10. What is derivative evidence, and what effect does the exclusionary rule have on it?

11. What is contained in a legally sufficient search warrant affidavit?

12. What is the role of voluntariness in obtaining consent to search?

13. What is the open-field exception to the warrant requirement, and what role does curtilage play in applying the exception?

14. How would a defense attorney try to attack the validity of a vehicle inventory?

15. What are the two quanta of cause that must be satisfied before an officer can engage in a legal stop and frisk?

16. What does the USA PATRIOT Act allow law enforcement to do that they could not do before?

17. What should always be contained in every search warrant affidavit?

REFERENCE

Clark, K. (2017). *Longmont police chief says housing authority is to blame for search confusion.* Retrieved July 7, 2017, from http://www.9news .com/news/local/next/longmont-police-chief -says-housing-authority-is-to-blame-for -search-confusion/446727711

KEY LEGAL CASES

Arizona v. Hicks, 480 U.S. 321 (1987).

Bumper v. North Carolina, 391 U.S. 543 (1968).

California v. Greenwood, 486 U.S. 35 (1988).

Chimel v. California, 395 U.S. 294 (1967).

City of Indianapolis v. Edmond, 531 U.S. 32 (2000).

Coolidge v. New Hampshire, 403 U.S. 443 (1971).

Delaware v. Prouse, 440 U.S. 648 (1979).

Florida v. Enio Jimeno, 499 U.S. 934 (1991).

Florida v. Royer, 460 U.S. 491 (1983).

Griswold v. Connecticut, 381 U.S. 479 (1965).

Mapp v. Ohio, 367 U.S. 643 (1961).

Michigan Department of State Police v. Sitz, 496 U.S. 444 (1990).

Mincey v. Arizona, 437 U.S. 385 (1978).

Miranda v. Arizona, 384 U.S. 436 (1966).

New York v. Belton, 453 U.S. 454 (1981).

Nix v. Williams, 467 U.S. 431 (1984).

Oliver v. United States, 466 U.S. 170 (1984).

Payton v. New York, 455 U.S. 573 (1980).

Pennsylvania v. Muniz, 496 U.S. 582 (1990).

Schneckloth v. Bustamonte, 412 U.S. 218 (1973).

Terry v. Ohio, 392 U.S. 1 (1968).

United States v. Leon, 468 U.S. 897 (1984).

United States v. Martinez-Fuerte, 428 U.S. 543 (1976).

United States v. Ross, 456 U.S. 798 (1982).

Weeks v. United States, 232 U.S. 383 (1914).

Wolf v. Colorado, 338 U.S. 25 (1949).

chapter 3

Managing Criminal Investigations and Cultivating Sources of Information

...I cannot live without brain-work. What else is there to live for?...What is the use of having powers, when one has no field upon which to exert them? Crime is commonplace, existence is commonplace, and no qualities, save those which are commonplace, have any function upon earth.

Sherlock Holmes
"The Sign of Four"

KEY TERMS

acquisition technology

circumstantial evidence

electronic communication

enhancement technology

follow-up investigation

hearsay

incident command system (ICS)

informant

intelligence

interrogation

interview

leads

managing criminal investigations (MCI)

National Incident Management System (NIMS)

preliminary investigation

signature

snitch

solvability factors

stakeout

tail

totality of the circumstances

Violent Criminal Apprehension Program (VICAP)

STUDENT LEARNING OUTCOMES

Upon completion of this chapter, students will be able to:

- Explain how crime scenes can be managed
- Recognize the national incident management system
- Examine the role of informants in the investigative process
- Evaluate how surveillance is conducted

Managing the Criminal Investigation

Traditionally, the detective who was on duty and took the call for investigative assistance conducted the investigation. Whoever was present became the owner of the new case. In departments where specialists investigated crimes, each detective would be in the rotation and responsible chronologically for the next case. For example, all burglary detectives would remain in the rotation, adding new cases as they were received. Each detective's caseload continued to increase and was lightened only when the detective cleared a case or determined that the case could not be solved with the available evidence and information.

The major source of motivation for investigating cases in this system was the probability of clearing the case quickly, thus removing it from one's caseload. Administrators evaluated the success of various investigators by the rate at which they cleared cases. It should not be surprising that those cases with the greatest potential for arrest were the ones on which investigators focused their time and energy. **Managing criminal investigations (MCIs)** accomplishes the same thing. MCIs are designed to determine which crimes are most solvable and to use limited investigative resources to solve them. However, it does not rely on traditional notions of ease of solvability as the primary indicators.

All successful investigations can be evaluated based on one of five possible outcomes:

1. Arrest
2. Cleared offense
3. Accepted for prosecution
4. Plea-bargained
5. Conviction

All of these outcomes also depend on the management of the investigation and the allocation of available resources.

MCI begins with recognizing that the way detectives—and patrol officers—are utilized at crime scenes is a waste of resources and manpower. Much of what is done during a preliminary investigation lays the foundation for a successful investigation. However, much of what needs to be done initially at a crime scene does not require the attention of a detective and could easily be accomplished by the first-responding patrol officer or officers.

Preliminary Investigation

In managing crime scenes, the **preliminary investigation** is the most important aspect of any investigation. The preliminary investigation is the police agency's first response to a report that a crime has been committed. As in every investigation, the primary objectives include the following:

- Determine who committed the crime, while making sure not to contaminate, lose, or destroy evidence.
- Ensure that all evidence discovered is handled to foster admissibility at the time of trial.
- Apprehend the perpetrator(s).
- Obtain a conviction.

In MCI, the first-responding officer collects evidence that will help identify the individual responsible for the crime and that will lead to the subsequent arrest and conviction of that person, thus relieving the investigative team of the responsibility of gathering relevant crime scene evidence.

Generally, first-responding officers render assistance to victims, take names, secure the crime scene, and restrain witnesses and suspects. First-responding officers record their perceptions and conduct interviews, which can be vital to the success of the investigation. Investigators then arrive on the scene, debrief the first-responding personnel, and release them to return to their duties. Investigators launch a structured examination of the premises and either supervise the recovery and processing of evidence or recover and process it themselves. They determine the nature of the crime, attempt to identify the victim, and make an informal assessment of the factors that will be helpful in solving the crime. Detectives devote substantial time and effort to processing the crime scene time that could be better used in pursuing the investigatory steps that might lead to solving the crime. Thus, MCI is designed to address these initial activities. Patrol personnel could conduct this preliminary investigation as readily as investigators. Giving the patrol officers responsibility for the preliminary investigation frees investigators to investigate. Included within this proposition is the idea that patrol personnel receive proper training in the recognition, discovery, recovery, and preservation of all evidence that may be obtained at a crime scene.

preliminary investigation
The police agency's first response to a report that a crime has been committed

managing criminal investigations (MCIs)
Concept designed to determine which crimes are most solvable and to use limited investigative resources to solve them

INVESTIGATOR'S NOTEBOOK

Crucial Elements of the Preliminary Investigation

The framework of the preliminary investigation is based on several major areas that the first-responding officer must address. The officer must:

- Decide if an offense has actually occurred and, if so, which offense.
- Determine if the time lapse between the crime's occurrence and when the police were notified was normal.
- Note any discrepancies in witness or victim statements.
- Determine if the facts provided by the victim and witnesses are supported by the physical facts.
- Identify the victim and the time and place the crime took place.
- Identify any solvability factors that could lead to the successful conclusion of the investigation.

Solvability Factors

As stated in earlier chapters, not all crimes can be solved. The sheer number of crimes is such that most metropolitan police agencies cannot field sufficient personnel to conduct the necessary investigations. In allocating investigatory personnel, more can be accomplished with less if patrol staff do preliminary investigations and gather input regarding solvability. Solvability input is used to determine where to best employ investigators and investigative resources.

The Rochester, New York, Police Department has identified 12 **solvability factors**:

1. Were there any eyewitnesses to the crime?
2. Has the suspect been identified by name?
3. Has the location of the suspect been determined?
4. Has a description of the suspect been obtained?
5. Has the suspect been identified?
6. Did the property that was taken have recognizable marks, numbers, or identifiable characteristics?
7. Has a modus operandi (MO) been discovered and identified?
8. Is there significant physical evidence left at the crime scene?
   a. Blood
   b. Body fluids
9. Was a vehicle involved?
   a. Was a description obtained?
   b. Was a license number obtained?
10. Did the search of the crime scene disclose anything that could be connected to an identifiable suspect?
11. Will additional investigation or media assistance increase the probability of solving the crime?
12. Is it possible that someone other than the suspect committed the crime (Leonard & More, 2000)?

During the preliminary investigation, the responsible officer processes the crime scene while keeping in mind these 12 solvability factors; crimes are seldom solved unless one or more of these factors exists. Their existence is of little consequence, however, if the preliminary investigator is not prepared to discover them.

The discovery of solvability factors determines whether a **follow-up investigation** is conducted and what direction that follow-up investigation will take. The absence of solvability factors at the time of the preliminary investigation may be overcome at a later date with the acquisition of information that was not available or not discovered at the time of the preliminary investigation. In other words, a closed case can be reopened.

The key to success in a preliminary investigation is the same as in any investigation: documentation. The decision to halt or continue the investigation is based on the documentation provided by the preliminary investigator. An incomplete preliminary investigation is of no value to the managers of the investigation in determining what resources to deploy. It is

---

solvability factors
Information about a crime that can provide the basis for determining who committed the crime

follow-up investigation
Investigation of a crime that is conducted if solvability factors are found during the preliminary investigation

imperative that preliminary investigators not only have the necessary investigative skills to ferret out solvability factors but also the discipline to document their findings correctly. It is often easier to find personnel who can identify the findings of an investigation than it is to find personnel who can identify and document investigative findings. It deserves repeating that in the world of criminal trials, if it is not documented, it does not exist. If evidence is not documented, it cannot be included in unchallenged courtroom testimony; thus, it makes little sense to conduct an investigation whose outcome will not be admissible at the time of trial.

Upon completion of the preliminary investigation, the case is submitted along with a recommendation, either for further action or that no further action will be taken. The recommendation has value if the following are met:

- All potential witnesses have been interviewed or accounted for.

- A thorough search of the crime scene has been conducted.

- All solvability factors that are present have been identified.

- Every reasonable investigative effort has been made.

- Documentation reflects the investigative effort and the basis for the discovered solvability factors.

Crime Scene Processing During the Preliminary Investigation

Students often ask how much evidence should be collected at a crime scene (**FIGURE 3.1**). The usual response is to err on the part of collecting too much as opposed to too little, but not all

FIGURE 3.1: Crime Scene Processing.
© Couperfield/Shutterstock, Inc.

investigations warrant full crime scene processing. Violent crimes should and will receive more attention than nonviolent crimes solely because of limited manpower and resources. What follows is a set of guidelines for managers of criminal investigations to use in determining how much evidence to collect at a given crime scene and how much effort should be applied in collecting that evidence.

- If a suspect is arrested at or near the scene, any physical evidence from the crime scene will be useful in the prosecution.

- If a suspect has been identified but not arrested, any physical evidence can be used to corroborate the identification.

- If there are sufficient leads to make it possible that the suspect will be identified, any physical evidence should be collected to corroborate any future identification.

- If there are peculiar circumstances to the crime, it may indicate a pattern. Physical evidence may be useful in corroborating the identification of a suspect traced through investigation of other crimes in the series.

Conviction Is the Objective

As mentioned in earlier chapters, the relationship between police and prosecutors is not always cordial. It is of little value to place blame for this historic development other than to recognize that it exists and that it must be overcome for investigations to have meaning. MCI requires investigating patrol officers to communicate with criminal investigators; who communicate with their supervisors; who manage investigations; who, in turn, communicate with the prosecutor's office. If MCI is to prove effective, there must be a change in investigatory procedure as described, but there also must be a change in how cases are prepared for trial. Prosecutors must be involved in those cases that have sufficient solvability factors to warrant additional investigation. That prosecutorial input can direct and assess the handling of the investigation, witnesses, and evidence. With early intervention by the prosecutor's office, there should be no surprises in initiating criminal proceedings, preparing the case for trial, or negotiating a plea agreement. In Costa Rica, prosecutors attend any felony crime scene as it is being processed. Costa Rican prosecutors are more intimately involved in their cases than their counterparts in the United States. Having a prosecutor present as a legal resource helps prevent constitutional violations that may jeopardize the introduction of evidence or statements. Additionally, prosecutors have a working relationship with criminal investigators as well as a first-person understanding of the crime, the crime scene, the evidence, and the people involved. Prosecutors may also provide legal counsel that reduces the incidence of errors that jeopardize the case.

With oversight from and communication with the prosecutor's office, it should be routine to evaluate the case periodically to assess progress toward obtaining evidence, witness statements, suspect identification, and, ultimately, conviction.

Advantages of Managing Criminal Investigations

There are a number of potential benefits associated with MCI:

1. *An increase in arrests and in case clearance.* With investigators focusing their attention on follow-up investigations of cases, with sufficient information to support a successful outcome and not wasting time on unsolvable cases, arrests and clearances should increase.

2. *A readily available cohort from which to draw future detectives.* Preliminary investigators will have demonstrated the temperament, patience, and discipline required of criminal investigators and will have served in a proving ground for promotion into those positions.

3. *Reallocation of personnel and resources.* Investigators will be able to focus on solvable cases.

Incident Command System

The **incident command system (ICS)** is a management tool designed to enable effective domestic incident management by integrating a combination of facilities, equipment, personnel, procedures, and communications in a common organizational structure. An incident command system is used to organize near-term and long-term field-level operations for a broad spectrum of emergencies, from small to complex incidents. It is normally structured to facilitate activities in six major functional areas:

- Command
- Operations

National Incident Management System (NIMS) A method of coordinating the supervision of multiple agencies working together

incident command system (ICS) A management tool that integrates multiple resources

- Planning
- Logistics
- Finance
- Administration (Department of Homeland Security, 2017)

Acts of biological, chemical, radiological, and nuclear terrorism represent particular challenges for the traditional ICS structure. Events that are geographically dispersed will require extraordinary coordination among federal, state, local, and nongovernmental organizations. The initial response to most domestic incidents is typically handled by local 911 dispatch centers and emergency responders in a single jurisdiction. In other instances, incidents that begin with a single response in a single jurisdiction may expand rapidly to multidiscipline, multijurisdictional incidents requiring significant additional resources and operational support. In such cases, ICS provides a flexible core mechanism for coordinated and collaborative incident management. When a single incident covers a large geographical area, multiple local ICS organizations may be required. Effective crossjurisdictional coordination is vital.

National Incident Management System

On February 28, 2003, President Bush issued Homeland Security Presidential Directive (HSPD)-5, which directed the Secretary of Homeland Security to develop and administer a **National Incident Management System (NIMS)** (**FIGURE 3.2**). According to HSPD-5, this system provides a consistent nationwide approach for federal, state, and local governments to work effectively and efficiently together to prepare for, respond to, and recover from domestic incidents, regardless of cause, size, or complexity.

FIGURE 3.2: National Incident Management System.
FEMA; FEMA/Jeannie Mooney.

To provide for interoperability and compatibility among federal, state, and local capabilities, NIMS includes a core set of concepts, principles, terminology, and technologies covering the incident command system; multiagency coordination systems; unified command; training; identification and management of resources (including systems for classifying types of resources); qualifications and certification; and the collection, tracking, and reporting of incident information and incident resources (Department of Homeland Security, 2017).

NIMS uses a systems approach to integrate the best of existing processes and methods into a unified national framework for incident management. This framework forms the basis for interoperability and compatibility that, in turn, enable a diverse set of public and private organizations to conduct well-integrated and effective incident-management operations. The core set of concepts and principles includes:

- Utilizing an incident command system for command and management

- Preparedness, including cross-agency training and agreements

- Resource management, which involves vulnerability studies and resource inventories

- Communications and information management, including using open lines and computers dedicated to the response to an incident

- Supporting technologies, including voice and data communication systems, information management systems, and data display systems (Department of Homeland Security, 2017)

ICS and NIMS facilitate the management of crime scenes that require a multijurisdictional response. All state public safety agencies should be conversant in the language of NIMS and ICS, because all grants are predicated on the premise that the agency submitting the proposal is NIMS and ICS qualified. Training in NIMS can be obtained through public safety agencies or online through a variety of websites, including an independent study at the Department of Homeland Security, Federal Emergency Management Agency, Emergency Management Institute.

The Follow-Up Investigation

Once the initial report of a crime is received, it is routed to the applicable department, assigned to an investigator, and a follow-up investigation is begun. Before the victim is revisited, all statements and evidence are reviewed. Any impressions, omissions, or inaccuracies in the report are noted and provide areas of inquiry for the investigator. Any evidence collected as part of the investigation will be logged and kept in the evidence room. On occasion, the crime laboratory may have evidence scheduled for comparison or testing. Most crime labs are backed up, so it may be impractical to wait for lab results. If lab results are available, they too should be reviewed in anticipation of further investigation. In homicide investigations, the medical examiner's report also takes time; however, cause and mechanism of death determinations are extremely valuable, and any speculation gathered at the crime scene should be confirmed by the medical examiner's report.

Once all statements have been reviewed, evidence examined, and reports digested, the investigator is prepared to contact the victim(s), witnesses, and suspects. This initial investigatory contact can be very emotional; even victims of nonviolent crimes may feel violated. Tact and patience can go a long way in letting victims relax and in establishing rapport. Establishing rapport does not mean that the investigator believes everything the victim says. People lie, not only suspects but also victims and witnesses. The motivation for a lie may not be apparent, but careful consideration of prior statements can sometimes indicate an inconsistency or lapse that, when revisited, can produce additional information. The name of the follow-up investigation game is information. In many investigations, the amount of information gathered can become overwhelming. Good note-taking is the only solution.

The Interview

Armed with a wealth of information, the investigator will arrange to interview the victim. It is best to get the victim's statement nailed down before talking to the witnesses. The perspective of the parties is different, and the statements made should reflect that difference. Witness and victim statements that are identical are generally a product of fabrication. No two people experience the same event in the same way, and although the similarities will be greater than the disparities, there should be differences.

Going over the crime a second time with a victim is a tedious process for the victim. In most instances, the victim wants the police to "do something." After the initial report, victims believe that the investigation has begun and progress is being made in capturing the offender. Having to go over the confrontation a second time is not exactly what the victim has in mind. Often a few days have passed, the original trauma has dissipated, and he or she would rather not revisit the offense. It is important to assure the victim that the follow-up visit is an integral part of every investigation and that only by talking to those involved can the investigator develop an appreciation for the dynamics of the people, places, and crime.

Preliminary statements are made under the influence of the offense that is still fresh and can be painful. The initial statements may have greater detail than the follow-up interviews. The lapse in time and the reduced chemistry provides for a more relaxed statement that may be in a different order than the original statement and may be missing events, times, and dates. All of this should be expected and is not necessarily indicative of lies but more than likely, a product of the victim's efforts to forget about the incident and not dwell on the particulars. The interview with the victim should be recorded and transcribed. The transcribed interview should be compared with the preliminary statement for any inconsistencies.

After the interview with the victim, the investigator should run a records check on the victim, witnesses, and suspect(s). A records check can give the investigator insight and leverage in dealing with those who have information about the crime under investigation. An understanding of the time of day, the weather, lighting conditions, and noise and traffic levels all may provide insight into the position and vantage point of witnesses and the reliability of the information they might provide. Once background information about each witness has been gathered and all witness statements have been read and noted, it is time to interview the witnesses.

Before interviewing witnesses, it is a best practice speaking with the first-responding officer, as this can provide clarity and continuity. The information gathered from that officer may not be entirely reflected in the initial reports. First-responding officer impressions of the crime scene, witnesses, and suspects can give a fresh perspective to the flatly described information in the various statements filed.

Witnesses can be invited to the police department, placed in an interview room, and interviewed by the investigator. Often, the most expedient approach is to interview the witness at a location that is likely to allow uninterrupted discourse. Sometimes, the turmoil in a household makes it impossible to carry on a discussion. Interview rooms provide privacy, but they do not provide warmth or comfort. Witnesses may respond in a hostile manner to being required to travel to the police department. Using interview rooms should be the exception rather than the rule. The best use of witnesses is to have them describe what they saw or heard from the vantage point of where they saw and heard it. There is no other way to obtain a real-world perspective of what and how the witness saw or heard what they say they have.

If a witness's statement is worthy of preservation, it should be preserved in three ways:

- By audio recording
- By video recording
- By written statement

The audio recording is to preserve the tone and tenor of the interview to avoid any allegations of coercion or coaching. Most witnesses will agree to allow their statements to be recorded. Most agencies have interview forms that assist the investigator in gathering information. They may differ in style and length, but most have the same substantive content. Victim interview forms usually contain provisions for:

- Name, address, and phone number of the victim
- Time and date of the offense
- A multiple-choice offender descriptive section, which includes:
  - Height
  - Weight
  - Age
  - Hair color
  - Eye color
  - Build
  - Clothing description
- A multiple-choice vehicle descriptive section
- A multiple-choice lighting descriptive section
- Name, address, and phone number of any known witnesses
- A multiple-choice location descriptive section, which includes:
  - City
  - Country
  - Building proximity
  - Roadway description
  - Business proximity
- A large section for a handwritten victim narrative

The witness narrative is labeled with the date and time of the statement. Once the statement is complete, the victim is asked to read it over, making any necessary changes. All changes should be initialed by the victim. The investigator reads the statement and asks questions about parts of the statement that need to be fleshed out. The additions are placed at the end of the original statement or on a supplemental statement. All additions are also initialed. The initialing serves an important purpose. It defuses any contentions by a defense lawyer that the statement was written by the police and never read by the victim. Once witness and victim statements have been taken and corroborated, an affidavit for an arrest warrant should be drafted.

The Search and the Arrest

Once witness and victim statements have been confirmed or systematically dissected, the next step in the follow-up investigation is to use the information gathered to fashion an affidavit in support of a search or arrest warrant. Service of the warrant should be a straightforward matter with sufficient additional personnel to facilitate a search or effect an arrest. Suspects, regardless of the crime under investigation, have the capacity for violence. That capacity is diminished by the way the arrest or search is made. Suspects should be treated with respect, as should their property. In spite of the damage done in movie searches, excessive damage done can give rise to a lawsuit that may result in the agency or the individual officers paying for the damage done.

Suspects injured in the arrest process will not be accepted for booking until first taken for medical intervention. Overly aggressive arrests ultimately lead to allegations of unreasonable use of force. Any evidence of unreasonable force goes a long way in challenging the legality of the arrest and the seizure of the evidence. When conducting a lawful search pursuant to a search warrant, the usual process is to include in the affidavit that which is expected to be found that is significant to the case under investigation. It is important to keep in mind that the "plain view" exception to the warrant requirement can operate during a search incident to a lawful warrant. There are two requirements for a constitutionally permissible plain-view seizure:

1. The officer is legally on the premise.

2. The officer has probable cause to believe that what is viewed is illegal to possess.

Keep in mind that when a warrant affidavit is being filled out, the courts have been consistent in ruling that not everything an officer expects to find on the premises needs to be included in the affidavit; however, it is important that the officer include the smallest thing expected to be found during the search. The size of the objects sought legally determines the parameters of the search. For example, if a warrant includes a rifle, only places where a rifle may be secreted can be searched. If the warrant includes firearms instead of just a rifle, the purview of the search now extends to places that a handgun can be secreted. If ammunition is included in the warrant, the areas that can be legally searched become smaller, giving a greater opportunity for the plain-view warrant exception to work. As a matter of course, since the courts do not require that everything an officer has probable cause to believe might be present at a residence be included in the warrant, the warrant should always include the smallest thing that can legitimately be sought.

Preparing for Trial

The culmination of investigative efforts may be the setting of a trial date. In many cases, the case never gets to a trial but is plea-bargained. Plea bargains are often frowned upon by the public. The truth is that the wheels of justice would grind to a screeching halt if all cases had to be tried. The most common avenue of disposing of criminal cases is through plea agreements. The word "bargain" gives a negative connotation to the process. Perhaps the use of the word "agreement" would lessen the poor image of the plea bargain process. As far as investigators are concerned, there are two types of plea agreements: good ones and not-as-good ones. If an investigation has been conducted properly, all leads have been pursued, witnesses have been properly handled, an abundance of evidence has been obtained, and all documentation reflects investigative efforts, the prosecutor can conduct a "take-it-or-leave-it" plea—the prosecution does not make deals, it makes a one-time offer. This is in no way a poor reflection on the quality of the investigation and should be seen as a success by the investigator and his or her supervisor. This kind of plea does not diminish the career prospects of an investigator and allows the wheels to keep turning. There is another type of plea that has an entirely different purpose and impact on the investigator. When a prosecutor receives a case that is poorly organized, has incomprehensible documentation, or has poorly conducted searches or seizures, the prosecutor can dismiss the case or reduce the charges to enhance the probability of a plea agreement. Presuming that the original charge was the correct one, reducing the charge to facilitate an agreement is a failure for everyone who is connected to the investigation. Should the case progress to trial, the key to success is well-documented cases based on constitutional searches and seizures. The second step in a successful prosecution is preparation. Every word written and every piece of evidence with its accompanying chain of custody logs must be reviewed in detail; any problems should be identified prior to setting the case for trial. Preparing for trial is not the time to discover that there are problems with documentation or evidence. Serious problems should be discovered long before the trial date. The easiest way to alienate a prosecutor is to bring a case to trial that has serious flaws in the investigation.

Revisiting each witness and the victim prior to trial is good practice. It helps to refresh memories about what was written in the past when the event was still clear in their minds. An investigator needs to be careful when revisiting witnesses and victims because they may occasionally want to supplement their statements with something they had forgotten at the time that the statement was written. If the original statements were sufficient to establish probable cause, changes can only complicate the matter. At the time of the trial, the defense will challenge any changes as a product of police coaching, claiming that if the forgotten addition was important enough to add, it should have been important enough to include in the first place. The jury is left with the idea that perhaps the witness or victim was coached and that the statement was not a recollection as much as a fabrication by the police to bolster their case.

The key to successful testimony is for investigators to testify honestly and professionally, recognizing that they must provide the defense with the same courtesy that they provide the prosecution. It is easy to get into a confrontation with a defense lawyer. Attacking the testifying investigator is often a ploy used by the defense in an effort to solicit an angry or unprofessional response. Such a response is meant to create the impression of volatility and the absence of professionalism in the minds of the jurors. A well-prepared investigator who testifies honestly and professionally goes a long way in securing a proper conviction.

Sources of Information

One of the most important tasks performed by police investigators is to gather **intelligence** (information). Although gathering intelligence has traditionally been viewed as a military

function, police investigators understand the need to discover and cultivate sources of information for cases under investigation as well as crimes yet to be committed. Many agencies have an intelligence organization or department whose sole responsibility is to gather information. Most police investigators gather information on a much less-formal basis. This less-formal process is discussed in this chapter.

Every crime has an abundance of information that can be gathered, from forensic evidence to witness, victim, and suspect input. The investigator's job is to recognize the prospective sources of information. If an investigation runs into an information dead end, the reason may be that the investigator has overlooked a source of information or has not recognized the importance of information already gathered.

Community Policing and Criminal Investigation

When we think of community policing, we often think of police on foot, walking beats. In truth, community policing is as diverse as the communities served. In any community, law enforcement personnel can assist in maintaining safety. One of the creative uses of community policing involves using community police teams to address all of the needs of a given community: traffic enforcement, emergency response, first response, and investigation of all crimes (as opposed to utilizing various felony departments within an agency). The team is managed from within rather than by an external hierarchical structure, which enables immediate decision making and direct accountability. People in a given community get to know the community team that provides services for them. In fact, the team becomes part of the community's resources, problem solvers, and leaders. Responses to problems are almost immediate, and responding team members have a pretty good idea of what to expect at any given location, because they most probably have been there before. This approach to community policing streamlines police services, including crime scene investigation.

Eyewitnesses and Victims

The most common sources of information are witnesses and victims. What someone sees, hears, smells, or touches carries great weight in the courtroom. Defense lawyers challenge all circumstantial evidence as unreliable. **Circumstantial evidence** is all evidence other than eyewitness testimony. The reality is that eyewitness testimony is the least reliable

intelligence
Information used to investigate a crime or compiled on related individuals to the crime

circumstantial evidence
All evidence other than eyewitness testimony

evidence available to the investigator and prosecutor. The inconsistencies in eyewitness testimony are the materials from which defense lawyers build cross-examinations. An investigator should begin to worry when eyewitness information does not bear any inconsistencies. No two people experience an event using the same senses. No two perspectives are ever the same. Gross descriptions should be very similar in content, but the fine details will vary from witness to witness.

An investigator turns first to witnesses and victims as sources of information when beginning to attempt to answer the who, what, when, where, and sometimes why and how of a crime. Witnesses and victims provide the first **leads** of the investigation—the descriptions of persons, places, events, and things. As hard as witnesses and victims may try to provide the information that the investigator seeks, they are not trained observers, and their recall may be sporadic and general rather than concise and specific. Of course, recollection is often a product of the inquiry that gives rise to it (see Investigator's Notebook).

Informants

The word **informant** has taken on negative connotations, although any citizen providing information to police, including witnesses and victims, is an informant. Although an informant is simply one who provides information, the use of informants can become legally complex when the motivation for providing information to the police is added to the mix. Most citizens will provide information readily and voluntarily. The problem is that the average citizen does not have the ties to the criminal community that would garner inside information about past and future crimes. Doctors, bakers, and candlestick makers generally do not travel in the same circles as criminals and their associates. The question, therefore, is how investigators can get a criminal or a criminal's affiliate to provide the investigators with information. There are two ways in which such information and people come to the assistance of the police: if the informants have a separate agenda to further, or if they are products of cultivation.

■ Informants with an Agenda

An informant may be motivated by a personal agenda that will somehow be furthered if the police act on the information provided. That agenda may include vengeance for past grievances (real or imagined) suffered by the informant and his or her crew or operation. Although information gained through this motive may be highly suspect, it nonetheless deserves a response. Information of serious criminal wrongdoing coming into the hands of the police should not be ignored, regardless of

leads
The initial descriptions of persons, places, events, and things related to an investigation

informant
One who provides information

INVESTIGATOR'S NOTEBOOK

© Shutterstock, Inc./Janaka Dharmasena

Working with Witnesses and Victims

The skills of a successful intelligence gatherer are a lifetime in the making. In gleaning information from citizens, it is best to use language that is familiar to those being interviewed and that is free of jargon.

Kilometers and meters (or yards and feet) may be foreign terminology to a witness, for example. Using measurement terms familiar to the witness will result in more accurate results. When asking questions about a vehicle, the investigator may be able to discover only the color and vehicle type. Requesting the witness to compare the vehicle in question with vehicles currently in the vicinity can be more helpful than asking if the vehicle was a compact, subcompact, mid-sized car, sedan, and so on. Likewise, when asking questions about a suspect's body type, the investigator should consider having the witness compare it with the body types of those present. The resulting information is likely to be more accurate than if the witness is required to guess the suspect's weight and height and express them in pounds and in feet and inches. The most efficient way of obtaining a good physical description is to construct a composite drawing. Most people are more comfortable thinking graphically than linearly or physiologically.

As for weapons, the unsophisticated witness may be able to distinguish between a pistol (semiautomatic) and a revolver but may be unable to provide much else in the way of information. With prompting and with visual guidance, the witness may be able to guess the barrel length as well as the caliber (a finger-sized hole as opposed to a pencil-sized hole) and possibly the color. It should be kept in mind that the witness's attention was on the gaping hole in the barrel, perhaps to the exclusion of everything else.

© Shutterstock, Inc./Nutink.

the source. Informants acting out of vengeance usually require anonymity, and it becomes the responsibility of the investigator to corroborate the information provided, if possible.

Sometimes, an informant provides information about a competitor as a way of weakening or dispensing with the competitor. Although the police may be reluctant to help one criminal against another, the information is often about a crime of such seriousness that a response is required. It would be a mistake to presume that the informant with an agenda has been cultivated. The informant is using the police and is not inclined to provide information that does not result in some personal advantage.

■ Cultivating Informants

There are many terms used to refer to informants: *confidential informant (CI); person providing information (PPI); cooperating person, party,* or *individual;* or simply *informant.* As noted, the most valuable informants are criminals and their associates; they are valuable in terms of the volume of information provided to the police. These informants often place themselves in situations that compromise their ability to keep secrets. When arrested, often the only thing a criminal has to trade is information about acquaintances involved in or planning criminal activities.

Every experienced investigator has **snitches** on the street for whom he or she is willing to go a long way to protect their identity and longevity. These street sources provide the bulk of information to police. How does someone become a snitch? Many snitches travel the edges of criminality without actually committing a crime, but by rubbing shoulders with those who do. These same individuals also may fantasize about being a police officer or assisting the police and may voluntarily assist an investigator once approached and identified as a non-player. The problem with informants of this type is that they are easily influenced and may turn over on the investigator as easily as they did on the criminal. Reliability is a perennial problem with informants.

A common motivation for someone to begin acting as a snitch is survival. Contrary to popular belief, the police do not arrest every criminal for every crime committed in their presence. Some criminals are informally worked by an investigator or an officer. Patrol officers often provide investigators with leads or information about past or pending crimes. Occasionally, a suspect will be taken into custody for a relatively minor offense. Drug users, in particular, suffer greatly during periods of incarceration

because of the pain of withdrawing from the substance to which they are addicted. An occupational hazard of addiction is the possibility of having to provide police with information or face a weekend in jail. In lieu of processing the offense for which a suspect has been arrested, the investigator will offer a deal to the suspect: As long as the suspect provides an ongoing flow of information to the investigator, the investigator will continue to hold the charges in abeyance. Most misdemeanors have a statute of limitations of 2 years and allow leverage to be applied during that period. Obviously, informants of this type are highly unreliable and can disappear or align themselves with a criminal element that can provide a modicum of protection or pose a greater threat than the offense being used as leverage.

The most useful information is an offer during ongoing investigations in which serious charges can be brought. Federal grand juries often conduct investigations over long periods of time, especially investigations that involve drug traffickers or organized crime. Persons caught up in the international narcotics trade or in the web of crime-family homicides may be given the opportunity to accept immunity for the information they can provide. Investigations on the state level often result in plea bargaining or in getting an informant to introduce an undercover agent to criminals at a certain rung on the criminal ladder. There is great danger inherent in these operations, in that the informant may choose to compromise the information provided or compromise the officer, given the introduction. Yet, informants, for all their inherent problems, are an indispensable element in the war on crime, especially the war on drugs.

■ Informant Reliability

If information provided by an informant is to be used to establish probable cause, it must first meet certain legal requirements. The history of **hearsay** in providing probable cause is illustrative of the courts' distrust of hearsay and informants. To understand the courts' lack of appreciation for informants and hearsay, it is necessary to consider three cases dealing with these issues: *Draper v. United States* (1959), *Spinelli v. United States* (1969), and *Illinois v. Gates* (1983).

As a result of *Spinelli v. United States,* hearsay upon which police could rely in establishing probable cause must have continued to meet the test set forth in *Aguilar v. Texas* (1964), now commonly known as the two-pronged test. Both prongs need to be satisfied before informant

snitch
Criminal or person who associates with criminals who gives information to police about acquaintances involved in or planning criminal activities

hearsay
Any out-of-court statement made by someone other than the person testifying

— Ripped from the Headlines —

Trouble with Using Police Informants in the U.S.

There are some estimates that put the number of U.S. drug cases utilizing informants as 90% or higher. However, there is a groundswell of calls for system reform due to surprisingly few rules governing how informants are used.

"Snitches' are staple fare in Hollywood crime dramas, often working secretly with the police to bring down mafia godfathers or powerful drug cartels." However, informants are used at nearly all levels of law enforcement and investigations. State, local and federal agencies all make use of informants within their investigative processes. "The use of criminal informants is often very helpful in penetrating organized crime, but that's not how we use criminal informants in this country—we use them everywhere," says Alexandra Natapoff, professor of law at Loyola Law School in Los Angeles. The number of informants has exploded in the past few decades. The main reason is the tough mandatory minimum sentences introduced in the 1980s for even relatively minor drug crimes.

Snitching offers one of the few escape hatches.

"Every defendant facing a mandatory minimum sentence will be confronted with the reality that becoming an informant may be the only way to get out from under those very high sentences," says Natapoff. However, "There are almost no rules constraining the government in its effort to persuade people to co-operate, the threats they can make to induce people to become informants, and how they are handled after that," she argues.

There is call to reform the laws on mandatory sentences for drug crimes for a variety of reasons, but one of them is pertaining to the issues brought up within this article. "You bust the little man, the little man snitches on the bigger man, he faces 25 years, so he turns round and snitches on a bigger man. That's the way this law was written, for the drug cartel and the mafia," he says.

"It was written so you could go up the chain of command. But that's not what it's doing. It's all the little guys at street level that are fighting each other."

"What snitching does is it rewards the informed, so the lower you are on the totem pole of criminal activity, the less useful you are to the government," says Natapoff. "The higher up in the hierarchy you are, the more you have to offer."

Data from Walker, R. (2013, March 27). The trouble with using police informants in the U.S. *BBC News*. Retrieved July 7, 2017, from http://www.bbc.com /news/magazine-21939453

© Shutterstock, Inc./rzarek.

CASE IN POINT

© Shutterstock, Inc./Vlastas.

Draper v. United States, 1959

A Denver narcotics agent had received word from an informant that Draper was going to Chicago to bring back heroin. He was to travel by train the morning of September 8 or 9. The informant, who had previously provided reliable information, gave a detailed description of Draper, including the clothes he would be wearing, and said that he would be walking fast. Denver police set up surveillance of all trains arriving on the two mornings in question. On the second day, police observed a person matching the description of Draper. He exited the train and walked fast. He was arrested. Heroin and a syringe were seized in a search pursuant to the arrest. Draper was convicted of transporting heroin.

The question of first impression to the U.S. Supreme Court was: Can information that would not be admissible at the time of trial, because it was hearsay, be used to establish probable cause to effect an arrest? There was no doubt that the information provided by the informant was hearsay. Hearsay evidence is any out-of-court statement made by someone other than the person testifying. The officer cannot testify at trial as to what he has been told without violating the hearsay rule. The Court in the Draper case said that the corroboration of the information by the police and the fact that the informant had proven reliable in the past allowed the information to be used in forming probable cause for the purposes of a search. The Court said that there was probable cause in this case because the informant had been employed specifically for that purpose and had provided reliable information in the past. The Court thus felt it would have been dereliction of duty to have ignored the information.

© Shutterstock, Inc./Nutink.

CASE IN POINT

© Shutterstock, Inc./Viastas.

Spinelli v. United States, 1969

Spinelli came to the attention of the Federal Bureau of Investigation (FBI), who placed him under surveillance. He was watched entering an apartment building. A check of the phone records at the apartment confirmed what an informant had said about phone numbers being used by Spinelli in a bookmaking operation.

A search warrant affidavit was written as a result of the informant's bookmaking tip and the investigators' corroboration of that tip. A warrant was issued based on the affidavit, and evidence of Spinelli's racketeering was discovered that laid the foundation for his conviction for interstate travel in aid of racketeering.

It was this case that the U.S. Supreme Court used to promulgate its two-pronged test for informant reliability. Keeping in mind the misgivings the courts had of this type of hearsay information, it is not surprising that the Supreme Court was concerned with the credibility not only of the informant but also of the information provided. It held that the evidence gathered from the surveillance was insufficient to establish probable cause and that the information provided by the informant lacked indices of reliability.

© Shutterstock, Inc./Nutink.

information can be used to establish probable cause—that is, the informant must be reliable and the information must be reliable. It seemed that the Court believed that any citizen providing information to the police must have done so on a prior occasion, and independent corroboration of the information by the police was to be expected. A failure of either prong of the two-pronged test rendered the information legally unusable.

The Supreme Court did not leave us with the *Aguilar/Spinelli* two-pronged standard. Although the test is still a good place to start in determining informant reliability, the Court set it aside in the case of *Illinois v. Gates* (1983). The Court had to come to grips with the reality of a drug war that was neither being won nor waged effectively. Law enforcement was provided more latitude in its battle against drugs, and the Court provided one more weapon by abrogating the *Spinelli* standard. The Court recognized that, on the street, police needed to consider all of the circumstances in determining informant reliability. Therefore, the "totality of circumstances" standard was the test to be applied. In essence, this standard asks: Is it more likely than not that the information being provided by the informant is reliable?

Surveillance

Watching people, places, and things may not always be exciting, but it is a necessary component of many criminal investigations. Perhaps the most tedious of all investigative tasks, surveillance is nonetheless an important source of information and can also corroborate information that would otherwise be useless for

establishing probable cause and confirming suspicions. Surveillance may be part of an ongoing investigation or an operation to prevent a crime from occurring (**FIGURE 3.3**). The most common reason for placing a person, a place, or a thing under surveillance is to locate a suspect. Surveillance may be continuous or periodic, intense or casual. The type of surveillance best chosen is determined by the seriousness of the situation (offense), the availability of personnel, and the sophistication of the suspect.

The key to successful surveillance is planning. The Navy SEALs refer to the seven Ps: "Prior proper planning prevents piss-poor performance." Although indecorous, the saying does bring home the importance of planning in any team operation. Experience is needed to conduct proper surveillance. Being able to react spontaneously to an unforeseen development requires imagination, stamina, and courage.

FIGURE 3.3: Conducting Surveillance.

© Dmitry Kalinovsky/Shutterstock, Inc.

CASE IN POINT

Illinois v. Gates, 1983

The Bloomingdale, Illinois, police department received an anonymous letter dated May 3, 1978, containing information that Gates was planning to fly to Florida and his wife was planning to drive her car to Florida on May 3 so that she and Gates could drive back to Bloomingdale with large quantities of drugs. The letter also indicated that Gates and his wife had more than $100,000 worth of drugs in their home. Acting on this tip from an anonymous and never-before-used informant, the police discovered that Gates had made reservations for a May 5 flight to Florida. The Drug Enforcement Administration (DEA) placed Gates and his wife under surveillance and discovered that he had taken the May 5 flight and had stayed in a hotel room registered to his wife. The couple left the following morning, and a search warrant for Gates's home and car was issued based on the informant's tip and the corroboration of the officers.

Upon arriving home, Gates found the police waiting. A search of the house and car disclosed marijuana and other illegal items. Gates was convicted of violating state drug laws. The court abandoned the two-pronged test of *Spinelli* and replaced it with a more flexible **totality of the circumstances** test. The court ruled that the task of the police in drafting an affidavit for a search warrant and of a magistrate in issuing that warrant is to determine whether, given all of the circumstances, "there is a fair probability that the evidence sought will be found in a particular place."

totality of the circumstances
Test used to determine if information supplied by an informant is legally usable; it states that such information is legal if, given all the circumstances, there is a fair probability that the evidence sought will be found in a particular place

The most common type of surveillance involves a suspect on the move, either on foot, in a car, or in the air. Usually, police use an automobile in conducting surveillance. A lack of personnel and resources means that only one automobile might be available. Unfortunately, it is fairly easy to detect a single surveillance automobile, because it must stay behind the subject and within view. Career criminals check periodically for **tails** and are often successful in eluding (shaking) a tail. Important cases justify using multiple automobiles for surveillance and expending the required resources.

Following someone on foot is a tricky business. The unaware or unsophisticated suspect is easy to follow if the surveillance is from afar and the tail understands the basic rules of foot surveillance. The suspect may enter a building or a vehicle to test for a tail. In one-car or one-person surveillance, when the suspect enters a building, it is best not to follow the suspect into the edifice but rather await his or her exit. Should there be more than one entrance, the officer should watch the entrance that the suspect used. Generally, people will exit through the same portal they entered—unless suspicious of a tail, in which case, the entry into the building may have been for the sole purpose of shaking the tail.

A **stakeout** is a type of surveillance that requires great patience and many departmental resources. Places and things are generally the focus of a stationary surveillance. Houses, automobiles, or hidden contraband may draw the attention of investigators.

Deciding the vantage point for fixed surveillance requires imagination and an appreciation of the characteristics of the setting and the people who live and work in the area. Police observers must be unobtrusive and draw no attention to themselves or their positions. Fixed surveillance is generally conducted for the following reasons (Lyon, 2007):

- To gather evidence pertaining to a person, place, or activities

- To establish probable cause for a search or arrest warrant

- To apprehend suspects

- To corroborate information provided by an informant

- To assess access routes for a tactical response

- To protect undercover operatives

Often, police will conduct a fixed surveillance and make audio recordings through the use of wiretaps or bugs. Whichever device is used, a warrant for the use of the device may be necessary. The two cases that provide the answers to questions involving intrusions into someone's spoken word are *Katz v. United States* (1967) and *On Lee v. United States* (1952).

The Katz decision overruled a prior decision in *Olmstead v. United States* (1928), which held that wiretapping did not violate the Fourth Amendment unless there was some trespass into a "constitutionally protected area." According

tail
Mobile or moving surveillance of a suspect

stakeout
A type of stationary surveillance that generally focuses on places and things and requires great patience and many departmental resources

INVESTIGATOR'S NOTEBOOK

Multivehicle Surveillance

In planning multivehicle surveillance, all participants must be aware of the various techniques employed by suspects to detect a tail and the methods of foiling such efforts. Changes of direction by the suspect to run a "square" in order to watch following vehicles can be dealt with by maintaining automobiles on parallel routes. When the vehicle turns, a radio message conveys to operatives that a parallel vehicle should take up the surveillance. Entry into a parking lot or garage requires a vehicle to watch the entrance and/or exit while the tailing vehicle either drives by the parked suspect or parks with the suspect vehicle in view. The surveillance should then be continued by a trailing vehicle at the entrance or exit.

The suspect may ignore traffic control devices or double back along his or her route of travel. Both tactics are generally unsuccessful in multivehicle surveillance if the officers involved have planned for this possibility. Obviously, in multivehicle and multiofficer surveillance, radio communications become an important element of the operation. More and more citizens have police scanners and monitor radio traffic. A secure channel should be maintained or cell phones should be used for communication.

© Shutterstock, Inc./Nutink.

INVESTIGATOR'S NOTEBOOK

Essential Considerations When Planning Surveillance

1. Who will watch?
2. When will watching take place?
3. What will be watched?
4. How long will the person, place, or thing be watched?
5. Will surveillance be sporadic or continuous?
6. Who will pay for the watching?
7. When will the watching cease?
8. Under what circumstances should watching be forsaken?
9. From where will watching take place?
10. What information is to be recorded?
    a. Documentary
    b. Audio
    c. Video (photographic)
11. What are the team members' roles?
    a. Watchers
    b. Gofers (errand runners)
        i. Food and drink
        ii. Equipment
    c. Problem solvers
    d. Recorders
        i. Notes
        ii. Photos
        iii. Videos
        iv. Audio recordings

© Shutterstock, Inc./Nutink.

to the Katz test, a search has been conducted whenever there is a reasonable expectation of privacy and that expectation has been breached. The Constitution protects people rather than places, and the Fourth Amendment is portable.

The *Katz* case established the basis for all wiretaps. All states have specific procedural statutes governing the issuance of wiretap orders as does the federal government. There is a widely recognized exception to the *Katz* standard, however—an exception that has also been codified in most states. This issue is seen in the case *On Lee v. United States*.

Legal Trends in Surveillance

As a result of innovations in electronic technology, there is virtually nothing today's police officers cannot hear, see, or follow. Parabolic microphones, sonic wave detectors, digital audio bugs, and "bionic ears" allow officers to listen to conversations just about anywhere. Even wiretaps have become much more sophisticated: They can now intercept conversations occurring over cell phones or satellite phones and between computers. Officers can also utilize night vision technology, thermal infrared imaging, helicopter surveillance with forward-looking infrared (FLIR) devices, and tiny video cameras that can be hidden in such things as eyeglasses and smoke detectors.

As a general rule, court authorization is not required to use **enhancement technology** to obtain better picture or sound quality provided that police are legitimately situated when the interception is made. As the U.S. Supreme Court observed, there is nothing in the Fourth Amendment that prohibits police from augmenting the sensory faculties bestowed upon them at birth with such enhancement as science and technology affords them (*People v. Arno*, 1979).

Acquisition technology surveillance devices do not merely enhance sights or sounds; they actually permit officers to acquire sights and sounds that they would not otherwise have been able to perceive from a legitimate vantage point. Examples include hidden listening devices and

enhancement technology
Technical devices that allow augmentation of sound or picture quality; such technology does not require a warrant or other court authorization

acquisition technology
Technical devices that permit officers to acquire sights and sounds that they would not otherwise have been able to perceive from a legal vantage point; such technology requires a warrant or other court order

— Ripped from the Headlines —

Drone Use in Police Surveillance

A 2014 presentation by a professor from Pepperdine University School of Law assembled some considerations for legislatures as concerns the use of drones and aerial surveillance (**FIGURE A**). The expanded use of unmanned aerial vehicles (commonly referred to as "drones") have led many to call for legislation mandating prohibition of drone use unless a warrant has been obtained.

"The first drone-related legislation appeared in 2013 in Florida, Idaho, Montana, Oregon, North Carolina, Tennessee, Virginia, and Texas. In 2014, Wisconsin, Illinois, Indiana, Utah, and Iowa also passed laws seeking to address the use of drones by law enforcement." Privacy advocates are concerned because they contend that the use of drones will increase surveillance efforts and could result in "widespread pervasive surveillance because drones are cheaper to operate than their manned counterparts."

However, according to the legal decision *Florida v. Riley*, the Supreme Court held that "the Fourth Amendment does not require the police traveling in the public airways to an altitude of 400 feet to obtain a warrant in order to observe what is visible to the naked eye." Thus, the law for almost the past 30 years has allowed law enforcement to fly above private property and observe citizens and property. It remains to be seen what the cheaper and more prevalent use of aerial surveillance will mean as it pertains to legislation and court rulings in the near future…

Data from McNeal, G. (2014, November). Drones and aerial surveillance: Considerations for legislatures. *Brookings.edu*. Retrieved July 7, 2017, from https://www.brookings.edu/research/drones-and-aerial-surveillance-considerations-for-legislatures/

FIGURE A: Unmanned Aerial Surveillance Vehicle (drone).
© Capture PB/Shutterstock, Inc.

© Shutterstock, Inc./rzarek.

CASE IN POINT

Katz v. United States, 1967

Defendant Katz was a bookmaker running a "wire" operation. He used a public telephone booth to call in street wagers to a site nearby that had a phone bank for accepting illegal wagers. The FBI suspected Katz of bookmaking and had him under surveillance. His routine use of the public telephone gave rise to additional suspicion, although it lacked probable cause. The FBI determined that because the telephone booth was visible to the public, there was no Fourth Amendment protection for those using the telephone inside. They placed a listening device on the outside of the booth without physically trespassing into the booth and recorded the defendant's conversations. Katz was convicted of transmitting wagering information across state lines.

The U.S. Supreme Court determined that any type of wiretapping that violated a person's reasonable expectation of privacy was a search under the Fourth Amendment and must be accompanied by a warrant or an exception to the warrant requirement. The Court held that Katz did not give up his right to Fourth Amendment protection because he made his call from a public place. One who uses a public telephone and shuts the door has demonstrated an expectation that conversations taking place therein are to be kept private. Considering the circumstances of this case, the Court felt that Katz should have been able to presume that the words he uttered into the mouthpiece were not to be broadcast to the world.

wiretaps. As a general rule, a warrant or other court order is required to use acquisition technology (*Katz v. United States*, 1967).

Some devices coming onto the market are so technologically sophisticated that a reasonable person could not envision that they would be able to enhance or acquire that which was intercepted. Defendants may argue that a warrant is required whenever officers want to utilize surveillance equipment that is highly sophisticated, regardless of whether it is also highly intrusive. At present, the courts have rejected the argument that a warrant is required to utilize a surveillance device merely because it is "sophisticated" or technologically complex (*United States v. Knotts*, 1983). In dealing with new technology, it would be wise to remember that the more sophisticated a form of technology, the greater the likelihood that warrantless use will

constitute an unreasonable intrusion. What is considered sophisticated today, however, will be on the journey to obsolescence tomorrow.

Police also rely on vehicle tracking devices to follow cars driven on public streets. These devices can be attached secretly to the suspect's vehicle or personal property. A warrant is not required to attach a tracking device to a car if the car is parked in a public place. A warrant is not required to follow a tracking device placed on a vehicle as long as the vehicle remains on public streets or in public places. In *United States v. Knotts* (1983), the Supreme Court held that "a person traveling in an automobile on public thoroughfares has no reasonable expectation of privacy in his movements from one place to another."

If a tracking device has been hidden inside a movable item, a warrant is not required to track it as it is carried to the home. Once the item is

CASE IN POINT

On Lee v. United States, 1952

On Lee was suspected of selling opium. A federal undercover agent and former acquaintance of On Lee entered On Lee's laundry wearing a radio transmitter while engaging him in conversation, all of which was being monitored by offsite federal agents. The conversations played a significant role at trial in winning a conviction of On Lee for selling opium. The Court held that there was no trespass onto On Lee's premises, in that it was open to the public and entry was invited. No trespass occurred, but was there a breach of On Lee's reasonable expectation of privacy? The Court felt that as long as the police have the permission of one of the parties to the conversation, eavesdropping on or recording the conversation is not a Fourth Amendment violation. Because a person assumes the risk that whatever is said to another person may be reported to the police, it follows that if the police are invited to share in that conversation, there is no violation of the suspect's constitutional rights.

carried into the residence, however, a warrant is required to continue tracking its movements because the tracking device is transmitting information "that could not have been obtained through visual surveillance" (*United States v. Knotts*, 1983).

One of the most effective methods of conducting surveillance is to do so from an airplane or helicopter. A warrant is not required to conduct aerial surveillance over public or private property, because air traffic is such a common part of our daily lives that people cannot reasonably expect privacy from the air unless the flight is being conducted in an unusually intrusive manner (*Florida v. Riley*, 1989). Surveillance from aircraft or helicopters may be conducted without a warrant as long as the following are true:

1. The aircraft has a legal right to be at the altitude, permitted by Federal Aviation Administration (FAA) regulations.

2. The flight is conducted in a "physically non-intrusive manner."

3. If a helicopter is used, it is not flown at unusually low altitudes, absent exigent circumstances.

Officers who are conducting aerial surveillance are free to use binoculars, camera equipment, or other surveillance technology to enhance that which is visible from the air.

Thermal imaging forward-looking infrared devices, commonly known as FLIRs, are mounted under aircraft in gimbaled housings and are used to detect heat sources. The most common use is in nighttime high-speed pursuits. Thermal imaging devices have also been used in cases where the police have reason to believe that marijuana is being grown inside a home, business, or other structure. The U.S. Supreme Court has held that the government may not use a device that is not in general public use to explore details of a private home that would previously have been unknowable without physical intrusion, ruling that such surveillance would be a Fourth Amendment search and, therefore, presumptively unreasonable without a warrant (*Kyllo v. United States*, 2001). It would appear that the use of FLIRs for identifying marijuana in open fields and unenclosed areas of curtilage would be constitutionally acceptable.

Binoculars and telescopes can function as either enhancement or acquisition devices, depending on their proximity to the target. If they are used merely to enlarge or clarify something visible to the naked eye, they are enhancement devices that require no legal authorization. On the other hand, a warrant may be required to utilize devices that acquire images that could not be seen from a suitable vantage point. Regarding night-vision binoculars, the courts have agreed that the use of artificial means to illuminate a darkened area does not constitute a search (*Oregon v. Wacker*, 1993).

Thanks to modern technology, officers can overhear people talking just about anywhere; however, an intercept order is required if the parties to the conversation reasonably expect privacy. Like wiretaps, listening devices are considered acquisition technology; thus, a court order or the consent of a party to the conversation is required if the device has been hidden inside the suspect's home, private office, or any other place in which a reasonable expectation of privacy exists (*United States v. McIntyre*, 1978).

In this vein, although the courts have not yet decided, it would appear that the use of parabolic microphones would be constitutionally permissible if the conversations that were being listened to or recorded were taking place in public subject to being overheard by the casual listener. Similarly, under federal law, the term **electronic communication** means in-transit electronic impulses, sounds, and other signals transmitted over wire, radio, or microwave. Absent issues of national security or investigation of organized crime, a federal court order or consent is necessary to intercept electronic communications if the transmission is not "readily accessible to the general public."

Police may take video images of anything that occurs in a public place, open fields, or any place not subject to a recognized expectation of privacy (*Lopez v. United States*, 1963). Similarly, although looking through windows may not be nice, it is lawful under certain circumstances:

1. The window is uncovered or only partially covered.

2. The police are in a place they have a legal right to be or are invited to be.

3. The officers' observations are made with the naked eye or enhanced by binoculars (*People v. Camacho*, 2000).

The use of dogs to detect drugs, explosives, or other contraband does not constitute a search as long as the activity takes place in a public forum. In addition, the warrantless inspection of garbage left for pickup in a public place does not constitute a search. Once the garbage is placed outside the curtilage of the home, it no longer enjoys the protection of the Fourth Amendment (*California v. Greenwood*, 1988).

electronic communication
In-transit electronic impulses, sounds, and other signals transmitted over wire, radio, or microwave

Useful information is available from the phone company, namely, information dealing with incoming calls, outgoing calls, addresses, payment histories, and residential histories. There is no recognized expectation of privacy in these records in that the phone company and not the suspect keeps them (*Smith v. Maryland*, 1979).

Modus Operandi

The identification of a suspect may be the product of how the crime was committed. The methods employed by the perpetrator to commit the crime may be so unusual as to bear noting. It is these methods, or MOs, that

signature
A factor or factors that make the crime atypical and distinguishable from other crimes and other criminals

may be an unintended clue to the offender's identity. Most crimes are so typical in terms of motive or methods as to be indistinguishable from one another. (In such cases, only evidence particular to the suspect, victim, or their relationship is likely to be useful.) Determining the MO in these types of cases will provide little information apart from generalizations that will not lead to a suspect or his or her identity. It is the uniqueness of a crime that qualifies an MO as workable.

Experienced investigators have encountered criminals whose MOs are so identifiable as to serve as a **signature** for the offender. The FBI

CASE IN POINT

© Shutterstock, Inc./Viastas.

Rooftop Slaying

Francine Elveson was a 26-year-old teacher of handicapped children at a local daycare center. Weighing 90 pounds and standing less than 5 feet tall, she brought a rare empathy and sensitivity to her students, being mildly handicapped herself with kyphoscoliosis (curvature of the spine). Shy and not very socially oriented, she lived with her parents in the Pelham Parkway House apartments in the Bronx, New York.

On May 1, 1963, she left for work as usual at 6:30 in the morning. At about 8:20, a 12-year-old boy who also lived in the building found her wallet in the stairwell between the third and fourth floors. He had no time to do anything with it and still be on time for school, so he kept it until he came home for lunch and then gave it to his father. The father went to the Elveson apartment a little before 3:00 that afternoon and gave the wallet to Francine's mother, who then called the daycare to let Francine know her wallet had been found. Mrs. Elveson was told her daughter had not shown up for work that day. Instantly alarmed, she and her other daughter and a neighbor began a search of the building.

On the roof landing at the top of the stairwell, they came upon Francine's nude body, beaten by blunt-force trauma so severely that the medical examiner later found that her jaw, nose, and cheeks had been fractured and her teeth loosened. She lay spread eagle and was tied with her own belt and nylon stockings around her wrists and ankles, though the medical examiner determined she was already dead when this was done. Her nipples had been cut off after death and placed on her chest. Her underpants had been pulled over her head to cover her face, and bite marks were on her thighs and knees. The several lacerations on the body, all of them shallow, suggested a small pocketknife. Her umbrella and pen had been forced into her vagina and her comb was placed in her pubic hair. Her earrings had been placed on the ground symmetrically on either side of her head. The cause of death was determined to be ligature strangulation with the strap of the victim's own pocketbook. On her thigh the killer had scrawled, "You can't stop me," and on her stomach, he had written, "Fuck you"—both with the pen that had been inserted into her vagina. The other significant feature of the scene was that the killer had defecated near the body and covered the excrement with some of Francine's clothing.

Traces of semen were found on her body. There were no defensive wounds on the hands or blood traces or skin fragments under her fingernails. The only tangible piece of forensic evidence was a single hair found on the body during the autopsy.

The initial attack occurred when Francine walked down the stairs. After she was battered unconscious, she was carried up to the roof landing. The autopsy indicated that she had not been raped.

Francine's parents said she sometimes took the elevator, sometimes the stairs, with no particular regularity. The occupants of the dwelling were about 40% African American, 40% white, and 20% Hispanic.

Based on the information provided in this chapter:

- Was this an organized or disorganized crime scene? Why?

- Who would you want to talk to? Why?

Source: Douglas, J. E., & Olshaker, M. (1996). *Mind hunter: Inside the FBI's elite serial unit*. New York: Pocket Books.

© Shutterstock, Inc./Nutink.

developed the **Violent Criminal Apprehension Program (VICAP)** in an effort to collect into databases, crime scene information unique enough to be identifiably the work of particular offenders. Although the database contains information that surpasses that contained in an offender's MO, there is little question that MO is included and was probably the starting point for the collection of the data. Most agencies have a rogues' gallery of photographs of past offenders. In the old days, these photographs were placed in books, and victims were asked to examine mug shots of prior offenders in the hopes of identifying the perpetrator. Today, it should be no surprise that many agencies have their rogues' gallery digitally entered into a computer system that includes information about a particular criminal's MO. The gallery can be searched by criteria, such as gender, race, age, name, height, weight, hair color, visible markings, eye color, or MO.

Modus operandi is further subdivided into the following elements:

- Time of day
- Location
- Property at issue
- Indoor versus outdoor
- Types of buildings involved (commercial or residential)
- Signatures

- Particular entry methodology or words
- Particular exit methodology or words
- Clothing
- Weapon
- Soiled scene
- Disguise
- Con (pretending to be on the premises legitimately relative to a particular job or status)
- Victim targeting
- Branding (whatever is left or taken unrelated to the commission of the crime)

Coupling faces with MOs allows the database to serve a dual purpose as a compilation of mug shots and as a database of MOs and their association with particular individuals, particular behaviors, and particular places with a criminal history.

Crime Mapping

Crimes are not geographically random. For a moment in time, crimes, victims, and offenders all exist at the same place at the same time. The lure of targets and their geographic availability determine where people decide to commit crimes. Mapping crimes provides insight into the where and, derivatively, perhaps the why of crimes (**FIGURE 3.4**). Mapping can help law enforcement officials identify the areas in which citizens need protection. The simplest

Violent Criminal Apprehension Program (VICAP) Program that collects, sorts, analyzes, and categorizes data on serial homicides in an effort to uncover hidden relationships among homicides, victims, and modi operandi

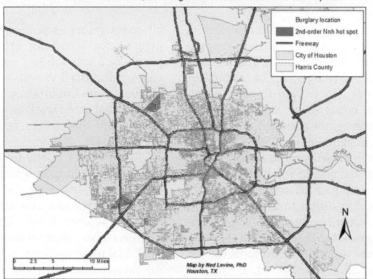

FIGURE 3.4: Crime Mapping.
Map produced by Ned Levine & Associates, Houston, TX; 2017.

of maps can be used to direct patrols to where concentrations of crimes suggest the most help is needed. Police administrators use maps to record criminal trends and to assist in the allocation of staff and resources. Criminal investigators use maps to help develop profiles of serial offenders and to geographically isolate a serial offender's comfort zone (Miller, Vandome, & McBrewster, 2010).

Crime mapping, in essence, is not new; police have long used pushpins in maps to isolate areas of criminal activity and to delineate the working area for particular offenders. Today, however, geographic information system (GIS) software allows police to produce digital maps. The same GIS software used to map crime locations can be used to calculate crime density (number of crimes per square mile). These density values can be used to create a map that uses color to represent different values among land units in the study area.

Data from sources other than law enforcement can be used in crime mapping and analysis. Census data can be used to examine a particular crime and the locations at which it is occurring with respect to demographic factors. A large cluster of homicides in high-population areas allows a correlation to be drawn between homicides and population density. Data pertaining to vacant housing units may represent a concentration of certain drug, violent, or property crimes. Police departments use computer-mapped crime locations to pinpoint hot spots,

that is, areas with high concentrations of crime. Hot-spot analysis can be conducted using spatial and temporal analysis of crime (STAC) software. The Illinois Criminal Justice Information Authority developed this software, which draws ellipses based on the densest concentrations of mapped incidents (Miller et al., 2010).

As with all computer-generated data, the end result is only as good as the information going in—garbage in, garbage out. Databases are tools that assist law enforcement officers in the management of information. No matter how sophisticated the instrument used to manage, organize, or manipulate information, the usefulness of the analysis is directly proportionate to the time, care, quantity, and reliability of the data on which the analysis is based.

Interviewing

An additional part of managing nearly any investigation, and a component that very much involves the cultivation of sources of information; pertains to interviewing; and sometimes, with luck, interrogation. Investigators **interview** witnesses or persons with information; after a suspect is in custody, the investigator moves from interviewing to **interrogation**. Whereas the goal of interviewing is to gather information, the goal of interrogation is to establish the truth. Because interviewing and interrogation is such a crucial part of an investigation, this topic is addressed as its own chapter (Chapter 7).

interview
A conversation with witnesses or victims in order to elicit information

interrogation
The formal questioning of a suspect conducted in a controlled environment and performed in an accusatory manner in order to learn the truth

CONCLUSION

When we watch investigations on television, everyone appears to know what their responsibilities are and addresses them. There seems to be no clear-cut management or leadership. Contrary to what is portrayed through entertainment, each crime scene is the responsibility of the investigator assigned to the case. Within it, that assignment includes the understanding that the investigator in charge knows how to manage the people who will be assisting in the processing of the crime scene, from the first-responding officer to forensic personnel working at his or her direction. The assignment also assumes that the investigator knows how to apply the appropriate protocol for the type of crime being investigated. In the old days, that skill came from on-the-job training; today, crime scene management is taught to

all investigators as police recruits and during investigator schooling. Effectively managing people or a location is a learned process. This chapter discussed various management methods but, more importantly, draws attention to the fact that those working on a crime scene do not manage themselves, nor does the location manage itself.

This chapter briefly touched on interrogation. The next chapter discusses the subject in depth. Today, many people believe that most crimes are cleared through the use of forensic evidence. While it is not a bad thing to believe, it is inaccurate. Most serious crimes are cleared by skillful interrogations, and the key to a skillful interrogation involves preparation. The next chapter reveals the secrets to a successful interrogation.

QUESTIONS FOR REVIEW

1. In MCI, who conducts the preliminary investigation?

2. In MCI, how is it determined if a follow-up investigation is to be conducted?

3. In MCI, who conducts the follow-up investigation?

4. What are solvability factors?

5. What risks or limitations are inherent in dealing with informants?

6. What is hearsay evidence, and how does the exclusion of hearsay evidence apply to information provided by informants?

7. What three cases have played a role in determining whether information from informants can be used to establish prob-able cause? Discuss the importance of each case.

8. What is GIS, and how is law enforcement using it?

9. When interviewing children, what effect do leading questions have on the credibility of the interview?

10. List four ways that suggestibility may influence the results of an interview with a child.

11. Explain how someone else might influence a child's testimony during an interview.

12. Discuss ways to avoid the hazards associated with child interviews.

13. List the core principles of NIMS.

REFERENCES

Department of Homeland Security. (2017). *National incident management system.* Retrieved July 13, 2017, from https://www.fema.gov/national-incident-management-system

Douglas, J. E., & Olshaker, M. (1996). *Mind hunter: Inside the FBI's elite serial unit.* New York, NY: Pocket Books.

Leonard, V. A., & More, H. W. (2000). *Police organization and management.* New York, NY: Foundation Press.

Lyon, D. (2007). *Surveillance studies: An overview.* Malden, MA: Polity Press.

McNeal, G. (2014, November). Drones and aerial surveillance: Considerations for legislatures. *Brookings.edu.* Retrieved July 7, 2017, from https://www.brookings.edu/research/drones-and-aerial-surveillance-considerations-for-legislatures/

Miller, F. B., Vandome, A. F., & McBrewster, J. (2010). *Crime mapping.* Mauritius: VDM Publishing.

Walker, R. (2013, March 27). The trouble with using police informants in the U.S. *BBC News.* Retrieved July 7, 2017, from http://www.bbc.com/news/magazine-21939453

KEY LEGAL CASES

Aguilar v. Texas, 378 U.S. 108 (1964).
California v. Greenwood, 486 U.S. 35 (1988).
Draper v. United States, 358 U.S. 307 (1959).
Florida v. Riley, 488 U.S. 445 (1989).
Illinois v. Gates, 462 U.S. 213 (1983).
Katz v. United States, 389 U.S. 347 (1967).
Kyllo v. United States, 533 U.S. 27 (2001).
Lopez v. United States, 373 U.S. 427 (1963).
Olmstead v. United States, 277 U.S. 438 (1928).
On Lee v. United States, 343 U.S. 747 (1952).
Oregon v. Wacker, 317 Or. 419 (1993).
People v. Arno, 90 Cal. App. 3d 505 (1979).
People v. Camacho, 23 Cal. App. 4th 824 (2000).
Smith v. Maryland, 442 U.S. 735 (1979).
Spinelli v. United States, 393 U.S. 410 (1969).
United States v. Knotts, 460 U.S. 276 (1983).
United States v. McIntyre, 582 F.2d 1221 (9th Cir. 1978).

chapter 4 The Crime Scene

> "Crime is common. Logic is rare. Therefore, it is upon logic rather than upon crime that you should dwell."
>
> **Sherlock Holmes**
> *"The Adventures of the Copper Beeches"*

KEY TERMS

ABFO scale
baseline
circle search
close-up photographs
contamination
crime scene processing plan
crime scene sketch
final sketch
first-responding officers
global positioning system (GPS)
grid search
killer's signature
lane/strip search
legend
line search
mapping
midrange photographs
overall photographs
photo log
photo placard
preliminary scene survey
press pool
rough sketch
spiral search
swath
trace evidence
triangulation
trophy
zone search

STUDENT LEARNING OUTCOMES

Upon completion of this chapter, students will be able to:

- Recognize the responsibilities of all members of the crime scene team
- Describe how to process crime scenes, big and small
- Explain the use of templates and virtual photography in constructing crime-scene sketches
- Construct crime-scene notes
- Appreciate the importance of recording/documenting the crime scene

Introduction to Crime Scenes

No matter what the crime or where the location, no two crime scenes are ever the same. Each crime scene encompasses not only the geographic area but also persons and things. Protecting the area is pointless if what is contained within it is not also protected. The entryways and exits and travel routes to and from the scene must similarly be guarded against contamination. The geographic area and the material objects within it usually can be secured easily. More difficult is preserving the people on the crime scene. Yet, they must be preserved as meticulously as any other evidence.

All crime scenes contain physical evidence, that is, evidence that can be touched, seen, or otherwise perceived using unaided senses or forensic techniques. The difficult task is to determine what is evidence and what is not. However, it is better to process too much evidence than too little. Experience will help an investigator begin to pare down what is taken from a crime scene. Each crime has its own set of evidence parameters that help in distinguishing evidence from nonevidence.

Anything taken from the crime scene should be instrumental in discovering the facts. Keep in mind that the evidence reveals the facts; when the evidence is inconsistent with a hypothesis, the hypothesis must be changed to fit the evidence—not the other way around. Numerous court cases have reduced the significance of suspects' confessions and highlighted the key role of evidentiary corroboration. The importance of crime scene processing continues to increase. Not all evidence is recognized readily as such. Seemingly insignificant material left at a crime scene can increase in importance as the trial approaches or during the trial. The skills of the investigator may come into play anywhere or at any time.

The crime scene includes all areas through which the participants moved while entering to commit the crime, while committing the crime, and while exiting the crime scene. Generally, the crime scene is a single, well-defined area, but it may encompass several noncontiguous areas. Because most human activity takes place in sheltered places, the majority of crimes occur inside. Buildings and vehicles are the most common crime scenes, so most crime scene processing involves these locations. However, as more and more people seek outdoor recreation, investigators will need to develop the ability to deal with outdoor crime scenes as well. For example, the roadways driven, the areas adjacent to a crime scene that facilitate parking, and the pathways leading to and away from an exterior scene may contain evidence of crime-related passage.

First Response

The investigative team's most valuable investigative tool consists of the officers who arrive first on the scene (**FIGURE 4.1**). Too often, these officers are excluded from the investigative "club," treated as underlings, and denied services and training that could increase the chance of investigative success. It is imperative that **first-responding officers** possess an understanding of the investigative process, including a familiarity with and an appreciation for forensic evidence and its location, processing, and handling. A telephone at a crime scene may be the most convenient phone to use, but getting to the phone and picking up the handset may destroy essential evidence. Ambling through the crime scene is preventable through education about the nature of the first-response function.

Protection of the crime scene will reduce crime scene **contamination**. All crime scenes and all evidence retrieved from a crime scene are contaminated; the goal is not to add to the contamination. Only materials handled in contamination-free laboratories can be said to be truly uncontaminated. The trick is to prevent any untoward or unnecessary contamination from occurring once the scene and its contents come into the possession of the police. Anyone entering a crime scene leaves something; anyone departing a crime scene

first-responding officers
First officers to arrive at the crime scene. They are responsible for protecting the crime scene from any avoidable contamination in order to preserve it for investigation purposes

contamination
Materials and other factors added to crime scenes that were not there at the time of the crime and can negatively affect the proper collection and interpretation of evidence

FIGURE 4.1: First responder.
© Ryan J. Lane/Getty Images.

takes something along. This theory is what prompts forensic scientists to search for minute materials that may have been left at the scene of the crime.

First-responding officers must protect the scene by:

- Conceptualizing the crime scene
- Establishing the boundaries of the crime scene
- Keeping out unauthorized personnel and the curious
- Detaining and separating any eyewitnesses
- Continuing security until properly relieved

While doing this, they must also obtain medical assistance for anyone at the crime scene who is injured.

The most difficult situations to deal with are those involving other agencies and media representatives. Medical examiners, emergency medical personnel, and coroners all have duties to perform. Bodies cannot be released until officials have completed their investigative analysis. Often, there will be someone making a demand for entry who may be upset by being excluded from the scene. It is vital that the police and all persons associated with a crime scene in any capacity be aware of and comply with the written policies and procedures that apply to crime scene security. Media representatives often attempt to gain access and information by invoking the First Amendment (**EXHIBIT 4.1**) and the people's right to know. Some police officers are only vaguely aware of

---

EXHIBIT 4.1

The First Amendment to the U.S. Constitution

Congress shall make no law respecting an establishment of religion, or prohibiting the free exercise thereof; or abridging the freedom of speech, or of the press; or the right of the people peaceably to assemble, and to petition the government for a redress of grievances.

U.S. Constitution. Art./Amend. I.

© Shutterstock, Inc./Africa Studio.

---

the amendment and have little understanding of the cases that have established First Amendment limitations. Nowhere does the First Amendment refer to the people's right to know, nor does it refer to extraordinary rights of the press. It simply refers to the abridgment of freedom of the press. The purpose of the First Amendment is to protect the press and the public from a strong central government and the temptation that it would have to censor the press. Denial of access to a crime scene does not abridge freedom of the press; journalists are free to write whatever they wish, within the confines of laws that govern the media.

In managing the press, it is important to attempt to maintain a good rapport with all representatives of the media. First responders do not have the responsibility to make any

---

INVESTIGATOR'S NOTEBOOK

© Shutterstock, Inc./Janaka Dharmasena.

Dos and Don'ts for Dealing with the Media

Do	*Don't*
Be firm	Be unnecessarily gruff
Be specific	Be pedantic
Be courteous	Make any on-record statements
Designate a press pool area	Apologize or make exceptions
Escort media representatives from the crime scene	Make press releases
Advise media representatives of press releases	Assist in coverage
Encourage coverage	Allow photos to be taken
Recognize First Amendment rights	Allow access to witnesses
Encourage investigative reporting	Take no for an answer
Keep lines of movement open	Allow media to be obstructive
Keep lines of communication open	

© Shutterstock, Inc./Nutink.

INVESTIGATOR'S NOTEBOOK

Media Checklist

- Do not contact the media unless you are trained and designated as the public information officer (PIO) or you are cleared through the PIO's office

- Be courteous at all times. An angry press does not serve the interests of law enforcement

- Bar all media from a crime scene and advise media representatives that an area will be set aside from which all information will be disseminated

- "No comment" is often the standard refrain of police. It is irritating to the press and should be replaced with a more rapport-building standard, such as "The public information officer will make a statement to all press representatives as soon as the situation allows."

- Avoid all contact with the media off duty as well as on duty, unless specifically charged with that responsibility

- Unauthorized statements quoted by the press are often claimed by the police to be misquotations or taken out of context; in reality, they are usually accurate, although uttered thoughtlessly or in haste. Think before you speak, and realize that anything you say can be recorded and broadcast.

- If you are the subject of press coverage, do not fall victim to believing the image that the press is attempting to portray

© Shutterstock, Inc./Nutink.

statements to the press. The public information officer should make all statements to the press, and all requests for access or statements should be referred to that officer. Media representatives have no greater right to enter a secured area than any other citizen, nor have they any greater right to information. Under no circumstances are media representatives to be allowed access to a crime scene. All information provided to the press regarding an investigation should be managed through **press pools** and public statements.

Once the boundaries of the scene have been determined and made secure, evidence must be discovered and collected and the crime reconstructed. Most evidence at a crime scene is vulnerable, and often the most effective evidence is the most easily damaged. **Trace evidence** is extremely fragile and susceptible to contamination. It is usually undetectable by the naked eye and must undergo extensive laboratory procedures before it can be preserved and used later at trial. Items of evidence, such as blood, fingerprints, hairs, fibers, footwear, broken glass, paint scrapings, tread marks, footprints, and toolmarks, are easily destroyed, altered, or contaminated. Only people authorized by written policy to help process the crime scene should be allowed on the scene.

As important as first responders are in securing the usual crime scene, they play an even more significant role in handling witnesses and securing the area in an underwater investigation. They may have to cordon off high-use areas and contact agencies that possess authority over the area.

Methodical Approach to Crime Scene Processing

Crime scenes can be complex and confusing. The first step in crime-scene processing is to establish a plan. All steps of crime scene response should be calculated and methodical to ensure the most positive result. It is for this reason that investigative personnel should take the information garnered from their preliminary scene survey and develop a systematic plan for proceeding with the processing efforts. A systematic **crime scene processing plan** will ensure that nothing is overlooked and no pertinent evidence is lost in the course of the subsequent investigation.

All crime scenes are different, but there are guidelines that exist in all cases that serve as a framework for the processing efforts. However, often, these tasks are not separate from one another but may overlap. This will be addressed

press pool
A group of journalists authorized to cover an event

trace evidence
Evidence left at the scene of a crime that usually cannot be seen with the naked eye and that requires the assistance of lights or reagents to visualize

crime scene processing plan
Plan created to carry out a systematic investigation of a crime scene

as the chapter unfolds. In any case, investigative and processing efforts should start in the least intrusive and destructive manners and progress to the most intrusive and destructive. Processing the scene this way will ensure evidence integrity for as long as possible. The first phase is documentation.

Documenting the Crime Scene

Documentation efforts at the crime scene begin the moment an officer gets a call and continue until the case is closed. This is often the most time-consuming but also the most important step in crime scene investigation (CSI). It is the purpose of crime scene documentation to record and preserve the location and relationship of discovered evidence as well as the condition of the crime scene as it was when the documenter was observing it. For the purposes of this text, there are four primary methods of documentation that are involved in CSI. These are:

1. Reports and note taking

2. Photographs

3. Videography

4. Crime-scene sketching and mapping (**FIGURE 4.2**)

The end purpose of documentation should be the successful notation of all observations made at the scene of the crime, which will ensure that the individual engaged in the documentation efforts will best be able to recall the events in the future. Importantly, this information may be presented in court.

Each of these methods is an integral part of crime scene documentation. None is a substitute for another. While some of the methods might appear to be redundant, this serves to corroborate the other methods and ensures that nothing is overlooked and that all areas are accounted for. Notes and reports are not sufficient by themselves because they do not accurately portray the scene in detail in the way that photographs can. However, photographs are not sufficient by themselves, as they often need more explanation, which is the purpose of reports and notes. Sometimes, notes are dictated into a tape or digital recording device; then, at some point, they are transcribed into a written format for court purposes. For that reason, notes and reports are defined as being both audio and written. Although photographs are a good tool for documenting the visual aspects of a scene, nothing brings the scene to life as much as videotaping. However, videos cannot be used in the same manner as photographs from a forensic analysis standpoint when documenting physical evidence.

Documentation/Reports

There is an adage in police work that, "if it's not written down, it didn't happen." To a large extent, this is true. It is important that each step of the process and every action taken be documented extensively using notes, photographs, sketches, and reports. The written notes begin with the first responder and continue throughout the investigative process. At each step, those individuals involved in the process are responsible for documenting all observations they made and all actions they performed. This includes documentation of efforts that resulted in negative findings. An example of a negative finding is a search for latent fingerprints that yielded nothing.

Each department typically has its own format and requirements for various levels of documentation in the investigative process. At the very basic level, written documentation consists of:

- Notification information

- Arrival information

- Scene description

- Victim description

- Crime scene team

Essentially, there are two types of written documentation. The first is notes. *Notes* are brief—often written in a bullet-point format—documentation of efforts, observations, and actions. Notes are taken at the time of the

FIGURE 4.2: Documenting the crime scene.

© Blitznetzov/Getty Images.

incident and are informal. The second type of written documentation is a report.

Reports can be either narratives or fill-in-the-blank forms that are utilized to record pertinent information relating to a case. These are formal and are typically unique to a particular department and specific to a certain type of scene or case. Narrative reports are formally written, usually in the first person, active voice, and past tense. They document all actions taken by the report's author and all observations he or she made.

Taking Notes

Note takers should record field notes while they are still under the stimuli that made something seem noteworthy, not later (**FIGURE 4.3**). Field notes constitute the most readily available and reliable record of the crime scene. They do not form a logical flow of events but make up a hodgepodge of information gleaned from numerous perceptions, interviews, and measurements. In large investigations, the task of note taking can seem overwhelming, but the basic principles remain the same (see Investigator's Notebook).

Field notes are the building blocks that the investigator uses to develop hypotheses and, later, a theory of the crime. Field notes also can stimulate the investigator's memory if and when the case goes to court. They provide the basic information for the official report, which is the foundation for trial testimony. The official report will contain numerous entries. The investigator will produce an initial report early in the investigation; as the investigation develops and new information is discovered, the investigator will add supplemental reports to the original. The compilation of these reports, in conjunction with the field notes, allows the investigator

to recollect the investigation in detail and thus form the backbone of the prosecution and the defense.

All courtroom testimony is balanced against the documentation that the investigator has accumulated, including his or her field notes. At the time of trial, the investigator may use the field notes to refresh his or her memory, but doing so allows the defense an opportunity to examine the notes and conduct a cross-examination of the witness pertaining to the notes. With that risk in mind, the investigator should put nothing in the notes that he or she would not be willing to share with the defense, the judge, or the jury. An additional caveat: All notes are available to the defense upon request, and the officer testifying is not allowed to remove anything from the notebook. Each notebook should contain notes about one investigation only, so that sensitive material from another investigation is not publicized inadvertently.

In some states, there is a rule of procedure that allows the defense to inquire of the witness whether there are any other writings or statements taken or made by the witness that are not included in the official report. An affirmative answer allows the defense to request a recess and an order directing the witness to obtain the documentation and return immediately with it to the courtroom. Even if the witness is not using the notes to refresh his or her memory, the defense may still obtain them if they exist.

Use of Notes

Notes are useful for the following reasons:

1. As the investigation progresses, suspects and witnesses make statements that may seem insignificant at the time but later may prove to be important. Field notes allow retrieval of those statements.

2. If a witness or suspect makes a statement and later adds information inconsistent with that statement, the notes will assist in impeaching the new statement and may lead to a confession.

3. It is through gathering, correlating, organizing, and comparing information that the crime scene is reconstructed and derivative evidence is developed.

4. Notes are important in preparing for interviews of witnesses, interrogation of suspects, and testifying before the court.

5. Attorneys for the state and the defendant will be interested in the time, date, and

FIGURE 4.3: An officer makes field notes.

INVESTIGATOR'S
NOTEBOOK
Elements of Field Notes
The Five Ws and an H

Who

- committed the crime?
- had a motive to commit the crime?
- was the victim?
- saw what happened?
- reported the crime?
- might know something?
- were the first people on the scene?

What

- was the relationship between victim and perpetrator?
- crime was committed?
- was said and by whom?
- evidence might there be?
- evidence has been discovered?
- is missing?
- was left?
- was moved?
- was touched?

Where

- did the crime occur?
- was evidence located?
- are all the witnesses?
- were all the witnesses?
- do witnesses live?
- is the suspect?
- was entry made?
- was exit made?

When

- was the crime committed?
- was the crime reported?
- was evidence discovered?
- did the first responder arrive?

- was the scene secured?

- was the scene released?

Why

- was the crime committed?

- was the victim chosen?

- was the location chosen?

- were the criminal implements chosen?

How

- did the perpetrator gain entry?

- was the crime committed?

- did the perpetrator depart?

Important Information

Field notes should also contain the following:

- *Identification of date and time* (the date and time of assignment to the case; the date and time of arrival on the scene).

- *Description of the location* (description of the scene on arrival, including weather, lighting, approaches, and geographic location). Information regarding the location can be useful in establishing lines of sight and the distance of visibility.

- *Description of the crime scene* (broad overview that narrows to specific noticeable details, such as forced entry, disarranged furniture, bloodstains, blood spatter, and the condition of doors and windows).

- *Listing of absent items*. What should be at the crime scene but is missing often reveals something about the perpetrator and the nature of the crime. A serial killer might take a souvenir or **trophy** that features prominently in fantasies associated with the killings. Such a souvenir or trophy may be helpful in establishing a profile of the killer and figuring out the **killer's signature** (the pattern associated with his or her killings).

- *Description of wounds on the victim*. The types and locations of wounds should be recorded. If discoloration is present, its location and color should be included.

- *Photograph log*. The photographer should keep a separate photo log; if the investigator takes the photos, he or she should place an entry in the field notes for each entry. The entry should include a description of the content of the photo; the speed of the film; the shutter speed; the distance from the object photographed; the location and direction from which the photo was taken; and the date, time, and case number or name.

- *Video log*. If the investigator is taking the video, the following information should be recorded: The type of recording device, the type of film (if not using digital), the type of lens or lenses, and whether artificial light was used.

- *Identification of the evidence recovered and its location*. All evidence must be geographically and temporally located. It is the investigator's job to record sufficient information to adequately place each piece of evidence. All measurements should be recorded, as well as the identity of the person who discovered the evidence. To identify evidence, the investigator should provide a description of the evidence and note its location, the time discovered, who discovered it, the type of container used to store it, the method of sealing the container, the markings used on tags and evidence, and where the evidence is being kept (maintenance log).

trophy
Remembrance or souvenir of a conquest, such as a body part

killer's signature
The pattern associated with a person's killings

INVESTIGATOR'S NOTEBOOK

Field Notes Best Practices

- Write legibly

- Write complete thoughts

- Indicate date and time for all entries.

- For each case, create one set of notes in one or more notebooks

- Share information with other investigators

- Corroborate all information

- Not everything is important, but err on the side of recording too much rather than too little

- Periodically transcribe your notes in type (they make more sense and patterns emerge more clearly)

- Organize transcriptions into categories, such as persons, places, and things; physical evidence; forensic evidence; and so on

- Use a matrix to assist in identifying information. Variations in witness statements regarding height, weight, hair color, stature, eye color, and car color or make can be recorded in a matrix to arrive at a range for each of the identifying characteristics, to compute an average, or to discover the most common response.

manner in which evidence and information were gathered and will have a vested interest in the quality and thoroughness of all reports, notes, and entries.

6. Memory is always suspect and subject to extrapolation and interpolation, the grist of cross-examination. Memory corroborated by reports and notes takes on a believability not possessed by unaided memory.

Conducting a Preliminary Scene Survey

preliminary scene survey
A careful walk through a crime scene, conducted to develop a perspective on the nature of the crime, its commission, the type of evidence that will be expected, and the types of resources necessary to properly process the scene

A **preliminary scene survey** (sometimes called a walk-through) of the crime scene is conducted to develop a perspective on the nature of the crime, its commission, and the type of evidence that will be expected and searched for. Once the scene is secure, investigative personnel should conduct a preliminary scene survey. The preliminary scene survey will have the greatest informational possibilities if the first responder is available to accompany the investigative personnel. This is because it is the first responder who has

the most direct knowledge of what the scene originally looked like when law enforcement responded to the event. He or she should also know of any changes made to the scene since that initial response. It is very important that investigators are well briefed by first responders regarding the case before conducting their examination of the scene. This ensures that the preliminary scene survey will result in maximum information gathering, while minimizing scene contamination and evidence destruction. The primary purpose of the preliminary scene survey is to assess the scene for logistic and safety considerations. During the preliminary site survey, the investigator visually locates evidence or prospective sites for trace evidence. The site survey will assist the investigator in determining the boundaries of the search, identifying focal points for the search, and discovering important evidentiary items that may need special photographic or forensic attention. Evidence that deteriorates over time or with exposure should be given processing priority. Experts may need to be invited to the scene to interpret bloodstain patterns or to process trace evidence.

The following list contains ten suggested matters to consider while conducting a preliminary site survey:

1. As with first responder efforts, make note of transient evidence present within the scene and efforts needed to properly document, collect, and preserve such evidence. If steps have not already been taken to do so, it may be necessary at this point to document, collect, package, and preserve such evidence.

2. Make note of weather and climate conditions (both indoors and outdoors).

3. Note whether lights are turned on or off.

4. Document whether doors and windows are locked, unlocked, open, closed, or if there appears to be evidence of forced entry.

5. Note the presence of any particular odors that may be connected to an individual (perfume, cologne) or an event (gas, smoke, chemicals, etc.).

6. Look for signs of activity (meal preparation, house tidy or disheveled, etc.) or struggle.

7. If timing is of great concern, look for date and time indicators such as on food, newspapers, mail, etc.

8. Attempt to locate the most probable point of entry, point of exit, paths between them, and any other areas of apparent action within the scene. These areas should be noted to ensure that processing personnel will reduce their movements in such areas to allow for the optimum opportunity to discover and collect physical evidence within the scene.

9. Attempt to answer the questions of: Who? What? When? Where? How? and Why? as they pertain to the scene and the crime in question.

10. Assess the scene for personnel (How many? Specialized?), equipment (How much? What kind?), and logistical concerns (How long? Food needs for personnel? Bathroom needs? Media considerations? Budgetary issues?). [National Forensic Science Technology Center. (2013).]

The preliminary site survey should be conducted in a cautious and aware manner. This is a minimally invasive information-gathering event and not an evidence search or collection effort.

There are two schools of thought about whether investigative personnel should wear gloves while conducting this scene survey. One view is that if personnel wear protective gloves, they will be more inclined to touch items and, therefore, they should not wear gloves and should adhere to the "hands in pockets" approach. The other view is that personnel should always wear gloves whenever they are inside a crime scene. The author agrees with the latter line of thinking for several reasons. First, the purpose of gloves is to both protect the wearer from contamination and to protect any item touched from contamination by the wearer. While it is true that in the preliminary scene survey there should be no touching of items, this is not to say that transient evidence will not be discovered that necessitates movement or collection. Having gloves on will ensure that such evidence is minimally damaged if such contact is necessary. Also, a "hands in the pocket approach" is not realistic because the point of a preliminary scene survey is to document conditions present throughout the scene. The investigator most certainly will have his or her hands outside of any pockets and will be writing and pointing throughout the process. It is best to have personnel wear gloves with the thought in the forefront of his or her mind that nothing is to be touched unless it is absolutely imperative.

After the preliminary scene survey has been conducted, investigative personnel should have the information they need to apprise supervisors of the situation and to lay out the crime scene processing strategy. At this stage, there may be a call for more specialized personnel. Some of these personnel may be from within the ranks of law enforcement. Other specialists, such as entomologists or engineers, may be necessary to provide technical assistance that is outside of the training and education of those in law enforcement. Agencies are encouraged to think broadly and utilize sources such as local universities and other private, local, state, and federal agencies to maximize the investigatory potential. If an individual has not been trained to collect or document certain evidence, they should not; instead, they should rely upon experts to do so.

A brief, and by no means all-inclusive, list of personnel who may be called upon to assist with the investigative effort is given in this section (**TABLE 4.1**).

TABLE 4.1 Personnel Associates with Investigations

Personnel	Function
Crime Scene Investigator/Crime Scene Technician	Police or civilian personnel who are specially trained to process a crime scene. Their purpose is twofold: to collect and preserve physical evidence.
Identification (ID) Officers	Responsible for photographing the scene and searching for latent fingerprints but not responsible for other types of physical evidence. Often, these individuals are fingerprint experts who later will perform comparative analyses.
Evidence Technician	Police or civilian personnel responsible for maintaining the custodial integrity of evidence. Duties and responsibilities typically include responding to and processing crime scenes, ensuring proper packaging of collected and submitted evidence, proper storage, maintaining the evidence management system to ensure proper chain of custody, and also eventual disposal and purging of evidence.
Forensic Surveyors	Often used to provide an accurate architectural rendition of the crime scene. They typically utilize Computer-Aided Drafting (CAD) to assist them with their documentation efforts.
Forensic Photographers	Specialized photography (low light, aerial, infrared, underwater, etc.) demands specific skills. These photographers have advanced training in photographic concepts and specialized situations.
Forensic Scientist/ Criminalist	Has gained specialized training and education in chemistry and biology as applied to the recognition, ID, collection, and preservation of physical evidence.
Medical Examiner/ Coroner	Forensic pathologist responsible for performing autopsies in criminal cases. This may include providing an ID of the deceased; determining cause, manner, and time of death; and taking custody of the remains.
Forensic Nurse	Licensed nurse with specialized training in proper evidence collection, and most often, is utilized in sexual assault investigations. Such nurses are usually certified sexual assault nurse examiners (SANE).
District Attorney	When called upon, provides a search warrant or a court order to obtain known specimens from a defendant. A district attorney may operate in an advisory capacity when a case involves a police officer (e.g., a police-related shooting, in-custody death of suspect, etc).
Hazardous Materials Specialists	Experts assist with recognition, collection, destruction, clean up, disposal, and preservation of hazardous materials at the crime scene.
Forensic Engineers	Engineer who analyzes the structural integrity of a building or other structures in accident investigations.
Firearms Examiners	Expert who assists in crime scene ballistic recovery and can assess the trajectory of fired weapons. He or she may also assist in determining whether a shooting was accidental or intentional.
K-9 Officers	Sworn officer and trained dog may be called upon to assist with searches and tracking of individuals; if the individual is believed to be dead or buried, cadaver dogs may be utilized. Cadaver dogs are specially trained to recognize the scent of decaying remains.
Federal Authorities	Numerous federal agencies can be called in to assist or take over a crime scene involving mass disasters, terrorist acts, bombings, major fires, and bank robberies. Some examples of these agencies include: the Federal Bureau of Investigation (FBI), the Drug Enforcement Administration (DEA), the Bureau of Alcohol Tobacco Firearms and Explosives (ATF), and the United States Secret Service (USSS).

— Ripped from the Headlines —

Civilianizing Crime Scene Duties

There is movement afoot pertaining to crime scene processing duties and who is responsible for them. A growing number of departments are finding that civilianizing crime scene duties, (having nonsworn, nonbadge, nongun carrying individuals) responsible for crime scene efforts is fiscally and strategically beneficial. The ability to hire and train civilians for specific crime scene processing efforts is more easily accomplished than the required training and education necessary to certify, hire, and train an officer. It also allows the officers to be freed up to conduct the other duties that the job calls for, which a civilian would not be able to handle.

The civilian positions are typically tasked with any situations where evidence is being collected. However, it has been increasingly recognized that a person neither needs a badge nor a gun to identify, document, collect, and preserve physical evidence. In cases where there is specific knowledge or certifications required (processing fingerprints, taking photographs, documenting blood spatter evidence, the additional training and education previously given to sworn investigative personnel can instead be given to civilians.

Keep your eyes open for these changes coming soon to a department near you!

Recording the Crime Scene

The crime scene is first recorded through photography or videography or both. The video camera is a popular tool for recording crime scenes. If used, this should be conducted either during or immediately after the preliminary scene survey and before anything is touched, examined, or moved. The result is a permanent historical record of how the scene appeared at the time of the documentation. Moving anything prior to recording the crime scene is a gross error, for a trial court will usually exclude any photograph or videotape that does not reflect the scene as it was found.

Crime Scene Photography

Entire texts have been written solely on this topic. This introduction comprises a succinct but thorough overview of the purpose and skills involved in crime scene photography. Photographers are urged to seek out books and courses that will help them to continually refine their skills.

The purpose of crime scene photography is to capture adequate images for the best possible documentation and reproduction of the reality present at the moment in time when the scene was photographed. When attempting to shoot precisely, one must remember that photography is a mechanical means of retaining vision. When properly taken, a photograph is one of the only ways to capture an instant of time. However, the camera was never intended to replace vision, because it certainly cannot (Weiss, 2009).

Crime scene photography is visual storytelling, and as such, the photographs should be a fair and accurate representation of the scene about which the story is being told.

Photographs are almost universally accepted by the courts and allowed into evidence irrespective of their image quality as long as the images contained in them are not inflammatory or prejudicial in nature (Weiss, 2009). Although it used to be necessary for a person to also be able to testify as to how a photo was developed or processed, this is rarely the case nowadays, as the images themselves are not the evidence but, rather, represent the evidence.

Photographers often may attempt to create photographs of objects or scenes "as seen" by someone else. Undoubtedly, this is an impossible undertaking, as no one can accurately document an item or moment as someone else saw it. Instead, it is an appropriate step to document the image or scene from the perspective of the viewer in approximately the same position, although not at the same moment in time (Weiss, 2009). Attention to a few simple rules can make photos acceptable to most judges.

Photographic Ranges and Perspectives

In keeping with the storytelling theme, the first photos taken at a scene should not be of gore or an item of physical evidence. Instead, they should be of the overall crime scene. They should set the stage for the beginning of the story. As such, there are three important ranges of photographs that are taken at the scene

Cityville Police Department

Case #: _____

Date: _____

Location: _____

Photographer Name: _____

Photographer ID: _____

Roll # (if applicable): _____

FIGURE 4.4: Example of a photo placard.

of a crime: overall photographs, midrange/evidence-establishing photographs, and close-up/comparison/examination photographs.

Also, it is important to remember to take a photograph of a **photo placard** as the first photo taken at the crime scene. A photo placard is a handwritten or agency-developed sheet (**FIGURE 4.4**) that lists pertinent case information for the photographs to follow. Taking a photo of this as the first photo on a roll of film or as the first digital photo of a case will ensure that personnel are familiar with which photographs pertain to which case, and the name of the photographer. Only one case should be photographed on a roll of film; however, with today's digital media, often, several (if not more) cases are photographed on a single digital media card prior to downloading onto a computer. Photographing a photo placard will serve as a separator between the cases, so that case photos will not become commingled.

■ Overall Photographs

Overall photographs (**FIGURE 4.5**) are exposed with a wide-angle lens or in such a fashion that allows the viewer to see a large area

in the scene at eye level. Their function is to document the condition and layout of the scene as it was found. They help eliminate issues of subsequent contamination (e.g., tracked blood, movement of items). Typically, these are shot from the four corners of the crime scene. If indoors, usually, they are taken from the corners of the room, shooting toward the center. If outdoors, they are often shot from the direction of a cardinal heading (north, south, east, and west). These four photographs most likely will capture the entire scene. If not, additional photographs from an appropriate vantage point can be taken. These overall photographs set the scene and should include street signs and addresses, if possible. Also, it may be necessary to not only take overall photos facing the building or scene in question but also overall photos facing away from the scene to show the surrounding area.

■ Midrange/Evidence-Establishing Photographs

The function of **midrange photographs** (**FIGURE 4.6**) is to frame the item of evidence with an easily recognized landmark. This visually

photo placard
A handwritten or agency-developed sheet that lists pertinent case information for the photographs that follow

overall photographs
Photos that show a large area of the crime scene at eye level, typically shot from the four corners of the scene; used to document the condition and layout of the scene as found

midrange photographs
Photos that frame the item of evidence with an easily recognized landmark to visually establish its position in the crime scene but not intended to show details; also called *evidence-establishing* photographs

FIGURE 4.5: Example of an overall photograph.
© South Agency/Getty Images.

FIGURE 4.6: Example of a mid-range photograph.
© Couperfield/Shutterstock, Inc.

establishes the position of the evidence in the scene in relation to the item's surroundings. These types of photographs are the most overlooked in crime scene work. They are taken of the evidence prior to movement or manipulation and should never include a scale of reference in the photo. The evidence-establishing photograph is not intended to show details, but simply to frame the item with a known landmark in the scene. The close-up and the evidence-establishing photograph go hand-in-hand.

■ Close-Up/Comparison/Examination Photographs

The function of **close-up photographs** (also called comparison, examination, or macro photographs) is to allow the viewer to see all evident details on the item of evidence (**FIGURE 4.7**). This photo should be close and fill the frame with the evidence itself. They are taken with and without a scale. It is extremely important that photographs of this type are first taken without a scale of reference and then with a scale of reference. The first photo shows the scene prior to contamination or manipulation by the photographer or crime scene personnel. The second includes a scale of reference with which the viewer is able to gauge the size of the item presented within the photograph. This scale will allow for a 1:1 ratio reproduction of the photograph (i.e., 1 inch equals 1 inch). Failure to photograph the close-up without a scale prior to incorporating a scale in the photo could result in the photo being inadmissible because of the allegation of scene tampering.

The preceding photographic ranges are used any time there is an important item of evidence that will have a bearing on the investigation. While there might be a variety of perspectives photographed, any photograph taken at a crime scene will fall under one of the preceding ranges. For instance, photographs taken from the reported position of a witness would fall into the overall range category. Those taken to show the address of a residence would fall into the mid-range category if they showed more than simply the numbers/letters and included the façade of the house or entry to the home. However, if it were only of the letters/numbers, this photograph would fall into the close-up range.

Proper Use of Forensic Scales

It is not enough for a photographer to simply make use of a scale of reference within a macro-photograph (**FIGURE 4.8**). He or she must also do so properly, or else it defeats the use of and intent behind the use of the scale of reference. In order for a scale to be of benefit, it must be possible to determine the size and/or dimension of the object(s) within the image. Forensic scales contain circles that will appear to elongate if photographed from an improper angle. Also, the lines representing termination of each centimeter can be extended to match up and intersect with the lines of the perpendicular centimeter intersection lines. If the lines do not meet and form a right angle, the photography angle was not directly overhead or parallel to the subject matter.

An **ABFO scale** is an example of a specific type of forensic scale of reference (seen within

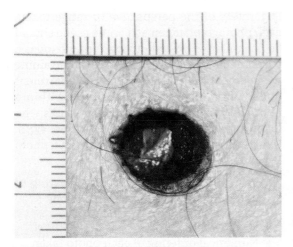

FIGURE 4.7: Example of a close-up/comparison/examination photograph.

© D. Willoughby/CMSP.

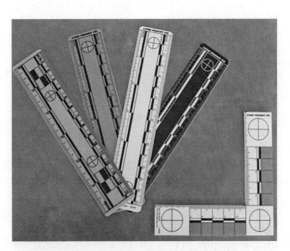

FIGURE 4.8: Examples of forensic scales of reference.

Dutelle, A.W. (2015). *Basic Crime Scene Photography*, 2nd Ed.

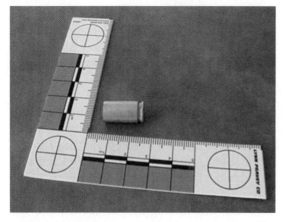

FIGURE 4.9: Improper use of ABFO scale as to evidence plane and camera angle.

Dutelle, A.W. (2015). *Basic Crime Scene Photography*, 2nd Ed.

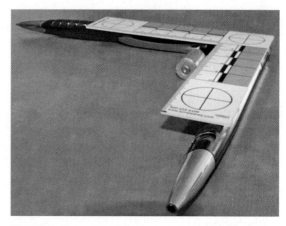

FIGURE 4.11: Use of props to raise ABFO scale to proper plane.

Dutelle, A.W. (2015). *Basic Crime Scene Photography*, 2nd Ed.

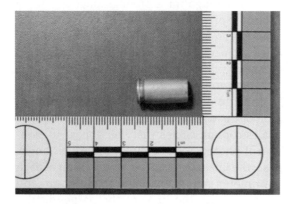

FIGURE 4.10: Proper use of ABFO scale as to plane and camera angle (props used to raise scale).

Dutelle, A.W. (2015). *Basic Crime Scene Photography*, 2nd Ed.

photo log
Recording of the people involved, equipment used, and conditions under which crime scene photographs were taken

FIGURES 4.9–4.11). An ABFO (American Board of Forensic Odontology) scale is an L-shaped piece of plastic used in photography that is marked with circles, black and white bars, and 18% gray bars to assist in distortion compensation and provide exposure determination (Figure 4.9). For measurement, the plastic piece is marked in millimeters. Note how the circles tend to look elongated and elliptical as well as how the imaginary centimeter termination lines do not result in right angles.

However, simply being at the correct angle is not sufficient to count as proper use of a scale of reference. The scale must also be present at the proper plane in order to be of the greatest benefit. If the scale is not presented at the proper plane, there will be distortion present. This is especially important when photographing impression evidence and

items of evidence exhibiting 3D characteristics (Figures 4.9–4.11).

As displayed in the previous figures, sometimes it may be necessary to raise a scale of reference in order to have it be of correct use. The opposite is also true. In the event that there is impression evidence, such as footwear or tire impressions, it will be necessary to arrange that the scale be at the same plane as the impression. Therefore, a small trench will need to be dug to the same depth as the impression, (after photographing the evidence prior to disturbing the surroundings) and the scale of reference placed within the excavated area, ensuring that the scale of reference is present on the same plane as the intended subject matter. This will result in the greatest forensic benefit of the resulting image.

Photo Logs

Regardless of the perspective or range taken, each photograph taken at a crime scene should be documented on a photo log. A **photo log** is a permanent record of all information pertaining to documentation by photographs. Department policy often dictates what is found within a photo log; however, if no policy exists, the following suggestions are offered (**FIGURE 4.12**). Information that should be included in a photo log includes:

- Title and information block consisting of date/time/case number/agency name
- Photo equipment used
- Numerical ordering of each photo taken
- Brief description of each photo taken
- Direction facing for each photo taken

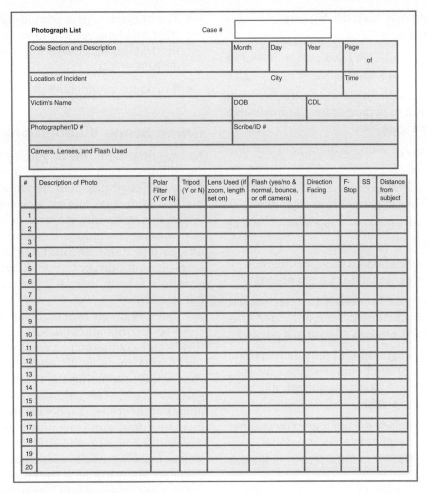

Photograph List				Case #						

Code Section and Description			Month	Day		Year		Page		of

Location of Incident				City				Time		

Victim's Name			DOB			CDL				

Photographer/ID #				Scribe/ID #						

Camera, Lenses, and Flash Used										

#	Description of Photo	Polar Filter (Y or N)	Tripod (Y or N)	Lens Used (if zoom, length set on)	Flash (yes/no & normal, bounce, or off camera)	Direction Facing	F-Stop	SS	Distance from subject
1									
2									
3									
4									
5									
6									
7									
8									
9									
10									
11									
12									
13									
14									
15									
16									
17									
18									
19									
20									

FIGURE 4.12: Example of a photo log.

- Approximate distance from subject matter in each photo taken
- Shutter speed, aperture setting, and ISO for each photo. If photographed with conventional photography, pertinent photographic information should be included for each. If photographs are taken in a digital format, documenting such information is not as imperative because it will be digitally recorded when each photo is taken as part of the digital file for each photo.

The photo log should be a documentation of visual storytelling that flows from the general to the specific. The log itself is not always constructed at the crime scene, but rather the foregoing information will sometimes be included on a rough copy of a photo log or within the field notebook of the photographer and transferred onto a photo sheet at a later time, to include information pertaining to the digital properties of each photo, retrieved from the camera or computer at the time of download. Most agencies use pre-printed log sheets divided into categories for ease of recording efforts.

Order of Taking Photographs

While this manner of documentation is listed near the beginning, taking overall photos is obviously much less intrusive to a crime scene than taking close-up photos (due to movement of items and the addition of scales of reference). Therefore, it is important that you realize that although these are listed together, not all ranges of photographs are taken together or at the same time during a crime scene investigation. After the initial scene survey has been conducted, but before a detailed search or examination is undertaken, the crime scene should be photographed. However, usually, this only includes the overall photographs, but if items of evidence have been located, mid-ranges can be taken from a safe position. Closeups are not typically taken until a thorough search of the scene has been conducted, unless the item is of a transient nature.

Guidelines for Crime Scene Photography

The following strategies have proven useful in crime scene investigations.

- Always use a photo placard on the first shot of each roll to demonstrate administrative data (see Figure 4.4)

- Always use a crime scene photo log (see Figure 4.12)

- Document the entire scene in situ as soon as possible using overall photographs

- Photograph all fragile evidence as soon as possible

- In the documentation stage, photograph all known evidence using closeup photos

- As items are discovered in later stages, return and document them fully, including additional overall photographs, if needed

- Create photographs that fully demonstrate the results of additional examinations (e.g., latent prints, bloodstain pattern analysis, trajectory analysis)

- Try not to include the photographer or other people in the photographs, if possible

- Shoot all close-up photographs with the use of a tripod

- Close-up photos should be taken with and without a scale of reference

- Be sure that the scale is on the same plane as the item of evidence being photographed

- The subject matter should be parallel to the film plane/camera to eliminate distortion caused by skewed angle photographs (**FIGURE 4.13**)

- If in doubt, photograph it!

Crime Scene Videography

As a result of digital media gaining widespread acceptance within U.S. courts, in the last few years, videography has become a routine method of documenting major crime scenes. While this is an obvious and useful method of providing visual documentation of the conditions and items encountered at the crime scene, it is important to remember that doing so is not a substitute for still photography. Each has its merits.

Video is taken to record the scene in as close to its original condition as possible, as this is an easy method to employ and is relatively quick in its application. Often, video is shot while conducting the preliminary scene survey as a way of recording the layout and conditions of the scene. This documentation is useful to supervisors and investigative personnel in determining logistic and equipment needs, as well as reducing official visitors by giving them the opportunity to look at the crime scene without actually entering into it themselves. It also enables investigative personnel to later "enter" the scene as often as necessary through viewing the video without the need for a search warrant. This is especially useful if the crime scene is no longer available to personnel.

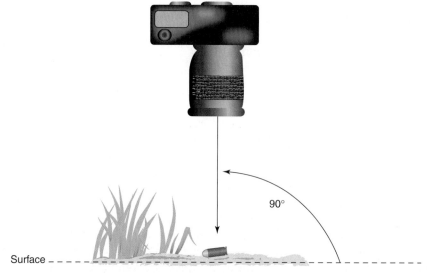

FIGURE 4.13: Example of correct camera angle for close-up photographs.

Courtesy of Dana Gevelinger.

Videography is a useful method for documenting a crime scene. It can provide a perspective that is more easily understood and perceived by the viewer than those offered by notes, sketches, or still photographs. However, it is important to remember that this is a supplemental method and not a replacement for still photography or other documentation methods.

■ Guidelines for Digital Video Recording a Crime Scene

While some of these points are similar to those for photography, a few key points are important to remember when shooting a moving data stream:

- Begin with an introductory placard that states case number, date, time, location, and other pertinent case and chain of custody information

- This video should be a storytelling event. Start with a general view of the area surrounding the crime scene. Following this should be an overview of the crime scene itself. It is a good idea to take overall photographs from the cardinal compass directions (north, south, east, west) for orientation purposes

- Turn off the audio on the digital recorder unless you intend to narrate

- Do not move the camera too quickly by panning (moving side to side), or zooming (moving in for a closeup view) as this results in abrupt motion and bad focus

- Unless in sunlight, always use a video strobe. Never use a flashlight to illuminate the scene.

- Do not use the zoom unless it is necessary because of an inability to get physically closer to the subject matter, or, if it is unsafe to do so. The human eye cannot zoom. If the video is to be a fair and accurate representation of how the videographer observed the scene, no zoom should be used.

- Video never should be edited or altered in any manner following the initial taping. The original copy should be kept as evidence, and duplicate copies should be made for viewing purposes.

Searching the Crime Scene

A variety of factors can affect a search method and these will determine the best, most accurate way to approach the scene:

- *Environment.* Environmental conditions, such as wind, rain, snow, heat, and cold will have an impact on the method chosen due to how they affect the scene and the personnel involved

- *Object being searched for.* Obviously, a larger item will not entail the same level of searching detail as a smaller item (e.g., a handgun versus a bullet)

- *Number of available personnel.* Some search methods are designed to incorporate a greater number of searchers in order to be most effective. If such personnel are not available, a method that utilizes fewer personnel needs to be considered.

- *Terrain.* Obstructions (trees, buildings), ground cover (asphalt, grass), and grade (steep, flat) will all impact the type of method employed, as they will have a bearing on the ability of searchers to perform the task, and the ability to properly locate the necessary items of evidence.

- *Exigency.* In cases of lost children, a search for a loaded handgun (public safety issue), and other events, there is often the need for exigency that trumps the more detailed search patterns that would be preferable. Therefore, a quick and efficient method should be chosen, making use of the maximum number of resources available in the quickest manner possible.

Swath Size

A **swath** is the effective area that a searcher can cover while conducting a search. Swath is affected by all of the aforementioned matters and is itself a consideration in the determination of the proper search method to employ. If looking for a firearm, a larger swath would be more possible in a parking lot than in high grass, for instance. Also, a search conducted at night or in low light would affect the swath due to the ability of a flashlight to illuminate the area of responsibility.

swath
The effective area that a searcher can cover while conducting a search

Types of Crime Scene Search Patterns

Depending on the aforementioned factors, a variety of crime scene search patterns exists that can be employed at a crime scene. Regardless of the search pattern chosen, the crime scene investigator must be sure that the search is conducted in a systematic and thorough manner. This will ensure that all evidence is properly located, documented, and collected.

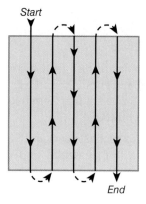

FIGURE 4.14: Example of a lane/strip search.

Courtesy of Dana Gevelinger.

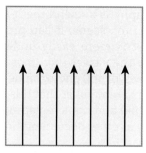

FIGURE 4.15: Example of a line search.

Courtesy of Dana Gevelinger.

■ Lane/Strip Search

A **lane/strip search** pattern divides the scene into manageable lanes in which the searcher(s) proceed back and forth, in a slightly overlapping fashion. This is similar to mowing a lawn. This method is typically conducted by only one person. (See **FIGURE 4.14**.)

■ Line Search

A **line search** is used when there are a large number of personnel available, often volunteers. In this method, searchers assemble in a line that runs along a chosen edge of the crime scene. Searchers stand side by side and spread apart, maintaining a manageable swath distance between each person. A search coordinator should place him- or herself in the middle of this line to make certain that everyone walks forward in as straight a line as possible.

If one end begins to lag, the other end is requested to slow down. At no point should anyone be encouraged to search faster! Keeping all searchers in a straight line reduces the possibility of missing an area and thus not discovering potential evidence. This method is the most commonly employed type during an exigent search for an item or person, especially when a large number of people are available. (See **FIGURE 4.15**.)

■ Grid Search

A **grid search** is sometimes referred to as a *double strip* or *double lane* method. In this method, a lane is searched in one direction, similar to the lane search method. However, at the lane's terminus, a 90° direction change is made and another lane is searched. This can either occur through the use of two searchers (one responsible for one direction and the other for the perpendicular direction), or it can utilize

a large number of searchers, incorporating the line method as described earlier and then turning 90° and performing a second line search perpendicular to the original lane. While quite time-consuming, this method allows the same area to be searched two separate times and at different angles. This redundancy will reduce searcher boredom and will change the lighting and obstruction conditions present, thus increasing the ability of the searchers to locate evidence. (See **FIGURE 4.16**.)

■ Zone Search

A **zone search** (also called a quadrant search) is typically utilized in an area that is already broken up into defined or manageable zones (e.g., a house or car). It is typically used indoors but may be used outdoors if the areas are broken down into defined zones. Zones can be searched independently and later re-searched by different search personnel to ensure that no evidence has been overlooked. This method also can be used as a way to break up a larger crime scene, so the search coordinator can then choose from any of the search methods to cover a zone area. Some choose to assemble a grid from of this method, so it is often referred to as "gridding" an area, which confuses it with the previously mentioned grid method. In this instance, an area to be searched is divided into smaller squares, each

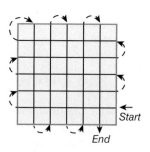

FIGURE 4.16: Example of a grid search.

Courtesy of Dana Gevelinger.

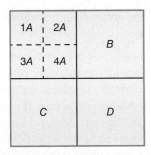

FIGURE 4.17: Example of a zone/quadrant search.

Courtesy of Ellie Blazer.

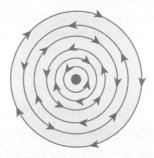

FIGURE 4.18: Example of a circle/spiral search.

Courtesy of Dana Gevelinger.

of which is further subdivided into four smaller squares. The search begins in the northernmost part of the smaller squares and progresses as one would read a book until the grid has been examined completely. (See **FIGURE 4.17.**)

■ Circle/Spiral Search

A **circle search** (also called a **spiral search**) is a specialized search pattern method that is seldom utilized; however, it does have its usefulness and merit. In this method, searchers can either start at a defined outer boundary and circle or spiral in toward the defined critical point, or they can begin at the critical point and circle or spiral outward toward the crime scene perimeter. However, physical obstructions and barriers in the scene will present problems with this method. This method is typically employed in bomb or explosive scenes with a defined seat of explosion. It may be used in underwater or open-water searches where there was a last known location for an item, vessel, or victim. If using a circling rather than a spiraling pattern, to ensure thoroughness, it is suggested that a central point and an effective swath width be determined. Once this is done, searchers should move out in concentric circles, often using a lanyard affixed to a point at the center of the scene. The searchers proceed to search in a 360° manner, around the central point, and once they reach the end of their circuit, they let out the lanyard a predetermined amount, using a manageable swath width, and then proceed to conduct another 360° circuit of the scene. It is suggested that this new circuit be in the opposite direction of the previous circuit both to reduce the possibility of entanglement and to reduce the searcher's vertigo issues from walking in a continuous circle. (See **FIGURE 4.18.**)

The physical nature of a crime scene will suggest what type of search is best to employ, but the characteristics of the scene should have no effect on the quality of the search. Obviously,

there will be exceptions. Large-area searches in mass-disaster investigations may have to sacrifice some quality for expedience, but in the average investigation, there is no excuse for haphazard searches. Proceed slowly, for evidence not only can be contaminated by being stepped on but can be destroyed easily or overlooked entirely by the unwary. An experienced investigator will have completed the preliminary scene survey before beginning the search, and the preliminary scene survey must be conducted with trace evidence foremost in the investigator's mind.

Important things to remember when conducting a search are:

■ Do not touch, handle, or move evidence

■ Mark or designate found items without altering them

■ Found evidence must be documented before any evidence can be moved or collected

Sketching and Mapping the Scene

Sketching

A **crime scene sketch** is a permanent record of the size and distance relationship of the crime scene and the physical evidence within it. The sketch serves to clarify the special information that is present in the photographs and video documentation, because the other methods do not allow the viewer to easily gauge distances and dimensions. A sketch is the most simplistic manner in which to present crime scene layout and measurements. Often, photographer/camera positions may also be noted in a sketch.

Why is a sketch important to crime scene documentation?

■ It accurately portrays the physical facts

■ It relates to the sequence of events at the scene

circle search
A specialized search pattern method in which searchers can either start at a defined outer boundary and circle or spiral in toward the defined critical point or begin at the critical point and circle or spiral outward toward the crime scene perimeter; *see spiral search*

spiral search
A search method that involves moving in an ever-tightening or ever-expanding spiral; it can be used indoors or out

crime scene sketch
A measured drawing showing the location of all important items, landmarks, permanent fixtures, and physical evidence at a crime scene

- It establishes the precise location and relationship of objects and evidence at the scene
- It helps to create a mental picture of the scene for those not present
- It is a permanent record of the scene
- It usually is admissible in court
- It assists in interviewing and interrogating
- It assists in preparing the written investigative report
- It assists in presenting the case in court. Well-prepared sketches and drawings help judges, juries, witnesses, and others to visualize the crime scene.

When should sketches be made?

- Sketch all serious crimes and accident scenes after photographs have been taken and before anything is moved
- Sketch the entire scene, the objects, and the evidence

Two types of sketches are produced with regard to crime scene documentation: rough sketches and final/finished sketches. **Rough sketches** are developed while on scene, typically during the crime scene assessment/preliminary scene evaluation phase to assist with development of a strategic plan for processing. The sketch is not done to scale, can be drawn with any implement (crayon, chalk, pencil, pen, etc.), and is very rough, artistically. As work progresses at the crime scene, the sketch will include not only the crude crime scene layout but also will be used to record measurements of items and structures, and distances among items. (See **FIGURE 4.19**.)

A **final sketch** (see **FIGURES 4.20** and **4.21**) is a finished rendition of the rough sketch. It is usually prepared for courtroom presentation and often will not show all measurements

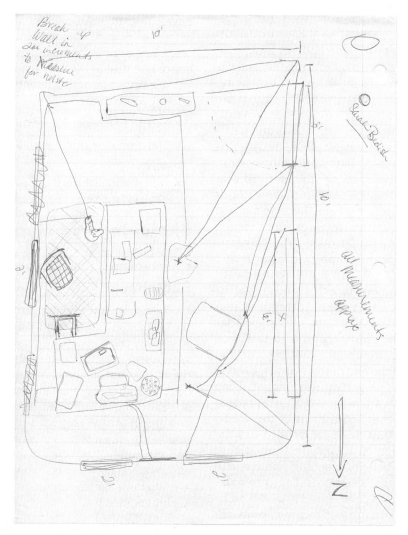

FIGURE 4.19: Example of a rough sketch.

Courtesy of Sarah Bedish.

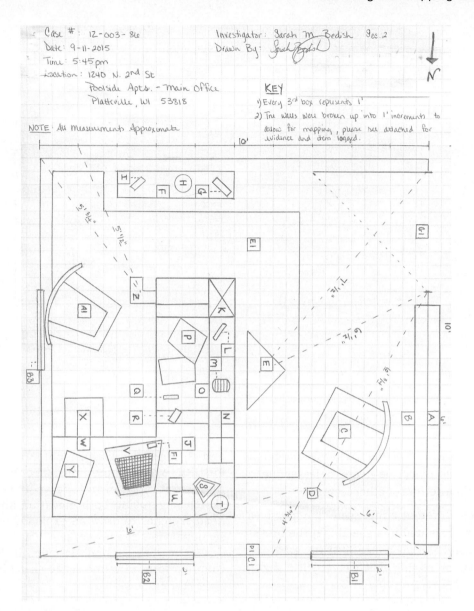

FIGURE 4.20: Example of a final hand-drawn sketch.

Courtesy of Sarah Bedish.

and distances originally recorded on the rough sketch. Only significant items and structures are typically present in a final sketch. A final sketch is either produced in ink or on a computer, in a manner that is not able to be modified (i.e., not in pencil!). The sketch should be clutter-free and should accurately depict all pertinent items of evidence, typically using an accompanying legend. A **legend** is a note of explanation, outside of the sketch area, which relates to a specific item, symbol, or information contained in the graphic representation of a sketch. A final sketch should include:

- Title (What does the sketch represent? For example, Sketch of Bank ABC Robbery)
- Legend (What do symbols in the sketch mean?)

- Case information (i.e., date, time, place, case number)
- Initials/name (person who drew the sketch)
- Indication of direction (e.g., north)
- Scale (e.g., 1 inch = 1 foot)
- Measurement table (i.e., if measurements are not represented within the confines of the sketch, an accompanying measurement table should be included to explain the distances and measurements associated with it)
- A notation following the scale or measurement table stating that all measurements are approximate. This will ensure that the sketch's author does not get into a credibility argument in court that a measurement

legend
A note of explanation that defines or labels specific information in a sketch

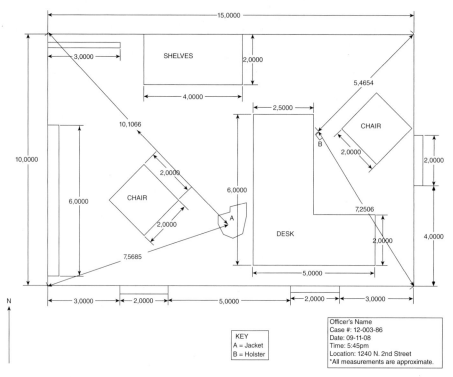

FIGURE 4.21: Example of a final computer-generated sketch.

Modified from an original illustration by Alex Albright.

is documented as the listed measurement but could, in fact, be greater or lesser due to rounding errors or other factors.

Three different crime scene perspectives can be represented in a sketch: (1) the bird's-eye or overhead view (see **FIGURE 4.22**), (2) the elevation or side view (see **FIGURE 4.23**),

and (3) the three-dimensional (3D) view (see **FIGURE 4.24**). Sometimes, people choose to incorporate several perspectives in a sketch (e.g., using both elevation and overhead sketches to draw an exploded or cross-sectional view of a scene; see **FIGURE 4.25**).

An overhead or bird's-eye view is the most common form of crime scene sketching. It is

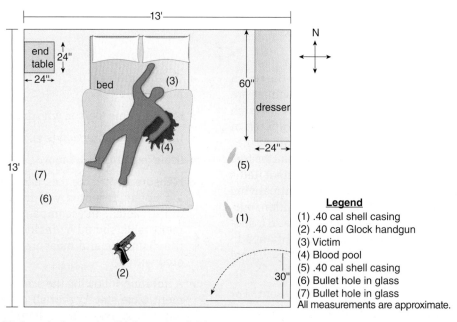

FIGURE 4.22: Example of an overhead/bird's-eye view sketch.

Courtesy of Dana Gevelinger.

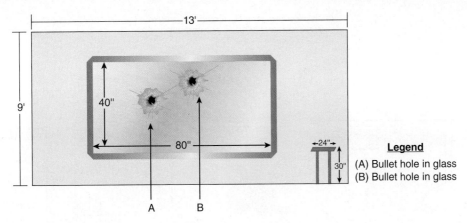

FIGURE 4.23: Example of an elevation/side-view sketch.

Courtesy of Dana Gevelinger.

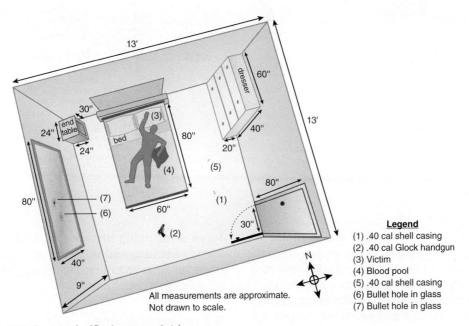

FIGURE 4.24: Example of a 3D crime scene sketch.

Modified from an original illustration by Alex Albright.

prepared as though its author were looking down on the scene from above. This type of view shows the floor layout but cannot represent heights of items or show associated evidence on walls. In order to show such information, a person must use an elevation or side-view sketch to show evidence located on a building facade or interior wall, or any item for which height is an important aspect (e.g., death involving a hanging). A 3-D crime scene perspective is created with the aid of computers. Its primary function is crime scene activity reconstruction—that is, to help explain what happened and in what order.

Everything that is included in the sketch must be located geographically (measuring distance from permanent features is one method of doing this). Eliminate all unnecessary detail from the sketch, and include only items necessary for locating evidence and establishing scene parameters.

To be useful, a crime scene sketch must contain accurate measurements. Artistic content is not a concern. All measurements should be made from permanent objects. For indoor sketches, walls, doorframes, window frames, and corners serve well as anchors for measurements. For outdoor sketches, buildings, utility poles, roadways, and, less optimally, trees are generally reliable. Keep in mind that anything to which a measurement is anchored must withstand the vagaries of time. The trial may occur years after the offense.

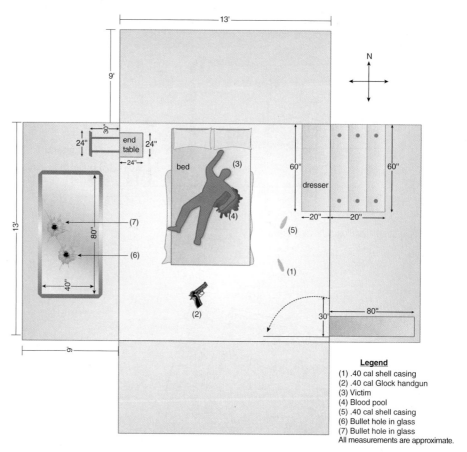

Legend
(1) .40 cal shell casing
(2) .40 cal Glock handgun
(3) Victim
(4) Blood pool
(5) .40 cal shell casing
(6) Bullet hole in glass
(7) Bullet hole in glass
All measurements are approximate.

FIGURE 4.25: Example of a cross-sectional/exploded sketch.

Courtesy of Dana Gevelinger.

Crime scene templates are available for many different types of crime scenes. Once the crime scene has been measured and those measurements are transferred to a sketch, those measurements will be used in reconstructing a more elaborate and architecturally correct diagram. Very little sophistication is required to use these templates, but a professional end product is possible.

Crime Scene Mapping

Mapping is the term associated with crime scene measurements. Sometimes, a person may sketch but not map, meaning that he or she draws a sketch of an area but does not apply measurements to the sketch produced and items represented. Rarely, however, will one map without sketching (i.e., record measurements with no graphic representation for what the measurements represent). Sometimes, this step is referred to as *measuring*. There are a variety of methods for mapping a crime scene, depending on whether the crime scene is an interior or exterior scene. As this is an introductory text, only the most basic and most often used methods are covered here. The basic

types of mapping methods utilized for crime scene sketching and mapping are (a) baseline, (b) rectangular coordinate, (c) triangulation, and (d) polar/grid coordinate.

■ Baseline Mapping

This is the most basic—and least accurate—form of crime scene mapping. For this method, a **baseline** is developed or identified from which to conduct measurements. This can be an existing area, such as the edge of a roadway, a wall, or fence; or it can be developed by personnel, such as by placing a string or tape measure through the scene and conducting measurements from there. In the case of the latter, the line should be run between two known fixed points, such as trees or other identifiable items, so that the points can be found in the future and the scene can be reconstructed, if necessary. Once the baseline is established, measurements are taken from it at an approximate 90° angle from the baseline to a point on the identified item or area of the crime scene. Typically, most measurements are made either to center mass of the item or to the nearest point of the item to the baseline. Because it is impossible to

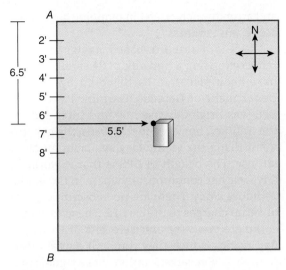

FIGURE 4.26: Example of the baseline mapping technique.

Courtesy of Dana Gevelinger.

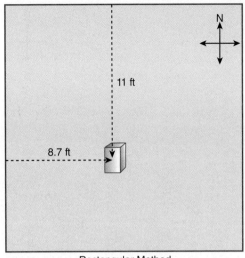

Rectangular Method

FIGURE 4.27: Example of the rectangular coordinate technique.

Courtesy of Dana Gevelinger.

ensure that the measurement was taken at 90°, the possibility exists that the measurement will be longer if the measurement was more than 90° from the baseline or if it was less than 90° from the baseline. For this reason, this method is not as accurate as some of the other methods; however, it is quick and extremely easy to use. (See **FIGURE 4.26.**)

■ Rectangular Coordinate Mapping

The rectangular coordinate mapping method is a slightly more accurate variation of the baseline method because it utilizes two such baselines instead of one. Two measurements are taken to a point on an item or location at the scene: one from each identified baseline. Some personnel choose to measure to two or more points on an item, using multiple rectangular measurements as a way of increasing accuracy, while others simply choose to measure to an arbitrarily identified center mass of the object in question or point to which measurements are being taken. As with the baseline method, it cannot be determined that such measurements are taken precisely at 90° angles from the baseline, so there exists a greater possibility of errors than with some of the other methods. However, because this method uses two measurements, it has much greater accuracy than the single baseline method. This method is especially useful in confined spaces and smaller interior scenes. (See **FIGURE 4.27**).

■ Triangulation Mapping

This is the most accurate method that does not make use of advanced technology. While

triangulation is quite a bit more laborious and time-consuming than other methods, it is worth the effort because it is sufficiently more accurate than the aforementioned methods of mapping. The accuracy for this method comes from its foundation: two fixed points. From these two fixed points, measurements are taken to specified points on an item or within the crime scene. There is no need to worry about whether measurements have been made at a right angle because the points derive from a known fixed point, such as the corner of a room or the edge of a doorframe. From these fixed points, a minimum of two measurements are made to each identified point. If the object has a fixed or constant shape (e.g., a firearm or item of furniture), the object is measured to two points, from the two fixed points, for a total of four measurements. If the object has a variable shape or size (e.g., a puddle of water, pool of blood, or pile of clothes), the object is measured to an approximate center of mass. (See **FIGURE 4.28.**)

■ Polar/Grid Coordinate Mapping

Utilizing polar coordinates is the fourth method of crime scene mapping used to document evidence location at a crime scene. Like those previously mentioned, this is a two-dimensional (2D) system that indicates the location of an object by providing the angle and distance from a fixed or known point. Obviously, in order to conduct measurements by this method, a transit or compass is necessary to measure the angles and polar directions. This method is best utilized in large outdoor scenes with very few

triangulation
Basic measurement technique used for geographically locating evidence; in this technique, three angles are measured—those of a triangle formed by the item of interest and two permanent objects (fixed points)

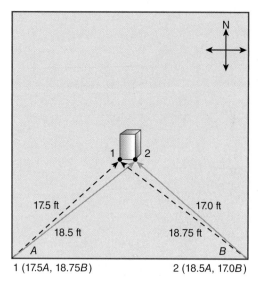

FIGURE 4.28: Example of the triangulation coordinate technique.

Courtesy of Dana Gevelinger.

landmarks (e.g., a plane crash in a forest or large field). [See **FIGURE 4.29**]

■ Advanced Mapping Techniques

Some departments may have the ability to better utilize modern technology, such as a **global positioning system (GPS)**, Total Stations, and 3-D crime scene mapping systems, which are mapping systems that can take measurements in polar coordinates and then convert the measurements into grid coordinates. The benefit of these technologies is that they are able to provide precise electronic distance measurements

global positioning system (GPS)
A device that uses satellites to compute position

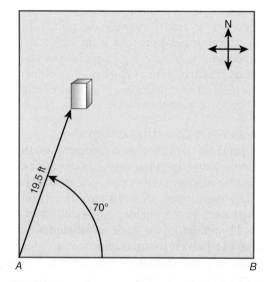

FIGURE 4.29: Example of the polar coordinate technique.

Courtesy of Dana Gevelinger.

and are extremely useful in mapping large-scale scenes and events.

GPS is a satellite-based navigation system comprising a network of 24 satellites that have been placed in Earth's orbit by the U.S. Department of Defense (Garmin, 1996–2011). GPS was originally used by and intended for the military; however, in the 1980s, the government made the technology available for civilian use. The benefit of GPS is that it works in any weather condition, anywhere in the world, 24 hours a day. There are no subscription fees or setup charges to utilize GPS. These satellites complete two very precise orbits of Earth per day, during which they transmit signal information. GPS receivers gather these signals and then use triangulation to calculate the user's location. A GPS receiver must be locked onto the position signal of at least three satellites in order to calculate a 2D position (latitude and longitude) and track movements of an object. If the GPS receiver is able to lock onto four or more satellites, the receiver can determine the user's 3D location (latitude, longitude, and altitude), along with object movement. The more satellites the GPS is locked onto, the greater the accuracy of the position. Once the user's position has been determined, calculation of movement can provide GPS users with the ability to record information, such as speed, bearing, track, trip distance, distance to destination, sunrise, sunset, time, and much more (Garmin, 1996–2011).

How accurate is GPS? In most cases, commercially available GPS receivers are accurate to approximately 12 yards, with higher-end units capable of accuracy in the 3- to 5-yards range. This is sufficiently accurate for large crime scenes that have no known or fixed landmarks. A GPS reading is typically used to "mark" a known point, and then measurements are made from that location, thereby ensuring that any measurements taken will all be "off" by the same amount because they all originate from the same location.

A Total Station is an electronic surveying instrument that has an integrated computer and can measure angles in the horizontal and vertical planes, utilizing a laser rangefinder instead of the more archaic method of a manual tape measure. This is especially useful because changes in elevation are difficult to measure and depict on a crime scene sketch. The Total Station is capable of recording evidence positions in three dimensions, thus simplifying this otherwise complicated situation.

Within the past several years, several vendors (i.e., Panoscan and Leica) have developed 3-D, panoramic crime scene photography and mapping systems. (**FIGURE 4.30**) "This results in a 3D representation of the scene from which any measurement can be made even after the scene has been released" (Leica, 2015). This enables such technology to be utilized for pre-event planning, crime scene documentation, and postevent analysis. Another benefit of this new technology is that it is capable of accurate crime scene documentation efforts in both bright sunshine and total darkness, often at a distance of up to 900 feet.

Crime Scene Measurements in Court

As with all other crime scene measurements, all measurements are approximate and are never documented as or testified to as being 100% accurate. Crime scene mapping is about producing the best possible documentation with the resources available, realizing that rounding and other factors inhibit the ability to be completely accurate.

A crime scene sketch is of little value if it cannot be admitted at the time of trial. As in the case of photos and audio recordings, there is a particular evidentiary foundation (predicate) that must be established in order to use sketches, maps, or diagrams:

Q: Did you participate in the preparation of the diagram that you have identified as State's Exhibit Number 2?
A: Yes.

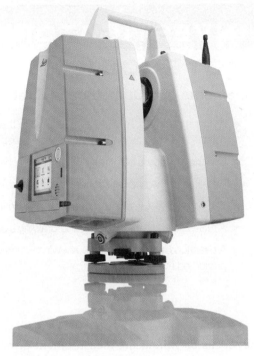

FIGURE 4.30: Example of 3D crime scene scanning equipment.

Courtesy of Leica Geosystems.

Q: Are you personally familiar with the objects and locations contained in the diagram?
A: Yes.
Q: Is this a fair and accurate representation of the [search site, recovery site, location of evidence found] as you recall it?
A: Yes.
Q: Is this diagram drawn to scale?
A: No.

Generally, it is easier to testify about a diagram that is not drawn to scale. Defense lawyers

— Ripped from the Headlines —

Using Drones to Map Crime Scenes

The day may soon come when investigators, and those tasked with processing crime scenes, will be making use of unmanned aerial vehicles, often termed "drones," as a way of conducting 3D mapping of the area.

One of the most impactful benefits of the use of drone technology is the area to move around (above) the crime scene, without touching or disturbing anything within the scene. As the technology improves, the ability to hover and stabilize a drone, while taking the necessary closeup, midrange, and overall photographs, which are required to properly document

a scene, will be possible. Also, due to the current technology, the photos are able to be digitally stitched together to provide a 3D virtual map of the crime scene, from nearly every angle. This allows for investigators (and even the jury) to be able to move around the scene freely, without ever having been to the scene or having disturbed anything within the scene.

INVESTIGATOR'S NOTEBOOK

Elements of a Crime Scene Sketch

- A scene identifier. That identifier, placed in the title box, should be either the case number or a recognizable title associated with the offense being investigated.

- Descriptive words identifying where the scene is situated

- The date of the original sketch (rough sketch)

- The name of the investigator and the person who drew the sketch, even if they are one and the same

- A written statement indicating the drawing's scale or noting the absence of scale

- A directional rosette (an arrow showing which direction is north). In orienting the drawing, it is generally presumed that north is up.

© Shutterstock, Inc./Janaka Dharmasena.

© Shutterstock, Inc./Nutink.

may focus on minuscule measurement errors to try to undermine the credibility of the entire diagram. Reasonable approximations are much easier to defend. However, if all measurements are linked to a permanent landmark that was located on the diagram with the aid of surveying instruments, having a scale drawing may not be a problem.

Collecting, Handling, and Preserving Evidence

After an intensive crime scene search and documentation, collection and preservation of evidence should begin. The objective of all criminal investigations is to discover the truth through the gathering of evidence in a forensically sound and constitutionally permissible manner—presuming that the determination has been made that a crime has, in fact, been committed. Evidence is of little value if it has been handled, tagged, or stored improperly. Once each item of evidence has been photographed and included in a crime scene sketch, it must be collected, preserved, transported, and stored. Improperly collected, preserved, transported, or stored evidence will be inadmissible at trial once the defense discovers any improprieties.

The handling and packaging of evidence is a lengthy subject. Each item of evidence at the scene should be placed in an appropriate container, which should be tagged to identify it and differentiate it from all other evidence taken at the scene as well as all other

evidence ever taken anywhere. Commercial evidence tags and labels are available and provide places for entering pertinent information. Once bagged and tagged, the evidence must be transported to the police evidence room. As mentioned in the chapter on chain of custody, every moment of the existence of a piece of evidence must be accounted for once that piece of evidence has been seized. Appropriate documentation will deflect any suggestion that the evidence in question has been misplaced, manipulated, or replaced. It is the evidence custodian's responsibility to ensure that any access to evidence placed in storage is legitimate and documented.

The following guidelines should be adhered to in order to ensure the most thorough and accurate investigation:

- Designate one person as the evidence collector/custodian (this ensures that nothing is missed)

- Document, collect, package, mark, seal, and preserve

- Collect all transient, fragile, or easily lost evidence first

- Use paper, which is the preferred packaging

- Package items separately

- Properly mark containers.

- Properly seal containers

- Mark seals with initials, date, and time

In all crashes, the specter of a human-caused explosion hovers. All clothing, personal

CASE IN POINT

© Shutterstock, Inc./Vlastas.

Large Crime Scenes

On April 19, 1995, at 9:03 am CST, calls were received by Emergency Medical Services (EMS) Authority Oklahoma City that a bomb had been detonated in the Alfred Murrah Federal Building. EMS ambulances, police, and firefighters had already been dispatched.

The State Emergency Operations Center was set up, including personnel from military, civil defense, and public safety along with the responding fire and police services. The governor called out the Oklahoma National Guard and members of the Department of Civil Emergency Management. Within the first hour, 50 people were rescued from the Murrah building. By the end of the day, more than 180 survivors were being treated at hospitals around the city. The last survivor, a 15-year-old girl, was found under the base of the collapsed building.

Three hundred and fifty tons of rubble were removed from the site each day until April 29. All of the debris was examined for body parts, explosive residue, and detonators. Canine units searched for survivors and located bodies among the building refuse. Rescue and recovery efforts were concluded on May 4, with the bodies of all but three victims recovered. For several days after the building's demolition, trucks hauled 800 tons of debris a day away from the site. Some of the debris was used as evidence in the trials of the conspirators.

It is important to understand that the bomb blast to the Murrah building was not devastating by itself; it just so happened that the blast was located at a critical point that undermined the whole structure of the building. Most of the damage and a vast majority of the fatalities were caused by the collapse of the building.

The FBI was on the scene immediately, because the building was under federal jurisdiction. Agents found a truck axle with a vehicle identification number (VIN). It was determined that the explosion had been contained in a 1993 Ford truck owned by Ryder Rentals of Miami, Florida. Ryder Rentals informed the FBI that the truck was assigned to a rental company known as Elliot's Body Shop in Junction City, Kansas. The FBI interviewed a rental agent at Elliot's Body Shop in Junction City on April 19, 1995. The individual who signed the rental agreement provided his name, Social Security number, South Dakota driver's license, a South Dakota home address, and a destination in Omaha; the FBI's investigation determined that all of the information was false.

On April 20, 1995, the rental agent was contacted again and assisted in the creation of a composite drawing. On the same day, agents interviewed three witnesses who were near the scene of the explosion prior to the detonation. The witnesses were shown a copy of the composite drawing and identified him as the person they had seen in front of the Murrah building. The composite drawing was shown to employees at various motels and commercial establishments in the Junction City area. Employees of the Dreamland Motel in Junction City told agents that the individual in the composite drawing had been a guest at the motel from April 14 through April 18, 1995. This individual had registered at the motel under the name of Timothy McVeigh, listed his automobile as bearing an Oklahoma license plate with an illegible plate number, and provided a home address on North Van Dyke Road in Decker, Michigan; he drove a car described as a 1970 Mercury.

A check of the Michigan Department of Motor Vehicle records showed a license in the name of Timothy J. McVeigh, date of birth April 23, 1968, with an address of 3616 North Van Dyke Road, Decker, Michigan. Further investigation showed that James Douglas Nichols and his brother Terry Lynn Nichols owned the property at that address and that the property was a working farm.

A relative of James Nichols told the FBI that Timothy McVeigh was a friend of James Nichols, who had been involved in constructing explosives and who possessed large quantities of fuel oil and fertilizer. On April 21, 1995, a former coworker of Timothy McVeigh's reported that he had seen the composite drawing on television and recognized the drawing to be Timothy McVeigh. He told the investigators that McVeigh was known to hold extreme right-wing views, was a military veteran, and was so agitated about the conduct of the federal government in Waco, Texas, in 1993, that he personally visited the site.

On April 21, 1995, investigators learned that Timothy McVeigh was arrested at 10:30 am on April 19, 1995, in Perry, Oklahoma, for not having a license plate and for possession of a weapon approximately 1.5 hours after the explosion at the Alfred P. Murrah Federal Building. (See **FIGURE A**) McVeigh, who had been

(continues)

(continued)

FIGURE A: Alfred P. Murrah Federal Building. Courtesy of FEMA.

held in custody since his arrest on April 19, 1995, listed his home address as 3616 North Van Dyke Road, Decker, Michigan; listed James Nichols of Decker as a reference; and was stopped driving a yellow 1977 Mercury Marquis.

As a result of the investigation conducted by the FBI, Timothy McVeigh was indicted, tried, found guilty, sentenced to death, and executed.

effects, and body parts should be handled in the same fashion as for a known bombing. Any investigation should search for detonator components. Aircraft parts should be recovered and documented like any other evidence. Even in the case of a crash with confirmation of accidental causes, those causes will be best discovered and corroborated by treating the recovery operation as a criminal investigation.

CONCLUSION

Scientific crime scene investigation is the best methodology to ensure that an investigation is properly conducted and that justice is served. Use of this methodology will prevent the abrupt end of an incomplete investigation and allow for the best use of the physical evidence found at crime scenes. The general rule relating to crime scene documentation is "if it isn't written down, it didn't happen." This is important to remember when conducting the various steps of crime scene documentation. It reminds the individual to be as thorough and precise as possible to correctly retain and be able to recall the events, items, and locations involved with a crime scene.

QUESTIONS FOR REVIEW

1. Why is it important to secure the crime scene?

2. What is physical evidence?

3. What is meant geographically by the term *crime scene?*

4. What is crime scene contamination, and what role does it play in the processing of a crime scene?

5. What is transfer, and what is its significance to a crime scene?

6. What are the eight elements of an appropriately protected crime scene?

7. What are field notes, and what role do they play in a criminal investigation?

8. What kind of information should be recorded pertaining to recovered evidence?

9. What is a preliminary scene survey and what purpose does it serve?

10. Where does photography come into play in processing a crime scene? What is photographed, and when is it photographed?

11. What information is included in a crime scene photo log?

12. What information should be included on a crime scene sketch?

13. How does processing a complex crime scene differ from processing a less complex crime scene?

14. What should the presumption be in a mass disaster?

15. List three rules of crime scene photography.

16. Discuss the types of photographs that should be taken at a crime scene.

17. Why photograph bloodstains?

18. How should a violent crime scene be photographed?

19. When should a crime scene be photographed?

REFERENCES

Dutelle, A. W. (2015). *Basic crime scene photography* (2nd ed.). Seattle, WA: CreateSpace Publishing.

Garmin. (1996–2011). *What is GPS?* Retrieved August 15, 2011, from http://www8.garmin.com/aboutGPS/

Leica. (2015). Leica Scanning Station C10. Retrieved April 27, 2015, from http://www.leica-geosystems.us/forensic/downloads/LeicaScanStationC10.pdf

National Forensic Science Technology Center. (2013, December). *Crime scene investigation: A guide for law enforcement.* Retrieved April 25, 2015, from http://www.nfstc.org/bja-programs/crime-scene-investigation-guide/

Weiss, S. L. (2009). *Forensic photography: The importance of accuracy.* Upper Saddle River, NJ: Prentice Hall.

chapter 5

Physical Evidence

"There is nothing like first-hand evidence."

Sherlock Holmes
"A Study in Scarlet"

KEY TERMS

- 3R rule
- agglutination
- angle of impact
- antibody
- antigens
- area of convergence
- area of origin
- arterial gushing (spurting)
- associative evidence
- backspatter
- barrel blowback (drawback)
- bloodstain pattern analysis
- blood type
- cast-off pattern
- circular distortion
- circumstantial evidence
- concentric fractures
- conchoidal fractures
- directionality
- drip pattern
- flow pattern
- forward spatter
- free-falling blood
- high-velocity-impact pattern
- Locard's Exchange Principle
- medium-velocity blood spatter
- Paint Data Query
- physical evidence
- probability
- product rule
- projected
- primary packaging
- primary transfer
- radial fractures
- ricochet
- secondary packaging
- secondary transfer
- spine
- splash
- surface texture
- SWGSTAIN
- target surface
- terminal velocity
- testimonial evidence
- transfer
- transfer evidence

STUDENT LEARNING OUTCOMES

Upon completion of this chapter, students will be able to:

- Identify the various types of evidence
- Understand the role of trace evidence
- Recognize bloodstain pattern analysis
- Demonstrate bloodstain mechanics
- Describe how to field test for blood
- Discuss how blood evidence is packaged and handled
- Understand the role that trace evidence plays in criminal investigations
- Discuss how trace evidence is packaged and handled

Physical Evidence

For the purposes of our discussion in this chapter, we can break criminal evidence into two broad categories: physical evidence and testimonial evidence. **Physical evidence** is evidence that can be handled, examined, tested, seen, felt, and tactually evaluated. It can be as small as a gene or as large as an automobile (**FIGURE 5.1**). **Testimonial evidence** encompasses the testimony of witnesses and defendants. All physical evidence is **circumstantial evidence** and is only partial proof of a crime. Indeed, all evidence is circumstantial except eyewitness identification or a confession by the defendant. The closer to certainty evidence brings us, the more it loses its circumstantial nature.

From an investigative viewpoint, the most important aspect of physical evidence is its transferability. **Transfer** of evidence provides the basis for much of what forensic technicians and forensic laboratories do. Whenever two objects meet, some evidence of the meeting remains to establish that, in fact, a meeting did occur. In particular, whenever a person comes in contact with a crime scene, something is left and something is taken away. Often, what is left or taken away is microscopic (trace evidence) and requires forensic skills to discover, handle, and evaluate.

Not all investigators can be forensic scientists, but all investigators must appreciate the potential loci of forensic evidence. These loci depend on the nature of the crime and the evidence left at the scene of the crime. The lack of an understanding of the potential loci of evidence at a crime scene can result in contamination or destruction of the trace evidence. Types of evidence that may transfer include the following:

- A vehicular collision may leave visible paint on the fender of each vehicle. Even if the paint is visible to the naked eye, forensic analysis will be needed to verify that the residues discovered are of the same paint. The color alone is not sufficient.

- In a kidnapping case, fibers from the interior of a suspect's automobile may match those taken from the clothing of the abductee. Again, color comparison is only the beginning; fiber analysis must be used to establish that the fibers came from the same source.

- Burglary tools, like other tools, leave distinctive marks on surfaces when applied with force. Microscopic examination of surface marks and of the face of a suspected tool may convince a jury that the tool was the one used in breaking into the burglarized premises.

physical evidence
Evidence that can be handled, examined, tested, seen, felt, and tactually evaluated

testimonial evidence
Evidence that encompasses the testimony of witnesses and of defendants

circumstantial evidence
All evidence other than eyewitness testimony

transfer
The process whereby a person entering and exiting a crime scene leaves something and takes something

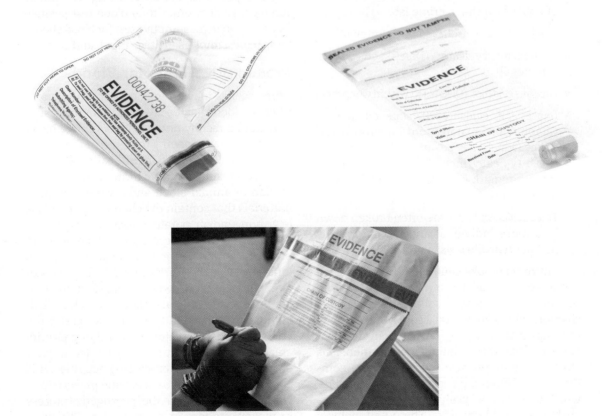

FIGURE 5.1: Examples of packaged evidence.

Investigators have the responsibility to determine what crime was committed, the avenues of entrance and exit used by the criminal, and the possible location of forensic evidence. It is the forensic evidence left behind that will allow the investigators to place both the suspect and the victim at the scene of the crime and to reconstruct the events that led up to and occurred during and after the offense. Thus, every investigator needs to appreciate what forensic technicians and laboratory scientists do, how they do it, and where they do it, for they are an important part of the investigative team and may make the difference between a successful and failed investigation as well as a successful and failed prosecution.

Types of Physical Evidence

While there is a myriad of possibilities for what one could encounter as physical evidence during the course of a criminal investigation, most can be categorized within one of the following areas:

- *Biological evidence:* (Discussed within this chapter, as well as Chapter 11) These can include blood, saliva, semen, urine, vaginal secretions, and other bodily fluids. DNA is also included as biological evidence, although it is typically its own area of analysis within a crime lab.

- *Drug evidence:* (Discussed in Chapter 14)

- *Fingerprint evidence:* (Discussed within Chapter 6)

- *Firearms evidence:* (Discussed within Chapter 8)

- *Impression evidence:* (Discussed within Chapter 10) Separate from fingerprint evidence (which may be impression evidence); these typically include toolmark impressions, tiremark impressions, and footwear impressions.

- *Trace evidence:* These are often broken down into more individual areas, but typically include, hair, fiber, glass, and paint evidence.

Entire textbooks could be written on each of the above areas. For our purposes, we will concentrate on just a couple here. Various chapters (noted above) have some discussion of the impact that various types of physical evidence can have on a criminal investigation. This chapter will emphasize the other more commonly encountered types of physical evidence, which do not fit as nicely into one of the previously mentioned chapters. These will include: blood evidence and trace evidence. The first type that we will look at is blood evidence.

Blood Evidence

Because of the violent nature of criminal events, blood is commonly found at the crime scene. The investigator may encounter blood evidence in one or more of four general areas:

1. On the victim

2. At the crime scene

3. On a weapon

4. On the assailant

When confronted with potential blood evidence, or material at a crime scene that the investigator believes may be blood, the following questions must be answered:

- Could it be blood?

- Is it human blood?

- Was there blood here at one time?

- If the blood is of human origin, how closely can it be associated with a particular individual?

These questions are answered using a variety of methods. The first step is to test to see whether the evidence in question is in fact blood.

In answering the first question, forensic scientists can use a variety of chemical tests known as *presumptive determinants* (presumptive because some substances other than blood test positive as well). A good presumptive test for blood should be specific, simple, sensitive, rapid, and safe.

Presumptive Tests for Blood

Crime scenes may often contain minute quantities of blood that, because of their small size, may not be readily noticed. Presumptive blood tests are initial screening tools that indicate, but are not specific for, the identification of blood. A positive result can come from the presence of human or animal blood and a variety of plant materials that contain the chemical peroxidase (e.g., horseradish, potatoes, etc).

In some cases, presumptive blood tests are used as a search method. They can also help to differentiate blood from things like rust, chocolate, tar, or other brownish-colored stains that are often incorrectly assumed to be blood. Utilizing a presumptive test can also assist the crime scene investigator in identifying priority areas or evidence that must be tended to prior to other crime scene-processing activities. It is extremely important to collect and preserve biological evidence early in the investigative process to prevent its loss or deterioration. The most commonly used reagents for presumptive blood tests are BlueStar, o-toluidine, phenolphthalein,

FIGURE 5.2: Use of BlueStar to search for blood.

Photo Copyright (©) BLUESTAR®.

luminol, and leucomalachite green. A positive result serves as a preliminary step in determining the origin of the stain. (**FIGURE 5.2**)

If it is discovered that the stain is blood, then the next step is to determine if it is of human origin. This step can only be performed at the forensic laboratory. Upon confirmation that the blood is of human origin, the next step would be to attempt to source the blood to a particular individual. This may or may not be possible, depending on the evidence available. In either event, there will be both class and individual identification options that may assist the investigator in developing leads or identifying the individual. Blood typing is one method of including or excluding individuals from consideration within a criminal investigation. The information derived from the analysis is class characteristic in nature. In order for blood to identify an individual, DNA analysis must be used. This and other methods of identification of suspects will be discussed in Chapter 6.

Blood Typing

In 1901, Dr. Karl Lansteiner discovered that blood could be grouped into four different categories, called *types*: A, B, AB, and O. This finding intrigued Dr. Leone Lattes, and in 1915, he devised a procedure for determining the blood group of a dried bloodstain. However, blood typing is not individualized but is considered to be class information. This can assist in either including or excluding individuals from consideration but will not specifically identify them.

■ Characteristics of Blood Types

Antigens are chemical structures residing on the surface of each red blood cell. **Blood types** are determined by the kind of antigen on the surface of these cells. Although numerous antigens exist on the surface of each red blood cell, the ones used for typing are the A, B, O, and Rh antigens (**FIGURE 5.3**).

ABO blood group

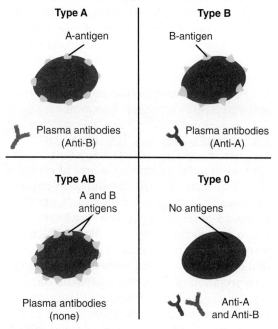

FIGURE 5.3: Blood types.

- Blood types are distinguished by the following antigens:
  - Type A blood has A antigens on its surface
  - Type B blood has B antigens on its surface
  - Type AB blood has both A and B antigens on its surface
  - Type O blood does not have either A or B antigens on its surface
  - Rh-positive blood has D antigens on its surface
  - Rh-negative blood does not have D antigens on its surface

For every antigen, there is an **antibody.** Each antibody name has the prefix "anti-" followed by the name of the corresponding antigen. An antibody will react with its specific antigen. If serum-containing anti-B is added to red blood cells carrying the antigen B, the antibodies will attach themselves to the cells, creating a network of linked cells through a process called **agglutination.**

- Type A blood has A antigens and anti-B antibodies
- Type B blood has B antigens and anti-A antibodies
- Type AB blood has AB antigens and neither anti-A nor anti-B antibodies
- Type O blood has neither A nor B antigens and both anti-A and anti-B antibodies

antibody
Substance that will react with its specific antigen

agglutination
The process by which blood cells link together to form clumps

antigens
Chemical structures residing on the surface of each red blood cell

blood types
The type of antigens found on red blood cells

The process of cell linking allows blood to be typed. In typing blood, only anti-A and anti-B serum are required. Blood of type A will be agglutinated by anti-A serum, blood of type B will be agglutinated by anti-B serum, AB blood will be agglutinated by both anti-A and anti-B serum, and blood of type O will not be agglutinated by either anti-A or anti-B serum. Both anti-A serum and anti-B serum are available commercially.

Bloodstains as Evidence

Because blood is a common source of evidence at a crime scene, it must be handled as physical evidence to be tagged and bagged. In addition, everyone entering the scene must take care not to disturb the patterns of blood, which can reveal as much to the trained eye as the results of the laboratory testing of the blood itself. The interpretation of bloodstain patterns requires careful, planned experiments utilizing surface materials comparable to those found at the crime scene. Whoever is assigned the responsibility of interpreting these stains must be given first access to the crime scene so that the blood patterns may be photographed before other crime scene-processing activities obscure them.

Bloodstain Pattern Analysis

The examination and analysis of bloodstains cannot occur at a scene that has not been preserved or through which the first-responding police officers have trod unnecessarily. Bloodstain pattern analysis may be accomplished by direct examination of the crime scene or by careful examination of color crime scene photographs by those with training in the methodologies associated with bloodstain pattern analysis. Investigators who examine photographs must also examine clothing and weapons along with any other physical evidence. Autopsy reports can also be helpful. However, analysis should leave hospital records, postmortem examinations, autopsy reports, and autopsy photographs for last. Often, these reports contain conjectural statements that may affect the interpretation. Once the investigators begin analysis, they should rely on these secondary resources for corroboration rather than formulation.

Bloodstain pattern analysis can provide a myriad of information, including:

- The origin of the blood drops
- The distance from origin to impact
- The direction of the impact
- The type of impact

- The number of blows, stabs, or shots
- The position of the victim and the assailant at the time of the bloodshed
- The movement of the victim and the assailant during the bloodshed
- The movement of the victim and the assailant after the bloodshed

The study of fluids in motion forms the basis for hypotheses regarding the location, shape, size, and **directionality** of bloodstains relative to the forces that produced them.

History of Bloodstain Pattern Analysis

Much like track impression evidence, the historic origin and skill development of **bloodstain pattern analysis** (BSPA) most likely dates back to the earliest of mankind's hunting efforts. Paleolithic art documents the skill of early human hunters and shows the use of blood tracks to locate prey. Biblical passages connect bloodstains with injury and with mortality. So, it is reasonable to assume that humans have been analyzing bloodstain patterns for well over 4,000 years. Investigators have been attempting to interpret bloodstains for as long as there have been criminal investigations; however, bloodstain analysis as a distinct area of forensic science and crime scene investigation appears to be a more modern occurrence.

The early 1900s saw several prominent scholars and scientists researching and experimenting with blood dynamics and properties of human blood. While numerous individuals recognized the importance of such matters, historically, BSPA as a forensic discipline is credited to Dr. Paul Leland Kirk of the University of California at Berkeley. In his book, *Crime Investigation* (1974, originally published in 1952), Kirk's chapter, "Blood: Physical Investigation," explains the benefits of and application of BSPA in criminal investigations. Kirk put his teachings into practice when submitting an affidavit of his examination of bloodstain evidence and findings in the case of the *State of Ohio v. Samuel H. Sheppard*, in 1955. In this case, Dr. Kirk testified as to the consideration of drying times for blood and pattern evaluation in an effort to explain the events that had occurred at the Sheppard residence, leading to the death of his wife.

This case and Dr. Kirk's textbook are considered an impetus for the modern forensic study of bloodstain pattern analysis. Afterward, the number of authors postulating on such matters began to increase in a dramatic fashion. One

directionality
The direction of a drop of blood from point of origin to point of impact

bloodstain pattern analysis
The FBI nomenclature for analyzing bloodstains left at a crime scene

such author was Herbert Leon MacDonell, whose research recreated bloodstains observed at crime scenes; his first book was *Flight Characteristics of Human Blood and Stain Patterns* (1971a). Although numerous texts have been published on the topic since, MacDonell is credited with reawakening the discipline and providing the stimulus for professional organizations such as the International Association of Bloodstain Pattern Analysts (IABPA) and International Association of Identification (IAI) to develop and/or begin to offer training and certification in this field. As a result of this professional and academic growth, the discipline, on the whole, has gained far greater acceptance in courtrooms across the United States.

Herbert L. MacDonell (1971a) has made an in-depth study of bloodstain patterns. The following are a few sample findings:

- **Surface texture** provides the foundation for blood pattern interpretation. The harder and less porous a surface, the more contained the pattern.

- When a drop of blood hits a hard, smooth surface, it breaks up, splashing smaller droplets about it. These smaller droplets travel in the same direction as the original drop, leaving a pattern that is teardrop shaped, with the pointed end directed toward the place of origin.

- The **circular distortion** of a stain on a flat surface will allow determination of the angle of impact. The more nearly perpendicular the angle of impact, the more circular the blood drop stain. As the angle increases, the stain becomes more elongated. The elongation allows a trigonometric determination of the point of origin (MacDonell, 1993).

There is a computer program that greatly simplifies the data handling and computations necessary to apply the formulas devised by MacDonell and others. This program can graphically represent the position of the victim at the instant that blood was shed, making manual reconstruction of the point of origin unnecessary. The program can analyze blood spatter on floors and walls; it cannot reconstruct a three-dimensional (3D) point of origin from patterns on surfaces of oblique orientation (Eckert & James, 1993).

Bloodstain Mechanics

■ Free-Falling Blood

As a drop of blood falls, the surface tension of the drop minimizes surface area, causing the drop to acquire a spherical shape. A spherical drop will not break up until acted upon by a force other than gravity. When a drop of **free-falling blood** strikes a nonporous, smooth, horizontal surface, the result is a circular bloodstain. A rough-textured surface will cause the surface tension to rupture and create a stain with **spines.** The degree of distortion of the stain is a product of the texture of the impact surface, not the distance that the blood falls (Laber, 1985). The diameter of the stain is a product of the volume of the drop, the distance fallen, and the texture of the impact surface.

Maximum diameters are achieved when the height of the blood source allows the blood drop to reach its **terminal velocity.** MacDonell (1971b) has established that for a 0.05 mL drop of free-falling blood, the terminal velocity is 25 feet per second, which is achieved after the blood falls a distance of about 20 feet. Drops of smaller volume have smaller terminal velocities, and drops of larger volume have higher velocities. Blood drops in excess of 0.05 mL will produce bloodstains with a greater diameter at a shorter falling distance. Investigators should derive conservative estimates as a result of experimentation that uses comparable surface textures and angles of impact. Investigators are able to recognize the types of bloodstains resulting from free-falling blood drops based on their size, shape, and distribution at a crime scene. The interpretation process can incorporate information about velocity, possible source, and movement.

■ Impact Angles

Free-falling blood dropping vertically and striking a horizontal surface at 90 degrees will produce circular bloodstains. (See **FIGURE 5.4.**)

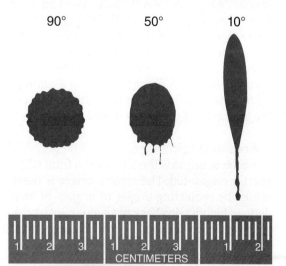

FIGURE 5.4: Shape of bloodstain as a result of angle of impact.

Courtesy of Erica Lawler.

free-falling blood
Blood that has not been acted on by a force other than gravity; when a drop of free-falling blood strikes a nonporous, smooth, horizontal surface, the result is a circular bloodstain

spines
The pointed-edge pattern that radiates away from a drop of blood that has struck a target surface

terminal velocity
The maximum speed to which a free-falling drop of blood can accelerate in air; this velocity is approximately 25.1 feet per second

surface texture
Composition of materials in a given surface that provides the foundation for blood pattern interpretation

circular distortion
The stain that results from blood striking a flat surface at an angle; the more nearly perpendicular the angle of impact, the more circular the blood drop stain

angle of impact

Angle at which a blood drop hits a surface, relative to the horizontal plane of that surface; the angle can be calculated by measuring the width and length of the bloodstain

area of convergence

The area containing the intersections generated by lines drawn through the long axes of individual stains that indicate in two dimensions the location of the blood source

SWGSTAIN

The Scientific Working Group on Bloodstain Pattern Analysis; was created to promote quality forensic bloodstain pattern analysis practices by government labs, law enforcement, private industry, and academia

area of origin

By establishing the impact angles of representative bloodstains and projecting their trajectories back to a common axis (Z), extended at 90 degrees from the area of convergence, an approximate location of where the blood source was when it was impacted may be established

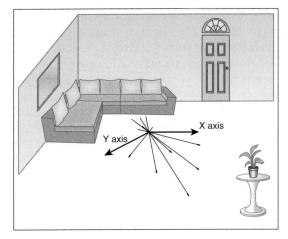

FIGURE 5.5: Determining the area of convergence from blood spatter evidence.

Courtesy of Dana Gevelinger.

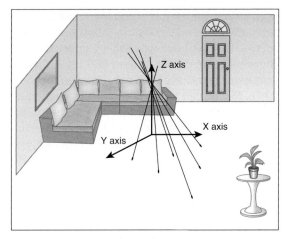

FIGURE 5.6: Determining the area of origin for blood spatter.

Courtesy of Dana Gevelinger.

Blood dropping on a nonhorizontal surface produces elongated, oval-shaped stains—the greater the angle, the greater the elongation. The narrowest end of the stain will point in the direction of travel and away from the point of origin. This angle can be calculated by measuring the width and length of the bloodstain. **Angle of impact** calculations are now usually done with the help of computer software.

■ Area of Convergence

When a body is subjected to a force sufficient to cause bleeding, the blood released will strike various surfaces at a variety of angles. The **area of convergence** is the area containing the intersections generated by lines drawn through the long axes of individual stains that indicate in two dimensions the location of the blood source (**SWGSTAIN**). (See **FIGURE 5.5**). Stains on a surface, when traced through their long axes, will come together at a point on that surface, showing the direction from which they came and their direction of travel. For example, bloodstains on a floor will lead back along the floor to a common point—the point at which lines drawn through the long axes of the stains would intersect.

■ Area of Origin

The **area of origin** is the 3D location from which spatter originated. The area of origin is determined by projecting angles of impact of well-defined bloodstains back to an axis constructed through the established area of convergence. In other words, the area of origin shows the general direction that the blood traveled. By examining the bloodstains, one can see a distortion in the shape of the drop due not to the surface texture but to the angle at which the blood drop hit the surface. This distortion reveals the impact angle of the blood. Strings can be projected from

each measured bloodstain at its angle of impact back to an axis perpendicular to the plane on which the bloodstains are located and passing through their point of convergence. The place where these strings come together is the point or the set of points in space from which the bloodstains are likely to have originated. (See **FIGURE 5.6**.)

■ Low-Velocity-Impact Bloodstains

When blood drips from a stationary object or falls as a result of no other force acting upon it other than inertia, low-velocity-impact bloodstains are created. (See **FIGURE 5.7**.) Secondary blood splashing (**ricochet**) may occur as a result of the deflection of large volumes of blood after impact on a **target surface. Splashed** bloodstain patterns usually have a large central area and peripheral spattering, with the spatter appearing as elongated, oval-shaped spots. These patterns are often produced when pools of blood are disturbed by objects such as shod feet, or when large volumes of blood fall from a source such as a victim's wound. The larger the quantity of splashed blood, the greater the spatter.

FIGURE 5.7: Example of a low-velocity-impact bloodstain.

Courtesy of Dana Gevelinger.

FIGURE 5.8: Example of a medium-velocity-impact bloodstain.

Courtesy of Dana Gevelinger.

FIGURE 5.9: Example of a projected bloodstain pattern.

Courtesy of Dana Gevelinger.

■ Medium-Velocity-Impact Bloodstains

When a strong force strikes an exposed source of blood, the blood is broken up into many small droplets. When these droplets strike a target surface, they produce bloodstain patterns that are readily distinguishable from **drip patterns,** which are associated with low-velocity force or impact (Eckert & James, 1993). These types of stains are typically produced as a result of blunt-force trauma and stabbings. (See **FIGURE 5.8.**)

■ Projected Blood

When large quantities of blood undergo medium- or high-velocity impact, the blood is forcibly **projected** on a target surface or surfaces and creates distinctive patterns. When blood is directed horizontally or vertically downward with more force than gravity alone would exert, the resulting pattern has a periphery of spine-like extensions and a streaking secondary spatter. Blood released under arterial pressure forms this type of pattern, and the process of release is referred to as **arterial gushing** (or **spurting**). The resulting stains are characteristic and readily identified by appearance and shape. Arterial gushing is common at crime scenes where a shooting or stabbing has occurred. (See **FIGURE 5.9.**)

■ Cast-Off Blood

In blunt trauma cases, often, the assailant swings a weapon repeatedly at the victim. These repeated blows may create a pattern as blood is flung from the weapon on each successive blow. If a weapon has produced blood, it will often adhere to that weapon. During the backswing away from the victim, the blood on the weapon will be thrown off and travel tangentially to the arc of the swing, striking nearby surfaces, such as walls, ceilings, floors, and other objects in its path. The initial blood that

is cast from a weapon during the backswing may strike a target surface and produce circular stains at 90 degrees. These stains often appear on walls or ceilings. As the backswing continues past its apex, the remaining blood is cast off a greater distance at a greater angle and will produce oval-shaped stains. Determination of the angle of impact and the convergence of these cast-off bloodstains allows a reconstruction of the position of the victim and assailant.

Numerous **cast-off patterns** will allow a reconstruction of the movements of the victim and assailant as well as their relative positions at the time that the cast-off patterns were produced. (See **FIGURE 5.10.**) They also allow an estimation of the minimum number of blows struck. The number of distinct patterns or trails

FIGURE 5.10: Example of a cast-off bloodstain pattern.

Courtesy of Dana Gevelinger.

ricochet
Secondary blood splashing that may occur as a result of the deflection of large volumes of blood after impact with a primary target surface to a secondary target surface

target surface
Surface onto which blood is deposited

splashed
A (projected) pattern created by a low-velocity impact on the surface of a pool of blood with a volume of 0.10 mL or greater

drip patterns
The pattern created by blood dripping into blood; in this pattern, round blood spatters occur at the periphery of the central bloodstain

cast-off patterns
The pattern produced by a bloody object in motion (such as a weapon) resulting in blood projected (thrown) onto a surface other than the impact site

projected
Directed forcefully onto a surface

arterial gushing (spurting)
Blood exiting under pressure from a breached artery

of cast-off stains equals the minimum number of blows struck plus one, because the first blow does not produce a cast-off pattern. If more than one blow was struck on the same plane, the cast-off patterns may overlap, which is the reason only the minimum number of blows struck may be estimated (MacDonell, 1971b).

■ Flow Patterns

Flow patterns indicate the direction of travel of flowing blood. Pooled blood behaves like pooled water. The direction of travel of either is dependent on gravity. Flow patterns may be seen on the body of the victim as well as on the surface upon which the victim is lying. Flow patterns and blood pooling may reveal movement of a victim during or after bloodshed or alteration of the crime scene. Blood flow patterns on the victim should be consistent with the victim's injuries and subsequent pooling. Any inconsistencies suggest that the injuries were not sustained at the crime scene and that the victim was transported there after injury or death.

A blood source that collides with an object moving at a speed between 5 and 25 feet per second will produce **medium-velocity blood spatter**. In order to create a medium-velocity blood pattern, the blood source must be exposed prior to impact. Medium-velocity bloodstains range from 1 mm to 4 mm in diameter and are often characterized by a pattern in which streaks radiate away from the area of impact. Interrupted radial patterns suggest that the assailant's body and clothing may have intercepted part of the splashing blood.

■ High-Velocity-Impact Bloodstains

A collision between a blood source and an object moving in excess of 100 feet per second will create a **high-velocity-impact pattern.** (See **FIGURE 5.11**.) The high-velocity impact creates a mist of showering blood that, because of its low density, does not travel far. High-velocity-impact bloodstains are generally associated with gunshot injuries. Spatter from a gunshot is multidirectional. **Backspatter** may occur if the assailant and weapon are proximate to the victim upon impact. The assailant and the weapon may bear evidence of blood spatter. The amount of backspatter is affected by the type of weapon and ammunition, the muzzle-to-target distance, the position of the victim at the time of impact, and the physiological characteristics of the struck area (Stephens & Allen, 1983). In the case of contact wounds, the barrel of the weapon may contain flesh,

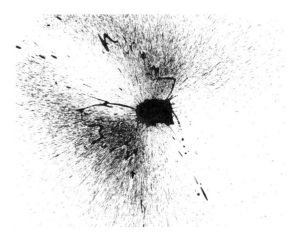

FIGURE 5.11: Example of a high-velocity-impact bloodstain. Courtesy of Dana Gevelinger.

bone, and blood residue from **barrel blowback** (or **drawback**). Barrel blowback may also cause backspatter on hands and clothing. High-velocity **forward spatter** is generally a product of a gunshot exit wound. This type of spatter can assist in determining the location of the victim at the time of the wounding.

Handling Blood Evidence

In crime scenes at which a violent crime occurred, blood is often transferred from the victim to the assailant. It is the probability of this type of transfer that makes homicide investigators pay special attention to blood and bloodstained clothing. In an effort to preserve what may become important evidence, investigators collect all of the clothing from the victim as well as samples of the underlying strata upon which the body rested. Even what appear to be unstained portions of clothing may be gathered. In many cases, blood may not be visible but may still respond to appropriate laboratory testing. All bloodstains should be measured and photographed prior to handling.

Packaging of bloodstained clothing is critical. Heat and moisture can reduce the viability of antigens. Time is of the essence. Bloodstains should be submitted for laboratory testing immediately. Not only does the passage of time corrupt bloodstains, but it also raises serious questions about efficiency and the chain of custody. Airtight containers may cause condensation of moisture in the container and result in the growth of bacteria that can destroy blood. Thus, bloody items should be packaged in paper or cardboard to allow the item to breathe and not degrade. (See **FIGURE 5.12**.)

FIGURE 5.12: Examples of improperly and properly packaged evidence containing blood.

Courtesy of Nicholas Vesper.

FIGURE 5.13: Example of collection of wet blood evidence.

Courtesy of Nicholas Vesper.

Collection of Blood Evidence

In crimes of violence, blood is usually found in the form of dried stains. Blood can frequently be identified and genetically compared with blood standards from individuals if a sufficient quantity is properly collected and submitted. In addition to identification and comparison testing, the shape and pattern of the bloodstaining may provide information concerning how the blood was deposited. Record the following:

- Physical state (fluid, moist, dry)
- Amount present (few drops, small pool, etc.)
- Shape (smear, round drops)
- Exact location in relation to fixed objects
- Pattern of stains (all in one spot, trail)
- Atmosphere conditions (temperature, humidity)
- Date and time of observation
- Scaled and unscaled photographs of stains

Liquid Blood

If wet blood or a pool of fluid blood is present, collection should be made in the following manner (see **FIGURES 5.13, 5.14,** and **5.15**):

- Wear gloves, mask, and eye protection while soaking up samples
- Soak the suspected blood onto cotton swabs
- Continue collecting the stain until it is either completely collected or until five swabs have been saturated
- Make sure to avoid contamination of swabs
- Consider changing gloves frequently, and change them immediately if contamination of gloves occurs

FIGURE 5.14: Example of collection of control sample relating to blood evidence. Courtesy of Nicholas Vesper.

Courtesy of Nicholas Vesper.

FIGURE 5.15: Example of blood evidence sample packaging.

Courtesy of Nicholas Vesper.

- Allow the swabs to dry in place or place them on a nonporous surface, like a glass microscope slide, and allow them to air dry thoroughly

- Package the dried swabs in a paper container (e.g., white slide box, envelope, paper bag). Use separate containers for each area recovered.

- Properly label and seal each container, including labeling the paper container with a "bio-hazard" sign

- Select an unstained area adjacent to the suspected bloodstain and collect a sample from this area, as before. This sample will serve as a control. Package, label, and seal this control separately from the stained material.

Dried or Moist Bloodstain Recovery

If the stained object is transportable, submit the item intact. If the suspected blood is still moist, allow it to thoroughly air dry in a well-ventilated but draft-free area prior to packaging. Label the area with "biohazard" signs. Package the item in a clean paper container, seal, and label. If it is impractical to submit the blood-stained item to the laboratory or it is not possible to cut or remove a portion of the stained and unstained area of the item, collect in the following manner:

- Wear gloves, mask, and eye protection while collecting samples

- Moisten a sufficient number of cotton swabs to collect the stain. It is better to underestimate the amount of swabs required as additional swabs can always be used.

- Wet the swabs using distilled water; clean tap water can be used if distilled water is not available

- Do not allow the swabs to come into contact with any other object

- Gently swab the stain with the moistened swabs until the swabs thoroughly absorb the blood and are a dark, reddish-brown color

- Continue collecting the stain until it is either completely collected or five swabs have been saturated

- Allow the stained swabs to thoroughly air dry, either directly on the stained object or on a clean glass microscope slide. To avoid contamination, swabs can also be dried by making a small perforation in a pillbox and placing the swab into the perforation. This will allow the swab to dry without contacting any other surfaces.

- Package, label, and seal the air-dried swabs in a paper container (e.g., white slide box, envelope). Label with a "biohazard" sign.

- Select an unstained area adjacent to the suspected bloodstain and collect a sample from this area as before. This sample will serve as a control. Package, label, and seal this control separately from the stained material.

Handling Guidelines

Unnecessary exposure of blood to heat, moisture, and bacterial contamination will shorten the survival time of its antigens. It is important that all bloodstained material be submitted for testing without delay. Each moment the material is not delivered to the laboratory must be accounted for and explained. Because of the importance of blood evidence, the investigators should devise a delivery protocol to get blood-stained material from the crime scene to the laboratory as quickly as possible. Such a protocol will prevent embarrassing questions on cross-examination and reduce the risk of a challenge to evidence based on deterioration of the specimen.

All containers in which blood is placed should be saved and available at the time of trial

INVESTIGATOR'S

© Shutterstock, Inc./Janaka Dharmasena

NOTEBOOK

Collecting Bloodstained Samples

All bloodstained clothing should be packaged separately in paper bags. If stains are wet, they should be air dried prior to packaging. Blood deposited on surfaces that do not lend themselves to packaging should be allowed to dry and then scraped onto a clean piece of paper. A control sample must also be submitted to prove that the positive results of any testing were from the sample submitted and not something previously deposited on the surface and lying under the sample.

© Shutterstock, Inc./Nutink.

CASE IN POINT

A Telling Drop

In one case involving an open-field death, the female victim was found face down with knife wounds to the front of her body. A cursory examination of the body revealed a single circular dried blood droplet on her buttocks. Investigators discussed various ways of retrieving the blood after having photographed it.

Determining that the blood would probably not survive handling and moving of the body, they decided to remove it prior to moving the body. The circumference of the blood drop indicated that it fell perpendicular to the victim's reclining body, probably as a result of a wound to the assailant. Mutilating the body was thought to be the only option until an evidence technician suggested lifting the droplet like a fingerprint. The efforts to lift it were successful, and analysis of the droplet played a prominent role in the identification and subsequent conviction of the murderer.

in case of questions pertaining to the collection and handling of the evidence. It is important that as much of the blood as possible be preserved at the scene and at the laboratory. The defense may request court permission to conduct independent tests, especially if DNA testing has been performed.

Other Biological Fluids

In addition to blood at crime scenes, there are numerous other biological fluids that may be collected and identified in order to explain what occurred at the scene of the crime. Most will yield the ability to identify DNA from them also. Other fluids that are present at crime scenes, and for which identification is sometimes necessary include but are not limited to semen, saliva, vomitus, perspiration, urine, and fecal matter.

Semen

In 1935, Kutscher and Wolbergs discovered that human semen contains uniquely high levels of

seminal acid phosphatase (SAP) compared with other body fluids and plant tissues. SAP is produced by the prostate and is, therefore, found in both animals and humans. However, it is 20 to 400 times more concentrated within humans than in any other body fluid (Saferstein, 2014). This is the scientific basis for the presumptive ID of semen. Many methods for the presumptive ID of semen have been devised.

One method is utilizing an ALS because seminal fluid contains an acriflavine, which fluoresces bluish-white when exposed to the light from an ALS, with a proper barrier filter. However, this test is not sufficient to presumptively identify semen, as there are numerous other substances that have the same fluorescence. These include: fabric softeners, toothpaste, cosmetics, sweat, and urine. This is a good starting point, however. There are presumptive field test kits to screen for SAP that are more isolating in nature. This test is performed by promoting a color reaction within the sample. In forensic laboratories, alphanaphthyl phosphate is the preferred substrate and Brentamine Fast

— Ripped from the Headlines —

Blood Evidence Used to Convict Boston Marathon Bomber

On April 8, 2015, Dzhokhar Tsarnaev was convicted of the 2013 Boston Marathon bombing, which killed three and injured 260. Blood evidence and DNA analysis featured prominently within the case investigation and litigation. Prosecutors presented DNA evidence and blood to tie in the involvement of both Tsarnaev brothers in the event, although only Dzhokhar was prosecuted for the crime, since Tamerlan died during the course of subsequent events.

Blue the color developer. However, Brentamine Fast Blue B is potentially carcinogenic, so liberal applications made directly onto items of clothing or areas of flooring are not recommended.

Confirmatory tests for the presence of semen can only be made at the forensic laboratory. Microscopic identification of spermatozoa is one type of confirmatory test for semen. At the lab, the criminalist will stain the prepared sample using a "Christmas tree" stain test that stains the head of spermatozoa red and their tails (flagella) green. This then provides unambiguous proof that the stain in question contains semen.

Another method to confirm the presence of semen in a sample is for the forensic lab to perform what is known as a p30 test. This test is performed when no sperm are found to be present within the sample (e.g., vasectomized male). p30 is a prostate-specific antigen produced in the human male. There have been cases where p30 was detected in samples stored at room temperature for up to 10 years. In fact, sperm can be located within an oral sample for up to 24 hours and inside of the vagina for up to 72 hours. This provides a finite window of collection opportunities for a crime scene investigator (Saferstein, 2014).

■ Procedure for the Collection of Seminal Stains

Where a sexual offense has occurred, stains may be found on clothing, bedding, rags, upholstery, or other objects. Seminal stains can be helpful in establishing whether or not an alleged sexual act occurred and can also provide information concerning the man who contributed the semen.

Carefully recover all suspected stained material, including the clothing worn by the victim and the suspect at the time of the offense. Each item of evidence should be packaged separately, labeled, and sealed. Air dry all damp stains in a well-ventilated but draft-free area.

Clean paper should be spread under the item to catch any debris that may be dislodged during the drying process. Package, label, and seal each item along with the paper upon which the item dried. Use only paper containers for packaging (e.g., paper bags). If the suspected seminal stain is on an object that cannot be transported, collect utilizing swabs and distilled water, as with blood evidence.

Standard blood samples are normally used for comparison purposes, rather than collecting semen standards for comparison.

Saliva

Humans produce 1 to 1.3 liters of saliva per day. Its primary purpose is to aid in the initial stages of digestion by lubricating food for ease of swallowing and to begin the process of digestion. However, no test is specific for saliva. Presumptive tests will test for presence of amylase (found in saliva, perspiration, semen, vaginal secretions, and breast milk). However, amylase is found in 50 times higher concentration within saliva. There have been cases where activity has been detected for up to approximately 28 months (Saferstein, 2014).

Saliva stains are not usually evident from a visual examination. However, certain types of evidence frequently contain traces of saliva (e.g., cigarette butts, gummed surfaces of envelopes, stamps, bite marks, areas where oral contact may have occurred, etc.) and sometimes the amount of saliva present is sufficient to determine the DNA type of the individual who is the source of the saliva.

■ Procedure for the Collection of Evidential Forms of Saliva

Easily transportable objects, such as individual cigarette butts and envelopes, should be placed in a paper container (e.g., paper bag or envelopes) and the container should be properly labeled and sealed. If transporting the object is not practical, such as in the case of bite marks on the body of sexual assault victims, the saliva can be collected as follows:

- Moisten a cotton swab with distilled water
- Shake the swab to eliminate excess water
- Gently swab the suspected saliva stain. Using a dry swab, go over the stained area to absorb any remaining moisture.
- Allow the swabs to thoroughly air dry prior to packaging, labeling, and sealing in a paper envelope. Air drying can be accomplished by making a perforation in the center of a pillbox, inserting the swab into the perforation and allowing the swab to air dry.
- Select an unstained area and collect as before. Package, label, and seal separately from the stained material. This swab will serve as a control.

Standard blood samples are normally used for comparison purposes, rather than collecting saliva standards for comparison.

Other Types of Biological Evidence

■ Urine

This is a rarely identified biological fluid. The presumptive test for urine by the forensic laboratory tests for the presence of creatinine, which is found in heavy concentrations in urine. It is also found, however, in high concentrations in sweat. There is no confirmatory test that is regularly utilized.

■ Vomitus

There is no presumptive or confirmatory test for vomitus. However, the material can be tested to determine food content and to compare pH levels.

■ Vaginal Secretions

In order to meet the elements of sexual assault, often, it is necessary to prove that an object was placed within the vagina. In these cases, it is necessary for the forensic laboratory to make use of microscopy in order to identify fluids and cells associated with vaginal secretions.

Vaginal secretions in the form of a foreign DNA (DNA that did not originate from the individual swabbed) can sometimes be attributed to another individual when the penis of a suspected sexual perpetrator is swabbed at the time of apprehension. The sample is collected by wetting a cotton swab with distilled water and swabbing the external area of the penis. This type of analysis is most successful when the perpetrator is apprehended shortly after the alleged occurrence of sexual activity, generally within 24 hours and prior to bathing. The outer area of condoms also can yield this type of DNA.

Preservation of Dried Biological Evidence

The ideal way to preserve biological evidence is to freeze it. This can become impractical with large amounts of evidence. Evidence with dried biological stains can be stored in a temperature-controlled room, which is maintained at normal room temperature or colder. Large fluctuations in temperature should be avoided. When biological evidence is returned after processing by the DNA unit of the crime laboratory, it frequently will contain a manila envelope labeled "DNA packet." This packet contains cuttings of stains and extracts of those stains. This packet needs to be frozen. If this packet is included with the evidence, it will be noted on the return release form and the evidence will be labeled "Biological Evidence Enclosed, Please Remove and Freeze."

Introduction to Trace Evidence

Connection of an object or person to a specific location or item is often paramount to establishing guilt or innocence. **Locard's Exchange Principle** states that, "whenever two objects come into contact with one another, there will be a cross-transfer of material, which will occur" (Gale, 2005). This theory is the underlying premise behind the documentation, collection, preservation, and identification of trace evidence. While the types are limitless, the term trace evidence typically refers to any evidence that is small in size, such as hairs, fibers, paint, glass, and soil, which would require microscopic analysis in order to identify it. The purpose of microscopic analysis is to determine whether or not an association between persons, places, and things can be established, and the subsequent strength of such an association. This association would be as a result of **associative evidence**. However, sometimes, enough uniqueness is present within the trace evidence to allow for an individualized association.

Probability/Product Rule

Another way to approach the level of individualization is through association with numerous levels of class characteristics. This association brings to light a mathematical concept known as **probability**. Probability is most simply defined as the frequency with which an event will occur, sometimes referred to as the *odds of occurrence*. For instance, if one were to flip a coin 10 times, the probability of the coin landing heads down will be 5 in 10. The concept of probability is important to comprehend from a forensic aspect because it is this frequency of occurrence that an examiner is depending upon to limit potential suspect items or individuals and to explain the odds of such occurrences to the potential jury.

The concept of probability can be taken a step further when considering all aspects of probability associated with an event in an effort to determine a statistical probability for the event or item in question, using classical or frequentist statistics. For instance, if all eye witnesses agree that a white male suspect over the age of 30 committed a crime, utilizing the **product rule** would lend statistical support to such matters and explain the frequency of such an event occurring. The product rule is when the frequencies of independently occurring variables are multiplied together to obtain an

TABLE 5.1 Utilizing the Product Rule

Demographic	Statistic	Percentage	Equation
Number of people in the United States (est.)	295,734,134		
Population that is white	241,614,787	81.70%	(241,624,787 ÷ 295,734,134)
Population that is white male	118,705,344	49.13%	(118,705,344 ÷ 241,614,787)
Population of white males over age 30	42,401,549	35.72%	(42,401,549 ÷ 118,705,344)

Using the product rule, 0.817 × 0.4913 × 0.3572 = 0.1433, or 14.33%, or 1 in 7 persons could have been involved in the commission of the crime. Data from the Central Intelligence Agency. (2006). The World Factbook. Retrieved August 4, 2009, from https://www.cia.gov/library/publications/resources/the-world-factbook/index.html.

overall frequency of occurrence for the event or item. **TABLE 5.1** shows the product rule applied to the case example given here.

Most evidence is not truly individualistic; instead, it is looked at as being individual in nature because the probability of a match between any other item is so remote (so large a number). However, the establishment of probabilities relating to evidence is typically the duty of the criminalist who analyzes or interprets the evidence, or of the attorneys or other forensic expert presenting the evidence within court, rather than of the crime scene investigator. Criminalists will determine probability and utilize the product rule during their analysis, interpretation, and, eventually, within their testimony. They will do this in order to attempt to explain the probability of a person's DNA matching that of the evidence presented (e.g., 1 in 1,476,565,780), or the frequency of another carpet fiber matching the one discovered at the crime scene (e.g., 1 in 7,896). Their utilization of such a statistical analysis does not, by any means, define an absolute but instead presents the trier of fact with an educated extrapolation of a number that a reasonable person would infer as being sufficient to believe that the probability of a more likely match being present is extremely remote.

Collection of Trace Evidence

Trace evidence is collected in a variety of ways, including with the use of a forceps, tweezers, by hand, tape lift, or even vacuuming. If possible, the entire item containing the suspected evidence should be collected and preserved for later analysis. If conditions do not allow for this, on-scene steps must be taken to properly collect and preserve the trace evidence (**FIGURE 5.16**).

When collecting trace evidence, the crime scene investigator must document and collect not only the questioned samples but also collect known samples for comparison purposes. For example, if a suspect is located in a burglary case involving entry through a broken glass window, the crime scene investigator should document and collect trace glass evidence from the clothing, or submit the clothing to the lab for trace glass analysis. The crime scene investigator must also collect known samples of the glass from the broken window for comparative analysis. Failure to collect the known/comparison sample will almost always result in the forensic lab declining to conduct an analysis, although this is dependent upon the expertise of the laboratory and analysts within the lab. The possibility exists that, with proper experience, the

FIGURE 5.16: Collection of trace evidence from crime scene.

CASE IN POINT

© Shutterstock, Inc./Vlastas.

The Product Rule at Work

While investigating a cold hit-and-run accident, a crime scene investigator located a piece of plastic that appeared to be from a turn signal of a vehicle. The plastic did not match the struck vehicle and was believed to have belonged to the vehicle that fled the scene. The plastic piece had a number stamped on it, along with the Chrysler logo. This led the investigator to contact a local Chrysler dealer's parts department, which was able to give the investigator information that the plastic piece belonged to a 2012 Dodge Ram pickup truck. The dealership was confident in this because that part was only placed into that specific year and model. The crime scene investigator knew that the vehicle that fled the scene was a white-colored vehicle due to paint transfer found on the red Chevy S-10 that was struck.

The crime scene investigator contacted local body shops and asked that if they had anyone who showed up with a 2012 white Dodge Ram pickup truck with right front-end damage, that they call the investigating officer. Within one week, a body shop called to report that an individual was requesting bodywork be done on the front of a damaged vehicle that had resulted from "accidentally striking their garage." The crime scene investigator responded to the body shop and noted red transfer paint on the damaged portion of the vehicle. Photographs were taken, and eventually hit-and-run charges were filed against the registered owner for the accident.

In court, the evidence was presented and the prosecution brought up the probability of a Dodge Ram pickup truck being the vehicle involved. It was determined through contact with Chrysler that there were 1,196, 2012 Dodge pickup trucks sold within 100 miles of the accident scene. Of those, 257 were white. This meant that the probability of the fleeing vehicle having been a 2012 white Dodge Ram pickup truck was 21.48%. The prosecution took this a step further and looked at the number of registered vehicles within a 100-mile radius through information derived from the Department of Motor Vehicles. It was determined that there were 175,765 validly registered vehicles within the defined area. Utilizing the product rule, the frequency of a 2012 white Dodge pickup being the vehicle involved in the incident was explained as follows:

2012 Dodge pickup (1,196 out of 120,125) 0.99%
2012 white-colored Dodge pickup (257 out of 1,196) 21.48%

Therefore, $0.0099 \times 0.2148 = 0.0021$, or 0.21%, or 1 in 500 vehicles on the road were 2012 white, Dodge Ram pickups.

This was a very large number and the jury took this as evidence of there being a very remote chance that another vehicle matching the description of the defendant's vehicle also sustained front-end damage consistent with the crash.

© Shutterstock, Inc./Nutink.

possible sources for the glass may be narrowed down by the analyst. Ultimately, the crime scene investigator is attempting to show that Locard's Exchange Principle is alive and well, and that the broken glass from the window can be used to show transfer and thus connectivity to the suspect, and vice versa.

It is important for crime scene investigators to understand the mechanisms of primary and secondary transfer. As trace evidence can be transferred during the commission of a crime, it can also be transferred during the search process. Not only can investigators inadvertently pick up hairs and fibers, they can also be inadvertently deposited at the crime scene. The following are important considerations to keep in mind at the crime scene:

- Elimination hair and/or fiber samples may need to be obtained from personnel conducting the search

- Prioritize the order of evidence collection. Collect large items first and then proceed to the trace evidence. Use caution when walking the crime scene.

- Once the trace evidence is collected via vacuuming, taping, or tweezing, take blood samples, remove bullets, dust for fingerprints, and so on

- Processing the crime scene for fingerprints prior to trace evidence collection is not recommended because it can inadvertently transfer trace evidence onto the clothing of the technicians, move trace evidence, and/or contaminate trace evidence with dusting powder.

When collecting most types of trace evidence, personnel typically make use of a druggist/pharmacist fold or bindle as a primary method of evidence preservation (**FIGURE 5.17**).

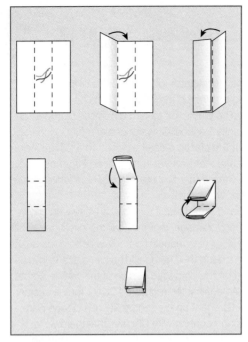

FIGURE 5.17: Example of how to fold and use a pharmacist/druggist fold for primary packaging of trace evidence.

Courtesy of Dana Gevelinger.

The trace evidence is placed onto a clean sheet of paper and the paper is then folded into thirds and then into thirds again, with one end of the paper tucked back into itself so as to safely encapsulate the trace material. This is referred to as primary packaging. This is not sufficient in itself. The **primary packaging** should then be placed into secondary packaging, such as a paper envelope or paper bag, or into a plastic bag if drug materials that will not be analyzed for biological material and then sealed appropriately. The **secondary packaging** serves to protect the primary packaging from damage and ensures that no trace material will be added to or lost from the initial evidence that was collected.

Glass Evidence

Because glass is so prevalent, breaks easily, and, when fragmented, has a tendency to adhere to clothing and body surfaces, it is frequently encountered within the context of crime scene investigation as **transfer evidence**.

Fracture Analysis

Examination of glass that has been fractured can lead the crime scene investigator to determine from which direction the impact originated. This can be useful in determining whether or not a window was broken from the inside or outside (e.g., in attempting to identify whether or not a window was broken to cover up an employee theft and disguise it as a burglary). To make this determination, the crime scene investigator must understand what happens when glass fractures. First of all, a crime scene investigator can observe the **radial fractures**, those originating from the point of impact and moving away from that point, and other fractures that appear to make a typically broken series of concentric circles around the impact point, known as **concentric fractures**. Next, the crime scene investigator can observe the edges of the glass and will see that the glass shows characteristics referred to as **conchoidal fractures** (**FIGURE 5.18**). These stress marks are shaped like arches that are perpendicular to one side of the glass surface and curved nearly parallel to the opposite glass surface. This is telling to a crime scene investigator because for radial fractures, the perpendicular edge is always opposite the direction from which the force was applied to the glass surface. In concentric fractures, the perpendicular end always faces the direction to which the force was applied to the glass surface. One way to remember this is the **3R rule**: Radial fractures form a Right angle on the Reverse side to which force was applied.

An investigator can also determine glass breakage sequence through careful analysis of present characteristics (**FIGURE 5.19**). By taking note that some cracks reach a termination point at their intersection with other fractures, the crime scene investigator can conclude that fractures that terminate occurred after those that do not. This will give an idea as to the glass break sequence. Impact direction can be gauged if enough of the initial impact point is still present. At the point of impact, a crime scene investigator will note that there will be

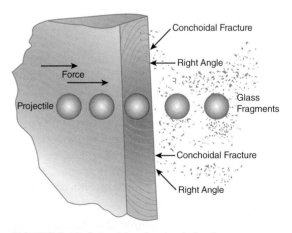

FIGURE 5.18: Determining glass break direction.

Courtesy of Ellie Blazer.

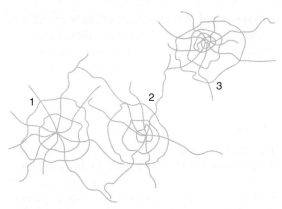

FIGURE 5.19: Determining glass break sequence.
Courtesy of Ellie Blazer.

evidence of a cone-like core ejection from the exit side of the glass. An example of when this would be used is in determining which bullet hole was made first within a window pane. If a suspect was shooting out of a glass picture window at police, and the police were shooting into the picture window from outside, a court will want to know who fired the first shot. Careful analysis of the glass fractures will help determine this fact.

Collecting and Packaging Glass Evidence

In order for glass evidence to serve an evidentiary purpose, it must be properly collected and preserved. The gathering of glass evidence at the crime scene and from a suspect or victim must be thorough if the forensic lab is to have a chance to attempt analysis that would individualize the glass fragments as being from a common source. This requires that the crime scene investigator have a working knowledge of what kinds of information can be derived from glass evidence.

First, glass evidence is typically viewed as class evidence and is only rarely able to be individualized. This can result in both inclusions and exclusions of persons and glass surfaces, which although not unique, are certainly advantageous within the context of a criminal investigation.

Depending on the crime, and the scene of the crime, it may be necessary for the crime scene investigator to attempt to collect all of the glass evidence located at the scene. In other cases, it may only be necessary for the crime scene investigator to collect a known sample of the glass. For instance, in a vehicle versus pedestrian hit-and-run accident, a crime scene investigator may find it necessary to recover all related headlight and reflector lens glass so that if a vehicle is later identified, the pieces can be puzzled together to show the uniqueness and thus include the vehicle as a suspect vehicle. Simply collecting a known sample of the glass at the scene would only result in glass analysis being able to determine that the suspect vehicle had glass components consistent with the glass found at the scene, which would typically be the

secondary packaging
Serves to protect the primary packaging from damage and ensures that no trace material will be added to nor lost from the initial evidence that was collected. Typically comprised of a paper envelope, paper bag, a plastic bag or other type of box or container

transfer evidence
A type of evidence that is passed from one item to another, typically as a result of contact or action. Careful analysis of this evidence can associate the questioned evidence with a known source

— Ripped from the Headlines —

FBI Performs Glass Fracture Analysis on Amtrak Train

On May 12, 2015, a Manhattan-bound Amtrak train derailed, killing eight people and injuring at least 200 others. During the course of the subsequent investigation, it was determined that the train was going twice the speed limit at the time that it derailed, and damage to the windows of the derailed train, as well as two other passing trains during the same night, raised suspicions of projectiles being thrown at trains in a deliberate manner. The NTSB subsequently requested the FBI to conduct glass-fracture analysis on the train windshield to determine if a projectile had indeed struck the train and if it was able to be determined if the glass fractures happened prior to the derailment or subsequent to the derailment. By analyzing the fractures that were present, it could be determined that a large item (projectile other than a bullet) had impacted the windshield and that the fractures had occurred prior to the subsequent damage caused by the derailment. At the time of the publication of this text, the NTSB has as of yet not released a formal reason for the crash.

Madhani, A., Onyanga-Omara, J., & Jansen, B. (2015). FBI: Amtrak train not hit by gunfire. *USA Today.* Retrieved on August 20, 2015, from http://www.usatoday.com/story/news/nation/2015/05/18/amtrak-resumes-service/27519113/

© Shutterstock, Inc./rzarek.

case for any such make and model vehicle having the same automotive parts. This would be enough to include the vehicle as a possible suspect vehicle but not sufficient to individualize it, as would be the puzzling together of all related glass and showing the corresponding match.

However, when an individual fit is not likely or necessary, the crime scene investigator should collect a reference sample of broken glass found at the scene of the crime, and then properly collect and package the suspect or victim's clothes for comparative analysis.

The reference sample should be collected as near the point of impact as possible. Approximately one square inch of material is all that will be required for forensic analysis relating to this comparison. Therefore, there is no need to collect an abundance of glass from the scene.

The fragment(s) should be packaged in solid containers, which will avoid breaking the glass further while in transit, and it will also not allow the glass to protrude from the packaging and injure personnel handling the evidence. If there are suspect or victim clothes that will be submitted to the lab for glass analysis, they should be wrapped individually in paper to ensure that the trace evidence is not lost in transport and then packaged in a porous material, such as paper bags or cardboard boxes. When the item is wrapped in the paper, the item should be folded within the paper in such a way that no surface of the clothing touches another surface of the same clothing, but instead has paper between them. This will ensure that there is no transfer or contamination of trace evidence and that the trace evidence is properly contained. The crime scene investigator should not attempt to shake the clothes to dislodge and thus collect the glass particles but should instead leave the discovery, collection, and analysis of glass evidence to forensic lab personnel.

If direction of force analysis is to be determined by the forensic lab, the crime scene investigator should attempt to collect as much of the glass evidence at the scene as possible. Also, if possible, the crime scene investigator should note which side of the glass was interior and which was exterior. If unknown, dirt, residue, etc., may be used to assist with the determination.

Paint Evidence

Paint chips and fragments of other protective coatings, such as varnishes, sealers, lacquers, enamels, and plastics, are frequently recovered at scenes of burglaries, hit-and-run vehicles and scenes, forced entries, and other crime scenes.

Paint Data Query

(Also known as the "International Forensic Automotive Paint Data Query") The world's largest international searchable database of chemical and color information of original automotive paints. The PDQ is used by forensic laboratories around the world to assist with criminal investigations requiring vehicle identification

A determination of common origin is possible in cases where irregularly shaped adjoining edges of paint chips can be physically joined to form a fracture match. However, the value of a single-layered paint chip or paint smear should not be overlooked.

Paint Evidence Analysis

The International Forensic Automotive **Paint Data Query** (PDQ) is the world's largest international, searchable database of chemical and color information of original automotive paints. The database represents 35 years of accumulated information provided by automotive companies and samples of vehicles submitted by other forensic laboratories or police. The PDQ contains information about the make, model, year, and assembly plant for many vehicles.

The PDQ is used by forensic laboratories around the world to assist with criminal investigations requiring vehicle identification. FLS maintains the database so that forensic laboratories can provide timely and effective support to police investigations. Police agencies do not access the PDQ directly.

The PDQ is one of the most collaborative ventures to be found in forensic science. Accredited users are given a free copy of the PDQ in exchange for submitting 60 new automotive paint samples per year. The paint samples are collected from vehicles at body shops or junkyards as well as from automobile manufacturers. Contributors to the PDQ include the Royal Canadian Mounted Police (RCMP), provincial forensic laboratories in Ontario and Quebec, 40 American forensic laboratories, and police agencies in 21 other countries. Over 1,500 samples of paint are collected each year and over 500 samples are selected for analysis and inclusion within the database. According to the RCMP, as of November 2013, the PDQ contained information on more than 20,000 samples of paint systems, which represent over 74,000 individual paint layers that are used on the majority of domestic and foreign vehicles that are sold within North America and Australasia. (RCMP, 2013).

Paint samples provided by automotive manufacturers are analyzed for their chemical composition. The chemical components and proportions are coded into the database. An automotive paint job usually consists of four layers. These known paint samples are then available for comparison against paint samples taken from a crime scene or from suspect vehicles.

The PDQ team samples each paint layer and the chemical composition of each layer is determined by an infrared microspectrometer, which outputs a spectrum containing the unique chemical information pertinent to each layer. Once unknown vehicles are potentially identified within the database, police can use the possible make, model, and year information to search for the vehicle involved in the criminal activity, most often a hit-and-run.

The PDQ serves to narrow the search for vehicles to enable further investigation. Once a suspected vehicle is located, the comparison of paint from the crime scene with paint of the suspected vehicle can be conducted to associate the vehicle more conclusively with the crime.

Soil Evidence

Soil is a generic term for any disintegrated surface material, natural or man-made, which lies on or near the earth's surface (Saferstein, 2014). This is important for a crime scene investigator to realize because forensic analysis of soil not only relates to such naturally occurring components as rocks, vegetation, pollen, minerals, and animal matter, but it also includes the identification and examination of such man-made components as paint particles, glass, asphalt, concrete, and other items present that may assist in characterizing the soil as being unique to a specific or definable location.

The evidentiary value of soil has its foundation in its prevalence at crime scenes and the ease with which it is transferred between the scene and the suspect. Thus, soil or the dried remains of mud found adhered to a suspect's clothing or footwear, when compared with soil samples collected from the crime scene, may provide an associative link between a suspect or an object and the crime scene. As with most physical evidence, soil analysis is comparative in nature. This means that soil that is located in the possession of a suspect must be carefully collected in order to be compared with soil samples from the crime scene and its surroundings. However, even if the scene of a crime has not been determined, the crime scene investigator should not overlook the evidentiary value of soil. For instance, a forensic geologist who is educated in the local geology may be capable of using his or her knowledge along with geological maps to direct law enforcement to the possible vicinity where the soil most likely originated from, and thus provide a possibility as to the area where the crime was committed.

Sand or soil is encountered in many types of investigations and should not be overlooked by the investigating officer. The following items frequently have soil related to the crime scene adhering to their surfaces: footwear, clothing, tool containers, vehicle operating pedals, undercarriages, or wheel wells. Soil found on the floor of a vehicle also may become valuable evidence. Most soil adhering to such objects is representative of the upper one-fourth inch of surface soil from which it originated and may be associated with its source, if proper known samples are recovered.

Most times, soil can be distinguished through a gross examination, primarily based upon coloration. It is estimated that there are approximately 1,100 different soil colors; thus, comparison of soil color is a logical first step in soil analysis. A crime scene investigator should note, however, that soil is darker when it is wet and, therefore, color comparisons should always be made when the samples are dry.

Collecting and Packaging Soil Evidence

Because soil variation is the fundamental consideration in soil analysis, establishing such variation must be considered when gathering soil specimens. It is suggested that standard/reference samples of soils are collected at various intervals within a 100-yardsradius of the crime scene, in addition to collection at the site of the crime, for comparison to the questioned soil. All samples should be dried and then packaged as discussed in the box.

Hair and Fiber Evidence

In crimes where personal contact has occurred, especially if there was physical force, hair and fibers are frequently found as evidence.

A cross-transfer of hair and/or fibers between a victim and an assailant can provide supportive evidence of an association. In addition, hair recovered from the scene may serve to associate an individual with the scene. Fibers recovered from the clothing of the victim, suspect, and crime scene can be compared with known textile materials to determine possible sources of origin.

If a hair is deemed probative to a case (be it animal or human), DNA analyses may be performed on the root (if present) of the hair. If DNA is obtained from a questioned hair root, this DNA can be compared with DNA from a standard blood sample from an individual. Identification may be the result. Mitochondrial DNA (mtDNA) could possibly be extracted and analyzed on a hair that does not contain a root. However, the information obtained from mtNDA is much more limited.

— Ripped from the Headlines —

Police Use Cat DNA to Convict

In August of 2013, British investigators used DNA analysis of cat hair to help convict a man of manslaughter. The case illustrated how the genetic material of animals, and not simply of humans, could be used by crime scene investigators to successfully solve a case. It was the first time that feline DNA had been used in the U.K. within a criminal trial. The Veterinary Genetics Laboratory at the University of California, Davis, has been providing DNA analysis of animals, to assist with criminal cases for over a decade. Knowing this, British investigators requested the assistance of the lab to identify cat hair, which had been discovered around the dismembered body of a victim, found concealed within a trash bag on a British beach over a year prior. As a result, investigators were able to match the cat hair as likely originating from a cat owned by the victim's friend.

The Associated Press, Wednesday, August 14, 2013. "British cops use cat DNA to help convict a killer", www.nydailynews.com

© Shutterstock, Inc./rzarek.

The significance of hair examination results is dependent on the method of evidence collection used at the crime scene, the evidence processing techniques employed, the methodology of the hair examination process, and the experience of the hair examiner. Head hairs and pubic hairs are routinely held as more significant than hairs from other body areas.

Collection of Hair and Fiber Standards

It is necessary to obtain standard hair and fiber samples from all possible sources (suspect, victim, and scene) for comparison with questioned hairs and fibers. DNA analysis on hair roots has replaced microscopic hair comparisons. Pubic and head hair standards are still necessary for determining which foreign, questioned hairs may be subjected to DNA analysis. Due to the ease of head hair transfer and potential limited probative value, DNA analysis on hairs will be limited.

Collecting and Packaging Hair Evidence

Submit individual hairs and fibers in clean paper or in an envelope with sealed corners. The primary paper or envelope should be placed inside a secondary sealed envelope with all corners taped. Many times, individual hairs identified on items of clothing are not removed or secured. These hairs may move or be lost, so it is recommended that they be removed and placed in an envelope (first noting where they were removed). If a floor surface is vacuumed, the debris should be placed on a white sheet of paper (8 × 11 inches) and folded at the corners. This paper should be placed in a heat-sealed or re-sealable plastic bag.

Fiber Evidence

A fiber is the smallest unit of a textile material that has a length many times greater than its diameter. Fibers can occur naturally as plant and animal fibers, but they can also be man-made. A fiber can be spun with other fibers to form a yarn that can be woven or knitted to form a fabric. The type and length of fiber used, the type of spinning method, and the type of fabric construction all affect the transfer of fibers and the significance of fiber associations. This becomes very important when there is a possibility of fiber transfer between a suspect and a victim during the commission of a crime.

As discussed previously, fibers are considered a form of trace evidence that can be transferred from the clothing of a suspect to the clothing of a victim during the commission of a crime. Fibers can also transfer from a fabric source such as a carpet, bed, or furniture at a crime scene. These transfers can either be direct (primary) or indirect (secondary). A **primary transfer** occurs when a fiber is transferred from a fabric directly onto a victim's clothing, whereas a **secondary transfer** occurs when already transferred fibers on the clothing of a suspect transfer to the clothing of a victim. An understanding of the mechanics of primary and secondary transfer is important when reconstructing the events of a crime.

primary transfer
Occurs when a fiber is transferred from a fabric directly onto a victim's clothing

secondary transfer
Occurs when already transferred fibers on the clothing of a suspect transfer to the clothing of a victim

When two people come in contact or when contact occurs with an item from the crime scene, the possibility exists that a fiber transfer will take place. This does not mean that a fiber transfer will always take place. Certain types of fabric do not shed well (donor garments), and some fabrics do not hold fibers well (recipient garments). The construction and fiber composition of the fabric, the duration and force of contact, and the condition of the garment with regard to damage are important considerations.

Another important consideration is the length of time between the actual physical contact and the collection of clothing items from the suspect or victim. If the victim is immobile, very little fiber loss will take place, whereas the suspect's clothing will lose transferred fibers quickly. The likelihood of finding transferred fibers on the clothing of the suspect a day after the alleged contact may be remote, depending on the subsequent use or handling of that clothing.

Collecting and Packaging Fiber Evidence

Collection and preservation of fiber evidence is quite similar to the methodology for collection of hair evidence. Reference and elimination samples must be collected, and each must be properly documented and packaged, as mentioned previously in regard to hair evidence (**FIGURE 5.20**).

FIGURE 5.20: Scaled photo of fiber evidence.

CASE IN POINT

© Shutterstock, Inc./Vlastas

Fiber Evidence in the Atlanta Murders

In February 1982, in Fulton County, Georgia, a jury returned a guilty verdict on two counts of criminal homicide against Wayne Bertram Williams. During the course of the trial, evidence was admitted linking Williams to the murder of Nathaniel Cater and Jimmy Payne in April and May 1981 as well as to the murder of 10 other young men. The telling evidence in the case was the association of fibrous debris removed from the bodies of 12 murder victims with objects from Williams's environment. Fiber evidence can corroborate other evidence in a case; it is used to support other testimony and validate other evidence presented at a trial. This was not the situation in the Williams trial. Other evidence and other aspects of the trial were important but were used to support and complement the fiber evidence, not the other way around. The hair and fiber matches between Williams's environment and 11 of 12 murder victims discussed at the trial were so significant that these victims were positively linked to both the residence and automobiles that were a part of the world of Wayne Williams.

Before Williams became a suspect in the Nathaniel Cater murder case, the Georgia State Crime Laboratory located a number of yellowish-green nylon fibers and some violet acetate fibers on the bodies and clothing of the murder victims whose bodies had been recovered during the period between July 1979 and May 1981. The yellowish-green nylon fibers were generally similar to each other in appearance and properties and were considered to have originated from a single source. This was also true of the violet acetate fibers.

Initially, the major concern with the yellowish-green nylon fibers was determining what type of object could have been their source. The fibers were coarse and had an oval cross-sectional appearance, tending to indicate that they originated from a carpet or a rug. The oval cross-sectional shape of these fibers, however, was unique, and initially the manufacturer of these fibers could not be determined. A number of different chemists agreed that the yellowish-green nylon fiber was very unusual in its cross sectional shape and was consistent with being a carpet fiber.

In February 1981, an Atlanta newspaper article publicized that several different fiber types had been found on two murder victims. Following the publication of this article, bodies recovered from rivers in the Atlanta metropolitan area were either nude or clothed only in undershorts. It appeared the article had forewarned the murderer, and victims were now being disposed of in rivers in this undressed state to prevent fibers from being found on their bodies. On May 22, 1981, a four-man surveillance team of personnel from

(continues)

(continued)

the Atlanta Police Department and the Atlanta office of the FBI were situated under and at both ends of the James Jackson Parkway Bridge over the Chattahoochee River in northwest Atlanta. Around 2:00 am, a loud splash alerted the surveillance team to the presence of an automobile being driven slowly off the bridge. The driver was stopped and identified as Wayne Bertram Williams.

Two days after Williams's presence on the bridge, the nude body of Nathaniel Cater was pulled from the Chattahoochee River, approximately 1 mile downstream from the James Jackson Parkway Bridge. A yellowish-green nylon carpet-type fiber, similar to the nylon fibers discussed earlier, was recovered from the head hair of Nathaniel Cater. Search warrants for Williams's home and automobile were issued and executed. An initial association of fibers from Cater and other murder victims was made with a green carpet in the home of Williams. Associations with a bedspread from Williams's bed and with the Williams family dog were also made at that time. An apparent source of the yellowish-green nylon fibers had been found. Because of the unusual cross-sectional appearance of the nylon fiber and the difficulty in determining the manufacturer, it was believed that this was a relatively rare type and, therefore, would not be present in large amounts (or in a large number of carpets).

It was determined that the yellowish-green nylon fiber was manufactured by Wellman Corporation and no others. It was also determined that fibers having this cross sectional shape were manufactured and sold during the years 1967 through 1974.

Through numerous contacts with yarn spinners and carpet manufacturers, it was determined that the West Point Pepperell Corporation of Dalton, Georgia, had manufactured a line of carpet called "Luxaire," which was constructed in the same manner as Williams's carpet. One of the colors offered in the Luxaire line was called "English Olive," and this color was the same as that of the Williams carpet (both visually and by the use of discriminating chemical and instrumental tests).

It was learned that the West Point Pepperell Corporation had manufactured the Luxaire line for a 5-year period from December 1970 through 1975; however, it had only purchased Wellman 181B fiber for this line during 1970 and 1971. In December 1971, the West Point Pepperell Corporation changed the fiber composition of the Luxaire line to a different nylon fiber, one that was dissimilar to the Wellman 181B fiber in appearance. Accordingly, Luxaire carpet like Williams's carpet was only manufactured for a 1-year period. This change of carpet fiber after only 1 year in production was yet another factor that made the Williams carpet unusual.

To any experienced forensic fiber examiner, the fiber evidence linking Williams to the murder victims was overwhelming. But regardless of the apparent validity of the fiber findings, it was during the trial that its true weight would be determined. Unless it could be conveyed meaningfully to a jury, its effect would be lost. Juries are not usually composed of individuals with a scientific background, and, therefore, it was necessary to educate the jury in what procedures were followed and the significance of the fiber results. In the Williams case, more than 40 charts with more than 350 photographs were prepared to illustrate exactly what the crime laboratory examiners had observed.

During the course of the trial, the fiber matches made between fibers in Williams's environment and fibers from victims Payne and Cater were discussed. In discussing the significance or strength of an association based on textile fibers, it was emphasized that the more uncommon the fibers, the stronger the association. None of the fiber types from the items in Williams's environment by definition were commonly found fiber types:

1. Station wagon

2. Throw rug

3. Blue rayon fibers

4. Bedroom bedspread

5. Bedroom carpet

6. Williams family dog

7. Backroom carpet square (yellowish-green synthetic fibers)

One of the fibers linking the body of Jimmy Ray Payne to the carpet in the 1970 station wagon driven by Williams was a small rayon fiber fragment recovered from Payne's shorts. Data were obtained from the station wagon's manufacturer concerning which automobile models produced prior to 1973 contained carpet made of this fiber type. These data were coupled with additional information from Georgia concerning the number of these models registered in the Atlanta metropolitan area during 1981. This allowed a calculation to be made relating to the probability of randomly selecting an automobile having carpet like that in the 1970 Chevrolet station wagon from the 2,373,512 cars registered in the Atlanta metropolitan area. This probability was 1 chance in 3,828, a very low probability representing a significant association.

Another factor to consider when assessing the significance of fiber evidence is the increased strength of the association when multiple fiber matches become the basis of the association. As the number of different objects increases, the strength of an association increases dramatically.

Studies have been conducted in England that show that transferred fibers are usually lost rapidly as people go about their daily routine (Pounds & Smalldon, 1995). Therefore, the foreign fibers present on a person are most often from recent surroundings. The fibrous debris found on a murder victim reflects the body's more recent surroundings, especially important if the body was moved after the killing. Accordingly, the victims' bodies in this particular case were not only associated with Williams but were apparently associated with Williams shortly before or after their deaths.

Although from these findings it would appear that the victims were in the residence of Williams, there was one other location that contained many of the same fibers as those in the composition of various objects in his residence: Williams's station wagon. The environment of a family automobile might be expected to reflect, to some extent, fibers from objects located in the residence. This was true of the 1970 station wagon. The automobile would be the most logical source of the foreign fibers found on both Payne and Cater if they were associated with Williams shortly before or after their deaths. It should also be pointed out that two objects, the bedspread and the blanket, were portable and could have at one time been present inside the station wagon. Both Payne and Cater were recovered from the Chattahoochee River. Their bodies had been in the water for several days. Some of the fibers found on these victims were like fibers in the compositions of the bedroom carpet and bedspread except for color intensity. They appeared to have been bleached. By subjecting various known fibers to small amounts of Chattahoochee River water for different periods of time, it was found that bleaching did occur.

Two crime laboratory examiners testified during the trial and concluded that it was highly unlikely that any environment other than that present in Wayne Williams's house and car could have resulted in the combination of fibers and hairs found on the victims and that it would be virtually impossible to have matched so many fibers found on Cater and Payne to items in Williams's house and car unless the victims were in contact with or in some way associated with the environment of Wayne Williams. Of the nine victims who were killed during the time period when Williams had access to the 1970 station wagon, fibers consistent with having originated from both the station wagon carpet and the bedroom carpet were recovered from six of the victims. The finding of many of the same fiber types on the remaining victims, who were recovered from many different locations, refutes the possibility that Payne's and Cater's bodies picked up foreign fibers from the river. The fact that many of the victims were involved with so many of the same fiber types, all of which linked the victims to Williams's environment, is the basis for arguing conclusively against these fibers originating from a source other than Williams's environment.

Source: This account of the use of fiber evidence in the Wayne Williams trial, by Harold A. Deadman, Special Agent, Microscopic Analysis Unit, Laboratory Division, Federal Bureau of Investigation, Washington, DC, is reprinted in part from the *FBI Law Enforcement Bulletin*, March and May 1984.

CONCLUSION

The documentation, collection and preservation of physical evidence is of paramount importance to a successful criminal investigation. While there are infinite types of physical evidence that will be encountered during investigative processing efforts, a number of areas of physical evidence type lend themselves to particular mention. Of those not covered in other chapters, biological evidence, specifically as it relates to blood evidence, and trace evidence (including glass, paint, hairs and fibers) are especially important to take note of.

What was once called blood spatter analysis is now referred to by the Federal Bureau of Investigation as bloodstain pattern analysis. Bloodstain pattern analysis is one of the staples of crime scene investigation that requires specific expertise in interpretation and collection. The role of the investigator is to recognize it and bring to bear the appropriate expertise to identify, analyze, and preserve bloodstain evidence. The amount of information that can be obtained from bloodstain analysis is only possible if the stains have been preserved in the condition in which they were deposited. In the beginning of this chapter, it was noted that blood at crime scenes is common. Just as common is the destruction of those stains. The primary responsibility of all parties to a crime wherein blood stain evidence is present is to preserve it and to record it.

Blood stains on clothing can be a way to identify a suspect; the next chapter discusses other ways of identifying a suspect, including fingerprints, composite drawings, lineups, and DNA evidence.

Edmond Locard dedicated his life to the microscopic analysis of trace evidence in an effort to prove that one's actions could be traced back to a particular item or location. It is this study that the forensic value of trace evidence is based upon. While most trace evidence is not individualistic in nature, this does not minimize its forensic importance. Such matters are up to the analyst who is performing the analysis of the evidence. What is imperative is that the investigator knows the proper method for documenting, collecting, and preserving the various types of trace evidence to ensure his or her ability to undergo proper forensic analysis.

QUESTIONS FOR REVIEW

1. What role does surface texture play in a blood pattern deposit?

2. If a blood drop stain is perfectly round, what can be said about the direction from which it fell?

3. What is the bloodstain impact angle and what does it say about the crime?

4. How does point of convergence differ from the point of origin?

5. Is it necessary to know the point of convergence to determine the point of origin? Why?

6. What is ricochet blood?

7. What are the differences among high-, medium-, and low-velocity bloodstains?

8. What are the various tests for determining whether a blood sample is, in fact, blood and, if so, whether it is human blood?

9. How is blood typed?

10. Can dried blood be typed and, if so, how?

11. How is phenolphthalein used to test for blood?

12. How is luminol used to test for blood?

13. Discuss crime scene DNA contamination.

14. What is STR?

15. How does mitochondrial DNA differ from nuclear DNA?

16. List the considerations in the handling and packaging of items that may bear DNA evidence.

REFERENCES

Eckert, W. G., & James S. H. (1993). *Interpretation of bloodstain evidence at crime scenes*. Boca Raton, FL: CRC Press.

Gale, T. (2005). Locard's Exchange Principle. *World of Forensic Science*. Retrieved September 1, 2017, from http://www.encyclopedia.com/doc.1G2-3448300354.html

Kirk, P. L. (1974). *Crime investigation* (2nd ed.). New York, NY: John Wiley & Sons.

Laber, T. L. (1985). Diameter of a bloodstain as a function of origin, distance fallen and volume of drop. *International Association of Blood Pattern Analysts News*, 2(1), 12–16.

MacDonell, H. L. (1971a). *Flight characteristics of human blood and stain patterns*. Washington, DC: National Institute of Law Enforcement and Criminal Justice.

MacDonell, H. L. (1971b). *Interpretation of bloodstains: Physical considerations*. In C. Wecht (Ed.), *Legal medicine annual*. New York, NY: Appleton-Century-Crofts.

MacDonell, H. L. (1993). *Bloodstain patterns*. Corning, NY: Laboratory of Forensic Science.

Pounds, C. A., & Smalldon, K. W. (1995). The transfer of fibers between clothing materials during simulated contacts and their persistence during wear. *Journal of the Forensic Science Society, 15,* 29–37.

Royal Canadian Mounted Police (RCMP). (2013). Retrieved June 27, 2015, from http://www.rcmp-grc.gc.ca

Saferstein, R. (2014). *Criminalistics: An introduction to forensic science* (11th ed.). Upper Saddle River, NJ: Pearson Prentice Hall.

Stephens, B. G., & Allen T. B. (1983). Backspatter of blood from gunshot wounds: Observations and experimental simulation. *Journal of Forensic Sciences, 23,* 437–439.

KEY LEGAL CASE

State of Ohio v. Samuel H. Sheppard, 352 U.S. 910 (1956).

chapter 6

Suspect Identification

> "He rushed out into the road, but, although several passers-by declared that they had noticed a man run out of the shop, he could neither see anyone nor could he find any means of identifying the rascal. It seemed to be one of those senseless acts of Hooliganism which occur from time to time, and it was reported to the constable on the beat as such."
>
> **Sherlock Holmes**
> *The Adventure of the Six Napoleons"*

KEY TERMS

accidental whorl

ACE-V

arches

automated fingerprint identification system (AFIS)

biometric identification

classification

Combined DNA Index System (CODIS)

composite picture

core

delta

developing prints

fingerprint individuality

fingerprints

friction ridges

immutable

latent prints

lifting

loops

minutiae

ninhydrin

patent prints

plastic impressions

post-indictment lineups

rogues' gallery

sketch artist

small particle reagent (SPR)

superglue fuming

visualized

whorls

STUDENT LEARNING OUTCOMES

Upon completion of this chapter, students will be able to:

- Recall a basic history of the evolution of fingerprinting
- Apply the various methods of developing fingerprints
- Recognize the two CODIS databases
- Create a lineup that is not unconstitutionally suggestive

Making Evidence Personal

Often, an investigator is confronted with a plethora of physical evidence but no suspect to whom the evidence relates. When this occurs, technicians and laboratory equipment form the front lines of the investigation battle. Many identification methods, such as fingerprint comparison, DNA analysis, and composite rendering, require the services of a forensic or investigative specialist. A more common identification method, the police lineup, involves investigators, witnesses or victims, and a known suspect. This chapter discusses the investigative, scientific, and legal aspects of the most common suspect identification methods.

The previous chapter discussed the forensic value of blood-related evidence. Included within the forensic value of all biological evidence, is the presence of DNA. As the single most reliable method of individualization, it is the first method of suspect identification, which we will discuss within this chapter.

Deoxyribonucleic Acid (DNA)

There was a time when the closest that one could get to identifying blood to a person was through blood type, which was class evidence and not at all individualistic. While blood typing offered forensic significance for the analysis of crime scene–related blood, it only offered the investigators the ability to isolate the evidence to a particular group but not to an individual. It was not until 1984, when Sir Alec Jeffreys made the revolutionary discovery of *deoxyribonucleic acid fingerprinting,* that the ability to isolate a specific individual (or individuals, in the case of identical twins) through blood (and other human tissues) was possible (**FIGURE 6.1**).

Value of DNA Evidence

DNA is a powerful investigative tool because, with the exception of identical twins and other multiples, no two people have the same DNA. Therefore, DNA evidence collected from a crime scene can be linked to a suspect or can eliminate a suspect from suspicion. During a sexual assault, for example, biological evidence, such as hair, skin cells, semen, or blood can be left on the victim's body or other parts of the crime scene.

Properly collected DNA can be compared with known samples to place a suspect at the scene of

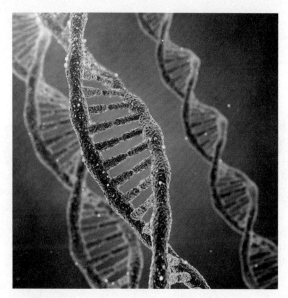

FIGURE 6.1: The double-helix structure of DNA.

© Nobeastoffierce/Shutterstock, Inc.

the crime. In addition, if no suspect exists, a DNA profile from crime scene evidence can be entered into the Federal Bureau of Investigation's (FBI) Combined DNA Index System (CODIS) to identify a suspect anywhere in the United States or to link serial crimes to each other.

The effective use of DNA as evidence also may require the collection and analysis of elimination samples to determine the exact source of the DNA. Elimination samples may be taken from anyone who had lawful access to the crime scene and who may have left biological material. When investigating a rape case, for example, it may be necessary to obtain an elimination sample from everyone who had consensual intercourse with the victim within 72 hours of the alleged assault to account for all of the DNA found on the victim or at the crime scene. Comparing DNA profiles from the evidence with elimination samples may help clarify the results.

Basics of DNA Typing

Only one-tenth of a single percent of DNA (about 3 million bases) differs from one person to the next. Scientists can use these variable regions to generate a DNA profile of an individual, using samples from blood, bone, hair, and other body tissues and products.

In criminal cases, this generally involves obtaining samples from crime scene evidence and a suspect, extracting the DNA, and analyzing it for the presence of a set of specific DNA regions (markers). If the sample profiles

— Ripped from the Headlines —

Using Ancestry Services for Law Enforcement Purposes

It sounds as if it is ripped directly out of a science fiction novel, but it is today's reality. Individuals making use out of ancestry DNA services, which are purported to provide the submitter with his or her genetic ancestry based on his or her submitted saliva (DNA) sample, found that such submissions place themselves or a family member in criminal jeopardy.

The concept is intriguing to many. First, spit into a vial and then mail the vial to a company that subsequently conducts DNA analysis, coupled with genetic comparison to known DNA markers associated with ancestry. The sender then receives a report, which provides ethic makeup and a family tree of ancestral history based on the genetic analysis. The DNA sample provider then celebrates his or her heritage. End of story.

But the story does not necessarily end there. In today's increasingly complex and technologically advanced world, law enforcement agencies are calling on every available resource to combat crime. In fact, law enforcement agencies may even be referring to databases of private genetics companies to help track down a suspect. Companies such as Ancestry® and 23andMe® typically have terms and conditions, which a submitter agrees to, that states something along the lines of "…we will not share your genetic data with employers, insurance providers or third party marketers without first getting your consent" (Ancestry, n.d.). However, an individual is perhaps not so quick to note the exclusion of "law enforcement agencies" from that list. In fact, on the very same website, "Ancestry Guide for Law Enforcement," the company outlines the processes that need to be followed and the information release that will be permitted, on receipt of a valid request from law enforcement.

With the advancements in DNA analysis, it is now possible to analyze a sample of DNA quickly and reliably and determine either maternal or paternal relationships. Therefore, while an individual may have no criminal concerns

themselves, and know that he or she is an upstanding citizen who has no reason to believe that his or her DNA would be associated with a crime, could in fact be assisting law enforcement with solving active or cold cases associated with a wanted family member as a result of his or her being lured by historical and ancestral curiosity.

"As the cost of DNA analysis gets cheaper and the amount of DNA companies have continues to grow, the use of familial DNA searching is only going to increase" (Maldarelli, 2015). Only time will tell how the legislation governing the use of DNA databases maintained by private companies for criminal justice purposes will play out. But for now, law enforcement agencies will continue to pursue any available and legal avenue to locate suspects and arrest those associated with major crimes.

Ancestry. (n.d.). Ancestry Guide for Law Enforcement. Retrieved November 6, 2017, from http://www.ancestry.com/cs/legal/lawenforcement

Maldarelli, C. (2015, October 16). Could having your DNA tested land you in court? *Popular Science*. Retrieved November 7, 2017, from https://www.popsci.com/could-submitting-your-dna-to-private-genetics-companies-land-you-in-court

© Shutterstock, Inc./rzarek.

do not match, the person did not contribute the DNA at the crime scene. If the patterns match, the suspect may have contributed the evidence sample. DNA from crime scenes also can be compared with profiles stored in a database.

DNA analysis is a powerful tool because each person's DNA is unique (with the exception of identical twins and multiples). Therefore, DNA evidence collected from a crime scene can implicate or eliminate a suspect, similar to the use of fingerprints. It also can analyze unidentified remains through comparisons with DNA from relatives. DNA is also a powerful tool because when biological evidence from crime scenes is collected and stored properly, forensically valuable DNA can be found on evidence that may be

decades old. Therefore, old cases that were previously thought unsolvable may contain valuable DNA evidence capable of identifying the perpetrator.

In every creature, DNA carries the coded messages of heredity, governing everything from eye color to toe length. It is present in every one of the trillions of nucleated cells in the human body. Based on the work of Alec Jeffreys at the University of Leicester, a method was developed to extract DNA from a specimen of blood, semen, or other tissue; slice it into fragments; and tag the fragments with a radioactive probe so that they expose x-ray film. The resulting pattern of stripes on the film is a so-called DNA fingerprint, and the process for isolating and reading DNA markers is known as DNA fingerprinting.

CASE IN POINT

© Shutterstock, Inc./Vlastas.

DNA Solves an Early Case

Based on his groundbreaking research and publications, Alec Jeffreys at the University of Leicester was called upon to resolve an immigration case involving a boy who was living in Africa with his father but who had been born in Britain to Ghanaian parents. The boy wanted to return to Britain and live with a woman he claimed was his mother, but the immigration service believed the woman to be his aunt and denied him British residency. Jeffreys had to somehow match the genetic fingerprint of the child with that of a father who was not present to supply a DNA sample. The genetic fingerprints of the undisputed children of the woman in question were taken. The intent was to match those fingerprints with those of the mother, thereby establishing the fingerprint of the absent father. When Jeffreys compared the pattern of the boy with those of his ostensible brothers and sisters, the reasonable conclusion was that the man had fathered all of the children (Wambaugh, 1985).

© Shutterstock, Inc./Nutink.

Handling DNA Evidence

DNA evidence may be abundant at a crime scene, but the contamination of any of it contaminates all of it. From a defense lawyer's perspective, there is no such thing as a partially contaminated crime scene. It is the easiest evidence to mishandle and requires specialized training to be able to handle it correctly.

■ Sample Contamination

Any crime scene is unlikely to meet the hygienic standards characteristic of research and medical laboratories. Defendants tend to believe that anything less than absolute purity in body samples raises questions as to the reliability of the DNA typing process. (See **TABLE 6.1**.) The word *contamination* raises the specter of something unnatural or careless happening to the samples before they reach the laboratory. It is imperative for an expert in DNA analysis who is called as a witness to address the nature of the environment in which DNA samples were deposited and to explain that contamination and age are an integral part of the nonsterile real world. Possible questions that could be asked of the expert in court include the following:

- The question is not one of contamination but rather of how much contamination, is it not?
- Can the contaminants be removed from the sample without altering the sample?
- Were the contaminants removed before the typing protocol began?

TABLE 6.1 DNA Defenses and Responsible Parties

Defense	Responsible Party
Contaminated crime scene	The nature of the crime
Improper labeling	Investigator (technician)
Improper handling	Investigator (technician)
Improper packaging	Investigator (technician)
Broken chain of custody	Investigator (technician, laboratory)
Contaminated lab sample	Laboratory
Improper lab protocol	Laboratory
Acceptability of protocol	Laboratory witness
Acceptability of expert	Laboratory witness

INVESTIGATOR'S NOTEBOOK

Guidelines for Handling DNA-Bearing Evidence

- Wear gloves; Change them between handling each item of evidence
- Use disposable instruments or clean the instruments thoroughly before and after handling each evidence sample
- Avoid touching the area where you believe DNA may exist
- Avoid touching your face, nose, and mouth when examining and packaging evidence
- Put dry evidence into new paper bags or envelopes; do not use plastic bags
- Do not use staples
- Handle all evidence as though a jury were watching
- Photograph or take video of the handling and packaging process

© Shutterstock, Inc./Nutink.

- Could you describe the nature of the contaminants present and the method of removal?
- How was the sample contaminated?
- Where did the contamination occur?
- Was the contamination a result of laboratory handling?
- Was the contamination a result of police handling?
- Was there enough of the sample to run more than one test?
- Were additional tests run?
- Were the results the same?
- Were known samples that were contaminated with similar contaminants cleaned and typed?
- Were the results consistent with the results for uncontaminated samples?

Contamination is a problem only if left to the defendant to use as an issue with which to obfuscate or confuse. The jury should be comfortable with the idea that all forensic DNA

CASE IN POINT

© Shutterstock, Inc./Vlastas.

The Innocence Project

The Innocence Project at the Benjamin N. Cardozo School of Law, created by Barry C. Scheck and Peter J. Neufeld in 1992, is a nonprofit legal clinic. The project only handles cases in which postconviction DNA testing of evidence can yield conclusive proof of innocence. Because it is a clinic, students handle the casework while being supervised by a team of attorneys and clinic staff.

Most of the clients are poor and forgotten and have used up all of their legal avenues for relief. The hope they all have is that biological evidence from their cases still exists and can be subjected to DNA testing. All Innocence Project clients go through an extensive screening process to determine whether DNA testing of evidence could prove their claims of innocence. Thousands currently await evaluation of their cases.

As a forerunner in the field of wrongful convictions, the Innocence Project has grown to become much more than the court of last resort for inmates who have exhausted their appeals and their means. The project is helping to organize the Innocence Network, a group of law schools, journalism schools, and public defender offices across the country that assists inmates trying to prove their innocence, whether or not the cases involve biological evidence that can be subjected to DNA testing. Project managers consult with legislators and law enforcement officials at the state, local, and federal levels; conduct research and training; produce scholarship; and propose a wide range of remedies to prevent wrongful convictions while continuing work to free innocent inmates through the use of postconviction DNA testing (Innocence Project, n.d.).

© Shutterstock, Inc./Nutink.

samples are contaminated and that nothing unique or unusual happened to the samples in question.

Identification Through DNA

It is important to realize that DNA evidence is only of evidentiary value if it is properly collected and preserved. If accomplished in both a scientific and legal manner, DNA is the most powerful tool in the suspect identification toolbox as a result of advances in digital technology that allow for the cataloging and identification of DNA profiles. The **Combined DNA Index System (CODIS)** is a computer network that connects forensic DNA laboratories at the local, state, and national levels (**FIGURE 6.2**). Every state in the nation has a statutory provision for the establishment of a DNA database that allows for the collection of DNA profiles from offenders convicted of particular crimes. CODIS software enables state, local, and national law enforcement crime laboratories to compare DNA profiles electronically, thereby linking serial crimes and identifying suspects by matching DNA profiles from crime scenes with profiles from convicted offenders.

DNA database systems that use CODIS contain two main criminal indices (the convicted offender index and the forensic index) and a missing persons index. The convicted offender index contains DNA profiles of individuals convicted of specific crimes, ranging from certain misdemeanors to sexual assault and murder. Each state has different qualifying offenses for which persons convicted of the offense must submit a biological sample for inclusion in the DNA database. The forensic index contains DNA profiles obtained from crime scene evidence, such as semen, saliva, or blood.

FIGURE 6.2: CODIS database.

Courtesy of the FBI.

When a DNA profile is developed from crime scene evidence and entered into the forensic (crime scene) index of CODIS, the database software searches thousands of DNA profiles of individuals convicted of offenses, such as rape and murder. CODIS can aid investigations by efficiently comparing a DNA profile generated from biological evidence left at a crime scene against convicted offender DNA profiles and forensic evidence from other cases contained in CODIS.

CODIS can also aid investigations by searching the missing persons index, which consists of the unidentified persons index and the reference index. The unidentified persons index contains DNA profiles from recovered remains, such as bone, teeth, or hair. The reference index contains DNA profiles from related individuals of missing persons so that they can be periodically compared with the unidentified persons index.

A match made between profiles in the forensic index can link crime scenes to each other, possibly identifying serial offenders. Based on these forensic matches, police in multiple jurisdictions or states can coordinate their respective investigations and share their leads. Matches made between the forensic and convicted offender indices can provide investigators with the identity of a suspect or suspects. It is important to note that an offender hit typically is used as probable cause to obtain a new DNA sample from that suspect so the match can be confirmed by the crime laboratory before an arrest is made.

Design of CODIS

CODIS is implemented as a distributed database with three hierarchical levels (or tiers): local, state, and national. All three levels contain forensic and convicted offender indices and a population file (used to generate statistics). The hierarchical design provides state and local laboratories with the flexibility to configure CODIS to meet their specific legislative and technical needs.

- *Local DNA Index System (LDIS):* Typically, the LDIS installed at crime laboratories is operated by police departments or sheriffs' offices. DNA profiles originated at the local level can be transmitted to the state and national levels.

Combined DNA Index System (CODIS) Database system that can aid investigations by efficiently comparing a DNA profile generated from biological evidence left at a crime scene against convicted offender DNA profiles and forensic evidence from other cases contained in the database

- *State DNA Index System (SDIS)*: Each state has a designated laboratory that operates the SDIS, which allows local laboratories in that state to compare DNA profiles. SDIS also is the communication path between the local and national tiers.

- *National DNA Index System (NDIS)*: The NDIS is the highest level of the CODIS hierarchy and enables qualified state laboratories that are actively participating in CODIS to compare DNA profiles. NDIS is maintained by the FBI under the authority of the DNA Identification Act of 1994.

Limitations of Using CODIS

The more data contained in the forensic and offender indices of CODIS, the more powerful a tool it becomes for law enforcement, especially in its application to unsolved case investigation. However, because many jurisdictions are in the process of developing and populating their DNA databases, there are convicted offender and forensic casework backlogs that continue to grow. As states recognize the crime-solving potential of DNA databases, they continue to expand the scope of their convicted offender legislation, which increases the number of samples to be collected and analyzed by the DNA laboratory. As a result, more than 1 million uncollected convicted offender DNA profiles are "owed" to the system.

Fingerprints

Fingerprinting is the most widespread biometric technology and the one favored by most government agencies. Fingerprint identification began more than 4,000 years ago when King Hammurabi of the Babylonian Empire used fingerprint seals on contracts. Nearly 600 years before Marco Polo visited China, the lawbook of Yung-Hwui required that a husband in a divorce decree had to seal the document with a fingerprint. In 1823, a graduate student named Johannes Purkinje described fingerprint types in his doctoral thesis and classified them into nine major groups.

Until the late 19th century, there was no unified system of physical identification beyond a general description of age, weight, marks, and scars. However, Alphonse Bertillon's new measurement system (see Chapter 1) helped spawn more interest in ways to catalog suspects. In 1888, Sir Francis Galton of England met with Sir William Herschel of India. Out of that meeting arose a classification system based on

various points of identification in a fingerprint, known as *Galton details*. In the 1890s, Sir Edward Richard Henry, Inspector General of Police in Bengal, India, experimented with Sir William Herschel's system of using Indian natives' palm prints on contracts. Henry eventually joined the Metropolitan Police of London and initiated his fingerprint identification system, which is the basis for the modern American fingerprint system.

Friction skin is made up of ridges running parallel to one another and is found on the soles of the feet and the palms of the hands. These **friction ridges** run in parallel rows that form patterns. The individual ridges form various shapes or characteristics that do not appear in the same place or sequence from one finger to another.

A close examination of the friction ridges reveals that all along their length, the surface is broken in an irregular fashion by sweat pores. The pores are openings for the ducts leading from the sweat glands found in the subcutaneous tissue. The human body has three kinds of sweat glands:

- Eccrine glands are found on all parts of the body and are the only sweat glands found on the palms of the hands and the soles of the feet.

- Apocrine glands are located in the pubic, mammary, and anal areas.

- Sebaceous glands are located on the forehead, chest, back, and abdomen and produce an oily secretion called sebum.

All three kinds of glands secrete water as well as many different organic and inorganic substances. Water is excreted to help control body temperature. As the water moves to the surface, it evaporates and picks up waste products from other parts of the body. Only the sebaceous glands secrete oily substances; fingers touching those areas are likely to pick up oily residues and transfer them on contact, leaving fingerprints.

Fingerprint Individuality

No two fingers have yet been found that have identical characteristics. **Fingerprint individuality** is not dependent on age, size, gender, or race. The identifiable aspects of a fingerprint are called **minutiae** (ridge characteristics). The shape, location, and number of minutiae individualize a fingerprint.

There is no agreement as to how many ridge characteristics must be shared by a discovered

---

friction ridges
Ridges on fingers that are the identifiable characteristics of fingerprints

fingerprint individuality
The shape, location, and number of minutiae that individualize a fingerprint

minutiae
Points where a finger friction ridge ends or splits in two; these are highly individualized

print and the fingerprint of a suspect before they can be said to be a match. After a 3-year study, the International Association for Identification determined that "no valid basis exists for requiring a predetermined minimum number of friction ridge characters, which must be present in two impressions in order to establish positive identification" (Saferstein, 2014). In each and every instance when identification is made between two impressions, that identification is the product of a comparison done by an expert. The value of the expert opinion is based on the following criteria:

- The number of comparable ridge characteristics

- The knowledge of the expert

- The experience of the expert

- The ability of the expert to explain how the comparison was done

- The quality of the testimony of the adverse expert

Fingerprint Immutability

From birth to death, a person's fingerprints retain their classifiable characteristics. The hands and fingers will grow and the print will enlarge with that growth, but the ridge characteristics remain **immutable**. Efforts to eradicate prints are futile, and the scar tissue that results from attempts to do so is as individual as the small number of ridge characteristics that may have been destroyed.

Fingerprints are mirror images of the friction ridge skin of the palm, fingers, and thumb. The black lines of an inked fingerprint impression are a reproduction of the friction ridges. When examined under a microscope, the friction ridges of the fingers reveal a single row of pores that are ducts through which sweat is deposited. That sweat, along with body oils that have been picked up when the fingers touch other parts of the body, may be deposited on a touched surface. The touching may result in a transfer of sweat and oils in the shape of finger friction ridges (a fingerprint) onto the surface touched.

Prints deposited onto a surface but invisible to the naked eye are known as **latent prints**. Technically, only prints that cannot be readily seen with the unassisted eye are latent prints, yet police frequently use the term *latent* to refer to any fingerprint left at a crime scene, whether visible or not. Fingerprint characteristics must be gleaned by

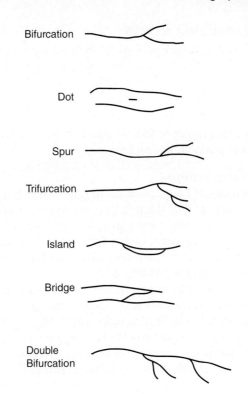

FIGURE 6.3: Fingerprint characteristics.

computer or by an individual examination of the pattern. (See **FIGURE 6.3**.) A magnified examination of the pattern will reveal the individual characteristics that make up the pattern. (See **FIGURE 6.4**) When done by hand, the work of determining fingerprint characteristics is tedious and painstaking.

FIGURE 6.4: Example of a fingerprint magnifier used for fingerprint identification.

Courtesy of SIRCHIE Finger Print Laboratories, Inc.

immutable
Unchangeable; refers to the retention of fingerprint characteristics throughout a person's life

fingerprints
Mirror images of the friction ridge skin of the palm, fingers, and thumb

latent prints
Prints deposited on a surface that are invisible to the naked eye

Classifying Prints

Fingerprints fall into three classes based on general patterns. The most common class is the loop; approximately 65% of the population has loop patterns on at least one finger. Approximately 30% of the population has a whorl pattern on a finger or thumb, and only about 5% of the population has arches.

■ Loop Patterns

Loops must have one or more ridges that enter from one side of the print, curve, and exit from the same side. Loops are divided into two groups: ulnar loops, which open toward the little finger, and radial loops, which open toward the thumb. (See **FIGURE 6.5**.)

Additionally, a loop pattern must have a core and a delta. The **core** is the centermost point of the loop at the apex of the innermost ridge of the loop. The **delta** is a two-sided triangular shape to one side of the loop that resembles a river delta (loop prints have only one delta per print). These two points are necessary for classifying a print based on the number of friction ridges between the delta and the core of the loop.

■ Whorl Patterns

As is often the case with things technical, the classification of **whorls** is confusing. (See **FIGURE 6.6**.) The confusion arises as a result of the four groupings into which a whorl pattern may fall: (1) plain whorl, (2) central pocket loop whorl, (3) double loop whorl, and (4) accidental whorl. The problem, for those unaccustomed to fingerprint classification,

FIGURE 6.6: Whorl pattern.
Courtesy of the Federal Bureau of Investigation.

is that the word *loop* is used in distinguishing among whorl patterns but is also used as the name of a non-whorl pattern. It helps to keep in mind that the names of the two loop patterns, radial and ulnar, are related to the radial and ulnar bones in the arm. The terms *central pocket loop* and *double loop* refer to loops occurring inside whorls—central pocket loop whorls and double loop whorls. However, radial and ulnar loops each have only one delta, and any whorl pattern has a minimum of two deltas. What appears to be a loop having two deltas is a double loop whorl or a central pocket loop whorl. Any pattern that is not covered by one of the categories or is a combination of two patterns is called an **accidental whorl**.

■ Arch Patterns

The least common pattern is also the simplest to classify. **Arches** are either plain or tented. (See **FIGURE 6.7**.) A plain arch is formed by friction ridges entering from one side of the print and exiting on the opposite side, rising to a

FIGURE 6.5: Loop pattern.
© Kevin L. Chesson/Shutterstock, Inc.

FIGURE 6.7: Arch pattern.
Courtesy of the Federal Bureau of Investigation.

---

loops
Fingerprint pattern that has one or more ridges that enter from one side of the print, curve, and exit from the same side; includes a core and a delta

core
In fingerprints, the centermost point of the loop at the apex of the innermost ridge of the loop; this shape is always found in a loop pattern

delta
A two-sided triangular shape found to one side of a loop that resembles a river delta; this shape is always found in a loop pattern

whorls
Fingerprint pattern having a minimum of two deltas; this pattern is classified into four groupings: (1) plain whorl, (2) central pocket loop whorl, (3) double loop whorl, and (4) accidental whorl

accidental whorl
Any fingerprint pattern that is not covered by one of the categories or is a combination of two patterns

arches
The least common fingerprint patterns; they are either plain or tented

peak in the center of the ridge to form a hill-like pattern. A tented arch, instead of rising gently to the center and sloping easily away, thrusts up in the center and falls quickly away.

Understanding fingerprint patterns is essential for doing fingerprint comparisons. Once two prints are seen to have the same pattern, they can be examined further for similarities in ridge numbers and configuration.

Detecting Prints

Although police often use the term *latent print* to describe all fingerprints found at a crime scene, many of the prints discovered are visible and should not be called latent. Any investigator, lawyer, or expert who inartfully uses "latent" to describe a visible print can expect to be challenged on competent cross-examination. Such a simple point is not lost on jurors, who generally are swayed by simple reasons to find one witness more believable than another.

There are three distinct types of prints found at a crime scene: (1) patent prints (2) plastic prints and (3) latent prints. Just as a photographic print is a representation of, but not identical to, the original scene, a fingerprint is a representation of, but not identical to, the actual finger skin friction ridges.

■ Patent Prints

Patent prints are readily identifiable as fingerprints, by the unassisted eye. Fingers that have been in contact with a colored material such, as toner, ink, blood, paint, oil, or chocolate leave visible prints. Once the material has soiled the fingers, the material may be transferred to a surface with which the ridges come into contact.

■ Plastic Prints

If fingers come into contact with a soft material, such as soap, wet putty, wet cement, wet plaster, or dust, a ridge impression may be left sufficient for performing comparisons. As children, most of us placed hand, foot, or finger impressions in wet cement. In Hollywood, a cultural artifact has been built around celebrities embedding their hands and feet in wet cement, leaving handprints and footprints. These are **plastic impressions**, and they can be used for fingerprint comparisons. If a movie star were a suspect in a crime and refused to allow inked impressions to be taken by the police, the star's concrete hand impression could probably be compared with a print at the scene of the crime to help determine the star's guilt or innocence.

■ Latent Prints

Body perspiration and oils might leave invisible residues on surfaces that, if **visualized** (made visible), would constitute a usable impression of the finger skin friction ridges. Visualizing latent prints requires the use of techniques, chemicals, and powders appropriate for the type of surface upon which the prints repose. **Developing prints** on a nonabsorbent surface requires a different approach than developing prints on a softer, more absorbent surface. The following section provides details.

Developing Prints

Fingerprints discovered on absorbent surfaces can be made visible through the application of powder. The type of powder to use depends on a number of variables.

■ Powders

Latent prints may be developed (visualized) by applying one of a variety of fingerprint powders available from distributors of fingerprinting equipment. These powders differ in color, consistency, density, and polarity. Whatever powder is selected may be applied by brush or by magnetic wand or blown onto the latent print. The powder will cling to the fluids that created the fingerprint. Excess powder can be removed with a feather brush. (See **FIGURE 6.8**.) On backgrounds that are complicated or distracting,

FIGURE 6.8: Fingerprint brush and the use of a brush and powder to develop latent prints.

Courtesy of SIRCHIE Finger Print Laboratories, Inc.

---

visualized
To make visible

developing prints
Making fingerprints visible by applying a powder or chemical

patent prints
Prints that are readily identifiable as fingerprints, by the unassisted eye

plastic impressions
Fingerprints left on soft materials such as soap, wet cement, or dust that can be used for fingerprint comparisons

FIGURE 6.9: Flourescent powder.

Courtesy of SIRCHIE Finger Print Laboratories, Inc.

FIGURE 6.11: Close-up of a latent print processed using ninhydrin.

ninhydrin
The most common chemical used for developing latent prints on porous surfaces; it reacts chemically with the amino acids in sweat and renders a purple-blue print

fluorescent powders offer advantages over conventional powders. They are applied in the same fashion, but ultraviolet light is necessary to view them. Using ultraviolet light requires an orange filter to see the fluorescent prints. The print can be lifted as any other powdered print but must use a specialized camera and lights to be photographed. (See **FIGURES 6.9** and **6.10**.)

■ Chemical Development

The most common chemical used for developing latent prints on porous surfaces, such as paper and cloth is **ninhydrin**. (See **FIGURE 6.11**.) Ninhydrin chemically reacts with the amino acids in sweat and renders a purple-blue print. (The color is similar to that of old-fashioned mimeographed handouts.) Ninhydrin (formerly known as triketohydrindene hydrate) is sprayed on the surface that is being checked for prints. The chemical is commercially available in fuming spray cans and wet wipes for ease of application. The development time, which ranges between 1 and 24 hours, can be hastened by heating the

FIGURE 6.10: Flourescent prints.

Courtesy of Maine State Police Crime Laboratory.

INVESTIGATOR'S NOTEBOOK

Handling Visible Prints

It is important that visible prints be photographed immediately. They can often be preserved by bagging the object on which they were found, by rendering the surface on which they were found small enough to be bagged, or by being lifted (see the description of the lifting of latent prints later in this chapter). A dry, bloody fingerprint on the body of a victim can be lifted using lift tape, avoiding mutilation of the body in an attempt to preserve the print. Any efforts to lift prints should be preceded by taking a set of photographs in case the lifting procedure is not successful.

© Shutterstock, Inc./Janaka Dharmasena.

© Shutterstock, Inc./Nutink.

specimen to 100°C. Diazafluoren one (DFO) can produce a similar result and is more reliable. It is a fluorescing ninhydrin analog and is useful on porous surfaces, including paper. DFO is also used to develop weak bloodstains but requires ultraviolet light for fluorescing.

Superglue fuming is widely acceptable in technical circles for the development of fingerprints on nonporous surfaces, such as Formica, metal, or plastic bags. Superglue is cyanoacrylate ester, which is the chemical that develops the print. Cyanoacrylate fumes are created when superglue is heated or placed on a piece of cotton with sodium hydroxide. (See **FIGURE 6.12**.) The item upon which the latent print is impressed must be placed, along with the superglue, in an airtight container and allowed to work. After a period of time, depending on humidity and heat, the fumes will begin to adhere to the latent print and produce a hard, whitish deposit in the form of the deposited print. A handheld cyanoacrylate wand can be used at the crime scene to develop latent prints in lieu of powder. (See **FIGURE 6.13**.) Superglue is useful on nonporous surfaces and works well on Styrofoam and plastic bags. The

FIGURE 6.13: Cyanoacrylate fuming wand and cartridges.

> **Superglue fuming**
> Technique used for the development of fingerprints on non-porous surfaces

developed prints can be dusted with powders and photographed in place.

To process items that are wet or have been in water, one may use the application of small particle reagent (SPR). SPR is a suspension of fine molybdenum disulfide particles that adhere to the fatty components of skin secretions, forming a black, gray, or white deposit. The reagent is sprayed on the suspect surface, given a few seconds to develop then gently washed away. Wherever a print resides, it can be developed further by additional applications of SPR until the print is of photographic quality. Conventional lifting methods can be used to lift and preserve the developed prints.

In homicide crime scenes, duct tape is a common type of evidence; often, the perpetrator leaves prints on overlapping tape on a victim or balled-up, discarded tape. Submersion in water does not necessarily destroy the prints. For instance, balled-up and folded pieces of duct tape submerged in water can be removed from the water and allowed to

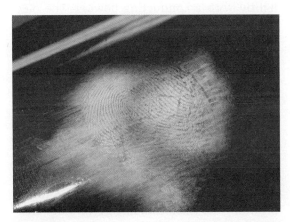

FIGURE 6.12: An example of a latent print processed using cyanoacrylate fuming.

INVESTIGATOR'S NOTEBOOK

Capturing Prints with Powders

Technical expertise is needed for the selection of the appropriate powder for the fingerprint, surface composition, and surface color. Light powders are best for dark surfaces, and dark powders are best for light surfaces. The method whereby the print is visualized is referred to as the development of the print.

Once developed and tagged, the print should be photographed. What may seem like an obsession with photography will make sense to anyone who has lost a print during the lift process or misplaced a print once lifted. Also, photographs of prints found at the crime scene and taken from the suspect can be enlarged and presented to the jury during expert testimony to assist the jury in understanding why the defendant and only the defendant could have left the print.

dry. Once dry, the tape can be untangled and unfolded using an adhesive remover (such as un-du). The tape is then left to dry and weighted on the ends to prevent it from curling as it dries. Once dried, a commercially available product such, as Wetwop or adhesive-side developer, is applied to the adhesive side of the tape. (See **FIGURE 6.14**.) The mixture should be applied with a camel-hair brush and allowed to sit for about 10 seconds, after which the mixture is washed from the tape with a slow, steady stream of water. Using this method, it is possible to recover fingerprints placed on the tape. It is not necessary to lift the prints when they have been developed; they can be preserved by placing lift tape over the developed prints on the adhesive side of the duct tape. Once dried, the tape can be preserved by applying a transparent tape over the developed prints and then photographed. **TABLE 6.2** provides information about the development

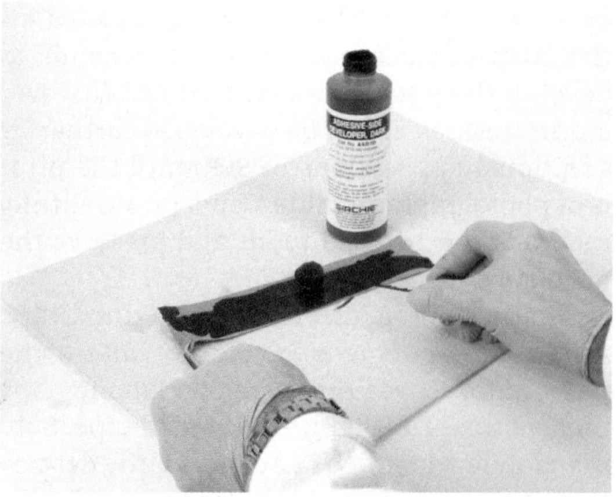

FIGURE 6.14: Duct tape developed prints.

Courtesy of SIRCHIE Finger Print Laboratories, Inc.

methods that are appropriate for surfaces with different characteristics.

■ Developing Fingerprints from Shell Casings and Bomb Fragments

Dr. John Bond of the University of Leicester and the Scientific Support Unit of the Northamptonshire Police discovered a new method to recover fingerprints from fired shell casings and exploded bomb fragments. The salts from sweat are sufficiently corrosive that shell casings handled with the bare hand may etch the finger's friction ridges into the metal of the shell casing and other soft metals. Although the metal may be exposed to extremely high temperatures or explosive forces, the etched prints may remain. In effect, the etched impression remains on the metal's surface long after the surface latent prints have been lost. The heat from being discharged or detonated causes the chemical reaction to accelerate. To develop the etched prints, it is necessary to pass 2,500 volts through the metal while dusting the surface lightly with a conducting powder. The electricity causes the powder to stick to the corroded ridges. The only way that the prints can be removed once corroded into the surface is by grinding them from the surface. (Bond, 2009, p. 1034)

■ Developing Fingerprints from Bodies

Prints on bodies can be developed using cyanoacrylate ester (superglue) or powder. Research conducted at the FBI laboratories assisted in responding to law enforcement inquiries regarding the viability of fingerprint ridge characteristics on dead bodies. In order to determine the likelihood of developable fingerprints

TABLE 6.2 Guide to Surfaces and Development Methods

Surface Characteristics	Development Methods
Smooth, nonporous	Powders, iodine, SPR, superglue
Rough, nonporous	SPR, superglue
Paper, cardboard	Iodine, ninhydrin, DFO, silver nitrate, powders
Vinyl, rubber, leather	Iodine, SPR, superglue, powders
Unfinished wood	Ninhydrin, powders, silver nitrate
Wax and waxed surfaces	Powder, superglue
Adhesive surfaces	Adhesive-side powders

Courtesy of SIRCHIE Finger Print Laboratories, Inc.

on a body, the researchers developed a protocol different from previous efforts. They used only unembalmed cadavers and placed latent prints.

Areas of skin were sectioned into numbered squares drawn on a body. A latent was placed in each square. The researchers then tried to develop the latent prints by employing several methods, including the use of lasers, alternate light sources, iodine/silver transfer, cyanoacrylate fuming, regular and fluorescent powders, specially formulated powders, and regular and fluorescent magnetic powders. Most methods failed to provide consistent results. The one technique that developed identifiable latent prints most often was glue fuming in conjunction with regular magnetic fingerprint powder.

As they continued their research, the scientists realized that they needed an improved method for spreading glue fumes over the skin. The earlier method used—forming an airtight plastic tent over a small area of skin or over an entire body—did not always work. It was impossible to distribute glue fumes evenly over the skin and extremely difficult to confine all of the fumes to the tent. In addition, when they removed the plastic tent at the end of the fuming process, the fumes often forced the researchers out of the work area. To alleviate these problems, one of the researchers developed a portable glue fuming chamber. Using the portable fuming chamber, researchers obtained identifiable latent prints most often with fuming times between 10 and 15 seconds.

In the early testing, it seemed that particular types and brands of fingerprint powders provided the best results. More than 30 brands and several types of powders and applicators were tested. In the end, researchers determined that powder selection was less critical than ensuring that the glue fuming process was performed correctly. Standard black magnetic powder produced more useful prints than other powders and was the least expensive.

To replicate field conditions, researchers developed prints on cadavers that had been exposed to the elements and placed in extreme environments. The single key to success was the rigorous application of the created procedures. The results showed that by following proper procedures, investigators could develop identifiable latent prints even under harsh conditions (Futrell, 1996). The results obtained and methods developed as a result of this research continue to impact criminal investigations today.

For the underwater crime scene, a process that can be used on wet metal and glass surfaces would be an advantage. One such process is the application of **small particle reagent (SPR)**. SPR is a suspension of fine molybdenum disulfide particles that adhere to the fatty components of skin secretions, forming a gray deposit. The reagent is sprayed on the suspect surface, given a few seconds to develop, then gently washed away. Wherever a print resides, it can be developed further by additional applications of SPR until the print is of photographic quality. Conventional lifting

small particle reagent (SPR) A suspension of fine molybdenum disulfide particles that adhere to the fatty components of skin secretions. Typically used to process latent prints found in wet environments

methods can be used to lift and preserve the developed prints.

Postmortem Fingerprint Impressions

On recently deceased bodies, fingerprinting is relatively easy, although it does require some specialized equipment. Ten-print cards can be cut into strips, or commercially manufactured card strips for postmortem fingerprinting can be used. Most technicians have a fingerprint spoon that they use in conjunction with the 10-card strips. Each finger is inked with a roller separately and impressed on a strip separately. Bodies with evidence of rigor mortis pose a bit more of a challenge but judiciously applied pressure will straighten a rigored finger, making it available for inking and printing. This is a procedure most commonly employed by the medical examiner's office.

When friction ridge skin is compromised by death and decomposition, it may break down into skin with no visible friction ridges. Boiling water can recondition friction ridge skin. This reconditioning process rehydrates the skin, visualizing friction ridge detail. As a result, impressions can be lifted and recorded. The process begins with heating water hot enough to boil. Once the water has reached the boiling point, the hand can be briefly immersed in the hot water. The submersion should last no longer than 5 to 10 seconds. If friction ridges are not recognizable, the process can be repeated but should not be repeated more than three times. Once the ridges are visible, the hand can be dried by pouring isopropyl alcohol onto the fingers and then dried with a warm, clean cloth. Once the fingers have been dried, the prints can be lifted by applying black silk fingerprint powder to the finger pads with a light dusting of powder. The powder can be lifted using a hinged or adhesive lifter. The lift can then be applied to the appropriate location on a 10-print card. Attempting to ink the fragile ridges will result in their disappearance, hence the fingerprint powder procedure.

■ Fluorescence and Alternate Light Sources

The earliest use of fluorescence to visualize fingerprints occurred when it was discovered that the blue-green light of the argonion laser made sweat fluoresce (like the black-light posters of the 1960s). It was later discovered that the treatment of fingerprints with ninhydrin and then zinc chloride or with the dye rhodamine 6G after superglue fuming caused fluorescence and sensitivity to laser light. Further experimentation focused on the use of alternate light sources as a method of visualizing fingerprints (Saferstein, 2014). Today, there are numerous products that use light to visualize fingerprints, and they have decreased the time and effort necessary to find and develop fingerprints.

One word of caution: The use of various powders and chemicals to develop fingerprints can interfere with the gathering of blood-related evidence. All common fingerprint developers affect the tests used to classify bloodstains.

Handling and Preserving Prints

As with plastic and visible prints, once an investigator has developed a latent print, he or she must prepare and preserve it for possible use in the laboratory and courtroom. First, it must be photographed. Next, the investigator should attempt to remove the print from the crime scene, either by preserving the item upon which the print lies or by **lifting** the print. Numerous manufacturers provide specialized adhesive lifters. (See **FIGURE 6.15**.)

A lifter is a transparent tape that is placed on the powdered print with the adhesive side down. When the tape is removed, the fingerprint powder is removed with it. The lifter is provided with a black or white card on which the transparent tape and powdered print can then be placed, adhesive side down. The colored card provides contrast to the colored powder used, helping to visualize the print. Lift tape comes in a variety of sizes and configurations so that the right type can be chosen for the size, number, and location of the prints to be lifted. Lifted fingerprints can be checked against the fingerprints of a suspect by sending both to the crime laboratory for classification and comparison.

Recent advances have allowed for the use of DNA analysis with regard to latent print lifts. Some chemical processes may prohibit the ability of this area of forensic analysis to be performed. If it is anticipated that DNA analysis of print residue will be used, the crime scene investigator is encouraged to contact the appropriate crime lab prior to utilizing chemical methods of processing so that any contamination or damage of DNA-related evidence can be avoided.

Identifying Fingerprints

Fingerprint individuality, and, therefore, fingerprint identification, rests on four premises:

1. Friction ridges develop in their definitive form when humans are still in the womb.

---

lifting
Removing a fingerprint from a crime scene by sticking a print developed with powder to transparent tape and then placing the tape (adhesive side down) on a black or white card

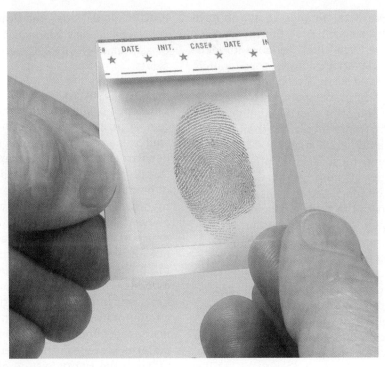

FIGURE 6.15: Lifting a fingerprint using an adhesive lifter.
Courtesy of SIRCHIE Finger Print Laboratories, Inc.

2. Friction ridges remain unchanged throughout life with the exception of permanent scars.

3. Friction ridge patterns and their details are unique.

4. Ridge patterns vary within certain boundaries that allow the patterns to be classified.

The entire purpose of recognizing and collecting fingerprints is to identify them in order to find a suspect or identify a person. However, most people have never given much thought to the process by which fingerprint identification is actually done. When prints are found, an expert

— Ripped from the Headlines —

Selfie Identification

Detectives in Florida recently used a popular method of self-photography to identify and convict a suspect. Dannie Horner, 34 was arrested for sexually abusing a 1-year old boy. As part of the postarrest evidence gathering, to support the charges, police confiscated and analyzed his cell phone. On the phone were a number of selfies, which did not show the photographer's face, but which showed the suspect holding the camera and conducting his abuse in front of a mirror. Detectives were able to use the images displayed in the mirror to isolate the suspect's fingers and fingerprints and compare them to the inked images collected at the time of his arrest. They were a direct match to one another. According to an interview conducted by the New York Daily News, the evidence was of paramount importance.

"We didn't have a face of an individual in a photo, but this was even better," Capt. Charlie Thorpe, head of the department's Investigations Bureau, told the Daily News. "In this case, you are looking at the actual print on the actual finger in an image. If the ridge detail is there, without the physical finger, what could be better? It made it a clear conviction," Thorpe said. "(The jurors) had no doubt in their mind."

A jury found Horner guilty of 26 charges, including capital sexual battery, molestation and possession and transmission of child pornography. The modern method can be more reliable than lifting prints off of an object, which can become problematic if there are smudges and debris on the print, the investigators said.

Data from http://www.nydailynews.com/news/national/detectives-fingerprints-photo-perp-hand-id-article-1.2268308 compares them with samples known to have been made by a suspect. First, the expert compares overall patterns and then looks for identical ridge characteristics. When these match, they are known as *points of comparison*. Current training in fingerprint comparison stresses that the quality of the print and the quality of the comparison are more important than placing emphasis on a numerical match.

The examiner must decide if sufficient quality and quantity of the ridge detail is present. If not, it may be concluded that there is "insufficient ridge detail to form a conclusion." The print is analyzed to determine its proper orientation and suitability before the comparison proceeds. Sometimes, inked prints may be compared with a set of inked prints on file. More commonly, the examiner compares a developed latent print with inked prints from a known person. The overall pattern and ridge flow are examined. Next, the minutiae are compared, point by point, as to type and location. Finally, pore shape, locations, numbers, and relationships, and the shape and size of edge features are compared. Any unexplained differences between known and latent prints during this process result in the conclusion that the known is "excluded as a source." If every compared feature is consistent with the known, and enough features are sufficiently unique when considered as a whole, the examiner makes an identification (ID). Therefore, in fingerprint identification, there are three possible conclusions that can be drawn from an analysis:

1. Insufficient ridge detail to form a conclusion

2. Print exclusion

3. Print identification

In law enforcement, IDs are always made by trained, and often by certified, examiners. Fingerprint examiners are trained extensively and are required to accumulate significant experience before being entrusted with this responsibility. In addition to the general principles and approaches used, therefore, the knowledge, training, and experience are also considered. Most examiners are certified or have been declared an "expert" by a court of law.

Classification of Fingerprints

A classification system is necessary if large sets of fingerprint files are to be useful for criminal identification. **Classification** is a formula given to a complete set of ten fingers as they appear on a fingerprint card generally based on pattern type, ridge count, or ridge tracing. (See FIGURE 6.16.) Today, the *Henry System* and the *FBI National Crime Information Center–Fingerprint Classification* (NCIC–FPC) are used to classify prints.

■ Henry System

Developed by Sir Edward Henry, the Henry System of print classification has been used for well over a century and remains in use in many departments today. This system requires the complete classification of all 10 fingers of an individual in order to properly file the information. When this system was developed, it allowed for efficient searching and maintenance of large fingerprint files. However, it did not allow for manually searching for a single print. The system was built around whether an individual had whorl patterns present in his or her prints (primary classification) and then had a series of five extensions to the primary classification, dependent on the type and size of the patterns present in the fingers. An example of utilizing the Henry System of classification is shown **EXHIBIT 6.1**.

■ National Crime Information Center–Fingerprint Classification (NCIC–FPC)

This system of classification, developed by the FBI, assigns a 20-character string of letters and numbers to a person's fingerprints. Every print entered into the FBI system is classified by this method, and it allows trained law enforcement personnel in the field to determine fingerprint compatibility with fingerprints on record, along with providing an efficient and effective way for filing fingerprints. The following is an example of an NCIC–FPC:

POAA05TT19CISR58DIXX

PO: Right thumb is a plain whorl with an outer tracing.

AA: Right index finger is a plain arch.

05: Right middle finger is an ulnar loop with a ridge count of 5.

TT: Right ring finger is a tented arch.

19: Right little finger is an ulnar loop with a ridge count of 19.

CI: Left thumb is a central pocket loop whorl with an inner tracing.

SR: Left index finger is unclassifiable due to scarring.

58: Left middle finger is a radial loop with a ridge count of 8.

DI: Left ring finger is a double loop whorl with an inner tracing.

XX: Left little finger is missing (possibly amputated, or missing since birth).

classification
A formula given to a complete set of ten fingers as they appear on a fingerprint card generally based on pattern type, ridge count, or ridge tracing

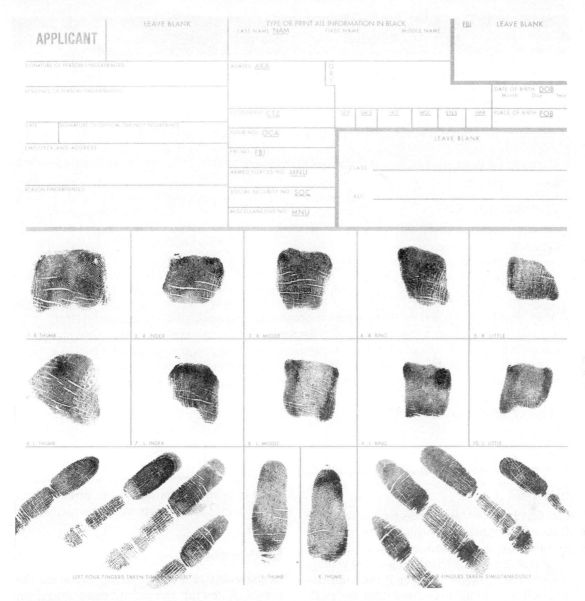

FIGURE 6.16: An example of a 10-print fingerprint card.

Courtesy of Nicholas Vesper.

Fingerprints and the Scientific Method

As was discussed in Chapters 1 and 4, a systematic and thorough approach to crime scene processing means employing the scientific method in investigative efforts. The scientific method is utilized to reduce the subjectivity in scientific experimentation.

The scientific method includes:

1. Making an observation
2. Stating the question
3. Generating a hypothesis
4. Experimentation
5. Arriving at a conclusion
6. Replication (others receive the same results employing the same process)
7. Recordation

A similar methodology is utilized with reference to the comparison and identification process of latent fingerprints. David R. Ashbaugh, a scientist with the Royal Canadian Mounted Police, developed a formal method known as **ACE-V** for the scientific comparison of prints. The acronym stands for analysis, comparison, evaluation, and verification. The purpose of this comparison methodology is to either identify a print via individualization as having originated from the same source or to exclude impressions as having no common origin (Coppock, 2007).

ACE-V
A formula given to a complete set of ten fingers as they appear on a fingerprint card generally based on pattern type, ridge count, or ridge tracing

EXHIBIT 6.1

Henry System of Classification

10	I	1	R	–	r	2
	S	17	U	2 a		

The above Henry classification is representative of the following:

Primary: 1/17

Secondary: R/U

Subsecondary/small letter group: – r/2a

Major: I/S

Key: 10

Final: 2

When trained to understand the Henry System of classification, the examiner is able to determine that there is one whorl pattern present in the hand (in the right thumb), a radial loop with a ridge count of 10 is present in the right index finger, a radial loop is present in the right ring finger, ulnar loops are present in the right middle finger, the right little finger (with ridge count of 2), the left thumb, the left index finger, and the left little finger. There are also arches present in the middle and ring finger of the left hand.

Although recognized the world over as an effective method for fingerprint filing, with the increased efficiency and affordability of computer systems, many departments are choosing to file and classify prints using a method developed by the FBI.

Analysis

The first level of this process begins with the study of the questioned print to determine the overall print orientation, quality, shape, and ridge flow. The comparison (or known) print is analyzed in the same manner. If the information derived is found to be consistent, the analysis proceeds to the next level. If nonmatching characteristics are observed, the examination is terminated, which results in an exclusion.

Comparison

If the analysis portion of the process yields sufficient information to warrant a further investigation, the next level begins with orienting the questioned and known prints in the same manner and identifying a common unique point in each print to utilize as a starting point. The examination will continue from this common starting point and progress along with recognition of other areas of commonalities between the prints, with regard to ridge characteristics, beginning with the most distinctive feature identified and continuing until all of the characteristics are accounted for and there are no unexplainable variances. Differences may exist due to print quality; however, what is being compared are the print characteristics that are present, not necessarily their clarity.

Evaluation

In the event of a clear variance between the prints, following the comparison stage, an exclusion would be made. However, if the information appears consistent between the two prints, an ID can be made. Typically, this ID is based on the degree of ridge detail. If the print is lacking in sufficient print detail, then pore distribution and ridge shapes and edges may be utilized instead or in combination.

Verification

Regardless of the conclusion reached—exclusion or identification—another examiner re-examines the print for verification utilizing the aforementioned process. Under ideal conditions, the examiner making the identification or exclusion should be an analyst who is in no way associated with the case, or who had any significant knowledge of the case. This could impart bias to the decision process.

One important case of misidentification was the FBI's arrest of American citizen Brandon

Mayfield in 2004 in connection with the Madrid bombings that killed 191 people and injured more than 2,000. It wasn't until the Spanish government identified a different man from the fingerprint evidence that Mayfield was released. (See **EXHIBIT 6.2**.)

Automated Fingerprint Identification Systems

Television, books, and movies often emphasize the value of fingerprints in solving serious crimes. Until the advent of computer technology, however, that value was mostly mythical. Fingerprints were used to inculpate or exculpate based on a suspect group. A search of fingerprint files for the match to a fingerprint found at the scene of a crime occurred only in fiction. The classification system used in categorizing stored fingerprints and the large number of fingerprints stored made it impossible to check through a fingerprint collection manually looking for a match. Computers have turned art into reality. Automated fingerprint identification systems now allow police to do what screenwriters and movie directors have long pretended they could.

An **automated fingerprint identification system (AFIS)** is an automatic pattern recognition system that consists of three fundamental stages:

1. *Data acquisition*: The fingerprint to be recognized is sensed.

2. *Feature extraction*: A machine representation (pattern) is extracted from the sensed image.

3. *Decision making*: The representations derived from the sensed image are compared with a representation stored in the system (**FIGURE 6.17**).

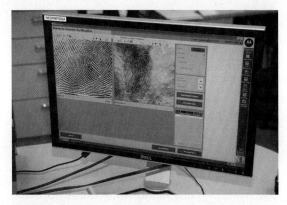

FIGURE 6.17: An example of an AFIS terminal.
© Mikael Karlsson/Alamy Stock Photo.

Different systems may use different numbers of available fingerprints (multiple impressions of a single finger or single impressions of multiple fingers) for person identification. The feature extraction stage may involve manual override and editing by experts. Image enhancement may be used for poor-quality images. Depending on whether the acquisition process is offline or online, a fingerprint may be one of three types: an inked fingerprint, a latent fingerprint, or a live-scan fingerprint.

Fingerprints no longer need to be manually matched to files. Time is often the critical factor in determining the success of a criminal investigation. The use of this computer technology not only saves time but significantly increases the accuracy match rate compared with manual comparisons. Because of this, and due to the systems becoming more affordable, AFIS is rapidly being implemented throughout law enforcement agencies.

Ten-print cards are scanned into the system. They are run against current latent prints in the system from "unknowns." AFIS

> **automated fingerprint identification system (AFIS)** An automatic pattern recognition system that consists of three fundamental stages: data acquisition, feature extraction, and decision making

EXHIBIT 6.2

The FBI Makes a Latent Fingerprint Misidentification

In the aftermath of the March 11, 2004, train bombing in Madrid, Spain, personnel from the FBI Latent Print Unit performed a fingerprint analysis and reported an individualization of a latent print with a candidate print from an Integrated Automated Fingerprint Identification Search (IAFIS). It was subsequently determined that the individualization was in error, and the latent print was ultimately identified with a different subject.

As part of the corrective action process, an international committee of distinguished latent print examiners and forensic experts was formed. Their task was to review the analysis performed by the FBI laboratory and make recommendations that would prevent this type of error from occurring in the future.

also can scan in latent prints and compare them with the 10-print cards on file. The computer assigns a percentage of probability on the matches generated. Searches can be conducted in seconds to minutes versus months for manual searches. It should be noted, however, that final determination is always left up to a professional print examiner and *not* the computer.

For AFIS to pull up candidates for a "match," an examiner must first ensure that minutiae points are properly identified; sometimes, these must be added or edited manually, which can be time consuming. However, if not performed, and minutiae points are incorrectly identified, or unidentified altogether, the chances of finding a proper match decrease dramatically.

This often tedious and problematic situation saw a dramatic improvement when, in April 2009, the National Institute of Standards and Technology (NIST) released results of biometric research that they had conducted with reference to Automatic Feature Extraction and Matching (AFEM). Utilizing automated fingerprint feature extraction, most of the tested prints' identities were found in the top 10 prints listed as possible matches. This shows a dramatic increase in efficiency of automation and bodes well for accelerating fingerprint data input and identification (Indovina et al., 2009).

Today, the FBI has in place an integrated automated fingerprint identification system (IAFIS). This system allows agencies to be linked together and compare and share evidence. However, not all systems are integrated. The majority of time, when someone thinks of an AFIS, they believe the system to be an IAFIS system, but that is not necessarily the case. An AFIS system accepts and stores input data in that system alone and is not integrated with outside systems. Therefore, if a comparison to other prints outside the agency's own system is to take place, the print must be emailed or otherwise sent digitally to an agency that has IAFIS capabilities. Agencies that are integrated—whether to the FBI's IAFIS system or simply to a larger network, such as one of several interstate crime laboratories—are able to run a print against all prints in the integrated system.

The possibilities offered by this technology can only be appreciated when we consider the size of the fingerprint database that the federal government has collected. The FBI has been receiving copies of fingerprint cards from all state and federal agencies that require employees to be fingerprinted. It has copies of all the prints of persons who served in wars from Korea to Iraq and Afghanistan. Additionally, the FBI has copies of the prints of all persons arrested and booked, as a juvenile or an adult, for a misdemeanor or a felony.

Palm Prints

The palms of the hands (as well as the soles of the feet) yield the same volar skin, and thus friction ridge skin, as that of the fingers (and toes). However, the large-scale classification of palm impressions relating to data entry or archiving is a relatively new concept. Until recently, the technology necessary to document and compare such information was not available on a large scale. Most AFIS computer databases allow only searches of fingerprints. A select few will allow for the input of and comparison of palm print impressions. (See **FIGURE 6.18**.)

Although palm prints are relatively new for AFIS systems, latent print comparisons are not new. One of the earliest latent print identifications, possibly the first in a criminal case in this country, was a palm print identification. Palm print and footprint identifications have been part of the friction ridge identification process for many years. Palm print identifications at the Secret Service, for example, historically have been very high because of the large number of forged U.S. Treasury Checks that were processed. This was especially true before forgery and general financial fraud became mostly electronic in nature. Quite often, prints of the side of the palm are developed under the signature area. This area of the palm is sometimes referred to as the *writer's palm* because it contacts the document when a person is writing (C. Artone, personal communication, October 25, 2008).

Palm prints often are found during crime scene search efforts. The most commonly encountered areas of friction skin impressions typically correspond to the large padded areas of the palmar surface. As technology continues to improve, comparison and identification efforts will also improve. A crime scene investigator should not let this deter him or her from the collection of the friction ridge evidence. To a crime scene investigator, all prints should be viewed as potentially identifiable. Such identification efforts are left up to the experience and technology of the forensic laboratory.

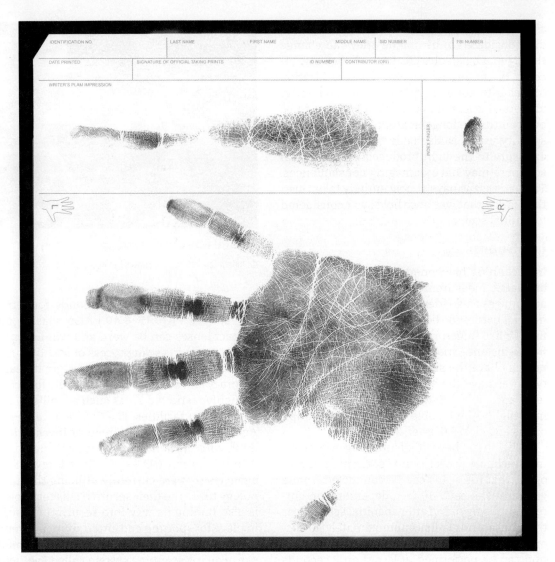

FIGURE 6.18: An example of a palm print card.

Courtesy of Nicholas Vesper.

Biometric Identification

The government has long attempted to identify people by biological characteristics, from bumps on a person's head to the ridges on his or her fingers. Recent trends in identification involve the use of retinal and iris pattern recognition systems. Banking and government agencies are the primary users of **biometric identification** systems, and biometrics has become a major growth industry.

All biometric systems require similar equipment, including a high-resolution scanning device to digitize an image of some part of the human body and a computer to run the pattern-recognition and sorting software for the specific type of identification in use. Various biometric systems scan human body parts, including fingerprints, irises and retinas, faces, and hands, and software and scanning devices are also being developed to identify signatures and voices.

Retinal Scans

Retinal scans are founded on the presence of the network of capillaries that supply the retina of the eye. The capillaries absorb light and are capable of visualization through proper illumination. Thus, retinal scans require close contact of the subject and the scanning technology. In addition, there must be nearly perfect alignment of the eye with the equipment and little or no movement of the eye. This can be extremely difficult to use in a passive identification system. Another drawback is that

biometric identification
Identifying people by biological characteristics

although retinal capillary patterns are generally considered to be unique, they can change throughout a person's life due to diabetes, glaucoma, or cataracts. This also makes utilization for security screening purposes difficult. Overall, retinal scans are considered by most to be overly intrusive for general access purposes and security use. It is also believed that prolonged exposure to the light produced by the retinal scanners may have damaging consequences. Thus, iris scans have almost entirely taken over the market that was once held by or considered for retinal scans.

Iris Scanning

Iris scanning has generated much interest in biometric measurement. The iris has several advantages as an identifying body part: It is an integral part of the body and is not easily modified. Unlike fingerprints, the iris can be imaged from a distance. Iris patterns are unique. No two persons have the same iris pattern; in fact, no two eyes have the same iris pattern. The patterns are stable throughout life and only change in a highly predictable manner as the pupil opens and closes (Lerner, 2000).

The main benefit of utilizing iris scanning technology over retinal scanning technology is that iris scans can be conducted from a greater distance (5–10 feet, depending on current technology), and after an initial scan of less than 20 seconds (versus approximately 40 seconds for retinal scans), subsequent identification can be performed in less than 2 seconds

FIGURE 6.19: Iris scan technology.

© Andrew Brookes/National Physics Laboratory/Science Source.

(versus approximately 20 seconds for retinal scans). (See **FIGURE 6.19.**) Also, glasses and contact lenses can be worn and will not interfere with the iris scan process or identification.

Retinal and iris scans offer a great deal of accuracy and are thus used primarily for access to highly restricted areas such as military and government facilities. The Central Intelligence Agency (CIA), Federal Bureau of Investigation (FBI), and National Aeronautics and Space Administration (NASA) are just a few of the agencies that are currently utilizing this technology to ensure their security. This technology is also finding its way into security measures in place for sporting and entertainment events. For example, the 2002 Sydney Olympics made use of an iris scanning system called Eye Ticket

— Ripped from the Headlines —

Airline Group Unveils New "Iris Scan" Technology

Long, annoying airport security screenings could soon be replaced by iris scans and microchips, if the International Air Transport Association has its way. The airline industry group has introduced a new biometric system to save passengers time that

calls for putting a microchip in passports. "Passengers should be able to get from curb to boarding gate with dignity," IATA Director General Giovanni Bisignani said. "That means without stopping, stripping, or unpacking, and certainly not groping."

Under the new system, passengers would undergo an iris scan, which would be matched against information on that chip. Then travelers would be sent through one of three 20-foot tunnels. Depending on the level of security risk, passengers

would be subjected to different degrees of searches. Airlines are hoping to have the new system in place within 5 years. "It's something that's long overdue," Transportation Security Administration Chief John Pistole said. "We're not at the checkpoint of the future yet, but we're working toward that. I think eventually we will see something similar."

Source: CBN News. (2011). Airline group unveils new 'iris scan' technology. Retrieved August 31, 2011, from http://www.cbn.com/cbnnews/us/2011/June/Airline-Group-Unveils-New-Iris-Scan-Technology/

© Shutterstock, Inc./rzarek.

to control access to venues and high-security areas. This technology is no longer simply a Hollywood dream; it is infiltrating a great many areas of daily life and will continue to develop and expand as technology improves.

Composite Identifications

Often, the only way to identify a suspect is to translate a verbal description into something police and the media can use easily. Although all-points bulletins historically have provided a verbal description of the suspect sought, a more elaborate method of identification is available through the services of artists, computers, and kits with interchangeable facial features.

A **sketch artist**, given a description, can create a picture that, through continual refinement based on witness input, begins to bear a strong resemblance to the suspect. Most agencies do not have the financial resources to employ a person with the artistic skills necessary to provide an artist's rendition, and so a number of manufacturers have produced kits that offer predrawn facial features from which to choose. By selecting the one feature that best meets the witness's verbal description, a nonartist can begin to construct a **composite picture** (**FIGURE 6.20**).

Not surprisingly, there are software programs that render composite drawings by means of mouse commands and pull-down menus. These programs pose queries to which the witness provides a response. Because, the questions are not suggestive of an answer, the final product tends to be more objective than an artist's sketch. A computer program such as Compusketch provides more than 100,000 selections from which the witness can choose, and the choices can be superimposed

to the satisfaction of the witness. The final product is a laser-printed computer rendition of the facial features of the suspect, ready to be distributed. Often, such images are photo quality.

There are obvious advantages to distributing sketches rather than verbal descriptions to a patrol force. Most agencies require that a photograph and the fingerprints of every arrested adult suspect be taken and stored. The mug shots make up an agency's **rogues' gallery**, a ready supply of photographs for witnesses to leaf through in the attempt to identify a perpetrator. The gallery is generally divided into either offense categories or categories based on modus operandi (the method employed by the perpetrator). The gallery may be further divided into patrol areas, precincts, or neighborhoods. In addition to a photo, identification information is also recorded, such as scars, hair color, height, weight, tattoos, and age. Computer programs can retrieve photos that meet a set of typewritten descriptors or are similar to a composite drawing. When a typewritten description or a composite drawing is entered into the computer, a search is made of the computer's database, and mug shot matches are identified. One of the problems associated with looking at mug shots is the viewer burnout that is bound to occur. Restricting the number of mug shots a witness has to peruse avoids—or at least postpones—viewer overload.

Lineups

In virtually every criminal trial, there must be an identification of the suspect. The prosecution has a responsibility to identify the defendant as the person who perpetrated the offense or was arrested for the offense charged. Often, a prior identification has taken place at the hands of a witness or victim. That pretrial identification generally occurs in one of two ways: a review of the rogues' gallery or a viewing of a police lineup. The controlling case pertaining to police pretrial lineups is *United States v. Wade* (1967). It should be noted that the requirement from *Wade* that counsel be present applies to **post-indictment lineups**, not to pre-indictment lineups (lineups conducted before an indictment is handed down).

Lineups traditionally have been used by police to identify suspects. Their format is generally the same, although the number of participants varies (the range is from 4 to 10). The participants are selected on the basis of

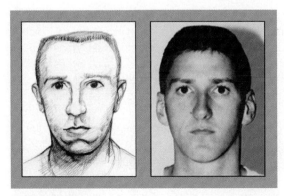

FIGURE 6.20: Forensic artist's composite of a suspect.

Courtesy of the FBI.

rogues' gallery
A ready supply of photographs for witnesses to leaf through in the attempt to identify a perpetrator

sketch artist
Person who can create a picture that, through continual refinement based on witness input, begins to bear a strong resemblance to a suspect

composite picture
Picture drawn of a suspect by selecting the one feature that best meets the witness's verbal description and continuing refinement based on witness input

post-indictment lineups
Lineup conducted after an indictment is handed down, during which counsel must be present

FIGURE 6.21: Example of a suspect lineup.

© Rich Legg/Getty Images.

their similarity to the suspect in gender, age, race, build, coloring, and other characteristics (**FIGURE 6.21**). The participants are allowed to select the position in which they stand. Each position is designated by a number, and the background is calibrated to allow witnesses to better assess height and weight. The idea behind requiring legal representation at lineups is that the presence of counsel averts prejudice in the selection and display of the participants.

Some investigators believe that the presence of legal counsel at post-indictment lineups serves as an obstacle to the successful completion of the investigation. The prudent investigator will welcome the input of defense counsel and recognize that such input will assist in conducting a constitutionally permissible lineup. It is better to find out during the lineup what objections, if any, the defendant's lawyer might raise than to wait until trial and discover that an impermissible lineup was conducted.

CASE IN POINT

© Shutterstock, Inc./Viastas.

United States v. Wade, 1967

Officials were conducting an investigation of the robbery of a federally insured bank in which two men with pieces of tape affixed to their faces stuffed money from the bank into a pillowcase and fled. A federal indictment was returned prior to the arrest of Wade. Fifteen days later, without notice to his counsel, Wade was placed in a lineup to be viewed by bank personnel. Wade was identified as the robber. At trial, witnesses who had made the lineup identification testified that they had seen Wade earlier in the custody of officials. At trial, the witnesses identified Wade and reconfirmed their lineup identification. Wade was convicted of robbery.

The U.S. Supreme Court concluded that there was grave potential for prejudice, intentional or not, in the pretrial lineup. The Court stated that counsel itself can often avert prejudice and ensure a meaningful confrontation at trial. For Wade, the post-indictment lineup was a critical stage of the prosecution and, therefore, one at which he was entitled to counsel. The Court said that both Wade and his counsel should have been notified of the impending lineup, and counsel's presence should have been a prerequisite for conducting a lineup, absent an intelligent waiver.

© Shutterstock, Inc./Nutink.

INVESTIGATOR'S NOTEBOOK

Crucial Factors in Lineup Identification

The following questions are relevant to both pre-indictment and post-indictment lineups:

- Did the witness have the opportunity to get a good look at the suspect at the time of the offense? Various ingredients come together to make an adequate opportunity: time viewed, weather conditions, visibility, lighting, and the visual acumen of the viewer.

- How much attention was the witness paying to what was happening and to what he or she was seeing at the time of the offense?

- How certain is the witness that the suspect is the same person perceived at the crime scene?

- How much time has passed from the commission of the crime to the identification?

- How consistent is the identification with the original report provided to the police?

- Was there anything about the lineup that pointed to the suspect as the person to choose?

The last issue is the one of most concern to the courts. If there was something that suggested one participant over another—position, clothing, or another factor—any further inquiry into the quality of the lineup would be preempted, because suggestibility is fatal to a lineup whenever it may occur.

Identifying the Deceased

Most criminal homicide investigations involve readily identifiable victims. Sometimes, however, a body is not readily identifiable because it has been disfigured or dismembered or has deteriorated over time due to putrefaction. A disfigured, dismembered, or decaying body may be identified through scientific assessment of the body parts. A victim's height, age, sex, and race may be determined by a forensic anthropologist if enough of the right bones have been uncovered. Sex can be assessed from the overall size of the bones or the skeleton. The width and structure of the pubic bone provide added evidence regarding the victim's sex. Race can best be assessed by examining the skull, because skull formation varies with race. (If the victim was of racially mixed parentage, the constellation of physical characteristics of the skull may be of little help in determining race.) The long bones of the leg may also assist in racial classification, because the femur bones of African Americans tend to be relatively straight whereas the femur bones of whites are somewhat arched. Age can be determined by dental development of the skull, skeletal size, and whether the epiphysis of the long bones in the legs is fused.

Dental work is distinctive and useful in identifying bodies that are otherwise unidentifiable.

Dental identifications can be accomplished if a tentative identification of the body has been made and dental records are available to confirm that identification. Missing-person reports often give the initial impetus for a dental or medical comparison.

Physicians and hospitals can provide medical records once a tentative identification of the body has been made. Even skeletal remains can disclose identity if bone fractures are observed. Radiographs (X-rays) may assist in identifying the deceased if corresponding medical records are available. The body is much like a history book, cataloging life's physical traumas. Many people, in the course of life, have had bone fractures, surgery, or herniated discs for which they have sought medical treatment. Many have received dental treatment regularly. Medical and dental records constitute a repository of identifying information waiting to be discovered.

Other physical features may assist in identifying the deceased, such as tattoos, birthmarks, scars, physical deformities, or handicaps. Many citizens have been fingerprinted sometime during their lives. The number includes all those who have served in the military, been arrested, or worked for a government agency. The investigator should obtain a legible and classifiable full set of fingerprints and palm prints to be forwarded to the FBI's identification division.

— Ripped from the Headlines —

Identification of Missing in Action Personnel

Hickam Air Force Base, Hawaii, is home to the Joint POW/MIA Accounting Command (JPAC). According to the JPAC Website, the "mission of the Joint POW/MIA Accounting Command (JPAC) is to achieve the fullest possible accounting of all Americans missing as a result of the nation's past conflicts. The highest priority of the organization is the return of any living Americans that remain prisoners of war." This mission dates back to World War II. While most countries throughout the world bury their war dead where they fall or are found, the United States vows that it will do everything in its power to bring service members remains home (JPAC, 2009).

This promise results in joint-service teams traveling to burial and crash sites around the world. Once teams have recovered remains and they are repatriated within the United States, the command's forensic laboratory attempts to identify them. The laboratory portion of JPAC, referred to as the Central Identification Laboratory (CIL), is the largest forensic anthropology laboratory in the world. The lab consists of state-of-the-art instrumental and analytical techniques to determine identity from the remains. DNA sampling and other cutting edge forensic equipment is advancing JPAC experts' ability to make positive identifications that were once impossible.

According to JPAC, since its inception, on average, JPAC identifies about six MIAs each month. To date, the U.S. government has identified over 1,300 individuals. At any given time, there are more than 1,000 active case files under investigation (JPAC, 2009).

Data from Joint POW/MIA Accounting Command (JPAC), United States Department of Defense. (2009). Mission overview. Retrieved October 2, 2012, from http://www.jpac.pacom.mil/index.php?page=mission_overview

© Shutterstock, Inc./rzarek.

Not all fingerprint searches will be successful; although a sizable portion of Americans has been fingerprinted, the majority has not. For obvious reasons, women are poorly represented in the fingerprint records maintained by the FBI (fewer women than men have been arrested, served in the military, or been in government service).

CONCLUSION

Next to determination of whether a crime has occurred, identification of the perpetrator is of paramount concern. Law enforcement has a myriad of tools available to assist with this task. Fingerprints, DNA, and many other possibilities exist not only to attempt to determine the identity of suspects but also to assist with determination of victims. Lineups and composite drawings have historically been the foundation of offender identification and also responsible for the greatest number of misidentifications. Both depend on eyewitness testimony, which has continued to prove faulty, but they still play an important part in getting information to the investigator.

In every instance in which fingerprints are left at a crime scene, it becomes a game of hide and seek to ferret out where they may have been left. Because most fingerprints are invisible, it becomes important to preserve the entire scene for those with the expertise in locating, developing, photographing, and lifting such prints. It is important to remember that no matter how expert the processing, fingerprints will be destroyed during development and lifting; that is why photographing fingerprints is part of the protocol.

One of the skills every investigator must have is the ability to manage people at a crime scene. It might be said that a crime scene is processed only as well as the investigator in charge can manage people. The next chapter introduces the concept of crime scene management and the ways in which those management skills might be employed.

QUESTIONS FOR REVIEW

1. What is it about fingerprints that suggests individuality?

2. Why is it incorrect to refer to visible fingerprints at a crime scene as latent prints?

3. What are fingerprint patterns, and of what value are they to the criminal investigator?

4. How is a latent print visualized, developed, and lifted?

5. Why is it important to photograph a fingerprint that the investigator plans to lift anyway?

6. What is superglue fuming?

7. For what is ninhydrin spray used?

8. How would you develop fingerprints on the sticky side of duct tape?

9. What is small particle reagent used for?

10. What are iodine crystals used for?

11. What chemical is used to test for blood that luminesces under ultraviolet light?

12. What is a composite picture, and in what ways might an investigator obtain one?

13. What is a suggestive lineup?

14. What is CODIS? Describe the three-tiered identification system.

15. What does ACE-V stand for?

16. What was the cause of the Madrid, Spain, fingerprint misidentification?

17. Is it possible to develop fingerprints from a corpse? If yes, describe the process; if not, why not?

18. Explain how fingerprints corroded in a brass shell casing can be recovered.

REFERENCES

Ancestry. (n.d.). Ancestry Guide for Law Enforcement. Retrieved November 6, 2017, from http://www.ancestry.com/cs/legal/lawenforcement

Bond, J. W. (2009, July). Visualization of latent fingerprint corrosion of brass. *Journal of Forensic Sciences*, 1034–1041.

Coppock, C. A. (2007). *Contrast* (2nd ed.). Springfield, IL: Charles C. Thomas.

Futrell, I. R. (1996). Hidden evidence: Latent print on human skin. *FBI Law Enforcement Bulletin*, April.

Indovina, M., Dvorychenko, V., Tabassi, E., Quinn, G., Grother, P., et al., & National Institute of Standards and Technology (NISTIR). (2009). *An evaluation of automated latent fingerprint identification technologies* (NISTIR 7577). Retrieved August 1, 2009, from http://fingerprint.nist.gov/latent/NISTIR_7577_ELFT_PhaseII.pdf

Innocence Project. (n.d.). http:www.innocenceproject.org/. Retrieved September 1, 2017.

Joint POW/MIA Accounting Command (JPAC), United States Department of Defense. (2009). Mission overview. Retrieved October 2, 2012, from http://www.jpac.pacom.mil/index.php?page=mission_overview

Lerner, E. (2000). Biometric identification. *Industrial Physicist*, 6(1), 18–21.

Maldarelli, C. (2015, October 16). Could having your DNA tested land you in court? *Popular Science*. Retrieved November 7, 2017, from https://www.popsci.com/could-submitting-your-dna-to-private-genetics-companies-land-you-in-court

Saferstein, R. (2014). *Criminalistics: An introduction to forensic science* (11th ed.). Upper Saddle River, NJ: Pearson Prentice Hall.

Wambaugh, J. (1985). *The Blooding*. New York, NY: Bantam.

KEY LEGAL CASE

United States v. Wade, 388 U.S. 218 (1967).

chapter

7 Interviewing and Interrogation

"*How often have I said to you that when you have eliminated the impossible, whatever remains, however improbable, must be the truth?*"

Sherlock Holmes
"The Sign of Four"

KEY TERMS

active listening	cognitive interview	preparation
alternative question	descriptives	Reid technique
confession	follow-up interview	theme
confession law	interrogation	waiver

STUDENT LEARNING OUTCOMES

Upon completion of this chapter, students will be able to:

- Distinguish the difference between an interrogation and an interview
- Explain the cognitive interview
- Discuss the cases leading to *Miranda v. Arizona*
- Employ the Supreme Court's holding in *Miranda v. Arizona*
- Conduct a successful interrogation
- Distinguish between an interview and an interrogation

Introduction

It may be useful to begin this chapter by distinguishing the difference between an interview and an interrogation. An interview conducted by the police remains an interview no matter how aggressively it is conducted. It has been said that the tone and content of an interview may change the nature of the interaction to an interrogation. From a legal perspective, an interview remains an interview until:

1. The focus of the inquiry singles out the suspect from all others AND

2. The suspect is not free to depart.

The second component may not be as apparent as the first. The standard as to whether or not a person is in custody is a subjective one: Would a reasonable person in the same or similar situation believe that his or her freedom to come and go has been circumscribed. In the following section, you will learn that Miranda warnings are required whenever police initiate communication with a person in custody. Therefore, a person subject to an interview who is free to depart is not subject to the Miranda requirements.

The interview is the method whereby information regarding the crime, crime scene, suspect, victim, and witnesses is obtained. It is our most valuable investigative tool. Being able to talk to people and have them talk to us is a skill that, in most instances, requires practice and development. Crimes occur in all communities and learning to communicate with people, even those who would prefer not to speak with us, is difficult, at best.

The Interview

Armed with a wealth of information, the investigator will arrange to interview the victim. It is best to get the victim's statement nailed down before talking to the witnesses. The perspective of the parties is different, and the statements made should reflect those differences. Witness and victim statements that are identical are generally a product of fabrication. No two people experience the same event in the same way, and although the similarities will be greater than the disparities, there should be differences.

Keeping witnesses isolated from one another is an important part of the interview process. If they are allowed to communicate, they will undoubtedly discuss what each has seen, heard, and felt. Unconsciously, the witnesses' perception of the event will change as they seek unanimity in what they have sensed

and experienced. We often corroborate our experiences by comparing them to others who have had similar experiences. Consequently, change is inevitable. That is why it is absolutely imperative to separate witnesses at a crime scene.

The same phenomenon can apply to the victim if given access to friends or relatives. Although they mean to commiserate with the victim, they may unwittingly alter his/her perspective of events and the order in which they occurred. We want the statements of all witnesses in as pristine a condition as they can possibly be had.

Going over the crime a second time with a victim is a tedious process for the victim. In most instances, the victim wants the police to "do something." After the initial report, victims believe that the investigation has begun and progress is being made in capturing the offender. Having to go over the confrontation a second time is not exactly what they have in mind. Often, a few days have passed, the original trauma has dissipated, and they would rather not revisit the offense. It is important to assure them that the follow-up visit is an integral part of every investigation and that only by speaking to those involved can the investigator develop an appreciation for the dynamics of the people, places, and crime. The **follow-up interview** allows for quiet retrospection and an opportunity to consider the event from some distance. It allows us to review the facts, compare them with the original statement, ferret out fabrications and exaggerations, and perhaps discover something that was left out of the original interview.

Preliminary statements are made under the influence of the offense that is still fresh and can be painful. The initial statements may have greater detail than the follow-up interviews. The lapse in time and the reduced chemistry provides for a more relaxed statement that may be in a different order than the original statement and may be missing events, times, and dates. All of this should be expected and is not necessarily indicative of lies but is more than likely a product of the victim's efforts to forget about the incident and not dwell on the particulars. The interview with the victim should be recorded and transcribed. The transcribed interview should be compared with the preliminary statement for any inconsistencies.

After the interview with the victim, the investigator should run a records check on the victim, witnesses, and suspect(s). A records check can give the investigator insight and leverage in dealing with those who have information about the crime under investigation. An understanding

follow-up interview
Allows for quiet retrospection and an opportunity to consider the event from some distance. It allows a review of the facts, and a comparison to the original statement, to ferret out fabrications and exaggerations and perhaps discover something that was left out of the original interview

of the time of day, the weather, lighting conditions, and noise and traffic levels may all provide insight into the position and vantage point of witnesses and the reliability of the information they might provide. Once background information about each witness has been gathered and all witness statements have been read and noted, it is time to interview the witnesses.

Before interviewing witnesses, it is a best practice to talk with the first-responding officer, as this can provide clarity and continuity. The information gathered from that officer may not be entirely reflected in the initial reports. First-responding officer impressions of the crime scene, witnesses, and suspects can provide a fresh perspective to the flatly described information in the various statements filed.

Witnesses can be invited to the police department, placed in an interview room, and interviewed by the investigator (**FIGURE 7.1**). Often, the most expedient approach is to interview the witness at a location that is likely to allow uninterrupted discourse. Sometimes, the turmoil in a household makes it impossible to carry on a discussion. Interview rooms provide privacy, but they do not provide warmth or comfort. Witnesses may respond hostilely to being required to travel to the police department. Using interview rooms should be the exception rather than the rule. The best use of witnesses is to have them describe what they saw or heard from the vantage point of where they saw and heard it. There is no other way to obtain a real-world perspective of what and how the witness saw or heard what they say they have.

If a witness's statement is worthy of preservation, it should be preserved in three ways:

- Audio recording
- Video recording
- Written statement

FIGURE 7.1: Interview occurring at police department.
© Mikael Karlsson/Alamy Stock Photo.

The audio record is to preserve the tone and tenor of the interview to avoid any allegations of coercion or coaching. Most witnesses will agree to allow their statements to be recorded.

Most agencies have interview forms that assist the investigator in gathering information. They may differ in style and length, but most have the same substantive content. Victim interview forms usually contain provisions for:

- Name, address, and phone number of the victim
- Time and date of the offense
- A multiple-choice offender descriptive section, which includes:
  - Height
  - Weight
  - Age
  - Hair color
  - Eye color
  - Build
  - Clothing description
- A multiple-choice vehicle descriptive section
- A multiple-choice lighting descriptive section
- Name, address, and phone number of any known witnesses
- A multiple-choice location descriptive section, which includes:
  - City
  - Country
  - Building proximity
  - Roadway description
  - Business proximity
- A large section for a handwritten victim narrative

The witness narrative is labeled with the date and time of the statement. Once the statement is complete, the victim is asked to read it over, making any necessary changes. All changes should be initialed by the person making the statement. The investigator reads the statement and asks questions about parts of the statement that need to be fleshed out. The additions are placed at the end of the original statement or in a supplemental statement. All additions are also initialed. The initialing serves an important purpose. It defuses any contentions by a defense lawyer that the statement was written by the police and never read by the victim.

Interview Techniques

When considering the array of skills evident in good interviewers, a short list seems to cover them. They have the ability to:

- Plan and prepare the interview
- Establish rapport with the subject of the interview
- Listen actively (to what is said, how it is said, to what is not said and accompanying body language)
- Ask leading questions
- Be patient (let the subject get to the heart of the matter in their own time)

■ Planning and Preparing the Interview

Studies have shown that officers often make interruptions during the course of the interview with little concern for the impact that the interruption may have on the subject's narrative. Any pauses or interruptions by the persons conducting the interview should not be random but calculated for specific impact. Some reasons for a calculated interruption might include:

- A break to relieve the emotional context of the subject matter
- An opportunity to bring the interview back on course if it has strayed too far
- A pause to suggest that what has just been said is not consistent with the evidence or prior statements

All other interruptions should be avoided.

■ Establish Rapport

No matter the nature of the crime or the heinousness of the offense, people know when the person with whom they are speaking likes them. Children are especially intuitive and will not respond to someone with whom they are not comfortable. The ultimate objective of every interview is to gather as many facts pertaining to the offense being investigated. However, immediate fact finding is often threatening to the subject of the interview, especially to victims of violent crimes. Everyone likes to talk about themselves; no matter how irrelevant background information may seem, in interviews, as in interrogations, once the subject begins to speak, he or she is inclined to continue. By allowing him or her to continue, that

person begins to believe that you see him or her as someone worth listening to (have value) and that person will begin to trust you. So, get the person to talk, let him or her talk and once he or she seems comfortable, ease him or her into the discussion that you want to have.

■ Active Listening

During normal discourse, it is not necessary to attend to the complete discussion. We usually understand what is being conveyed after a few words and we then begin to fashion a response, we add to it and subtract from it as we tune in and out what is being said, and then simply wait for a lull in the conversation to interject a thought. The closest we come to **active listening** is when we are lost and our auto global positioning system (GPS) is giving instructions to get us back on track. Listening hard and listening to everything that is said is the first part of active listening. In investigative active listening, we not only listen to what is said, we listen to:

- How it is said
- What is not said
- The body language and posture accompanying the communication

Active listening does not come easily and requires both mental and physical concentration. Hostage negotiators actively listen to the things listed above and also to all of the background noises and conversations as well as input from their listening mental health professional and backup negotiator. Their listening or lack thereof can result in the loss of lives. It is not unusual to see them soaked in sweat in air conditioned command centers. Active listening does not come easily.

■ Asking Leading Questions

The same studies that showed officers interrupting subjects during interviews also reported that officers often used too many short-answer questions. Questions that can be answered with a simple yes or no should be avoided once the substance of the interview has been reached. A certain amount of background information may need to be gathered and can best be accomplished by specific questions seeking specifically short answers but once recall of the event begins, every opportunity should be given the subject to couch the narrative in the way that is most comfortable to him or her.

■ Patience

There are different personality types that gravitate toward varying types of work. Those

active listening
Listening not only to what is said, but what is not said, how it is said and observing the body language associated therewith

individuals who like activity and find it difficult to be quiet and contemplative do not make good interviewers or good interrogators. Conducting interviews that must be completed in a particular time frame are seldom successful and interviewers who are more concerned with the approach of quitting time will not gather all of the information that is potentially available. Being patient is much like active listening in that not everyone is comfortable or competent in doing it. There is no doubt that we all can learn to be more patient and better active listeners but it is also apparent that some people excel at both. Interviews are an energy exchange between subject and interviewer. Whatever behavior the interviewer brings into the interview will most likely be mirrored by the subject. An anxious subject will not become less anxious simply by telling him/her that there is no need to be anxious, but may well become less anxious in the hands of a patient and active listening interviewer.

Patience is crucial in dealing with children and victims of violent crimes. These people generally need to be given the opportunity to "vent." They may talk about things that are unrelated or manifest anger and/or fear. Only through patience and rapport will the interviewer get them to discuss the material germane to the investigation.

Patience is not just waiting. Patience is empathy and, when necessary, sympathy. People, especially children, can tell when people like them.

■ The Cognitive Interview

One interview technique that has promise for police investigators is the **cognitive interview**, which incorporates all of the things discussed to this point and organizes them in a recommended approach to conducting an investigative interview.

Step:

1. Greet the subject and make him or her comfortable. Personalize the situation by making it apparent that the interview is about the subject, not the crime or the perpetrator.

2. Explain what the interviewer is attempting to accomplish and solicit the subject's help in accomplishing it.

3. Insure that the statement is voluntary and not the product of efforts to please the interviewer:

   a. Ask open-ended questions

   b. Use pauses to allow the subject respite from the inquiry and relief from the intensity of the interview

cognitive interview
an organized approach to an interview conducted through a psychological perspective

c. Make sure that all nonverbal behavior of the interviewer is open and encouraging

4. Ask questions that require the subject to tell the story in reverse order (easier to detect fabrications when trying to recall untrue facts backwards)

5. Vary the method and style of questions

6. Have the subject place him- or herself, mentally, in the environment in which he or she saw what he or she saw or heard what he or she heard (ask the person to describe the environment and those in it)

7. Summarize the interview and ask for corroboration, correction, or elaboration

8. Close the interview, allowing the subject to believe that he or she has been helpful (Fisher & McCauley, 2013)

Victim Interviews

In preparing for a victim interview, the investigator must factor into the equation the emotional state of the victim. The preparation should include any and all information gathered by the officers who were first on the scene. Their written reports may give some insight into the nature of the crime, the background of the crime, and the emotional condition of the victim. It would be a mistake to rely solely on the written information. A person-to-person conversation with the responding officers could prove useful. It is a wise investigator who checks the criminal history of victims and all other sources of information to assess the credibility of the information about to be received.

The first meeting with the witness can be fruitful or disastrous, depending on the effort that the investigator has put into preparing for the interview. The nature of the offense can tell a great deal about the likely mental state of the victim. When dealing with property crimes, an investigator can generally expect to find a very angry victim. The frustration that the victim has experienced in attempting to protect his or her property and in attempting to understand how this could have happened to him or her often manifests as anger. The perpetrator is unavailable as a subject on which to vent hostility, so it often falls to the investigator to field the victim's anger. This is not an easy thing to do, but a sympathetic, patient, and non-accusatory demeanor can go a long way toward defusing the anger and establishing rapport.

It is impossible to be irrational and rational simultaneously. Thus, an effective approach in dealing with emotionally distraught people is to ask questions that require processing of information rather than simple, automatic responses. Focusing questions away from the victim and the offense will require the victim to focus on providing factual information. The first question or questions may be ignored, but continued efforts to elicit factual information will likely be successful.

Crimes against a person usually result in a broader range of emotions, some of which may be hard to defuse. Sexual assault victims, assault victims, and relatives of homicide victims have an array of responses that may require professional help to sort out; sometimes, only time can begin to heal the emotional wounds that the victim suffered. It takes an experienced investigator to know when to push and when to allow time to do its healing. If the victim needs professional help, the investigator may be most successful in gathering information by recognizing this fact and by giving the victim the names of resources that can provide that help.

Interviewing Reluctant Witnesses

People are reluctant to talk to the police for a variety of reasons: prior experience with the police, culturally influenced views regarding the police and cooperation with the police, fear of the police or of those who may be pursued by the police, language barriers, or alignment with the criminal element in the community. When encountering a reluctant witness, the investigator must attempt to discover the basis for the reluctance and determine what approach, if any, might mitigate the underlying reasons for the lack of cooperation.

Most commonly, people simply prefer not to get involved. Giving information to the police, although only minimally disruptive to their routines, may eventually result in injury to them or to family members. Pleas for help that focus on the civic responsibility of citizens may be useful. An explanation of the importance of cooperating may ring true. One might suggest that if the witness were the victim, he or she would want others to assist in the apprehension of the offender. It is generally a bad ploy to try to intimidate a person into cooperation. This tactic will usually result in more antagonism and perhaps escalate into an unnecessary confrontation.

The victim of certain types of crimes may be reluctant to cooperate with the police. The elderly, who do not wish to appear senile or naïve, may disguise their concerns with ambivalence or lack of cooperation. Assurance that the type of victimization to which they fell prey is not at all unusual or a reflection on them or their age may open closed doors. A female rape victim may harbor resentment toward men generally as a result of her experience and may flatly refuse to talk to male police and investigators. A male officer may arrange for the assistance of a female officer and thus provide the victim with a listener with whom she is comfortable. Before presuming that a female rape victim is uncooperative, a male investigator might ask if she would prefer to talk to a female officer or a doctor. Should she request a physician, the male investigator should spend some time with the interviewer beforehand, discussing the types of information the investigator would like to

INVESTIGATOR'S NOTEBOOK

Examples of Data Processing Questions

The following are typical data processing questions:

- Do you live here alone? What is your home phone number? What is your work number? Who else lives with you? How long have you lived here? Where did you live prior to this location? Who are the members of your family? What are their names?

- Are you employed? Who is your employer? How long have you worked there? What do you do there? Is any special training required to do your job?

- Do you know your neighbors? Are they home? Do you know their names and telephone numbers?

It is difficult to answer such questions appropriately (i.e., by providing the right kind of information) and to be hysterical simultaneously. Perseverance may be necessary for many victims, but once the bridge has been crossed, the anger level should be reduced to levels that will allow offense-specific questions to be asked.

obtain. If she requests a female officer, the male officer should inform the interviewer about the crime. When dealing with any witness who is highly emotional, the investigator should gather the information carefully and with sensitivity and treat it skeptically. All information should be documented and corroborated later through a follow-up interview.

Interviewing Children

Children are notorious for telling investigators more than they want to know. No matter what age a child witness is, the investigator must be an active listener—not someone who is merely asking specific questions and wants only specific answers, but someone who is genuinely interested in the child and what the child has to say. In addition, the interview should be conducted in a place that provides the child with a sense of comfort, familiarity, and security. It is best to have a parent in attendance during the interview, and many states have statutes that require a parent to be in attendance throughout the interview. Preschool children have difficulty thinking in measured units, be they units of time, weight, or distance. They often talk with a free flow of consciousness and touch on material that ranges far and wide from the matter under investigation. An investigator needs to exhibit great patience and care in managing the course of the interview. Patience and an appreciation of children are the basic prerequisites for interviewing children; the rest can be learned.

Children process information differently than do adults. They think in concrete rather than abstract terms, they do not organize their thoughts, and their narratives wander. Also, they may not understand why lying is bad or why the truth is important. A child's world revolves around him- or herself; thus, the more the questions that pertain to the child, the more information will be provided. Keep in mind also that children have a limited attention span (it lengthens with age). Questions should be kept short and the questioning period brief. If necessary, conduct the interview in sessions. Finally, children know when interviewers like them and are comfortable with them. If an interviewer is not comfortable, the child will not be comfortable.

Investigators who conduct interviews with children should understand the basics of how a child's memory works, which is different from that of adults. Memory-associated development occurs over time and includes attention, language, conversational tracking, scripting, and source monitoring (Mallon & Hess, 2014).

Because perception relies on attention, attention plays a large part in governing what aspects of an event a child will remember, what parts of an interview he or she will understand, and to which questions a child will respond. Attention is affected not only by brain development but also by a child's interest in and familiarity with a task, which affect the amount and duration of attention they give to it (Reisberg, 2001). Interviewers should not only seek to eliminate distractions (such as toys and clutter) when talking to children, but should also make sure that the child is familiar with and understands the purpose and form of the interview.

A child's verbal repertoire has a huge impact on conversational ability. The more words a child knows, the more options the interviewer has in forming questions and the more options the child has in crafting responses. Crafting questions in language that a child of a particular age and developmental stage can comprehend is a skill unto itself. The ability to remember and report is linked to the ability to speak. The younger the child, the more limited the vocabulary, which results in very limited communication and very limited response and imagery (Howe, Goodman, & Cicchetti, 2008).

Many researchers who have studied children's autobiographical accounts comment on how difficult it can be to get children to talk about the desired subject in response to open-ended questions. Although it is recognized that open-ended questions are a more reliable interviewing technique that provides less suggestibility for generating a particular answer, it may be an exercise in futility in getting a child to respond to such questions and, if responding, to respond to the specific topic of interest to the interviewer. Children may need a prompt to initiate focus on the subject. The question "What happened today?" may not precipitate a response or may precipitate a response irrelevant to the subject of interest. Achieving relevance may require mild prompting, such as, "What happened at school during spelling today?" Such prompting questions should only be used to begin the conversation; open-ended questions are the method of choice once the child begins to respond (Poole & Lindsay, 2001). A child may not be able to maintain focus on the subject of the inquiry and may drift to other, more interesting topics. If the interviewer does not recognize topic drift when it happens, there is a great opportunity for misunderstanding or misinterpretation of a child's responses (Poole & Lindsay, 2001).

INVESTIGATOR'S
NOTEBOOK

© Shutterstock, Inc./Janaka Dharmasena.

Tips for Interviewing Children

It is important that a child be given an explanation for the interview as well as certain ground rules. A child witness should be told the following:

- Who is going to conduct the interview

- What is going to be sought

- Why it is being sought

- Why it may be necessary to tell the story more than once (to police, psychologists, social workers, investigators, and so on)

- What happens with the information gathered

- What more may be expected of the child

- That police, investigators, prosecutors, and judges are there to protect the child

The interviewer should select his or her words carefully, with an emphasis on clarity and understandability. The interview should begin with questions the child can answer easily and successfully and progress to the more nebulous queries only after the child has been put at his or her ease.

- Conduct the interview in an environment that is comfortable for the child being interviewed

- Establish rapport. Allow a brief period of introduction.

- Pay attention—both to what is being said and what is not

- Listen actively

- Do not interrupt

- Allow a free flow of information, even if the information is irrelevant

- Encourage narrative responses

- Ask open-ended questions

- Give the impression that time is not of the essence

- Be patient

- Be courteous

- Be professional

© Shutterstock, Inc./Nutink.

A script is an understanding of what is supposed to happen based on what has happened in the past. It provides some security, in that for much of what we encounter on a daily basis, we either have encountered it before or have encountered something similar enough to allow us to fashion a generalized workable response. Scripts reduce the effort needed to get through routine events. Schemata can produce automatic expectations of what will happen in a familiar context; therefore, when actual events contradict expectations, scripts can also cause inaccurate reconstructive recollection of events (Principie, Ceci, & Bruck, 2010).

Children who are interviewed multiple times may develop scripts about the subject matter of the interviews even if they had no actual experience with the event in question. If children are exposed repeatedly to suggestive information about the investigation during interviews or conversations with family or others, their developing scripts may cause them to give progressively more complete and believable testimony about an event they may not have experienced (Principie et al., 2010). The effects of scripting make it crucial that interviewers resist conducting suggestive and repetitive interviews and learn to gather the information they need in as few

— Ripped from the Headlines —

Asking the Hard Questions

The Dr. Bill Lewis Center for Children is a neutral, welcoming, non-threatening location where child victims of abuse can be forensically interviewed about their abuse. Children arrive with their parents or guardian, after having been referred to the center by law enforcement, social services, medical personnel, or others. "The idea of a Child Advocacy Center (CAC) is to minimize the number of times we interview the child, and to only have that child interviewed one time. This eliminates the need for children to be interviewed by several agencies, investigators or individuals, which can be especially traumatizing to the individual.

"After an alleged assault, the child and his or her parents or guardian will enter through the front, while other agency representatives enter through the rear door of the building. Together, they sit at a large table in a "team room" as they watch and listen to the interview on a closed-circuit television. In case there are any specific questions, each representative is able to communicate with the interviewer, who wears an earpiece.

The forensic interviewers that are employed by the CAC are well-trained and are dedicated to maintaining their neutrality as to the investigation and legal proceedings. It is not a job for everyone. "A lot of people say there's no way I could listen to that," says Fox, who says she has interviewed children who have witnessed homicides or have been physically abused.

"I've seen the marks, and I see the fear in the child, because that child truly is traumatized because they were hurt and they were afraid. That makes it difficult for me. When I see fear or shame in a child, that's what bothers me. ...

"What gets me through the interview is I know that there is a police officer with a gun in the other room, and a prosecutor that, when I walk out, they're going to go get 'em, and I had a part of that. I don't want to affect or to hurt that investigation in any possible way because I don't want to see somebody walk because of us not doing our job correctly."

Data from Warden, S. (2017). Asking the hard questions. *The Journal Gazette*. Retrieved July 9, 2017, from www.journalgazette.net/features/20170709/asking-the-hard-questions

interviews with as few questions and prompts as possible.

The boundaries between a child's concept of reality and fantasy are not rigidly defined. For instance, children may believe that something pretend can become real, so it is difficult for them to decide with certainty whether an event was real or imagined (Principie et al., 2010). Identifying the source of memories for real events is challenging, but is a necessary component of nonsuggestive interviewing.

One source-monitoring task that is particularly difficult for children is discriminating between information they received through their own experience and that received through other sources. Source-monitoring skills have major implications for interviewing children. To give accurate testimony, children need to be able to distinguish whether they or someone else really did something or just pretended and whether their information about it comes from their experience or from a conversation or other source. Interviewers need to keep their questions grounded in reality and to question sources of information whenever possible. The first step in source monitoring is to interview

those who have interacted with the child prior to and in anticipation of the interview. From medical personnel to teachers and parents, it is important to learn what such sources know and what and how they are related to the child (Poole & Lindsay, 2001).

No two child witnesses will respond the same way to interviewers or interview techniques. Police interviewers must appreciate the typical developmental cognitive skills of each child witness to better determine how to interview a particular child. Along with that information, they should develop an instinct for the potential hazards that can befall the unsuspecting interviewer.

There are many ways in which interviewing procedures can be suggestive. Through word choice, praise and punishment, and disproportionately attending to some information, interviewers can have a significant effect on the responses they get from children they interview. Interviewers' choices of words can reveal important information and assumptions even in questions that sound ordinary. Poole and Lindsay (2001) recommend that interviewers use neutral language and avoid words such as "abuse," "bad," and "hurt" when investigating allegations of abuse.

Another common form of suggestion or leading in interviews comes from the attention that interviewers pay to or withdraw from certain topics. When children say something inconsistent with the interviewer's hypothesis or bias, it frequently gets ignored. The method of attending, ignoring, rewarding, and punishing can heavily sway children's testimony. Interviewers should practice reinforcing children for any information they give, including saying, "I don't know" (Poole & Lindsay, 2001). Also, interviewers should think through their assumptions about a case and challenge them so that they will be more likely to entertain multiple hypotheses and conduct non-leading interviews. Time considerations are also a potential hazard. The longer a child has to wait between witnessing an event and being interviewed about it, the less complete and accurate his or her report will be (Poole & Lindsay, 2001).

Although children may need direct prompts to begin speaking about an event, it is best to use open-ended lines of questioning whenever possible. Interviewers often have suspicions about the event they are asking a child about and intentionally or unintentionally ask close-ended questions that guide the child to confirm their suspicions. Interviewers should orient children to the topic of the interview, using specific prompts if needed. They should also check periodically to confirm that the child is still on topic and that his or her responses pertain to the event in question (Poole & Lindsay, 2001). Beyond any directive questions or prompts needed to orient children to the topic at hand, interviewers should rely on open-ended questions (Ceci & Bruck, 1995).

Avoid repeated questions and interviews. Children involved in investigative interviews often undergo 6 to 12 or more official interviews during the course of an investigation. Children can develop a script for an event they may not have experienced just by undergoing a series of interviews about it. Furthermore, repeated closed and specific questions often lead children to change their answers. Social rules about conversation dictate that when someone asks you a question a second time, it is generally because you failed to answer it satisfactorily the first time. Children may not understand that, in some contexts, a question is repeated to generate more information, not to encourage recantation of the original answer (Poole & Lindsay, 2001).

It is not hard to imagine that after multiple interviews, children's testimony could be contaminated easily, even though it may not be possible to gather all the information available in only one interview. If numerous interviews are necessary, it is critical that interviewers use non-leading and open-ended questions and limit the number of interviews as much as possible.

In addition to the interviews to which children may be subjected, they may also talk with their parents, friends, and teachers about the event or the interview. Suggestion, leading questions, and misinformation can come from sources other than the investigator's interview. It is important for the interviewer to return to the source of the answers being offered by the child. It might prove useful to begin with questioning the child about what he or she has been told about the event in discussions with parents, friends, teachers, and so forth. Once it has been determined that other sources may have shaped the child's perspective, it helps to query the child often as to the source of the information; for example, "Is that what your mom told you?"

The Interrogation

One of the most effective tools in law enforcement is a **confession**. A confession that is properly obtained provides the prosecution the leverage to obtain a guilty plea saving time and resources. The impact of this type of evidence is one of the reasons that the U.S. Supreme Court promulgated guidelines for law enforcement agents eliciting confessions. Confessions are obtained through **interrogations**.

This is when a criminal investigator demonstrates his or her real skill as an investigator. The best-planned interrogations, like the best-planned trials, often go awry. It is when an interrogation does go awry that a novice interrogator begins to understand what the interrogation process really is.

Preplanned opening moves may serve well with new offenders or in establishing rapport with career criminals, but the preparation for the interrogation is what carries an investigator beyond the opening. An investigator's familiarity with the crime, the modus operandi of the crime, the suspect, the evidence to date, and the crime scene determines whether he or she can make it to the end game when playing against a seasoned, hostile, or psychopathic offender. Seasoned offenders and psychopaths often enjoy doing battle with police, whom they believe to be intellectually inferior. Too often, the interrogator's lack of preparation proves them correct (Gilbert, 2010).

Interrogations usually take place at the police station, in a sparsely furnished room with

confession
A statement acknowledging personal responsibility for a crime, including details only the guilty person would know

interrogation
The formal questioning of a suspect conducted in a controlled environment and performed in an accusatory manner in order to learn the truth

no windows or distractions. This Spartan environment is designed to disarm the suspect and place him or her at a disadvantage. Separation from the things he or she is familiar with can be traumatic for the uninitiated. For the experienced offender, it is just one more in a long series of places he or she would rather not be.

Interrogative technique is unique to the interrogator. Successful interrogators, however, tend to:

- Show respect for the suspect's constitutional rights
- Show respect for the dignity of the worst among us
- Possess an understanding of human and conversational dynamics
- Maintain control over passions and prejudice
- Exhibit confidence and professionalism
- Exhibit self-respect as well as respect for the law and the criminal justice system

The interrogation environment created by police is inherently intimidating. The Supreme Court has been concerned with the intimidating aspects of interrogation in determining whether confessions obtained by investigators are voluntary. One case demonstrates the Court's concern and establishes guidelines for ensuring that statements obtained from suspects are voluntary and not a product of coercion.

Massiah v. United States (1964) added to our understanding of the when and where the Sixth Amendment right to counsel attaches. Prior to Massiah, the prevailing procedure was that individuals were entitled to counsel once the trial and pre-trial processes began. In *Massiah* the Court recognized that once having been indicted and having retained counsel, no further communications could be had with the suspect without the presence of counsel. It took the *Massiah* case to carry the Sixth Amendment from the courtroom to the police station.

Recognizing the intimidating nature of the interrogation the Court in *Miranda v. Arizona* (1966) proscribed safeguards to assure that any statement made while in custody would be of the suspect's free will. The two elements giving rise to the need for Miranda warnings are *custody* and *interrogation*. The absence of either removes the need to provide such warnings. There are a number of cases of which every investigator should be aware. These cases, briefly described here, define the boundaries of interrogation and the types of situations in which Miranda warnings are not required.

- *Frazier v. Cupp*, 394 U.S. 731, (1969). Telling a co-conspirator that his accomplice has already confessed thereby obtaining the suspects confession does not render the statement inadmissible.

- *New York v. Quarles*, 467 U.S. 649 (1987). Public safety concerns exempt police from having to provide Miranda warnings. A response to an inquiry about the location of an abandoned weapon may be incriminatory, but it also serves the public interest because it pertains to safety; therefore, it does not raise the need for Miranda warnings.

- *McNeil v. Wisconsin*, 501 U.S. 171 (1990). A suspect's invocation of the Fifth Amendment right to remain silent with regard to a particular offense does not constitute an invocation for other offenses for which the suspect has not yet been charged. The invocation of the Fifth Amendment right to remain silent prohibits police from inquiring into any aspects of the offense in question, but they may initiate further interrogation about unrelated offenses until the right to remain silent is again invoked. The invocation of the Fifth Amendment right against self-incrimination is specific to an offense.

- *Oregon v. Elstad*, 470 U.S. 298 (1985). Miranda warnings may "cure" a previously voluntarily provided unwarned confession if the warnings are provided prior to the elicitation of a subsequent statement.

- *Connecticut v. Barrett*, 479 U.S. 523 (1987). A suspect who has refused to give a written confession may still be urged to provide an oral confession as long as he or she has not invoked the right to remain silent.

- *Duckworth v. Eagan*, 492 U.S. 195 (1989). The Miranda warnings need not be given exactly as suggested by the Supreme Court or as written in police procedural manuals as long as they convey to the suspect his or her Fifth and Sixth Amendment rights.

- *Pennsylvania v. Muniz*, 496 U.S. 582 (1990). Because the Fifth Amendment provides testimonial protection—that is, protection regarding a person's testimony—behavior and communications designed to gather non-evidentiary information are not covered. Driving while intoxicated (DWI) roadblocks typically involve routine questioning of a stopped motorist. The questions may elicit responses that eventually prove incriminating, but they are designed to gather routine information. Answering such questions is not considered to be self-incriminatory and therefore is not protected by the Constitution. Should videotape recordings of responses to these routine questions be made, they too are constitutionally permissible.

- *Davis v. United States*, 114 S.Ct. 2350 (1994). After a suspect voluntarily waives his or her rights as described in *Miranda*, investigators may continue the interrogation until the accused affirmatively asserts his or her rights.

- *Brewer v. Williams*, 430 U.S. 387 (1977). Interrogations may be direct or indirect, explicit or implicit. An investigator cannot attempt to accomplish indirectly what he or she cannot accomplish directly. In *Brewer*, a conversation between officers in a police vehicle was intended to and did elicit an incriminating statement from the suspect in the backseat. The court held that the statement was the functional equivalent of a confession because of the officers' knowledge of the suspect's sensitivity toward religious issues; absent his lawyer, the subject's statement was inadmissible.

- *Arizona v. Mauro*, 481 U.S. (1987). Recorded self-incriminatory conversations between two persons, one of whom gives consent for the recording, do not rise to the level of an interrogation and do not require Miranda warnings.

- *Texas v. Cobb*, 532 U.S. 162 (2001). A suspect's invocation of the Sixth Amendment right to counsel with regard to a particular offense does not constitute an invocation for other offenses for which the suspect has not yet been charged. The invocation of the Sixth Amendment right to counsel prohibits police from inquiring into any aspects of the offense in question, but they may initiate further interrogation about unrelated offenses until the right to counsel is again invoked. The invocation applies to the offense in question and any factually related offenses.

- *United States v. Patane*, 542 U.S. 630 (2004). Evidence discovered as the result of a voluntary but unwarned statement is admissible.

- *Missouri v. Seibert*, 542 U.S. 600 (2004). Securing an inadmissible unwarned confession then providing Miranda Warnings and obtaining a second confession does not break the taint from the original statement unless sufficient time has transpired to assure the second statement is a new and voluntary statement made without the influence of the prior confession.

- *Berghuis v. Thompkins*, 560 U.S. 370 (2011). Police may interrogate a suspect who has neither invoked nor waived his or her Miranda rights.

It is not unusual for the defense attorney, during trial, to request the testifying officer to recite the Miranda warnings to the jury just as they were provided to the defendant the night in question. The best practice is to read the warnings from a card. The defense attorney may ask whether the reason it is necessary to read them is because of the officer's inability to recall them, or the attorney may request to see the card (which he or she is entitled to do) and then ask the witness to recite the warnings. The reason for reading the warnings is simply to ensure that no misunderstanding occurs as the result of a possible misstatement of the warnings. In response to the request to recite the warnings without benefit of the card, the witness should state that it would not be his common practice or departmental policy and explain why if given the opportunity.

To see the problem, consider the following version of the warnings:

> *You have the right to remain silent. Anything you say may be used against you in a court of law. You have the right to consult an attorney before speaking to the police and to have an attorney present during questioning now or in the future. If you cannot afford a lawyer, one will be appointed for you before any questioning if you wish. If you decide to answer questions now without a lawyer present you will still have the right to stop answering until you talk to an attorney. Knowing and understanding your rights as I have explained them to you, are you willing to answer my questions without an attorney present?*

If you recognized that the word "may" in the second sentence could be problematic, you are right. The word "may" suggests an alternative and constitutes a hint of impermissible coercion through unauthorized bargaining. The defense would make the most of it by intimating that if this error were made, many other serious errors might have been at the time the warning were given before the beginning of the interrogation. It is prudent to read Miranda warnings both on the street and in the courtroom. Those who do read the warnings will not risk falling victim to a skillful cross-examiner.

INVESTIGATOR'S NOTEBOOK

Miranda Warnings

You have the right to remain silent.

Anything you say can be used against you in a court of law.

You have the right to consult an attorney before speaking to the police and to have an attorney present during questioning now or in the future.

If you cannot afford a lawyer, one will be appointed for you before any questioning if you wish.

If you decide to answer questions now without a lawyer present you will still have the right to stop answering until you talk to an attorney.

Knowing and understanding your rights as I have explained them to you, are you willing to answer my questions without an attorney present?

INVESTIGATOR'S NOTEBOOK

Interrogation Tips

- Pick the time—to suit the investigator.
- Pick the place—to isolate the person being interrogated.
- Provide Miranda warnings, even if they have been provided in the past.
- Maintain eye contact. The eyes are the "windows to the soul," and penetrating eye contact is disconcerting to the guilty.
- Record the interrogation, including the Miranda warnings.
- Transcribe the interrogation and have the person interrogated sign the transcription, making any corrections he or she feels necessary.
- Treat the person being interrogated with respect and dignity.
- Be patient.
- Be professional.
- Be honest.
- Do not play games.
- Do not deprive the person being interrogated of sleep, food, cigarettes, or the use of toilet facilities.
- Do not say or do anything you would not want a jury to hear.
- BE PREPARED

Successful Interrogations

A successful interrogation results in the guilty criminal suspect making a confession or admitting participation in an illegal activity - voluntarily. Often, guilty suspects leave the interrogation room without making an admission. Interrogations can fail for many reasons. Some are foreseeable. Once investigators have identified these factors, they can consider and act upon them to increase the probability of successful outcomes.

Certain components are crucial to every successful interrogation. These major components are:

- Preparing for the interrogation
- Distinguishing between interrogations and interviews

- Developing persuasive themes and arguments
- Establishing a set plan
- Building a good relationship with the interrogation subject
- Allowing enough time for the interrogation

Preparing for the Interrogation

Preparation is the most important factor in conducting a successful interrogation. Factors to consider when preparing interrogations include:

- The setting and environmental considerations
- Knowledge of case facts
  - Familiarity with the evidence
  - Familiarity with the crime scene
- Knowledge of the subject's background (including criminal history)
- The method used to document the confession

■ Setting and Environmental Factors

Successful interrogations require that interrogators, not subjects, control not only the topics of discussion but also the physical environment. Officers should conduct interrogations only when they can ensure privacy and control of the environment. A good setting is a small, controlled, sound-insulated room void of distractions (**FIGURE 7.2**). A setting free from diversions forces the subject to respond only to the interrogator's inquiries. It also gives investigators a much better opportunity to observe the subject's verbal and nonverbal responses to the questions. The further the situation gets from a controlled setting, the higher the chance that the interrogation will fail. Often, only one

FIGURE 7.2: A controlled environment for an interrogation.
Courtesy of the Law Enforcement Resource Center.

good interrogation opportunity exists. Risking that opportunity in an unacceptable environment may be a poor investigative decision (Wolf, Mesloh & Wood, 2013).

■ Knowledge of Case Facts

Understanding case facts remains critical to any interrogation, but some facts may prove more important than others. Knowing how a crime occurred can be an effective tool of persuasion. If investigators can tell a suspect how a crime was committed, the suspect may give the reasons for his or her involvement in the incident. Often the understanding of every aspect of the crime and the evidence may convince the suspect that the interrogator knows more than s/he actually does. Keep in mind that the suspect's guilt will lead them to presume the worse. Examining the evidence gathered in the case and all documentation accompanying the evidence is crucial. It is imperative to have visited the crime scene whenever possible. Only by mastering the available information can the suspect be convinced that the interrogator knows as much about the crime as the person who committed it allowing a guilty imagination to work in the interrogator's favor.

■ Familiarity with the Subject's Background

Acquiring adequate background information about a suspect is another critical factor in achieving a successful outcome. A subject's feelings, attitudes, and personal values directly affect the nature and outcome of an interrogation. Individuals often make the choice to confess based on their emotions, and then defend their positions or choices with logic. When interrogators understand a suspect's goals, needs, and conflicts, they can use this information to persuade a suspect that confessing the truth is in the suspect's best interest (Moak & Carlson, 2015). At some point during the interrogation the good interrogator is going to interject an option that appears less egregious to the suspect. This alternative explanation will allow the suspect to see the crime as less serious or his/her motives more justified. Having information about the suspect insures that this option is couched in the most favorable terms.

■ Documenting Confessions

Investigators should plan the details of documenting the confession before beginning the interrogation. Best practice for interrogation is for all interactions with a suspect to be recorded with sound and video. Any allegations of coercion or overreaching can best be rebutted

<aside>
preparation
The most important factor in conducting a successful interrogation; it involves considering the setting and environment, knowing the case facts, being familiar with the subject's background, and determining the method used to document the confession
</aside>

INVESTIGATOR'S NOTEBOOK
Elements of a Plan for Documenting a Confession

- Who will obtain the waiver of rights?
  - Get the waiver in writing.
- Will the confession be a stenographic recording?
- Will the suspect write out the statement?
- Will the statement be recorded with audio/video?
  - Obtaining both a videoed oral and written confession are the best options.
- Who will witness the statement?
- Will the statement be a narrative or in question-and-answer format?

by providing a complete video recording of what transpired before, during, and after a suspect made an incriminating statement. Additionally, a verbatim transcript of the entire interrogation should be made—not a transcript of only the incriminating statement but of every word that transpired between interrogators and the suspect.

Once the entire process has been recorded and transcribed, the portion containing the incriminating statement can be cut from the transcript. All this is necessary in the event that the confessing suspect recants the confession and alleges coercion.

Distinguishing Between Interrogations and Interviews

Investigators must understand the distinction between interviewing and interrogating suspects. Interviews are the pathways to interrogations: an interview should precede every interrogation when possible. Through the interview, investigators learn about the suspect and his or her needs and fears. The information gathered during the interview will be used to fashion the arguments and themes used throughout the interrogation.

In interrogations, investigators lead, and subjects follow. Investigators do not seek information. They do not take notes. They only want to obtain truthful admissions or confessions. Continuing to obtain erroneous or fabricated facts while trying to secure truthful admissions causes investigators to lose the advantage in the interrogation process. Once investigators determine that interrogation is warranted, obtaining the truth from the subject becomes their only goal (Moak & Carlson, 2015).

Developing Persuasive Themes and Arguments

Lack of arguments and themes to persuade subjects to tell the truth is a major cause of interrogation failure. Experience provides investigators with an ever-increasing supply of arguments. Conducting more interrogations gives investigators additional ideas and a wider variety of themes to pursue. Preparation allows investigators to plan their themes and arguments before interrogating subjects.

Certain themes and arguments remain universally available, including the following:

- Minimizing the crime
- Blaming the victim
- Decreasing the shamefulness of the act
- Increasing guilt feelings
- Appealing to the subject's hope for a better outcome

Knowing what is important to a suspect gives interrogators plenty of topics to pursue, helping them avoid running out of subjects.

Building a Good Relationship

Suspects may confess for no other reason than their respect for and trust in their interrogators. Investigators must build a good relationship with suspects. Anything that appears more important than the suspect or the relationship may prove detrimental to the interrogation process.

The perspectives, values, and goals of suspects and investigators diverge dramatically. It is necessary for an investigator to view an interrogation, a crime, and life experiences from the suspect's point of view. As investigators realize and understand these differences, interrogations become more personal and more effective.

Allowing Enough Time

Successful interrogations require a certain amount of time to complete. That time is unique to each investigation and to each suspect. Suspects make critical life decisions based on their personal needs and wants and their perceived ideas about their situations balanced against the themes, arguments, and facts presented by interrogators. Such a complicated process requires ample time to develop and conclude successfully. Do not rush an interrogation.

The Reid Technique

John E. Reid, who established a private polygraph firm in 1947 in Chicago, developed the **Reid technique**. The technique represents the cumulative experiences of dozens of associates who used the technique successfully to solve thousands of crimes since 1947. The training was first made available to the public in 1974, and more than 200,000 investigators have been trained in these techniques.

The Reid technique describes a three-part process for conducting a successful interrogation:

1. *Factual analysis*. This stage represents the collection and analysis of information relative to a crime scene, the victim, and possible suspects. Factual analysis helps determine the direction an investigation should take and offers insight regarding the possible offender.

2. *Interview of possible suspects*. This highly structured interview, referred to as a behavioral analysis interview, is a non-accusatory, question-and-answer session intended to elicit information from the subject in a controlled environment. The clinical nature of the interview—including the asking of specific behavior-provoking questions—is designed to provide the investigator with verbal and nonverbal behavioral clues that support either probable truthfulness or deception.

3. *Accusatory interrogation*. If the investigator believes that the subject has not told the truth during the non-accusatory interview, the third part of the technique is employed, which is the accusatory interrogation.

The purpose of an interrogation is to elicit a confession; less concern is placed on finding the truth. However, the persuasive efforts used during an interrogation must be balanced against the possibility that the suspect is innocent of the offense. The techniques must be effective enough to persuade a guilty suspect to tell the truth, but not so powerful as to cause an innocent person to confess.

All deception is motivated by the desire to avoid the consequences of telling the truth. These consequences may be social (going to prison, losing a job, paying a fine) or personal (feelings of embarrassment, shame, or humiliation). The investigator who tells a suspect, "You're in a lot of trouble and face the rest of your life behind bars," has made it psychologically very difficult for the suspect to tell the truth. The common technique, used by interrogators nationwide, of informing the suspect about the possible sentence facing him or her if convicted should be avoided.

The interrogator should also refrain from using hard **descriptives** such as *murder, rape*, and *theft* in favor of the less harsh concepts of *taking a human life, nonconsensual sex*, and *taking*, respectively. It is psychologically much easier to admit causing a person's death than it is to admit to murdering that person. In addition, the investigator should portray an understanding and compassionate demeanor toward the suspect that allows the suspect to feel better about himself/herself and less guilty about the crime s/he has committed. Another technique to reduce the perceived consequences of a crime involves more active persuasion. In this instance, the suspect is told that his or her crime could have been much worse and that it is fortunate that the suspect did not engage in the more serious activity.

Every person who has committed a crime will have justified that crime in some way. A crime against a person is often justified by blaming the victim. Crimes against property may be justified in a variety of ways. The employee who steals may justify the theft because she is underpaid and overworked; the auto thief blames society for not providing him a sufficient standard of living. Over time, criminals develop a victim's mentality. Criminals convince themselves and each other that they are the casualties of an unjust world and an unjust and unfair criminal justice system. Although the criminal may accept that what he did was wrong, the criminal believes he deserves special consideration because of his unique situation. An important part of the victim mentality is the urge to protect this victim image, to the extent of making a self-serving yet incriminating statement.

Reid technique
Technique for conducting a successful interrogation that describes a three-part process to be used during the interrogation

descriptives
Words that yield vivid mental images

The procedures employed in the Reid technique reinforce the guilty suspect's own justification for the crime and culminate by taking advantage of the suspect's victim mentality.

Steps of the Reid Technique

John Reid divided interrogation into different steps because he observed that suspects often go through identifiable stages during a successful interrogation. Suspects often begin by denying involvement in the offense. The guilty suspect eventually becomes quiet and withdrawn. At some point, the guilty suspect starts to mentally debate whether to confess. It is at this stage that the investigator seeks the first admission of guilt. Once this admission is offered, the suspect is generally willing to disclose the details of his or her crime through standard questioning procedures.

■ Step 1: Direct, Positive Confrontation

In the first step, the investigator advises the suspect that the investigation clearly indicates that he or she is responsible for the commission of a crime. This, of course, may not be a true statement. However, to persuade a guilty suspect to tell the truth, the investigator must often exaggerate his or her confidence in the suspect's guilt and the evidence and information in the possession of the police.

Following this direct positive confrontation, the investigator makes a transition statement. An example of a transition statement is, "We have everything we need to tie you to this crime; now's the chance to tell your side of the story." The transition statement is psychologically important in that it offers a pretense for the interrogation other than to elicit a confession. The concept of understanding why the crime was committed is attractive to the guilty suspect, who believes outside circumstances were responsible for his committing the crime. Finally, the transition statement allows the investigator to become more understanding and compassionate, encouraging the suspect to respond.

■ Step 2: Theme Development

A **theme** is a monologue in which the investigator offers moral or psychological excuses for the suspect's criminal behavior. The theme is not designed to plant new ideas in the suspect's mind but merely to reinforce the justifications that already exist in the guilty suspect's mind.

Criminals mentally distort the motives and circumstances surrounding their crimes. They

theme
Monologue in which the investigator offers moral or psychological excuses for the suspect's criminal behavior

do not accept the true reasons behind their behavior. They have found some justification that, in their minds, either excuses or excepts their behavior, often with a victim-mentality embellishment. It is the investigator's job to determine what this fallacious justification might be and turn it into a theme that will allow the suspect to buy in, reducing in his or her mind the criminal consequences of his or her behavior.

■ Steps 3 and 4: Handling Denials & Overcoming Objections

Most guilty suspects will offer denials during theme development. An important principle with respect to denials is that the more often a suspect denies involvement in an offense, the more difficult it is for that person to tell the truth. If a suspect is permitted to voice too many denials, he becomes committed to that position and no amount of persuasion will allow him or her to save enough face while telling the truth. For this reason, the investigator will discourage the suspect from offering weak denials by simply maintaining a flow of words (**FIGURE 7.3**).

It is important to recognize that the interrogator does not prevent a suspect from offering a denial; he or she simply makes the suspect socially uncomfortable when denials are made. A guilty suspect's denials become weaker and less persistent as the investigator continues on with his or her theme. Once the suspect recognizes that his denials are not dissuading the investigator's confidence in his guilt, he often psychologically withdraws. His mind is focused on the consequences of his crime, and he is content to allow the investigator to continue to talk and simply tunes him or her out.

FIGURE 7.3: Discouraging weak denial.
Courtesy of the Law Enforcement Resource Center.

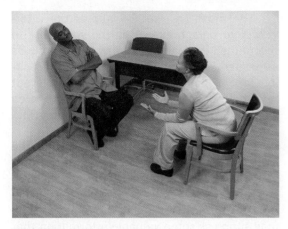

FIGURE 7.4 Withdrawn suspect.

Courtesy of the Law Enforcement Resource Center.

■ Step 5: Procurement and Retention of the Suspect's Attention

Once the suspect begins to withdraw (**FIGURE 7.4**), it is important for the interrogator to redefine the suspect's focus. That focal change should be directed toward the interrogator. The change in focus should be gradual, not abrupt. For the first time during the interrogation, the suspect may begin to think about telling the truth. The behavioral signs at this stage of an interrogation include dropped barriers (uncrossing arms or legs), a less tense posture, and an inability to maintain eye contact.

■ Step 6: Handling the Suspect's Passive Mood

The tempo of the interrogation slows. The investigator condenses theme concepts to one or two central elements and moves to the next step of the process, which is designed to elicit the initial admission of guilt.

■ Step 7: Presenting an Alternative Question

This step is the point to which the interrogator has been heading since the beginning. There is but one time during the course of an interrogation where an **alternative question** will elicit a truthful response. It is the skillful investigator who recognizes that point in time. The question presents two choices to the suspect regarding the crime he or she has committed. The choices generally contrast a positive and a negative choice. Accepting either choice, of course, results in an admission of guilt. The psychology of the alternative question relies on the guilty suspect's victim mentality. An example of an alternative question in a homicide case might be, "Did you plan on doing this since the day you got married, or did it pretty much happen

on the spur of the moment because of the fight you had?" or "Did you pull the trigger, or did your partner?"

■ Step 8: Having the Suspect Relate Details of the Offense

In those instances in which a suspect accepts the positive side of the alternative question, the suspect's agreement with the investigator's question is an admission of guilt that must be preserved.

■ Step 9: Converting an Oral Confession Into a Written Confession

The admission should lead to an oral confession, which in turn should result in a recorded or written confession. A confession is a statement acknowledging personal responsibility for a crime, including details only the guilty person would know.

Recent research regarding the Reid method suggests that it is the most popular and frequently used interrogation technique in the United States (Bull & Soukara, 2010). The authors of the technique claim an 80% confession rate, although this has not been scientifically verified. Concerns have arisen in the United Kingdom and elsewhere that the technique may solicit false confessions. These concerns, however, do not suggest that the method should not be employed. In the hands of well-trained and monitored interrogators, the technique may be non-coercively applied (Bull & Soukara, 2010).

Critics have recommended that the presumptive and confrontational aspects of the Reid method be replaced with a non-confrontational model. A common approach used in the United Kingdom is called the PEACE model. PEACE is an acronym for Preparation and Planning, Engage and Explain, Account and Clarification, Closure, and Evaluation. The PEACE model has been in use in the United Kingdom since the early 1990s. It is included in all police academy curricula. Its primary purpose is to minimize the risk of false confessions (Kapardis, 2014).

The preparation and planning stage of the PEACE method is based on interrogators knowing as much as possible about the evidence, suspect, witness(es), and victim(s). Any lapses in preparation and planning will become apparent during the course of the interrogation and may prove an impediment to a successful interrogation. The other stages focus on fact finding rather than the obtaining of a confession per se. The other phases of the process focus on the interrogation process, closing the interrogation,

alternative question
A two-pronged question that presents two choices (generally a positive and a negative choice) to the suspect regarding the crime he or she has committed; accepting either choice results in an admission of guilt

a final evaluation of the interrogator, the interrogative process, and the end result. UK police are not allowed to lie or present false evidence to a suspect during an interrogation as are their American counterparts. During UK police interrogations, interrogators are taught to center their interrogation on fairness, accountability, and openness. They do not use leading questions, pressure, or psychological manipulation. Their objective is to obtain a confession under circumstances that remove the likelihood or hints of a false confession (Kassin et al., 2010).

Written Statements and Confessions

waiver
Conscious act of giving up rights or privileges

Written statements are permanent records of the pretrial testimony of accused persons. They may be used in court as evidence attesting to what was told to investigators, to refresh the memory of the people who made the statements, and to refresh the memory of investigators.

confession law
Area of law dealing with the proper technique for legally obtaining a confession, and the rights guaranteed a suspect when he or she is deciding whether to give a confession

The suspect must receive Miranda warnings and sign a **waiver** form stating that the suspect understands his or her rights pursuant to *Miranda v. Arizona* and voluntarily waives those rights in making any written statements before providing a written confession. The confession is generally recorded using one of three accepted methods: narrative, question-and-answer, or a combination of narrative and question-and-answer.

The narrative method allows the interviewee or person executing the statement to record the information in his or her own words as desired. That is ideal if the person is articulate and does not compile a mass of irrelevant information. The narrative is used more often with a complainant or witness than with a victim or suspect.

In the question-and-answer method, the investigator can limit the information presented to that which is pertinent. Two disadvantages of using this method are: (1) it is time consuming for the investigator, and (2) it may suppress some valuable information that might have been volunteered had the narrative method been used.

A combination of the preceding two methods normally produces the best results. The person being questioned is first allowed to tell his or her story, and then the investigator elicits specific information previously omitted. This method or the question-and-answer method is most often used when taking a statement from an accused suspect.

Confession Law

Confession law is the area of law dealing with the proper technique for legally obtaining a confession, and the rights guaranteed a suspect when he or she is deciding whether to give a confession. Key developments in this area are summarized in **TABLE 7.1**.

TABLE 7.1 Key Developments in Confession Law

Case	Ruling
Brown v. Mississippi (1936)	Physical coercion violates the Fourth Amendment.
Chambers v. Florida (1940)	Psychological coercion violates the Fourth Amendment.
Ashcraft v. Tennessee (1944)	Psychological coercion is not admissible.
Haley v. Ohio (1948)	Relay teams of interrogators are inherently coercive.
Payne v. Arkansas (1958)	Holding a suspect incommunicado is coercive.
Miranda v. Arizona (1966)	Suspects must be read their rights before questioning.
United States v. Ferrara (1967)	Promises of light bail may be permissible.
Frazier v. Cupp (1969)	Police can say that an accomplice is cooperating.
Harris v. New York (1971)	Confession can be used in court to impeach testimony.

(continues)

TABLE 7.1 *(continued)*

Case	Ruling
United States v. Arcediano (1974)	Promises of federal instead of state prison are approved.
Beckwith v. United States (1976)	Custody, not focus of suspicion, triggers the need to read the Miranda warning.
Brewer v. Williams (1977)	Established functional equivalence test for custody.
United States v. Fike (1977)	No need to re-Mirandize a suspect unless day(s) have passed.
North Carolina v. Butler (1979)	Waiver of Miranda does not have to be written.
California v. Braeseke (1980)	Requests to speak off the record must be honored.
Rhode Island v. Innes (1980)	No functional equivalent if police talk to each other.
California v. Prysock (1981)	Miranda warnings do not have to be read ritually.
Edwards v. Arizona (1981)	Miranda is waived if suspect initiates conversation.
New York v. Quarles (1987)	Established public safety exception.
Duckworth v. Eagan (1989)	Miranda warnings do not have to be read precisely.
Illinois v. Perkins (1990)	Police can pose as inmates to extract confessions.
Minnick v. Mississippi (1990)	Interrogation stops when the suspect requests an attorney.
Pennsylvania v. Muniz (1990)	Miranda warnings do not apply to sobriety checkpoints
Arizona v. Fulminate (1991)	Technically deficient confessions do not overturn convictions.
Davis v. United States (1994)	Suspect must make an unambiguous request for an attorney.

CONCLUSION

Interrogations have always been a concern to the American people, whose collective historical experience with England during the colonial period, as reflected in the Declaration of Independence and later in the Bill of Rights, highlights the major grievances that the colonists had with the English government. Prominently situated in the Fifth Amendment is the prohibition against self-incrimination. Although national emphasis has changed the law enforcement focus to forensic evidence, the confession that is a product of understanding constitutional constraints is still the grist that makes the law enforcement mill turn.

In the next chapter, we discuss firearm and cartridge class characteristics and the methods used by firearms examiners to identify and compare firearms, cartridges, cartridge cases, and projectiles. In the United States, the handgun is commonly employed in armed robberies, aggravated assaults, and homicides. Handling firearm evidence requires an appreciation for what forensic personnel are looking for and making sure that the handling and packaging assists in the preservation of any trace evidence.

QUESTIONS FOR REVIEW

1. When does an interview become and interrogation?

2. Why are Miranda Warnings not necessary in an interview?

3. What is a cognitive interview?

4. Of what value might a cognitive interview be over common police interview practices?

5. What role did the case of *Massiah v. United States* play in the evolution of confession law?

6. List the cases that contributed to the evolution of confession law. What was their contribution?

7. Under what circumstances must a person be given the warnings pursuant to *Miranda v. Arizona?*

8. Is it necessary to provide Miranda Warning prior to conducting field sobriety tests?

9. Is it necessary for an undercover police officer to provide Miranda Warnings prior to soliciting an incriminating statement?

10. May police lie to a suspect to encourage an incriminating statement?

11. List four themes that an interrogator may incorporate into an interrogation.

12. Discuss the method of documenting a confession.

13. What is a waiver, and how is one obtained?

14. What are some researchers' concerns about the using the Reid interrogation technique?

15. What is the PEACE interrogation method, and in what ways is it more successful than the Reid technique?

REFERENCES

Bull, R., & Soukara, S. (2010). Four studies of what really happens in police interviews. In G. D. Lassiter & C. A. Meissner (Eds.), *Police interrogations and false confessions* (pp. 81–95). New York, NY: American Psychological Association.

Ceci, S. J., & Bruck, M. (1995). *Jeopardy in the courtroom: A scientific analysis of children's testimony.* Washington, DC: American Psychological Association.

Fisher, R. P., & McCauley, M. R. (2013). Information retrieval: Interviewing witnesses. *Psychology and Policing.* Brewer, N. & Wilson, C., eds.

Gilbert, J. N. (2010). *Criminal investigation* (8th ed.). Englewood Cliffs, NJ: Prentice Hall.

Howe. M. L., Goodman, G. S., & Cicchetti, D. (2008). *Stress trauma and children's memory development.* New York, NY: Oxford University Press.

Inbau, F. E., Reid, J. E., Buckley, J. P., & Jayne, B. C. (2015). *Essentials of the Reid technique: Criminal interrogation and confessions* (2nd ed.). Burlington, MA: Jones & Bartlett Learning.

Kapardis, A. (2014). *Psychology and law: A critical introduction.* New York, NY: Cambridge University Press.

Kassin, S. M., Drizin, S. A., Grisso, T., Gudjonsson, G. H., Leo, R. A., & Redlich, A. P. (2010). Police-induced confessions: Risk factors and recommendations. *Law and Human Behavior,* 34, 3–38.

Mallon, G. P., & Hess, P. M. (2014). *Child welfare for the twenty-first century: A handbook of practices, policies and programs* (2nd ed.). New York, NY: Columbia University Press.

Moak, S. C., & Carlson, R. L. (2015). *Criminal justice procedure.* New York, NY: Routledge.

Pool, D. A., & Lindsay, D. S. (2001). Children's eyewitness reports after exposure to misinformation from parents. *Journal of Experimental Psychology Applied,* 7(1), 27–50.

Principie, G. F., Ceci, S. J., & Bruck, M. (2010). *Children's memory: Psychology and the law.* San Francisco, CA: Wiley-Blackwell.

Reisberg, D. (2001). *Cognition* (2nd ed.). New York, NY: W.W. Norton.

Warden, S. (2017). Asking the hard questions. *The Journal Gazette.* Retrieved July 9, 2017, from www.journalgazette.net/features/20170709/asking-the-hard-questions

Wolf, R., Mesloh, C., & Wood, R. H. (2013). *Constitutional limitations of interviewing and interrogations in American policing.* Durham, NC: Carolina Academic Press.

KEY LEGAL CASES

Arizona v. Fulminate, 499 U.S. 279 (1991).

Arizona v. Mauro, 481 U.S. 520 (1987).

Ashcraft v. Tennessee, 322 U.S. 143 (1944).

Beckwith v. United States, 425 U.S. 341 (1976).

Berghuis v. Thompkins, 560 U.S. 370 (2011).

Brewer v. Williams, 430 U.S. 387 (1977).

Brown v. Mississippi, 297 U.S. 278, 279 (1936).

California v. Braeseke, 444 U.S. 1309 (1980).

California v. Prysock, 453 U.S. 355 (1981).

Chambers v. Florida, 309 U.S. 227, 228–229 (1940).

Connecticut v. Barrett, 479 U.S. 523 (1987).

Davis v. United States, 114 S.Ct. 2350 (1994).

Duckworth v. Eagan, 492 U.S. 195 (1989).

Edwards v. Arizona, 451 U.S. 477 (1981).

Frazier v. Cupp, 394 U.S. 731 (1969)

Haley v. Ohio, 332 US 596 (1948).

Harris v. New York, 401 U.S. 222 (1971).

Illinois v. Perkins, 496 U.S. 292 (1990).

Massiah v. United States, 377 U.S. 201 (1964).

Minnick v. Mississippi, 498 U.S. 146 (1990).

McNeil v. Wisconsin, 501 U.S. 171 (1990).

Miranda v. Arizona, 384 U.S. 436 (1966).

Missouri v. Seibert, 542 U.S. 600 (2004)

New York v. Quarles, 467 U.S. 649 (1987).

North Carolina v. Butler, 441 U.S. 369 (1979).

Oregon v. Elstad, 470 U.S. 298 (1985).

Payne v. Arkansas, 356 U.S. 560 (1958).

Pennsylvania v. Muniz, 496 U.S. 582 (1990).

Rhode Island v. Innes, 446 U.S. 291 (1980).

Texas v. Cobb, 532 U.S. 162 (2001).

United States v. Ferrara, 377 F.2d 16 (1967).

United States v. Arcediano, 371 F. Supp. 452 (1974).

United States v. Fike, 563 F2d 809 (1977).

United States v. Patane, 542 U.S. 630 (2004).

PART 3

SPECIALIZED INVESTIGATIONS

chapter
8

Firearms Investigation

"*Somebody killed the man, and whoever it was, I could clearly prove to you that he should have done it some other way…What does he mean by using a shotgun when silence was his one chance of escape?*"

Sherlock Holmes
"The Valley of Fear"

KEY TERMS

ballistics

breechblock

caliber

class characteristics

comparison microscope

degree of twist

firearms

firearms examination

firing pin

gauge

grooves

handgun

jacketed bullet

lands

National Firearms Act of 1968

primer

propellant

rifle

rifled firearm

smoothbore firearm

zones of possibility

STUDENT LEARNING OUTCOMES

Upon completion of this chapter, students will be able to:

- Distinguish the difference between ballistics and firearms examinations
- Recognize the types of firearms used by offenders
- Describe the class characteristics of firearms
- Discuss the class characteristics of cartridges, cartridge cases, and projectiles
- Explain the issues associated with the introduction of firearms evidence at the time of trial

Introduction to Firearms

Whether because of American heritage or movie exploits, firearms play a large role in American society. Some believe that there are too many guns, while others believe that everyone has the right to own a gun for self-defense. Whatever the case, there are millions of them within the United States that help account for the large number of crimes committed daily. According to the United States Department of Justice, the most recent research indicates that:

- According to the 2013 National Crime Victimization Survey, 332,950 victims of violent crimes stated that they faced an offender with a firearm.

- Incidents involving a firearm represented 8% of violent crimes of rape and sexual assault, robbery, and aggravated and simple assault between 2002 and 2011.

- The Federal Bureau of Investigation's (FBI) Crime in the United States estimated that 69% of the 14,196 murders in 2013 were committed with firearms (Bureau of Justice, 2014).

- Firearms were used in 40% of robberies and 22% of aggravated assaults in 2013.

The Early History of the Examination of Firearms

The history of contemporary **firearms examination** may have begun with the work of Dr. Albert Llewellyn Hall, a practicing physician in Buffalo, NY. In 1931, Hall published an article in the *American Journal of Police Science* titled, "The Missile and the Weapon" (Hall, 1931). This article concerned the possibility of matching fired bullets to the weapon that fired them based on microscopic examination of the striations on the bullets.

The first firearms case in the United States should have established the precedent for the admissibility of firearm comparison testimony. In *Commonwealth v. Best* (1902), the Supreme Judicial Court of the Commonwealth of Massachusetts permitted the introduction of the results of comparative examinations of markings on bullets. The case was ignored until the 1930s. The widespread acceptance of comparisons of bullet markings took more than a quarter of a century. Courts seemed willing to allow the introduction of cartridge case comparisons but were extremely reluctant to allow the admission of testimony pertaining to comparison of bullets, firing-pin impressions, or extractor marks. The readiness of courts to accept comparisons of marks on cartridges but not rifling marks on bullets may have been due to the greater visibility of the marks on cartridges and to the absence of a comparison microscope. The first use of firing pin impressions and extractor marks as evidence occurred during the investigation of the Brownsville massacre.

Often, the physical evidence found at a crime scene includes a firearm or firearm components. It is imperative that personnel tasked with processing and investigating a crime scene understand the forensic potential of such evidence. For the purposes of this text, a **firearm** is any device that expels a projectile or projectiles as a result of an explosive or propellant charge. Crime scene personnel and firearms examiners typically will come into contact with three types of firearms: handguns, rifles, and shotguns. However, it is useful to know that within each category, there are several subcategories. This is important because each category and subcategory of firearm operates differently, and each may require different concerns as far as documentation and preservation methods are concerned.

firearm
Weapon from which a shot is discharged; firearms examiners generally come into contact with five types of firearms: pistols, rifles, assault rifles, machine guns, and shotguns

firearms examination
Examination of the fired bullets and cartridges of a firearm to determine the weapon that fired them

CASE IN POINT

© Shutterstock, Inc./Viastas.

The Brownsville Shooting

On the night of August 13, 1906, unknown persons shot up downtown Brownsville, Texas, killing a local barkeeper. Local civilian witnesses claimed that black soldiers carried out the shooting. During the ensuing Senate investigation, an Army officer and a civilian technician from the U.S. arsenal in Springfield, Massachusetts, examined the firing impressions and extractor marks on cartridges found in the streets of Brownsville the day after. These examiners found that most of the cartridges had been fired from rifles of B Company, 25th Infantry. Being unable to assign blame to a specific soldier and believing that a conspiracy of silence existed among the personnel of the 25th Infantry, the War Department dishonorably discharged all 167 enlisted men in the battalion (Lane, 1971).

© Shutterstock, Inc./Nutink.

Modern Firearms Investigation

Cases involving the use of firearms are multi-layered and extremely complex in nature. In addition to determining what type(s) of firearm(s) was/were involved in the crime, there are other aspects which directly impact the case. These typically include shooter preparation, shooter location, shooter egress, shooter status, and post-shooting activities both by the shooter and by law enforcement or other responding personnel. The recent, highly chaotic and tragic shooting in Las Vegas is an example of a shooting incident where it is not always as simple as shooter, victim, witness(s) and law enforcement. Oftentimes, there are many other factors, resources and elements in play. In these instances, it is imperative for investigators to call upon all resources and potential sources of information to develop a richer picture of the entire picture of the incident.

The questions which need be answered go beyond those of "Why did this occur?" The questions of "Who else was involved?", "How did the shooter acquire the firearm(s)?", "How can this be prevented in the future (if at all)?"

and "How much information do we release or else run the risk of doing the homework for and assisting future perpetrators of such incidents?" are all questions which need be considered by investigators.

The onion that is a highly public and devastating shooting incident, is a complex scenario which will call upon all of an investigator's experience and resources. Firearms examination, ballistics, trajectory analysis, victim interviews, suspect interview and interrogation, incident preparation and planning, and a working understanding of firearms are all components which will be included within the process, and which must be considered by the investigator. As such, each of these areas will be further addressed.

Rifled Firearms

The most common firearms used in the commission of a crime are those which would be classified as **rifled firearms**. Their barrels (**FIGURE 8.1**) have a set of spiraling lands and grooves in them, referred to as rifling. The **lands** of the rifling are the raised ridges that bite into the surface of the bullet and give it a rotational

rifled firearm
Type of firearm whose barrel has a set of spiraling lands and grooves

lands
The raised ridges of the rifling that bite into the surface of the bullet and give it a rotational motion as it moves down the barrel

— Ripped from the Headlines —

Mass Shooting in Las Vegas

At approximately 10:00pm on October 1, 2017, Stephen Paddock opened fire on a crowd attending the Route 91 Harvest music festival, occurring on the Las Vegas Strip, in Las Vegas, Nevada. Firing hundreds of rounds from the 32nd floor of his Mandalay Bay hotel suite, he killed 58 and injured at least 546 people. It was to be the deadliest mass shooting committed by a single individual, within the United States, to date.

The subsequent investigation into the shooting revealed a cache of 23 firearms, including both handguns and assault rifles. It also revealed a significant amount of planning and preparation

upon the shooter's part, having literally stockpiled firearms and ammunition for decades, and methodically transported them to his hotel room. From evidence collected at the scene, the shooter was also found to have conducted targeting calculations to maximize his shooting effectiveness, accounting for distance and drop and environmental conditions. The shooter also had removed his laptop hard drive and taken steps to destroy or conceal other digital evidence.

The shooting would also ignite a renewed debate concerning firearms legislation and availability within the U.S., especially as concerned bump-stocks, which the shooter made use of, effectively converting his semi-automatic rifles so as to operate at a rate similar to that of a fully automatic rifle.

Due to the massive number of casualties, victims, witnesses, first responders, and hotel personnel involved, the investigation proved to be an extremely complex event. Law enforcement struggled with controlling the flow of information and it became necessary to modify timelines and information released a number of times. The lessons learned from the response to and the investigation of the incident will almost certainly be as voluminous and impactful on the public and on law enforcement as were the massacre at Columbine High School (1999) and the North Hollywood bank robbery (1997).

Source: Hanna, J., Almasy, S., McKirdy, E., & Rehbein, M. (2017). Las Vegas shooter left behind calculations for targeting crowd. CNN. Retrieved October 27, 2017, from http://edition.cnn.com/2017/10/07/us/las-vegas-shooting-investigation/index.html

© Shutterstock, Inc./rzarek

FIGURE 8.1: Rifled barrel.

FIGURE 8.2: Semiautomatic pistol (top) and Revolver (bottom).
© Woods North Photo/Shutterstock, Inc.

motion as it moves down the barrel; the **grooves** of the rifling are the recessed areas between the lands. The rifling grips the fired bullet and engraves its surface with land and groove impressions. The microscopic imperfections of the rifling produce patterns of parallel scratches called striations (or striae). Rifled firearms may be characterized by their **caliber**, or bore diameter. The bore diameter of a rifled barrel is the diameter measured from the tops of opposing lands. The caliber and bore diameters of American weapons normally are given in inches, whereas those of other weapons are given in millimeters. Many manufacturers and users express caliber in both inches and millimeters.

Handguns

A **handgun** is a weapon designed to be held in and fired with one hand. However, anyone familiar with firearm usage will agree that the most accurate way in which to fire a handgun is through the use of two hands, as that position creates a stable shooting platform. There are two primary subcategories of handguns: pistols (semi-automatic and automatic) and revolvers (**FIGURE 8.2**).

■ Pistols

Most nonrevolver types of handguns are of the semi-automatic variety. A semi-automatic firearm will fire each time the trigger is depressed and subsequently released for as long as there is ammunition remaining within the firearm. These firearms typically include a spring-loaded magazine, which holds the cartridges and feeds them into the awaiting

chamber after the previously spent shell casing has been extracted and ejected as a result of the slide action of the semi-automatic handgun. In some extremely rare cases, a pistol may be of the automatic variety. In this case, the weapon will continue to fire (unless interrupted by a malfunction) as long as the trigger is depressed and there is ammunition within the weapon. In either case (semi-automatic or automatic pistols), expended shell casings will be expelled from the firearm and will remain at the scene unless retrieved by the shooter (**FIGURE 8.3**).

grooves
The recessed areas between the lands of the rifling

caliber
The diameter of the bore of a gun

handgun
A type of weapon designed to be held in and fired with one hand; two primary subcategories are pistols and revolvers

Colt 10mm, Semi-automatic Pistol

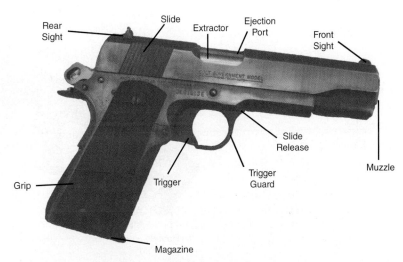

FIGURE 8.3: Characteristics of modern firearms (handgun).
Courtesy of Erica Milks.

Double-Action Revolver

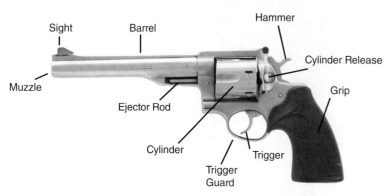

FIGURE 8.4: Characteristics of modern firearms (revolver).
Courtesy of Dana Gevelinger.

FIGURE 8.5: Example of an assault rifle.
© Pro 3D Artt/Shutterstock, Inc.

rifle
Weapon designed to be used with two hands and fired from the shoulder position

■ Revolvers

A revolver is a type of handgun that incorporates a revolving cylinder as the method of containing ammunition and of cycling the ammunition into battery. There are no interchangeable magazines and shell casings of expended ammunition are contained within the cylinder rather than being expelled as in a semi-automatic pistol. At a crime scene involving the use of a firearm, therefore, failure to find expended shell casings might mean that the perpetrator made use of a revolver or he or she picked up the shell casings (**FIGURE 8.4**).

There are two types of revolvers: single action or double action. A user of a single-action revolver must manually cock it each time before firing. The user of a double-action revolver only needs to pull the trigger, which, in turn, cocks the firearm and then subsequently fires it.

Rifles

A **rifle** is a weapon designed to be held in two hands when being fired from the shoulder. As with handguns, there are various types (**FIGURE 8.5**). Some rifles are single-shot, slide-action types that will fire one round and then, through manipulation of a bolt, will extract the spent shell casing and either load another round or the user will have to manually load another. Some are semi-automatic versions, which operate similarly to semi-automatic pistols, firing one round for each depression of the trigger as long as there is ammunition available. Automatic rifles will continue to fire as long as the trigger is depressed and ammunition is available (**FIGURE 8.6**).

Colt AR-15 Semiautomatic Rifle

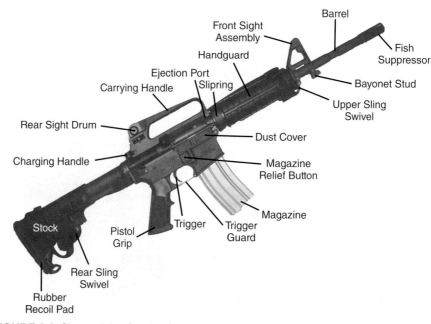

FIGURE 8.6: Characteristics of modern firearms (rifle).
Courtesy of Erica Milks.

FIGURE 8.7: Smoothbore barrel.

(A)

(B)

(C)

FIGURE 8.8: Shotguns: (A) pump action, (B) double barrel (side by side), double barrel (over and under), and (C) semiautomatic.
© Strannik 72/Shutterstock, Inc.; ATF; Guy Sagi/Alamy Stock Photo.

Smoothbore Firearms

As discussed earlier, if there is no rifling present within the firearm bore, the firearm is referred to as being a **smoothbore firearm** (**FIGURE 8.7**). The most common example of a smoothbore firearm is a shotgun. A *shotgun* is a firearm that, as with a rifle, is designed to be held in two hands and fired from the shoulder (**FIGURES 8.8** and **8.9**). They are most commonly used to fire pellet loads rather than single projectiles (slugs). While some shotguns are able to interchange and have rifled barrels for firing slugs, the shotgun was originally designed to fire multiple projectiles (shot) that are typically fired through a smoothbore barrel.

There are other types of smoothbore weapons that typically include antique blackpowder type weapons. However, because not many crime scenes involve such firearms, they are not a focus within the confines of this text.

Just as rifled weapons are referred to by their caliber, smoothbore weapons are referred to by their **gauge**. Gauge is the number of spherical lead balls that have the diameter of the interior of the barrel of the firearm that add up to weigh one pound. For example, 12 lead balls having the diameter of the interior of a 12-gauge shotgun barrel (roughly .75 inches) would weigh approximately 1 pound (**FIGURE 8.10**). An exception to this rule is the .410 gauge, which has an actual bore diameter of .410 inches. This is not meant to confuse the reader, but rather to recognize that referring to "gauge" is not an absolute measure with regard to smoothbore weapons.

smoothbore firearm
firearm that has no rifling present within the firearm bore

gauge
The number of spherical lead balls that have the diameter of the interior of the barrel of the firearm that add up to weigh one pound (e.g., 10 lead balls having the same diameter as the interior of the barrel of a 10-gauge shotgun should weigh 1 pound)

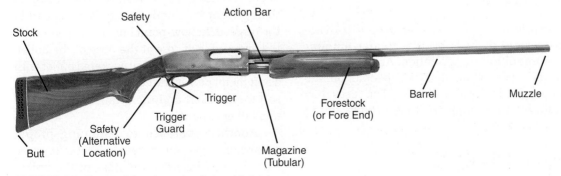

FIGURE 8.9: Characteristics of a modern firearm (shotgun).
Courtesy of Dana Gevelinger.

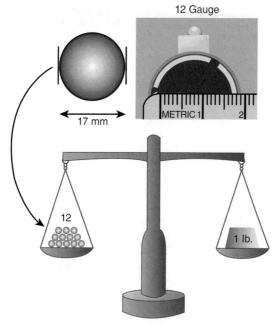
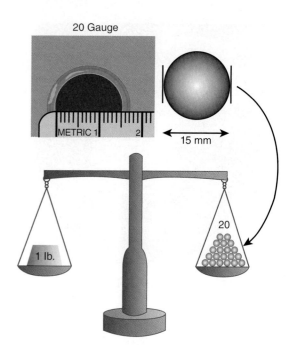

FIGURE 8.10: Explanation of how gauge is determined.

Courtesy of Nick Vesper.

The Firing Mechanism

The firearms examiner needs to know how certain components of a firearm's firing mechanism perform. The **breechblock** is the part of a firearm's action that supports the base of the cartridge in the chamber when it is fired. The **firing pin** is the part of the firearm's action that strikes the cartridge primer in order to fire it. Breechblocks may be finished with an end mill, by turning on a lathe, or by hand filing. The breechblocks of semiautomatic pistols are usually finished by filing vertically down through the ejector slot in the slide. This gives a characteristic direction to the striations imparted to the soft metal of the primer caps of fired cartridges. Firing pins are turned on lathes or filed flat by hand (Sommerville et al., 2006).

Ammunition

As many handguns as there are in private possession, there is even a greater amount of ammunition in circulation. An old bumper sticker reads, "Guns don't kill people, bullets kill people." Projectiles and cartridge cases may retain information of great importance to the firearms examiner.

Types of Bullets

The three most commonly used bullets (**FIGURE 8.11**) in rifled firearms are lead-alloy

bullets, semi-jacketed bullets, and fully jacketed bullets. Lead-alloy bullets are harder than pure lead bullets and are less likely to produce lead fouling of the rifling. Pure lead .22-caliber bullets may be coated with a very thin film of copper. This film has a tendency to flake off the surface of the bullet, removing the striations produced by the rifling (Heard, 2008).

Jacketed bullets consist of a lead core surrounded by a jacket of harder material. Jackets are commonly made of a copper-nickel alloy or mild steel. Semiautomatic pistols use fully jacketed bullets because the noses of the bullets must slide up a ramp as rounds are chambered (Sommerville et al., 2006).

A semi-jacketed bullet has a copper-alloy or aluminum jacket that covers only the side of the bullet, leaving the nose exposed. This type of bullet is designed to mushroom on impact so that most of its kinetic energy is expended in the target. A hollow-point bullet has a hollow in the exposed lead core at the nose of the bullet. A soft-point bullet is a semi-jacketed bullet with a soft metal plug inserted into its nose. Both the soft metal insert and the thinner jacket facilitate bullet expansion.

Another approach to obtaining proper expansion of a semi-jacketed bullet is to place a hard metal insert in the nose of the bullet. Bronze-point bullets are special bullets intended for hunting. Upon impact, the bronze point is

---

breechblock

The part of a firearm's action that supports the base of the cartridge in the chamber when it is fired

firing pin

The part of the firearm's action that strikes the cartridge primer in order to fire it

jacketed bullets

Bullets that consist of a lead core surrounded by a jacket of harder material, commonly a copper-nickel alloy or mild steel

FIGURE 8.11: Examples of different bullet types in ammunition.
© Jeffrey R. Banke/Shuttterstock, Inc.

forced back into the bullet's core, causing it to mushroom.

Frangible bullets are composed of powdered iron or powdered iron with an organic binder. These bullets are used in shooting galleries and in urban law enforcement because they disintegrate on impact without the danger of a ricochet or penetration through thin walls.

Steel-jacketed, armor-piercing bullets have an extremely hard steel jacket surrounding a tungsten carbide core. The hardness of the jacket generally prevents the rifling of the weapon from marking the projectile.

A special-purpose bullet called an accelerator cartridge has been developed by Remington. The projectile is a normal .223-caliber soft-point bullet pressed into a .30-caliber plastic grommet (sabot). Upon firing, the bullet and the sabot exit the barrel, and at some distance from the muzzle, the bullet separates from the sabot and continues along its trajectory as the sabot falls away. There are no identifiable rifling marks on such a bullet.

Bullets may have round noses, pointed noses, or flat noses. Their bases may be flat or boat tailed. The shape of a bullet is dictated by a number of considerations, including aerodynamics. Boat-tailed bullets are designed to reduce turbulence in the wake of the bullet, thereby reducing bullet drag.

The media has given much coverage to a Teflon-coated bullet that is reputed to be a cop killer. It is a green projectile, supposedly covered with a Teflon substance that will allow penetration of police body armor. In truth, the cartridge is an armor-piercing round, and the Teflon coats the projectile to protect the hard metal of the projectile from damaging the lands and grooves in the barrel. The Teflon has nothing to do with the penetrating characteristics of the projectile.

Propellants

Smokeless powders are classified as degressive burning, neutral burning, or progressive burning. Degressive-burning powder grains burn from the outside in; the surface area consequently decreases, as does the burning rate of the grain. Solid, uncoated powder grains burn in a degressive manner. Neutral-burning powders have perforations so that the burning of the outside of the grains is balanced by the burning on the interiors of the perforations; the net effect is that the surface area remains relatively constant, as does the burning rate. Progressive-burning powders are coated with a deterrent material that slows down the initial burning of the powder grains; once the deterrent coating is burned off, the burning rate goes up (The Diagram Group, 2007).

The manipulation of powder burning rates through variations in grain size, shape, and coating is necessary because of the variations in caliber, barrel length, and chamber size among firearms. When a weapon is fired, the **propellant** begins to burn, generating hot gases. These gases expand, forcing the bullet from the cartridge casing into the barrel. Once the bullet begins to move, the volume available to the gases generated by the burning propellant increases. If the production of gases stopped immediately after the unseating of the bullet into the barrel, further travel of the bullet down the barrel would cause the pressure behind it to fall. At the point where the pressure exerted on the bullet was balanced by the frictional force acting between

propellant
Powder that begins to burn when a firearm is fired; the pressure increase caused by the burning powder propels the bullet from the firearm

the bullet and the barrel, the bullet would come to a stop. To prevent this, the powder must continue to burn as the bullet proceeds down the barrel. Burning of powder after the bullet exits the barrel wastes energy because none of the energy released after the bullet exits the barrel can be converted into kinetic energy. The weight (amount), grain size, and burning rate of a cartridge's propellant must be adapted to the type of firearm intended to fire it.

Primers

The centerfire cartridge is a 19th-century invention. Eventually, it supplanted the rim fire cartridge in all but the smallest calibers. Centerfire ammunition manufactured in the United States uses the Boxer primer (named for its inventor, E. M. Boxer, a colonel in the British army). This **primer** consists of a metal cup containing a small amount of primer material placed between the cup and a small metal anvil. When the weapon is fired, its firing pin crushes the primer material between the cup and anvil; the flame from the primer's explosion reaches the propellant through a large flash hole in the base of the cartridge. Centerfire cartridges manufactured outside of the United States use the Berdan primer (named after its inventor, Hiram Berdan, a colonel in the Union army during the American Civil War). Cartridge cases that accept the Berdan primer have a conical anvil as an integral part of their bases. The primer cap is simply a small metal cup containing a pellet of primer compound. Two or three small holes spaced evenly around the anvil communicate the flash of the primer through the base of the casing to the propellant (The Diagram Group, 2007).

Beginning in 1900, primers based on potassium chlorate began to appear as replacements for mercury fulminate primers, but their

primer
A metal cup containing a small amount of primer material placed between the cup and a small metal anvil

residue proved as corrosive as the residue of the latter. Modern primers are exclusively nonmercurial and noncorrosive. A typical centerfire primer produced today will contain lead styphnate, antimony sulfide, barium nitrate, and tetracene.

Cartridge Cases

Cartridge cases are available in a wide variety of shapes and sizes (**FIGURE 8.12**). Differently shaped cases are intended for use in different types of firearms. Revolvers fire straight-rimmed cartridges; the rims prevent the cartridges from falling through the revolver's cylinder. Self-loading pistols fire straight rimless cartridges; because they are clip fed, there is no need for a rim. Cartridge cases may have cannelures rolled into them near their mouths; these cannelures prevent the bullets from inadvertently being pushed back into the cases. A bullet may also be held in place by crimping the mouth of the cartridge onto the surface of the bullet.

The heads of cartridges frequently bear stampings that provide information about the maker of the cartridges. For instance, the letters R-P on the head of a cartridge case indicate that Remington-Peters made it. A cartridge also may carry markings identifying the nominal caliber of its bullet.

Shot Shells

Most shotgun ammunition contains pellets, although some commercially available shot shells either have a single-round ball or a rifled slug. Shotgun pellets come in a variety of sizes, from 000 buckshot (0.36-inch diameter) down to Number 12 birdshot (0.05-inch diameter). The larger the shot number, the smaller the shot. The number of pellets of each size making up the load of a shot shell

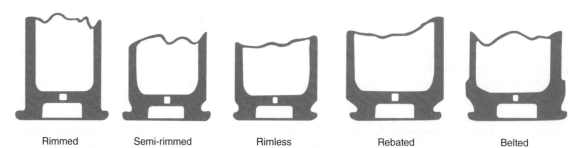

FIGURE 8.12: Types of cartridge rims.

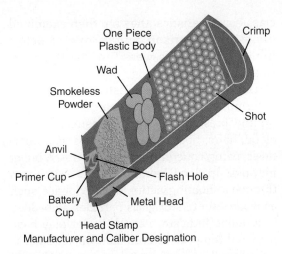

FIGURE 8.13: Shot shell components: primer, powder, wadding, and shot.

depends on its gauge. For example, 12-gauge Number 1 buckshot cartridges generally contain 16 pellets, whereas a 16-gauge Number 1 buckshot cartridge generally contains 12 pellets. Shotgun pellets may be lead, lead alloy, or soft steel. Concern that waterfowl might eat toxic lead pellets has generated a movement to replace all lead-based shot with the more environmentally sound nontoxic soft steel shot. At one time, shot shells were made completely of brass. These brass shells have disappeared and have been replaced by shells with brass bases and paper or plastic sides.

The pellets in the shot shell are separated from the propellant by one or more over-powder wads (**FIGURE 8.13**). These wads are used to separate the propellant gases from the shot and to cushion the pellets during their acceleration up the barrel. Wadding is made of cardboard, felt, or plastic. In modern shot shells, the pellets are held in a plastic cup that prevents their deformation through contact with the interior of the shotgun barrel. The plastic cup in some applications also serves as a wad.

Ballistics and Firearms Identification

The examination and identification of firearms is often incorrectly referred to as ballistics. **Ballistics** is actually the study of projectiles in motion. Ballistic studies involve four discrete areas:

- *Interior ballistics* is the study of the motion of projectiles in the gun barrel and the conversion of the chemical energy of the cartridge propellant into the kinetic energy of the projectile.

- *Transitional ballistics* deals with the transition from the projectile's passage through the gun barrel to the projectile's flight through the air.

- *Exterior ballistics* deals with projectile flight from the muzzle end to the target (taking into account air resistance, gravity, wind, and elevation).

- *Terminal ballistics* is the study of the interaction of the projectile with the target (Heard, 2008).

Firearms identification, on the other hand, is concerned primarily with the identification of firearms through the examination of related firearms components, such as fired bullets, cartridge cases, and firearm bore interior analysis. Such examination and analysis is only tangentially related to ballistics.

Examination of Weapons

As an examination protocol, test firing is not necessarily the first step. There is a possibility that the weapon was last used in a homicide involving a contact wound. If the barrel was in contact with the body upon firing, there may be blood and tissue in the barrel as a result of barrel blowback. The weapon's bore may also have fibers from its owner's pockets. There is also a possibility that the weapon, its components, and its ammunition may retain fingerprints.

Once the firearm has been processed for fingerprints and trace evidence, a complete identification of the weapon should be made. The identification should include the following class characteristics:

- Make or manufacturer
- Type (revolver, pistol, etc.)
- Caliber
- Serial number
- Model
- Number of shots
- Barrel length

The make, manufacturer, and model are determined from names, trademarks, and proof marks placed on various components of the weapon. The caliber of the weapon may be indicated by the name or by trademark

ballistics
The study of projectiles in motion

comparison microscope

Microscope that can be used to examine two or more fired bullets that exhibit the same class characteristics and determine whether the bullets were fired by the same weapon

National Firearms Act of 1968

Act that requires retailers to record the serial number of a weapon and the name of its purchaser

class characteristics

Characteristics used to identify a firearm, including caliber, direction of twist of the rifling, degree of twist, number of lands and grooves, and width of the lands and grooves

degree of twist

The grooves inside the barrel of a gun spiral at a particular angle, with some steeper (greater) than others; degree of twist is an identifying characteristic of the firearm that includes the number of twists, the angle of the twist, and whether the twist is to the left or the right

information. A weapon may be modified by fitting a different-caliber barrel to the weapon's frame.

The **National Firearms Act of 1968** requires retailers to record the serial number of a weapon and the name of its purchaser. Because of the importance of the serial number for tracing a firearm's owner, a criminal may remove the stamped serial number by grinding. If the grinding does not go deep enough into the metal, a stamped serial number may still be recovered by chemical etching, electrochemical etching, or ultrasonic cavitation. Many firearms have parts of the serial number stamped into internal components. Handguns often have the serial number stamped at different locations on the frame.

In a case involving an accidental firing or a firing that occurred during a fight or struggle, the amount of force required to pull the trigger may be important. The trigger pull may be measured by gradually increasing the amount of weight hanging from the weapon's trigger while the weapon is held vertically with the mechanism cocked. The measurement should be made with the actuating force applied to the trigger at the same spot that the finger of a person firing the weapon would be placed.

Examination of Bullets

In the absence of a suspect weapon, a firearms examination is confined to the determination of **class characteristics** of the bullets, such as caliber, direction of twist of the rifling, **degree of twist**, number of lands and grooves, and width of the lands and grooves (**FIGURE 8.14**). With these data, the firearms examiner may be able to determine the make and model of the firearm that fired the bullets. If there are two or more fired bullets that exhibit the same

class characteristics, they are then examined under a **comparison microscope** to determine if the bullets were fired by the same weapon.

Before class characteristics of bullets are determined, the bullets should be examined for the presence of trace evidence, such as blood, hairs, fibers, wood splinters, glass particles, paint, concrete, or soil particles. A bullet may pick up blood, hairs, and fibers as it passes through a shooting victim. Trace evidence, such as wood splinters or glass particles embedded in a bullet, indicate that the bullet may have passed through an intermediate object, such as a door, wall, or window. Paint, concrete, or soil particles may be found if a bullet ricochets off of a hard surface.

■ Caliber

The caliber of an undeformed fired bullet may be measured with a micrometer. The diameter of interest is the diameter across the land impressions (which, on the expended bullet, will be indentations made by the barrel lands). Allowance must be made for the fact that firearm calibers are merely nominal indications of the true bore diameters. The author measured the bores of a group of Colt pistols, part of his personal collection, all nominally .38-caliber weapons, and found bore diameters ranging from 0.348 to 0.395 inch.

The caliber of an intact but badly deformed bullet may be estimated from its weight. The determination of caliber by weight will rarely allow the examiner to specify a particular caliber for the bullet, but certain calibers may be eliminated as possibilities. When the bullet is fragmented, an accurate weight can no longer be obtained. In such a case, the caliber of the bullet may be estimated by measuring the widths of a land impression and

CASE IN POINT

© Shutterstock, Inc./Viastas.

St. Valentine's Day Massacre

In 1929, Calvin Goddard was called to Chicago to examine the fired bullets and cartridges in the St. Valentine's Day massacre. He was able to determine that the victims of the gangland execution had been killed with two different Thompson submachine guns, one with a 20-round magazine and the other with a 50-round drum magazine (Goddard, 1930). Goddard's impressive performance led to the establishment of a private forensic laboratory in Chicago under Goddard's direction. This laboratory later became the Chicago Police Department Crime Laboratory. Also in 1929, Goddard testified in *Evans v. Commonwealth* (1929), which became the precedent-setting case for the admissibility of comparisons of rifling marks.

© Shutterstock, Inc./Nutink.

FIGURE 8.14: Bullet comparisons.

Courtesy of Austin Police Department, Austin, Texas.

an adjacent groove impression (The Diagram Group, 2007).

■ Number of Lands and Grooves

In bullets recovered intact, the number of lands and grooves can be determined by counting them. In cases where bullets are badly deformed, measurement of the width of the land and groove impressions may be combined with knowledge of the caliber of the bullet to calculate the number of lands and grooves. Because manufacturers use a specific number of grooves in their firearms and this number is generally constant for a given make and model, the number of lands and grooves is an important class characteristic.

■ Rifling Twists

The direction of twist of the rifling may be determined by inspection of the fired bullet if it is not badly deformed. The rifling may spiral either to the left or to the right. Left-hand twist rifling is often referred to as Colt-type rifling, and right-hand twist rifling is often referred to as Smith and Wesson-type rifling.

■ Land and Groove Width

The width of the land and groove impressions may be measured using a filar micrometer, traveling microscope, or toolmaker's microscope. Measurements are made perpendicular to the axis of the bullet. Observing that the land impressions on a bullet are wider than the groove impressions allows the firearms examiner to eliminate certain makes and models of firearms. Land and groove impressions that are of a markedly different width than the other impressions on the bullet may reflect a defect in manufacture that is extremely rare (The Diagram Group, 2007).

■ Bullet Comparisons

Bullet comparisons are made using a comparison microscope. A comparison microscope consists of two compound microscopes, each with its own objectives, stage, and focusing adjustments. The microscopes are joined by a comparison bridge—a system of prism mirrors that brings the images of the two microscopes together so that they may be compared side by side through a single ocular. The images of the two microscopes may be superimposed, or they may be viewed side by side, with the field of view divided equally between the two microscopes. The bullets to be compared are attached to short, cylindrical bullet holders. The bullet holders slip onto the shafts of the bullet-manipulating mechanisms, which, in turn, are attached to the microscope stages. The bullet-manipulating mechanisms are provided with universal joints so that the bullets may be oriented at any angle.

Once the bullets are mounted, the examiner begins the search for matching patterns of striations. The limited expansion of jacketed bullets leads to only occasional contact with the bottoms of the grooves, and only the base may be upset sufficiently to seat well in the barrel's rifling. Therefore, the initial examination is most likely to discover a pattern of striations near the base of the bullet. A land impression on a test-fired bullet is compared successively to each land impression on the suspect bullet until a match is obtained or it is determined that no match is possible. Once a match has been made with a pair of land impressions, the bullets are rotated synchronously to see if other matching striation patterns may be observed. If both bullets were fired from the same barrel, numerous matching patterns will be evident. Marks other than land and groove striations may be observed.

Skid marks are caused by the bullet sliding over the beginnings of the lands at the breech end of the barrel. Shaving marks occur when a revolver bullet in the cylinder is not lined up perfectly with the barrel. The bullet will strike the edge of the forcing cone (the flared opening in the revolver's frame in front of the cylinder where the fired bullet enters the barrel), and a portion of the bullet will be shaved off on the side striking the forcing cone. Comparing shaved spots on a bullet may be difficult. Test firing may not always result in a similar shaving, and many shots may have to be fired before a similarly shaved bullet can be obtained.

In an effort to avoid detection, criminals may flatten, bend, or shorten the barrel of a firearm. Flattened barrels may be restored to round, bent barrels may be straightened, or bullets may be forced through the barrels. The marks on bullets fired through the barrel at its original length may not match the marks on bullets fired through a shortened barrel.

The examination of fired bullets may lead to any one of three conclusions:

1. The bullet in question was fired from the suspect weapon.

2. The bullet in question was not fired from the suspect weapon.

3. The results of the examinations are insufficient to reach a final determination.

■ **Examination of Cartridges**

In examining a fired cartridge case, the examiner using a low-power microscope will note the following:

- Size
- Shape
- Type (rimmed, semi-rimmed, rimless, belted, rim fire, centerfire)
- Size of firing pin impression
- Position of firing pin impression
- Location of extractor marks
- Location of ejector marks
- Any other accidental marks (any mark other than those caused in the manufacturing process)

The shape and location of the firing pin impression on the cartridges of bullets shot from a .22-caliber, single-shot, breech-loading rifle can serve to identify the make and model of the rifle. The relative positions of the extractor and ejector marks on cartridges from self-loading pistols allow the same determination (Girard, 2017). If a suspect firearm is available and if the class characteristics of cartridges from that weapon match those of the questioned cartridge, the examiner fires test shots with the suspect weapon in order to obtain fired cartridges for comparison purposes. The cartridges are then placed inside an iris diaphragm that attaches to the bullet-mounting devices in the comparison microscope. Comparison of the various marks on the fired cartridges begins with the firing pin impressions, firing pin drag marks, and breechblock marks. A match of these marks would show that the same weapon fired both cartridges.

After the examiner evaluates these marks, he or she compares the extractor marks, ejector marks, chambering marks, and magazine (clip) marks. A match of any of these types of marks indicates that the two cartridges have been run through the action of the same weapon but does not establish that they ever passed through the barrel. Cartridge case class characteristics include:

- Caliber (headstamped)
- Manufacturer (headstamped)
- Composition (copper, cupronickel)
- Rim type (rimless, rimmed, semi-rimmed, belted)
- Primer (center fire, rim fire)

Examination Objectives

Whenever a firearm is discharged in the commission of a crime, physical evidence is likely to be available. Such evidence in the hands of a competent firearms examiner may prove valuable in answering a number of questions. Residue from firing a firearm will remain on surfaces until removed. Barrel blowback will deposit unignited powder, which is expended as a black cloud, on the firearm and the hand and forearm of the individual firing it. Gunshot residue tests can be conducted to determine if residue is present on an assailant's or victim's hand. Although the FBI no longer tests for gunshot residue because of lack of demand and expense, gunshot-residue testing in the field is still an important investigative tool.

Generally speaking, the objective of firearms examination includes:

- Matching/identifying projectiles
- Matching/identifying cartridge cases
- Matching/identifying cartridges
- Matching/identifying extractor marks
- Matching/identifying ejector marks
- Matching/identifying lands and grooves
- Matching/identifying firearms
- Matching firing pin impressions
- Matching machine marks on cartridge case heads
- Matching striations on projectiles
- Assessing trigger pull
- Examining powder residue

Firearms Evidence Handling and Packaging

To ensure the maximum value of firearms evidence, it first must be properly identified, preserved, and packaged. These steps should be properly documented by notes and photographs. When practicable, always render a weapon safe to handle before proceeding with further investigation or examination. When unloading a revolver, it must first be ascertained that the weapon is not cocked. Decocking must be done carefully before any further handling. Once decocked, the revolver can be opened and the ammunition removed. Each cartridge in the cylinder should be first photographed in place and then removed; the investigator should take care to document where each cartridge resided. The method most commonly used for documenting the cartridges is to mark one cylinder opening with a small mark, indicating that documentation begins at this spot and that the cylinder well becomes number one. Continuing in a clockwise fashion from the well-marked and designated one, each well then becomes the next successive number. The cartridge in each numbered well is then tagged with the corresponding numbered cylinder well. Dealing with a semiautomatic pistol requires detailed notes and photographs of the weapon and the magazine. The first step is to ensure that the weapon is unloaded. This is done by removing the clip/magazine and opening the action. Once the action has been opened, the investigator can clear the weapon of any ammunition that may be in the barrel. If possible, the slide on the pistol should be left in the open position so that anyone with a need to handle it can immediately tell the weapon is unloaded. Many jurisdictions require investigators to mark the weapon in some unique fashion to be able to identify the weapon to the exclusion of all others.

If marking is required, it should be done to a place that is not readily removable from the weapon. Most agencies have moved away from engraving an identifying mark on firearms and use serial numbers for identification purposes. Now that fingerprints can be etched into the brass of ammunition, crime laboratories may instruct investigators not to remove cartridges from semiautomatic weapons.

Delivery of firearms is always best accomplished by transporting the evidence as quickly

INVESTIGATOR'S NOTEBOOK

© Shutterstock, Inc./Janaka Dharmasena

Questions a Firearms Examiner Aims to Answer

- Can the crime scene bullet or cartridge casing be linked to a suspected weapon?
- Is the recovered weapon capable of being fired?
- Can the weapon be accidentally fired?
- What is the trigger pull?
- Can the serial number be restored?
- Can the type of gun be determined from an examination of the class characteristics of a bullet or cartridge case recovered at the crime scene?

© Shutterstock, Inc./Nutink.

as possible after discovery by the person discovering it. Chain of custody issues can be avoided by keeping the number of people in the chain to an absolute minimum. All firearms should be packaged pursuant to agency protocol, which generally includes boxes, manila envelopes, and paper wrapping. Plastic containers are not good repositories in that they may "sweat," causing damage to the contents. Firearms recovered in water should be submitted in the same water in a watertight container. However, a firearms examiner must be contacted prior to submission if it is unknown whether the firearm is loaded.

Projectiles may carry microscopic striations. Cartridge cases may contain ejector and extractor marks along with etched fingerprints. The microscopic nature of this evidence requires that these evidentiary items be handled with the utmost of care, so as not to destroy or contaminate trace evidence. They should be packed and sealed in paper or paper boxes made for the purpose. The projectile, cartridge, or cartridge case should not be marked in any way. The container can be marked with identifying information (Girard, 2017).

National Integrated Ballistics Information Network

Developed in 1999, the National Integrated Ballistics Information Network (NIBIN) is a nationally interconnected, computer-assisted ballistics imaging system operated by the Bureau of Alcohol, Tobacco, Firearms and Explosives (ATF&E) and used by firearms examiners to obtain computerized images of bullets and cartridge cases. It "is the only national network that allows for the capture and comparison of ballistic evidence to aid in solving and preventing violent crimes involving firearms" (atf.gov). NIBIN is composed of several computer-connected networks, and the goal is for NIBIN data to be shared nationally. To meet that goal, the ATF&E has more than 80 offices around the country, which serve as repositories for the deposit and retrieval of ballistic images, assisted by 172 sites and 3,500 agencies nationwide.

Prior to the creation of NIBIN, comparisons of bullet and cartridge case marks were historically accomplished by firearms examiners using comparison microscopes. This process was accurate but slow and labor intensive. In the early 1990s, the ballistics imaging and matching process was computerized. Digital cameras were used to photograph bullets and

cartridge cases and scan them into a computer. These images were then analyzed by a software program and stored in a database, making ballistics matching faster. When the computerized system was connected across numerous law enforcement agencies through a telecommunications system, it allowed the rapid comparison of bullets and cartridge cases used in crimes from different jurisdictions. The use of computerized images of bullets and cartridge cases streamlines chains of custody for those bullets and cartridge cases that are to be used in court.

Presently, the participation of federal, state, and local law enforcement agencies in NIBIN is restricted by law to the ballistics imaging of data associated only with those guns used in crimes. "NIBIN acquisitions are expressly limited to ballistic information from recovered firearms and fired ammunition components pursuant to a criminal investigation. Therefore, NIBIN cannot capture or store ballistic information acquired at the point of manufacture, importation, or sale; nor purchaser or date of manufacture or sale information" (atf.gov). Recent bills introduced in Congress (but not yet enacted as law) would require all manufacturers to supply a spent cartridge and bullet for inclusion in the system before being allowed to sell or import the firearm. This would significantly increase the ability to trace firearms used in crimes.

Integrated Ballistic Identification System

The heart of NIBIN is the Integrated Ballistic Identification System (IBIS), comprised of a comparison microscope (paired with a digital camera) and a computer unit that enables an image to be captured digitally for subsequent analysis (**FIGURE 8.15**). These images can then

FIGURE 8.15: An example of a NIBIN station.

be compared with images already entered within the system. The system is maintained by the ATF&E and the IBIS sites are electronically joined to multistate regions, thus making up the integrated federal network.

NIBIN was originally introduced in all 50 U.S. states, although it was later cut back and/or redistributed due to a lack of use in some areas. There are currently IBIS sites within 40 of the U.S. states, as well as the District of Columbia, the U.S. Virgin Islands, and Puerto Rico. The states that do not currently have an IBIS site within them include: Arkansas, Idaho, Maine, Montana, New Hampshire, North Dakota, South Dakota, Utah, West Virginia, and Wyoming. However, although these states do not have IBIS sites within them, they are able to have their firearms-related evidence documented through other sites within their various regions, as a result of agreements with bordering states and the ATF.

The technology that comprises IBIS was developed by a Canadian company in 1991. Forensic Technology created IBIS and partnered with public safety agencies around the globe to provide ballistics and firearms identification solutions. In 2011, Forensic Technology acquired Projectina Ltd, a Swiss company specializing in computation and the development and manufacture of optical and opto-electronic components, which enabled for robust growth and maturation of the IBIS systems. In 2014, Forensic Technology was acquired by Ultra Electronics, an internationally successful defense, security, and transport company (www.ultra-forensictechnology.com/about). Ultra Electronics continues to be the sole source for IBIS components associated with the ATF NIBIS network.

The IBIS consists of two separate work stations:

- *Digital Acquisition Station (DAS):* Used to collect image data. It does not retrieve and compare images. Composed of a microscope and a computer unit that allows image acquisition or evaluation; these systems are linked to a regional server, where the images are stored and bullet cartridge case comparison or correlation requests are sent. There are presently two primary types of DAS, which are used by the IBIS sites:
  - *BrassTRAX:* Fully automated cartridge case imaging station. For centerfire cartridge cases, this includes the breech face and firing pin impressions on the primer, and the ejector mark. For rim-fire cartridge cases, this includes the firing pin impression.
  - *BulletTRAX:* Bullet imaging station (available in either 2D or 3D technology). Captures topographic information of a bullet's lands and grooves. It produces an image strip representing a bullet's 360-degree circumference, or a combination of regions from a bullet's fragments (**FIGURE 8.16**).
- *Image Analysis Station:* Used by the trained firearms examiner to examine entered images and compare them with others on file and determine whether a match or hit exists.
  - *Match Point Plus:* This is the primary comparative analysis station for examining 2D and 3D images of potential matches

— Ripped from the Headlines —

Mobile NIBIN

At the end of March, 2017, the ATF rolled out a mobile forensics lab that was introduced as being a mobile addition to the NIBIN network. This technology is essentially a portable cartridge casing system that allows on-site digital capture of fired cartridge cases and bullets for transmission to a central IBIS for processing, comparison, and storage. The van is intended to deploy to locations where law enforcement may not currently have resources that are dedicated to the analysis of firearms-related evidence. The large van, replete with large digital flat screens, numerous computers, and a comparison microscope paired with a digital camera, is also equipped with an attachable trailer. The trailer will give investigators and forensics personnel the ability to test fire-associated firearms, enter the collected firearms evidence into the IBIS terminal located within the van, and subsequently upload all of the information into NIBIN.

© Shutterstock, Inc./rzarek.

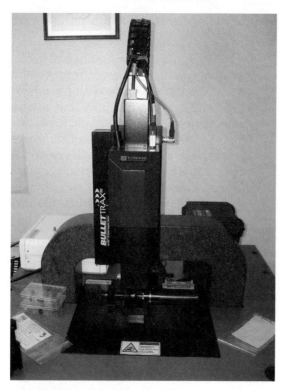

FIGURE 8.16: 3D Bullet trax.

being returned to the DAS remote. The images are transmitted to the regional server for comparison to the region's database. Again, a hit results in the correlation data being returned to the cooperating DAS, and the RBI user is notified either by email or telephone. Ejected cartridge cases found at a crime scene can be digitized at the scene. The information can be transmitted to a laboratory, where a technician can use the system to conduct a search. If a hit is found, results can be returned to the personnel at the scene while the investigation is still in progress. The IBIS analysis system does not provide matches; as with AFIS, it provides correlations—a short list of possible matches. The final analysis for a match is conducted by a firearms examiner through a comparison microscope.

Improved Technology

Technology has enhanced firearm examination analytical possibilities through the use of three-dimensional (3D) imaging technology. Two-dimensional images are limited in detail and depth. IBIS TRAX-HD3D is a 3D IBIS system, which allows for documentation and examination of the entire surface of a cartridge, cartridge case, or projectile. 3D software makes a mathematical model of the item viewed and stores the digital model in a database. The technician or examiner can subsequently view a 3D rendering of the item upon a high-definition, flat-screen computer monitor. According to firearms examiners, the IBIS technology upgrades have led to stronger correlations to possible matching fired evidence already logged within the system. The movement to 3D analysis also allows system users to view additional areas on the discharged cartridge cases for comparison, which allows the user to further compare images on

obtained from IBIS correlation algorithms.

IBIS technology is designed to be used without extensive computer training or sophistication. Once entered, a sample that results in a hit (a possible match with a database record) provides demographic information about the crime; images of the correlated cartridge case, which includes the breech face, firing pin, and ejector marks; and images of the correlated bullet, including lands and accidentals.

If the image is captured at a DAS remote, the data is sent to the regional server for comparison. A hit results in the correlation data

INVESTIGATOR'S NOTEBOOK
NIBIN Hit Process

- Fired ammunition components are recovered from a shooting scene
- Imaged onto the network
- Firearm recovered from a suspect and test fired
- NIBIN identifies possible hit and microscopic comparison confirms hit
- NIBIN partner notifies law enforcement agencies of hit

screen before requesting the fired evidence for comparison on the comparison microscope.

■ Defining a "Hit"

A "hit" is defined as "the linkage of two different crime investigations by a user of the NIBIN technology, where previously there had been no known connection between the investigations." It is a linkage of cases, not of individual pieces of evidence. However, in the case of multiple bullet or casing entries, each is entered as part of the same case record and each discovered linkage to an additional case constitutes a "hit" (atf.gov).

A hit must subsequently be confirmed by a trained firearms examiner. Hunches, investigative leads, or previously identified laboratory examinations do not classify as "hits" for NIBIN purposes. The agency responsible for initiating and confirming the microscopic comparison of the case evidence is credited for the "hit."

■ Success of NIBIN

Some would say that success is subjective, but the statistics are certainly encouraging. NIBIN has seen an increase from approximately 10,000 entries to 25,000 entries a month, within the past 2 years. As a result of the increase in the numbers of exhibits being entered, there has been an increase in associated "hits" as well.

Much of the success of NIBIN is attributed to the training and operational policies of its users. According to the ATF, NIBIN success requires adherence to four critical steps:

1. **Comprehensive Collection and Entry:** Partner agencies must collect and submit all evidence suitable for entry into NIBIN, regardless of the crime. Evidence includes both cartridge cases recovered from crime scenes and test fires from recovered crime guns.

2. **Timely Turnaround:** Violent crime investigations can go cold very quickly, so the goal is to enter the evidence into the network as quickly as possible in order to identify potential NIBIN leads, and subsequently provide the relevant and actionable intelligence to investigators.

3. **Investigative Follow-up and Prosecution:** Linking otherwise unassociated crimes gives investigators a better chance to identify and arrest shooters before they reoffend.

4. **Feedback Loop:** Without feedback, NIBIN partners cannot know how their efforts are making the community safer, which is necessary for sustained success.

■ Investigative Tool or Evidence Analysis

Some view NIBIN as an intelligence-gathering tool. Many of the agencies that are responsible for the analysis of firearms-related evidence are not responsible for investigating crimes. Rather, they are responsible for processing and analyzing evidence. Since NIBIN is essentially comparing digital pictures, rather than evidence, it is not necessarily "evidence analysis." Any time a "match" or "hit" is made on NIBIN, it is considered an investigative lead only. The actual case evidence must then be put under a digital comparison microscope and analyzed by a firearms examiner to make an identification for court purposes. Therefore, NIBIN is essentially a technologic filter.

For instance, firearm evidence may be uploaded (and possibly even analyzed) associated with a shots-fired incident, involving no witnesses and having no leads or possibility of criminal prosecution. The same would occur in a case where a firearm was used in the commission of a homicide, and which had a plethora of witnesses and other evidence, having a

---

— Ripped from the Headlines —

NIBIN Statistics

As of March of 2017:

- The ATF has certified more than 1,000 NIBIN users

- Nationwide, approximately 25,000 items are entered into NIBIN each month

- There are currently 172 sites and 3,500 agencies contributing to NIBIN

- NIBIN partners have captured approximately 2.8 million images of firearm-related evidence

- NIBIN partners have confirmed over 74,000 NIBIN hits

— Ripped from the Headlines —

Future Issues with Bullet Path Determination

In April of 2015, the world was made aware of a startling development in the world of ballistics. According to the United States Defense Advanced Research Projects Agency (DARPA), the military has developed a self-steering bullet. Intended for long-distance application, the bullet is capable of changing course in order to strike moving targets. In February, the "smart bullet" (a .50-caliber projectile equipped with optical sensors) had successfully concluded a live-fire test. During the test, an experienced marksman "repeatedly hit moving and evading targets. Additionally, a novice shooter using the system for the first time hit a moving target. " Although tested with a .50-caliber projectile, it is anticipated that the technology "opens the door to what could be possible in future guided projectiles across all calibers."

From a crime scene investigation standpoint, the new technology will add an interesting wrinkle to crime scene processing techniques. Traditional bullet path determination, using such things as trajectory analysis, will not be possible. Are we reaching a day when determining where the shooter was and what path the bullet took will be impossible? Or will there simply be the development of new and exciting technology that defies traditional thinking and will allow for possible modeling that will keep pace with this new development in technology?

Melvin, D. (2015). No more dodging a bullet, as U.S. develops self-guided ammunition. *CNN*. Retrived July 31, 2015, from http://www.cnn .com/2015/04/29/us/us-military-self-guided-bullet/ index.html

high likelihood of successful criminal prosecution. In either case, the same workload would be present from an IBIS/NIBIN standpoint. However, in the first case, this would rarely be an example of evidence sent to a crime lab for analysis. Whereas the second example would nearly always go to a crime lab for analysis. And yet, both examples would be cases that agencies would want to enter related information into NIBIN for the inherent possibility of connecting the events to other firearm-related incidents.

As a result of the aforementioned, some of the IBIS units that comprise NIBIN have moved to within police intelligence centers. This has been deemed to speed up the process of entry and also to make the best use of the derived information, and within its proper context, as a tool to generate investigative leads, but not necessarily as an evidence identification tool. In some instances, this has also helped to reduce case backlog within the crime laboratories.

In the end, as with most tools in the investigative toolbox, NIBIN (and its associated information) is only as good as the information that is loaded into it and as good as the examiner who is examining and analyzing it. Firearms-related evidence analysis remains an area of forensics that is accentuated by technology, but which continues to have as its foundation, the properly trained and educated humans, who are ultimately responsible for making the "match."

Bullet Path Determination

Defining a bullet's path at a shooting scene is a useful element of crime scene reconstruction. A shooter's position and final bullet location can both be defined by determining the path of a bullet or bullets through a sequence of materials. Such reconstructions are most accurate when a bullet has created both a bullet hole and a subsequent impact site or two or more bullet holes appear in successive planes of material, for example, in sheet rock on both sides of an interior wall. Inserting rods through the bullet holes (or from bullet hole to impact site) will define a bullet path that can direct the investigator to the shooter's position or to the bullet's likely location. Rods should not be inserted in any bullet hole until documentation and examination of the bullet hole has been completed. Over short distances, string can be attached to the rods to project the bullet path. This technique is especially useful in reconstructing shootings involving vehicles due to their double-panel construction. However, because the projected bullet path increases in distance from the bullet hole, greater imprecision will be introduced into the reconstruction. For bullet path

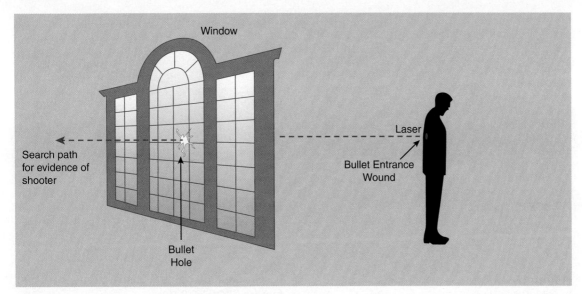

FIGURE 8.17: Determining discharge trajectory and location of shooter.

Courtesy of Dana Gevelinger.

reconstructions over long distances, a combination of spacer cones, rods, and lasers will offer much better precision, especially if meaningful diagramming of the reconstruction is desired (**FIGURE 8.17**).

Unless a bullet passes through a significant thickness of material, a single bullet hole will usually not allow useful reconstruction of the bullet path. However, bullet direction can be determined from through-and-through bullet holes in many materials. The passage of a bullet through metal will create an indentation on the metal surface facing the bullet origin and metal stretch on the surface in the direction away from bullet origin, clearly defining the direction of the bullet through the metal. Bullets that pass through auto glass, skull, and some plastics will create a crater on the side of the material away from the bullet origin. In other words, the crater opens up in the direction of bullet travel. Even a portion of a bullet hole in a destructively fractured skull can define the direction of the bullet and subsequently establish exit and entrance. The combination of glass cratering and radial glass fracture in a window can even define the sequence of shots through the window, particularly when working with vehicle shootings.

Evaluating and Documenting Zones of Possibility

While observing and documenting the crime scene, personnel begin to develop theories of possibilities and potential areas from which the shooting event could have originated. It is important to narrow down areas of possibility and areas of impossibility regarding the event, so as to reduce the suspect pool, tighten the story, and come as close as possible to the truthful events that transpired. While determining a trajectory may not definitively place an individual in a specific position or location, it can serve to eliminate individuals or locations, and exclusions are just as important to investigative efforts as inclusions. What is essential to determine in such a case would be what is referred to as **zones of possibility**. These zones of possibility are documented to establish limits as to what is likely, what is possible, and what is impossible, based upon the evidence presented (Moran, 2001). The zones are commonly identified as follows.

■ Zone 1

Probable: The area of greatest probability. The location of this zone is typically at a point along the identified trajectory that is at or lower than the likely shooter's shoulder height, and which is considered most comfortable and most logical, given the context of the scene being evaluated. This zone is further established and narrowed through inclusion of other scene-related shooting incident evidence, such as muzzle-to-target data evaluation (**FIGURE 8.18**).

zones of possibility
Used to establish limits as to what is likely, what is possible, and what is impossible, based upon the evidence presented

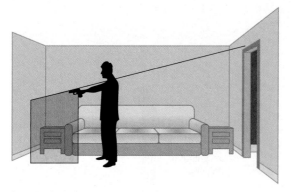

FIGURE 8.18: Zone 1: Probable.

Courtesy of Gabbie Mears.

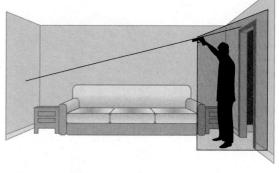

FIGURE 8.20: Zone 3: Impossible.

Courtesy of Gabbie Mears.

▪ Zone 2

Possible: This zone includes possible locations where a shooter could have been when the shot was fired but which would include an awkward stance or position. This typically involves any position along the identified trajectory path that is higher than the likely shooter's shoulders but which could still be reached by the shooter. For instance, it may be possible for a shooter to reach his or her arms up to the ceiling and bend his or her wrist so as to place the firearm on the trajectory, but such a position would not likely be a logical firing position unless there was an obstruction, a struggle, or some event that necessitated the awkward angle and positioning (**FIGURE 8.19**).

▪ Zone 3

Impossible: This zone includes the areas within the identified shooting area that would be impossible for the shooter to have stood and fired the shot. In this area, the shooter would be physically incapable of aligning the firearm along the identified trajectory. Such impossibilities could

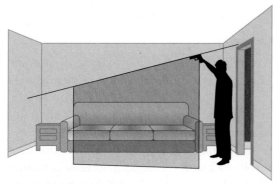

FIGURE 8.19: Zone 2: Possible.

Courtesy of Gabbie Mears.

be a result of height, obstructions, or other factors (**FIGURE 8.20**).

Not all shooting-related incidents will have all three zones of possibility present. For instance, in an event involving level flight, no higher than a possible shooter's shoulders, there would only be two zones present. Zone 1 would include the probable area and Zone 3 would include the area outside of the room or vicinity from which the shot could not have originated. There would be no Zone 2.

Range-of-Fire Estimation from Powder and Pellet Patterns

In the reconstruction of shooting incidents, the range and direction of fire are of paramount importance. Gunshot residue is typically used to measure these patterns. Gunshot residue consists of particles from the gun barrel, particles from the bullet surface, particles originating from the propellant, and particles originating from the primer. This residue is projected in a roughly conical cloud in the direction of the target (**FIGURE 8.21**).

A widely used rule-of-thumb is that the pellets spread one inch for each yard down range. The sizes of shotgun pellet patterns are affected by the choke of the shotgun barrel. Sawing off the barrel of a shotgun may increase the size of the pellet patterns that it will fire.

Legal Aspects

A Virginia case decided in 1897, *Dean v. Commonwealth*, was the first in which an appellate court approved of testimony regarding the similarity

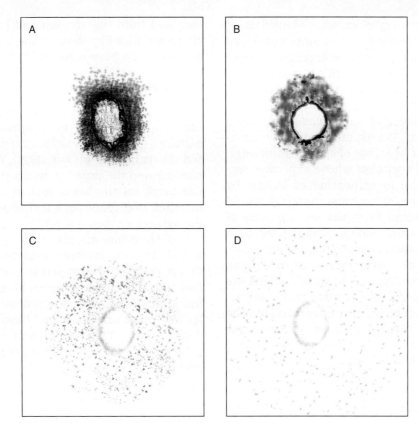

FIGURE 8.21: Determining proximity of firearm at the time of discharge.

Courtesy of Ellie Blazer.

INVESTIGATOR'S
NOTEBOOK
Range-of-Fire Estimation

Forensic pathologists usually place the range from which a GSW was inflicted into one of several categories:

1. **Distant:** No detectable GSR reaches the skin or clothing of the victim. GSWs consist of a circular or elliptical defect in the skin, which is surrounded by a "marginal abrasion ring" where the skin has been stretched and torn by the bullet entry.

2. **Close Range/Intermediate Range:** GSR reaches the skin/clothing of the victim and stippling /tattooing is present.

3. **Near Contact/Contact:** Often produces a *stellate defect*, which is an irregular, blown-out entrance wound. This type of wound is caused by the propellant gases separating the soft tissue from the bone and creating a temporary pocket of hot gas between the bone and the muzzle of the weapon. Blood and other tissue may be blown back into the muzzle of the weapon and onto the hand and forearm of the shooter.

between fatal and test bullets (weight was the compared variable). Beginning with *Jack v. Commonwealth*, a Kentucky case decided in 1928, expert testimony concerning firearms identification began to receive objective appellate appraisal. A year later, this same court, in *Evans v. Commonwealth* (1929), rendered the first exhaustive opinion treating firearms identification as a science and sanctioned its use for the purpose of establishing the guilt of the accused.

Today, the accuracy of firearms identification is common knowledge, and ample case law upholds the admissibility of firearms evidence when presented by a qualified expert.

As with other expert testimony, the witness is permitted to testify that in his or her opinion, a particular bullet was fired from a certain weapon. The expert's testimony is confined to his or her areas of special knowledge. For example, a witness whose expertise concerns only the identification of bullets by means of their microscopic markings would not be permitted to testify on the issue of whether a certain wound was caused by a particular weapon or whether the bullet traveled a particular trajectory prior to striking the victim. In situations in which bullets are mutilated beyond identification or the suspect weapon cannot be fired, an expert still may be permitted to testify regarding other relevant matters. Even though the condition of fatal bullets may preclude an identification of the evidence weapon, an identification is permissible on the basis of cartridge case breech face imprints, firing pin impressions, or ejector and extractor marks (*Williams v. State*, 1960).

Class Characteristics

A firearms expert may be able to identify only the class characteristics of a badly deformed bullet. That expert may still testify to the fact that the fatal bullets were fired from a gun having characteristics similar to those of the gun obtained from the accused and had physical characteristics like those of the bullets in the accused's gun (*State v. Bayless*, 1976).

Cartridge Evidence

Identification based on a comparison of breech face imprints, firing pin impressions, and extractor and ejector marks was recognized by the courts in *State v. Clark* (1921). This Oregon case allowed the expert to testify that "a peculiar mark on the brass part of the primer" matched that found on a cartridge fired from the suspect weapon.

In Montana, another case was decided based on comparative evidence (*State v. Vuckovich*, 1921). The expert in this case testified that a peculiar crimp on an empty shell found at the scene of the murder was similar to a mark on shells fired from the defendant's pistol. Evidence was introduced to show that the "firing marks made by the lands and grooves of the barrel of the pistol were the same" on both the test and the fatal bullets. This decision confirmed the acceptability of using shells and bullets as comparative evidence.

Chain of Custody

As with all evidence, the chain of custody of weapons, shells, and bullets must be unbroken and documented. If it is necessary for more than one examiner to handle the evidence,

CASE IN POINT

Examination of the Weapon Used to Assassinate President Lincoln

In 1997, a U.S. Park Captain and a curator of the National Park Service retrieved the Derringer pistol that had been allegedly used by John Wilkes Booth to assassinate President Abraham Lincoln. The pistol had been on display at the Ford Theater and was turned over to the FBI for nondestructive testing to determine if the artifact was truly the weapon used by Booth in the slaying of the President.

In addition to the Derringer, the FBI was provided photographs of the pistol, taken at the time of the shooting. The FBI's Firearms-Toolmarks Unit recorded the physical characteristics of the weapon and compared it with others of the period. Using modern digital photography, they superimposed pictures of the artifact over the pictures taken at the time of the assassination. The photographs matched perfectly. The physical characteristics of the pistol were examined and the wood of the stock bore distinctive patterning. The barrel displayed pit marks that were distinctive. Both the wood grain and the pit marks matched the photographic evidence. The FBI determined beyond a reasonable doubt, based on the examination of the firearm, that it was the weapon used by Booth in his assassination of President Abraham Lincoln.

Source: Schehl, S. A., & Rosati, C. J. (2001, January). The Booth Derringer: Genuine artifact or replica. *Forensic Science Communications*, 3(1), 42–44.

that should be recorded and the documentation should be available to the defendant upon request. Every moment of the existence of the evidence from the time it entered into the possession of the state (through the hands of law enforcement personnel) to its introduction at the time of trial must be accounted for and supported by the appropriate chain-of-custody documentation.

Long periods of time may elapse between the time that shots are fired and the time that the bullets or shells are collected. In *State v. Boccadoro* (1929), a bullet fired into the ground a year or two prior to the commission of the murder under investigation was recovered and identified as having been fired by the murder weapon. In *State v. Lane* (1951), shells dropped into a river during target practice months before their recovery were admitted. The time that the shells spent underwater was to be considered when assigning weight to the evidence, but it was not detrimental to admissibility. In *Commonwealth v. Ellis* (1977), bullets that had been fired into an oak tree 4 months prior to the homicide were recovered and matched to the bullets found at the scene of the crime.

The destruction of firearm evidence before the defendant has had an opportunity to conduct his or her own tests may be a violation of a defendant's constitutional rights to due process and of the confrontation assurances of the Sixth Amendment. Where the destruction is inadvertent, the courts have been unsympathetic to such claims. The state inadvertently destroyed the alleged murder weapon and bullets in the case of *People v. Triplett* (1965), and the defendant contended that this destruction denied him his right to confront the state's firearms expert with his own expert's analysis of the physical evidence. The court rejected this assertion, refusing to take an absolutist view of the confrontation clause.

CONCLUSION

Firearms are the most common weapon used in homicides in the United States. The historic relationship with firearms and violent confrontation of our Western past is alive and well in the American proclivity to use firearms to commit crimes and resolve conflict. The good news is that firearm evidence at crime scenes is readily found and recovered and is easily identifiable. National ballistics databases make the identification of firearms evidence quicker and more accessible.

Confrontation to resolve a dispute may result in death. The next chapter introduces us to the specific nature of death investigations in all of its manifestations from manslaughter to capital murder.

QUESTIONS FOR REVIEW

1. What are the differences among physical evidence, testimonial evidence, and circumstantial evidence?

2. Transferability is an important forensic concept for investigators to understand. Why?

3. What is the difference between firearms examination and ballistics?

4. Why is a pistol that fires each time the trigger is pulled misnamed if referred to as an "automatic"?

5. What role do lands and grooves play in a bullet's flight and in the examination of a suspect bullet?

6. What is the measure for expressing the size of a shotgun or a shotgun shell? How is it determined?

7. Who was Calvin Goddard, and what did he contribute to the field of firearms examination?

REFERENCES

Bureau of Alcohol, Tobacco, Firearms, and Explosives (ATF). (n.d.). Retrieved June 29, 2017, from https://www.atf.gov/resource-center/data-statistics

Bureau of Justice Statistics. (2014). *Firearms and crime statistics.* Retrieved July 28, 2015, from http://bjs.ojp.usdoj.gov/content/guns.cfm

Dutelle, A. W. (2017). *An introduction to crime scene investigation* (3rd ed.). Burlington, MA: Jones & Bartlett Learning.

Girard, J. E. (2017). *Criminalistics: Forensic science, crime and terrorism* (4th ed.). Burlington, MA: Jones & Bartlett Learning.

Goddard, C. H. (1930). St. Valentine's Day massacre: A study in ammunition tracing. *American Journal of Police Science, 1,* 60–78.

Hall, A. L. (1931). The missile and the weapon. *American Journal of Police Science, 2,* 311–321.

Heard, B. J. (2008). *Handbook of firearms and ballistics: Examining and interpreting forensic evidence.* Hoboken, NJ: Frank Willey.

Lane, A. J. (1971). *The Brownsville affair: National crisis and black reaction.* Port Washington, NY: Kennikat.

Melvin, D. (2015). No more dodging a bullet, as U.S. develops self-guided ammunition. *CNN.* Retrieved July 31, 2015, from http://www.cnn.com/2015/04/29/us/us-military-self-guided-bullet/index.html

Moran, B. (2001). *Shooting incident reconstruction,* presentation to the Association of Crime Scene Reconstruction. Las Vegas, NV. October 2001.

Schehl, S. A., & Rosati, C. J. (2001, January). The Booth Derringer: Genuine artifact or replica. *Forensic Science Communications, 3*(1), 42–44.

Sommerville, J., Hatcher, J. S., Jury, F. J., & Weller, J. (2006). *Firearms: Investigation, identification and evidence.* Schnecksville, PA: Ray Riling Arms Books.

The Diagram Group. (2007). *The new weapons of the World Encyclopedia.* New York, NY: St. Martin's.

Ultra Electronics Forensic Technology. (n.d.). Retrieved June 29, 2017, from http://www.ultra-forensictechnology.com/about

KEY LEGAL CASES

Commonwealth v. Best, 62 N.E. 748 (1902).
Commonwealth v. Ellis, 364 N.E.2d 808 (1977).
Dean v. Commonwealth, 32 Gratt (V.) 912 (1897).
Evans v. Commonwealth, 19 S.W.2d 1091 (1929).
Jack v. Commonwealth, 222 Ky. 546, 1 S.W.2d 961 (1928).
People v. Triplett, 243 N.W.2d 665 (1965).
State v. Bayless, 357 N.E.2d 1035 (1976).
State v. Boccadoro, 144 A. 612 (1929).
State v. Clark, 196 P. 360 (1921).
State v. Lane, 223 P.2d 437 (1951).
State v. Vuckovich, 203 P. 491 (1921).
Williams v. State, 333 S.W.2d 846 (1960).

Death Investigation

KEY TERMS

abrasion ring

adipocere

algor mortis

antemortem

asphyxia

autopsy

burial indicators

causation

corneal clouding

corpus delicti

death

decomposition

direction of fire

entry wound

excusable homicide

exit wound

exsanguination

forensic entomology

fouling

gloving

homicide

hyperspectral imaging

justifiable homicide

laceration

lividity

livor mortis

mummification

murder

penetrating wound

perforating wound

perimortem

petechial hemorrhage

postmortem

postmortem interval (PMI)

proximate cause

putrefaction

rigor mortis

stippling

stocking

taphonomy

Virchow method

"Was there any clue, may I ask, as to the exact hour that the man met his death?

He had been there since one o'clock. There was rain about that time, and his death had certainly been before the rain."

Sherlock Holmes
"A Reminiscence of Mr. Sherlock Holmes"

STUDENT LEARNING OUTCOMES

Upon completion of this chapter, students will be able to:

- Distinguish the different types of homicides
- Apply a homicide investigative protocol
- Recognize the types of wounds made by firearms
- List the postmortem changes in a decedent

Introduction to Death Investigation

For the purposes of this text, and most criminal investigations, **death** is the irreversible cessation of circulatory and respiratory functions. No crime scene and subsequent investigation will require as much from investigative personnel as a death investigation. Personnel will be called upon to use all aspects of their training and education in an effort to determine whether the death was natural or unnatural. However, not every death scene is a homicide, and not every homicide is a murder. It is important to understand the distinction between the various classifications of death (**FIGURE 9.1**).

Challenges in the Investigation

Death investigations have added difficulty due to a number of challenges that exist compared with other types of investigations. One of the largest is pressure by the media and the public. The public has a desire and a right to feel safe. It is up to the police to ensure that the community is safe and that the reason for the death is determined in an effort to alleviate community concerns for future safety.

Sometimes, this is not as easy as it would appear, however. Although there might be a death, there also might be difficulty establishing that the death is not from natural causes or that a crime has been committed. If the death involves advanced decomposition of remains or is particularly gruesome, it may be difficult to identify the victim. Lastly, as will be discussed further in this chapter, establishing the cause, manner, and time of death is not always as simplistic as is shown in modern forensic television and film dramas and, in many cases, is particularly difficult.

FIGURE 9.1: Coroner personnel remove a body.
© Zuma Press Inc./Alamy Stock Photo.

Homicide

Homicide is the killing of one person by another. A basic requirement in a homicide investigation is to establish whether death was caused by a criminal action. Murder and homicide are not synonymous. All murders are homicides (and criminal); however, not all homicides are murders (or criminal). Although the term *homicide* is usually associated with a crime, not all homicides are crimes.

Excusable homicide is the unintentional, truly accidental killing of another person. It is the result of an act that, under normal conditions, would not cause death, or from an act committed with due caution that, because of negligence on the part of the victim, results in death (i.e., running in front of a car).

Justifiable homicide is the killing of a person under authority of the law. This includes killing in self-defense or in the defense of another person if the victim's actions and capability present imminent danger of serious injury or death. It also includes killing an enemy during wartime, capital punishment, and deaths caused by police officers while attempting to prevent a dangerous felon's escape or to recapture a dangerous felon who has escaped or is resisting arrest.

Not all homicides require the attention of the police. The circumstances of the homicide determine if it was justifiable or if it was **murder**, the killing of another with *malice aforethought*. Criminal homicide is defined by state statute and may be further subdivided into categories such as capital murder (murders for which, due to the circumstances of the murder, capital punishment may be imposed), murder (homicide with malice aforethought), and manslaughter (homicide with the absence of malice aforethought). Many states still use degrees to distinguish one type of homicide from another, with first-degree murder being murder with malice aforethought.

Every murder has specific elements that must be proven at the time of trial, referred to as the **corpus delicti** of the offense. The use of this Latin term, which means *body of the crime*, often misleads the public and the media into thinking that the state must produce a corpse in order to convict someone for murder. In fact, the term is used in law to refer to the material evidence in a criminal homicide case that shows that a crime has been committed (evidence that may include the victim's corpse, of course). All criminal homicides require the state to prove the following:

- There has been a death of a human being (which may be difficult to prove absent a body—this fact, in turn, explains the tendency of perpetrators of premeditated murders to try to dispose of the body).

- The death was caused by another person's illegal act or failure to act.

The legal questions that often plague a homicide investigation usually revolve around **proximate cause** and **causation**. The question of proximate cause concerns the conduct of the agent and the consequences of that conduct. The illegal act must be close in time and space to the death of the deceased. There is no problem in determining that a person who shot a gun was responsible for the consequences when the projectile struck the person at whom the gun was aimed. Proximate cause may become an issue, however, in more convoluted scenarios. Consider this example: Someone fires a shot into a construction site for the purpose of shooting a personal enemy but instead causes a person on the construction site to jump instinctively and drop a concrete block, which, in turn, strikes and kills another person two stories below. This scenario may be tragic, but the person firing the shot has not murdered the person upon whom the block has fallen. The chain of cause and effect is too tenuous to establish the causal element of the corpus delicti of murder.

The question of causation most often arises in situations in which an individual is seriously injured by another but does not die immediately or shortly after the assault. The greater the time from the illegally caused injury until death, the more attenuated the relationship between the injuring act and the death becomes. Most states address the causation question by statute, requiring that the death occurs within a particular timeframe after the illegal act causes the injury.

Most police agencies do not have homicide investigators and evidence technicians, although most metropolitan agencies do. Therefore, it is necessary in many small or rural agencies for all patrol officers to process their own crime scenes. Assignment is on a first-come, first-served basis, and the responding officer is also the officer responsible for the investigation and preparation of the case for trial.

Suicide Versus Homicide

More Americans die by suicide than by homicide. Research studies have shown that 85% of suicides are premeditated and that 90% of those who take their lives communicate their intentions to someone they know (Bennett & Hess,

2010). Three basic considerations to establish that a death might be a suicide include:

1. The presence of the weapon or means of death at the scene.
2. Injuries or wounds that are obviously self-inflicted or that could have been inflicted by the deceased.
3. The existence of a motive or intent on the part of the victim to take his or her own life.

All death investigations should be treated as homicide investigations, regardless of the initial reporting or theory that the death is a suicide. This ensures that the investigation does not become narrowly focused or only documents evidence that supports the theory of suicide.

Who Kills?

Americans report more than 16,000 murders each year, most of which occur in large cities. Most murder victims are white; however, in proportion to the population, blacks are more often both victims and offenders. Criminal homicide is the leading cause of death among black males 25 to 34 years of age. Most murders are committed using a firearm and are perpetrated by the young, those 20 to 24 years old. Men are more likely to be killed in the kitchen, whereas women are more likely to be killed in the bedroom. Criminal homicide is predominantly the domain of men; women commit only 10% of criminal homicides. To the advantage of the police, only 20% of homicides are committed by strangers; the rest are homicides in which a casual or close personal relationship exists between victim and offender. The number of stranger murders is growing, presumably as a result of increased gang- and drug-related violence (Federal Bureau of Investigation [FBI], 1975–2009).

Preliminary Investigation

Regardless of what is reported, at any scene, the first priority is to give emergency aid to the victim, if he or she is still alive, or to determine that death has occurred. Signs of death include lack of breathing, lack of heartbeat, lack of flushing of the fingernail bed when pressure is applied to the nail and then released, and failure of the eyelids to close after being gently lifted. Another quite obvious sign of death is advanced decomposition and related insect activity. If there are remains with insects coming and going from the body, it does not require one to be a physician to determine that the person is dead.

proximate cause
A cause that directly produces an event and without which the event would not have occurred; a cause that is legally sufficient to result in liability

causation
The production of an effect

In cases of sudden, unexpected, suspicious, or unnatural death (homicide, accident, or suicide), the coroner or medical examiner (ME) must be notified and his or her representative will be responsible for the body remains and the subsequent death investigation. The crime leading to the death, and the investigation concerned with such, remains the responsibility of law enforcement. It is imperative that the agencies work together in an effort to ensure the proper investigatory outcome. It is the responsibility of the coroner or ME to establish the cause and manner of death.

Numerous persons will be in a hurry to move the deceased, but any movement of the deceased should be done by the investigators or by medical personnel under the direction of the investigators. Once the coroner or ME arrives, the medical personnel will likely ask to remove the body—for their own convenience. They have better things to do than hang around a crime scene. The body should not be removed until the investigator has gathered whatever information he or she is seeking, regardless of how long that may take.

Once the scene has been cleared of unnecessary personnel (there should have been none to start with), the investigator can begin a closer examination of the body and the crime scene and may uncover relationships between the positioning or location of the body and other aspects of the crime scene.

The Investigative Protocol

Until it has been conclusively determined that the death in question was accidental or a product of natural causes, the investigator should follow the protocol outlined in the Investigator's Notebook. In jurisdictions that have homicide investigators and departments, it may prove helpful to remember who is on the investigative team.

The Investigative Team

The first responder maintains crime scene integrity, retains and segregates witnesses, and arrests suspects. It is important to remember that the first responder is a team member and to acknowledge the contribution that he or she makes toward attaining the objective of

INVESTIGATOR'S NOTEBOOK

Protocol at the Scene of a Death

1. Preserve the crime scene.
2. Retain and segregate witnesses.
3. Conduct a preliminary scene survey of the crime scene.
   a. Mentally locate evidence.
   b. Mentally locate access and exit points and look for evidence of forced entry.
   c. Navigate the crime scene without damaging or contaminating trace or blood evidence. (If this is not possible, ensure that trace and blood evidence are photographed and tagged and bagged, or arrange for blood specialists to evaluate blood-pattern evidence.)
   d. Determine what is to be photographed.
   e. Determine from what vantage point the best photos can be obtained.
   f. Determine what, if anything, appears to be missing.
   g. Attempt to construct a scenario based on your observations.
4. Search the premises for evidence.
   a. Navigate the crime scene without damaging or contaminating trace or blood evidence.
   b. Locate all evidence (mark the location of evidence with distinctive markers in order to relocate the evidence and to prevent its destruction or contamination during further searching).
5. Record the crime scene.
   a. Take field notes that reflect your first impressions and construct an overall description of the crime scene and the evidence.
   b. Photograph the scene based on impressions gathered during the preliminary scene survey.

6. Locate all evidence geographically and temporally. The measurements should be taken without disturbing the evidence. If this is not possible, they should be taken after collection of the evidence, using evidence markers placed in the same positions as the evidence collected.

7. Collect and preserve all evidence.

   a. Maintain an evidence log.
   b. Bag and tag all evidence.
   c. Where necessary, place an identifying mark on the evidence itself.

8. Identify the victim.

   a. Search for identifying documentation on the victim's body and confirm identification by talking with friends and relatives.
   b. If the victim is not readily identifiable, seek secondary evidence of identification and appropriate tools, such as:
      i. Medical records
      ii. Dental records
      iii. Radiographs
      iv. Composite drawings
      v. Assistance from a forensic anthropologist
      vi. Fingerprints
      vii. Jewelry

9. Ascertain cause and mechanism of death, utilizing documents, such as the following:

   a. Autopsy report
   b. Medical examiner's report
   c. Pathologist's report
   d. Toxicological report

10. Gather information.

    a. Conduct interviews with the following:
       i. Relatives
       ii. Neighbors
       iii. Employers
       iv. Coworkers
    b. Run a criminal history.
    c. Check business records.
    d. Compare the modus operandi to that of other crimes and criminals.
    e. Collect samples of writing, voice, hair, blood, and so on from the pool of suspects.

11. Interrogate suspects.

    a. Corroborate all statements using existing information.
    b. Allow a free flow of information.
    c. Do not express or imply any intimidation.
    d. Provide Miranda warnings.

all criminal investigations, which is winning a conviction.

The medical examiner pronounces the deceased dead, determines the cause and mechanism of death, and provides medico-legal information pertaining to death (the events that occurred prior to, during, and after death). A show of appreciation for the work done by the medical examiner may go a long way toward creating a good working relationship. The first place and time that the investigator and medical examiner talk about the case should not be at the courthouse just prior to trial.

Forensic scientists provide technical information about evidence obtained at the crime scene and may collect evidence at the crime scene. Knowing what forensic scientists do and how they do it will assist the investigator in searching, processing, and interpreting crime scenes.

Investigators analyze, process, and synthesize information for the purpose of providing legally sufficient evidence at the time of trial. Prosecutors utilize the work product of the rest of the team to convict the guilty party. Too often, other team members view prosecutors as adversaries or as people who will derail an investigation because of legal niceties or technicalities. The duty of all team members is to work together to obtain the conviction of criminals. Without the other members, the efforts of the investigator would be rendered useless. Each member of the team will make a contribution that will ultimately allow the investigator and trier of fact to determine the cause of death, the nature of the death (homicide, either justifiable or mitigated; natural causes; accident; or self-inflicted injury), and who caused the death.

Time of Death Determination

Most criminal homicide investigations try to establish a time of death in order to:

- Establish the victim's movements prior to death
- Establish the victim's activities prior to death
- Establish a suspect and witness pool
- Corroborate suspects' alibis
- Establish some parameters for the investigation
- Clarify anomalies at the crime scene

No problem in forensic medicine has been investigated as thoroughly as that of determining the time of death on the basis of postmortem findings. An effort to find the moment of death for a person dates back to as early as 1247 AD with the first known forensic handbook written by Sung Tz'u (Sachs, 2001). In his book, *The Washing Away of Wrongs*, Tz'u noted that decomposition rates change between seasons, even stating that winter decomposition rates will be five times slower than that of summer and that decomposition occurs at a different rate in heavier people.

Repeated experience teaches the investigator to be wary of relying on any single observation for estimating the time of death. Factors

that help in estimating the time of death include:

- Hypostasis/postmortem lividity/livor mortis
- Rigor mortis
- Algor mortis
- Vitreous draw
- Appearance of the eyes
- Stomach contents
- Stage of decomposition
- Evidence suggesting a change in the victim's normal routine

Many methods remain in use today to help investigators estimate the time of death, which is usually referred to as the **postmortem interval (PMI)** of a victim. The PMI is the time that has elapsed since a person has died. While only an estimate, it assists in narrowing the interval between death and discovery, providing a timeline for investigators to begin the search for the suspect. The PMI is estimated through various scientific observations of the changes that occur to a body after death. The scientific observations are based on the biologic processes of the body when it is both living and dead. The heart circulates oxygen-rich blood throughout the body but also has the important role of removing bacteria and waste from the body. With death, the heart stops pumping, gravity causes blood to settle, and the bacteria remain in the body. Although their host is deceased, bacteria continue to thrive. These physiological events all contribute to the beginning of the decomposition process.

Hypostasis / Postmortem Lividity / Livor Mortis

Livor mortis is another aid in PMI estimations when combined with both algor mortis and rigor mortis. Also known as postmortem lividity, **livor mortis** is the visible color change that occurs from the pooling of blood once the heart stops pumping. The onset of **lividity** begins within half an hour after death (**FIGURE 9.2**). Until the point in which lividity is set, blanching may occur, and the lividity may shift if the victim's body position is changed. Blanching can be noticed when applying pressure to an area where lividity is present; if the lividity temporarily disappears upon the application of pressure, lividity is not yet set but becomes set once the blood clots. The timeframe in which lividity sets varies, but typically occurs between 8 and 12 hours. After 8 to 12 hours, the blood

postmortem interval (PMI) The time that has elapsed since a person has died; while only an estimate, it assists in narrowing the interval between death and discovery

livor mortis The gravitational movement of blood to the lowest point after deaths occurring other than as a result of drowning

lividity A purplish-blue discoloration on the lowest points of the body that are not in contact with a hard surface, associated with the onset of livor mortis...

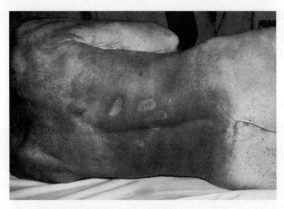

FIGURE 9.2: Example of post-mortem lividity.

Courtesy of Dr. Edward T. McDonough.

will congeal in the capillaries or diffuse into the surrounding tissues, both of which will result in a lack of blanching being present, and the inability for displacement of blood to occur. In some cases of advanced stages of lividity, the capillaries may burst and cause what appear to be small, pinpoint hemorrhages, which are termed *Tardieu spots*. This is especially common in the lower extremities in situations involving hanging.

Lividity appears purple in color, which is caused by the dying, deoxygenated blood. The color of lividity presents several problems. In some instances, lividity may be mistaken for bruising or injuries that occurred prior to death, and in other instances may be undetectable due to the color of a victim's skin or blood loss. Once again, because of the disparity in the timeframe and the difficulty in detecting it, lividity is simply another tool to be used in combination with algor mortis and rigor mortis to estimate a timeframe for death. Together, these three methods can be used to help investigators estimate the

time of death, but at the most, these are only present for up to 60 hours (Bennett & Hess, 2010).

Rigor Mortis

Rigor mortis, or the stiffening of the body, is another factor to consider when estimating the PMI. Rigor mortis begins within 1 to 4 hours after death (**FIGURE 9.3**). Ultimately, rigor mortis is the contraction of body muscles; it begins in the smaller muscle groups and progresses to the larger groups and may be found first in the jaw and neck. It is the direct result of chemical changes that occur in the body upon death. Adenosine 59-triphosphate (ATP) nucleotide in cells is the chemical "energy" that allows muscles to contract and relax. Following death, the body's supply of ATP is depleted and lactic acid is produced, which results in the contraction of muscles. This chemical reaction is responsible for the fixation of a body in its position of rigor (stiffened muscles).

Because ATP is affected by muscle movement, there is no standard for the amount present in the body. Strenuous exercise, excitement, or a struggle before death will affect the amount of ATP present, which, in turn, directly affects the onset of rigor mortis. This is because muscles that were used extensively just prior to death will contain more lactic acid, which expedites the rigor process.

In temperate climates, rigor mortis becomes completely set by approximately 12 hours after death. It will then remain in place for approximately 12 hours, at which time it will begin to dissipate, disappearing after approximately another 12 hours. Rigor mortis has many other factors that affect the time of onset and duration in a cadaver, including temperature and body size. Warmer temperatures may accelerate the progression of

rigor mortis
Stiffness of the muscles after death, which eventually freezes the joints

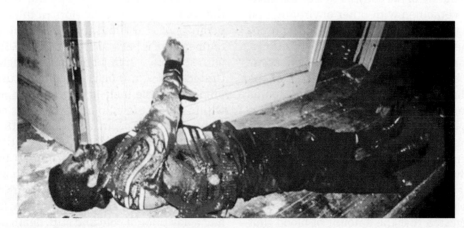

FIGURE 9.3: Example of rigor mortis (note unnatural positioning of victim).

Courtesy of Dr. Edward T. McDonough.

INVESTIGATOR'S NOTEBOOK

Hypostasis / Postmortem Lividity/Livor Mortis

- The medical condition that occurs after death and results in the settling of blood in areas of the body closest to the ground.
- The skin will appear as a dark blue or purple color in these areas.
- Onset is immediate and continues for up to 12 hours after death.
- The skin will not appear discolored in areas where the body is restricted by either clothing or an object pressing against the body but will, instead, lack coloring due to blanching.
- Can be useful in determining if the victim's position was changed after death occurred.

© Shutterstock, Inc./Janaka Dharmasena.

© Shutterstock, Inc./Nutink.

INVESTIGATOR'S NOTEBOOK

Rigor Mortis

- The medical condition occurs after death and results in the shortening of muscle tissue and the stiffening of body parts in the position they were in when death occurred.
- Appears within the first 24 hours and disappears within 36 hours.
- This can be useful in determining if the victim's position was changed after death occurred.

© Shutterstock, Inc./Janaka Dharmasena.

© Shutterstock, Inc./Nutink.

rigor mortis, while a colder temperature may significantly slow down the progression; rigor mortis may never develop in obese people, but it may be expedited in lean people. These disparities clearly demonstrate that PMI estimations must be combined with other means in order to find a more accurate timeframe.

Algor Mortis

The temperature of the body, as well as the environment, combined with other environmental and biologic factors, affect the rate of decomposition. The body's loss of heat, or **algor mortis**, is based on simple physics: heat loss will occur until the body reaches the temperature of the surrounding environment (ambient temperature). Numerous environmental factors can significantly alter the rate of heat loss. Humidity, wind, ambient temperature, body temperature at the time of death, the surface that the body is on, body position, body size and composition (fat acts as an insulator), and clothing can all affect the rate of heat loss of a body. It has even been suggested that the amount of blood that has been lost from a body may drastically affect this rate, because, essentially, the blood will be at the same temperature as the body, and less

blood remaining in the body is one less source of heat (Sachs, 2001).

Although there are what seem to be endless numbers of variables that affect the body temperature, algor mortis is still widely used throughout the United States as a beginning estimation of time of death. Algor mortis is best used as a predictor within the first 10 hours after death, where the heat is lost at approximately 1.5°F per hour. This is based on the assumption that the body was at the normal internal temperature of 98.6°F and that the environmental temperature is between 70°F and 75°F. However, with so many varying climates throughout the United States, a touch test is often used as a predictor. If the body is warm, death occurred within the last few hours; if a body is cold and clammy, death occurred between 18 and 24 hours ago (Geberth, 2006). This method may also be combined with rigor mortis to give a closer timeframe: if the body is warm and flexible, death occurred within a few hours; if warm and stiff, death occurred from a few hours to half a day prior; if cold and stiff, death occurred from half a day to 2 days prior; and finally, if the body is cold and not stiff, death occurred more than 2 days prior (Sachs, 2001).

algor mortis
Postmortem drop in body temperature

INVESTIGATOR'S NOTEBOOK

Algor Mortis

- Postmortem changes cause a body to lose heat. The process in which the body temperature continually cools after death until it reaches the ambient or room temperature is algor mortis.

- It is influenced by factors such as the location and size of the body, the victim's clothing, and weather conditions.

- As a general rule, beginning an hour after death, the body will lose heat at a rate of approximately 1° to 1.5°F per hour until reaching ambient temperature. However, this is only an estimate.

© Shutterstock, Inc./Nutink.

Vitreous Draw

A relatively recent method of assisting with determination of PMI is to use a syringe to take a sample of ocular fluid (vitreous humor) from the eye to determine potassium levels. This is referred to as a *vitreous draw*. Studies have shown that following death, cells on the inner surface of the eyeball will begin to release potassium into the ocular fluid. Through the collection and analysis of the amount of potassium present at various intervals after death, the forensic pathologist can determine the rate at which potassium is released into the vitreous humor. This allows the time of death to be approximated.

Stomach Contents

The theme of variance continues when examining stomach contents. Stomach contents have been examined in the hope of determining the PMI. This may even include the contents throughout the gastrointestinal tract. Like the heart, digestion halts after death occurs and, therefore, the amount of food in the stomach, combined with the knowledge of when the victim's last meal was eaten, should be able to present a narrow timeframe for death. Digestion occurs as a process, and the presence of food or digested materials in the stomach and small intestines can give a timeframe for death. Digestion rates may have extreme variance from victim to victim, however, due to metabolism, activity prior to death, or narcotics.

Evidence Suggesting a Change in the Victim's Normal Routine

Yet another indicator of PMI involves evidence in a victim's home; place of business; car; or another place the victim frequents that suggests

an interruption or break in behavior, or aids in isolating specific dates. Examples include:

- Dated items in a fridge
- Newspapers or mail
- Answering machine / voicemail messages
- Computer activity (email)
- Receipts
- Calendars / date books

Appearance of the Eyes

The eyes are often the first part of the body to exhibit the earliest signs of postmortem change. This can include **corneal clouding** due to the eyes remaining open following death (**FIGURE 9.4**). A thin film can often be observed within minutes of death, converting to complete cornea clouding within 2 to 3 hours postmortem. If, however, the individual's eyes are closed, the corneal film development may be delayed by several hours and corneal cloudiness may not be present for more than 24 hours.

corneal clouding
A thickening of the thin film seen on the corneal surface within minutes after death; clouding occurs 2 to 3 hours after death

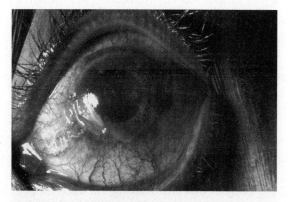

FIGURE 9.4: Example of corneal clouding.

© Dr. M.A. Ansary/Science Source.

If the individual dies in an arid environment, and his or her eyes are open at the time of death, the exposed area of the eyeball (sclera) may develop a brownish-black line known as *tache noire* (black spot).

Eyeball collapse, resulting from absence of intraocular fluid in the eyeball, typically will occur after 24 hours; however, it may take as long as 4 or 5 days following death.

Decomposition

The postmortem breakdown of body tissues is referred to as **decomposition**. During this process, the components that make up the tissues of the body will begin to leak and break down. The bacteria and other microorganisms present in the body (mouth, digestive tract, etc.) thrive on the newly unprotected organic components of the body, resulting in **putrefaction** (postmortem changes produced as a result of actions by bacteria and microorganisms).

Putrefaction

These decompositional changes are entirely dependent upon environmental conditions and the health of the victim prior to death. From an environmental standpoint, changes that occur in temperate climates in a matter of days may be evident in a warm environment within only hours. Additional considerations, such as the victim's proximity to a heat source, may also exacerbate putrefaction, while exposure to cold will significantly retard the process. Proximity to a heat source is not the only concern with regard to positioning and location of a victim. The rate of putrefaction is also dependent on whether the victim is exposed to air, buried, or in water. In general, putrefaction is more rapid in air than in water and more rapid in water than in soil. Approximately 1 week in air is the equivalent of 2 weeks in water and approximately 7 to 8 weeks in a soil environment. Putrefaction is more accelerated in obese victims and significantly slower in infants and thin individuals.

Under normal conditions, decomposition will initially be visually present within 24 to 30 hours. Early forms will manifest themselves as bluish-green discoloration of the abdomen region, due to the thriving bacterial present in the colon and digestive tract. The area of greatest discoloration is typically the lower right area of the abdomen.

The next phase of putrefactive changes to the body is gaseous bloating. As bacteria proceed to break down body tissues and organic material in the body, methane is produced, which causes certain areas of the body to swell and bloat. This is especially true of the abdominal area but is often found in the breasts and scrotum as well.

Next, dark purple and green discoloration of the face is common, along with purging of decomposition fluids from the orifices of the body. The discoloration of the face typically will spread to the chest and extremities within 36 to 48 hours after death. This period is characterized by venous marbling, a breakdown of the walls of the veins and arteries of the body with the seepage of blood into the surrounding tissues.

Decomposition will continue to progress with the separation of the epidermal and dermal skin layers, resulting in what is commonly referred gloving to as **gloving** (on the hands) or **stocking** slippage (on the legs or feet). This is especially true for bodies that have been immersed in water for a considerable amount of time, or bodies with second-degree burns.

Insect Activity

Insects are a foreign contributor to the process of decomposition, and yet, their contribution is an increasingly effective manner of estimating the PMI of a victim. **Forensic entomology** is the study of insects as they relate to a criminal investigation. Forensic entomology is a relatively new area of study in determining the PMI that has been gaining credibility since the 1980s. Entomology may prove useful in identifying previous locations of a body, but most importantly, how long a body has been dead. Through progression of insect eggs and presence on a body or even insect bite marks left postmortem, a PMI may start to be established. As a body continues to decompose, different odors attract different insects. Although the specific type of the insect may vary, insects within the same family tend to appear on a carcass at the same stage. The stages of decomposition harbor conditions that are good for different families of insects, which make the order of their appearance, regardless of the region, fairly predictable.

Insects found on a body are characterized into the following categories: (a) scavengers of the body, (b) predators and parasites of the scavengers and the body, (c) predators and parasites of only the scavengers, and (d) insects that use the body as a shelter. The first insects typically present on a body are flies, which will show up soon after death occurs and inhabit the body until the advanced decay stage. Soon after they arrive, the flies lay eggs on the body, typically in the corners of the eyes, mouth, and other mucous membrane areas, as well as in open wounds

---

decomposition
The postmortem breakdown of body tissues

gloving
The shedding of the skin of the hands, including the fingernails

stocking
The shedding of the skin around the feet and legs

putrefaction
The decomposition of the body

forensic entomology
The analysis of insects and other invertebrates that sequentially colonize a decomposing body and of the rates at which various stages of their offspring develop

FIGURE 9.5: Example of decompositional insect activity.

(**FIGURE 9.5**). Flies are still present through the advanced decay stage, but the fresh stage is the only stage in which the flies mate, which gives an important timeline toward the determination of a time of death for a carcass. A minimum time of death can be established once the eggs develop into maggots. The maggots will proceed to rapidly consume the soft tissues of the body and will concentrate on body openings and wounds or perforations to the body. Therefore, any time a decomposing body is found with a high concentration of maggot activity in a certain area, it sometimes can be deduced that the area was most likely the site of a wound to the individual (defensive wounds on hands, gunshot wound [GSW] in chest, etc.). In cases of contact or close-range firearm injuries, it is common for the maggots to consume the surrounding flesh but leave soot-covered flesh or bone untouched.

The succession of insects continues as beetles and other predators, such as bees, arrive to prey on the maggots. This continues in a predictable manner, allowing forensic entomologists to determine the time of death of the victim by determining the insect present on the carcass and the current stage of development of the insect.

Many insect inhabitants occupy the carcass in overlapping periods with other insects, making the PMI estimation much easier.

CASE IN POINT

© Shutterstock, Inc./Viastas

Insects Can Tell a Story

Sixty specimens of insects were found in two separate seizures of cannabis (marijuana) in New Zealand. Only one species was known to occur in New Zealand. Eight other species were native only to Asia:

COLEOPTERA

- *Bruchidius mendosus (Bruchidae):* Distributed throughout Southeast Asia but not known in Indonesia or the southern tip of the Malayan Peninsula.

- *Tachys species (Carabidae):* An abundant tropical genus normally found along the banks of streams or lakes.

- *Stenus basicornis (Staphylinidae):* Distributed throughout Southeast Asia; usually found on the banks of streams or lakes.

- *Azarelius sculpticollis (Tenebrionidae):* A rare species known only in Sumatra and Borneo. It lives as a "guest" in the nests of termites.

- *Gonocnemis minutus (Tenebrionidae):* Found in Thailand; lives as a "guest" in the nests of termites.

HYMENOPTERA

- *Parapristina verticellata:* A pollinator of the fig (*Ficus microcarpa*), that is distributed throughout the Indo Australian region, from India and South China to New Caledonia.

- *Tropimeris monodon (Chalcididae):* Known from northwest India to Sumbawa in Indonesia.

- *Pheidologeton diversus (Formicidae):* Restricted in distribution to Southeast Asia from India to Indochina, including Singapore and West Indonesia. It is most common in the Indo-Malaysian region, including Thailand. By plotting the distribution of these species and studying the degree of overlap, it was possible to suggest that the cannabis originated in the Tenasserim region between the Andaman Sea to the west and Thailand in the east. From the known habits of the insects, it was surmised that the cannabis was harvested near a stream or lake with fig trees and termite nests nearby.

Source: Goff, M. L. (2001). *A fly for the prosecution.* New York: Harvard University Press.

© Shutterstock, Inc./Nutink.

INVESTIGATOR'S NOTEBOOK

Handling Insect Evidence

Representative samples of all adult and immature insects should be collected from the corpse as well as from inside and beneath the body. Once collected, adult flying insects can be placed immediately in 70% ethanol or isopropyl alcohol diluted with water to a ratio of 1:1. Crawling insects from the surface and within the body should be collected using forceps or fingers. Insects on the ground beneath the corpse can be collected most easily by scooping up the top few centimeters of soil and placing it in a plastic bag. The plastic bag containing the soil should be chilled to prevent further growth of the insects before they are extracted and preserved. A careful examination of the soil beneath the corpse is important, particularly in cases of advanced decay. When skeletal remains are encountered in a field, examination of the bones and surrounding soil must be made prior to skeletal removal. Close examination of bone cavities should produce insect remains, and examination of the cranial vault should prove fruitful.

Representative samples of the fly larvae, including the largest individuals present, should be collected and immediately divided into two subsamples. One subsample can be preserved immediately in ethanol; the other should be saved alive for raising to the adult stage. Sufficient numbers of individuals should be collected to ensure that a representative sample of the insect population is present. Specimens for rearing should be placed alive in small cups filled with vermiculite or a similar inert substance. Living specimens to be reared should not be placed in sealed plastic bags or sealed vials for longer than 12 hours.

Containers holding the preserved and living specimens should be labeled with the appropriate data, such as date and time collected, location of the remains, area of the body from which removed; and the name, agency, and telephone number of the collector. Because climatic conditions have a profound effect on the development of immature insects, acquiring the most accurate available weather data describing conditions at the location where the corpse was found is critical. Whenever possible, maximum and minimum temperatures at the scene should be recorded (Amendt & Goff, 2009).

---

mummification
The dehydration of soft tissues as a result of high temperatures, low humidity, and wind or other form of ventilation

adipocere
The hydration and dehydrogenation of the body's fat, which results in an off-white, waxy, clay-like substance that in many cases preserves the body and retards the decomposition process

---

Although this method of PMI estimations has many benefits, insects are very sensitive to environmental changes as well as the manner of death. As with other areas of PMI estimation, temperature and humidity both affect the activity of insects on a body: while warmer temperatures accelerate insect activity, cooler temperatures retard insect activity, with activity even ceasing during periods of extreme cold.

Mummification

Mummification is the dehydration of soft tissues as a result of high temperatures, low humidity, and wind or other form of ventilation. The skin will appear brown, leather-like, and tight. The mummification process begins at the tips of the fingers and toes and progresses toward the hands and feet, face, and other extremities. Fingers found in a mummified state cannot be inked and fingerprinted. In such a case, the fingers first must be soaked in warm water so that the tissues will rehydrate, which allows them to be more pliable and closer to their original texture so that the ridge detail can be documented correctly.

In cases where mummification is allowed to become fully developed, a body will be preserved for a relatively long period of time. The rate at which mummification develops is a factor of environmental elements and conditions in the vicinity of the body, but often will require a postmortem interval of longer than 3 months to develop fully. This, of course, can be exacerbated by extreme heat and low humidity, for example, being present indoors during the winter months with the furnace on or being present in an arid, desert climate.

Adipocere

When a body is exposed to conditions of high humidity and high temperatures, it will often exhibit signs of **adipocere**. Adipocere is the hydration and dehydrogenation of the body's fat, which results in an off-white, waxy, clay-like substance that, in many cases, preserves the body and retards the decomposition process. It is especially common in the subcutaneous tissues of body extremities, the face, buttocks, and breasts, and in individuals with a high percentage of body fat.

Taphonomy

In order to study human remains, knowledge about the human physical form and function must be combined with scientific input regarding postmortem changes. The combined information is essentially the postmortem history of the body, which is referred to as **taphonomy**. Examples of postmortem changes include normal decomposition, alteration and scattering by scavengers, and movement and modification by flowing water, freezing, or mummification.

The study of taphonomy requires input from forensic experts in a variety of fields. Essentially, all of the biological and geological sciences overlap in the study of taphonomy. Anthropologists, entomologists, botanists, biologists, geologists, archeologists, pathologists, and many others are often called to contribute to telling the story or giving the history of a body following death. Assembling a taphonomic history of a body involves accounting for information relating to the circumstances of the death event itself as well as the interval of time between death and discovery and the collection of the body. This includes any modifications to the hard and soft tissues of a body by environment, activity, event, and scavengers. While it has already been discussed that it is a difficult process to collect accurate data and determine PMI, this difficulty is significantly compounded by the activities of weather, insects, rodents, and other animals. Small gnaw marks on bone by rodents sometimes can be mistaken for tool or weapon marks by an untrained eye. Cockroaches, ants, and other insects will sometimes leave postmortem bite marks on a body that will be mistaken for defensive wounds or other perimortem-related trauma. This natural scavenging activity can add a greater degree of difficulty for the investigative process when the involved scavenger removes a bone, limb, or other portion of a body and drags it away to its burrow or den. Often, these components will go undiscovered, even after a thorough search.

One of the largest parts of a taphonomic history involves the interpretation of traumatic injuries to the body. It must be determined whether the injuries were made before death and were beginning the healing process, whether they occurred at or near the time of death, or whether there were injuries to the body after death.

Antemortem Trauma

Antemortem injuries are those sustained prior to death that have healed or begun to heal. These can include injuries, such as broken bones that have been cast or set, cuts that have been stitched or begun healing on their own, or other injury activities where evidence of healing is shown.

Postmortem Trauma

A body may be subjected to modification by an assortment of taphonomic methods after death. These injuries are referred to as occurring **postmortem**. These can include injuries caused by carnivores, freezing and thawing, transport by flowing water, and many other events that may damage bone or soft tissue. Such postmortem damage is not related to the cause of death and must be differentiated from perimortem trauma. This is accomplished by noting the patterns of bone breakage and identifying modifications made by scavengers, plants, or other weather-related or geological processes.

Perimortem Trauma

Perimortem injuries are those that show evidence of having occurred at or near the time of death. These show no signs of healing, but do show signs that the body was still alive at the time of injury (as evidenced by hemorrhaging, subcutaneous blood, etc.). This type of injury can occur with hard tissues (bones) as well. However, unlike soft tissue, bone will not exhibit a vital reaction and requires several days of healing time in order to see evidence of healing. Therefore, bone damage that shows no signs of healing and for which no postmortem explanation exists often is considered to be related to perimortem causes. There are several classifications of perimortem-related injuries. These include mechanical trauma (sharp-force injuries and blunt-force injuries), thermal trauma, chemical trauma, and electric trauma.

Sharp Force Injuries

A sharp force injury is a subcategory of mechanical trauma that refers to injuries received from sharp implements, such as knives, machetes,

antemortem
Occurring before death

taphonomy
The study of postmortem changes to the body. Examples include: normal decomposition; alteration and scattering by scavengers; and movement and modification by flowing water, as well as freezing or mummification

postmortem
Occurring after death

perimortem
Occurring around the time of death

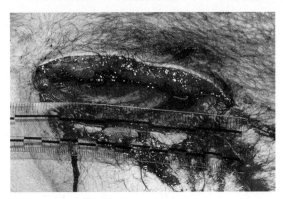

FIGURE 9.6: Example of sharp force injury.

laceration
A cut caused by blunt trauma

exsanguination
Death due to loss of blood/bleeding out

penetrating wound
A gunshot wound that does not exit the body

perforating wound
A gunshot wound that exits the body

saws, and axes (**FIGURE 9.6**). The amount of mechanical force required for a sharpened instrument to exceed the tensile strength of tissue is significantly less than the force required with a blunt object. Sharp objects produce incised wounds, known as *incisions*. In deaths resulting from sharp trauma, the cause is typically due to **exsanguination**—death due to loss of blood / bleeding out.

Defensive Wounds

In cases involving sharp force injuries, it may be necessary to determine whether the person sustained defensive wounds during the altercation, resulting in death. Persons who are beaten or stabbed to death typically will have defensive wounds on the little finger side of the forearm and palm of the hand, sometimes resulting in the severing of fingers in sharp-force injury instances. However, the absence of such injuries does not necessarily mean that the victim did not see his or her attacker or was suicidal. If the victim is restrained by physical or chemical means, no defensive wounds will be present. One of the most common methods of chemical restraint is alcohol.

Blunt-Force Injury

Another subcategory of mechanical trauma is blunt-force injury. Blunt objects produce **lacerations**. Blunt traumas are further subdivided into nonfirearm and firearm groups. Typically, deaths due to blunt trauma are the result of significant damage to the brain or from laceration to the heart or aorta, which then leads to exsanguination.

Firearm Injuries

Injuries by firearm are the most common suicidal and homicidal wounds in the United States. They may be classified as close / near contact, intermediate range, or long range. Firearm injuries can be further classified as **penetrating wounds** or **perforating wounds**. A penetrating gunshot wound has an entrance wound but no exit and, therefore, a projectile should be recovered at autopsy for every penetrating GSW. A perforating GSW has an entrance wound and an exit wound. This means that generally, no projectile will be recovered by a pathologist at autopsy. This is important information to relay to those responsible for processing the crime scene because a projectile should be recovered on scene for each identified exit wound.

INVESTIGATOR'S NOTEBOOK
Suicide Versus Homicide Sharp Injuries

Suicide Indicators
- Hesitation wounds
- Wounds under clothing
- Weapon present, especially if tightly clutched
- Usually wounds at throat, wrists, or ankles
- Seldom disfigurement
- Body not moved

Homicide Indicators
- Defense wounds
- Wounds through clothing
- No weapon present
- Usually injuries to vital organs
- Disfigurement
- Body moved

Contact Wounds

When a firearm is fired with the muzzle against a clothed part of the body, the bullet hole in the fabric touching the muzzle sometimes is surrounded by a flat ring caused by the heated barrel. The loose fringes of fabric in the center of the bullet hole usually are turned outward, away from the body, as a result of the expanding gases escaping back through the wound. Soot in varying amounts also is deposited behind the clothing on the body. Not only will the outer surface of the garment show gun smoke deposits, but the inner surface of the garment may also, even if there are no apparent gun smoke deposits on the outside surface. The deposits on the inner surface of clothing result from the muzzle blast spreading smoke between the skin and the clothing; deposits are most likely to occur if the shot passes through several layers of fabric or if the shot was fired through a pocket. Each layer is blackened individually on both sides of the fabric, whereas the skin and wound may have no gunpowder or soot. The bright yellow flame extending from the muzzle at the time of discharge scorches clothing and adjacent skin and singes hair up to a distance of 3 inches. Soot, but little gunpowder, will be deposited (Spitz, 1993).

If clothing does not intervene between the firearm's muzzle and the skin, all the gun smoke will enter the wound—unless the firearm is a revolver whose cylinder fits loosely against the barrel, in which case gun smoke may spew from the cylinder as well as the muzzle. Additionally, if the cylinder does not fit correctly against the barrel and the alignment is not correct, particles of bullet shavings may be found on or may have penetrated the skin, even in the case of a contact wound. Small bullet fragments around a wound are referred to as **fouling**.

In contact wounds to the head, the wound may be star shaped because of tears radiating from the sides of the wound (**FIGURE 9.7**). These tears are the result of the sudden release of firearm gases into a confined space. When a high-powered rifle is fired while in contact with the head, the gas generated is so great that it causes massive cranial destruction. It may be impossible to identify the deceased through facial recognition. A high-powered discharge under the chin or in the mouth will cause an overexpansion or bloating of the head and face. Damage to the head is so severe that finding the entrance wound may be impossible (Spitz, 1993). The muzzle

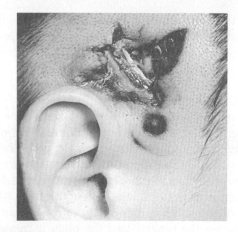

FIGURE 9.7: Contact wound to the head.

Photos courtesy of Steven Hanson, former Chief Investigator Bexar County MEO.

blast of a firearm discharged in contact with a body creates a negative pressure at the barrel following discharge, which may cause blood, hair, tissue, and fabric to be forced back up into the barrel.

Firearm injuries that are made at contact or near-contact range (less than 0.5 centimeters from the target) will exhibit signs of blackening and charring of the skin. Depending on the body location of the injury, the skin also may show stellate (star-like) lacerations that originate at and radiate away from the point of impact. These lacerations form because the gas blown into the wound results in the skin being torn apart. The gases associated with a firearm discharge will also cause red discoloration of the underlying tissue and hemoglobin present in a wound. This cherry-red discoloration is similar to that found in the skin and organs in carbon monoxide-related deaths.

Intermediate-Range Injury

As the distance between the barrel of a firearm and its target increases, the effect of the gas and associated unburned powder accompanying the event diminishes. Intermediate-range injuries are considered to be those occurring at a distance of between 0.5 centimeters and approximately 1 to 1.5 meters. At this distance, unburned powder that penetrates the skin produces a defect injury known as **stippling**. This injury occurs as the result of impact of burned and unburned particulates associated with the discharge of a firearm. They surround the bullet impact wound in a roughly circular pattern because gunpowder is discharged in a conical pattern as it exits a firearm. This pattern is seen to enlarge as the muzzle-to-target distance is increased. Such stippling

fouling
Small bullet fragments around a gunshot wound

stippling
Powder burns on the skin from a close contact wound

patterns are not typically observed at a range greater than 1 to 1.5 meters because the speed of the powder slows sufficiently so that it cannot penetrate the skin.

Determining the muzzle-to-target distance in close-range wounding requires testing the weapon originally used with the same type of ammunition originally used. Different ammunition will produce different results when fired from the same weapon. Gunpowder residue can be visible when the shot fired was twice the distance from the body as the length of the barrel of the weapon. Generally, as the distance between the muzzle and the body increases, the pattern of residue on the body increases in size and the particle density decreases. In the firing of a handgun, little gunpowder and soot are deposited on the body when the distance exceeds 7 inches. Gunpowder residue is distributed circumferentially around a wound. When more residue is discovered on one side than the other, it is possible that the shot was fired at an angle. Powder residue will be more densely deposited on the side from which the shot was fired.

Distant-Range Injury

A GSW that occurs at a muzzle-to-target distance greater than 1 to 1.5 meters will lack the characteristics exhibited by close-contact and intermediate-range injuries (i.e., soot damage and stippling). It is typical for a distant wound to exhibit a circular skin defect known as a marginal abrasion ring around the entrance wound edges. This is due to the stretching of the skin relating to the blunt force trauma.

Entrance and Exit Wounds

Conventional wisdom is that GSW exits are larger than entrance wounds; however, this is not always true. In most cases, it is advisable not to make assumptions as to entrance or exit wounds at the scene of a crime or in a report. The autopsy process will determine which wounds are associated with an entrance or an exit of a projectile.

Shotgun Wounds

Shotguns are used often in criminal homicides. Reconstruction of the distance of shotgun fire is similar to the process used for other firearms, although the diversity of shotgun ammunition and the use of pellets make the determination of firing distance more complex. The number of pellets in a shot shell depends on pellet size. The largest pellets are 00 Number 12 buckshot, and the smallest pellets are 270 Number 9 birdshot. The smallest shotgun is a .410, and the largest is a 10-gauge. The bore of a shotgun is smooth but may taper at the end or have affixed to the barrel end a cylinder smaller than the bore diameter. This small cylinder is called a choke and is designed to keep the pellets from spreading too quickly. In conducting tests for determining firing distance, it is imperative that the same type and number of shot be used as was used in the criminal homicide.

■ Shotgun Contact Wounds

Most wounds inflicted with a shotgun in contact with the body will result in a wound diameter approximately the same as the diameter of the shotgun's bore. Because the pellets have no time to spread and thus remain in a mass, they enter the body as a single projectile, creating marginal abrasion around the perimeter of the wound, as in the case of other contact firearm wounds. Contact wounds to the head cause remarkable damage, and skull fragmentation and tissue reorganization typically render the face unrecognizable. Head, brain, and bone tissue may be spread over a wide area. It

INVESTIGATOR'S NOTEBOOK

© Shutterstock, Inc./Janaka Dharmasena

Suicide Versus Homicide Gunshot Wounds

Suicide Indicators

- Gun held against skin

- Wound in mouth or in right temple if victim is right-handed and left temple if victim is left-handed

Homicide Indicators

- Gun fired from more than a few inches away

- Angle or location that rules out self-infliction

- Shot through clothing

- No weapon present

© Shutterstock, Inc./Nutink.

is necessary for all dispersed bone and tissue to be recovered, for it will be used in the facial reconstruction and will allow a more precise determination of the pellets' entryway. If the contact wound is somewhere other than the head, the muzzle flame may be large enough and intense enough to ignite clothing that is not fire retardant.

■ Close-Range Shotgun Wounds

A shotgun discharged at a distance of less than 5 feet will allow the pellets to remain in a single mass until they reach the body. As in contact wounds, the entry hole will be approximately the same size as the bore diameter. The margins of the wound will evince abrasions, but the pattern will be less concentric and more scalloped in appearance as a result of the pellets' tendency to separate. Because of the scalloping, the pattern is called a cookie-cutter pattern. At a firing distance beyond 6 feet, the diameter of the wound increases, because the pellets continue to spread out. At a firing distance of less than 6 feet, most shotguns will deposit powder and soot on the clothing or skin.

■ Distant Shotgun Wounds

The wound pattern that occurs when a shotgun is fired at distances greater than 6 feet depends on the length of the barrel, size of shot, powder load, gauge of the shotgun, and choke characteristics. With small shot, pellets entering the skin produce round wounds. With large shot, such as 00 buckshot or Number 4, the wounds cannot be distinguished by the naked eye from bullet wounds. Along with the small, penetrating holes caused by the pellets, there may be a larger, nonpenetrating abrasion caused by the shotgun wad. This wad is a component of all shotgun shells containing pellets and is often found in the wound or elsewhere at the scene. Investigators can derive a significant amount of information from the wadding. The diameter of the wad corresponds to the gauge of the shotgun and will often disclose manufacturing characteristics that help to identify the manufacturer of the shot shell (see **FIGURE 9.8**).

Direction of Fire

In determining the **direction of fire**, it is essential to properly identify the **entry wound** and the **exit wound**. The relationship between the entrance and exit wounds may reveal the direction from which the projectile was fired. Entrance wounds reveal a missing sphere of flesh carried into the wound by the projectile

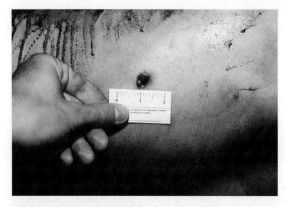

FIGURE 9.8: Shotgun wound.
© Charles Stewart & Associates.

(**FIGURE 9.9**). Exit wounds have no missing flesh; if the skin around the wound were replaced, including all of the jagged edges, there would be a complete covering of the exit hole. An entrance wound is often smaller than the caliber of the bullet that created the wound, whereas the exit wound is substantially larger. The skin at the point of entry is stretched by the penetrating bullet and returns to its original size after penetration. Any guess as to the caliber of a bullet based on the entrance wound diameter would be approximate and unreliable.

An entrance wound will have an **abrasion ring**—a circular or oval bruising of the tissue immediately around the bullet hole that results from the bullet scraping the skin as it penetrates (**FIGURE 9.10**). The abrasion will be circular and of uniform width if the bullet strikes the body perpendicularly, scraping all sides of the wound equally. If the bullet strikes the body at an angle, the hole itself will be round but the abrasions surrounding the wound will be oval because the length of the bullet has scraped along the skin

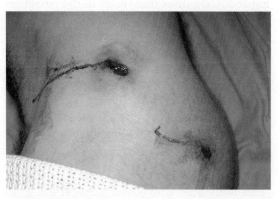

FIGURE 9.9: Entry wound.
© Mediscan/Alamy Photo.

abrasion ring
A circular or oval bruising of the tissue immediately around the bullet hole that results from the bullet scraping the skin as it penetrates

direction of fire
Direction from which the projectile was fired; the relationship between the entrance and exit wounds may reveal this information

entry wound
The wound that results when a projectile enters a body; such wounds reveal a missing sphere of flesh carried into the wound by the projectile

exit wound
The wound that results from a projectile exiting a body; such wounds have no missing flesh, and if the skin around the wound were replaced, including all the jagged edges, there would be a complete covering of the exit hole

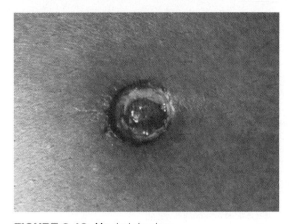

FIGURE 9.10: Marginal abrasions.

Photos courtesy of Steven Hanson, former Chief Investigator Bexar County MEO.

as the tip of the bullet penetrates. The length of the abrasion depends on the angle at which the projectile struck the body.

Medical examiners and pathologists often are asked to position the assailant and the victim relative to the bullet pathway (or pathways). It is at this point that the information provided by the investigator becomes important to the medical examiner. Notes, measurements, and sketches are crucial in determining the resting place of the deceased. A horizontal bullet track through the chest of the victim may have been inflicted while the parties were standing, with the assailant pointing the gun directly at the victim's chest parallel to the ground, or while the victim was lying face up on the ground, with the assailant pointing the weapon down at the victim's chest (Spitz, 1993).

Chemical Trauma Injuries

In approximately 50% of deaths, ethyl alcohol is a contributing factor (James & Nordby, 2005). In most cases of alcohol-related deaths, it is alcohol-induced comas that result in the cessation of respiratory functions, resulting in death. However, another common chemical injury is that of carbon monoxide–related poisoning, resulting in death. Carbon monoxide–related deaths are characterized by the victim's cherry-red skin. Carbon monoxide–related deaths are typically either accidental or suicidal deaths and are rarely associated with homicide.

Thermal Trauma Injuries

If an individual is exposed to excessive heat or cold, the result can be death. *Hypothermia*, the lowering of the body's core temperature,

asphyxia
The interruption of oxygenation of the brain

results from exposure to excessive cold. *Hyperthermia*, a rising of the body's core temperature, is the result of exposure to excessive heat. Persons who die at the scenes of fires most commonly succumb from the inhalation of carbon monoxide and/or other products of combustion rather than thermal-related injuries. Most thermal trauma is accidental or unintended.

Electrical Trauma Injuries

Electrical-related deaths are quite rare, resulting in approximately 1,000 fatalities a year in the United States (Spitz, 1993). High voltage–related deaths are quite evident and present little difficulty for the examining pathologist. High-voltage burns can result in poration, the flow of a current through tissues that creates holes in the membranes of the cells. This often leads to loss of limbs. High-voltage burns are characterized by ferning marks on the body.

Whereas the passage of low-voltage electricity through a person may cause cardiovascular-related difficulties, death can be due to the heart experiencing ventricular fibrillation that can lead to nonresuscitability within minutes. Low voltage may or may not produce electrical burns and will rarely exhibit signs of ferning (**FIGURE 9.11**). Most electrical trauma is accidental in nature and not typically associated with a homicide event.

Asphyxia-Related Deaths

Asphyxia is the interruption of oxygenation of the brain. There are a number of ways for this interruption to occur. These include, but

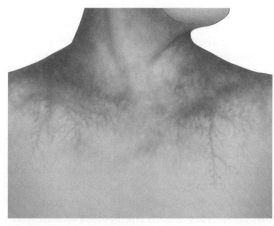

FIGURE 9.11: Example of ferning in electrical trauma-related death.

are not limited to, drowning and strangulation. Asphyxia-related deaths are most commonly associated with accidents but are also associated with suicide and homicide death scenes.

Drowning

Drowning is death by asphyxiation from immersion in water or other liquid. There are several forensic ways to determine whether a body recovered from water died as a result of drowning or was dead prior to entering the water. At autopsy, the forensic pathologist can conduct a lung "float test." If a person died due to drowning, his or her lungs will be heavier and will sink when exposed to this test. There is also the possibility of conducting microscopic examination and analysis of bone marrow collected from the victim, to look for the presence of microorganisms known as diatoms, which are present in water and, if ingested by the victim, will find their way into the marrow. This can also prove or disprove drowning.

Manual Strangulation and Hanging

Asphyxial deaths associated with strangulation will often necessitate determining whether the event was self-induced or homicidal in nature. To determine this, the hyoid bone of the neck is typically examined at autopsy to see if fracture has occurred. Fracturing of the hyoid typically will be found only in cases of manual strangulation. Manual strangulation constricts the airway by compressing the neck or crushing the airway. Ligature strangulation, when from hanging or garroting, characteristically does not involve fracture of the hyoid. In addition to the lack of fracturing of the hyoid bone, there are ligature differences between hanging- and strangulation-related deaths. Typically, the ligature marks made by hanging will be vertical, making a U-shape that extends under the victim's chin and around the back of the ears, whereas homicidal strangulation ligature marks typically will be horizontal marks extending from front to back and may include an area near the back of the victim's neck where the ligature material was crossed, tied, or pressed against the victim to ensure the constriction of airflow (**FIGURE 9.12**).

Hanging-related deaths typically involve the victim dying as a result of cutting off the blood supply (and oxygen) to the brain through pressure placed on the carotid arteries, versus strangulation, which compacts or crushes the trachea, thus depleting the intake of oxygen and thereby causing death. Not all hanging deaths

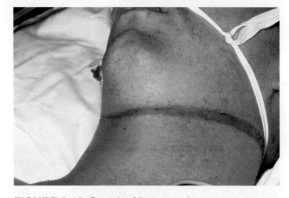

FIGURE 9.12: Example of ligature marks.

© Wellcome Trust Library/Custom Medical Stock Photo.

are suicidal. Child hangings are most commonly accidents, while adult hangings are most commonly suicidal.

One highly visible clue of asphyxia likely being the cause of death is the presence of **petechial hemorrhage**, the bursting of capillaries resulting from interference with venous blood flow (**FIGURE 9.13**). These hemorrhages can be found within the eyes and sometimes on the face, especially in fair-skinned individuals.

Homicide, Suicide, or Accidental?

In attempting to determine whether an asphyxial death was suicidal, accidental, or homicidal, the following are offered as suggestions:

- Most cases of choking, drowning, and smothering are accidental
- Most cases of hanging are suicides (except in the cases of children)
- Most cases of strangulation are murder

It must be remembered, however, that all deaths should be investigated as homicides

> **petechial hemorrhage**
> The bursting of capillaries resulting from interference with venous blood flow, typically due to pressure or asphyxiation, and often found in the sclera of the eye or surrounding tissue of the face

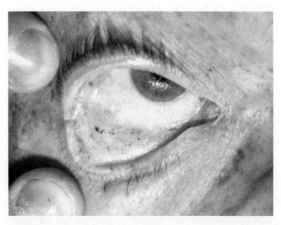

FIGURE 9.13: Example of petechial hemorrhage.

Courtesy of Dr. Edward T. McDonough.

until such point as the evidence determines otherwise.

Deaths Due to Drug Overdose

In some cases of drug overdose and drowning, the victim will exhibit signs of froth emanating from the mouth and nostrils. This froth is sometimes referred to as a *cone of foam*. It is a result of severe pulmonary edema and may initially appear off-white but will advance to pinkish in color as the decomposition process advances.

Public Assistance in Death Investigations

Death investigations are complex and often confusing undertakings. In some cases, it may be necessary to seek the assistance of the public in attempting to gain information that can assist in determining the activities associated with a death or the identity of a recovered victim. In these cases, a *biological profile* is developed that is distributed to the media through law enforcement channels. A biological profile is assembled by studying the remains and noting characteristics of shape and size, which may allow an estimation of height, build, age, sex, ancestry, and any individualistic features such as tattoos, jewelry, medical apparatus, and clothing. Stature is estimated by measuring total body (or skeletal) length. Unique antemortem characteristics, such as a healed bone fracture or an unusual dental configuration, are also included. The goal of developing a profile is to describe the individual in such a way that law enforcement or acquaintances can narrow the range of possible identities.

Forensic Pathology

Forensic medicine has been around for years because of the close relationship between law and medicine for the better part of the 20th century and onward. Pathology is the branch of medicine associated with the study of structural changes caused by disease or injury. The term *forensic pathology* simply adds the concept of unnatural or suspicious in front of the word denoting disease or injury.

There are actually two branches of pathology: anatomic, which deals with structural alterations of the human body; and clinical, which deals with laboratory examination of samples removed from the body. Most forensic

pathologists are experts in both branches. Such experts are certified to perform the following functions:

- Establish cause of death
- Estimate time of death
- Infer the type of weapon used
- Distinguish homicide from suicide
- Establish the identity of the deceased
- Determine the additive effect of trauma or preexisting conditions

The pathologist generally makes these determinations as a result of conducting a forensic autopsy.

Autopsy

The purpose of an **autopsy** is to observe and make a permanent legal record of the gross and minute anatomic peculiarities of a body as soon as possible after death. Anatomic examination may be sufficient to establish cause of death if the forensic pathologist has access to other information (such as surrounding circumstances, life history, psychiatric data, and other pertinent information). Clinical, or microscopic, examination of organ parts is often necessary to further bolster the forensic pathologist's conclusions. The examination of organ parts from the body is useful in toxicology cases as well as any time alcohol or drugs are suspected. The inspection of stomach contents is part of every postmortem exam, because it may provide information as to cause and time of death. Clinical examination also tends to confirm hunches about age, race, sex, height, weight, and general health condition in cases of unidentified remains.

Autopsy Interpretation

Generally, autopsy reports include a four-stage interpretive process.

1. *Contributing cause.* Usually a preexisting illness or condition. Examples are pneumonia or asthma, if the victim had either of those conditions. The preexisting illness could conceivably be the real cause of death.

2. *Mechanism.* Usually anything expressible only in medical jargon. For example, "lung sacs became obstructed and could no longer transport oxygen."

3. *Immediate cause.* This section usually gets at the cause of death. It can be expressed in medical jargon, such as "asphyxia," "contusion," and so on, or it can be expressed in

layman's terms, such as "perforating gun-shot wound to the head."

4. *Manner of death*. Whether the forensic pathologist thinks the death is a suicide, a homicide, or from accidental, natural, or unknown causes.

If the mechanism is undetermined, the death must be ruled as occurring in an unknown manner. This happens in some poisoning cases. If the immediate cause simply aggravated a significant preexisting condition (contributing cause), the pathologist must rule the death natural, but the law may consider the death a homicide. Most traffic fatalities are ruled accidental.

The Autopsy Procedure

The government can order an autopsy in every state when there is suspicion of foul play. In addition, in most states, an autopsy may be ordered if someone dies unattended by a physician or if the attending physician is uncomfortable signing the death certificate. Many autopsy services have a sign that reads, "This is the place where death rejoices to teach those who live" (usually it is written in Latin: "Hic locus est ubi mors gaudet succurrere vitae").

In performing an autopsy, a pathologist first examines the outside of the body (**FIGURE 9.14**). The pathologist opens the body with a Y-shaped incision from shoulders to mid-chest and down to the pubic region. These incisions cut deeply, down to the rib cage and breastbone. If the head is to be opened, the pathologist makes a second incision across the head; joining the bony prominences just below and behind the ears; this cut is deep enough to expose the skull. The scalp and the soft tissues in front of the chest are then retracted. To enter the chest cavity, the pathologist must cut the cartilages that join the ribs to the breastbone. The pathologist removes and examines the breastbone and attached rib cartilages. The skull vault is opened using two saw cuts, one in front and one in back. The top of the skull is removed, and the brain is very carefully cut free of its attachments from inside the skull.

The pathologist inspects chest organs, including the heart and lungs, and takes blood from the heart to check for bacteria in the blood. He or she may send blood, urine, bile, or the fluid of the eye for chemical study and to look for medicine, street drugs, alcohols, and/or poisons. The pathologist examines the heart; generally, the first step following its removal is sectioning the coronary arteries that supply the heart with blood.

The first dissection in the abdomen is usually done to free the large intestine. Using the **Virchow method**, the pathologist will begin removing organs individually. The pathologist saves a section of any removed organ in preservative solution. He or she weighs the major solid organs (heart, lung, brain, kidney, liver, spleen, and sometimes others) on a grocer's scale. The smaller organs (thyroid, adrenals) get weighed on a chemist's triple-beam balance.

The lungs are almost never normal at autopsy. Due to environmental conditions during life, and trauma coinciding with death, the lungs typically contain environmental contaminants and may or may not contain food particulates, foreign fluids or blood. The pathologist weighs both lungs together, then each one separately. Dissecting the lungs can be done in any of several ways. All methods reveal the surfaces of the large airways and the great arteries of the lungs. The air spaces of the lungs are evaluated based on their texture and appearance.

In order to examine the inner structure of the liver, the pathologist removes and weighs it, and then cuts it into 1-cm slices. The kidneys are weighed and dissected. The urinary system may be removed as one piece, and the digestive system down to the small intestine (the esophagus, stomach, pancreas, duodenum, and spleen) as another single piece. Once these organs are opened, a portion of the gastric contents is saved to check for poison.

Before the autopsy is over, the brain is usually suspended in fixative for a week so that the later dissection will be clean, neat, and accurate. When the internal organs have been examined, the pathologist may return all but the portions that have been saved to the body cavity. The pathologist usually replaces the breastbone and ribs in the body, sews the skull and trunk

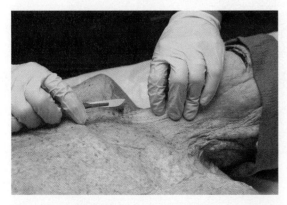

FIGURE 9.14 Preparing to begin the initial autopsy incision.
© Jones and Bartlett Publishers. Courtesy of MIEMSS.

Virchow method
Autopsy method developed by Rudolf Virchow that included the removal and examination of each organ

incisions shut, and then washes the body and forwards it to the funeral director.

The pathologist submits the saved tissue to the histology lab to be made into microscope slides. When these are ready, the pathologist examines the slide sections, looks at the results of any lab work, and reports his or her final conclusions. (The University of Leicester has a website that allows interactive autopsy education at www.le.ac.uk/pathology/teach/va/titlpag1.html.)

Recovering Human Remains*

Looking for buried human remains requires the recognition of **burial indicators**. Time since burial, ground moisture, and terrain will affect these indicators. In any search for buried remains, it may well be that the body was dismembered and that more than one burial site is involved. The search must consider large as well as multiple small burial sites (**FIGURE 9.15**).

Burial site indicators include the following:

- *Disturbed vegetation.* Whenever a hole is dug in the ground, the vegetation in and around the hole is disturbed. Adjacent areas that were disturbed during digging will also show signs of vegetation disturbance.

- *Soil compaction.* The natural decomposition of buried remains leaves a void in the soil. Time and rain cause the soil above the remains to sink to fill the void, forming a depression in the surface above the body.

This depression is sometimes called a compaction site. A secondary depression may also be noted inside the primary depression. This is caused by the deterioration of the corpse's abdominal cavity.

- *New vegetation.* The new growth will not be as mature as growth in the surrounding area.

- *Soil disturbance.* When a grave is dug, the layers of the soil are disturbed. The soil under the ground is layered. Some areas have very shallow layers or multiple layers within a very few inches from the surface, whereas others have layers several feet thick. At different depths, the soil varies in color. These different colors represent the different layers of soil. Once the layers are disturbed, no amount of effort and precision can replace them exactly. Digging not only disturbs the soil layers in the grave but also disturbs the surface soil around the grave. There will always be some residue left after refilling a hole. The residue will be a different color than the surrounding surface soil.

Multiple indicators may be present at any site.

Not all terrain lends itself to the discovery of visual burial indicators. In some instances, it may be necessary to utilize tools in the search.

- *Infrared photography.* Uses the difference in temperature between the buried body and the temperature of the soil around or on top of it. Infrared photography may also indi-

burial indicators
Indications of the presence of buried remains; these include disturbed vegetation, soil compaction, new vegetation, and soil disturbance

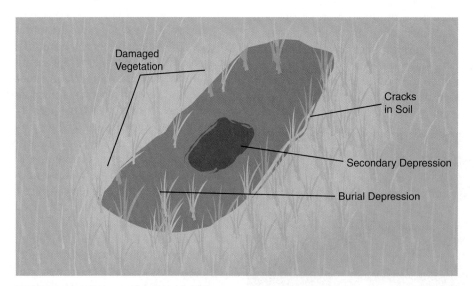

FIGURE 9.15: Examples of burial indicators.

Courtesy of Erica Milks.

---

* The material in this section was adapted from a series of lectures by Dr. M. L. Goff at his 2003 "Handling Human Remains Workshop," held each summer at Chaminade University of Honolulu.

cate the difference in temperature of disturbed and undisturbed soil.

- *Methane detector.* As organic objects decompose, they produce methane gases. The longer the body has been buried, the less likely it is that methane gas can be detected.

- *Aerial photography.* A comparison of aerial photographs of the suspected area taken over a period of years might disclose a possible burial site. Aerial photos could show a vegetation disturbance occurring where a body is buried.

- *Probe.* A 4-foot metal rod approximately 3/8 inch in diameter with a wooden T-shaped handle is poked into the ground. When pushing the probe into the ground, the investigator can feel a difference in the pressure needed to push the probe into undisturbed and disturbed soil.

Recent innovations in the detection of human remains include the work being done at McGill University in Montreal, Canada, by Andre Costopoulos and Margret Kalacska. Both are using hyperspectral imaging to detect individual and mass burial sites. **Hyperspectral imaging** collects visible and invisible light, including ultraviolet and infrared. As a body decays, the site becomes toxic and remains so for many years. The vegetation at a site affected by the soil toxicity does not reflect light the way nontoxic soil does. The plants do not reflect as much light, and this diminution in visible and invisible light can be detected using hyperspectral cameras. (For more information, see Bland, 2010.)

After approximately 5 years, the chlorophyll in the same plants increases. The body acts as compost or fertilizer, over time, providing more nitrogen and phosphorous than the surrounding vegetation. Nearly twice as much light is emitted from the "fertilized" plants than from the surrounding vegetation, and again, the hyperspectral cameras can pick that up. In soils devoid of plants, the soil itself can reveal that human remains lie beneath. A dead body can release a variety of substances that can stain the soil, and that stain is detectable through proper imaging (Bland, 2010).

Surface Recovery

Once the search is completed and the body is located, the recovery site must be defined. Extreme scattering of the bones, body parts, or physical evidence by animals frequently occurs. Therefore, the area encompassing the scattered remains may be a few feet or several yards. This area must be processed (see Investigator's Notebook).

Once the surface of the site has been cleared of all remains and evidence, the next step is to examine and excavate the top 6 inches of soil for any further evidence or bones. In some instances, the remains have gone through a self-burial. Objects placed on the surface of the ground may work their way into the ground. The extent to which this occurs will depend on the object's weight, the density of the ground, the terrain of the area, the time elapsed, and the weather conditions.

For example, the author investigated a homicide in Montana in which the victim was lured to the side of a mountain, ostensibly to participate in a party and to partake of drugs (LSD). He was struck from behind on a game trail some distance from the mountain road and was repeatedly hit with large rocks until dead. His body was then rolled off the trail and was left there. The murder went undiscovered for more than a year. The victim was an Alaska native who had been passing through the area. Because he was not a local resident, no one reported him missing. As criminals are likely to

hyperspectral imaging
Cameras can produce images of visible and invisible light used in the detection of burial sites

---

INVESTIGATOR'S NOTEBOOK

Processing the Burial Site

After the site is photographed and sketched and vegetation is cleared away, photos should be taken of the new "clean" site. Using rope or string, set up a grid for the purpose of locating the items by measurements and for ease in placing the items on a sketch. Take close-up photographs of all items prior to their removal. Package the remains of the deceased, and if the body has skeletonized and been disarticulated, bag body parts separately. If the body is intact, lace it on a backboard that is covered with a white sheet and then place in a new body bag.

© Shutterstock, Inc./Tandka Dharmasena.

© Shutterstock, Inc./Nutink.

do, the perpetrators talked to friends during parties and even acted out the murder. But no one reported the story to the police until a hunter discovered a human skull in a draw at the bottom of the same mountain where the deceased was dispatched. Investigators immediately cordoned off the area and planned and initiated a search. Various bones were strewn across the mountain, and human hair of the same color as the decedent's was found entangled in the brush. It was possible to trace the movement of the body down the hill by the hair and bones that were strewn from the trail to the bottom. Many of the bones had been gnawed and some cracked. Only about 30% of the body was actually recovered over a large area. The two young men who had committed the murder confessed when confronted with the evidence.

Excavation Techniques

Once the investigator has located and defined the burial site, he or she can choose the method of excavation. Three methods of excavating the ground around the body and, ultimately, the body itself, are recommended:

1. *Hole.* As the name indicates, a hole is dug, uncovering the remains as the soil is removed from over and around the body.

2. *Trench.* A trench is dug next to the remains to a depth of 2 feet below the upper body level. The trench must be at least the length of the body and approximately 2 feet wide. This trench will provide sufficient room to work and collect evidence and the remains. Using this method, three of the four walls of the grave can be defined.

3. *Table.* A table is dug by trenching all around the body, usually leaving a table approximately 4 feet wide by 7 feet long and extending 2 feet beyond the depth of the body. This method will leave all four walls of the grave intact and provide sufficient room to work around the body.

Regardless of which method the investigator uses, he or she must estimate the position of the body under the ground prior to excavation. With a generous estimate, excavating a hole, trench, or table can be done without fear of disturbing the remains.

With any of these methods, investigators should remove soil in strips approximately 12 inches wide and 6 inches in depth and should hand-check and sift the soil as the different layers are removed. Anything that is not soil could be evidence or bones.

Anthropological Considerations

Because the remains in question are usually badly decomposed or skeletonized to some degree and little soft tissue may remain, a forensic anthropologist is an essential member of any recovery team. Forensic anthropologists can assist investigators by answering several important questions:

1. Are the remains in question human?

2. Is there evidence of a homicide?

3. What are the ascertainable victim characteristics (e.g., age, gender, ethnic origin, stature)?

4. Do the remains exhibit any indications of premortem and/or postmortem trauma that may assist the medical examiner or coroner in determining the cause and/or manner of death?

5. Is there anything associated with the body that will assist in identifying it?

The ability of the forensic anthropologist to answer these questions depends on the amount of the skeleton recovered and the amount of damage done during the recovery.

The skull is typically the first part of the skeleton to decompose. As a result, the skull can often be found great distances from the main concentration of the remains. Gravity (if the body is on a sloping hill or any incline) and the activity of scavenging animals (such as rodents, bears, coyotes, wolves, or canines) can result in the skull being displaced after it has decomposed enough to be separated easily from the rest of the body.

Damage to important skeletal elements can occur if recovery personnel do not handle the remains appropriately. The skull and mandible are important in determining gender, laying the foundation for facial reconstruction, and determining ethnic origin. Inadvertent damage can occur to the bones during transportation. To avoid such damage, package all bones in separate bags.

CONCLUSION

In modern society, the taking of a human life is typically viewed as the most grievous of offenses. More human resources and money is spent on death investigations than on any other type of investigation, and it is the easiest of crime scenes to contaminate. Everything known about processing a crime scene and forensic protocols comes into play in the death investigation. It may seem highly unlikely that well-trained investigators and forensic staff would not bring their best game, but complacency, stress, fatigue, and other factors may significantly impact an individual's ability to perform his or her job. However, if personnel train and practice using proper methodologies and best practices, evidence contamination and improper scene documentation and processing will be minimized, and the successful outcome will be maximized.

QUESTIONS FOR REVIEW

1. What, if anything, is the difference between homicide and murder?
2. What is the corpus delicti of criminal homicide?
3. List two reasons for staging a crime scene.
4. What is the presumed attraction of auto-erotic hypoxia?
5. List four burial indicators.
6. Of what assistance is a forensic anthropologist in the recovery of human remains?
7. When is an autopsy performed?
8. How can time of death be ascertained?
9. What type of physicochemical changes does a body undergo after death? What are livor mortis, rigor mortis, and algor mortis?
10. What service might a forensic entomologist provide to a criminal investigator?
11. Explain what role insects can play in criminal homicide investigations.
12. What are the differences between contact wounds, close-range wounds, and distant wounds?
13. What is firearm smudging, tattooing, or stippling?
14. What are the characteristics of an entry wound, and how do they differ from the characteristics of an exit wound?
15. What is an abrasion ring?
16. How might stomach contents of the deceased be of use to the investigator?
17. How do hyperspectral images assist in the discovery of burial sites?

REFERENCES

Amendt, J., & Goff, M. L. (2009). *Current concepts in forensic entomology.* New York, NY: Springer.

Bennett, W. W., & Hess, K. M. (2010). *Criminal investigation* (9th ed.). Clifton Park, NY: Cengage Learning.

Bland, E. (2010). New tech sees dead people. Retrieved September 6, 2011, from http://msnbc.msn.com/id/36602201/ns/technology

Dutelle, A. W. (2016). *An introduction to crime scene investigation* (3rd ed.). Burlington, MA: Jones & Bartlett Learning.

Federal Bureau of Investigation. (1975–2009). *Uniform crime reports.* Washington, DC: U.S. Department of Justice.

Geberth, V. J. (2006). *Practical homicide investigation* (4th ed.). Boca Raton, FL: CRC Press.

Goff, M. L. (2001). *A fly for the prosecution.* New York, NY: Harvard University Press.

James, S. H., & Nordby, J. J. (2005). *Forensic science: An introduction to scientific and investigative techniques* (2nd ed.). Boca Raton, FL: CRC Press.

Sachs, J. S. (2001). *Corpse, nature, forensics and the struggle to pinpoint time of death.* Cambridge, MA: Perseus.

Spitz, W. U. (1993). Drowning. In W. U. Spitz (Ed.), *Medicolegal investigation of death* (3rd ed.). Springfield, IL: Charles C. Thomas.

chapter

10

Theft, Burglary, and Robbery

KEY TERMS

aggravated robbery
approach to entry
asportation
ATM robbery
bait money
bona fide
breaking and entering
bump-and-grab
burglary
career robber
carjacking
casing
chop
commercial robbery
conversion
delivery van robbery

departure signature
entry access
fence
habit pattern
jimmy
joyriding
larceny
method of entry
modus operandi (MO) (plural modi operandi)
opportunistic robbers
point of entry
residential robbery (home invasion)
show of force
smash-and-grab

sound suppressor
specialty robbery
specific intent
street robbery
stripped
substance-habituated robber
target selection
theft
tire impression
toolmark
tracing
truck hijacking
unauthorized use of a motor vehicle
vehicle identification number (VIN)

STUDENT LEARNING OUTCOMES

Upon completion of this chapter, students will be able to:

- Distinguish the different types of burglary
- Identify the entry techniques used to facilitate a burglary
- Distinguish the different types of robberies
- Identify the modus operandi of robbery
- Describe the difference between modus operandi and signature

Introduction

In common law, taking the property of another for the purpose of depriving that person of ownership was called **larceny**. It required three basic elements:

1. A taking
2. **Asportation** (movement of the items taken)
3. An intent to deprive the owner

All three elements are problematic in our contemporary understanding of theft. In many instances, a person may be convinced to voluntarily part with his or her property, which is obviously counter to the common-law notion of "taking." Some things are so large as to prohibit movement, such as a house, land, and trees, yet today, through fraud, a person may have his or her house, land, or trees stolen. Clearly, for larceny to make sense today, there must have been an evolution of the elements. Taking may now be real or constructive, and asportation may also be real or constructive.

In common law and presently in some jurisdictions, there are numerous types of theft, with different names and definitions, in which one of the traditional elements of theft is lacking. Theft by false pretext, for example, occurs when a person voluntarily relinquishes property under some pretext that allows the thief to deprive the owner of the property. Theft by embezzlement occurs when a person entrusted with property uses the property to his or her own advantage (**conversion**) and with the intent to deprive the owner of possession.

Over time, legislatures and the judiciary have recognized many related offenses that differ in some degree from basic theft, and the result has been an ever-expanding and confusing network of theft-related statutes. Many jurisdictions, aware of the imaginativeness of thieves, decided to consolidate the theft offenses into one statute, forsaking the categories of theft by false pretext, conversion by a bailee, shoplifting, theft from a person, acquisition of property by threat, swindling, swindling by worthless check, embezzlement, extortion, receiving or concealing embezzled property, receiving or concealing stolen property, credit card theft, theft of trade secrets, forgery, and fraud. These special types of theft indicate how earnestly criminals work to separate people from their property.

Theft has come to be defined as an unlawful intentional appropriation of property. Intent to deprive ownership is questionable as an element in only one type of theft: **joyriding**. Many jurisdictions have added a new section to their penal codes. In addition to statutes prohibiting theft of a motor vehicle, which involves intent to permanently deprive ownership, there are now statutes dealing with **unauthorized use of a motor vehicle**. The lesser deprivation reduces the seriousness of the offense in those jurisdictions that recognize joyriding as differing from outright theft.

Once theft offenses were consolidated, the magnitude of a theft offense became based on how much was taken. Excepted from this consolidation were the offenses of burglary and robbery. The elements of burglary differ in significant degree from those of theft, and burglary is still treated as a separate and more serious offense than theft. Because of the personal confrontation and threat of personal violence involved in robbery, it too is treated as a separate and more serious offense.

Burglary

There is an old joke about shooting burglars that goes like this: If you shoot a burglar outside your home, drag him back inside in order to avoid legal consequences. The conventional wisdom is that a homeowner can use deadly force in defense of his or her property. This may or may not be true, depending on state burglary penal codes. That is why it is in the best interest of investigators to not only understand the penal code definition of burglary but all the cases in a state that have added to or interpreted that code.

Types of Burglary

Most burglaries are products of opportunity perpetrated by noncareer burglars. Open doors and windows are an opportunist's invitation. Uncollected mail and newspapers are also an invitation. Originally, burglary was referred to as **breaking and entering** and may still be called that by investigators. Burglaries in common law required a breaking (forced entry) component and a physical entry into the premises. Today, neither element is required, but both generally are present. The breaking component is lacking when someone who is originally invited onto the premises extends the visit and secrets him- or herself onto the premises to await an opportunity to commit theft. It is also lacking when entry is made through openings inviting access. Finally, there are those cases in which the burglar does not physically intrude on the premises at all but, for example, pokes a stick through an open window to withdraw a purse on a nearby table.

larceny
In common law, taking the property of another for the purpose of depriving that person of ownership; it required three basic elements: a taking, asportation (movement of the items taken), and an intent to deprive the owner

unauthorized use of a motor vehicle
Use of a vehicle by someone other than the owner without the owner's permission

asportation
Movement of items taken from another; one of the three basic elements required for larceny in common law

conversion
Using property entrusted to a person by another for the former's advantage and with the intent to deprive the owner of possession

breaking and entering
Term that was originally used for burglary because it required a breaking (forced entry) component and a physical entry into the premises

theft
An unlawful intentional appropriation of property

joyriding
Stealing an automobile for personal enjoyment

Most officers understand the statutory elements of a burglary. In most jurisdictions, a **burglary** involves (1) a person who (2) enters or remains on the premises (3) of another (4) without effective consent of the owner (5) for the purpose of committing a felony or theft. Keep in mind that misdemeanor theft rises to a felony when coupled with an unlawful entry of a dwelling. Often, burglaries are further subdivided into burglaries of:

- Dwellings
- Dwellings with residents present
- Commercial establishments
- Other structures
- Vehicles

When charging a suspect, confusion may arise because of unspoken aspects of the burglary elements. For example, if a person, while supposedly on a business trip, entered his or her own home after the family was asleep and stole numerous valuable items so that an insurance claim could be made, was a burglary committed? Which element is missing? A person cannot burglarize his or her own home: It must be the premises of another. Where would you find the answer to that question? The statute only implies the answer. Try this one: A person trains a monkey to gather bright, shiny objects and throws the monkey through an open window. The animal returns with a cache of jewelry. Strictly speaking, entry by a person is required. A monkey is not a person. Has a burglary been committed? Where would you go to find the answer? The point of describing such scenarios is that statutory language and elements may not be sufficient to determine what crime has, in fact, been committed. It is necessary to be aware of various state court decisions that have interpreted the statute.

Penal codes come in two versions: annotated and unannotated. Annotations are short summaries of court decisions that have helped to interpret vague or ambiguous portions of a statute. Every investigator should have an annotated copy of the appropriate penal code and be familiar with the code elements as well as the court interpretations. How else would it be possible to figure out the crimes involved in a situation like the following? A man follows his wife to the home of a friend and sees her in an amorous tryst with the man of the house. The irate husband backs his pickup into the living room, hoping to crush the occupants. What crimes have been committed? Traffic violations, trespass, criminal mischief, disorderly conduct, reckless conduct, assault, aggravated assault,

attempted murder? The most serious offense will usually determine the charge ultimately brought. The most likely offense for the prosecution to prove would be aggravated assault. However, the behavior in question also constitutes a burglary. Did you get that? If not, go back to the elements of burglary and examine each with respect to the irate husband scenario.

Most burglaries occur at night, usually between 10:00 pm and 2:00 am. It is during this time that a burglar has the best chance of entering a dwelling without being identified. The career burglar will have ascertained that the dwelling is vacant and may look for clues that lead the burglar to believe that the occupants are not at home. Burglaries of residences are riskier than burglaries of commercial sites, because they may be interrupted by the arrival of the residents and they generally carry a higher statutory penalty than commercial burglaries. Less risk is associated with commercial burglaries, except for the security measures taken by the owners to prohibit unlawful entry. Commercial burglaries also require greater planning and may require specific expertise, such as knowledge of computer and security systems, lock picking, safe cracking, and the value of items to be stolen.

Residential burglars focus on homes, condominiums, and apartments in the affluent sections of a community. Most home security measures, short of electronic surveillance, can be overcome easily. The professional burglar generally will seek valuables that can be transported easily, preferring money, negotiable securities, jewelry, and small art objects of value. Some professionals may specialize in art or jewelry and use a network established to provide ready disposal of the stolen items. Drug addicts comprise a significant portion of household burglars and steal to support their habits. (A habit is often referred to in terms of a dollar amount, as in "I got a $250-a-day Jones [habit].") They will steal items for which a professional would not put him- or herself at risk. Amateur burglars do not specialize, nor do drug addicts. They steal whatever may be turned for a profit.

As much as the public deplores burglars and thieves, it supports their efforts, in a sense. Burglars would have no market if nonburglars refused to buy stolen merchandise. The **fence** (seller) is the middleman necessary to let the majority of people who purchase stolen property pretend they have not been involved. As in most con games, it is people's desire to get something for nothing that allows them to be conned and to blindly (or not so blindly) support the theft industry. If a deal looks too good to be true, it probably is too good to be true and involves either a con or stolen property. A too-good-to-be-believed deal should put the citizen on notice that it is something better passed by.

Juveniles form a subclass of amateur burglars. Amateurs are often armed and pose a serious threat of violence to unsuspecting returning residents. Juveniles characteristically resort to unnecessary destruction and bravado during the commission of their burglaries. Because the burglaries are usually committed by several juveniles working together, bravura is expected and displayed. They may eat the residents' food, drink their beverages, wear their clothes, use the phone, leave disparaging notes on mirrors or walls, and soil the house with feces or urine. Although the results of the juvenile burglars' gross behavior can be unpleasant, the tremendous amount of trace evidence left at the scene helps law enforcement to make positive identification of suspects.

The professional burglar plans his or her crime, its execution, the departure from the site, and the disposal of stolen goods. The nature and quality of the burglary will determine the level of detail required in the planning as well as the number of people needed to pull off the burglary. The most successful professional burglars work alone and hit big, infrequently, and discreetly.

Although there was no shortage of burglaries in 2009, there were an estimated 2,199,125 burglaries, which was a decrease of 1.3% compared with 2008 data. Of all burglaries, 61.0% involved forcible entry, 32.6% were unlawful entries (without force), and the remainder were forcible entry attempts. Victims of burglary offenses suffered an estimated $4.6 billion in lost property in 2009. Overall, the average dollar loss per burglary offense was $2,096 (Federal Bureau of Investigation, 2010).

Entry Techniques

Burglars use various tools in gaining entry to the premises or to locked containers (**FIGURE 10.1**). Some of the more common techniques to gain entry include the following:

- Doors and window faces can be pried using a **jimmy**, and locks can be picked using burglar picks or commercially designed pick systems that have a pistol-grip handle and interchangeable picks.

- The lock cylinder can be knocked out of a lock by using a slap hammer.

- Windows can be broken and doors kicked down.

- By smashing a store window, a burglar can grab the displayed items.

- By cutting out a glass pane with a glass cutter, a burglar can reach through, unlock, and open the window or door.

- Credit cards or other thin, flexible devices can be slipped between the lock and the doorjamb to force the lock back.

- Hinge pins on a door may be removed, allowing the whole door to be removed.

- Adjacent walls may be removed or penetrated to facilitate entry.

jimmy
Tool used to pry open doors and windows

FIGURE 10.1: Burglar gaining entrance to a residence.

- Explosives and heavy tools may be used to open safes.
- Bump keys can be used to jar loose the lock pins (Osterberg & Ward, 2010).

Toolmarks and entry evidence are important for identifying the modus operandi and the individual burglar.

Toolmarks and Other Impressions

toolmark
Any impression, cut, gouge, or abrasion caused by a tool coming into contact with another object

A **toolmark** is any impression, cut, gouge, or abrasion caused by a tool coming into contact with another object (Saferstein, 2014). Impressions can be found at burglary crime scenes on door and window frames through which entry was made. These impressions are made with screwdrivers, crowbars, or other devices used to pry doors and windows open. An impression itself usually renders only class characteristics indicating the type of tool, although it can have unique characteristics that allow it to be matched to a single tool. A tool retains machined marks from its manufacture, just as firearms. These marks and striations are changed as the result of nicks and breaks in the tool's working surface that occur as the tool is used and misused. The pattern and shape of these modifications are altered by continued use, further individualizing the imperfections. It is unlikely that any two tools will have manufacturing striations, wear markings, and breaks that are exactly the same. It is these small imperfections that allow the crime laboratory to determine that the impressions at the crime scene were left by a suspect tool.

If a tool edge is scraped against a surface that is softer than the metal of the tool, it will leave a series of markings that reflect the pattern of the tool edge. These markings and the imperfections on a suspect tool can be compared in a laboratory with a comparison microscope. The comparison may show an association between the marks and the tool. The more individualized the tool edge pattern, the more definitive the comparison.

In handling toolmark impressions, it is important to relegate the mark to a photographic record, first from an intermediate distance and then a close-up. Once the impression has been photographed, it is ready to be worked. A molded impression of the marks should be taken. If the portion of the entryway bearing a toolmark can be removed and transported to the laboratory, a molded impression may not be necessary. Do not examine the marking with the aid of a ballpoint or metal probe. Any marks made to the impression that were not a product of the original tool may render the impression inadmissible at the time of trial.

Forced entry is usually accomplished with the aid of tools, and the indentations left can be lifted and preserved with a casting compound similar to DUROCAST (manufactured by Sirchie Laboratories; see **FIGURE 10.2**). The putty-like material enables castings to be made

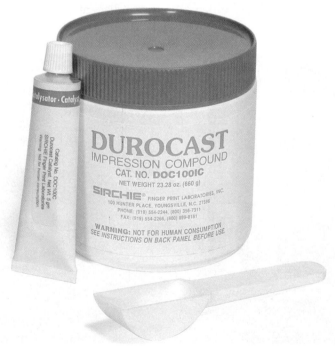

FIGURE 10.2: Durocast impression compound.
Courtesy of SIRCHIE Finger Print Laboratories, Inc.

on horizontal or vertical surfaces. The casting material can be molded into a piece long and wide enough to cover the toolmark. Once pressed gently into the toolmark and allowed to dry, the casting material can be removed, and a reverse impression of the toolmark will have been transferred to the casting material, which should then be bagged and tagged as any other evidence would be (**FIGURE 10.3**).

There may be impressions other than toolmarks left at a burglary crime scene, such as shoe or **tire impressions**. The major task of the investigator is to preserve a reproductive cast of any such impression until it can be transported to and examined by the crime laboratory. The first step in processing any impression, whether of a tool, shoe, or tire, is to preserve it through photography, bringing out as much detail from as many different angles and heights as possible. Photographs are not the preferred laboratory specimens but can supplement and support reproductive casts should the casts for lab comparisons be lost, damaged, or destroyed. Tire impressions can be duplicated by inking the suspect tread with fingerprint

impression ink and running the inked tire over paper (**FIGURE 10.4**). The best impression involves the entire circumference of the tire, not just the suspect location. A device is available from evidence equipment manufacturers that involves a print-out system. Some defects will not be visible unless the tire is under load. The system uses two sheets of paper affixed back to back. One sheet facing the other is treated with carbon (much like old typewriter carbon paper). Once the tire is run over the two sheets, the carbon side leaves an impression of the tire tread on the clean piece of paper opposite it (**FIGURE 10.5**). The carbon-treated side is then removed and the side with the transferred impression is treated as any other evidence (**FIGURE 10.6**).

Shoe impressions may be taken at a crime scene or from a suspect. Crime scene shoe impressions require that the investigator record the footprints photographically and then make a casting of the impression. Something needs to be placed around the footprint to serve as a dam. Anything that is immersed in the tread impression should not be removed, and any loose

tire impression
Imprint left by a tire

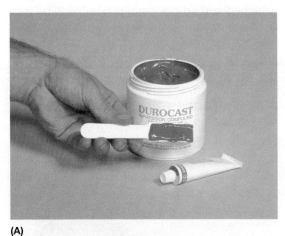
(A)

(B)

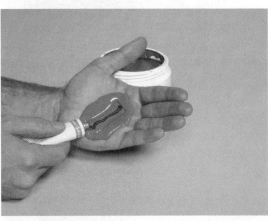
(C)

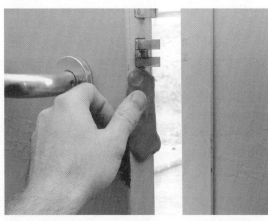
(D)

FIGURE 10.3: Durocast simulated application; in an actual case, gloves should be worn during the application process.

Courtesy of SIRCHIE Finger Print Laboratories, Inc.

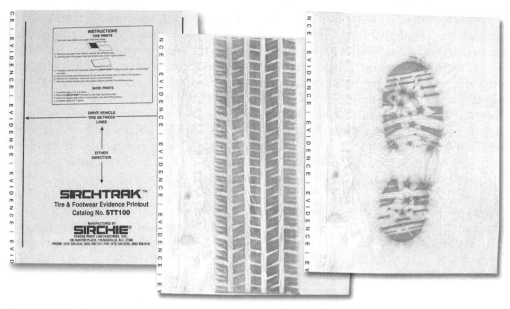

FIGURE 10.4: Sirchtrak.

Courtesy of SIRCHIE Finger Print Laboratories, Inc.

debris may be removed, but the margins of the shoe impression are fragile and must be avoided. The impression should be prepared by spraying a commercial hardener on the surface. After a few minutes to allow the hardener to dry, a light coating of release agent can be applied. This will allow removal of the cast without bringing attached soil. In the past, plaster of Paris was used to cast footprint impressions; it worked well but shrunk in the drying process by about 10%. New casting materials dry without shrinking. Many of these new casting solutions come premixed with a hardener embedded in the package (**FIGURE 10.7**). Shelf life is indefinite

(A)

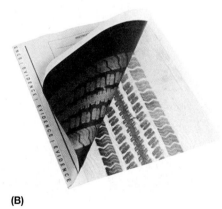

(B)

FIGURE 10.5: Tire impressions.

Courtesy of SIRCHIE Finger Print Laboratories, Inc.

FIGURE 10.6: Tire track.

Courtesy of SIRCHIE Finger Print Laboratories, Inc.

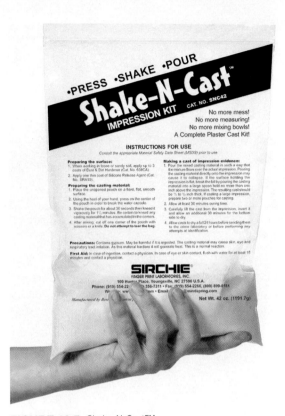

FIGURE 10.7: Shake-N-Cast™.

Courtesy of SIRCHIE Finger Print Laboratories, Inc.

as long as the hardener ampoule is not broken and mixed with the casting material. Breaking the hardener ampoule and mixing it makes the material time dependent.

It is important not to pour the mixture directly onto the impression; it can destroy ridge character. Pouring the mixture onto a spoon held close to the surface of the impression will prevent damage to the impression. Once the contents of the package have been poured over the impression to a depth of no more than half an inch (12.7 mm) and into the dam, all that is left to do is to wait for the casting material to dry. Once dry, the impression can be removed from the frame and tagged and bagged. Nothing should be removed from the bottom of the casting to avoid damage to the impression. The lab can remove it without causing damage.

Impressions in snow pose a real challenge to the investigator. Snow is highly fragile and subject to changes in the weather. Because most gypsum-based casting materials generate heat during the curing process, it is necessary to provide something to insulate the shoeprint from the casting material. Impression wax is sold in an aerosol applicator that can be sprayed over the print; once the impression is protected, the casting material can be poured (**FIGURES 10.8** through **10.10**).

FIGURE 10.8: Placement of the dam.

© By Ian Miles-Flashpoint Pictures/Alamy Images.

FIGURE 10.9: After pouring.

© Pablo Paul/Alamy Images.

FIGURE 10.10: Cast footprint (mud and sand).

© 67photo/Alamy Images.

FIGURE 10.11: Bio-foam box.

Courtesy of SIRCHIE Finger Print Laboratories, Inc.

FIGURE 10.12: Lifted dust print.

Courtesy of Maine State Police Crime Laboratory.

Making an impression of a suspect's shoe used to be done by inking the bottom of the shoe and pressing it onto paper; today, new methods are available. Once again, it is best to take an impression under load. Footwear impression lifts use a Styrofoam-like substance in a long box; the suspect steps into the box and onto the foam. The suspect's weight should be controlled so that the suspect does not step all the way through the foam to the bottom of the box, thereby losing the impression. Once the impression has been laid, the same procedure for casting a footprint is used (**FIGURE 10.11**). In this case, once the casting material has dried and hardened, the foam can be torn away from the cast. The remaining cast is then tagged and bagged.

Commercial electrostatic dust lifters consist of a high-voltage power supply, a nickel-plated steel ground plate, and a metallized lifting mat. In the past, it required two lifting mats: a positively charged mat and a negatively charged mat; today, only one sheet is used along with a metal ground plate. The mat is gently floated onto the dust print to be lifted. Once the mat is in place, a fingerprint ink roller can be used to smooth the surface of the mat. As high voltage is applied to the lifting mat, it takes on a negative charge and the ground plate becomes positive. Any dust present under the mat will take on a positive charge and will then be attracted to the negatively charged collection mat. A dust print that is transferred to the lifting mat will appear as a precise mirror image of the original print (**FIGURE 10.12**).

The value of a footprint is determined by the number of class characteristics that match the class characteristics of a suspect item. Agreement in size, shape, or design can only prove that the item in question may have made the impression; a definitive identification cannot be made on the basis of class characteristics alone. It is the presence of individual characteristics from wear, breaks, or tears that, if numerous, will support an opinion that the cast or recovered impression came from one source and one source only: the suspect item (Saferstein, 2014).

The Burglary Investigation

Patrol officers typically are the first responders to burglaries, and these officers consequently face the greatest risk. A burglary-in-progress call holds the potential for violence, although burglary is legally a property crime. Not until the initial call has been resolved does the investigator arrive on the scene. Once again, it is imperative that first responders be treated as members of the investigative team. Any investigation, if it is to be successful, depends largely on scene integrity, but none more so than a burglary investigation. In a homicide, the body and mess preclude rapid repopulation of the premises. In a burglary, the victims feel personally violated and hasten to remove evidence of that violation and determine how extensive it was and what was taken. It is the responding officers' responsibility to prevent anyone from degrading the integrity of the crime scene; that includes residents as well as patrol officers. The patrol officers can be of assistance to the investigator in a number of ways, including:

- Locating or notifying owners of the burglary and keeping them at a distance until the investigator arrives

- Locating witnesses (anyone who has seen or heard anything that may assist in the investigation)

- Locating the party reporting the burglary if other than the owner

- Listing items taken if owners have already assessed their losses

- Securing the crime scene

Once the investigator arrives on the scene, the primary objective is to recognize and preserve possible sites of forensic evidence. This objective, however, is not the first addressed. The investigator will want to determine the point and **method of entry** onto the premises. The **point of entry** will provide information about the method of entry and provide an indication as to the direction from which the burglar(s) approached the building. The area of approach may contain footprint, tire print, or eyewitness evidence that is easily destroyed, lost, or overlooked. Prior to examining the point

of entry, the investigator should examine this area to discover whatever evidence there is and prevent its irretrievable loss. Examining a window from the outside without examining the grounds first may lead to the trampling of footprints or tire impressions. Likewise, finding out where the burglars parked will allow identification and preservation of any tire impressions, cigarette butts, litter, or vehicular fluid deposits left by the burglars and will prevent haphazard parking by the police and others from contaminating this part of the crime scene. Once the approach areas have been processed, an examination of the interior part of the crime scene can begin.

The most obvious points of entry are windows and doors. An absence of evidence of forced entry suggests that the burglar gained entry by using a key, lock pick, jimmy, or bump keys, or by coming through an unsecured window or door. It should also raise the question of whether a member of the household assisted in or perpetrated the burglary. Burglaries are sometimes committed by a disenchanted or drug-using juvenile family member or by his or her friends and are also sometimes committed for the purpose of fraudulently acquiring an insurance payoff. Suspicions of household involvement must be handled tactfully and held in abeyance until they are corroborated by other evidence.

Once point of entry has been ascertained, the entry portal should be examined for toolmarks, fiber evidence, and fingerprints. Any evidence of toolmarks must be documented photographically and removed to the crime

method of entry
The manner and direction from which the burglar(s) approached the building; it is determined by looking at the evidence at the point of entry

point of entry
Place where the criminal entered the premises; it is a location where forensic evidence is likely to be found

INVESTIGATOR'S NOTEBOOK

© Shutterstock, Inc./Tanaka Dharmasena

Processing a Crime Scene in Which Toolmarks Are Apparent

It is an investigator's responsibility, whenever practical, to submit the entire object possessing the toolmarks to the laboratory. If the object cannot be removed for submission, then photographs and cast impressions need to be provided. Neither photographs nor cast impressions will allow as definitive a comparison as would the actual object.

Under no circumstances should a suspect tool be fit into the impression. An attempt to do so will alter the impression and raise serious questions as to crime scene integrity and the quality of any comparison information provided by the crime laboratory.

If both a suspect tool and impression are available at the crime scene, they should be packaged separately so as to avoid any contact between the two. Failure to separately package and protect the suspect tool and impression could result in a cursory contact that might alter or add to the imperfections of either, rendering a comparison more difficult or impossible. In addition, a tool may bear paint or fiber trace evidence that could be contaminated or destroyed in the handling.

© Shutterstock, Inc./Nutink.

INVESTIGATOR'S NOTEBOOK

© Shutterstock, Inc./Janaka Dharmasena.

Processing a Crime Scene in Which Footprints Are Found

Footprints made on surfaces that lend themselves to fingerprint lifting can be lifted in the same fashion as a latent fingerprint. Lift tape large enough to accommodate a footprint is available commercially. The tape should be placed carefully over the impression, just as it would be placed over a fingerprint. A fingerprint roller can be used to squeeze out any air bubbles created by the tape. The lifted footprint should be placed on a white or black backing, just as a fingerprint would be.

When shoe or tire impressions are left in dirt, preservation is achieved through photography first and a reproductive cast second. If dirt or debris adheres to the cast, it should not be removed but packaged with the cast and transported to the crime laboratory.

© Shutterstock, Inc./Nutink.

laboratory for examination. Reproductive casts are second best. Prior to making a cast or removing the tool-marked item, it should be examined for fibers and fingerprints. An alternative strategy is to handle the marked item as though it contains both and transport it to the crime laboratory to be processed for fibers and prints. A burglar crawling through a window will undoubtedly leave some fiber evidence; the trick is in finding it and processing it. Toolmarks are so forensically valuable, however, that nothing should be done with them that is not absolutely necessary, thereby avoiding the possibility of altering them.

Toolmarks are created when a tool causes a cut, scratch, or impression to be made on another surface. Any tool that can scratch a surface can leave a toolmark. Often burglaries are performed using screwdrivers or crowbars to gain entry to the location to be burgled. Cutting tools used to cut through metal may also leave marks. The marks left by these tools may be specific to the tool used. As tools are used and misused, they develop unique characteristics on their cutting surfaces. These characteristics can be the result of wear or chipping. In either case, the marks left by these characteristics can be matched to the tool that left them. The impressions left by tools with these types of characteristics may be matched to the tools themselves.

Once the point of entry and the **approach to entry** (the area that led to the entry of the crime scene) have been ascertained and processed, the investigator can turn to the interior of the crime scene. It is at this point that a preliminary scene survey with the owner can be instructive. The owner can point out the absence or presence of things that should or should not be there. A tool, used chewing gum, a cigarette butt, or other evidence might be otherwise over-

looked. The owner can also assist in determining what things the burglar might have touched as he or she traveled through the dwelling. The crime scene, including avenues of approach, should be portrayed in a drawing, along with appropriate measurements.

Witnesses should be identified and interviewed, and in-depth interviews should be conducted with the owner and the entire family. A list of family associates, especially juveniles, should be compiled. Neighbors should be contacted, routinely, to help narrow down the time of the burglary, based on what they may have heard or seen. Reducing the possible timeframe can indicate whether the burglary was planned. Narrow timeframes suggest two possibilities: the burglar was a very lucky amateur burglar, or the burglar was provided with information.

One successful method of catching burglars and reducing the threat of burglary is to stamp serial numbers on valuables and record the numbers. Serial-numbered items are more readily identifiable than items for which only physical descriptions are provided. The serial number of a stereo can be included in statewide and nationwide computer databases used to identify stolen property. In addition, when receivers or purchasers of stolen items are confronted with the irrefutability of a serial number, they may become much more cooperative and willingly identify the persons from whom the property was received.

Motor Vehicle Theft

Historically, cars have been stolen for five reasons: (1) joyriding, (2) parts, (3) resale, (4) insurance fraud, and (5) crime use. Temporarily depriving an owner of his or her vehicle, in many jurisdictions,

approach to entry
The area that led to the entry of the crime scene; often seen as a secondary crime scene, it may include parking areas, sidewalks, yards, and building exteriors

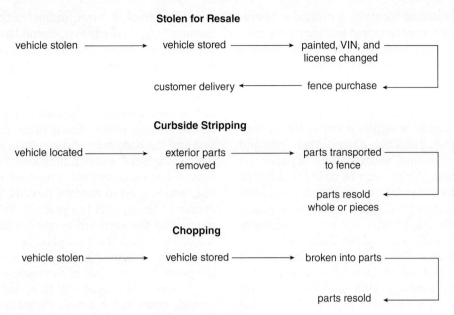

FIGURE 10.13: Stolen-for-resale, stripping, and chopping flowcharts.

does not rise to the level of auto theft. Most joyriding ends with the vehicle being abandoned and available for recovery. Not much in the way of investigation is required in joyriding cases if the culprits are not caught in possession of the vehicle. This section concentrates on the investigation of the remaining four types of auto theft.

Thefts generally occur at night, and auto thefts are no exception. The most commonly reported crime is a stolen vehicle. Other crime data may reflect underreporting, but auto thefts are reported universally, probably because of the statutory requirement that autos be insured and because a police report is required to collect on insurance policies for damages or loss or to get a replacement rental vehicle. Not surprisingly, young people have their vehicles stolen more often than the elderly. Most vehicles are stolen by juveniles who are often in places that are popular hangouts for other juveniles. About half of all stolen vehicles are recovered in part or whole (Harlow, 1988).

Autos stolen for parts are generally **stripped** of the easily removed, easily transported parts, which are resold to individuals or salvage yard dealers. (See **FIGURES 10.13** and **10.14**.) A vehicle may be stripped where parked, or it may be stolen and transported to a location where it can be stripped at leisure. The objective is to remove as many valuable parts as possible, except the engine block and body, and then abandon the vehicle. Air bags have become a choice item for thieves in the stripping business.

The vehicle is usually recovered close to the place where the removal of parts took place. Most auto components are not stamped with numbers based on a universal numbering system and are, therefore, virtually impossible to trace. Investigative efforts should focus on storage rental facilities, gas stations, and public and private garages in the area surrounding the spot where the vehicle was abandoned.

Thieves who **chop** a vehicle have in mind the same objective as those who strip a vehicle: the reduction of the vehicle to its parts. The focus is on the major body components, including doors, fenders, hood, bumpers, and windows—in fact, everything but the frame and the engine block. Auto body components histor-

chop
Stealing an automobile to remove the major body components, including doors, fenders, hood, bumpers, and windows, in order to sell them

FIGURE 10.14: Stripped automobile.
© Tonis Valing/Shutterstock, Inc.

stripped
Removing and stealing the most easily removable and transportable parts from an automobile in order to resell them to individuals or salvage yard dealers

ically have lacked identifying numbers. Manufacturers, aware of stripping and chopping, have begun putting a **vehicle identification number (VIN)** on auto components. The auto thief generally is not the individual who removes the parts. The thief sells the car to a chop shop, and a chopping team reduces it to rubble.

Occasionally, a vehicle is stolen for the purpose of resale. The VIN is altered, a new title and license are obtained, and the vehicle is put on the block for sale. Vehicles can be stolen to order, or they can be stolen by a criminal enterprise specializing in appropriating late-model luxury vehicles and altering, transporting, and selling them, both inside and outside of the United States.

A vehicle's VIN consists of 17 letters and numbers. Altered or false VINs can be recognized by someone who understands what the letters and numbers represent. The first symbol, which is a number, indicates the nation in which the vehicle was manufactured; the second symbol, a letter, indicates the manufacturer (e.g., G stands for General Motors); and the third, a number, indicates the make of the vehicle (e.g., Chevrolet). The next symbol indicates the type of restraints used in the vehicle (e.g., C for seatbelts). The next three symbols, all numbers, constitute the manufacturer's code for the position of the vehicle in the production line and the body type of the vehicle (e.g., van); the next symbol, a letter, indicates the type of engine. The ninth symbol, a number, is a check digit and is used to validate the VIN. The tenth symbol, a letter, tells the year the vehicle was made, and the eleventh symbol, a letter, tells the city in which the auto plant is located. The remaining six symbols, all numbers, constitute the production number of the vehicle.

The vehicle most likely to be subjected to forensic examination is the vehicle stolen for use in a crime. The automobile becomes a focal point of the investigation of the crime and is processed

INVESTIGATOR'S NOTEBOOK

Checklist for Use in Vehicle Theft Cases

1. Make, model, license number, and VIN of the vehicle
   - Names of all known operators of the vehicle
2. Where was the vehicle recovered?
3. How was entry made?
   - Break-in
   - Keyed
4. Who witnessed the theft?
5. When was the theft discovered?
   - By whom?
6. Where was the vehicle last legitimately used?
   - Who used it?
   - For what purpose?
7. Where was the operator at the time of the theft?
   - Witnesses to the operator's location and activities?
8. Where was the owner at the time of the theft?
   - Witnesses to the owner's location and activities?
9. Who has possession of keys to the vehicle?
   - Account for each set of keys.
10. Payment history?
11. Repair history?
12. Owner's financial circumstances?

for fingerprints, hair, fibers, and any other trace evidence that may linger. The automobile should be processed like any other crime scene.

Auto thefts are difficult to investigate. Those autos stolen for profit are usually stripped or disposed of with little evidence of their passing. Those taken for a joyride are abandoned quickly, leaving little usable evidence in their wake. The number of auto thefts occurring in any major metropolitan area is staggering and unmanageable. Thus, resources are best focused on autos used in other crimes. Most auto investigations proceed along the same lines. A checklist for such an investigation is given in the following Investigator's Notebook.

Applicable Case Law

Burglary is a specific intent crime. One cannot accidentally commit a burglary. Often, cases revolve around the intent of the suspect or ownership of the stolen items. The following cases address these two issues.

Ownership

Generally, a **bona fide** (innocent) buyer of stolen goods receives only those ownership rights possessed by the seller. If the seller has stolen the items sold, the buyer has no right to possession or ownership, because the thief had none. The caveat, "Let the buyer beware," puts a bona fide buyer on notice that if the seller is not the owner and has no title to the property transfers, the lawful owner may reclaim the stolen item as having the greater right to possession. This principle can be seen in the case of *Greek Orthodox Church of Cyprus v. Goldberg et al.* (1990).

Intent to Commit Theft

Theft or larceny requires a **specific intent** to deprive an owner of possession of property. The intent to steal may be proved by direct evidence or by circumstantial evidence. Generally, the jury or judge infers intent to steal from the conduct and acts of the defendant. Intent may be obvious or ambiguous. It is the responsibility

bona fide
Innocent, genuine; in Latin, translates as "in good faith"

specific intent
Unambiguous purpose or reason; this must be proved in order to convict a person of theft or larceny

---

CASE IN POINT

© Shutterstock, Inc./Vlastas.

Greek Orthodox Church of Cyprus v. Goldberg et al., 1990

Peg Goldberg, an art dealer traveling in Europe in search of art purchases, was told of four early-Christian mosaics that were said to have been found in the rubble of a church in Cyprus and exported to Germany with the permission of the Cyprus government. In fact, they were stolen from the Greek Orthodox Church of Cyprus. While in Germany, she made an offer of purchase and bought them for $1,080,000. They were shipped to the United States. The Orthodox Church made claim for possession based on the fact that they had been stolen and transported to Germany and sold by the thief, not the church. Possession of the mosaics was returned to the church despite the substantial payment made by Ms. Goldberg.

The court held that when circumstances are as suspicious as those that faced Peg Goldberg, prospective purchasers would do best to do more than make a few last-minute phone calls. In such cases, dealers should take steps to ensure that the seller has legal possession of the items being sold. Ms. Goldberg could have had an authenticity check or a full background search of the seller done, could have asked to be provided with the seller's claim to title, or could have purchased buyer's insurance. Had she done any of these things, she might have discovered that the church had a valid, superior, and enforceable claim to these mosaics and was entitled to have them returned.

© Shutterstock, Inc./Nutink.

CASE IN POINT

© Shutterstock, Inc./Vlastas.

People v. Jaso, 1979

The defendant, Jaso, left a Sears department store with a bag of merchandise for which he did not pay. He was stopped in the parking lot by security. When confronted, he said that he was simply returning to his vehicle to get his wallet from his auto and that he had intended to return to pay for the merchandise. A struggle ensued, and Jaso was subdued and handcuffed. He was convicted, but on appeal, it was determined that the instruction provided to the jury was defective, for it did not include an instruction that "in the crime of theft there must exist in the mind of the perpetrator the specific intent to take property of another and unless such intent so exists that crime is not committed."

© Shutterstock, Inc./Nutink.

CASE IN POINT

© Shutterstock, Inc./Viastas.

Commonwealth of Pennsylvania v. Muniem, 1973

Muniem was found leaving an empty warehouse. He was cooperative, had no loot, and did not resist police efforts to arrest him. He told police that he had to go to the toilet and had looked for a restroom in the empty building. The defendant had entered through an open door. Muniem was married, employed, and had no prior record. The Pennsylvania court ordered him released based on this reasoning:

> The only evidence produced against the appellant is his presence, perhaps as a trespasser, in a vacant building in daylight.... When found by the police, he was walking to the open door by which he testified he entered the building. The owner of the building testified that nothing was missing and there was no evidence of a forcible entry, or possession of any burglary tools, other tools or anything else.
>
> Each case must stand on its own facts in determining whether the Commonwealth has sustained its burden of proof. At best, the evidence of the Commonwealth may give rise to suspicion and conjecture of guilt but most certainly does not have such volume and quality capable of reasonably and naturally justifying an inference of a willful and malicious entry into a building with the intent to commit a felony so as to overcome the presumption of innocence and establish guilt beyond a reasonable doubt of the crime of burglary.

© Shutterstock, Inc./Nutink.

of the prosecution to prove intent by direct or circumstantial evidence.

Intent in the Case of Burglary

If a defendant is caught in the act of stealing during a burglary, proving intent to commit theft is a fairly straightforward matter. If, however, there is no evidence of theft or of commission of a felony, proof of illegal entry into a premise that has items worthy of theft meets the requirement of proof of theft.

The Illinois Supreme Court held in *People v. Johnson* (1963) that intent must be proved, usually by inference. Proof of unlawful entry into a building that contains property that could be the subject of theft gives rise to an inference that will support the intent requirement for the offense of burglary. It may be assumed that the unlawful entry was not without purpose and that theft was the most likely purpose. However, in the case of *Commonwealth of Pennsylvania v. Muniem* (1973), the court found that inconsistent evidence refuting theft after illegal entry was sufficient to dismiss the charge of burglary.

Robbery

The crime that visits urban streets and places the populace in fear for their safety consists primarily of robberies—not the gangland slayings and drive-by shootings that fill the evening news. Those most likely to be afraid of robbery are women and the elderly. Those most commonly robbed on the street are men and juveniles. Robbery, although defined differently in

different jurisdictions, has common elements. It involves the taking of the property of a person by another with the intentional, knowing, or reckless causing of bodily injury or the intentional or knowing threatening of imminent bodily injury or death (**TABLE 10.1**).

Robberies can be simple or aggravated. Jurisdictions may categorize robberies based on weapon use or injuries caused. Typically, a person is held to have committed **aggravated robbery** if he or she (1) commits robbery and (2) causes serious bodily injury to another or (3) uses or exhibits a deadly weapon or (4) causes

aggravated robbery
Robbery in which the person (1) commits robbery and (2) causes serious bodily injury to another or (3) uses or exhibits a deadly weapon or (4) causes bodily injury to another person or threatens or places another person in fear of imminent bodily injury or death if the person is 65 years of age or older or is disabled

TABLE 10.1 The Probability of Violence in Various Types of Robbery	
Type	Probability of Violence
Vehicle robbery	Low to moderate
Bump-and-grab	Low to moderate
ATM robbery	Low to moderate
Residential robbery	Low to moderate
Commercial robbery	Moderate to high
Carjacking	High
Street robbery	High

bodily injury to another person or threatens or places another person in fear of imminent bodily injury or death if the person is 65 years of age or older or is disabled.

Robberies fall into two broad categories, depending on the use or threat of the use of force:

- Strong-arm robbery, often referred to as common-law robbery, involves the use of physical force or the threat of the use of physical force absent a weapon.

- Armed robbery involves the use of a deadly weapon. The weapon does not have to be a firearm—it can be any weapon that, in its use or intended use, may cause serious bodily injury.

Robbery, in some jurisdictions, is considered to be a crime of property, because the basic objective is theft. The Federal Bureau of Investigation (FBI), for purposes of gathering data for its *Uniform Crime Reports*, regards it as a crime against the person, for the theft is from a person and the threat or use of violence is against the person, not the thing taken. No matter the category, robbery is a felony in all jurisdictions—and a higher-degree felony, if it is aggravated. It is interesting to note that the definition of aggravated robbery given earlier, taken from the Texas Penal Code, 2003, Title 7 Chapter 30, treats a robbery as aggravated if it is perpetrated upon the elderly or the disabled—the two kinds of victims least likely to be robbed but most in fear of being robbed because of media sensationalism.

Although there are more than 500,000 reported robberies a year, many more go unreported. National surveys (Federal Bureau of Investigation, 2010) suggest that the actual number is more than 1 million. Most are committed with a weapon, and the weapon of choice is the handgun. Only 25% of all robberies reported are cleared by arrest. Many crimes are reported to the police as robbery. Anyone who has had something stolen is likely to refer to the crime as a "robbery" when, by legal definition, it may be a theft or burglary. What people call the offense is irrelevant as long as police appropriately identify the offense and charge the offender.

In 2009, nationwide, there were an estimated 408,217 robberies. The 2009 estimated robbery rate of 133.0 per 100,000 inhabitants reflected a decrease of 8.8% compared with the 2008 rate. Robberies in the United States cost an estimated $508 million in losses. The average dollar value of property stolen per reported robbery in 2009

was $1,244. Firearms were used in 42.6% of the robberies and strong-arm tactics were used in 41.1%. Of the total number of robberies, knives and cutting instruments were used in 7.7% of reported robberies, and other dangerous weapons were used in 8.7% of robberies in 2009 (Federal Bureau of Investigation, 2010).

Robbers

Although robbers come from all walks of life and have a range of motivations, they fall into several broad categories. Perhaps the most frustrating category is the **career robber**, who has chosen robbery as his or her life's work. Career robbers are responsible for the majority of robberies committed. The tiresome aspect arises from the fact that these individuals are released again and again to re-offend. The capture of these robbers has been facilitated by the creation of police programs that keep track of repeat offenders and their **modus operandi (MO)**.

Opportunistic robbers are not necessarily lifetime offenders. They are amateurs who prey upon others as the opportunity presents itself. Victims are randomly and hastily selected more because of the favorable circumstances than the loot they may relinquish. Amateur robbers are often violent and reckless, attacking without warning, preparation, or consideration of profit potential. They focus on individuals who are in the wrong place at the wrong time and who are least likely to offer resistance. Women and the elderly are their preferred victims, but they tend to stay away from the isolated areas favored by opportunistic robbers (**FIGURE 10.15**). Most robberies occur in the early hours of the morning before daylight in dark, unprotected areas of cities.

FIGURE 10.15: Opportunistic robber.
© Sturti/Getty Images.

career robber
Criminal who has chosen robbery as his or her life's work; career robbers are responsible for the majority of robberies committed

modus operandi (MO)
Method of operation; robbers often repeat their MO, which can be useful in figuring out who committed a particular crime

opportunistic robbers
Amateurs who prey upon others as the opportunity presents itself; these robbers focus on individuals who are in the wrong place at the wrong time and who are least likely to offer resistance

Substance-habituated robbers commit robbery to support a habit. These robbers have graduated to robbery from other less-lucrative criminal activities. They seek immediate cash rather than stolen goods that must be fenced. Occasionally, they rob drugstores or dealers to obtain drugs directly, but, most often, they commit robberies as their need for a drug increases and their ability to purchase the drug decreases. The frequency of these robberies and the amount taken are often clues to the drug dependence that drives these robbers. They will not rob until their drug needs go unaddressed and they will attempt to steal enough to purchase the drug quantity necessary to sustain them. Drug users are generally not under the influence of drugs when they rob, for it is the absence of drugs that motivates the robberies. Alcohol abusers, on the contrary, are generally under the influence of alcohol when they rob (Burns, 2007).

Robberies

People often claim that they have been robbed when their car has been stolen or their homes have been burglarized. In this chapter, we will learn that robbery is a very specific crime involving theft from a person with the use of violence or the threat of the use of violence. If cars have been stolen, it is called auto theft. If homes have been burgled, it is called burglary. Only a person can be robbed.

Street Robberies

Most robberies occur on the streets of our cities (see Table 10.1 for a list of types of robberies and the attendant risk of violence). A typical attack involves a young robber and a vulnerable victim. Muggings and purse snatchings occur on the street. If a mugging or purse snatching includes violence or the threat of violence, it is a robbery. A **street robbery** often involves more than one offender. The mere presence of a number of menacing youths demanding money and jewelry is sufficient for the victim to produce all valuables. If a request for spare change is made from such a menacing group but with no threats accompanying the request, the victim may believe that violence is implied and volunteer all of his or her valuables; without a threat or **show of force**, however, the encounter does not rise to the level of a robbery or theft. The objective of a street robbery is to acquire the victim's money, wallet, credit cards, identification, or jewelry. A street robbery can occur so quickly that the victim, celebrating

his or her escape without injury, may not be able to provide much, if any, information to police (Deakin, Smithson, Spencer, & Medina-Ariza, 2007).

Automated teller machines (ATMs) are a fertile hunting ground for robbers, and ATM robbers have designed special methods to employ during **ATM robberies**. They may lie in wait for the victims to make a withdrawal and rob them upon completion of the transaction or abduct the victims and transport them to various locations to be able to maximize the amount of money stolen, because many machines restrict the amount that can be withdrawn at one time and the number of withdrawals in a 24-hour period. Fortunately, many banks provide security guards and video cameras at their ATM locations. These video cameras have assisted investigators in identifying and apprehending a variety of street thugs who, without knowing it, were filmed in passing by or across the street from an ATM. In investigating any kind of street crime, investigators should examine the environment for the presence of ATMs and their accompanying video cameras.

Residential Robberies (Home Invasions)

Often, a burglary that goes wrong becomes a residential robbery (home invasion), assault, or rape. Most burglars are content stealing from homes in which the occupants are absent. Occasionally, occupants return or the burglar was mistaken about the absence of the occupants. In such cases, what was intended to be a burglary now becomes a **residential robbery (home invasion)**—if force is used in dealing with the occupants and possessions are removed from the person of the occupants (Brown, 2010).

As the prevalence of ATM robbery demonstrates, crime adapts to changes in society. More and more people travel and take their valuables with them, and thus, criminals have developed a repertoire of techniques to take full advantage of people's mobility. For example, hotels and motels are common sites for robbery. Furthermore, the criminals committing these crimes enter when the travelers are in residence for the purpose of relieving them of their possessions, rather than burglarizing the rooms, because they have discovered that travelers generally carry their valuables on their forays.

As a variation on this theme, some robbers gain entrance to people's houses by misrepresenting themselves as repair persons, city inspectors, or police officers. The victims are selected based on the location and value of their homes. The occupants may be robbed, raped, assaulted, or killed. Some of these residential robberies may be drug-related, and in such robberies, drugs or large quantities of cash typically are targeted. The victim of a robbery in which a large stash of money or drugs were taken will be reluctant to admit the exact nature of the crime, but the criminal history of the victim may be helpful in determining motive.

Commercial Robberies

Most **commercial robbery** sites are small businesses, such as liquor stores and convenience stores (**FIGURE 10.16**). By far, the favorite sites are convenience stores, because they are operated by one or two persons, their high visibility allows ease of **casing**, public access makes entry simple and unremarkable, and their location on interstates and major thoroughfares makes escape easy (in some parts of the country, these robberies are called "stop and robs"). By casing the premises, robbers can determine peak business periods in an effort to avoid witnesses and logistical difficulties.

Experienced robbers eventually begin to weigh the risks against the benefits of small robberies and start to aim at higher targets. Robbers may progress from convenience stores to businesses that specialize in a product or service. The robbery of a jewelry store or a savings institution requires planning and associates, if it is to be done effectively. Occasionally, a lone offender will rob a bank—usually a branch office that has one employee. Generally, banks and jewelry stores require more manpower and planning. The planning makes the investigation more difficult, but the increase in the number of felons increases the probability that someone will make a mistake or speak about one of the robberies. The perpetrators of a **specialty robbery** may have received inside information from an accomplice or may have had firsthand employment experience in the particular business robbed or in the same industry.

Vehicle Robberies

Commercial vehicles are often robbery targets, especially taxicabs and delivery trucks. Taxicabs are most vulnerable, because they have cash readily available and the drivers may be lulled into taking a passenger to an isolated location where the offense can be committed. Taxicab robbers tend to be violent, and the drivers are often assaulted or murdered. Possibly because a robber has engaged in conversation and has been under visual scrutiny for a lengthy time, he or she might be concerned about identification by the driver and perceive murder as a prevention against prosecution (dead victims cannot testify). A **delivery van robbery** is typically a crime of opportunity perpetrated by a group of young men who have observed the van making a delivery and deduced that cash must have been received for products delivered. The group will often aggressively and violently attack the driver and remove valuables from the victim after seriously injuring him or her.

A **truck hijacking** is a specialty crime committed by well-armed and experienced offenders. In a truck hijacking, an entire transport vehicle and its cargo are taken. The vehicle is selected because of its cargo, and knowing what the cargo is generally requires inside information. The robbers park another truck at an isolated location and offload the stolen cargo into this truck. The driver is usually released unharmed and may have been the source of the inside information. Traditionally, liquor, cigarettes, and high-tech consumer goods are stolen (Fay, 2007).

Another specialty crime is the robbery of passengers in a vehicle. Two methods have developed. In the **bump-and-grab** method, robbers in a vehicle select a vehicle they think contains occupants with valuables. The victims' vehicle is selected based on its monetary value or the fact that it is a rental in a tourist area. The robbers bump the rear of the target vehicle and stop to examine the damage. When the occupants of the bumped vehicle exit, the robbery takes place. The prevalence of this practice in some tourist centers has prompted legislation prohibiting rental agencies from displaying anything on their vehicles that indicates that they are rented. Young robbers without a vehicle may pick a strategic location at a traffic intersection

FIGRE 10.16: Commercial robbery.
© Steve Cole images/Getty Images.

commercial robbery
Robbery at a place of business, typically convenience stores

casing
Evaluating a chosen robbery site in order to determine peak business periods in an effort to avoid witnesses and logistical difficulties

delivery van robbery
Typically a crime of opportunity perpetrated by a group of young men who have observed a van making a delivery and deduced that cash must have been received for products delivered; the group often will attack the driver aggressively and violently and remove valuables from the victim after seriously injuring him or her

truck hijacking
A specialty crime committed by well-armed and experienced offenders, in which an entire transport vehicle and its cargo are taken.

specialty robbery
Robbery in which the robber(s) may have received inside information from an accomplice or may have had firsthand employment experience in the particular business robbed or in the same industry

and await a potential target. Looking for an auto with a purse, briefcase, or laptop computer on the seat, the **smash-and-grab** thief uses a pipe or other device hidden in his or her clothing to break the passenger-side window and grab the valuable that was spotted.

An especially frightening type of vehicle robbery is a **carjacking**. Instead of smashing windows of vehicles stopped at intersections, robbers commandeer cars that have stopped and steal the vehicle and the possessions of the occupant(s). In some cases, the occupants are kidnapped, taken to an isolated location, and assaulted, raped, or murdered. Because of the fear of carjackings, Congress has made carjacking a federal crime punishable by up to 15 years in prison, or life imprisonment if death is the result of the carjacking.

Modus Operandi

Because of the confusion and psychological trauma associated with robberies, victims' perceptions are questionable and often not very helpful. The major tool of the investigator in identifying a robber is the method employed in the robbery, along with personal characteristics of the robber cited by witnesses (**TABLE 10.2**). Robbers tend to specialize and to develop a repertoire of behaviors that have proven successful in the past and that they believe will continue to be successful. It is their belief in methods of proven efficacy that is an investigator's greatest ally. The traits and techniques

developed early in a career of robbery remain with the robber in later stages. These include the following:

- Target selection procedure
- Robber's attire or disguise
- Method of entry (if not a street robbery)
- Words or notes employed
- Weapons chosen and used
- Type of force or intimidation used
- Manner of the loot grab
- Departure signatures (if any)
- Method of departure

Target Selection

In street robberies, targets are usually determined by opportunity, but there may be some selection process (e.g., women, the elderly, and the disabled may be the victims of choice). Robberies other than the street variety require some type of **target selection**. That selection may have taken minutes or months, depending on the sophistication and experience of the robber and the nature of the target selected. Hitting a convenience store does not require as much preparation as a bank or jewelry store robbery or a truck hijacking.

The selection criteria employed by the robber give the investigator a place to start. The answers to two questions—why and how was this target selected?—are the first insights into the robber's modus operandi. If the target could not have been selected without some pre-robbery scrutiny, the investigator must inquire throughout the community whether any strange persons or automobiles have been noticed (Jacobs, 2010).

Attire or Disguise

Robbers tend to select clothing and disguises that have proved functional and successful. Most robbers do not engage in extensive planning and restrict themselves to casing the places and persons to be robbed. Robbers have limited wardrobes and better things to do with their money than to buy an array of masks or disguises. Robbers are likely to select, consciously or subconsciously, clothing that hides a weapon, is comfortable, and allows a free range of motion. Just as we all have favorite clothing and just as professionals have preferred attire for specific tasks, so do robbers. A description of clothing is important when **tracing** the identity of offenders. The investigator depends on witnesses when gathering this

TABLE 10.2 Personal Traits and Methods of Operation of Robbers

Personal Traits	Methods of Operation
Age	Geographical domain
Gender	Target specialty
Socioeconomic class	Words used
Literacy	Weapon of choice
Predilection for violence	Method of entry
Power needs*	Clothing

*The power needs of a robber are reflected in how he or she treats victims. Robbery is a predator crime, and often, the power and control exercised over the victim are as much incentives to commit robbery as the valuables that can be obtained, especially in the case of the young, amateur robber.

information and should allow the witnesses to describe attire in his or her own way and in his or her own time. Such information may be helpful in uncovering patterns and connecting robberies.

Method of Entry

Entry access is significant in robberies, as it is in homicides and burglaries. Additionally, the behavior of the offender prior to and during entry may be unique. Entry behavior includes all conduct prior to entry up to the demand for valuables or a show of force. Habit creeps into all of our behaviors, and robbers are no exception. In convenience store robberies, the offender will often enter the store posing as a customer and may handle merchandise, engage in conversation with the clerk and witnesses, or use the restroom. Anything handled by the suspect should be processed for fingerprints. Convenience store video footage is not only useful in making a visual identification of the offender but may also assist the investigator in retracing the intruder's steps and reveal possible locations of fingerprints or footprints.

Words and Notes Employed

If a financial institution is the target of a robbery, the request for money must be conveyed in some fashion. The words used are important in figuring out the MO of the robber. The words may be written or spoken and may reveal more about the offender than he or she recognized. The type of paper used is informative. Was the note prewritten, typed, or handwritten, or was it a pasted collage? What type of paper was used? What does the note show about the robber's command of grammar and syntax? Did the robber use paper available at the crime scene? What words were chosen to convey the robber's demand, whether written or spoken?

Although not case determinative, answering these questions adds information that will assist the investigator in fashioning an MO for the robber. An MO is often as revealing as a criminal profile and may be thought of as information upon which a profile can be partly based. In essence, compiling information about a robber's MO allows the investigator to get into the mind of the robber and determine, with some certainty, whether the offender will rob again, the type of target that will be selected, the chance of violence during future robberies, and the geographic area within which the robber is comfortable operating. The information gathered by the investigator not only helps in tracing the identity of the offender but also helps sometimes in connecting the robber with prior robberies and allows limited predictions about his or her future conduct.

Weapons Chosen and Used

Robbers have a large range of weapons from which to choose. The choice of weapon may reflect amateur versus experienced status and planned versus opportunistic target selection. A knife is an amateur's weapon of choice, and its use suggests that the robber selects targets opportunistically and has limited resources and experience. If a firearm is used, the choice of weapon may reflect the sophistication and power needs of the robber. Sawed-off shotguns are intimidating, limited in firepower, and often selected out of a need to feel powerful and hence to carry a weapon capable of causing devastating tissue damage. They are chosen despite the fact that they are difficult to secrete upon one's person, difficult to transport, and less likely than handguns to be disposed of upon completion of the robbery. Handguns are the weapon of preference for most robberies, with semiautomatic firearms providing additional firepower and range. A revolver may be selected in the early stages of a robber's career because of its cost and simplicity. Amateurs will use the same weapons repeatedly, whereas a more professional robber will select weapons commonly owned by ordinary citizens (thereby reducing their identifiability) and will dispose of each weapon used immediately upon completion of the robbery (Wells & Horney, 2002).

Hollywood movies portray modern professional robbers as equipped with fully automatic submachine guns and **sound suppressors** (the correct name for a silencer). It should be noted that unless a handgun or submachine gun is equipped with an integral sound suppressor, dissipating the gases that cause the sound means dissipating the gases that operate the bolt, so only one shot can be fired before manually re-cocking the weapon. Also, sound suppressors are only effective when used with weapons that fire bullets at speeds less than the speed of sound. There are two sounds that occur as the result of a firearm discharge. In weapons that fire a round at speeds in excess of the speed of sound, one crack occurs at the barrel and the other where the bullet breaks the sound barrier. This second sound is impossible to suppress. Submachine guns are less available and less likely to be disposed of than more common weapons. If a submachine gun is used in the commission of a robbery, it is likely to be used again.

entry access
The entry point chosen by a robber to gain access to the site of the robbery

sound suppressor
The correct name for a silencer; it is only effective when used with weapons that fire bullets at speeds less than the speed of sound

Type of Force or Intimidation Used

The offender brings force to bear in some fashion during the course of a robbery. That show of force may also become part of the robber's **habit pattern**. All people relegate to habit those things that they do so often that thinking about them becomes unnecessary and a waste of time: which shoe to put on first, which arm to wash first in the shower, how to insert the key into the ignition of a vehicle, where to carry one's car keys, which buttons to button first on one's shirt. Many of one's habits can tell an observant person something about who and what someone is. So too do robbers fall victim to habit patterns that are specific to the offenses they commit. Such habits are considered a robber's MO, but they may be indicative of habits that transcend the crime and reflect who and what the offender is, independent of the offense being investigated.

The language used by a robber is such a habit pattern. The words selected for the purpose of committing the offense indicate the type of language with which the offender is most comfortable. The choice of words is not accidental; the robber has picked them and rehearsed them. The words said may be what the victim best remembers about the offender, or they may be the only thing upon which multiple victims can agree. It is a safe assumption that the words selected have been used in the past and will be used again in the future.

Conversations between offenders in multiple-person robberies can also reveal something about the offenders and their relationships. Professional robbers will keep conversation to a minimum and may restrict communication to nods and gestures. Their original demand may be a collage constructed on nondescript paper. Yet, most robberies are charged with excitement and require spontaneous decisions to address the ever-changing circumstances, eliciting verbal responses from the offenders. These responses may add to the profile that is developing of the offenders and their relationships with each other. Spontaneous comments may provide names and demonstrate that the robbers know the layout, the geographical area, the security system, or police procedures. It is important to glean every word uttered and every gesture made by the robbers. The investigator will want to ask each victim when that victim first realized that a robbery was in progress and what the robbers said or did to convey that message.

Manner of the Loot Grab

The loot (possessions) taken was obtained in a particular fashion—by request, demand, gesture, or self-help. It is important to determine exactly how the robber grabbed the loot. In the robbery of a bank, if the robber directed the teller not to include **bait money** (bills that have had their serial numbers recorded and have been set aside specifically to be given to robbers so they can be traced. They may also contain dye packs, which explode and color the bait money with dye upon exit from the location), several questions are raised:

- Has the robber worked in a financial institution?
- Has the robber learned about bait money through experience (suggesting the possibility of a criminal record)?
- Has the robber been provided with inside information?

Departure Signature

Every robbery comes to an end. Of potential significance is the manner in which the robber exits the premises and the robber's actions toward witnesses and victims—what he or she does to them or has them do. If they have been bound, trace evidence will be present. If they were directed to lie face down on the floor, a **departure signature** may be in the making. Any last comments or behaviors unnecessary to the completion of the robbery may become the robber's trademark or signature, as though he or she were signing a just finished letter or work of art. A signature is a part of the robber's MO and sometimes is the most obvious connection between the robbery being investigated and other crimes committed previously. A signature can occur at any time during the course of the robbery, depending on the imagination and psychological need for recognition of the offender. A kiss to female victims, a slap, or a beverage taken in celebration are examples of signatures left by robbers.

Method of Departure

One of the most valuable variables of the MO is how the robber escapes the scene—on foot, in a car, or on a motorcycle or bicycle. The most easily traceable element of the offense may be the method of escape. Victims may be able to provide the make, model, and color of the vehicle. They may even recognize the vehicle as one they have previously seen in the neighborhood. This is the type of information that may be gathered from a canvass of the neighborhood. Some people are reluctant to approach the police with information, even if they understand that the information is relevant. It is more difficult for a person to shirk his or her civic responsibility

---

bait money
Bills that have had their serial numbers recorded and have been set aside specifically to be given to robbers so they can be traced

habit pattern
Things done so often that thinking about them becomes unnecessary and a waste of time; when these habit patterns are a consistent part of a person's robberies, they are called the robber's modus operandi

departure signature
Any last comments or behaviors unnecessary to the completion of the robbery that become the robber's trademark or signature, as though he or she were signing a just-finished letter or work of art

INVESTIGATOR'S NOTEBOOK

© Shutterstock, Inc./Janaka Dharmasena.

Goals of Gathering Information

By gathering all of the information possible at a robbery crime scene, the investigator is working toward three separate but interdependent goals:

1. Reconstruction of the robbery
2. Identification of the robbers
3. Construction of the MO and comparison of it with those of other robberies

A complete MO is never forthcoming. The objective of the investigator is to gather as much information as possible in the hopes of being able to construct a working hypothesis as to the offender's MO. By comparing the MO in one case with those of similar robberies, the names of prior offenders may arise as possible suspects.

© Shutterstock, Inc./Nutink.

when looking into the eyes of a hardworking, courteous investigator who is trying to protect the neighborhood and its citizens. It should not be assumed that all witnesses have been rounded up by the first-responding officers, nor that all witnesses have come forth voluntarily.

Processing the Robbery Crime Scene

The crime scene in a robbery includes the robbers' modes of arrival and departure. It may extend to the area from which a vehicle used in a robbery was stolen and to the location of the vehicle after it has been abandoned. It may include a motel room where the robbers planned the crime and to which they returned to divide the spoils. It is necessary to see a robbery as a dynamic entity, with a beginning and end apart from the person robbed or from the place where the coerced transfer of money or goods occurred. Much of the investigative effort will be focused on determining the beginning point and end point of the robbery. Although not immediately apparent, they become evident during the course of the investigation.

The robbery scene itself may be of evidentiary value, based on what the offender or offenders did while at the scene. The possibility of finding fingerprints, footprints, trace evidence, or tire tracks depends on what the robbers did and whether the investigator discovers what they did. If the investigation revealed that a vehicle had been parked at a particular location for an extended period of time while robbers cased the site, there may be evidence of that wait. Tire tracks, litter, or footprints in adjacent soil may be the product of a lengthy surveillance, and the knowledgeable investigator may be able to discover such evidence and use it to good

effect. The doorway through which entry was made may reveal fingerprints. The cash register or display cases handled by the robbers may render fingerprints, as may any merchandise handled by an offender while posing as a customer. It is the investigator's job to determine which, if any, of these potential repositories of evidence may exist (Fish, Stout, & Wallace, 2011).

Vehicles recovered after a robbery may contain a wealth of forensic evidence. It is impossible to operate a motor vehicle without leaving some type of trace evidence. In one robbery homicide, for example, a black plastic bag was tied with a cord around the victim's head. Upon arrest of the suspect, a box of plastic garbage bags and a spool of cord were found in the trunk of his car. An examination of the striations imparted to the bags during the manufacturing process identified the bag in the homicide as having come from the box of unseparated bags. Also, the end of the rope at the crime scene had been cut, and when that rope and the rope on the spool in the suspect's trunk were viewed under a comparison microscope, there was little doubt that the former had been cut from the spool.

The discharge of firearms at a robbery opens up another realm of forensic evidence. The most common evidence will be shell casings and spent bullets. Both casings and bullets have substantial evidentiary value. Firearm identification, discussed in Chapter 8, is applicable in any investigation in which a firearm is used or suspected.

Robbery Checklist

Every crime is unique and requires an investigation tailored to the crime, the victim, and the situation. Yet, enough commonalities exist among investigations to allow the creation of

INVESTIGATOR'S NOTEBOOK

Examples of Trace Evidence to Look for in Vehicles

- Fibers (on seat backs, roof liner, and door frames)
- Soil
- Broken glass, asphalt, gravel (carried in the soles of the shoes)
- Hair on headrests and roof liner
- Fingerprints (on all glass surfaces, door handles, dashboard, and radio controls)
- Cigarettes and litter (in ashtray; on floor; in glove compartment; behind sun visors; on, under, and behind seats)
- Tire treads (impressions and residue, which may be identifiable in dirt or gravel)
- Saliva (left on cigarettes, cups, or discarded bandanas or other items used as a mask)
- Trace materials (fiber, blood, dirt, glass, any of which may be on both the robber and the victim if physical contact between them occurred)
- Toolmarks (identifiable characteristic marks left by knives, pry bars, and other instruments used at the crime scene)
- Rope and tape

© Shutterstock, Inc./Nutink.

a checklist for the purpose of ensuring that all investigative issues have been addressed. The checklist in the Investigator's Notebook is illustrative only, and the steps need not follow each other in the order given. The list is best used to determine if an investigation has addressed all of the potential sources of information that may be available.

INVESTIGATOR'S NOTEBOOK

Checklist for Processing the Scene of a Robbery

1. Triage the injured.
2. Provide first aid.
3. Contact emergency medical assistance.
4. Identify any victims.
   a. Ascertain that a robbery has occurred.
   b. Interview victims (sooner rather than later).
5. Separate witnesses.
   a. Identify witnesses.
   b. Interview witnesses.
   c. Canvass the community.
6. Provide a broadcast dispatch.
   a. Describe the suspect or suspects.
      i. Gender
      ii. Race
      iii. Clothing
      iv. Physical characteristics (height, weight, hair color)
      v. Identifiable characteristics (scars, tattoos)
      vi. Weapons

    b. Describe the vehicle.
      i. Direction of travel
      ii. Time of departure
      iii. Number of occupants
      iv. Make, model, year, and color
      v. License number
      vi. Stolen status

7. Search the surrounding area (if applicable). Contact hostage negotiators if hostages were taken or the situation becomes barricaded.

8. Process the crime scene.

    a. Locate the scene (which may include a wide geographic area).
    b. Protect the scene (including people, places, and things).
      i. Log all traffic in and out.
      ii. Handle and package evidence.

9. Identify MO.

10. Utilize street sources of information.

11. Prepare the case for trial (a case summary or prosecutorial summary is a good tool [see the following section]).

CONCLUSION

This chapter shows that theft, burglary, and robbery can take many forms and that the investigation of each requires attention to detail. Burglaries are the silent dread of everyone who has a lock on his or her door. We often think of burglaries as crimes of property but forget that much of what we have we worked hard for and many things of value are worth more because of the sentiment attached to them. Those who say burglary is a property crime have never been burglarized.

In most street robberies, the victim is traumatized to the extent that little useful information is generally available. Most victims of robbery are so pleased to be released unhurt that other considerations pale. In robberies, as in most other "stranger" crimes, the probability of apprehending the offender is remote, and as time passes, that probability lessens. We do know that robbers have turf and that in most cases, they will rob again. Absent genuine efforts to catch robbers through stings and surveillance, patrol response is likely to be of little help.

Because robberies occur predominately on the street, there is little useful evidence available to responding officers. The area surrounding the robbery should be canvassed for individuals who saw something or who recognized the offenders. In truth, most robbers are caught either in the act or in the act of selling or pawning items taken from their victims.

Often, these crimes are committed by people in search of or in need of drugs. Much of what is stolen in burglaries is fenced for as little as 10 cents on the dollar. That money, in many instances, is used to fuel a drug habit. In the next chapter, we will consider drugs: what they are, what they do, and how law enforcement carries on the war on drugs.

QUESTIONS FOR REVIEW

1. What is the definition of larceny?

2. How does larceny differ from theft?

3. What has been the impact of consolidating theft offenses?

4. How does someone convert property that is not his or hers?

5. How does unauthorized use of a motor vehicle differ from auto theft?

6. What role does a fence play in the theft business?

7. What is the value of toolmarks to a burglary investigator?

8. Of what value are the point of entry, method of entry, and approach to entry to the burglary investigator?

9. What is a VIN, and of what value is it to a burglary investigator?

10. How does stripping a vehicle differ from chopping a vehicle?

11. What right to possession has a bona fide purchaser of stolen goods? Why?

12. What propositions should come to the mind of the carjacking investigator?

13. Why might it be a good idea to photograph a tool impression prior to making a mold of it?

14. Why should tire impressions be taken with the tire still on the vehicle?

15. What is the difference between a simple robbery and an aggravated robbery?

16. What is an opportunistic robber, and how does an opportunistic robber differ from a career robber?

17. What is a street robbery?

18. How might one defend against a street robbery?

19. What social and technological changes have led to the creation of new types of robbery?

20. What are specialty robbers, and what do they specialize in?

21. What is the difference between a bump-and-grab robbery and a smash-and-grab robbery?

22. How is a carjacking conducted?

23. What does it mean to say that a robber has a modus operandi?

24. What is a case summary, and what value does it have?

25. What should be contained in a case summary?

26. What would be included in a robbery checklist? Why?

REFERENCES

Brown, D. L. (2010). *Home invasion: The fear is real.* Niles, OH: Parkway Press.

Burns, M. (2007). *Medical-legal aspects of drugs* (2nd ed.). Tucson, AZ: Lawyers and Judges.

Deakin, J., Smithson, H., Spencer, J., & Medina-Ariza, J. (2007, February). Taxing on the streets: Understanding the methods and process of street robberies. *Crime Prevention and Community Safety*, 9(1), 52–67.

Fay, J. J. (2007). *Encyclopedia of security management* (2nd ed.). Burlington, MA: Elsevier.

Federal Bureau of Investigation. (2010). *Uniform crime reports.* Washington, DC: U.S. Department of Justice.

Fish, J., Stout, R. N., & Wallace E. W. (2011). *Practical crime scene investigations for hot zones.* Boca Raton, FL: Taylor & Francis.

Harlow, C. W. (1988). *Motor vehicle theft.* Washington, DC: U.S. Department of Justice, Bureau of Justice Statistics.

Jacobs, B. A. (2010, May). Serendipity in robbery target selection. *The British Journal of Criminology*, 50(3), 514–529.

Osterberg, J. W., & Ward, R. H. (2010). *Criminal investigation: A method for reconstructing the past* (6th ed.). Cincinnati, OH: Anderson.

Saferstein, R. (2014). *Criminalistics: An introduction to forensic science* (11th ed.). Upper Saddle River, NJ: Pearson Prentice Hall.

Wells, W., & Horney, J. (2002, May). Weapon effects and individual intention to do harm: Influences on the escalation of violence. *Criminology*, 40(2), 265–296.

KEY LEGAL CASES

Commonwealth of Pennsylvania v. Muniem, 303 A.2d. 528 (Pa. Super. Ct. 1973).

Greek Orthodox Church of Cyprus v. Goldberg et al., 917 F.2d 278 (7th Cir. 1990).

People v. Jaso, 84 Cal. Rptr. 567 (Cal. Ct. App. 1979).

People v. Johnson, 28 Ill.2d 441, 192 N.E.2d 864 (1963).

Assault Investigation

KEY TERMS

aggravated assault

aggravated sexual assault

aspermia

assault and battery

attitude

battery

concealed handgun laws

deadly force

diaphorase

domestic assault

fallacy of innocence

fighting words

gender-specific

medical examination

mutual combat

photographic record

scrapings

seminal stains

sex crimes investigator

sexual assault evidence collection kit (SAE kit)

simple assault

spermatozoa

spousal immunity

standards of resistance

swabbings

trace evidence carriers

> "He had apparently been struck down first from behind, but his assailant had gone on beating him long after he was dead. It was a most furious assault. There are no footsteps nor any clue to the criminals."
>
> **Sherlock Holmes**
> *"A Reminiscence of Mr. Sherlock Holmes"*

STUDENT LEARNING OUTCOMES

Upon completion of this chapter, students will be able to:

■ Recognize what constitutes an assault

■ Describe the assault investigative protocol

■ Discuss how to investigate domestic violence and child abuse

■ Explain the legal justifications for the use of force

■ Demonstrate the gathering of evidence in a sexual assault investigation

domestic assault
Assault that occurs in the home, usually committed by a person's spouse

aggravated assault
A physical attack that results in serious bodily injury and that is perpetrated in the course of another felony or involves the use of a deadly weapon

simple assault
A threat to cause bodily injury, an offensive contact or touch, or an attack that does not cause serious bodily injury; the term is used in jurisdictions that have dropped the term *battery* from their penal codes

battery
An attack on another

assault and battery
The threat to commit an attack upon another, and then the attack

Introduction

The crime scene processing and criminal investigation of an assault are similar to those for a homicide. The major difference is that assaults do not result in death, even though that may have been the intent of the assailant. There are more than 1 million reported assaults committed each year (Federal Bureau of Investigation [FBI], 2016). More than 50% of reported aggravated assaults result in arrests. National victim surveys indicate that the actual number of assaults committed annually far exceeds the number reported to the police. First, there is general agreement as to what constitutes an **aggravated assault**. All jurisdictions treat a physical attack that results in serious bodily injury and that is perpetrated in the course of another felony or involves the use of a deadly weapon as an aggravated assault. The difficulty arises in defining a **simple assault**. Historically, attacks on another person have been called **battery**, and the threat to commit an attack upon another was called an assault. News commentators often report that the assailant committed **assault and battery**. Many jurisdictions have dropped the term *battery* from their penal codes and have replaced it with *simple assault*. Those jurisdictions define a simple assault as a threat to cause bodily injury, an offensive contact or touch, or an attack that does not cause serious bodily injury.

Assault arrests are generally made by patrol officers. These officers happen upon assaults in progress or respond to dispatches for assaults in progress. Their arrival and the circumstances often result in an arrest and extemporaneous investigation based on their observation of the assailant and victim, with little need for a subsequent investigation.

Most agencies do not expend tremendous time or resources on simple assaults unless they are a product of domestic violence. In the vast majority of cases, victims of assault know their assailants and often refuse to file a complaint against the attackers.

One of the most frustrating aspects of law enforcement is the reluctance of an assaulted spouse to file a formal complaint against his or her assailant. The call to police is made out of fear and panic. The service requested is protection and removal of the offending spouse. These **domestic assaults** often occur on weekends in the early hours of the morning. Once the offender has been removed from the home, the victim has time to reflect on the consequences of formal prosecution. Recognizing that the assailant may lose his or her job if he or she does not report for work on Monday or if the employer discovers that he or she has been charged with a criminal offense, the victim, who may have only limited financial resources, forgoes signing the necessary complaint. State legislatures have addressed this anomaly by not requiring spousal complaints in domestic violence situations and requiring that an arrest be made if there is any evidence of violence. The bulk of reported assaults are domestic in nature and do not require the services of an investigator or require much in the way of an investigation.

Aggravated Assault

The investigator in aggravated assault cases may confront a traditional crime that is accompanied by an assault. Rapes, drug deals gone awry, extortion, robberies, and burglaries frequently include an assault.

INVESTIGATOR'S NOTEBOOK

© Shutterstock, Inc./Janaka Dharmasena

Handling Aggravated Assault

In any investigation in which an aggravated assault is involved, the following steps should be taken in the indicated order.

1. Triage of the victim
2. Render first aid and summon medical assistance
3. Preserve the crime scene
4. Question the victim and witnesses
5. Process the crime scene

© Shutterstock, Inc./Nutink.

Triage of the Victim

Injuries are often deceptive. Although there may be no external evidence of bleeding, blunt weapon attacks may cause internal damage. It is not the role of the investigator to make a medical determination, but he or she should inquire into the type of injuries received and the method by which they were received. If blunt trauma has occurred, especially to the head, the victim should be examined by a medical professional. Keep in mind that an aggravated assault may easily be the product of a friendly dispute that escalated, especially if the dispute was accompanied by alcohol or drug use. The victim may not have the mental alacrity to assess the severity of the injuries suffered and may, therefore, refuse medical help.

Rendering First Aid and Summoning Medical Assistance

The first obstacle may be to convince the victim that medical assistance is necessary. Hollywood portrayals are to the contrary; the first responsibility of every officer arriving at a scene where injury has occurred is to provide first aid, even if the perpetrator is within arm's reach. This responsibility extends not only to victims injured at the hands of assailants but also to suspects and offenders injured by police. It may seem surprising, but a police officer who has just shot an assailant attempting to take the life of another police officer has an immediate responsibility, after disarming the assailant, to provide assistance for the injuries just inflicted (**FIGURE 11.1**).

Preserving the Crime Scene

All too often, by the time an investigator arrives at the scene of an aggravated assault, it has been rearranged and trampled upon by

FIGURE 11.1: The first responsibility of every officer arriving at a scene where injury has occurred is to provide first aid.

© Sir Travel A lot/Shutterstock, Inc.

a variety of people. One major obstacle to this type of investigation is the difficulty of assessing what damage occurred during the assault by the parties and what damage occurred by friends, police, and medical personnel. It is the first responders' responsibility to ensure that this type of damage is kept to a minimum and to record any changes to the scene occurring prior to and during their tenure at the scene. To preserve this type of scene, keep all admitted and possible witnesses available and sequestered.

Questioning the Victim and Witnesses

Assaults occurring in taverns and clubs are notorious for having no cooperative witnesses who will give statements associated with viewing the event. The major evidence in this type of investigation generally will come from the victim and the witnesses. It is important to determine if the victim was actually a victim of an assault or a perpetrator who did not fare well in his or her assaultive attempt. In virtually every assault that is not a domestic violence offense, the offender will raise the idea of self-defense at trial or during pretrial motions. The investigator should keep in mind that one object of the investigation is to anticipate this defense and defuse it by obtaining sufficient information and evidence to establish unequivocally who was the assaulter and who was the victim.

The victim's rendition of facts will be different from the suspect's and should be recorded if possible. Information about what preceded the assault must be gathered. This kind of information will help uncover the motive for the assault and also establish that an assault in fact occurred. Simply because two people were fighting and one was injured does not mean that an assault occurred. Some states allow a **mutual combat** defense. If two parties agreed to step into the parking lot for the purpose of involving themselves in an altercation, there may or may not have been an assault. In states with mutual combat statutes, an assault may have occurred if the following criteria were met:

- The terms of the agreement were exceeded (e.g., rather than engaging in an agreed-upon fistfight, one of the parties hits the other over the head with a beer bottle).

- One party attempted to withdraw from the combat and the other did not allow withdrawal (the shield of self-defense could

mutual combat
Defense to a charge of assault, contending that the two parties agreed to involve themselves in an altercation

CASE IN POINT

Medical Assistance Imperative

In 1996, the author provided expert testimony in a federal civil rights lawsuit filed against a local Texas police officer and agency. A Texas Department of Public Safety officer was involved in an altercation with a man who was intoxicated and was much bigger and stronger than the officer. The suspect attempted to subdue the officer with blows from a flashlight to his head. During the struggle, the suspect attempted to draw the officer's weapon. Repeated blows to the officer's head did not succeed in dislodging his grip. Wresting the weapon from the suspect, the officer fired. His call for assistance at the onset of the scuffle was answered, and local officers arrived on the scene.

The Texas Department of Public Safety officer was in shock and suffering from head injuries and was unable to render assistance to the offender. The local officers who arrived on the scene assessed the condition of the offender and decided to await the arrival of the emergency medical staff without offering any assistance to the offender, who bled to death before he was treated. Medical testimony established that basic first aid would have kept the offender alive until the emergency medical service arrived. The family of the deceased filed a federal civil rights suit against the local officers and their agency for failure to provide medical assistance to the deceased. The case is instructive, for not only is there a moral imperative to provide medical assistance to all who are injured, but there also may be legal repercussions for failing to do so.

be raised by the party who attempted to withdraw).

- One party attempted to terminate the combat and the other did not allow termination.

By interviewing the witnesses and gathering information about what preceded the assault, the investigator will flesh out his or her understanding of what took place and perhaps why it took place. Interviewing witnesses will assist in corroborating what the investigator has learned from the victim, the offender, or the crime scene. In those instances in which the authorities are unable to interview the victim, the only reliable information will be what the crime scene reveals and what the witnesses provide. If the investigator is lucky, the witnesses will help ascertain motive and assist in defusing any self-defense shield thrown up at a later date. The witnesses may also help make sense of a trampled crime scene and describe any weapons that were used.

Processing the Crime Scene

The scene itself should be handled as if it were the scene of a homicide—which it may end up being if the injuries are so severe that they cause death. The investigator should conduct a search focused on weapons, blood evidence, fingerprints, and trace evidence, and he or she should evaluate the scene based on the information that the witnesses, victim, and offender have given.

If possible, after processing the scene, the investigator should conduct a preliminary scene survey with the victim and the suspect, who can each provide a narrative of the events prior to, during, and after the assault from his or her unique perspective. It is important to remember that the victim's injuries and the clothing are evidence, and the investigator has the responsibility to obtain and process the clothing for forensic examination and to record all injuries photographically.

If the assault is committed with a firearm, the defendant will probably allege that the weapon was fired accidentally or during a struggle. Powder stippling, gun smoke residue, and barrel blowback will all assist in corroborating or negating the defendant's accidental firing claim. Additionally, the angle of entry may help in establishing the relative positions of the participants at the time of the shooting. Consequently, the **medical examination** must contain a forensic component out of the ordinary for the emergency room. The investigator may have to accompany the unconscious shooting victim to the hospital to retrieve clothing and to ensure that a forensic examination is made of the victim and the victim's injuries.

Photographs of the victim's injuries should be taken as soon as possible after their infliction. Injuries will heal, and the hospital may not make a **photographic record** of the injuries. A verbal description of injuries contained in the medical records is not as effective with a jury as photographs (preferably color photographs). The best advice that an investigator can receive about investigating aggravated assaults

medical examination Examination of the effects of an assault on the victim's body, in order to help determine the circumstances of the assault

photographic record Photographs (preferably color photographs) taken of an assault victim's injuries

is to view an aggravated assault as a murder that failed.

Elements of Proof

In prosecuting an aggravated assault, the state must prove that (1) the defendant was the aggressor, (2) the victim was seriously injured and/or (3) a deadly weapon was used, and (4) no justifications exist that excuse the assault.

Types of Abuse

Domestic violence is a pattern of coercive control founded on and supported by violence or the threat of violence. The abuse may take the form of physical violence, sexual violence, emotional abuse, psychological abuse, or some combination of these elements.

Emotional abuse takes the form of a systematic degrading of the victim's self-worth. This may be accomplished by calling the victim names, making derogatory or demeaning comments, forcing the victim to perform degrading or humiliating acts, threatening to kill the victim or the victim's family, controlling access to money, and acting in other ways that imply that the victim is crazy. Psychological battering involves all of the features of emotional abuse, but also consists of at least one violent episode or attack on the victim to maintain the impending threat of additional assaults. Destruction of property is violence directed at the victim even though no physical contact is made between the batterer and the victim. This includes destroying personal belongings, family heirlooms, or even the family pet.

Domestic Violence

Officers responding to domestic abuse calls need to have a full understanding of the complex social, economic, and psychological issues that surround acts of domestic violence. That understanding can only be obtained as the result of specific training pertaining to such issues as the following:

- The cycle of domestic violence
- Investigating domestic violence
- Providing resources for the domestically abused

The Cycle of Domestic Violence

Police generally become involved in a domestic abuse situation once it has reached a flash point. However, in most domestic abuse cases, physical abuse occurs during one of the three phases that make up the cycle of violence (Walker, 2009):

1. Tension building
2. Battering
3. Honeymoon

By becoming familiar with the features of each phase in this cycle, responding officers can help victims understand that the cycle of abuse is likely to continue if nothing is done to address the underlying causes.

■ Stage 1: Tension Building

During the first—and usually the longest—stage, tension escalates between the couple. Excessive drinking, illness, jealousy, and other factors may lead to name calling, hostility, and friction. Unless some type of professional intervention occurs at this point, the second phase of the cycle becomes virtually inevitable.

Many victims recognize these signs of impending violence and become more nurturing or compliant or just stay out of the way. Some victims will accept their partner's building anger as legitimately directed at them. Such victims may come to believe that if they play their part well, the aggressor will remain calm. However, if they fail, the resulting violence is their own fault.

■ Stage 2: Battering

Many batterers do not want to hurt their partners, only to control them. However, this is the stage where the victim, the batterer, or responding officers may be assaulted or killed. Unless the battering is interrupted, the violence during this phase will escalate beyond the level of violence used in prior abusive situations. The batterer intends to emphasize control through violence: If that control was not sufficiently created during the last battering session, then, in the mind of the batterer, not enough violence was used. Serious injury or death may occur because batterers may reach the point in their evolution at which they cannot or will not stop. After a battering episode, many victims consider themselves lucky that the abuse was not worse, no matter how severe their injuries. They often deny the seriousness of their injuries and refuse to seek medical attention.

Law enforcement officers who respond immediately after a violent episode may find an abusive perpetrator who appears extremely calm and rational. The batterer's calm demeanor is deceptive; he or she has just released anger and vented tensions at the victim. The batterer may point to the victim, who may be highly agitated or hysterical because of the abuse, and the batterer may attempt to blame the victim for the violence. The victim may, in fact, respond aggressively against officers who attempt to intervene. Officers should be aware that this reaction might be due to the victim's fear that more severe retaliation awaits if officers arrest the batterer. The victim also may feel desperate about the impending loss of financial support or even emotional support he or she receives from the abuser. Although officers should not make any false promises, they should reassure the victim that the mechanisms are in place for the criminal justice system to help. Officers have a responsibility to provide a complete, professional investigation so that the system will work. A haphazard investigation or a lack of concern by responding officers could result in a violent abuser's being released from jail to retaliate against a vulnerable victim.

■ Stage 3: Honeymoon

The last stage of the cycle is a period of calm, loving, contrite behavior on the part of the batterer. The victim wants to believe that his or her partner really can change. Victims feel responsible, at least in part, for causing the incident, and they feel responsible for their partners' well-being. It is at this stage that many victims request that complaints against batterers be dropped.

■ Handling The Cycle of Violence

The cyclic nature of domestic violence has prompted most states to pass laws requiring the following:

- In cases of obvious physical violence, police must effect an arrest.
- An inquiry must be made as to the availability of firearms on the premises.
- If firearms are on the premises, they must be taken into police custody.

INVESTIGATOR'S NOTEBOOK

© Shutterstock, Inc./Janaka Dharmasena

Tips for Interviewing Victims of Domestic Violence

- The introduction should be brief, making it clear who you are and why you are investigating.

- Once consent to the interview has been granted, spend some time "being human" and getting to know the victim.

- Once the victim is at ease, clearly lay out the parameters of the interview. It will help the victim focus his or her thoughts and serve as a tool for keeping the victim on track.

- Ask permission to take notes or record the interview. There are pluses and minuses to each method, but one way or another, the information must be documented.

- Try to focus the questioning in an organized fashion. Start with the first time the victim knew there were problems in the relationship and move forward from there. Get as much detailed information as possible. When this incident happened, was there anyone else present? Did the victim call the police?

- Tie down the date of prior incidents whenever possible. No one will remember exact dates, but ask what time of year it was. Was it winter or summer? Was it before the Christmas incident mentioned or after? Approximate dates can be critically important in locating documents and corroborating information with other witnesses.

- Always ask for the names and contact information of other people who may have information—friends of the victim, roommates, coworkers, social service agencies with whom he or she dealt, where he or she went to school. Each interview will likely yield four or five other potential witnesses, each of whom has a piece of the puzzle.

- Ask for permission to contact the victim if questions come up later, and ask him or her to contact investigators if anything else comes to mind. Often, the process of remembering will cause the victim to recall other details or incidents.

Source: Adapted from Tanya Brannan, Purple Berets, "Violence Against Women," http://www.purpleberets.org/violence_investigatingdv.html

© Shutterstock, Inc./Nutink.

- The victim must be provided written materials describing available support services.
- The victim must be told that he or she can be removed to a safe house.
- A complete investigation of the abusive circumstances must be made.
- A records check of the assailant must be performed; outstanding warrants must be executed.
- Interviews of neighbors, friends, coworkers, and relatives must be conducted.
- A signed medical record release and an examination of medical records to document prior incidents of suspected abuse are required.

It is the intent of legislatures and police agencies that the victim be protected and that the suspect be prosecuted. If that means the case must go forward with a reluctant victim, it is to the investigation and documentation that the prosecution must turn for a conviction. The goal of officers responding to domestic violence should be to develop a case that can be prosecuted, even if the victim becomes resistant to testifying. Although most domestic relationships involving violence include some type of cycle, not all violent relationships go through each phase as described previously.

Investigating Child Abuse

Investigation of potential incidents of child abuse is a critical and sensitive matter. Protection of children and fairness to parents are complementary, not mutually exclusive, ends. Balancing these interests is a difficult and challenging law enforcement responsibility. Physical and sexual abuse of children may be camouflaged as accidental injuries. Investigators frequently must determine whether a child's accident or illness was caused by a parent or caretaker. However, it is often difficult, even for medical personnel, to discriminate between injuries and illnesses that are accidental and those that are intentional. The information in this part of the chapter can help law enforcement personnel to determine if it is likely that abuse has occurred.

Identifying Child Abuse

Investigators must determine whether the explanation for an injury is believable. Police should begin their investigation by asking the caretaker for an explanation of the child's bruises or injuries. This is best done by asking the question, "How did the accident happen?"

All bruises must be investigated. If bruises are found on two or more planes of a child's body, investigators should be increasingly suspicious (e.g., a child has bruises on his buttocks and stomach). The caretaker's explanation is that the child fell backward in the living room of the family home. This might explain the bruises on the buttocks, but not the stomach bruises. If a discrepancy exists between the reported cause of an injury and the injuries seen, law enforcement personnel should investigate further.

Investigators should also keep in mind the following points:

1. All other children in the home should be examined for possible signs of child abuse.

2. Victims of physical abuse often have been intimidated and will usually support the abuser's version of how their injuries occurred to avoid further injury. They also feel that the abuse was just punishment because they were bad.

3. A physical examination of the child in suspected cases of maltreatment must be done and the data recorded precisely.

4. Laboratory data should be obtained to support or refute the evidence of abuse.

5. If the reported history of an injury or injuries changes during the course of an investigation, or if there is conflict between two adult caretakers as to the cause of injury, the likelihood of child maltreatment increases.

6. The demeanor of the child's parents or caretakers is sometimes revealing. For example, a mother's assessment of her pregnancy, labor, and delivery will often provide insight into her attitude about her child as well as give an indication of whether there is something about the child that is influencing her behavior.

7. Investigators should ask questions in an unobtrusive manner; for example:

   - Was this a planned pregnancy?
   - Did you want the baby?
   - Do you like the baby?
   - How did the accident happen?
   - What were you doing just before the accident?
   - Who was at home at the time of the accident?

- What do you feed the baby? How often? Who feeds the baby?

8. Information about a child's birth and his or her neonatal and medical history are critical elements in investigations. Hospital records can confirm or eliminate the existence of birth injuries.

9. Any child may be abused, and child abuse occurs in all levels of society. However, there are some factors that increase a child's risk of abuse. These include the following:

- Premature birth or low birth weight

- Being identified as "unusual" or perceived as "different" in terms of physical appearance or temperament

- Having a variety of diseases or congenital abnormalities

- Being physically, emotionally, or developmentally disabled (e.g., mentally retarded or learning disabled)

- Having a high level of motor activity, being fussy or irritable, or exhibiting behavior that is different from the parents' expectations

- Living in poverty or with a family that is unemployed

- Living in environments with substance abuse, high crime, and familial or community violence

A careful examination of the circumstances and types of injuries and an assessment of the child and family should be carried out.

Types of Injuries

■ Bruises

Bruises are caused by the leakage of blood into skin tissue and are produced by tissue damage from a direct blow or a crushing injury. Bruising is the earliest and most visible sign of child abuse. Early identification of bruises resulting from child abuse can allow for intervention and prevent further abuse.

Bruises seen in infants, especially on the face and buttocks, are suspicious and should be considered nonaccidental until proven otherwise. Injuries to children's upper arms (caused by efforts to defend themselves), the trunk, the front of their thighs, the sides of their faces, their ears and neck, genitalia, stomach, and buttocks are also more likely to be associated with nonaccidental injuries (**FIGURE 11.2**). Injuries to their shins, hips, lower arms, forehead,

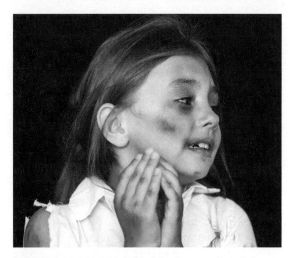

FIGURE 11.2: A child with bruising that most likely indicates nonaccidental injury.

© Sevilla/Shutterstock, Inc.

hands, or the bony prominences (the spine, knees, nose, chin, or elbows) are more likely to signify accidental injury.

It is important to determine the ages of bruises to see if their ages are consistent with the caretaker's explanation of the times of injury. Age dating of bruises can often be determined by looking at the color of the bruise. Bruises will sometimes have a specific configuration. This may enable law enforcement officers to determine whether bruises are accidental or nonaccidental. One of the easiest ways to identify the weapon used to inflict bruises is to ask the caretaker, "How were you punished as a child?"

The pattern of a skin lesion may suggest the type of instrument used. Bruise or wound configurations from objects can be divided into two main categories: those from fixed objects, which can only strike one of the body's planes at a time, and those from wraparound objects, which follow the contours of the body and strike more than one of the body's planes. Hands can make either kind of bruise, depending on the size of the offender's hands and the size of the child. Examples of fixed and wraparound objects include the following:

- Fixed objects: Coat hangers, handles, and paddles

- Wraparound objects: Belts, closed-end (looped) cords, open-end cords (closed-end cords leave a bruise in parallel lines; open-end cords leave a bruise in a single line)

Injuries inflicted by human hands, feet, or teeth or those inflicted by belts, ropes, electrical cords, knives, switches, gags, or other objects will often leave telltale marks (e.g., gags may leave down-turned lesions at the corners of the mouth). These marks may also help in the investigative process. For example, the size of bite marks may help to determine the biter's approximate age; their shape may help identify whose teeth made the marks.

In some cases, however, bruises are acquired innocently, through play and accidental falls, or when a child has a defect in his or her clotting mechanism. The medical diagnosis of clotting disorders requires blood tests and interpretation of those tests by qualified physicians. Investigators must never jump to conclusions and must make a complete investigation of all aspects of suspected child abuse. However, their first duty is to secure the safety of the child quickly.

■ Eye Injuries

External eye injuries are so common in children that they are seldom clear-cut evidence of abuse. Some types of eye injuries, however, may raise a red flag for the knowledgeable investigator:

- Two black eyes seldom occur together accidentally.

- The "raccoon eyes" associated with accidental and nonaccidental fractures at the base of the skull may look similar to each other, but raccoon eyes from nonaccidental trauma usually are associated with more swelling and skin injury (**FIGURE 11.3**). The history helps distinguish between them.

- Hyphema, the traumatic entry of blood into the front chamber of the eye, may be the result of a nonaccidental injury caused by striking the eye with a hard object, such as a belt buckle. The child will complain of pain in the eye and have visual problems.

FIGURE 11.3: "Raccoon eyes" associated with nonaccidental fractures at the base of the skull.

© Andy Dean Photography/Shutterstock, Inc.

- Retinal hemorrhages are the hallmark of shaken baby syndrome and are only rarely associated with some other mechanism of injury.

- Nonaccidental trauma must always be considered in a child under 3 years of age who has retinal hemorrhages or any traumatic disruption of the structures of the globe of the eye (e.g., the lens or retina) or the skin around the eye.

Investigating allegations of child abuse is a challenge, both in recognizing the abusive characteristics of the injuries children receive and in recognizing that kids are active, are prone to accidents, and are injured easily. Equally as challenging is the provincial notion that only poor people abuse their children. Child abuse is pervasive and knows no racial, gender, or socioeconomic boundaries.

Child abuse is difficult to investigate because children are reluctant to communicate the abuse to anyone. Although they are being abused by a parent that does not mean that they do not love that parent. Sadly, abusive parents may also love the child they abuse but not be able to manage their anger and violent response to the often loud and disconcerting behavior of children. Whatever happens from an investigative point of view, it is important to remember that psychological intervention is necessary for the child and, perhaps, the parent. The first responsibility is to remove children from abusive environments, followed as closely as possible by providing services that will reduce the impact of the child's abusive history.

Legal Justifications for the Use of Force

It should not be surprising that assault is one of the most common offenses committed. The adventure movies that are popular today typically have an antihero rather than a hero—a character with attitude.

One can purchase a beer with attitude, a car with attitude, or clothes with attitude; date a man or woman with attitude; or be a spectator at a sporting event whose participants exhibit attitude. **Attitude** may best be defined as an aspect of an individual's personality that immediately puts all others on notice that this individual "takes nothing from nobody at no time." Attitude has become so prevalent in our society that a woman without it is perceived as unliberated and a man without it is viewed as less than masculine. If two motorists with attitude arrive

attitude
An aspect of an individual's personality that immediately puts all others on notice that this individual "takes nothing from nobody at no time"

at an uncontrolled intersection, what might be the outcome? If two persons with attitude enter a dispute, what might be the outcome? It is no accident that the streets of our cities seem to be under siege, given the prevalence of street attitude (never relinquish the right of way), road rage (attitude with a car and gun), and leisure-time assaults (attitude hierarchies). Attitude has replaced courtesy, compassion, and consideration. It is a fuel that, lit with a spark, can flare up into an assault.

In the United States, legislators in some states have enacted **concealed handgun laws** and have defined the circumstances in which a person may use force, including **deadly force**, in defense of self and property. Concealed handgun laws and rights to use force add an element to homicide and aggravated assault investigations of which investigators must be aware.

An example of such legislation is found in the Texas Penal Code, "Justification Excluding Criminal Responsibility." In the section dealing with the use of force to protect persons, the code allows citizens to use reasonable and necessary force in self-defense to the degree that they reasonably believe the force is immediately necessary to protect themselves against others' use or attempted use of unlawful force (Vernon's Annotated Penal Code, 1997, Section 9.31(a)). Of course, the statute goes on to list the many situations in which such force cannot be used, including the following:

- In response to verbal provocation alone (in Texas, **fighting words** do not justify the use of force)

- Resisting an arrest or search, whether it is legal or illegal (unless unnecessary force is being used by the police)

- The actor consented to the exact force used by the other

Additionally, a person may use deadly force to protect his or her person if:

1. A reasonable person in the actor's position would not have retreated

2. It is reasonably believed that deadly force is necessary either

   - to protect against another's unlawful use of deadly force, or

   - to prevent the imminent commission of aggravated kidnapping, murder, sexual assault, aggravated sexual assault, robbery, or aggravated robbery

The Texas legislature also has provided for persons to use force to protect their property from trespass (for real property) or to retrieve stolen property if recovery of the property is possible. Unique to Texas is the provision that use of deadly force is justified to protect property in cases where the citizen is attempting to prevent arson, burglary, robbery, aggravated robbery, theft at night, or criminal mischief during the nighttime or the flight of an individual who has committed burglary, robbery, aggravated robbery, or theft during the nighttime and is escaping with property.

An investigator must not only know the elements that make up assault and aggravated assault but also have an understanding of the legal justifications for the use of force. The existence of a seriously injured victim does not always establish that an assault occurred. Furthermore, a breach of the statutes justifying the use of force could constitute an assault. Knowing what is and what is not an assault is not as easy as it might appear to be.

Sexual Assault

Human sexual conduct has historically been one of the dark corridors of human behavior. As human sexuality has become more open, it has received a certain amount of social and academic acceptance and has become the focus of intelligent discussion. It is no surprise that sexual repression and the absence of sexual candor have redounded to the disadvantage of women. Repressed sexuality has as its adjuncts ignorance and discrimination. Much of the sexually disordered thinking prevalent in our society is the result of hundreds of years of repressed human sexuality. Some of that repression continues to taint the way sexual assault is treated by society and by law enforcement.

The only thing more dangerous than humanity's history of sexual repression is the imagined segregation of men and women into two separate camps: potential rapists and potential victims. The data on rape that are bandied about and that form the foundation of political positions can be biased and misleading. Contributing to the bias is the difficulty of defining rape and the intentional skewing of the definition. In many surveys, women acknowledge that they have been victims of rape in amazingly large numbers. As serious as the problem is, it can be exaggerated by defining rape so as to advance a political agenda. Some unwanted, nonconsensual contact is not rape.

concealed handgun laws
Laws that allow the use of force, including deadly force, in defense of self and property

deadly force
Force that results in death

fighting words
Verbal provocation

Some unforced sexual intercourse is not consensual. Because of the reluctance in the past to honestly discuss sexual aberrations and illegal sexual conduct, we can easily be saddled with working definitions of rape that are not legally relevant.

Traditionally, sexual assault has required corroboration beyond the testimony of the victim. In common law, rape was defined as forced sexual penetration by a person other than a spouse. It was a male-specific crime and could not be committed by a husband upon his wife. Additionally, for the force element to apply, there had to be evidence of resistance. Two **standards of resistance** evolved: maximum and reasonable resistance.

Predominantly male investigators, judges, and juries saw death as preferable to succumbing to rape. A woman who survived rape was often shunned (socially ostracized) by her community and her family. It was forgivable for a husband to abandon a wife who had been raped and for a man to abrogate the marriage contract if his fiancée was raped.

As severe as these responses seem in retrospect, basic attitudes toward rape have carried over into contemporary society. Why is it necessary to protect the identity of a rape victim? What is it that we are protecting him or her from? Why is there still some stigma affixed to someone who has been raped that restrains disclosure of his or her identity?

Elements of Sexual Assault

Sexual assault generally involves penetration or contact without consent (or, in the case of a minor, with or without consent). Legislatures have removed the **gender-specific** aspects of prior legislation, recognizing that women can sexually assault men, women can sexually assault women, and men can sexually assault men. Most penal codes contain language that prohibits the following:

- Penetration of the anus or female organ of another person by any means without the person's consent

- Penetration of the mouth of another person by the sexual organ of the actor without the person's consent

When children are at issue, the statutes prohibit the following:

- Contact or penetration of the sexual organ of a child with the mouth, anus, or sexual organ of another person

- Contact or penetration of the mouth, anus, or sexual organ of a child with the anus or sexual organ of another person

The question of consent, when children are at issue, is not material. Adult consent (or lack thereof) is usually defined in detail by statute. Adult consent is generally held to be lacking in the presence of the following:

- Use of physical force or violence

- The threat of physical force or violence with the ability to carry out the threat

- Unconsciousness or inability to resist

- Mental disease or defect that affects the ability to give consent

- Alteration of a person's ability to resist through the covert introduction of drugs

The elements of sexual assault are multitudinous and complex. A proper investigation begins with understanding what the elements of a sexual assault are and assessing the evidence that may be available to support those elements. Sexual assault cases are difficult to prove, and many rapists have gone free because of lazy or half-hearted investigations that failed to substantiate the necessary elements of rape through corroborative evidence. The good news is that three of the most unacceptable common-law provisions regarding rape have been abolished: spousal immunity, the relevance of the victim's sexual history, and resistance requirements.

Spousal Immunity

Spousal immunity has died and been buried. Spousal abuse statutes now include provisions prohibiting nonconsensual sex between marriage partners. Some states include the prohibition in their rape or sexual assault statutes. There is little probability that the spousal relationship will provide a defense against a charge of nonconsensual intercourse. The notion that sex was a partner's right, or a partner's duty, is no longer accepted legally or socially.

Past Sexual Conduct

Additionally, most jurisdictions prohibit fishing exhibitions into the sexual past of the victim. It was not uncommon for the defense to argue that the survivor was "promiscuous," wore provocative clothing, or used suggestive language. Under contemporary legal standards, it does not matter what the victim has done. As a practical matter, the conduct of the victim at or near the

standards of resistance
Two standards, maximum and reasonable resistance, that evolved for the force element to apply in the common-law definition of rape

spousal immunity
The notion that sex was a husband's right and a wife's duty and, therefore, that sexual assault by a person against his spouse was not a crime

gender-specific
Limited to one gender

time of the assault will be paraded before the jury, as will the victim's behavior, language, and clothing. Some change in social standards has accompanied legal changes, and juries are less likely to find suggestive behavior, clothing, or language a substitute for consent.

Resistance

The resistance requirement has been dropped from the statutes of most jurisdictions. Nonetheless, the absence of injury or the absence of an application of force will be used to bolster the defendant's position that intercourse was consensual. The average juror still expects an unwilling participant to resist and further expects there to be evidence of that resistance. In acquaintance-rape cases, the absence of injury, torn clothing, or other evidence of rape is often seen as evidence of consent. In these cases, the evidence is generally the victim's word against the accused's word, and juries generally will not convict without corroborative evidence. Perhaps it is possible for a couple to date, have sex, and, the next morning, have differing opinions as to whether the sex was consensual. Given that many of these liaisons involve the ingestion of alcohol or drugs, good judgment is often missing and an accurate reconstruction of what happened by either party may be impossible. Juries are not immune to being influenced by the realities of today's dating protocol, and absent some suggestion of coercion, they will likely acquit the suspect accused of date rape. Bear in mind that a verdict of not guilty is not a finding that the defendant is innocent, only that there was insufficient evidence to convict.

Aggravated Sexual Assault

Sexual assault, in most jurisdictions, is raised to the level of **aggravated sexual assault** if serious bodily injury results, a deadly weapon was

aggravated sexual assault
Sexual assault in which serious bodily injury results, a deadly weapon was used, or the victim was kidnapped

used, or the victim was kidnapped. In some jurisdictions, the step up to aggravated sexual assault occurs if the assault was committed:

- By a public servant acting under color of law
- In retaliation against a public servant
- In retaliation against a witness, informant, or person reporting a crime

Sexual Assault Investigation

Sexual assault investigations are especially difficult investigations. The psychological well-being of the victim must be taken into consideration as well as his or her medical condition and needs. Throughout the process of attempting to attend to the victim's needs, the investigator must delicately balance evidence collection, both testimonial and physical. This is typically conducted by officers of the same sex as the victim/suspect and often with medical personnel present. Special attention to evidence collection and preservation methods, both testimonial and physical, will ensure the greatest opportunity to successfully prosecute the case.

Considerations for Processing the Scene

Sexual assault crimes involve physical contact between perpetrator and victim. This contact results in the transfer of materials, such as hairs, fibers, and body fluids, particularly seminal fluid and saliva. In many cases, the perpetrator is not known to the victim, and the assault occurs in seclusion or with no witnesses. As a result, there are some additional considerations that a crime scene investigator should take in order to ensure the proper documentation and collection of related evidence.

CASE IN POINT

© Shutterstock, Inc./Vlastas.

People v. Orenthal James Simpson

fallacy of innocence
The false belief that a person who is found not guilty in a trial is innocent

A perfect example of the **fallacy of innocence** is the O.J. Simpson case. The criminal jury reached a verdict of not guilty, but a civil jury based on the same evidence and testimony found him civilly responsible for the deaths of Nicole Simpson and Ronald Goldman. The difference can be found in the quantity of proof necessary to find culpability. In a criminal case, jurors have to convict based on evidence beyond a reasonable doubt (equivalent to a probability of more than 90%). In a civil case, a jury is instructed to render a verdict based on the preponderance of the evidence (more likely than not, or a probability equivalent to 51%). The criminal jury may not have believed Simpson was innocent, but only that the state had not provided sufficient evidence to find him guilty beyond a reasonable doubt.

© Shutterstock, Inc./Nutink.

The crime scene investigator should attempt to recover articles, such as handkerchiefs, rags, or tissues, that may have been used as a wipe after ejaculation. They should also recover and submit any articles that may have become stained during the offense or might have foreign hairs present (bedding, rugs, sofa cushions, etc.). When condoms are recovered in suspected sexual assault cases, they should be placed in a glass specimen jar and frozen until submitted to the crime laboratory.

Once the police have been notified of a sexual assault, they should follow a protocol that does not vary in its essential elements from investigation to investigation. The victim, although a person, should be treated as part of the crime scene and thus processed for forensic and **trace evidence carriers**. Failure to recognize the possibility of evidence on the victim's person may result in the destruction of valuable forensic evidence.

It is incumbent upon the police agency to ensure that all parties responding to a sexual assault dispatch be trained in applying the protocol. The absence of specialized training for officers responding to sexual assault cases has contributed to the historic reluctance that victims have exhibited to report sexual assaults. Police have not always been sensitive to the physical, psychological, and emotional needs of sexual assault victims and have inadvertently contributed to their victimization. Their insensitivity, coupled with the defense strategy of placing blame on the victim, explains why sexual assaults have so often gone unreported. Assault victims have been unwilling to be victimized by the police and the courts after having been victimized by their assailants.

In the past, sexual assault and child abuse cases were assigned to female officers or the newest person on the force. Men were not comfortable handling these types of cases and avoided assignment to them. It was thought that female officers, solely because of their gender, brought a level of sensitivity to sexual assault investigations that male officers could not. The truth is that there are women who are emotionally insensitive and poorly prepared to investigate sexual assaults, just as there are men who have the necessary skills. The abilities required to be a successful **sex crimes investigator** are not gender specific and can and must be learned.

Modern agencies have addressed past indiscretions and have trained their personnel to handle sexual assault victims. Many agencies have specially trained teams whose only responsibility is to respond to sexual assault cases. They, along with specially designated attorneys who have also undergone in-service training on how to prepare and prosecute sexual assault cases, understand what is required for the successful investigation of sexual assaults and the successful prosecution of the assailants.

Medical Attention and Examination of the Victim

As in all situations in which a victim has undergone a physical attack, the primary responsibility of the officer first responding to the scene is to triage the victim. That responsibility is greater in sexual assaults. The victim, fearing the perceived shame associated with being raped, may decline medical treatment. It is at this early juncture that the skill of the specially trained sex crimes investigator must come into play.

The medical attention sought is not only for the purpose of providing treatment but also for the purpose of collecting forensic evidence. To prove that sexual assault of an adult occurred, it must be shown that penetration took place. Showing this can only be accomplished through a medical examination and the collection of physical evidence from the person of the victim. Use of force may be proven by the presence of injuries to the body or ligature marks on the body. All injuries must be noted by the

sex crimes investigator Investigator who has been taught to be sensitive to the physical, psychological, and emotional needs of sexual assault victims and has been trained in what is required for the successful investigation of sexual assaults

trace evidence carriers Items on which trace evidence is likely to be found

INVESTIGATOR'S NOTEBOOK
Basic Elements of a Sexual Assault Investigation

1. Provide medical assistance to the victim
2. Protect the crime scene
3. Establish an evidentiary link between the assailant and the victim

examining physician and photographed. It should not be presumed by the investigator that the physician will take photographs of the injuries. A request should be made directly to the physician, and if necessary, a police photographer of the same sex as the victim should be provided to photographically record all relevant body markings under the supervision of the medical personnel.

Many people who are raped delay reporting the incident. Any delay can hinder the investigation because the victim may have showered or destroyed soiled clothing and bed linen. Not only do such actions remove corroborating evidence from the reach of the investigator, but the defense may question why the victim did not call police immediately. In an effort to defuse this tactic, the investigator should record the mental and emotional condition of the victim following evaluation by the examining doctor.

In a rape case, investigators may need to collect and analyze the DNA of every consensual sexual partner who the victim had up to 4 days prior to the assault. Testing can eliminate those partners as potential sources of DNA suspected to be from the rapist. A sample should also be taken from the victim. It is important to approach the victim with extreme sensitivity and to explain fully why the request is being made. A qualified victim advocate or forensic nurse examiner can be a great help.

In sexual assault cases, it is especially important that victims are told why they should not change clothes, shower, or wash any part of their body after an assault. Depending on the nature of the assault, semen may be found on bedding or clothing, or in the anal, oral, or vaginal region. Saliva found on an area where the victim was bitten or licked may contain valuable DNA. If the victim scratched the assailant, skin cells containing the attacker's DNA may sometimes be present under the victim's fingernails. Victims should be referred to a hospital, where an exam will be conducted by a physician or sexual assault nurse examiner.

In all cases, it is essential to have the victim(s) examined by a medical professional as soon as possible after the assault and before the affected areas (pubic area, vagina, rectum, etc.) or clothing are washed or cleaned.

Evidence on or inside a victim's body should be collected by a physician or sexual assault nurse examiner. A medical examination should be conducted immediately after the assault to treat any injuries, test for sexually transmitted diseases, and collect forensic evidence, such as

fingernail scrapings and hair. Typically, the vaginal cavity, mouth, anus, or other parts of the body that may have come into contact with the assailant are examined.

The examiner should also take a reference sample of blood or saliva from the victim to serve as a control standard. Reference samples of the victim's head and pubic hair may be collected if hair analysis is required. A control standard is used to compare known DNA from the victim with that of other DNA evidence found at the crime scene to determine possible suspect(s).

Today, all hospitals and emergency rooms are aware of the procedure to be employed in examining a sexual assault victim and will have a **sexual assault evidence collection kit (SAE kit)** available that can assist the investigator and attending medical professional in properly collecting the specimens required (**FIGURE 11.4**). This kit can be used to collect appropriate samples from both male and female sexual assault victims and suspects.

Each kit gives specific collection methods for various types of evidence that must be collected and documented. These include:

- Clothing
- Pubic hair combings
- Vaginal swabs (four) and smear (one)
- Cervical swabs (two) and smear (one)
- Rectal swabs (two) and smear (one)
- Oral swabs (two) and smear (one)
- Pubic hair standards
- Penile swab (one)
- Buccal cell standard (cheek or mouthwash)
- Fingernail scraping (if indicated)
- Bite marks (if indicated)
- Toxicology specimens

Interviewing the Victim

■ Initial Interview

The initial interview must address the who, what, and where of the assault. A description of the assailant will be valuable in communicating a description to patrol officers. What was done during the assault will provide a perspective to the investigator for the examination that is to be conducted by medical staff and the accompanying gathering of physical evidence from the body of the victim. Where the assault occurred will lend further structure to the investigation and the possible locations of forensic evidence left at the scene of the assault.

sexual assault evidence collection kit (SAE kit) Assortment of equipment that is useful for collecting evidence of a sex crime from a victim

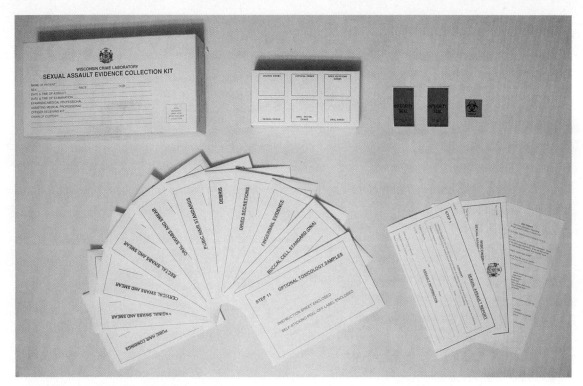

FIGURE 11.4: Sexual Assault Examination Kit.

Courtesy of Nick Vesper.

Interviewing sexual assault victims is a delicate process and requires special training for the interviewer or interviewing team. In most instances, a woman who has been sexually assaulted harbors residual fear that may generalize to all adult males. Many agencies with crisis intervention teams have men and women on the team with the necessary training and empathy required to conduct the first interview. It is this interview that is the most difficult and the most important. It will be the inclination of all concerned to forestall the interview, thereby reducing any additional emotional trauma to the victim. That is a luxury that is not available to the sexual assault investigator or team. Much of the evidence sought is fragile. It will dissipate, be destroyed, or be contaminated if not attended to immediately. Victim comfort is always a consideration, but it must be recognized that the investigation cannot go forward without some discomfort to the victim. The sooner and more professionally that discomfort is dealt with, the better. There are victims who are so traumatized that an immediate initial interview is impossible. It must be remembered that the initial interview is the first step in the investigation. The investigation cannot begin without it. Time is the friend of the assailant.

In most instances, the interview should be conducted in private with a healthcare worker present. Family and friends should be excluded unless the interview cannot be conducted without the presence of the third party (child victims are handled differently). Soliciting a narrative from the victim is the best approach but may be difficult in light of the trauma suffered. If questions are needed to prompt responses, those questions need to be considered very carefully to ensure that there are no suggestions of challenge to the victim's circumstances. Any inconsistencies in the victim's rendition should be attributed to the emotional state of the victim and not to conscious deception.

From the initial interview, the investigator will be able to suggest to medical personnel the scope and breadth of the physical examination that the victim must undergo. It is also from this interview that the parameters of the search will be constructed of the victim's person as well as the physical surroundings in which the assault occurred.

■ **Follow-Up Interview**

The initial interview will give police, investigators, and medical personnel a starting place. Once the investigation has been launched, numerous questions will arise that will require revisiting the victim and his or her story. Time will have allowed the victim to regain composure and dignity. The second interview should be more detailed, focusing on the specific words spoken and the specific acts in question. Questions of resistance can be

INVESTIGATOR'S NOTEBOOK

Elements Sought in the Interview of a Sexual Assault Victim

The initial interview should attempt to gather the following information:

1. A narrative of the assault
2. A description of the assailant
3. Any outstanding characteristics of the assailant that will assist in constructing a modus operandi (MO)
   a. Assault method
   b. Words spoken or threats made
   c. Weapons used
   d. Salutatory comments or gestures
4. What the victim was doing prior to the assault
5. What the victim was doing during the assault
6. What the victim did after the assault
7. What the assailant was doing during the assault
8. What the assailant did after the assault
9. Whether a vehicle was used
   a. Make
   b. Model
   c. License number
10. Where the assault took place (perform a preliminary scene survey addressing each point of contact during the assault)
11. The names of any persons who may have witnessed the entry or the exit of the assailant
12. The names of any persons who may have witnessed the assault
13. Any necessary medical information
    a. Points of penetration
    b. Injuries
14. Points of body-to-body physical contact

© Shutterstock, Inc./Nutink.

addressed. Issues of reputation will have to be pursued in an effort to defuse defense efforts at discrediting the victim based on prior relationships and reputation. Further descriptions of the events of the assault and of the assailant can be developed. Even the most thorough investigators will find themselves returning to the victim for any additional information that will help to clear the case. Interviews should be kept to a minimum and should be based on new perspectives rather than something that was overlooked in the initial or follow-up interview.

Gathering Evidence

The clothing of the victim and suspect(s) is the next most important type of evidence. Articles of clothing worn by the victim (and suspect, if possible) should be submitted to the laboratory for examination, as there may be seminal stains, bloodstains, foreign hairs and fibers, or other trace evidence adhering to the clothing. In addition, items at the crime scene may provide important evidence that associates either the victim, the suspect, or both with the scene.

The recommended procedure for the collection and preservation of clothing is as follows:

- Clothing of the victim must be kept separate from that of the suspect at all times.

- Clothing worn at the time of or immediately after the offense must be recovered and preserved. This includes undergarments, handkerchiefs, sanitary napkins, and/or tampons (only if used during or after the offense).

- Garments should be handled as little as possible to avoid the loss of trace evidence.

Each item should be packaged separately. Plastic bags should not be used. Paper bags will not affect the clothing or any evidence on the clothing. If the victim is conscious and wearing the clothing that he or she wore at the time of the rape, a "catch paper" should be used to capture any evidence that may be dislodged during disrobing. If the victim is unconscious, the catch paper should be placed beneath the body to accomplish the same objective. The catch paper should be folded, edges inward, to avoid loss of evidence and then packaged separately.

Clean paper should be spread under the item to catch any debris that may be dislodged while any wet evidence undergoes a drying process. Package, label, and seal each item along with the paper on which the item dried. Use only paper containers for packaging (i.e., paper bags). If a suspected seminal stain is on an object that cannot be transported, collect utilizing swabs and distilled water, as with blood evidence.

Proof of penetration is required to establish sexual assault. It will be necessary to obtain **swabbings** of the mouth, anus, and vaginal cavity in an effort to corroborate the victim's statement that penetration occurred. The victim is likely to recall what part of the body was penetrated, and the physician can focus the examination on that area. Occasionally, a victim is so badly injured that he or she either does not recall the entirety of the assault or is unconscious. In this case, all three areas need to be swabbed. The swabbing is done to detect the presence of seminal fluid or spermatozoa. For each swabbing taken, a separate package must be used. Along with the swab and any attached evidence, there must be a separately packaged unused swab as a laboratory control to defuse any suggestion that the swab that was used was contaminated. It is part of the medical protocol to prepare slide smears for microscopic examination from swabbings. These slides must also be packaged and appropriately marked. The physician may also obtain an oral and vaginal rinse. Each rinse should be placed in an evidence vial and appropriately labeled. Again, as with all forensic examinations, there should be a control sample of the rinsing material packaged separately.

Hair and fibers are commonly found at the sexual assault crime scene or on the person of the sexual assault victim. Proper processing and handling may provide corroborative evidence that will assist in the prosecution. Fiber or hair evidence alone seldom results in a conviction. Hair and fiber evidence are suggestive rather than determinative trace evidence. Fingerprints and DNA identifications are determinative, for only one person can have a particular fingerprint or DNA print. Typically, hair and fiber, however, cannot be so specifically identified. Only in instances where a hair, complete with root, is located will there be the possibility of recovering individualized DNA.

Fingernail and toenail **scrapings** may be obtained in an effort to detect hair, fibers, blood, or tissue from the assailant. Toenail scrapings may reveal dirt or fibers from a vehicle floor or assault location. Each hand and foot should be processed separately and the scrapings placed in separate bags. The instrument used to obtain the scrapings should be provided as a control and packaged separately.

Vaginal Secretions

In order to meet the criteria for sexual assault, it is often necessary to prove that an object was placed in the vagina. In these cases, it is necessary for the forensic laboratory to make use of microscopy in order to identify fluids and cells associated with vaginal secretions.

Vaginal secretions in the form of a foreign DNA (DNA that did not originate from the individual swabbed) can sometimes be attributed to another individual when the penis of a suspected sexual perpetrator is swabbed at the time of apprehension. The sample is collected by wetting a cotton swab with distilled water and swabbing the external area of the penis. This type of analysis is most successful when the perpetrator is apprehended shortly after the alleged occurrence of sexual activity, generally within 24 hours and prior to bathing. The outer area of condoms can also yield this type of DNA.

Semen

Semen is the reproductive fluid that normally contains **spermatozoa**, the male reproductive cells. The presence and appearance of spermatozoa are highly important to the value of semen as tracing evidence. Following their discharge from the male, spermatozoa may remain in an active state for up to 15 hours. **Seminal stains** not deposited in the body of the victim may remain intact for lengthy periods of time. Not all seminal samples contain spermatozoa. Some men have a condition called **aspermia**, which prevents spermatozoa from appearing in their seminal fluids. If a seminal sample is to be tested for DNA, the evidence must first be tested to determine if it contains sperm, since it is the sperm cell that contains the DNA.

scrapings
Particles under the fingernails and toenails that may be obtained in an effort to detect hair, fibers, blood, or tissue from the assailant

swabbings
Specimens taken with a swab from the mouth, anus, and vaginal cavity to detect the presence of seminal fluid or spermatozoa

spermatozoa
The male reproductive cells

seminal stains
Traces of semen that may be found in three localities: on the victim, at the crime scene, and on the suspect; use of an ultraviolet light is helpful for locating seminal stains

aspermia
A condition that prevents spermatozoa from appearing in a male's seminal fluids

Seminal stains may be found in three localities: on the victim, at the crime scene, and on the suspect. Semen located on the victim may be discovered on any exterior surface of the body or in any of the body orifices. An examination of the crime scene with ultraviolet light may reveal traces of semen, especially in areas and on things related to the assault, such as beds, towels, washcloths, paper towels, toilet paper, and carpeting. Most humans secrete blood into their other body fluids. Chemical analysis of a secretor's semen, saliva, or gastric juices may reveal blood type. Additionally, the enzyme **diaphorase** is only present in sperm in humans. It exists in three distinctive forms: The most common form appears in 50% of the male population, the second most common appears in 40%, and the least common is present in only 10%. The discovery of the enzyme is useful in eliminating innocent subjects and can be useful in tracing the assailant (Gilbert, 2009).

In 1935, Kutscher and Wolbergs discovered that human semen contains uniquely high levels of seminal acid phosphatase (SAP) compared with other body fluids and plant tissues. SAP is produced by the prostate and is, therefore, found in both animals and humans. However, it is 20 to 400 times more concentrated in human semen than in any other body fluid (Saferstein, 2014). This is the scientific basis for the presumptive identification (ID) of semen. Many methods for the presumptive ID of semen have been devised.

One method is utilizing an alternate light source (ALS) because seminal fluid contains

— Ripped from the Headlines —

Using CLU Fluorescence to Detect Semen Stains

The advent of DNA technology and databases have made semen stains found at the scene of a sexual assault the most valuable piece of evidence. The problvem is that the semen stains must first be located and sampled.

The conventional method—fluorescence detection—illuminates the crime scene with light from a high-intensity lamp while an investigator views the area through optical filter glasses. This method has a number of drawbacks. Although semen fluoresces, the light it emits is weak compared with surrounding room light, thereby hindering detection. If the crime scene is outdoors, investigators must wait until nightfall to use the technique. If the crime scene is indoors, investigators must turn off all lights and black out the windows to maximize the method's effectiveness. This takes time and effort and increases the possibility that investigators will contaminate the area.

Moreover, when blacking out a room, many other substances besides semen fluoresce, such as food spills and animal urine. In order to complete their search in a reasonable amount of time, investigators often collect all questionable fluorescing materials. Detecting and documenting semen stains thus become the task of technicians back at the crime lab. Typically, this involves photography of the items of evidence examined in addition to written documentation of all examinations conducted.

The use of a *criminalistics light-imaging unit (CLU)* at the crime scene offers significant improvements over conventional approaches (**FIGURE A**). CLU is a multispectral imaging system that uses various colors of light to view the substance or structure being examined. It can locate body fluids at crime scenes under normal lighting conditions. By using a strobe lamp, signal processing, and improved optics, CLU rejects surrounding light and thereby improves both the sensitivity and specificity of the area being viewed. CLU is five times more sensitive than current fluorescing methods. CLU allows investigators to find fluorescing evidence under normal lighting conditions and to easily view and highlight images of suspected evidence at the crime

FIGURE A: Criminalistics Light Imaging Unit (CLU).

© David R. Frazier Photolibrary, Inc./Alamy Stock Photo.

scene. Furthermore, CLU greatly reduces the chances of crime scene contamination.

Source: Information retrieved from the National Institute of Justice (NIJ). (2003, July). Without a trace? Advances in detecting trace evidence. *NIJ Journal, 249*, 2–3.

© Shutterstock, Inc./rzarek.

an acriflavine, which fluoresces bluish-white when exposed to the light from an ALS, with a proper barrier filter. However, this test is not sufficient to presumptively identify semen, as there are numerous other substances that have the same fluorescence. These include fabric softeners, toothpaste, cosmetics, sweat, and urine. This is a good starting point, however. There are presumptive field test kits to screen for SAP that are more isolating in nature. This test is performed by promoting a color reaction in the sample. In forensic laboratories, alpha-naphthyl phosphate is the preferred substrate and Brentamine Fast Blue Test is the color developer. However, Brentamine Fast Blue B is potentially carcinogenic, so liberal applications made directly onto items of clothing or areas of flooring is not recommended.

Confirmatory tests for the presence of semen can only be made at the forensic laboratory. Microscopic identification of spermatozoa is one type of confirmatory test for semen. At the lab, the criminalist will stain the prepared sample using a "Christmas tree" stain test, which stains the head of spermatozoa red and the tail (flagella) green. This then provides unambiguous proof that the stain in question contains semen.

Another method to confirm the presence of semen in a sample is for the forensic lab to perform what is known as a *p30 test*. This test is performed when no sperm are found to be present in the sample (e.g., sample is from a vasectomized male). p30 is a prostate-specific antigen produced in the human male. There have been cases where p30 was able to be detected in samples stored at room temperature for up to 10 years. In fact, semen cells can be located in an oral sample for up to 24 hours and inside the vagina for up to 72 hours. This provides a finite window of collection opportunities for a crime scene investigator (Saferstein, 2014).

■ **Procedure for the Collection of Seminal Stains**

Where a sexual offense has occurred, stains may be found on clothing, bedding, rags, upholstery, or other objects. Seminal stains can be helpful in establishing whether an alleged sexual act occurred and can also provide information concerning the man who contributed the semen.

Preservation of Dried Biological Evidence

The ideal way to preserve biological evidence is to freeze it. This can become impractical with large amounts of evidence. Evidence with dried biological stains can be stored in a temperature-controlled room, which is maintained at normal room temperature or colder. Large fluctuations in temperature should be avoided. When biological evidence is returned after processing by the DNA unit of the crime laboratory, it frequently will contain a manila envelope labeled "DNA packet." This packet contains cuttings of stains and extracts of those stains. This packet needs to be frozen. If this packet is included with the evidence, it will be noted on the return release form, and the evidence will be labeled "Biological Evidence Enclosed, Please Remove and Freeze."

CONCLUSION

It was once thought that domestic violence only occurred in the lower socioeconomic classes. We now know it happens at all levels of our society. In the real world of policing, it seems that assault calls occur at the same places, and that ultimately the call involves injury or death. That perspective is consistent with our understanding of the battering cycle for abused women and children. Today's disturbance is tomorrow's assault.

Recognizing that assaults leave as much evidence on the person assaulted as on the surrounding area is the first step in determining what to process at an assault crime scene. The first priority in any assault is to provide medical assistance where necessary. Pursuing the assailant is not part of the investigation. Protecting the victim as a person and as a crime scene is the most important part of the investigation.

The key to sexual assault investigations, as in all other investigations, is training. For the investigation of sexual assaults, those agencies that have specialized sexual assault investigation teams seem to fare better in the investigation and in gaining the trust and cooperation of the victim to ensure a knowledgeable, believable, and successful trial witness. No matter the quality of investigation, without a confident, competent witness, the trial outcome will not be satisfying to the state, the victim, or the investigator. When interviewing and collecting evidence from the victim, it is imperative that both are done with sensitivity while understanding the long-range goals of the investigation. Explaining to the victim what is going to happen and why goes a long way in procuring cooperation and trust. It would seem that one of the unspoken objectives of sexual investigations is to convince victims that they were not at fault and that what happened to them in no way diminishes them as persons or as citizens.

The next chapter discusses the various forms of robbery current in our society. Street muggings and robberies at gunpoint are the tried-and-true robbery methods. Burglaries and robberies are hard to clear, there is seldom a relationship between the robber and the robbed, and the police have little evidence with which to conduct an investigation.

QUESTIONS FOR REVIEW

1. What is simple assault?
2. What is aggravated assault?
3. What is triage? Why is it an important component of an assault investigation?
4. How does self-defense come into play in assault charges?
5. What can an investigator do to defuse the self-defense shield raised by the defense in assault cases?
6. Why is a medical examination important in an assault investigation?
7. Why is a photographic record of a victim's injuries important in an assault investigation?
8. What elements must the state prove in establishing that an aggravated assault took place?
9. What are fighting words, and do they legally justify a violent response?
10. What legal justifications are there for using force? Give examples of each.
11. What is spousal immunity?
12. What makes a sexual assault a case of aggravated sexual assault?
13. Why is it incorrect to view a jury's verdict of acquittal as establishing the defendant's innocence?
14. What is typically included in an SAE kit?

REFERENCES

Federal Bureau of Investigation. (2016). *Uniform crime reports*. Washington, DC: U.S. Government Printing Office.

Gilbert, J. N. (2009). *Criminal investigation*. Upper Saddle River, NJ: Prentice Hall.

Saferstein, R. (2014). *Criminalistics: An introduction to forensic science* (11th ed.). Upper Saddle River, NJ: Pearson Prentice Hall.

Vernon's Annotated Penal Code. (1997). Chapter 9, Section 9.31(a), Justification excluding criminal responsibility.

Walker, L. E. (2009). *The battered woman syndrome*. New York, NY: Springer.

Drug Offenses

chapter 12

KEY TERMS

amphetamines

barbiturates

club drugs

cocaine

codeine

color reactions

controlled substances

Controlled Substances Act

crack cocaine

designer drugs

Dille-Koppanyi test

dissociative drug

drug

Duquenois-Levine test

forensic chemist

hallucinogens

lysergic acid diethylamide (LSD)

Marquis test

methadone

narcotics

phencyclidine (PCP)

physiologic dependence

Scott test

screening test

self-propelled semi-submersible

tetrahydrocannabinol (THC)

> "Save for the occasional use of cocaine, he had no vices, and he only turned to the drug as a protest against the monotony of existence when cases were scanty and the papers uninteresting."
>
> **Sherlock Holmes**
> *"The Adventure of the Yellow Face"*

STUDENT LEARNING OUTCOMES

Upon completion of this chapter, students will be able to:

- Explain the various scheduling levels of controlled substances
- Describe the various classes of controlled substances
- Recognize the various field tests available to presumptively determine that a substance is a drug
- Distinguish the various types of laboratory tests available to determine that a substance is a drug
- Discuss the various types of designer drugs presently in vogue

© Shutterstock, Inc. / happykanppy

Drug-Related Evidence in Criminal Investigation

Typically, when one talks of "drugs," one is, in fact, referring to "controlled substances." However, it is important to differentiate between the two, because the distinctions between the two terms relate to the investigative importance and criminal wrongdoing associated with each.

A **drug** is any chemical substance, other than food, that is intended for use in the diagnosis, treatment, cure, mitigation, or prevention of disease or symptoms. These can be dispensed and used either by prescription or over the counter (OTC). Possession of an OTC drug does not require a prescription and is not illegal (except in bulk as is associated with the manufacture of methamphetamine, which is discussed later in this chapter).

Controlled substances, on the other hand, are those substances (typically drugs) whose possession or use is regulated by the government. Title 21 of the United States Code (21 USC) defines these substances (U.S. Department of Justice [USDOJ], 1990).

The Controlled Substances Act

The **Controlled Substances Act** (CSA) and Title II and Title III of the Comprehensive Drug Abuse Prevention and Control Act of 1970 are the legal foundation upon which the U.S. government's fight against the abuse of drugs and other substances is based. This law is actually a consolidation of numerous laws regulating the manufacture and distribution of narcotics, stimulants, depressants, hallucinogens, anabolic steroids, and chemicals that are used in the illicit production of controlled substances.

Drug Regulation

The CSA places all substances that were in some manner regulated under existing federal law in one of five *schedules*. This placement is based on the substance's medical use, potential for abuse, and safety or liability for psychological and/or physical dependence. The criminal penalties for the manufacture, sale, or possession of controlled dangerous substances are related to the schedule as well. The most severe penalties are for drugs listed in Schedules I and II.

drug
Any chemical substance, other than food, that is intended for use in the diagnosis, treatment, cure, mitigation, or prevention of disease or symptoms

controlled substances
Substances (typically drugs) whose possession or use is regulated by the government

Controlled Substances Act
An act that established five schedules of classification for dangerous substances on the basis of potential for abuse, potential for physical and psychological dependence, and medical value and that set forth criminal penalties for the manufacture, sale, or possession of these controlled dangerous substances

Scheduling of Controlled Substances

According to the most recent edition of the Drug Enforcement Administration (DEA) publication, *Drugs of Abuse*, the five schedules into which substances may be placed are as follows:

Schedule I

- The drug or other substance has a high potential for abuse.
- The drug or other substance has no currently accepted medical use in treatment in the United States.
- There is a lack of accepted safety for use of the drug or other substance under medical supervision.
- Examples: Heroin, lysergic acid diethylamide (LSD), marijuana (according to federal law), and 3,4-methylene-dioxymethamphetamine (MDMA).

Schedule II

- The drug or other substance has a high potential for abuse.
- The drug or other substance has a currently accepted medical use in treatment in the United States or a currently accepted medical use with severe restrictions.
- Abuse of the drug or other substance may lead to severe psychological or physical dependence.
- Examples: Morphine, phencyclidine (PCP), cocaine, methadone, and methamphetamine.

Schedule III

- The drug or other substance has less potential for abuse than the drugs or other substances in schedules I and II.
- The drug or other substance has a currently accepted medical use in treatment in the United States.
- Abuse of the drug or other substance may lead to moderate or low physical dependence or high psychological dependence.
- Examples: Anabolic steroids, codeine and hydrocodone with aspirin or Tylenol, and some barbiturates.

Schedule IV

- The drug or other substance has a low potential for abuse relative to the drugs or other substances in Schedule III.
- The drug or other substance has a currently accepted medical use in treatment in the United States.
- Abuse of the drug or other substance may lead to limited physical dependence or psychological dependence relative to the drugs or other substances in Schedule III.
- Examples: Valium and Xanax.

Schedule V

- The drug or other substance has a low potential for abuse relative to the drugs or other substances in Schedule IV.
- The drug or other substance has a currently accepted medical use in treatment in the United States.
- Abuse of the drug or other substances may lead to limited physical dependence or psychological dependence relative to the drugs or other substances in Schedule IV.
- Examples: Cough medicines with codeine.

Proceedings to add, delete, or change the schedule of a drug or other substance may be initiated by the Drug Enforcement Administration (DEA), the Department of Health and Human Services (DHHS), or by petition from any interested person. The scheduling is conducted by cooperation between the DHHS and the DEA, with the legal and scientific/medical communities weighing in on the process.

Introduction to Drug Classes

The CSA regulates five classes of drugs: narcotics, depressants, stimulants, hallucinogens, and anabolic steroids (**TABLE 12.1**). Each class has distinguishing properties, and drugs within each class often produce similar effects. However, all controlled substances, regardless of class, share a number of common features. It is the purpose of this chapter to familiarize the reader with some of these shared features and to give definition to terms frequently associated with these drugs.

All controlled substances have abuse potential or are immediate precursors to substances with abuse potential. With the exception of anabolic steroids, controlled substances are abused to alter mood, thought, and feeling through their actions on the central nervous system (brain and spinal cord). Some of these drugs alleviate pain, anxiety, or depression. Some induce sleep and others energize. Although therapeutically useful, the "feel good" effects of these drugs contribute to their abuse. The extent to which a substance is reliably capable of producing euphoria increases the likelihood of that substance being abused.

In legal terms, the nonsanctioned use of substances controlled in Schedules I through V of the CSA is considered drug abuse. While legal pharmaceuticals placed under control in the CSA are prescribed and used by patients for medical treatment, the use of these same pharmaceuticals outside the scope of sound medical practice is also considered drug abuse.

Individuals who abuse drugs often have a preferred drug that they use but may substitute other drugs that produce similar effects (often, these are found in the same drug class) when they have difficulty obtaining their drug of choice. Drugs within a class are often compared with each other in terms of *potency* and *efficacy*. Potency refers to the amount of a drug that must be taken to produce a certain effect, whereas efficacy refers to whether a drug is capable of producing a given effect, regardless of dose. Both the strength and the ability of a substance to produce certain effects play a role in whether that drug is selected by the drug abuser.

It is important to keep in mind that the effects produced by any drug can vary significantly and are largely dependent on the dose and route of administration. Concurrent use of other drugs can enhance or block an effect, and substance abusers often take more than one drug to boost the desired effects or counter unwanted side effects. The risks associated with drug abuse cannot be accurately predicted because each user has his or her unique sensitivity to a drug. There are a number of theories that attempt to explain these differences, and it is clear that a genetic component may predispose an individual to certain toxicities or even addictive behavior. In the sections that follow, commonly encountered drugs in each class are profiled. Although marijuana is classified in the CSA as

TABLE 12.1 Types of Controlled Substances

Types of Controlled Substances	Examples	Legitimate Uses
Stimulants	Cocaine, amphetamines, methamphetamine	Legitimate uses include increased alertness, reduced fatigue, weight control, and topical analgesic (pain-killing) action
Depressants	Barbiturates, sedatives, and tranquilizers	Legitimately used to obtain release from anxiety, for the treatment of psychological problems, and as mood elevators
Narcotics	Opium, morphine, heroin, methadone, codeine, Dilaudid	Legitimately used for pain relief, antidiarrheal action, and cough suppression
Anabolic steroids	Nandrolene, oxandrolene, oxymetholone, and stanoxolol	Used legitimately for weight gain; for treatment of arthritis, anemia, and cancer treatments
Inhalants	Nitrous oxide, super glue, gasoline, chloroform, freon, and toluene	Legitimately used for a variety of purposes, but very few of them related to inhalation
Cannabis	Marijuana, hashish, cannabis plants, sinsemilla, and hashish oil (all of which are collectively referred to as marijuana)	No legitimate use according to federal law
Hallucinogens	Lysergic acid diethylamide (LSD); phencyclidine (PCP); peyote; mescaline; psilocybin; 3,4methylene-dioxyamphetamine (MDA); methylenedioxy-methamphetamine (MDMA)	No legitimate use according to federal law

a hallucinogen, a separate section is dedicated to that topic.

There are also a number of substances that are abused but not regulated under the CSA. Alcohol and tobacco, for example, are specifically exempt from control by the CSA. In addition, a whole group of substances called inhalants are commonly available and widely abused by children. Control of these substances under the CSA would not only impede legitimate commerce, but would likely have little effect on the abuse of these substances by youngsters. An energetic campaign aimed at educating both adults and youth about inhalants is more likely to prevent their abuse.

narcotic
Analgesic that relieves pain by depressing the central nervous system; the source of most narcotics is opium, and their regular use leads to physical dependence

Narcotics

The word narcotic is derived from the Greek word *narkotikon*, which means "to numb" or "benumbing." It refers to the principal effect of opium, which is to relieve pain. The term narcotic was originally used to refer to opium-derived drugs that produce analgesia or stupor, but common usage and legal definitions have expanded the use of the term to include other pain-relieving and stupor-inducing drugs. For the purposes of this text, the term **narcotic** refers to drugs that produce morphine-like effects.

Narcotic drugs are analgesics that relieve pain by depressing the central nervous system. They are used therapeutically to treat pain, suppress cough, alleviate diarrhea, and induce anesthesia. Narcotics are administered in a variety of ways. Some are taken orally, transdermally (skin patches), intranasally, or injected. As drugs of abuse, they are often smoked, sniffed, or injected. Drug effects depend heavily on the dose, route of administration, and previous exposure to the drug. Their regular use will lead to physical dependence.

Aside from their medical use, narcotics produce a general sense of well-being by reducing tension, anxiety, and aggression. These effects are helpful in a therapeutic setting but contribute to their abuse. Narcotics produce languor or even a stupor. To an addict, all else pales next to the effect of the opiates. All other tasks and responsibilities take a distant second to obtaining additional narcotics. Individuals are lethargic while under the influence of a narcotic but may become extremely agitated when the drug begins to wear off and withdrawal sets in. It is at this point that rational behavior and communication become difficult.

The source of most narcotics is opium. Opium is extracted from the unripe pod of the opium poppy (**FIGURE 12.1**). The morphine content of the extracted opium is from 4% to 21%. The opium poppy will grow in a wide range of climates, but production of opium is labor intensive. The unripe seed pod is incised lightly multiple times. The milky fluid that collects on the surface is raw opium. After several hours, a collection of semi-dried material is taken from the surface. Each pod produces only a small amount of fluid, and thousands of pods have to be incised and harvested to produce a pound of raw opium. In 1945, more than 200 tons of opium were imported into the United States for legitimate medical needs, and it was estimated that several times that amount was imported for illicit drug use. Today, in spite of the extensive use of synthetic analgesics, more than 500 tons of opium or equivalents in poppy straw concentrate are legally imported into the United States annually for legitimate medical use (United Nations, 2010). The drug is primarily produced in Asia, where labor is relatively cheap. Much of the illegal opium produced today is from an area referred to as the Golden Triangle. Some estimate that 5,000 to 20,000 pounds or more of illegal opium products, such as heroin, are brought into the United States each year.

In 1803, a German pharmacist isolated morphine from opium. Opium contains

FIGURE 12.1: Poppy plant.
© Juri/Shutterstock, Inc.

approximately 10% morphine. The compound was named after Morpheus, the Greek god of dreams, because of its sleep-producing effect. Eventually, **codeine**, occurring in opium at levels of 0.5%, was isolated. Morphine and codeine are the principal opium-derived alkaloids used today. Codeine is used as an analgesic and cough suppressant, morphine is used in several forms as an analgesic, and opium is used in preparations to treat diarrhea.

All true narcotics have shown themselves to be addictive when abused, even though several were originally introduced with the suggestion that they were nonaddictive. Addiction is a combination of psychological and physical dependence on a drug. As tolerance to the drug develops, the user requires more than the usual amount to experience the same euphoric effect. When tolerance and habitual use develop, a **physiologic dependence** also occurs, so withdrawal of the drug leads to clinical signs, such as abdominal pains, nausea, and vomiting. Agitation and a feeling of distress generally resolve in several days. These physical signs can be prevented by renewing the drug levels or by substituting drugs, such as methadone. Addiction is evident when the drug user has an overpowering desire or compulsion to obtain and take the drug and when there are physiologic effects upon withdrawal. It should be noted that some narcotic users are not addicts.

codeine
Narcotic that is used as an analgesic and a cough suppressant

physiologic dependence
Dependence on the use of a drug such that withdrawal of the drug results in clinical signs such as abdominal pains, nausea, and vomiting

These users, known as chippers (because they "chip" away at a habit), moderate their dosage in quantity and frequency. Opium is most typically taken orally (in a tincture, such as laudanum) or smoked. Smoking vaporizes the opium, allowing morphine and other alkaloids to be absorbed from the smoke. Although the amount used initially is small, eventually, large amounts are required to achieve an effect.

Heroin

Much like opium, morphine and heroin enjoyed wide over-the-counter acceptance. By 1900, some estimated that there were 1 million addicts in the United States. Heroin, introduced in 1898, was immediately proclaimed the most effective analgesic known. Thought to be nonaddictive, heroin was recommended specifically as treatment for addiction to other opium derivatives. It was sold as an elixir and in patent medicines until the early 1900s, when the danger was recognized. In 1914, the Harrison Narcotic Act made heroin and heroin-based medicines illegal (Baden, 1980).

The concentration and nature of heroin vary widely from region to region, as does the form (**FIGURE 12.2**).

Heroin usually is sold as a fine, white powder in a glassine envelope or paper bundle, or as a tar wrapped in foil, in a balloon or condom,

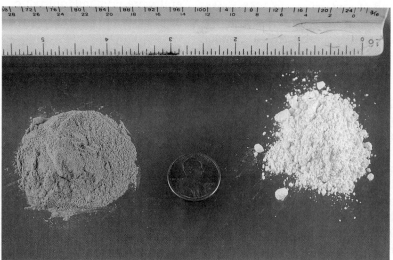

FIGURE 12.2: Varieties of heroin.

Courtesy of the DEA.

FIGURE 12.3: Hypodermic needles for disposal.
© Rusian Sitarchuk/Shutterstock, Inc.

FIGURE 12.4: Heroin volcanoes.
© Michael Newman/PhotoEdit, Inc.

or in a small plastic bundle. To use, the contents of the container are emptied into a cooker. The cooker can be a spoon or wire-held bottle cap; anything that will hold about 5 mL of fluid and allow heating over a flame will do. When water is added, most of the material is not dissolved immediately. A flame, usually from a match or cigarette lighter, is used to warm the solution to increase solubility. The liquid is aspirated into an insulin syringe (**FIGURE 12.3**), usually through a small piece of absorbent cotton, to remove insoluble material. The needle is inserted under the skin (skin popping) or into a vein, and a small amount of solution is injected as a test dose. The drug abuser subjectively interprets how powerful the drug is and how much will be injected. This process of injecting a small amount and withdrawing some blood to keep the lumen open is called registering, fooling, and booting.

Individuals who have difficulty finding a vein can employ another method of using heroin. Often, the needle marks fester. Heroin can be rubbed onto the festering blisters, allowing the heroin to be introduced into the system. The skin erupts in lesions called volcanoes (**FIGURE 12.4**).

Heroin is made by allowing morphine to react with anhydride or acetyl chloride. The solution is cooled and neutralized with sodium carbonate. The heroin freebase is then purified by adding concentrated hydrochloric acid (Saferstein, 2014). The high associated with the use of heroin is short-lived, lasting 3 to 4 hours. The impact of the body's withdrawal from the effects of the drug—known as "keeping the sickness off"—accounts for the user's pursuit of another fix as much as the high.

Four foreign source areas produce the heroin available in the United States: South America (Colombia), Mexico, Southeast Asia (principally Burma), and Southwest Asia (principally Afghanistan). However, South America and Mexico supply most of the illicit heroin marketed in the United States.

Methadone

Some narcotics are not derived from opium. These drugs are nonetheless referred to as opiates because of the narcotic effect of the drugs. **Methadone** is a synthetic opiate used in maintenance programs for heroin addicts. When taking 80 to 120 milligrams a day of methadone, heroin addicts will not experience the high associated with heroin or morphine use. The intent is for people attempting to kick a heroin habit to avoid the effects of withdrawal and the desire to get high.

Codeine

Codeine is also present in opium but is usually prepared synthetically from morphine. It is used as a cough suppressant and is only one-sixth as strong as morphine. Codeine is not a drug of choice for heroin users.

Hallucinogens

Hallucinogens are among the oldest known group of drugs used for their ability to alter human perception and mood. For centuries, many of the naturally occurring hallucinogens found in plants and fungi have been used for a variety of shamanistic practices. In more recent years, a number of synthetic hallucinogens have been produced, some of which are much more potent than their naturally occurring counterparts.

Hallucinogens are drugs that cause a distortion in thought processes and perceptions as

methadone
A synthetic opiate used to prevent the physical symptoms of narcotic withdrawal that would otherwise be felt by someone addicted to narcotics

hallucinogens
Drugs that cause a distortion in thought processes and perceptions as well as changes in moods

well as changes in moods. Prolonged use can bring about permanent personality changes and loss of contact with reality. Persons under the influence of strong hallucinogens might not respond to verbal communication and could hallucinate to the extent that they are completely removed from reality. Users can be dangerous when confronted because of the distortion in their perceptions and vision. Contact with individuals under the influence must be cautious and humane. Hospitalization is preferable to incarceration because of the continuing danger these people may pose to themselves or others.

The abuse of hallucinogens in the United States received much public attention in the 1960s and 1970s. A subsequent decline in their use in the 1980s may be attributed to real or perceived hazards associated with taking these drugs. However, a resurgence of the use of hallucinogens is cause for concern. Fortunately, the 2008 National Survey on Drug Use and Health reported that the prevalence of past-month hallucinogen use has remained relatively constant from 0.5% in 2002 to 0.4% in 2003, 2004, 2005, 2006, 2007, and 2008 (Substance Abuse and Mental Health Services Administration [SAMHSA], 2009). Hallucinogenic mushrooms, LSD, and MDMA are popular among junior and senior high school students who use hallucinogens.

Lysergic Acid Diethylamide

Lysergic acid diethylamide (LSD)—commonly called "acid"—is synthesized from a type of fungus that attacks certain grasses and grains. Albert Hoffman, a Swiss scientist, first described the hallucinogenic effects of LSD after accidentally ingesting it in 1943. LSD is manufactured in a variety of forms, each having its advocates. The chemical itself is colorless and tasteless and can be distributed through a variety of shapes and forms, such as the following:

- *Windowpane acid:* 1-millimeter by 2-millimeter rectangles of LSD-impregnated gelatin
- *Blotter acid:* An aqueous solution of LSD poured evenly over absorbent perforated paper, usually about 1 centimeter squared (**FIGURE 12.5**)
- *California sunshine:* Yellow tablets
- *Stamp acid:* Postage stamps with an aqueous solution of LSD dropped onto the adhesive surface
- *Sugar cubes* (**FIGURE 12.6**)

FIGURE 12.5: LSD paper designs.
© Darrin Jenkins/Alamy Stock Photo.

FIGURE 12.6: Sugar cube acid.
© Anette Linnea Rasmussen/Shutterstock, Inc.

The drug is very potent; as little as 25 micrograms is enough to start visual hallucinations that can last up to 12 hours. The acid trip is one of plateaus and peaks (periods of maximum hallucinations). The hallucinations begin 20 to 60 minutes after ingestion. More rapid absorption results when the material is dropped into the eye or injected. Subsequent dosages must be increased to obtain the same effects when LSD is used over an extended period. The drug might produce visual and auditory hallucinations as well as mood swings and feelings of anxiety, tension, and paranoia.

One common LSD-related legal problem is that the small amount of LSD in submitted samples makes analysis difficult. The most common spot test for LSD is Erlich's test, in which the reagent turns purple in the presence of LSD. This spot test can be used to visualize LSD after thin-layer chromatography, thereby allowing two tests to be conducted on the same sample. In some states, LSD is

— Ripped from the Headlines —

Bath Salts

Beginning in 2010, hallucinogens that were legally sold as "bath salts" for homeopathic remedies began taking the U.S. populace by storm and had law and drug enforcement officials scrambling for a response. The substances were available at area convenience stores and via the Internet, selling for approximately $20, and packaged as bath salts or plant food, but almost always marked "not for human consumption." "It's a derivative that's very similar to amphetamines, and its side effects are largely the same side effects we see with amphetamines in large dose," said Jeffrey Baldwin, Professor and Vice Chair of Pharmacy Practice and Pediatrics at the University of Nebraska Medical Center in Omaha. The drugs are typically snorted, smoked, or injected; however, some people are even mixing them in beverages. "If you take the very worst of some of the other drugs—LSD and MDMA with their hallucinogenic-delusional–type properties; PCP with extreme agitation, superhuman strength and combativeness; as well as the stimulant properties of cocaine and meth—if you take all the worst of those and put them together, this is what you get. It's ugly," added Mark Ryan, director of the Louisiana Poison Control Center.

"On Friday, October 21, 2011, DEA published a final order in the Federal Register exercising its emergency scheduling authority to control three synthetic stimulants that are used to make bath salts, including: Mephedrone, 3,4 Methylenedioxypyrovalerone (MDPV), and Methylone. Except as authorized by law, this action makes possessing and selling these chemicals, or the products that contain them, illegal in the United States. This emergency action was necessary to prevent an imminent threat to public safety. As a result of this order, these synthetic stimulants are designated as Schedule I substances under the Controlled Substances Act."

Information from Gardner, A. (2011). *Hallucinogens legally sold as "bath salts" a new threat.* Retrieved August 25, 2012, from http://www.womenshealth.gov/news/headlines/649596.cfm

© Shutterstock, Inc./rzarek.

---

proscribed, but isomers of LSD, such as lysergic acid methylpropylamine (LAMPA), are not. However, this issue is rendered moot in those jurisdictions that include LSD isomers in the proscriptive definition.

In instances of suspected LSD presence, first pass an ultraviolet lamp across the surface of the suspected material. Any areas that fluoresce purple under ultraviolet have LSD present. Each purple dot is a dose of LSD. Because of the possibility of absorbing LSD through the skin, only nitrile rubber gloves should be used. Nitrile gloves do not breathe and will not transmit LSD from the medium touched onto the investigator. Testing of suspected LSD is best left for the laboratory because of the ease of absorption.

Phencyclidine

Phencyclidine, once marketed by Parke-Davis as a large-animal tranquilizer, is a synthetic substance referred to on the street as PCP. PCP has appeared on the street in pill form (peace pills) and powder form (angel dust, tic, and dummy dust). Regardless of the delivery system, PCP is now generically referred to as angel dust. The preferred method of use is inhalation or ingestion. The drug can be placed in a solution (sherm) into which marijuana cigarettes can be dipped and sold individually. The dust can be sprinkled onto marijuana, which is then sold as an especially potent strain of marijuana.

PCP was developed as an intravenous surgical anesthetic. The drug is classified as a dissociative anesthetic and not as a hallucinogenic. Its effects can produce a trance-like and detached experience. That detachment is the reason why PCP is referred to as a **dissociative drug**. PCP was never approved for human use because of delirium, agitation, and detachment experienced by patients emerging from anesthesia. When snorted or smoked, PCP rapidly passes to the part of the brain responsible for the perception of pain, learning, memory, and emotion. Physical effects include shallow, rapid breathing; increased blood pressure and heart rate; and elevated temperature. Large doses may cause dangerous changes in blood pressure, heart rate, and respiration, and decreased awareness of pain. Muscles may contract, causing uncontrolled jerking or movement. The muscle contractions can be so strong that fractures,

dissociative drug
Those drugs that cause a distorted perception of space and time

phencyclidine (PCP)
A synthetic substance that has appeared on the street in pill form (peace pills) and powder form (angel dust, tic, and dummy dust); now generically referred to as angel dust, and the preferred method of use is inhalation or ingestion

convulsions, coma, and death may result. Repeated use of PCP can result in addiction, with withdrawal symptoms characteristic of heroin withdrawal.

A chemist may be called on to analyze material suspected of being PCP or to evaluate the manufacturing capabilities of a clandestine laboratory. A thorough knowledge of the chemistry used to manufacture PCP and any analogs of PCP will be necessary for the chemist to testify that PCP was being manufactured or was to be manufactured. The chemist will also need the ability to assess the production output of a clandestine laboratory based on the results of a police investigation and search.

PCP is a dissociative drug that should be treated as carefully as LSD. Absorption through standard rubber gloves is possible, so the default glove, again, is nitrile. PCP has a distinctive odor—similar to cat urine—in powder or liquid form, whether smoked in a marijuana cigarette or used as a powder. This is another of those substances that should be transported to the crime lab as quickly as possible to avoid an accidental dosage. A field test created just for PCP should render a solid blue color.

Marijuana

Marijuana is often classified as a hallucinogen. Although marijuana is sold as a green, leafy material and it is the leaves that are smoked by users, scientists and law enforcement have a broader definition of what constitutes marijuana.

The term marijuana encompasses all parts of the Cannabis sativa L. plant whether growing or not including seeds, resin extracted from any part of the plant, and any compound, manufacture, salt, derivative, mixture, or preparation of the plant, seeds, or resins. It doesn't include the mature stalk of the plant, fiber, compound, manufacture, salt derivative, mixture or preparation produced from the stalk, oil or cake made from the seeds, or sterilized seeds.

The marijuana preparation consists of crushed leaves mixed in varying proportions with the flowers (buds), stems, and seeds (**FIGURE 12.7**). Often, the quality of the marijuana is determined by the number of buds included in the bag (the more buds, the more potent the marijuana). Marijuana is usually smoked in a cigarette, or joint, or in a pipe or bong.

FIGURE 12.7: Marijuana.

Usual purchase amounts of marijuana include the following:

- A joint or blunt (one hand-rolled cigarette or cigar)
- A matchbox (a small paper matchbox, about four joints' worth)
- A lid (approximately one ounce contained in a plastic bag)
- A pound (sold in paper and plastic bags)
- A key (a kilogram, or roughly 2.2 pounds)

The marijuana plant secretes a sticky resin that is known as hashish (or hash). Hashish is sold by the gram or in compressed, 1-ounce bars about the size of a chocolate bar. The resinous material also can be extracted from the plant by soaking it in a solvent. Hashish oil is a resinous, viscous material, dark green to brown in color that has the consistency of tar. Hashish is smoked in a hash pipe (a metal or wooden device with a small bowl about the size of a dime) or a ceramic chillum (a straight-stemmed pipe without a filter but with a rock placed loosely over the hole in the bowl to prevent the hash from being sucked into the stem). Hash oil is dropped onto a marijuana cigarette to increase its potency, or it may be dropped onto a tobacco cigarette. Increases in the distribution of hashish appear to coincide with lapses in the leaf marijuana market. Marijuana users prefer leaves to the resinous hashish.

Marijuana was first introduced in the United States around 1920, most probably smuggled by Mexican laborers across the border into Texas (United Nations, 2010). By 1937, 46 states and the federal government had laws prohibiting the use or possession of marijuana. Marijuana is a weed (and is sometimes referred to as "weed") that grows under most climatic conditions but flourishes in hot, tropical areas. The size of the plant and the potency of the marijuana depend on the amount of sunlight and rain it receives. The plant grows to a height of 15 feet and is characterized by an odd number of leaflets on each leaf (**FIGURE 12.8**). Each leaf contains five to nine leaflets, all having characteristic serrated edges.

In 1964, scientists isolated the psychoactive ingredient in marijuana: **tetrahydrocannabinol (THC)**. The discovery of THC allowed scientists to determine the potency of marijuana preparations and the effect those preparations have on individual users. The THC content in cannabis varies in different parts of the plant, with the resin and buds having the greatest potency. Marijuana, as generally used, and hashish have a THC content of 3%

FIGURE 12.8: Marijuana leaf.

© underworld/Shutterstock, Inc.

tetrahydrocannabinol (THC)

The psychoactive ingredient in marijuana

to 4%. The THC-rich resin extracted from the marijuana plant in the form of hash oil may have a THC content of 20% to 65% (Thornton & Nakamura, 1972).

— Ripped from the Headlines —

Marijuana Legalization Issues

Recent policy changes to cannabis regulation in the United States of Oregon, Washington, and Colorado now make the authorized production, distribution and consumption of marijuana legal, under some conditions, such as purchasing age.

The International Narcotics Control Board has expressed concern that "a number of States are considering legislative proposals intended to regulate the use of cannabis for purposes other than medical and scientific ones" and it urged "all Governments and the international community to carefully consider the negative impact of such developments." In the Board's opinion, "the likely increase in the abuse of cannabis will lead to an increase in related public health costs." Although in those three jurisdictions, the purchase, possession, and consumption of cannabis are now legal, the details, design, and implementation of the new laws vary significantly. For example, in the State of Colorado, purchases of up to 1 oz (28 g) are

allowed per outlet, with no central registry of cumulative purchases per buyer nor any limit on the amount that can be purchased each month.

Because of these and other notable differences in each law, there is unlikely to be one uniform impact of these policy changes, but rather, measurable distinct changes reflecting the contexts of each jurisdiction. The impact of the new legislation could differ substantially from current cases of depenalization, decriminalization of "medical" cannabis laws by allowing the establishment of a licit supply chain, including large-scale licensing for production, personal cultivation and retail commercialization of the market. While it is not yet clear how the market will change, the commercialization of cannabis may also significantly affect drug-use behaviors. Commercialization implies motivated selling, which can lead to directed advertisements that promote and encourage consumption. For instance, in the case of tobacco companies, advertising was directed to attract new users, which resulted in effective marketing to youth. Because laws of this kind have

never before been enacted or implemented in a national or state jurisdiction, no previous case studies are available to predict what changes should be expected. Thus, monitoring and evaluation will provide critical data for policymakers. For this reason, it is important that the impacts of this legislation are measured against a number of factors, ranging from the impact on health and criminal justice (effects on the individual as well as institutions and society) to the balance of public revenues against costs and to other social impacts.

At this time, many of the states surrounding Oregon, Colorado, and Washington have not adopted similar regulatory or legislative measures. In consideration of this, additional outcomes that need to be monitored include drug tourism, cross-border leakage and access and availability to youth in neighboring jurisdictions.

Source Information from United Nations. (2014). Cannabis: overview. *World Drug Report 2014*, pp. 36–46. United Nations Office on Drugs and Crime. Retrieved August 3, 2015, from http://www.unodc.org/documents/wdr2014/Cannabis_2014_web.pdf

© Shutterstock, Inc./rzarek.

— Ripped from the Headlines —

DEA Moves Quickly to Control Synthetic Pot

In 2010, a blend of household herbs, laced with synthetic marijuana, became wildly popular. The herbal blend, known as "K2" or "Spice," was openly sold in head shops as well as over the Internet. As with most recreational drugs, little is known about the long-term impacts of the substances, but people who smoked it were often seen at hospitals with symptoms ranging from racing heart rates to paranoia to sometimes near-death experiences. According to a press release from the DEA, in March of 2011, "the United States Drug Enforcement Administration (DEA) exercised its emergency scheduling authority to control five chemicals (JWH-018, JWH-073, JWH-200, CP-47,497, and cannabicyclohexanol) used to make so-called 'fake pot' products. Except as authorized by law, this action makes possessing and selling these chemicals or the products that contain them illegal in the United States. This emergency action was necessary to prevent an imminent threat to public health and safety."

They are designated as Schedule I substances, the most restrictive category under the Controlled Substances Act. Schedule I substances are reserved for those substances with a high potential for abuse, no accepted medical use for treatment in the United States, and a lack of accepted safety for use of the drug under medical supervision.

"Young people are being harmed when they smoke these dangerous 'fake pot' products and wrongly equate the products' 'legal' retail availability with being 'safe,'" said DEA Administrator Michele M. Leonhart. "Parents and community leaders look to us to help them protect their kids, and we have not let them down. Today's action, while temporary, will reduce the number of young people being seen in hospital emergency rooms after ingesting these synthetic chemicals to get high."

Information from U.S. Drug Enforcement Administration (DEA). (March, 2011). Retrieved July 7, 2012, from http://www.justice.gov/dea/pubs/pressrel/pr030111.html

© Shutterstock, Inc./rzarek.

Depressants

Historically, people of almost every culture have used chemical agents to induce sleep, relieve stress, and allay anxiety. Although alcohol is one of the oldest and most universal agents used for these purposes, hundreds of substances have been developed that produce central nervous system depression. These drugs are called *depressants* and have also been referred to as downers, sedatives, hypnotics, minor tranquilizers, and anti-anxiety medications. Unlike most other classes of drugs of abuse, depressants are rarely produced in clandestine laboratories. Generally, legitimate pharmaceutical products are diverted to the illicit market. A notable exception to this is a gamma hydroxybutyric acid (GHB).

Barbiturates are one sub-classification of depressants. Because of the relaxing effects of barbiturates, they are generically referred to on the streets as downers. They act on the central nervous system and create a feeling of well-being and drowsiness. All barbiturates are derived from barbituric acid, first synthesized by a German chemist, Adolf Von Bauer. Of the 25 barbiturate derivatives used in medical practice, only five are common: amobarbital, secobarbital, phenobarbital, pentobarbital, and butabarbital (Saferstein, 2014). The withdrawal from physical dependence on barbiturates is more severe than that for any other drug. Because of the large number of barbiturate derivatives manufactured, it is difficult to determine which specific derivative is in question.

Barbiturates are available through prescription and are made by numerous manufacturers. The marking on a barbiturate reflects the name of the manufacturer, such as Lilly or Roche, or brand names such as Seconal, or a number/letter combination. Efforts to identify a particular tablet or capsule can include contacting the crime laboratory, consulting a pharmacist, or using the *Physician's Desk Reference*. The *Physician's Desk Reference* is a compendium of all manufactured drugs; it provides all or some of the following information pertaining to a particular manufactured drug:

- Controlled Substance Act schedule
- A photograph of the imprints on either side of the substance
- The name under which the substance is sold
- A list of all active ingredients in a substance

barbiturates
Depressants derived from barbituric acid that act on the central nervous system and create a feeling of well-being and drowsiness; they are generally taken orally in 10- to 70-milligram doses and are absorbed through the small intestines

INVESTIGATOR'S NOTEBOOK

Treatment of a Clandestine Drug Lab

Good practice dictates that the lab remain undisturbed until a chemist or the person expected to testify about the lab and its production has had an opportunity to examine the premises and the equipment found on the site. It may be necessary for the prosecution to change the charges from "possession" or "manufacture" to "attempted manufacture" or "conspiracy to manufacture" based on the chemist's analysis of the lab's readiness.

- Photographs of the drug in the forms in which it is sold
- The manufacturer
- The marketer

Gamma Hydroxybutyric Acid (GHB)

In recent years, gamma hydroxybutyric acid (GHB) has emerged as a significant drug of abuse throughout the United States. Abusers of this drug fall into three major groups: (1) users who take GHB for its intoxicant or euphoriant effects; (2) bodybuilders who abuse GHB for its alleged utility as an anabolic agent or as a sleep aid; and (3) individuals who use GHB as a weapon for sexual assault. These categories are not mutually exclusive, and an abuser may use the drug illicitly to produce several effects. GHB is frequently taken with alcohol or other drugs that heighten its effects and is often found at bars, nightclubs, rave parties, and gyms. Teenagers and young adults who frequent these establishments are the primary users. Like flunitrazepam (Rohypnol), GHB is often referred to as a "date-rape" drug.

GHB involvement in rape cases is likely to be unreported or unsubstantiated because GHB is quickly eliminated from the body, making detection in body fluids unlikely. Its fast onset of depressant effects may leave the victim with little memory of the details of the attack.

GHB produces a wide range of central nervous system effects, including dose-dependent drowsiness, dizziness, nausea, amnesia, visual hallucinations, hypotension, bradycardia, severe respiratory depression, and coma. The use of alcohol in combination with GHB greatly enhances its depressant effects. Overdose frequently requires emergency room care, and many GHB-related fatalities have been reported.

The abuse of GHB began to seriously escalate in the mid-1990s. For example, in 1994, there were 55 emergency room episodes involving GHB reported in the Drug Abuse Warning Network (DAWN) system. By 2006, there were 3,330 emergency room episodes. DAWN data also indicated that most users were male, younger than 25 years of age, and taking the drug orally for recreational use. GHB was placed in Schedule I of the CSA in March 2000 (SAMHSA, 2006).

INVESTIGATOR'S NOTEBOOK

GHB Usage as a Predatory Drug

GHB is a clear, odorless liquid, slightly thicker than water. Its only detection is that it has a salty taste, making it virtually undetectable by victims. Its effects are not felt for 2 to 4 hours, and users commonly do not remember what happened during that time. GHB can easily be slipped into any drink (most commonly alcoholic beverages). GHB causes the body's functions to slow dramatically. Breathing can decrease to six times per minute. Heart rate can slow to 25 beats per minute. Victims commonly pass out and are unaware of what has happened to them while they were unconscious.

Stimulants

As with all of the classifications of controlled substances, there are many subtypes. Each has its own history and associated dangers. There are also some that are medically beneficial, whereas others are simply street drugs with no medicinal purpose or benefit.

Amphetamines

amphetamines
Synthetic central nervous system stimulants

Amphetamines are synthetic central nervous system stimulants. Abusers collectively refer to them as uppers or speed and may inject the drug or take it orally. Injecting the drug provides for an immediate physiologic response (rush), followed by an intense feeling of pleasure. Individuals who prefer amphetamines to other drugs are called "speed freaks" and often binge, as do cocaine users. During a binge, a user may inject 500 to 1,000 milligrams of amphetamines every 2 to 3 hours. The binge usually continues until all of the drug has been injected. Users report an increase in perception, information processing, and body function. Binging may produce hallucinations and paranoia. As the drug begins to wear off, users slip into a depression and prolonged periods of sleep.

The drug is primarily known for its stimulating properties, for it imparts a prolonged feeling of strength and well-being. Because it increases physiologic activity, tiredness is replaced by a feeling of energy. Amphetamines were used in the 1940s to increase productivity and allow prolonged activities that normally would be very tiring or tedious. Bomber pilots during World War II, for example, were given amphetamines to help them stay alert on long flights. Methamphetamine has garnered much attention in the media. It is known on the street as meth, crystal, crank, and speed; most of the chemical components are regulated, and many chemical syntheses leading to the same compounds are possible (Derlet & Heischober, 1990).

Methamphetamine may be a pure white crystal powder, but differences in recipes and cooking techniques can cause differences in color; color is not equated with purity. Meth can turn out in powder or chunks, depending on the humidity during cooking and drying (**FIGURE 12.9**). The high moisture content of

(A)

(B)

(C)

(D)

FIGURE 12.9: Varieties of methamphetamines.

(A and D) Courtesy of DEA. (B and C) Courtesy of Orange County Police Department, Florida.

meth can cause problems in weighing. The substance can lose up to 50% of its weight in evaporation, which must be taken into account at trial.

Today, there are two primary methods of manufacture. One method (Red P) requires heat and is used to make large batches of meth; the other method utilizes anhydrous ammonia. Each method starts with ephedrine or pseudoephedrine. Both of these chemicals are used in diet pills and over-the-counter cold remedies. In order to separate the ephedrine from the medication, it must first be extracted. The tablets are crushed (e.g., in blenders) and placed on a coffee filter, and denatured alcohol is poured over the powder. The alcohol is allowed to evaporate, and what remains is ephedrine. The next step in the Red P recipe calls for red phosphorus (from which the process receives its name), which is used in match striker plates. By cutting the striker plates from the matches and soaking them in denatured alcohol, the red phosphorus can be extracted: Once the alcohol has evaporated, the remaining residue dries into red flakes of phosphorus. Solvents, such as iodine and acetone, are necessary to complete the process (**FIGURE 12.10**).

FIGURE 12.10: (A-D) Meth production; (E) phosphorus in solution.

© Shvaygert Ekaterina/Shutterstock, Inc.

There is yet another version of methamphetamine, which has been described as being more potent than the powder form. When volatile methamphetamine oil is allowed to crystallize slowly in a refrigerator, large crystals form. White or slightly yellow in color, they are usually the size of rock salt, about one-quarter to one-half inch across (**FIGURE 12.11**). "Ice," which is composed of crystal-like quantities of methamphetamine, is said to be more pure and thus more potent; however, it is composed of nearly the same ingredients and contains the same potency. There is simply an additional step taken to crystalize the powdered form. How potent or pure a batch of methamphetamine is depends on the experience of the cook and the quality of the ingredients; it does not matter whether it is produced in powder or crystal form.

The commonly used amphetamines can be smoked. The powder or crystals may be mixed with tobacco or marijuana, but more often, they are heated to vaporize on the screen of a pipe so that the fumes can be inhaled. The pipe is usually a glass bulb with a hole in the top and a tube on one side, which acts as the mouthpiece. The drug is placed in the pipe, and the pipe is heated until white vapor appears as the drug melts. The finger sealing the hole on the top of the pipe is removed and the user inhales from the tube as long as possible, holding the breath to allow absorption through the lungs. After inhalation, the pipe is immediately cooled with a wet cloth to condense the vaporized drug. A single crystal can be used several times before it is consumed completely, and considering the length of the high, it would seem to be more economical than cocaine. A used pipe will have carbon on the outside bottom and a coating of white to gray crystals on the inside walls.

cocaine
Stimulant drug derived from the coca plant

A significant problem associated with amphetamines is that they create, in users, a propensity toward paranoia and violent behavior, which may increase the likelihood that the user is carrying weapons. The major problems in analyzing amphetamines are in distinguishing between the various isomers of an amphetamine and in differentiating amphetamine from methamphetamine. Furthermore, a forensic chemist not only must be able to analyze the substances submitted but also may be called upon to determine the exact status of a clandestine laboratory at the time that it is seized. Investigators and police on the scene at the time of arrest must reduce the impact of their presence to a quantifiable minimum. Any changes in the scene resulting from the arrest will be noted by the defense. Photographs should be taken of the entire operation before, during, and after the processing of the crime scene. Gross changes in the features of these photos will require explanation by the investigators in charge and may provide means by which the defense may challenge statements regarding the production capabilities of the laboratory, possibly resulting in a reduced or dismissed charge.

Cocaine

■ History of Use

The word *coca* comes from the Aymara word *khoka*, meaning "the tree" (Karch, 2009). Measurable quantities of **cocaine** and nicotine have been detected in 3,000-year-old Egyptian mummies (Balbanova, Parsche, & Pirsig, 1992). Boerhave favorably mentioned coca in his textbook on medicinal plants, published in 1708 (Mortimer, 1901).

Two events in 1884 significantly changed the pattern of cocaine use in the United States and Europe. The first was the publication of Freud's paper on cocaine (Stephens, 1993). The second was Koller's discovery that cocaine was a local anesthetic (Noyes, 1884). The availability of an effective local anesthetic had tremendous impact. Cocaine was propelled into the limelight, and physicians around the world were soon experimenting with the use of cocaine in a wide range of conditions (Karch, 2009). The first reports of cocaine toxicity appeared less than 1 year after Koller's and Freud's papers were published. An article in the *British Medical Journal* described the toxic reactions associated with cocaine use in ophthalmologic surgery ("Toxic Action of Cocaine," 1885). None of the negative reports appeared to have much impact. Patent medicine manufacturers continued to cash in on the popularity of coca by replacing

FIGURE 12.11: Meth ice.

Courtesy of DEA.

low-concentration cocaine extracts with high concentrations of refined cocaine hydrochloride. Thousands of cocaine-containing patent medicines flooded the market (Karch, 2009).

Until the early 1900s, cocaine had been taken mainly by mouth or by injection. The fact that the first cases of septal perforation and collapse were not reported until 1904 suggests that inhalation (snorting) had only become popular a year or so earlier (Maier, 1926). Between 1928 and 1973, there was only one reported fatality, and it involved a surgical misadventure. Suarez, Arango, and Lester (1977) first described the "body packer" syndrome, in which death results from the rupture of cocaine-filled condoms in a smuggler's intestines. Significant toxicity from the use of the coca leaf and coca leaf extract was not a problem in the United States until purified cocaine became available (U.S. DEA, 2011). The small amounts of cocaine in patent medicines were apparently harmless, but the huge amounts of purified cocaine that could be ingested represented a quantum leap in dosage. With the appearance of crack cocaine in 1986, another order of magnitude increase in dosage occurred. Cocaine-related deaths and injuries are a product of more people using more of the drug in a more effective manner (Karch, 2009).

■ Production

The coca leaf has grown in the Andean subregion for thousands of years. Early explorers found it all along the eastern curve of the Andes, from the Straits of Magellan to the borders of the Caribbean. Coca grows best on the moist, warm slopes of mountains ranging from 1,500 to 5,000 feet. Coca shrubs grow to heights of 6 to 8 feet. Major growing areas in Bolivia share many characteristics. The Yungas Mountains, which are close to La Paz, have an average annual rainfall of 45 inches; and the Chapare River area, which is close to Cochabamba, has an annual rainfall of 102 inches. The coca plantations in the Yungas can be harvested three times a year. Each harvest yields from 1 to 1.5 tons of leaf per hectare (890 to 1,336 pounds per acre) per year. The Chapare plantations are harvested four times a year, with a yield of 2 to 3 tons per hectare (1,789 to 2,672 pounds per acre) per year.

Cocaine extraction is a two- or three-step process, carried out in a series of laboratories. The first steps occur immediately after harvesting, when leaves are placed in a shallow pit lined with heavy plastic and then soaked in a solution of water and lime for 3 or 4 days. Gasoline or kerosene is then added to the mixture to extract the nitrogenous alkaloids. The coca leaf

is discarded, and sulfuric acid is added to the extract. The gasoline or kerosene is removed, and the remaining solution is made alkaline by the addition of lime, causing the more basic alkaloids to precipitate out. This crude form of cocaine, called coca paste or pasta, is allowed to dry in the sun (Brewer & Allen, 1991).

The site where the initial steps occur is referred to as a pasta lab. Laborers, called pisacocas, keep the alkali-coca leaf mulch mixed by stirring it with their hands and feet. The fluid is very corrosive and causes ulcers. The pisacocas tolerate the ulcers only because they are given a constant supply of coca paste to smoke (Weatherford, 1988).

Once the pasta is prepared, the clandestine manufacturer has two options. The pasta may be further purified at a base lab, or the producer may go directly to a crystal lab. At base labs, pasta is dissolved in diluted sulfuric acid. Potassium permanganate is added until the solution turns pink, thereby destroying the cinnamoylcocaine isomers present as impurities in the pasta. The reddish-pink solution is allowed to stand; then it is filtered, and the filtrate is made basic with ammonia. The cocaine base precipitates out. The precipitate is filtered, washed with water, and then dried. Finally, it is dissolved in diethyl ether or acetone. After filtering, concentrated hydrochloric acid and acetone are added, causing purified cocaine hydrochloride to precipitate out. This final step may be done on site, or the semipurified cocaine may be transported to a crystal lab, usually located in larger cities.

As much as 50 kilograms may be processed at one time in a crystal lab. The semipurified cocaine is dissolved in a solvent, often ether. Hydrochloric acid is added, along with acetone, and white crystals precipitate out (**FIGURE 12.12**). The crystals are collected by filtration. Traces of the solvent remain, and their presence can sometimes be used to identify the origin of cocaine samples. In producing countries, there is a significant market for the semipurified paste itself. Paste is smoked rolled up in pieces of newspaper or packed into cigarettes. The purity of confiscated cocaine is considered to be a good general indicator of availability (Karch, 2009). It is apparent that the market is volatile with no restraints other than what the market will bear.

■ Crack Cocaine

In the early 1970s, the organized production of cocaine lowered its street cost and increased its availability just as a wave of increased drug acceptance spread across the United States. This combination led to a resurgence of cocaine

FIGURE 12.12: Powdered cocaine.

© Photopixel/Shutterstock, Inc.

crack cocaine
Form of cocaine that melts at 98°C and vaporizes; the vapor is absorbed by all mucous membranes and the lungs, rapidly producing a euphoric sensation that may last as long as 30 minutes

use (Musto, 1991). As an acid or hydrochloride salt, the drug could be snorted or injected but not smoked. From the user's point of view, it was still expensive—more expensive than heroin—and the pleasurable effects did not last as long.

Crack cocaine, on the other hand, can be smoked (**FIGURE 12.13**). Rather than chemically decomposing, crack cocaine melts at 98°C and vaporizes. The vapor is absorbed by all mucous membranes and the lungs, rapidly producing a euphoric sensation that may last as long as 30 minutes. For many people, this effect is so overwhelming that they will sell or do anything to get more of the drug. The euphoric effect depends on the release of dopamine and other neurotransmitters, especially in the pleasure centers of the brain. Drug abusers state that the drug induces a feeling of power, self-esteem, and sensual well-being or sexual prowess, although prolonged use at high dosages has an adverse effect on sexuality.

Cocaine hydrochloride has been snorted or injected for years. However, by mixing it with ammonium hydroxide and then extracting the cocaine with ethyl ether, it could be changed into basic form and smoked. Smoking imparts a faster high, a more powerful onset of the drug's effect, and a longer-lasting high than the hydrochloride salt gives by injection. Inexperienced or intoxicated persons handling flammable solvents and open flames as

(A)

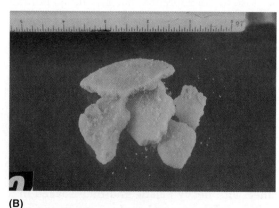

(B)

FIGURE 12.13: (A) Crack cocaine; (B) cocaine cookie crack (crack in the shape of the container in which it was formed).

(A) Courtesy of the DEA. (B) © Arthur Turner/Alamy Stock Photo.

they heated the extracted crystals of base on a pipe to vaporize and inhale the fumes suffered severe burns when the flammable solvent caught fire. As the amount of available cocaine became greater, prices dropped. A safer way to manufacture base cocaine using household chemicals was developed. Mixing the alkaline solution of cocaine with common sodium bicarbonate and heating the combination results in an opaque mass that is broken into chunks or rocks. Stoves were used to drive off the water and fix the base to the cocaine molecule, but microwave ovens are now commonly used for that purpose.

Many consider crack and freebase to be the same. They both begin as cocaine hydrochloride, and both can be smoked. There is a distinct difference between them, in that freebase is virtually pure cocaine hydrochloride, whereas crack has the original impurities imparted from the cut in the powdered cocaine plus the residue of any baking soda that has not been strained out.

There are various methods of making crack. For example, soda can crack requires 6 grams of cocaine hydrochloride, 2 grams of flour, 2 grams of baking soda, a pinch of yeast, a carbonated drink, and the bottom of a beverage can. The dry ingredients are added first into the can bottom, with the beverage added next to form a thick liquid. The entire solution in the can bottom is then cooked on low heat, stirring until the solution reduces into a thick paste. Once the paste dries, it can be removed from the bottom of the can into one large crack cookie. The color of the crack will take on the color of the beverage used in the manufacturing of the crack.

Whichever method of making crack is employed, it is important to remember that each was made with, and contains, cutting agents and adulterants. When field testing crack, it is best not to scoop the bottom of the container for a sample: rather, a chunk can be broken, thereby reducing the chances of just picking up loose cut in the bottom of the container.

■ Using Cocaine

Snorting involves making a line on a flat surface, such as glass or a mirror. The thin, 2- to 3-inch-long strip (the width of a matchstick) of cocaine powder is inhaled (snorted). Single-edged razor blades are used to finely chop the cocaine powder and to construct the line for snorting. A rolled dollar bill (the denomination of the bill may be status related), a soda straw, a glass, silver or gold tube, or a miniature spoon may be used for snorting (**FIGURE 12.14**). Regular users may grow the fingernail on the little finger of the dominant hand for use as a makeshift spoon.

The typical intravenous user injects the drug with an insulin syringe, leaving a pinprick-size puncture site. Because cutting agents are usually soluble, the skin reaction, granulomas, and needle tracks seen with other drugs are not common in the case of cocaine.

Crack cocaine can be smoked in any manner that results in vaporizing the drug. It may be

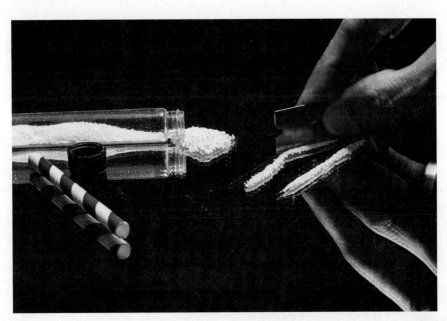

FIGURE 12.14: Cocaine powder, small bottle carrier and spoon lid, razor (to chop cocaine finely for inhalation), and metal straw (for inhalation "tooting").

© GillTeeShots/Getty Images.

mixed with tobacco in a cigarette, in a regular pipe, in a pipe with a screen to hold the tobacco and drug, or in a special crack pipe. Used by itself, the drug can be heated with a propane torch. Propane is preferred because other fuels are thought to impart an unpleasant taste to the vapors.

■ Self-Propelled Semi-Submersibles

Technology makes life easier for all of us. Advances in technology have spurred cocaine traffickers to experiment with a variety of delivery methods and systems. From cocaine dissolved in wine to cocaine inside tractor trailer semi-truck tires, traffickers have worked hard to stay ahead of law enforcement. One of the limitations that traffickers encounter in the distribution of cocaine is keeping up with the demand and finding new and clever ways to transport large quantities of cocaine. The latest innovation involves the mass transit of cocaine in a submarinelike vessel, the **self-propelled semi-submersible**. It does not completely submerge, but it submerges sufficiently to be virtually invisible from the sky. The partially submerged vessel is capable of stowing up to 4 tons of cocaine and attaining speeds in excess of 13 miles per hour. These vessels can be 60 feet long with crews of five (**FIGURE 12.15**).

The semi-submersibles are built with valves that open to the ocean, allowing the vessel to be scuttled by the crew, should there be a chance of apprehension. The U.S. Coast Guard and the Drug Enforcement Agency have been tasked with removing these vessels from the seas. The task

> **self-propelled semi-submersible**
> A submarine-like vessel that does not fully submerge and is used to transport cocaine

FIGURE 12.15: Cocaine submarine.
© AP Photos.

is made more difficult in that the range of these semi-submersibles may exceed 2,500 miles. Intercepting these vessels is a bit of a legal quagmire in that the present international and maritime law protects vessels in international waters.

Steroids

Concerns over a growing illicit market, abuse by teenagers, and the uncertainty of possible harmful, long-term effects of steroid use led Congress in 1991 to place anabolic steroids as a class of drugs in Schedule III of the CSA. The CSA defines anabolic steroids as any drug or hormonal substance chemically and pharmacologically related to testosterone (other than estrogens, progestins, and corticosteroids) that promotes muscle growth.

Once viewed as a problem associated only with professional and elite amateur athletes, various reports indicate that anabolic steroid abuse

— Ripped from the Headlines —

What's Next? Drones?

In January of 2015, the Associated Press reported that police in a Mexican border town city responded to the report of a drone, which had crash-landed and was reported to be carrying drugs. Upon arrival at the supermarket parking lot crash site, officials found a six-propeller drone aircraft with six packets of methamphetamine, weighing a little more than 6 pounds, attached to the drone by tape. Officials were unable to determine who had been controlling the aircraft at the time that it crashed.

This was not the only instance of newsworthy drone involvement in criminal activity. In April of 2015, authorities in South Carolina located a drone outside of a prison fence. The crashed drone was found to be carrying cellphones, marijuana, and tobacco.

It appears that drones may be the next mule-method for criminal enterprise and appear to be playing an increasingly significant role in the world of drug smuggling and investigation, on both sides. In an increasing number of instances, U.S. government officials from the FBI, ICE, DEA, and others have acknowledged the role that use of drones had played in conducting surveillance, locating and capturing drugs, individuals, and other property.

Source: Information from Associated Press. (2015). Meth-filled drone crashes in Mexican border town. *CBS News*. Retrieved August 8, 2015, from http://www.cbsnews.com/news/meth-filled-drone-crashes-in-mexican-border-town/

has increased significantly among adolescents. According to the 2003 Monitoring the Future Study, 2.5% of 8th graders, 3.0% of 10th graders, and 3.5% of 12th graders reported using steroids at least once in their lifetime (United Nations, 2010).

Most illicit anabolic steroids are sold at gyms, competitions, and through mail-order operations. For the most part, these substances are smuggled into the United States from many other countries. The illicit market includes various preparations intended for human and veterinary use as well as bogus and counterfeit products. The most commonly encountered anabolic steroids on the illicit market include testosterone, nandrolone, methenolone, stanozolol, and methandrostenolone.

A limited number of anabolic steroids have been approved for medical and veterinary use. The primary legitimate use of these drugs in humans is for the replacement of inadequate levels of testosterone resulting from a reduction or absence of functioning testes. Other indications include anemia and breast cancer. Experimentally, anabolic steroids have been used to treat a number of disorders, including AIDS wasting, erectile dysfunction, and osteoporosis. In veterinary practice, anabolic steroids are used to promote feed efficiency and to improve weight gain, vigor, and hair coat. They are also used in veterinary practice to treat anemia and counteract tissue breakdown during illness and trauma.

When used in combination with exercise training and a high-protein diet, anabolic steroids can promote increased size and strength of muscles, improve endurance, and decrease recovery time between workouts. They are taken orally or by intramuscular injection. Users concerned about drug tolerance often take steroids on a schedule called a cycle. A cycle is a period of between 6 and 14 weeks of steroid use, followed by a period of abstinence or reduction in use. Additionally, users tend to stack the drugs, using multiple drugs concurrently. Although the benefits of these practices are unsubstantiated, most users feel that cycling and stacking enhance the efficiency of the drugs and limit their side effects.

Another mode of steroid use is called pyramiding. With this method, users slowly escalate steroid use (increasing the number of drugs used at one time and/or the dose and frequency of one or more steroids), reach a peak amount at mid-cycle, and gradually taper the dose toward the end of the cycle. The escalation of steroid use can vary with different types of training. Body builders and weight lifters tend to escalate their dose to a much higher level than long distance runners or swimmers.

The long-term adverse health effects of anabolic steroid use are not definitely known. There is, however, increasing concern of possible serious health problems associated with the abuse of these agents, including cardiovascular damage, cerebrovascular toxicity, and liver damage.

Physical side effects include elevated blood pressure and cholesterol levels, severe acne, premature balding, reduced sexual function, and testicular atrophy. In males, abnormal breast development can occur. In females, anabolic steroids have a masculinizing effect, resulting in more body hair, a deeper voice, smaller breasts, and fewer menstrual cycles. Several of these effects are irreversible. In adolescents, abuse of these agents may prematurely stop the lengthening of bones, resulting in stunted growth. For some individuals, the use of anabolic steroids may be associated with psychotic reactions, manic episodes, feelings of anger or hostility, aggression, and violent behavior.

Over the last few years, a number of precursors to testosterone have been marketed as dietary supplements in the United States. New legislation has been introduced in Congress to add several steroids to the CSA and to alter the CSA requirements needed to place new steroids under control in the CSA.

Club Drugs

Club drugs is a general term used for certain illicit substances, primarily synthetic, that are usually found at nightclubs, bars, and raves (all-night dance parties). Substances used as club drugs include, but are not limited to, MDMA (methylenedioxymethamphetamine, known as "ecstasy"), GHB (gamma hydroxybutyrate—commonly used as a date-rape drug), Rohypnol (flunitrazepam—a date-rape drug), ketamine (Special K), dextromethorphan, and methamphetamine (discussed earlier). They too, like PCP, are dissociative drugs that can induce feelings of detachment and isolation and distortions in perception. These distortions often result in a misidentification of the substance as a hallucinogenic drug.

MDMA belongs to the family of amphetamines with effects very much like stimulants and hallucinogens (**FIGURE 12.16**). MDMA may result in a distorted perception of time and space. The drug is generally ingested and reaches its peak impact after 2 to 3 hours and begins to decline after 4 to 6 hours. During a night's activities, MDMA users may believe it necessary to repeat the original dosage to regain

club drugs
A general term used for certain illicit substances, primarily synthetic, that are usually found at nightclubs, bars, and raves

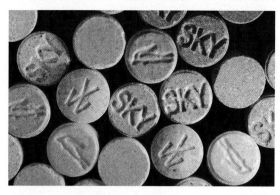

FIGURE 12.16: Examples of MDMA.

Courtesy of DEA.

the effects that they were seeking. MDMA works by increasing the activity of neurotransmitters in the brain—primarily serotonin, responsible for regulating moods, sleep, pain, emotion, and appetite—resulting in the brain taking time to rebuild serotonin levels and thereby requiring larger doses of MDMA to approximate the desired effect. In some users, there have been instances of increased body temperature and decreased heart-pumping efficiency. This drug is often used in conjunction with recreational activities and dancing, which contribute to increased body temperature and heart strain, which may result in cardiovascular problems among susceptible users. Repeated use of MDMA can result in depression, paranoia, anxiety, disturbed sleep, and mood swings.

The popular use of MDMA at places where young people gather and recreate has given rise to a new application of a strength-training supplement that can be used to induce inactivity and amnesia. Ketamine, also known as Special K or K, is a dissociative anesthetic that was produced to replace phencyclidine. Instead of use as a recreational drug, ketamine is used as a "rape drug." The chemical can be purchased via online stores that sell health supplements, or it can be produced from certain types of copy machine toner cleaners. It is colorless, odorless, and tasteless and can induce a temporary inactive state with concomitant amnesia. It has replaced Rohypnol as the date-rape drug of choice. If placed in a bottle of water, however, it is detectable by shaking the bottle and then setting the bottle on its side; any small bubbles forming at the surface may be an indication that ketamine is present.

Dextromethorphan, also called "DXM" or "robo," is a cough suppressant found in a number of nonprescription cold remedies. Users most commonly purchase "extra-strength" cough syrup, which contains a greater amount of the dextromethorphan than the regular strength. At high doses, the drug produces effects similar to PCP. Low doses produce distorted perception and act as a mild stimulant. In approximately 6 hours, these effects diminish. Since most of the cough remedies containing dextromethorphan also contain antihistamines and decongestants, dextromethorphan can be habit forming.

To some, club drugs seem harmless. Often, the raves where these drugs are used are promoted as alcohol-free events, giving parents a false sense of security that their children will be safe attending such parties. These parents are not aware that raves may actually be havens for the illicit sale and abuse of club drugs.

Because club drugs are illegal and are often produced in unsanitary laboratories, it is impossible for the user to know exactly what he or she is taking. The quality and potency of these substances can vary significantly from batch to batch. Additionally, substitute drugs are sometimes sold in place of club drugs without the user's knowledge. For example, PMA (paramethoxy-amphetamine) has been used as a substitute for MDMA. When users take PMA, thinking they are really ingesting MDMA, they often think they have taken weak ecstasy because PMA's effects take longer to appear. They then ingest more of the substance to attain a better high, which can result in death by overdose.

The Addict Myth

The media and Hollywood portray an epidemic of drug abuse in U.S. cities that is threatening law-abiding citizens. One result is that many people see themselves as victims of a lawless under-society that resorts to violence in its efforts to corner the market on illicit drugs. Adding to this view is the fact that prison populations are overflowing with those incarcerated for drug-related offenses.

The reality is that poor people do not provide the impetus for this country's multibillion-dollar-a-year drug industry. White polite society is irrevocably involved in the use of controlled substances. If addicts could be removed from our midst in the morning, there would still be a significant drug industry. When we examine the drug industry in all of its facets, we see that a large portion of the drugs that are available are not the types generally used by the socio-economically deprived. As Robin Williams, the actor and comedian, said, "Powdered cocaine is God's way of telling you that you have too much discretionary income." Hallucinogens, depressants, and stimulants are among the preferred recreational devices of the bored or jaded. Many doctors prescribe pharmaceuticals that are then easily abused and re-obtained. College campuses are hotbeds of experimentation for curious students looking for newer and bigger kicks.

Legislatures have passed stiff penalties for violent drug offenders, but they also provide funds for drug-abuse programs for those who qualify—generally people who are white, middle class, employed, educated, and financially secure. Two tiers of drug abuse have gripped our society; two tiers of enforcement strategies address the problem; and two tiers of legislation attempt to sanction the problem out of existence. Holding myopic views of drug abuse leads to draconian laws that hardly provide a sanction, depending on the socioeconomic status of the abuser.

Drug programs should not be a method for allowing individuals to avoid responsibility for their illegal behavior, nor should they be used in lieu of legal sanctions. If a war is to be waged (and there is no evidence that one has ever been conducted), all persons should be subjected to the same legal process and the same sanctions for the same offenses. Attempting to focus only on those who supply drugs is foolhardy, expensive, and not effective in a society based on supply and demand. Removing a supplier only results in increased prices, more violence, and an opportunity for another to fill the created void.

Substance abuse habituation should carry special status only if addressed prior to arrest. Many professional organizations provide substance habituation rehabilitation without personal cost to the professional member. No stigma or loss of professional status is associated with voluntarily participating in a professional organization's substance abuse program. National funds should be made available to provide drug rehabilitation programs for persons voluntarily committing themselves for treatment prior to arrest. Any citizen should be able to seek and get the same type of treatment that professional organizations afford their members. No stigma should be attached to drug abusers seeking help, and they should be returned to their community and their employment upon successful completion of the program.

As a result of the widespread experimentation with drugs by young people, many lawyers do not see recreational drug use by middle-class society as a problem and attempt to differentiate the casual social user from the violent pusher. Any such perspective undermines the war effort. All drug involvement ultimately redounds to the benefit of the same people. When drug offenders are presented with a panoply of legal options, it is not surprising that respect for the law and for law enforcement deteriorates.

Regardless of what the legislators from state to state reflect in state statutes, citizens from those same states are voting with their cash ballots. Given the amount of money spent yearly on drugs and the cavalier way drug humor is bandied about on television and movies, it makes little sense for police to die over laws that the citizens of this country do not appear to support.

In Texas in 1975, possession of marijuana was a felony punishable by life imprisonment. Some years thereafter, the legislature made the offense a citable misdemeanor. No one from the legislature bothered to explain the new policy to the spouses, parents, and children of those officers killed in the line of duty enforcing what came to be recognized as an unenforceable law. It is a shame that any law enforcement officer in this country should lose his or her life enforcing a law this country clearly vetoes every day with their cash ballots.

Forensic Analysis of Controlled Substances

Once at the forensic laboratory, the identification of controlled substances is divided into botanical and chemical examinations. Botanical exams identify physical characteristics specific to plants that are considered controlled substances. Chemical exams use wet chemical or instrumental techniques to identify specific substances that are controlled by statute. For each examination, a series of tests is administered to the sample. Each test is more specific than the last. At the end of the sequence, the examiner is able to determine if there is a controlled substance in the sample and identify it.

Botanical Analysis

These are the most common examinations performed in the controlled substance section of a forensics lab. Examinations are typically associated with such substances as marijuana, peyote, mushrooms, and opium. Marijuana examinations typically exceed 50% of the forensic laboratory's caseload. As a rule, by education and training, the examiner is a chemist, not a biologist or a botanist. The examiner has been trained in the identification of whether plant material is marijuana or another substance. Beyond that, the examiner should not render an opinion as to the identity of the substance.

Marijuana Analysis

The analysis of marijuana is a two-step process. The first step establishes the plant or plant material as marijuana through its physical characteristics (microscopic exam). The second step establishes the presence of the plant resin that contains the psychoactive components. A chemical color test is then used to confirm the presence of cannabinoids, specifically delta-9-tetrahydrocannabinol (THC), which is the primary psychoactive compound. This chemical color test is known as the Duquenois-Levine test. Additional confirmatory chemical and instrumental tests for marijuana resin include chromatographic exam, thin-layer chromatography (TLC), and gas chromatography (GC; Saferstein, 2014).

Chemical Analysis

The balance of the samples encountered by the controlled substance section requires the identification of specific compounds in a mixture. The composition of the samples may vary, but the procedure remains the same. Each sample requires a screening step, an extraction or sample preparation step, and a confirmatory step. Tests can be further subdivided into wet chemical and instrumental procedures. Wet chemical procedures are used as a screening method or for sample preparation. Instrumental procedures are used for screening or as a confirmation tool.

Forensic chemists are confronted with an array of substances in the specimens submitted to them for analysis. Their analyses must be specific and remove any doubt as to what drugs, if any, are involved. Furthermore, the identity of the drugs must be capable of being proven at

the time of trial. How does a chemist determine which drug is in a particular specimen? How does a chemist confirm that the probability of any other drug responding in an identical manner to the protocol selected is low enough not to be worth considering? He or she employs a two-stage protocol, consisting of screening tests and confirmatory tests.

Screening Tests

In a **screening test**, a specimen is subjected to a series of reagents that yield characteristic colors for commonly encountered drugs. Screening tests are used both in the lab and in the field. Ease of application makes color testing an efficient field-based method for achieving a tentative, presumptive identification of a drug. Color reactions are useful for screening purposes but do not result in a conclusive identification.

Five color test reagents are commonly used:

1. **Duquenois-Levine test** is a test for marijuana (**FIGURE 12.17**). When applied to marijuana, the reagent turns violet. The reagent is composed of three solutions: Solution A consists of 2% vanilla and 1% acetaldehyde in ethyl alcohol, solution B is concentrated hydrochloric acid, and solution C is chloroform.

2. The **Marquis test**, which screens for heroin, morphine, and opium derivatives, turns purple in their presence. The reagent can also be used for amphetamines and methamphetamines; in their presence, the mixture turns orange-brown. This reagent is composed of 2% formaldehyde in sulfuric acid.

3. Van Urk reagent, in the presence of LSD, turns blue-purple.

INVESTIGATOR'S NOTEBOOK

Important Precaution Regarding Drug Investigations

It is dangerous to taste any powder found at a crime scene, regardless of the media's common portrayal of police tasting suspected drug substances. There is no exception under the law justifying police ingestion of controlled substances for testing purposes. Such ingestion may be felonious and could ruin a promising career.

The amount of controlled substance in a sample is undetermined until tested, and a test-ingested, controlled substance thought to be one thing may turn out to be something else—something that might have an intense physiologic and psychological impact requiring medical assistance. The proper way to field test suspected controlled substances is discussed in the section "Screening Tests"; field testing does not include tasting, smelling, or tactile manipulation (LSD can be absorbed through tissues).

FIGURE 12.17: Duquenois-Levine Reagent System.

Courtesy of Forensics Source.

4. **Dille-Koppanyi test** is a test for barbiturates, in whose presence the reagent turns violet-blue.

5. The **Scott test** is a screen for cocaine (**FIGURE 12.18**). It renders a blue color upon application of solution A to a specimen containing cocaine. The blue transforms into pink upon application of solution B, and the blue color reappears in the chloroform layer upon addition of solution C.

Most labs and some field tests are completed using an open system with sealed bottles of solvents and reagents. The solvent dissolves and the reagent, an acid, causes a reaction. The color of that reaction has been recorded and can be expected of the appropriate solvent and reagent when placed on the questioned substance. The specimen to be tested is placed on a porcelain dish or in a petri dish. The appropriate amount of solvent is placed on the specimen and allowed a few minutes to do its work. Once the suspect material has been dissolved, the appropriate reagent is then dropped onto the specimen. If the solution turns a particular color and that color is consistent for the drug being tested, the test is positive. The test is recorded and the record is retained for further investigation and trial. The open containers of acid are broken or spilled easily, making the system hazardous; the Occupational Safety and Health Administration recognizes the procedure as highly hazardous.

A safer way to conduct field tests is to use commercial products that have solvent and reagent ampoules embedded into the package; the ampoules are broken in a particular sequence. This reaction takes place inside a sealed container, so the possibility of spills is eliminated from the testing equation. Each ampoule causes a reaction that is color coded to the drug for which the test is being conducted. The ampoules contain reagents that are acids and that when improperly broken, may cause stains, burns, and damage to clothes, so care must be taken when conducting the tests. Disposable rubber gloves are fundamental to drug testing (nitrile gloves are designed specifically for handling these types of substances).

Each drug testing kit provides the drug pouch or disposable chemical applicator, tubette, and a small, sterile, toothpick-sized drug scoop. When preparing the pouches or tubettes, it is important to use only a sterile device for picking up the suspect drug and placing it in the package. Often, investigators will use a knife or pen that is not sterile, thereby contaminating any test results. It is also important not to overload the pouch or tubette with the suspect drug; a very small quantity will produce the reaction. Whichever is being used, pouch or tubette, once the first ampoule is broken, after the test material has been added, it must be agitated for a minimum of 30 seconds to 1 minute. This agitation allows the solvent to dissolve the drug and the reagent to react with the dissolved drug. After each ampoule is broken, it must be agitated to facilitate the desired reaction.

Once the test is complete, it is important to document each step of the testing process. The tests themselves are only determinative

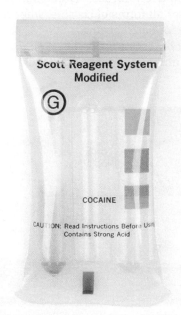

FIGURE 12.18: Scott Reagent System Modified.

Courtesy of Forensics Source.

Dille-Koppanyi test
A test for barbiturates, in whose presence the reagent turns violet-blue

Scott test
Test used to screen for cocaine

of probable cause and will dissipate over time. They will not be available for trial, because once the test is complete and recorded, the specimen is disposed of or destroyed. The only thing left reflecting the test will be the record made in writing at the time of the field test.

In using a drug field-testing pouch for marijuana (Duquenois-Levine), first make sure that the test label is correct for the substance being tested. Examine the pouch and be sure there are three intact ampoules. The top of the pouch is clipped shut; to use the pouch, the clip must be removed. After removing the clip, insert into the pouch the following (**FIGURE: 12.19**):

- Plant material: Three or four quarter-inch-long particles
- Hashish: 5–10 grams
- Hash oil: A pinhead's worth
- THC: A portion that fits on the tip of the loading device

Once the suspect material has been inserted, the pouch must be clipped closed and then tapped to force the materials to the bottom. When the material has descended

sufficiently, with the printed side of the pouch facing the user, the left ampoule can be broken and the pouch agitated for 1 minute. A very light tan color should form. When the middle ampoule is broken, the operator must pay close attention to the reaction, because, based on the quantity, quality, or freshness of the sample, the color may develop slowly or rapidly. As the purple color develops, there is a point at which the color will become darker. Too much development will spoil the reaction. Once the purple color has developed adequately, the third ampoule should be broken and the pouch agitated. By breaking the third ampoule, the color remains fixed.

When analyzing the color, it should be noted that there was little reaction upon the breaking of the first ampoule (**FIGURE 12.20**). After breaking the second ampoule, the color turned purple, and upon breaking the third ampoule, the solution turned blue. When the pouch is tipped at an angle with the solution trapped in one corner, close examination will reveal a gray layer on top of a blue/purple layer. This is presumptively positive for *Cannabis sativa* (marijuana and its extracts).

Make sure to select the right tubette when testing for cocaine (Scott test). Crush the material to be tested into a powder; use only the amount that will fit onto the loading device. Open the tubette, add the suspect substance, and tap it to the bottom. Breaking the first (bottom) ampoule should reveal a blue color when agitated. Breaking the top (second) ampoule will also cause a blue, sticky reaction. This reaction is presumptively cocaine hydrochloride. It can be used for all forms of cocaine, whether powder, crack, or base cocaine.

Color reactions differ based on the testing medium and method. The official definition of

FIGURE 12.19: Marijuana field test.
© Mikael Karlsson/Alamy Images.

FIGURE 12.20: First ampoule breaking in pouch.
© Mikael Karlsson/Alamy Images.

color reactions is a measurement and analysis of color by comparison with a standard—typically, the colors are on the front of the pouch. In tubes, the standard is the color of the printing on the box or the color of the printing on the caps. A match to the family of colors only, not the exact color shown, is sought.

There are three factors that affect the color reaction:

- Quality
- Quantity
- Agitation

The quality of the substance used for the test will affect the color intensity. A more pure substance may display darker colors and weaker substances may display lighter colors. The amount of the substance used will affect the intensity of the color reaction to varying degrees. It is necessary to agitate the sample vigorously to allow the chemistry to react properly with the substance itself. Depending on the agitation, color may increase or decrease.

Various cutting agents may create immediate heat and expansion in the test. If this reaction occurs, the clip on pouches can be canted 45°, thereby allowing any generated heat or expansion to escape the pouch. Venting the pouch should dissipate most of the expansion and heat without destroying or contaminating the sample being tested. Once the pressure and heat have been reduced, the pouch can be reclosed and the clamp pushed back into position, allowing the reaction to develop fully and color analysis to continue.

Preparing Materials for Field Testing

All substances must be prepared properly prior to testing to facilitate the best reaction. The investigator must wear nitrile gloves whenever testing or preparing to test, both for protection and to avoid allegations of cross-contamination. It is important to remember that the purity of what is being tested is always in question. If what is found is pure and in powder or liquid form, the unclad hand may absorb the drug, or the hands may transfer what has been picked up by the hands, to the face and eyes. Once absorbed, there is no way to anticipate the drug reaction, which may be from mild to lethal. That is why the protocol always includes nitrile gloves and field testing rather than bare-handed handling of drugs (or tasting them) as a field test. Only a fictional investigator would be so foolish as to taste something whose purity and identity has yet to be determined.

If the substance to be tested is in capsules, the capsule can be separated by twisting the two parts of the capsule in opposite directions, allowing the contents to pour onto paper or a sterile surface. Sometimes, the material in the capsule becomes caked and does not pour or comes out in chunks. Generally, rolling the capsule half between forefinger and thumb will dislodge the contents; the powder can be crushed with a gloved finger and then lifted and placed inside the testing package.

Tablets must be reduced to powder or small fragments prior to testing. This can be done by crushing the tablets with the thumb or with the heel of the hands. The powder will disperse beyond the hands, so it is important to have paper in place to capture as much of the powder as possible. Should it be necessary to use something harder than hand or fingers to crush the tablet, shroud the tool in an unused nitrile glove before applying pressure to the tablet. Using something to crush the tablet that is not sterile will lead to allegations of cross-contamination. Powders often arrive or are distributed in large chunks. Reduce chunks to powder for testing. Break off a piece from the large chunk to obtain a sample that can be crushed in the same manner as tablets.

Liquids are the most dangerous controlled substances that may require field testing. The liquid may be highly volatile, or it may interact with water or other substances to cause an explosive reaction. The best rule to follow when dealing with liquids is to take them to the lab to be tested. Should it be necessary to field test liquids, do it carefully and use very small amounts. Moisten a sterile cotton swab with the liquid and then allow it to dry. Once dried, the swab portion can be cut off and deposited into the testing medium.

Remember that any positive reaction is for probable-cause purposes only. Any evidence pertaining to the test at the time of trial will be based on the information recorded from the testing process.

Confirmatory Tests

Each screening test is insufficient enough by itself to prove a drug's identity, but the proper protocol will generate a combination of test results characteristic of only one chemical substance. Drug identification protocols generally rely on a combination of test types to confirm a drug's identity.

color reactions
Expected reactions to drug field tests

Drug Investigations

In a contraband drug investigation, the investigator is typically looking for evidence that has been hidden on the person, in a dwelling, or in a vehicle. When doing so, it is important to remember the rules of evidence and the requirements for establishing a chain of evidence. As with all aspects of evidence collection, it is imperative that the investigator be aware of current laws regulating search and seizure activities (Fisher, 2004).

The use of large amounts of unaccounted-for cash and the common arrest of persons who use or are addicted to controlled substances give the drug investigator a foothold in the fight against drugs. Most drug investigations are the result of police work, including the arrest of drug users who will cooperate with the police and the gathering of intelligence from the drug community. Information received from the drug community is always suspect. Informants do not provide information to police out of altruism. They generally have another agenda, apart from the enforcement of laws and the enhancement of community safety.

The most effective tool to date in combating drug cartels has been the use of the Racketeer Influenced Corrupt Organizations (RICO) Act, which provides for asset forfeiture. RICO laws were originally intended to combat organized criminal activity. Much of what is being done in contemporary drug distribution today fits the description of organized criminal activity. RICO prohibits investing the proceeds of a pattern of racketeering activity in an enterprise that engages in interstate or foreign commerce; acquiring or maintaining an interest in such an enterprise by means of a pattern of racketeering activity; using a pattern of such activity in conducting the affairs of such an enterprise; and conspiracy to do any of the preceding (Osterburg & Ward, 2010). If a drug dealer is arrested based on proper probable cause, the government can seize property that has been used or obtained in violation of the law. The legal procedure employed in the forfeiture of such assets is civil rather than criminal in nature, requiring that a standard of a preponderance of evidence be applied by the state or federal government in proving that the assets were the product of an organized criminal enterprise. Through asset forfeiture, state and federal police agencies have confiscated automobiles, money, houses, boats, airplanes, weapons, and other large consumer goods.

designer drugs
Substances that are chemically related to some controlled drugs and are pharmacologically potent

Clandestine Drug Laboratories

Illicit controlled substances, such as those discussed previously, are often manufactured in clandestine locations, known as clandestine laboratories. The investigation of clandestine laboratories is one of the most challenging efforts of law enforcement. No other law enforcement activity relies on forensic science as heavily. It is important in these situations that personnel take proper precautions while attempting to maximize physical evidence recovery efforts.

The Controlled Substances Act includes a provision stipulating that an offense involving a controlled substance analog (i.e., a chemical substance substantially similar in chemical structure to a controlled substance) shall trigger penalties as if it were a controlled substance listed in Schedule I. This section is designed to combat the proliferation of so-called **designer drugs**. Designer drugs are substances that are chemically related to some controlled drugs and are pharmacologically potent. These substances are manufactured in clandestine laboratories by skilled individuals who are aware that their products will not be covered by the schedules of the Controlled Substances Act.

Recent changes in the Controlled Substances Act constitute an effort to decrease the prevalence of clandestine drug laboratories designed to manufacture controlled substances. The act now regulates the manufacture and distribution of precursors, the chemical compounds used by clandestine drug laboratories to synthesize drugs of abuse.

Drug Prevention and Education

Many states are trying to change the message given to youths about drugs from "just do it" to "just say no." This latter message may fall on receptive ears if broadcast early enough. Teenagers, however, are listening to a different message conveyed by the media and the entertainment world. Late-night talk shows will invariably reveal comments about drugs, often flattering, frequently in jest. If we are facing an epidemic of drug abuse, if we are concerned about our children and their future, we need to change the perspective we bring to entertainment and education. Nothing is funny about drugs—about their use, their sale, and their consequences. Talk show guests do not jest about AIDS or breast cancer. The fact that

INVESTIGATOR'S NOTEBOOK

© Shutterstock, Inc./Janaka Dharmasena.

Following Up on Informants' Tips

Police receiving information from informants are at risk in two ways: First, by receiving information that may or may not be true; and second, by acting on information provided by people with ulterior motives. Yet, the characterization of the enforcement of drug laws as a "drug war" prompts police to invest time and effort in responding to leads provided by informants.

Surveillance is the tool most often used by investigators to corroborate information provided by informants. Electronic, aural, and visual surveillance are part of the investigator's arsenal. Using electronic aural enhancement (wiretaps) to gather information can be arduous. The vocabulary of the drug world is unique and ever changing. Investigators must have a working vocabulary that allows them to converse with drug-using informants as well as to interpret intercepted communications. Often, innocuous cell phone conversations carry the seeds of a drug transaction. The more sophisticated traffickers may use text messages containing code words or numbers in describing locations, drug types, and monetary values. Having an opportunity to examine cell phone records or messaging logs may reveal a repeating number or alphanumeric system that can be decrypted.

© Shutterstock, Inc./Nutink.

drugs are ripe for comedic exploitation implies two things: Drug use is more prevalent than we suspect, and drug use is more acceptable than we pretend.

One problem in educating young people about drugs is that the cast of characters we have fictionalized includes the evil drug user and the recreational drug user. It is a mistake to believe there is any difference between the two. The substances of abuse all come from the same place and support the same industry. Whether cocaine is abused in a crack house, dormitory, or penthouse is of little relevance to the cartel of drug producers and dealers who drive new autos and brandish 9 mm weapons. The purchase, regardless of location or use, contributes to the success of a growth industry as well as to the death of police fighting a winless war.

Current and Future Drug Trends

According to the United Nations (2010) Office on Drugs and Crime's *World Drug Report 2010*, the most recent estimates are that between 155 and 250 million people, or 3.9% to 5.7% of the population aged 15–64, has used illicit substances within the past year. Cannabis users comprise the largest number of illicit drug users (129–190 million people). Amphetamine-type stimulants are the second most prevalent, followed by opiates and cocaine. However, in terms of harm associated with use, opiates rank at the top.

There are, however, encouraging signs about drug use declining around the world. The first encouraging sign is that coca cultivation in the Andean countries continues to fall, driven by significant declines in Colombia. Global demand for cocaine has also stabilized, although the decline in the United States is offset by alarming increases in some European countries. Second, the production and consumption of amphetamine-type stimulants (ATS) has leveled off, with a clear downward trend in North America and, to a lesser degree, Europe. Third, the health warnings on higher potency cannabis, delivered in past *World Drug Reports*, appear to be getting through. For the first time in years, there is not an upward trend in the global production and consumption of cannabis. Fourth, opium production, while significant, is now highly concentrated in Afghanistan's southern provinces. Indeed, the Helmand province is on the verge of becoming the world's biggest drug supplier, with the dubious distinction of cultivating more drugs than entire countries such as Myanmar, Morocco, or even Colombia. Curing Helmand of its drug and insurgency cancer will rid the world of the most dangerous source of its most dangerous narcotic and go a long way toward bringing security to the region.

Another source of good news is that drug law enforcement has improved: Almost half of all cocaine produced is now being intercepted (up from 24% in 1999) and more than a quarter of all heroin (up 15% since 1999; United Nations, 2010).

CONCLUSION

Drugs are involved in the violation of virtually every criminal statute. Prisons fill, gangs proliferate, and street crime continues to rise—all fueled directly or indirectly by drugs. There are no casual users because the drug industry does not differentiate.

QUESTIONS FOR REVIEW

1. What is the "two tiers of law" concept, and how does it apply to sanctions for the possession of cocaine?

2. What are the various presumptive tests that forensic chemists use to help them identify controlled substances?

3. Describe the following laboratory procedures: microcrystalline tests, gas chromatography, thin-layer chromatography, and mass spectrometry.

4. How is heroin usually used, and from where does it come?

5. What makes a drug fall into the hallucinogenic classification?

6. What legal problems confront an investigator and a forensic scientist when dealing with a methamphetamine laboratory?

7. What was the result of the passage of the Controlled Substances Act?

8. What is crack cocaine?

9. Which drugs pose the most serious withdrawal risks for those habituated?

10. What is a club drug?

11. What are some of the dangers associated with the use of club drugs?

12. Why should police not use a pocket knife to scoop drugs into a test kit?

13. In drug testing, does the sequence of progressive color change matter?

14. What are the three most likely factors responsible for reagent coloring?

15. Why is it important to document drug test procedures and results?

16. What kinds of information about a drug might be obtained from a PDR?

17. When handling drugs, why are nitrile gloves preferable to common rubber gloves?

18. Describe the burn method for testing cocaine.

19. What is urine meth?

20. What is a dissociative drug? Give an example of one.

21. What role do self-propelled semi-submersibles play in the trafficking of cocaine?

REFERENCES

Associated Press. (2015). Meth-filled drone crashes in Mexican border town. *CBS News*. Retrieved August 8, 2015, from *http://www.cbsnews.com/news/meth-filled-drone-crashes-in-mexican-border-town/*

Baden, M. M. (1980). Investigation of deaths from drug abuse. In W. U. Spitz & R. S. Fisher (Eds.), *Medicolegal investigation of death* (2nd ed.). Springfield, IL: Charles C. Thomas.

Balbanova, S., Parsche, F., & Pirsig, W. (1992). First identification of drugs in Egyptian mummies. *Naturwissenschaften, 79*, 358–371.

Brewer, L., & Allen, A. (1991). N-formyl cocaine: A study of cocaine comparison parameters. *Journal of Forensic Science, 36*, 697–731.

Derlet, R. W., & Heischober, B. (1990, December). Methamphetamine: Stimulant of the 1990s? *Western Journal of Medicine, 153*(6), 625–628.

Drug Enforcement Administration. (2017). *Drugs of abuse*. Retrieved October 19, 2017, from https://www.dea.gov/pr/multimedia-library/publications/drug_of_abuse.pdf

Fisher, B.A. (2004). *Techniques of crime scene investigation* (7th ed.). Boca Raton, FL: CRC Press.

Gardner, A. (2011). *Hallucinogens legally sold as "bath salts" a new threat*. Retrieved August 25, 2012, from https://consumer.healthday.com/mental-health-information-25/addiction-news-6/hallucinogens-legally-sold-as-bath-salts-a-new-threat-649596.html

Karch, S. B. (2009). *The pathology of drug abuse* (4th ed.). Boca Raton, FL: CRC Press.

Maier, H. W. (1926). *Der Kokainismus* (O. J. Kalant, Trans.). Toronto, Ontario, Canada: Addiction Research Foundation.

Mortimer, W. G. (1901). Peru: The history and regulation of a dangerous drug. *Cornell Law Review*, 58, 537.

Musto, D. F. (1991). Opium, cocaine and marijuana in American history. *Scientific American*, 265(1), 40–47.

Noyes, H. (1884). Muriate of cocaine as a local anesthetic to the cornea: The ophthalmological congress in Heidelberg. *Medical Record*, 17, 418.

Osterburg, J. W., & Ward, R. H. (2010). *Criminal investigation: A method for reconstructing the past* (6th ed.). Cincinnati, OH: Anderson.

Saferstein, R. (2014). *Criminalistics: An introduction to forensic science* (11th ed.). Upper Saddle River, NJ: Prentice Hall.

Stephens, B. G. (1993). *Investigations of death from drug abuse*. In W. U. Spitz & R. S. Fisher (Eds.), Medicolegal investigations of death (3rd ed.). Springfield, IL: Charles C. Thomas.

Suarez, C., Arango, A., & Lester, J. (1977). Cocaine-condom ingestion. *Journal of the American Medical Association*, 238, 1391–1392.

Substance Abuse and Mental Health Services Administration. (2009). *Results from the 2008 National Survey on Drug Use and Health: National findings*. Rockville, MD: U.S. Department of Health and Human Services.

Thornton, J. I., & Nakamura, G. R. (1972). The identification of marijuana. *Journal of Forensic Science Society*, 12(3), 461.

"Toxic action of cocaine." (1885, November 21). *British Medical Journal*, 983.

United Nations. (2010). *World Drug Report 2010*. United Nations Office on Drugs and Crime. Retrieved September 20, 2011, from http://www.unodc.org/documents/wdr/WDR_2010/World_Drug_Report_2010_lo-res.pdf

U.S. Department of Justice. (1990, November 29). *Title 21 United States Code (USC) Controlled Substances Act*. Retrieved September 20, 2011, from http://www.deadiversion.usdoj.gov/21cfr/21usc/802.htm

U.S. Drug Enforcement Administration. (2011, March 1). *Chemicals used in "Spice" and "K2" type products now under federal control and regulation* (news release). Retrieved June 7, 2011, from http://www.justice.gov/dea/pubs/pressrel/pr030111.html

Weatherford, J. (1988). Indian givers. In *The drug connection*. New York, NY: Crown.

chapter
13

Arson and Explosives Investigation

> " *You will admit, Watson, that these facts are very suggestive. In each case there is evidence of a poisonous atmosphere. In each case, also, there is combustion going on in the room—in the one case a fire, in the other a lamp. The fire was needed, but the lamp was lit—as a comparison of the oil consumed will show—long after it was broad daylight. Why? Surely because there is some connection between three things—the burning, the stuffy atmosphere, and, finally, the madness or death of those unfortunate people. That is clear, is it not?* "
>
> **Sherlock Holmes**
> *"The Adventure of the Devil's Foot*

KEY TERMS

area of origin

arson

background sample

combustible liquid

deflagration

detonation

detonation point

direct evidence

explosion

explosive

flammable liquid

flammable range

flash point

high-order explosives

ignitable liquid

ignition temperature

ignitor

improvised explosive device (IED)

incendiary evidence

low-order explosive

masking fires

microtaggants

point of origin

pyrolysis

secondary device

spontaneous combustion

trailers

vapor detector (sniffer)

STUDENT LEARNING OUTCOMES

Upon completion of this chapter, students will be able to:

- Recognize what constitutes arson
- Distinguish some of the motives for committing arson
- Describe the types of evidence to be sought at an arson crime scene
- Identify the various classifications of explosives
- Identify the types of evidence to be sought in an explosion crime scene

FIGURE 13.1: Structure fire caused by arson.

Arson is usually divided into two categories: arson and aggravated arson. The latter involves risk of human injury, whereas the former does not. Many states have recognized a number of different types of arson and have provided specific statutory prohibitions and sanctions for them. In Texas, a person can commit arson upon a fence, pasture, tree, auto, unoccupied dwelling, building, or structure. States having hot, dry summers have passed arson laws pertaining to fires that get out of hand and cause extensive property damage; although not technically arson (because of the absence of intent), they are nonetheless prohibited and may be cause for the application of legal sanctions. The Federal Bureau of Investigation's (FBI) Uniform Crime Reporting (UCR) Program defines **arson** as "any willful or malicious burning or attempting to burn, with or without intent to defraud, a dwelling house, public building, motor vehicle or aircraft, or personal property of another" (FBI, 2015) **(FIGURE 13.1)**.

The most recent data reported by the FBI (2015) show that 15,222 law enforcement agencies reported 44,840 arsons. Arsons involving structures made up 45.9% of the total number of arsons reported. Mobile property comprised 23.8% of the reported arsons. "Other" types of property accounted for 30.3 % of reported arsons. The average dollar loss was $14,390. The number of arsons reported in 2013 was a 13.5% decrease over arsons reported in 2012. Nationwide, there were 16.1 arson offenses for every 100,000 inhabitants. (FBI, 2015).

Investigation of Arson

Traditionally, the responsibility for investigating fires fell to firefighters. Just as they had equipment to conduct water rescues and were, therefore, given the responsibility for recovering drowning victims, they had expertise in fighting fires and were, therefore, given the responsibility for investigating them. Time has shown that specialized skill, experience, and equipment are required to conduct an effective arson investigation, prompting many fire departments to do one of two things: (1) report suspected arson to the police for investigation, or (2) train firefighters as arson investigators.

The role of firefighters is generally to fight fires and, in the process, report anything suspicious that might indicate arson. They are not usually trained or equipped to investigate arson. Unfortunately, neither are most police investigators. The law enforcement community rarely paid much attention to deliberately set fires unless they were started to conceal a more serious offense, such as homicide or burglary. The thinking generally has been that the insurance industry would handle the investigation and there was no sense in duplicating efforts. Although the insurance carrier's adjuster or investigator may investigate a fire, he or she will arrive on the scene long after the fire has been extinguished and long after prospective witnesses have disappeared and prospective evidence has been destroyed or removed.

Fires and explosions provide little information on which an investigation can proceed. Available information is generally circumstantial, concentrating on the suspected **area of origin**. This is typically the large track of space or area where a fire likely started. Arson and bombings are committed with some degree of planning, and the arsonist or bomber is usually far from the scene when the crime is discovered and investigators respond. The extensive destruction at the scene renders most evidence unidentifiable or unusable. The laboratory can provide only limited assistance in identifying ignitable liquids that may have been deployed or in reconstructing igniting or detonating devices.

An **ignitable liquid** is any liquid that is capable of fueling a fire. Although forensic scientists may be able to identify minute amounts of an ignitable liquid in the materials provided for examination, there is no scientific test that will determine whether a particular arsonist used the ignitable liquid, unless a suspect is taken into custody with evidence of the ignitable liquid on clothing or in a container. Some jurisdictions may have access to accelerant-sniffing canines **(FIGURE 13.2)**, which may help investigators in locating accelerant use points and potentially identifying ignitable liquids used for igniting and maintaining an incendiary event.

The cause of a fire may be readily apparent or may require extensive examination. Fires may

arson
Any willful or malicious burning or attempting to burn, with or without intent to defraud, a dwelling house, public building, motor vehicle or aircraft, or personal property of another

area of origin
The large track of space or area where a fire would have started and can be located where the fire was able to grow and develop

ignitable liquid
Any liquid that is capable of fueling a fire

flammable range
The range in which air and a fuel will support combustion

spontaneous combustion
Combustion that is a product of a natural heat-producing process; it is caused and maintained by poor ventilation

ignitor
An item or phenomenon that can start a fire by providing temperatures in excess of the ignition temperature of most fuels

ignition temperature
Temperature provided by some outside source of heat that causes a fuel to ignite; the ignition temperature is always higher than the flash point

point of origin
Location where a fire began; it generally evidences the deepest charring;

flash point
The lowest temperature at which a liquid gives off sufficient vapor to form a mixture with air that will support combustion

flammable liquids
Liquids that have a flash point lower than 100°F

FIGURE 13.2: Ignitable liquid-sniffing canine being used to investigate a fire scene.

© Jones & Bartlett Learning. Photographed by Glen E. Ellman.

be caused by accident or by intent. One way of proving intent is by ruling out accidental causes of the fire. A final determination must take into consideration numerous factors and deserves a complete and meticulous investigation. Only properly trained and experienced investigators can conduct that type of investigation.

Normally, an ordinary match will ignite fuels. However, other **ignitors** must be considered; electric discharges, sparks, and chemicals may provide temperatures in excess of the **ignition temperature** of most fuels. A fuel will interact with oxygen to produce a flame only when the fuel is in a gaseous state. This is true even if the fuel feeding the flame is wood, paper, cloth, plastic, or gasoline. In the case of a liquid fuel, the temperature must be high enough to vaporize the fuel. The vapor that forms burns when it mixes with oxygen. The **flash point** is the lowest temperature at which a liquid gives off sufficient vapor to form a mixture with air that will support combustion. Ignitable liquids may be either flammable liquids or combustible liquids. **Flammable liquids** have a flash point lower than 100°F, whereas **combustible liquids** have a flash point higher than 100°F. Once the flash point is reached, the fuel can be ignited by an outside source of high temperature. The ignition temperature is always higher than the flash point. With a solid fuel, the process of generating vapor is more complex. Solid fuel will burn only when it is exposed to heat that is high enough to break down the solid into a gaseous product. The chemical decomposition is called **pyrolysis**. Gaseous fuel and air will only burn if their composition (the fuel-air mix) lies within certain limits. If the proportion of fuel to air is too low or too high (as in a flooded auto carburetor), combustion will not occur. The range in which air and fuel will

support combustion is called the **flammable range** (Chandler, 2009).

There are instances in which a fuel can burn without a flame. A burning cigarette or red-hot charcoal is an example of glowing combustion or smoldering. Combustion is taking place on the surface of a solid fuel in the absence of heat high enough to break down the fuel into a gaseous product (pyrolyze the fuel). This same phenomenon can be seen in wood fires once all of the gases have been expended; the wood continues to smolder until all of the carbonaceous residue has been consumed (Saferstein, 2014).

Tabloids and tabloid television spread the belief that fire can begin as the result of **spontaneous combustion**. Some have gone so far as to insist that humans can combust spontaneously. Regardless of what scriptwriters suggest, there is no documented case of a human spontaneously combusting. Spontaneous combustion of nonhuman materials is a product of a natural heat-producing process. This process is caused and maintained by poor ventilation. Hay stored in hot, unventilated areas is a conducive medium for the growth of bacteria that generate heat. If left unventilated at elevated temperatures long enough, the hay may be ignited by the activity of the bacteria. Paint, oily rags, and various chemicals left in a hot, unventilated area may also ignite. Spontaneous combustion is seldom the cause of a fire but often is invoked as the cause.

The focus of every arson investigation is the fire's **point of origin**. The investigation must begin as soon as possible after the fire has been reported, preferably while it is still burning. The fire itself may provide information about its nature and origin. The direction in which the fire travels will be helpful in determining where it began (**FIGURES 13.3, 13.4,** and **13.5**). If there are numerous fires spread out over a burning structure, arson should be presumed. Ignitable liquids that may have been used to start the fire have detectable odors and smoke coloring. The inability of firefighters to gain access to the building suggests that the fire began accidentally or that someone with a key started the fire. In addition to what the fire can tell, witnesses on the scene may be helpful in gathering information about the fire. Investigators will want to note the following:

- When the fire was first discovered
- The size of the fire upon discovery
- Who discovered the fire
- Who reported the fire

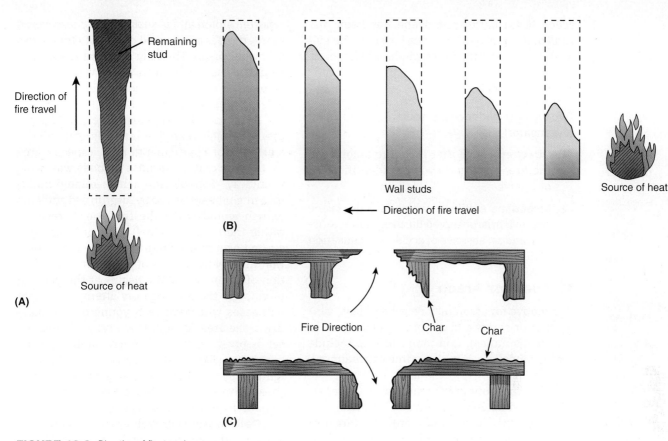

Remaining stud

Direction of fire travel

Source of heat

(A)

Wall studs

Direction of fire travel

Source of heat

(B)

Fire Direction   Char   Char

(C)

FIGURE 13.3: Direction of fire travel.

FIGURE 13.4: Direction of fire travel (couch burning).

Courtesy of Nick Vesper.

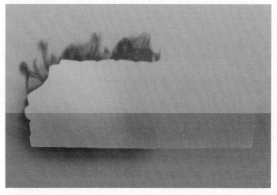

FIGURE 13.5: Direction of fire travel (couch moved).

Courtesy of Nick Vesper.

- Unusual activity around the premises before the fire

- Unusual or unidentified persons in the area (Chandler, 2009)

Often, an arsonist will return to the scene to enjoy the fruits of his or her labor. It is important to begin the investigation by taking photos of those watching the fire to identify any known fire starters or persons who neither work nor live in the area. Professional arsonists may linger to determine if the fire set will be sufficient to destroy the building and the evidence of arson.

Once the fire has been extinguished, entry should be made as soon as it is safe. Recording the scene photographically is the first priority. A thorough search of the premises is required, for subsequent entries may have to be based on probable cause and a search warrant. Time is working against the investigator. Most fires are started or accelerated with petroleum-based hydrocarbons. Any remaining residue can evaporate in a matter of hours. Salvage operations may begin quickly, or a search of the premises for survivors or bodies may be conducted. It is imperative that the examination of the crime

combustible liquids
Liquids that have a flash point higher than 100°F

pyrolysis
The chemical decomposition of a solid into a gaseous product

scene begin before the scene has been disturbed, if possible; if it is not possible, the evidentiary value of the photographs will increase.

Arson Evidence

Two types of evidence are available to the arson investigator:

1. **Direct evidence** that links the arsonist to the fire, such as eyewitness identification or motive

2. **Incendiary evidence**, which includes crime scene debris, observed burning characteristics, and an absence of accidental causation (Saferstein, 2014)

Motives for Arson

The motive for arson may be general (e.g., vandalism) or specific (e.g., commercial arson to collect insurance). Common motives include profit, vandalism, revenge, crime concealment, and thrill seeking (pyromania).

Fires for profit are common and are generally started as an alternative to financial failure or partner disenchantment. The target of the fire may not be the building alone. A thorough investigation of the paper trail associated with the business may not reveal anything confirming the fire. An absence of expanded or new insurance coverage might suggest that no profit motive exists. The relevant insurance, however, may be on the goods stored rather than the business itself. It is not unusual for fires to be set to rid the owner of a cumbersome or outdated inventory. There is usually some evidence to support the hypothesis that the fire was set to destroy the inventory. Valuable items that the owner does not wish to "liquidate" may be removed from the premises or replaced with outdated items that have been insured at new-merchandise prices.

Automobile owners plagued with mechanical difficulties or monthly payments that they can no longer maintain may burn their autos for the insurance coverage and the relief of getting rid of a lemon. The vehicle will be reported stolen after the fire is set so that the owner avoids being stopped in a reportedly stolen vehicle. The time at which the vehicle was torched and the time it was reported stolen may be useful in investigating the auto arson. Additionally, items of commercial or sentimental value may have been removed from the vehicle prior to the burning. It is much more common for a stolen vehicle to be abandoned in a watery depository than for the thieves to burn it. If a vehicle is reported stolen and is subsequently discovered burnt, there is a very good possibility that it was an owner arson. The only practical reason fire would be used to destroy a stolen vehicle would be to cover up a more serious offense (a homicide, a robbery, or a hit and run).

Fires started by vandals cause untold property loss each year. The intent is generally to start a fire of a particular thing in a specific area for the "fun of it" or because "nobody was using it anyway." Schools and school-related buildings might be set on fire by disgruntled students (which would make the fire one of revenge rather than pure mischief). Field or forest fires started as a prank often grow into major fires that destroy thousands of acres. The investigation of a vandalistic fire begins at the point of origin, and the investigators attempt to locate witnesses who have seen young people playing in the area. Most of these types of fires are set by juveniles without much planning, using a match or lighter as an igniter; sophisticated ignition systems are not going to be found at these crime scenes. Most vandal arsonists remain uncaught (Kolko, 2002).

Occasionally, a firefighter will set a fire that appears to be vandalism for the purpose of being part of the team called in to put out the fire. This type of arson, because of motive, falls in a category by itself. The ultimate objective may be for profit (fires keep firefighters employed) or self-aggrandizement (the firefighter has an opportunity to do something heroic). Obviously, a firefighter arsonist is the most difficult type to catch, because he or she has extensive knowledge of fires and their investigation.

Fires for revenge are cowardly but nonetheless lethal. The cast of potential characters range from spurned suitors to disgruntled employees, and the motives range from racism to anger caused by a neighborly dispute. Once revenge has been selected as a possible motive, the list of suspects should be short and illuminating. These fires may be the product of long-range planning or may be fairly spontaneous. The modus operandi, which can range from igniting drapery in a hotel to setting ignition devices around the perimeter of a building, will vary, but the motive will steer the investigation.

Masking fires set to mask the commission of other crimes (e.g., homicides) are the major focus of arson investigations conducted by police agencies. The investigator must not only conduct a thorough arson investigation but must also observe the rudiments of, say, a homicide investigation at the same time. The main question confronting an investigator in arson

direct evidence
Evidence that links the arsonist to the fire, such as eyewitness identification or motive

incendiary evidence
Evidence from the fire itself, including crime scene debris, observed burning characteristics, and an absence of accidental causation

masking fires
Fires set to mask the commission of other crimes

— Ripped from the Headlines —

Convicted Arsonist Commits Suicide in Court

On June 28, 2012, as the jury foreman of a Phoenix jury uttered the word "guilty" regarding defendant Michael Marin's trial for arson, the defendant placed his head in his hands and appeared to place something into his mouth and then retrieved a bottle of liquid from his briefcase and took a drink. Moments later, Marin collapsed, face first onto the courtroom floor. Attempts to revive him in the courtroom, by the same investigator who built the case against him, were unsuccessful and Marin was pronounced dead shortly after at an area hospital. Marin likely swallowed a poison pill as the verdict was read and he was found guilty of setting fire to his $3.5 million Phoenix mansion and faced from 10 to 21 years in prison. The subsequent arson investigation found Marin to have only $50 in his bank account, after having nearly $900,000 the year prior, and he faced a looming balloon payment on the property of $2.3 million within a matter of days. On July 5, 2009, Marin escaped an inferno at the 10,000 square-foot home using a rope ladder, while wearing a scuba mask and scuba tank to avoid inhaling smoke, which he just happened to have handy in his bedroom at the time of the blaze. Investigators eventually determined that there were several places within the residence where intentional fires were set and Marin was subsequently arrested for felony arson.

Information from AP. (2012, June 28). Myers, Amanda L. "Suicide by poison suspected in courtroom death." http://www.kmov.com/news/national/Suicide-by-poison-suspected-in-courtroom-death-160971445.html.

with human victims is whether the fire was set to effect the death of the victims or whether the deaths were unintended consequences of the arson.

People love fire. It is hypnotic and simultaneously warming and comforting, not to mention romantic. People will turn the air conditioner on to be able to have a fire in the fireplace to create an intimate environment. Folks gathered around a campfire share not only its warmth but also each other's. Our love affair with fire has brought us to the pinnacle of technologic refinement, but fire is also the source of a morbid fascination because of the havoc it can wreak when released. There are those among us who long to "release the beast"—those who set fires out of a sexual obsession and who will continue to set fires until stopped. Pyromaniacs—serial fire starters—are generally compulsive, and their fires are unplanned. Many believe that this type of fire starting is one of a trilogy of behaviors that together are characteristic of serial killers. (The other two are bedwetting and animal torture.)

CASE IN POINT

The Happy Land Social Club Fire

In November 1988, the Happy Land Social Club was ordered to close down as a fire hazard because it had no fire exits, no fire alarm, and no sprinkler system. After a brief hiatus, the club was reopened, although the violations had not been addressed. On a weekend in April 1990, Julio Gonzalez, a Marielito (a member of the 1980 Cuban boatlift), engaged in a quarrel with his ex-girlfriend Lydia Feliciano. A bouncer ordered Julio off the premises. He left, saying he would be back and would shut the place down. Gonzalez told police that he purchased a dollar's worth of gasoline in a plastic milk jug and returned to the club. He splashed the gasoline through the front door of the club and then ignited it with a match. Most of the occupants were on the second floor and rushed toward two narrow stairways leading to the ground floor. Many were trampled in the panic; those who were not trampled, found the front entrance blocked by flames. Ironically, the object of Julio's wrath managed to escape with four others. Eighty-seven people were killed, most from smoke inhalation. Gonzalez was indicted on 87 counts of felony murder (Magnuson, 1990).

Incendiary Evidence

Fires tend to move upward, and; therefore, the point of origin is often the lowest point that shows intense burn characteristics.

Arsonists may attempt to spread fire to other areas by intentionally linking them together with ignitable liquids, or other easily burned debris. These materials are referred to as **trailers**. Thus, one fire will, in turn, ignite other areas via use of the trailers. There are many common household items (gasoline, isopropyl alcohol, nail polish remover, etc.), which may be used as an ignitable liquid in combination with trailer items. The presence of such items at a fire scene is not necessarily indicative of a nefarious intent. It is important to remember that it is not the fuel that makes something a trailer, but rather, the manner and location in which the fuel was used that will speak to its intent and purpose. Personnel must look for and be observant of such items and item locations.

Gasoline-soaked rags, paper trails, or other devices used to ensure that fire starts and spreads may have not completely burned. Gasoline residue soaked into unburned furnishings or cracks in the flooring material may be retrievable, indicate the origin of the fire, and serve as evidence of arson (Chandler, 2009).

Igniter containers may be left at or near the scene. Most arson fires (except for those set by vandals) are started with the use of an igniter other than a simple match. An ignition device allows the arsonist to exit the building safely or provides for ample time to secure an alibi for the time the fire was set. Igniters can be very complex or deceptively simple. The more complex the igniting device, the more likely unburned remains will exist.

Collecting Evidence

The containers of choice for holding evidence in an arson investigation include unused paint cans (**FIGURE 13.6**) and mason jars. Both can be sealed airtight, and neither will react with suspect materials. Once evidence of arson has been discovered, the material should be placed in an airtight container, leaving one-third of the volume of the container empty. In order for the laboratory to run tests, three things are necessary:

1. An uncontaminated sample
2. A sufficient sample
3. A **background sample** (control)

Contamination is a byproduct of fire and the extinguishing of the fire. Additional contamination resulting from mishandling is what must be avoided. Containers made of plastic or polyethylene will react with hydrocarbons and may result in the destruction of hydrocarbon vapors. When gathering material for collection, the investigator should try to preserve sizable specimens. The point of origin should produce a gallon of porous material, soot, debris, and any other substances thought to contain ignitable liquid residue. It is important that all materials suspected of containing volatile liquids be accompanied by a thorough sampling of similar but relatively clean control specimens from an area of the fire in which ignitable liquids are thought to have been absent. The laboratory scientists will check the control materials to ensure that they are free from flammable

trailer
A lone trail of combustibles or ignitable liquids leading from the point of origin to some other area of the building; used to spread the fire

background sample
A control sample to compare against evidence found at the scene of a fire

FIGURE 13.6: Unused paint can for storing evidence.

Courtesy of SIRCHIE Finger Print Laboratories, Inc.

INVESTIGATOR'S NOTEBOOK

© Shutterstock, Inc./Janaka Dharmasena

Processing the Arson Scene

Once the point of origin has been located, it must be protected until a thorough examination has been completed. Again, photographs should be the first priority. The search for ignitable liquids should not be forsaken because of the abundance of water left after the fire. Water does not interfere with laboratory methods used to detect flammable liquid residues. A **vapor detector**, also called a **sniffer**, helps in the detection of flammable fluids. The device detects the presence of volatile residues by sucking in air around the suspect sample. The air passes over a heated filament. A combustible vapor oxidizes and increases the temperature of the heated filament, measured by the detector's meter. A positive finding by the sniffer, however, is not determinative, only presumptive. Its value is that suspect samples can be tested at the scene. Any questionable samples must be properly handled, packaged, and transported to the laboratory.

© Shutterstock, Inc./Nutink.

residues, thereby removing cleaning solvents or other household hydrocarbons as possible sources of contamination.

Explosions

For the purposes of this text, an **explosion** is an event that results in the release of mechanical or chemical energy in a violent manner in such a way that it generates great heat (high temperature) and the subsequent release of large quantities of associated gasses. Any chemical compound, mixture, or device, the primary or common purpose of which is to produce an explosion, is termed an **explosive**. Often, the explosive is held within a metal container, such as a sealed lead pipe. (However, a water heater is an example of a sealed metal container that is also capable of producing an explosion.) When an explosion occurs, the gasses produced within the sealed container cause the walls of the item to deform until such point that the pressure inside becomes so great as to fracture or rupture the walls of the container. This rupture results in fragments and debris being expelled in all directions, with great force and deadly consequences. Often, bomb makers will add tacks, nails, glass, etc., to produce additional shrapnel (other than the walls of the container item).

Investigating Explosions

At times, an investigator will respond to the scene of an explosion. Just as all fires are not criminal in nature, not all explosions are criminal. Construction accidents, defective home-heating devices, or a tanker truck hauling a volatile chemical can all potentially cause an explosion. However, there are explosions that do occur for criminal or terrorist reasons. Those that do occur for criminal or terrorist reasons typically make use of an explosive.

The steps employed in the investigation of an explosion are generally the same as for arson, but there are several additional considerations. The chances of finding a large amount of trace evidence are remote. Like fire, an explosion is the product of combustion accompanied by the creation of gases and heat. It is the sudden buildup of expanding gas pressure at the point of detonation that produces the disruption of the explosion. Chemical explosions can be classified on the basis of the velocity of energy waves transmitted upon detonation.

Categories of Explosives

According to the Department of Homeland Security (2008) Incident Response to Terrorist Bombings, explosives can be divided into three categories: pyrotechnics, propellants (both of which are called low explosives), and high explosives. These categorizations depend, in part, on the manner of use of the materials. Technically, explosives are categorized based on the speed at which they produce gas (which results in the explosive incident). A chemical explosion in which the reaction front moves through the explosive at less than the speed of sound is classified as a **deflagration**. Whereas, a chemical explosion in which the reaction front moves through the explosive at greater than the speed of sound, is classified as a **detonation**.

Low-order explosives (deflagrating explosives) involve a relatively slow rate of conversion to a gaseous state. The energy wave generated travels at a speed of less than 1,000 meters per second (**FIGURE 13.7**). The most widely used

---

vapor detector (sniffer) A device that detects the presence of volatile residues by sampling the air around a suspect area or sample

explosion An event that results in the release of mechanical or chemical energy in a violent manner in such a way that it generates great heat and the subsequent release of large quantities of associated gasses

explosive Any chemical compound, mixture, or device, the primary or common purpose of which is to function by explosion

deflagration A chemical explosion in which the reaction front moves through the explosive at less than the speed of sound

detonation A chemical explosion in which the reaction front moves through the explosive at greater than the speed of sound

low-order explosive Explosive that involves a relatively slow rate of conversion to a gaseous state; they can be ignited by heat and are usually ignited with a lighted fuse

FIGURE 13.7: Remnants of a low-order explosion (note glass blown out of windows).

© Chris Pole/Shutterstock, Inc.

FIGURE 13.9: Dynamite.

© Fer Gregory/Shutterstock, Inc.

explosives in the low-order group are black powder and smokeless powder. Low-order explosives can be ignited by heat and are usually ignited with a lighted fuse.

High-order explosives (detonating explosives) change rapidly to a gaseous state upon ignition. The energy wave created travels at a rate between 1,000 and 9,000 meters per second (**FIGURE 13.8**). Dynamite is the most common high-order explosive (**FIGURE 13.9**), although composition C-4 (made of RDX) is also used.

> **high-order explosive**
>
> Explosives that change rapidly to a gaseous state upon ignition; they must be detonated by an initiating device, such as a blasting cap

Unlike low-order explosives, high-order explosives must be detonated by initiating devices. The most common initiator is a blasting cap. However, the ignition switch on a boat can also be used to provide the spark necessary to detonate high-order explosives.

Dynamite

Nobel's invention made large-scale blasting available to the road-building and mining industry. Later, it was learned that replacing the clay filler with a porous combustible material, such as rice hulls or sawdust, improved dynamite's gas production and, as a result, its explosive power.

Ammonium Nitrate/Fuel Oil

Ammonium nitrate (AN) is a fertilizer that is widely used by farmers. Mining companies soon found that if ammonium nitrate was mixed with a source of carbon, it made a very cheap and effective explosive. Miners eventually found that fuel oil (home heating oil or diesel fuel) was easier to mix than powdered coal. Thus, ANFO was discovered. ANFO, a mixture containing approximately 94% ammonium nitrate and 6% fuel oil, is currently the most commonly used explosive material in the world today. As a result, dynamite production (and use) in the United States has greatly declined. (In 1959, there were 34 dynamite plants in this country; today, there is only one). Because ANFO requires a primer charge to initiate a blast, ANFO is technically classified as a blasting agent. Since blasting agents do not perform well when used in small quantities, ANFO is rarely encountered in small, improvised bombs. Large amounts of ANFO, however, have been used in terrorist bombings.

FIGURE 13.8: Remnants of a high-order explosion.

© urbancow/iStockphoto.com.

Military Explosives

Military explosives are manufactured for specific purposes. Because of the enormous quantity of explosives used in warfare, military explosives must be produced from cheap raw materials that are not strategic and are available in great quantity. In addition, the operations used to manufacture them must be reasonably simple, cheap, and safe. Finally, the density of military explosives needs to be as high as possible. Grenades, for example, are small military devices that can produce large explosions. TNT, RDX, and HMX are examples of military explosives. (Girard, 2017)

Improvised Explosives

Recent reports from the ATF reported that there are approximately 4,000 domestic bombings a year (in recent years), with most of these involving low explosives. The most common type of device is what is referred to as an **improvised explosive device (IED)**. An IED is a homemade (non-militarily/commercially produced) bomb or destructive device designed to destroy, incapacitate, harass, or distract. A low-explosive IED has two necessary components: a container to confine the explosive and a fuse or primer to detonate it. By contrast, a high explosive does not need confinement to explode. There are two types of improvised low explosives: commercially available products that are modified to act as explosives and combinations of chemicals (Girard, 2017). The pipe bomb is the most common type of improvised explosive that is used in the U.S. (**FIGURE 13.10**).

Explosive Investigation

While the majority of explosive investigations are typically handled by military and federal authorities, in today's world of increasing domestic terrorism activities, more often, local authorities are being placed in the position of being first responders to critical incidents relating to explosions. There are two types of bombing incidents: predetonation and postdetonation. Predetonation incidents include bomb threats, suspicious item incidents, and situations involving suspected suicide bombers. Postdetonation incidents, on the other hand, include situations in which explosives have already been detonated.

Predetonation

Although the nightly news typically teems with stories of suicide bombers and suspicious incidents, bomb threats are the most common

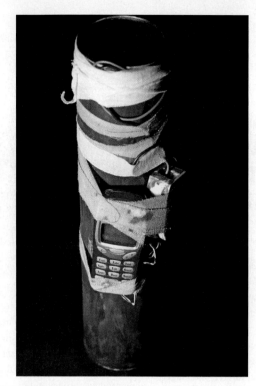

FIGURE 13.10: Pipe bomb.
© Adrian Britton/Shutterstock, Inc.

improvised explosive device (IED) A homemade (nonmilitarily/commercially produced) bomb or destructive device designed to destroy, incapacitate, harass, or distract

type of predetonation incident. Most of these are hoaxes and are reported simply as a prank. Sometimes, there are ulterior motives, such as cancelling school, work, a controversial community event, etc. However, many agencies and school districts now impose significant penalties on individuals who communicate bomb threats. Statutes covering these situations have been upgraded in many jurisdictions and callers now face large fines and even imprisonment.

The initial first responder at a suspicious item incident is typically a law enforcement officer. He or she should immediately evacuate persons from around the suspected item or areas where devices could be located. In no case should anyone other than a certified bomb technician attempt to handle or render safe any suspected explosive device. The Department of Homeland Security recommends the actions of first responders at a predetonation incident not be observed or recorded by personnel who do not have a legitimate requirement to document such actions. Written summaries, audio or video recordings, or police responses can be used by bombers in planning subsequent attacks.

Postdetonation

As with the response to all scenes, the first priority of the initial response to a postdetonation incident is the safety of the public and the first

— Ripped from the Headlines —

Low-explosive IEDs Used for Domestic Terror and Mischief

In 2013, the Boston Marathon bombers constructed their IEDs by placing smokeless powder and nails in a pressure cooker. As can be seen in **FIGURE A**, they used a timer to detonate the smokeless powder and the pressure cooker to contain the pressure buildup.

Homemade mixtures of (1) potassium nitrate with sugar and aluminum, (2) sulfur/charcoal, potassium chlorate, and sugar, and (3) potassium perchlorate with sugar and aluminum have all been used to construct pipe bombs. Swimming pool chlorinators often contain calcium hypochlorite;

when this chemical is mixed with automobile brake fluid, the mixture spontaneously ignites in a few minutes.

For mischief purposes, juveniles have found numerous inexpensive methods for assembling simple explosives. Although most are made with materials found in the home, the danger posed by these devices should not be underestimated. One such device is a chemical reaction bomb called the "MacGyver bomb" (named after the television character who was a master at improvising devices from common household items). Its main ingredients—toilet bowl cleaner and aluminum foil—are placed in a two-liter plastic soda bottle. When the aluminum and liquid react, they produce large amounts of oxygen gas, which quickly pressurizes the bottle. The plastic bottle can withstand only 80 pounds per square inch of pressure; when this level

FIGURE A: The IED used in the 2013 Boston Marathon bombing was constructed from a pressure cooker, smokeless powder, nails, and a timer that was attached to a detonator.

Courtesy of Federal Bureau of Investigation.

is exceeded, it bursts. MacGyver bombs have been placed in mailboxes, under vehicles, and in trash containers. Some have nails added to act as projectiles, causing severe injury. (Girard, 2017)

© Shutterstock, Inc./rzarek.

---

secondary device

A secondary explosive device placed at a scene to detonate after the original explosion. Typically, a place to target emergency responders and investigators at the scene of the initial bombing

responders. Every effort must be made to avoid additional casualties. All responders should be alert for any item that could be a **secondary device** or any location where a secondary device can be concealed. A secondary device is a second bomb placed at a scene to detonate after the original explosion. Secondary devices are typically placed to target emergency responders and investigators at the scene of a bombing. Law enforcement officers, firefighters, medical personnel, and other emergency response personnel should continually observe their opera-

INVESTIGATOR'S NOTEBOOK

Responses to Predetonation Situations

- Do not touch an item that could contain explosive material.
- Always move people away from a suspicious item—never try to move the item away from people.
- Never use a radio, cellular telephone, or other transmitter within a minimum of 300 feet of a location where there is a suspected or actual explosive device.
- Pay close attention to appropriate evacuation distances.
- Be aware of the potential for secondary devices.

Adapted from Department of Homeland Security. (2008). *Incident response to terrorist bombings*. Washington, DC: US Government Printing Office.

© Shutterstock, Inc./Nutink.

© Shutterstock, Inc./Sanaka Dharmasena.

tional areas for any signs of secondary devices. If a suspected secondary device is observed, the incident commander should be notified and recall procedures should be implemented immediately. The search for secondary devices should also include staging areas, command posts, rest and rehab areas, and triage areas.

Scene Search

The search should focus on locating the site of the device and identifying the type of explosive used. The point of detonation will often leave a gaping hole surrounded by scorching. The type of explosive used may be determined by inspecting the residue at the scene. Wood, metal, and fiberglass samples surrounding the **detonation point** should have sufficient residue to allow identification of the explosive. The entire area must be searched systematically to recover any trace of a detonating mechanism. Particles of explosives will be embedded in the pipe cap or threads of a pipe bomb. All

materials gathered from the site of an explosion must be packaged in separate containers and labeled with all pertinent information (International Association of Arson Investigators, 2012).

Many manufacturers of dynamite include magnetic **microtaggants** in each stick. These fluorescent, color-coded, multilayered particles identify the residue as dynamite and indicate the source of manufacture. The color should make the taggants visible to ultraviolet light, and their magnetism should make them susceptible to a magnet. Electric shunts from blasting caps, clock mechanisms, batteries, and pieces of wrapper may survive the explosion and concomitant fire. In those instances where humans have been the victims of a vessel fire, their remains should be bagged. Their clothing should not be removed (Girard, 2017).

Zones and Perimeters

Multilevel containment is often suggested as a scene preservation and containment method to ensure the integrity of evidence and safety of

microtaggants
Fluorescent, color-coded, multilayered particles that identify a residue as dynamite and indicate the source of manufacture

detonation point
Location where an explosive was detonated

INVESTIGATOR'S NOTEBOOK

© Shutterstock, Inc./Janaka Dharmasena.

Microtaggant™ by Microtrace

According to their website, Microtrace "provides identification, authentication and security solutions to companies and organizations worldwide, including foreign and domestic government agencies."

"Taggants are microscopic or nano-materials that are uniquely encoded and virtually impossible to duplicate—like a fingerprint. They can be incorporated into or applied to a wide variety of materials, surfaces, products and solutions." (*http://microtracesolutions.com/taggant-technologies/*)

"First engineered by 3M, the Microtaggant was originally developed for the postdetonation tracing of explosives." Microtrace has since refined the technology to make use of it in a dearth of applications.

"The Microtaggant Identification Particle is a microscopic, traceable, anti-counterfeit and identification technology."

Microtaggant Characteristics:

- Each coded particle is made of multiple colored layers which form a unique numeric code sequence (millions of code sequences available).
- Inert plastic material that is chemically and thermally stable.
- Pattern recognition can be utilized to create a unique "fingerprint" on each individual item that cannot be duplicated.

Reading/Detecting Microtaggants

- Undetectable to the untrained/unaided eye
- UV light can trigger a fluorescent response
- Can be detected with a handheld audible detector
- Can be read and identified through the use of a microscope

Source: Secure your future: Microtaggant Security Inks. Retrieved from http://www.flintgrp.com/en/documents/Packaging-and-Narrowweb/Narrowweb/Flint_Group_external_flyer_revised.pdf

© Shutterstock, Inc./Nutink.

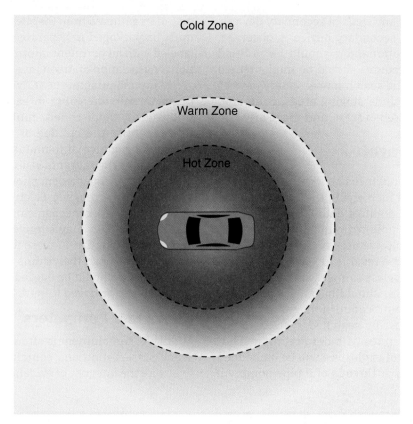

FIGURE 13.11: Example of multizone containment used in explosive investigations.

Courtesy of Nick Vesper.

personnel. The investigation and processing of a postdetonation incident is one that certainly calls for such a methodology to be employed. In such an instance, there will be the establishment of three specific zones within what will be considered the crime scene. These are broken down into hot, warm, and cold zones (**FIGURE 13.11**).

■ Hot Zone

The hot zone includes the area that encompasses significant structural collapse or damage and extends to the point where a person would be relatively safe from blast, fragmentation, or shrapnel from secondary devices, if they should prove to be present in the same location as the original device. This area can differ significantly in size and will shrink as the threat of secondary devices diminishes. The only personnel authorized in the area are first responders who have been trained and equipped to operate in the high-hazard environment and have a legitimate need to be in the area. This group includes firefighters and emergency medical personnel conducting rescue operations, bomb technicians, and specially trained law enforcement officers.

■ Warm Zone

The diameter (Y) of the warm zone is determined by identifying the distance from the seat of the explosion (or ground zero) to the farthest point where evidence can be visually identified (X), then adding half that distance (50% of X) (**FIGURE 13.12**). The formula is:

$$X + .50X = Y$$

■ Cold Zone

The cold zone encompasses the area required for the command post, staging areas, temporary morgue, and a designated area for victims' families. This special area for victims' families is typically used to discourage family members from trying to approach the target to assist in rescue operations or attempt to obtain information concerning their loved ones.

Relevant Case Law

Under what circumstances may investigators enter a building after a fire in the building has been extinguished? How long may they remain on the premises? How often may they return? What can be taken from the scene? These and other questions were

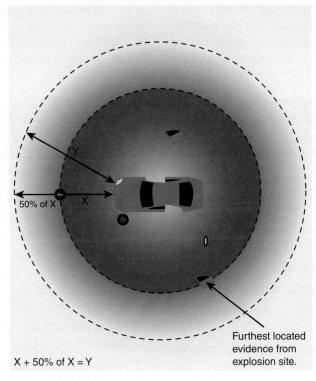

50% of X

X

Y

Furthest located evidence from explosion site.

X + 50% of X = Y

FIGURE 13.12: Example of how to calculate warm zone diameter.

Courtesy of Nick Vesper.

answered by the U.S. Supreme Court's decision in *Michigan v. Tyler* (1978):

> *Prompt determination of a fire's origin may be necessary to prevent its recurrence. Immediate investigation may also be necessary to preserve evidence from intentional or accidental destruction. The sooner that officials finish their duties, the less subsequent interference there will be in the privacy and recovery efforts of the victims. Officials need no warrant to remain in a building for a reasonable time to investigate the cause of a blaze after it has been extinguished. If the warrantless entry to put out the fire and determine its cause is constitutional, the warrantless seizure of evidence while inspecting the premises for these purposes also is constitutional.... In determining what constitutes a reasonable time to investigate, appropriate recognition must be given to the exigencies that confront officials serving under these conditions, as well as to individuals' reasonable expectations of privacy (p. 502).*

The Supreme Court used the terms *immediate* and *prompt* in describing the needs of investigators in examining the burnt premises. That language suggests that the examination should be conducted as soon as it is safe to enter the premises. Investigators may remain on the premises as long as is necessary to determine whether there is a possibility of the fire rekindling and to discover the cause of the fire. The court said that investigators can "remain in the building," which suggests that the investigation is an integral part of the firefighting effort. Their remaining in the building can only be for a "reasonable time"—the time necessary to complete the examination.

It appears from the language of this case that the examination of the premises must be conducted concomitantly with the extinguishing of the fire and its aftermath. Any subsequent visits must be accompanied by a warrant. During the initial examination, however, the investigators can take any evidence that they find.

CONCLUSION

Arson is a crime that is difficult to prevent and to investigate. Arson investigators need to know as much about fires as they do about

investigation and law enforcement. The investigator does not need to be a firefighter; however, a basic understanding of firefighting techniques will aid investigators in the interpretation of a fire scene. Fire and explosive scenes must be approached in the same, methodical manner as all other crime scenes. The crime scene investigator should approach the fire scene or scene of an explosion as though it were a criminal event and allow the physical evidence found to point them in the direction of classifying the fire or explosion as intentional, accident, or an act of God.

QUESTIONS FOR REVIEW

1. What distinguishes simple arson from aggravated arson?
2. How are igniters and delay devices used in arsons?
3. What makes something burn?
4. What is the value of smoke color and odor to the arson investigator?
5. How does spontaneous combustion occur?
6. What kinds of evidence are available to the arson investigator?
7. How does an arsonist's motive assist in an arson investigation?
8. What are the most common motives for arson?
9. What is a masking fire?
10. What is a pyromaniac, and what is the serial killer trilogy?
11. What are streamers used for?
12. Where does the arson investigation begin?
13. What is the significance of the point of origin of the fire?
14. Why is it necessary to provide the laboratory with a background sample from the fire?
15. Why do fire departments investigate boat arsons?
16. What is an alligator pattern, and what is its significance to an arson investigator?
17. What is the difference between a high-order and low-order explosive?
18. What service does the American Insurance Association provide arson investigators?
19. What is the detonation point?
20. What are microtaggants?

REFERENCES

Beveridge, A. (2011). *Forensic investigation of explosions* (2nd ed.). Boca Raton, FL: CRC Press.

Bolz, F., Dudonis, K. J., & Schulz, D. P. (2011). *The counterterrorism handbook: tactics, procedures, and techniques* (4th ed.). Boca Raton, FL: CRC Press.

Chandler, R. K. (2009). *Fire investigation.* Clifton Park, NY: Delmar.

Department of Homeland Security. (2008). *Incident response to terrorist bombings.* Washington, DC: U.S. Government Printing Office.

Department of Homeland Security. (2002). *Arson detection for the first responder: ADFR-student manual.* Washington, DC: U.S. Government Printing Office.

Federal Bureau of Investigation. (2015). *Uniform crime reports.* Washington, DC: U.S. Department of Justice.

Federal Bureau of Investigation. (2015). *Crime in the United States.* Washington, DC: U.S. Department of Justice.

Girard, J. E. (2017). *Criminalistics: Forensic science, crime and terrorism* (4th ed.). Burlington, MA: Jones & Bartlett Learning.

International Association of Arson Investigators. (2012). *Fire investigator: Principles and practice to NFPA 921 and 1033.* Sudbury, MA: Jones & Bartlett Learning.

Kolko, D. J. (2002). *Handbook on presetting in children and youth.* San Diego, CA: Academic Press.

Magnuson, E. (1990, April 9). "The devil made him do it." *Time*, 38.

Myers, A. L. (2012). Suicide by poison suspected in courtroom death. *Associated Press.* Retrieved July 6, 2012, from http://www.kmov.com /news/national/Suicide-by-poison-suspected -in-courtroom-death160971445.html

Saferstein, R. (2014). *Criminalistics: An introduction to forensic science* (11th ed.). Upper Saddle River, NJ: Prentice Hall.

KEY LEGAL CASE

Michigan v. Tyler, 436 U.S. 499 (1978).

Computer Crime and Digital Evidence

chapter 14

KEY TERMS

contraband

identity theft

independent
component doctrine

instrumentality

limiting phrase

off-site computer

phishing

utility software

> "Computers can figure out all kinds of problems, except the things in the world that just don't add up."
>
> Isaac Asimov

STUDENT LEARNING OUTCOMES

Upon completion of this chapter, students will be able to:

- Describe the basic steps involved in a computer investigation

- Appreciate the requirements of a legally valid search warrant for computers and related material

- Recognize proper steps for seizing and handling electronic evidence

- Identify how someone's identity can be stolen

- Understand how GPS technology can aid law enforcement with conducting investigations

- Understanding how social media plays a role in criminal investigations and evidence collection

Introduction to Computer Crimes and Digital Evidence

More and more frequently, computers and other digital devices are being used as a component of criminal activity, and when such devices are found at a crime scene, they should be regarded as a possible source of evidence. While the majority of agencies and departments cannot afford to train or equip personnel to specialize in the processing and analysis of digital evidence, it is important for a crime scene investigator to have basic knowledge of the forensic potential of digital evidence and how to proceed when confronted with such evidence. However, if, at any point, the investigator is unsure of the correct steps to take, a knowledgeable professional should be contacted.

Computers are being used to store records of drug transactions, money laundering, child pornography, prostitution, and many other criminal activities. The information presented in this chapter refers specifically to standalone digital components and computers. If the crime scene investigator suspects that a network, mainframe, or some other type of system may be involved, a computer specialist should be consulted prior to disturbing or seizing any of the components. Computer technology is constantly changing, and seizure methods may change in the future. Therefore, if the crime scene investigator has any questions, he or she should contact the forensic laboratory for technical assistance.

Computer crimes exceed our capacity to investigate them for a number of reasons. First, computer crimes are seldom discovered until after the fact. Accomplished computer criminals are capable of using computers to their financial advantage and disappearing before the crime comes to the attention of the victim and the police. In most instances, it is a question of recreating the crime to discover any clues that might lead to the identity or whereabouts of the perpetrator. Computers allow criminals to commit crimes for larger sums than traditional crimes with less risk of being caught. The proceeds from a typical computer crime far exceed what the average burglar or robber might obtain.

The computer criminals who are most often caught are habitual criminals who are not seeking financial gain and who persist in the use of their computers in illegal activity. The most commonly caught computer criminals are those trafficking in child pornography. The success of catching them depends on the fact that the perpetrator will continue until caught. The

jurisdiction for these crimes is federal, and protocols, tools, and expertise have been developed to ensure arrest, prosecution, and conviction of the perpetrator. The U.S. Code defines what constitutes a computer crime and provides the penalty for the offense in Title 18, Section 1030. The statute provides a definition but no investigative guidelines pertaining to the detection of computer crime or its investigation.

Computer Investigations

Computer investigations involve physical evidence and logical evidence. The key to the investigation is the appropriate seizure of both. Seizing physical evidence is by far the easier of the two but is still complex.

The major tool for investigators is the same as for any type of criminal investigator: the search warrant. Problems arising from search and seizure issues as they pertain to computers extend beyond the Fourth Amendment to embrace the free-speech and free-press guarantees contained in the First Amendment. The foundation upon which all searches and seizures are based is the "reasonableness" of police behavior. A search and seizure conducted within the parameters of a valid warrant is presumed reasonable. Conversely, any search and seizure conducted without the benefit of a warrant is presumed unreasonable (until proven otherwise). Warrant validity is based on the existence of probable cause as sufficiently stated in the affidavit supporting the warrant (particularity).

Criminal Use of Digital Equipment

The United States Department of Justice (USDOJ) categorizes computers that are used in a criminal manner in one of three ways: contraband, instrumentality, or "mere" evidence (NIJ, 2008). If a digital device is found to be illegally possessed or, for some legal reason, is illegal to possess, it is considered **contraband**. If a device, system, or its associated hardware played a significant role in the commission of a crime, it is considered an item of **instrumentality**. Any system or device that is termed "mere" evidence is often not seized, but instead, the goal is acquiring the data that are of evidentiary value from the device, while adhering to computer forensic principles. However, before this is done, it is important to first examine the manner in which crime scene investigators and first responders should treat digital evidence.

What follows is information assembled by the USDOJ's National Institute of Justice (NIJ)

contraband
An item that is found to be illegally possessed or for some legal reasons is illegal to possess

instrumentality
A device, system or its associated hardware playing a significant role in the commission of a crime

in a special report called *Electronic Crime Scene Investigation: A Guide for First Responders, Second Edition* (2008).

Computer Particularity and Probable Cause

When computers are the subjects of warrants, the areas of particularity and probable cause create new headaches for police investigators. Most computer investigations will be the result of considerable intelligence gathering and analysis.

Computer criminals must use devices that allow them access to other computers and databases. It is necessary to determine the computer's role in the alleged crime in order to meet probable cause requirements for a search and/or seizure. The computer's role will determine if the machine itself is to be seized or simply searched onsite. It will also determine whether the peripherals (printer, modem, keyboard, etc.) are to be seized or searched onsite. The determination of these issues can only be made based on extensive information about the crime that has been committed and the way that it was committed. That information will establish the probable cause upon which the investigator may act.

A probable cause affidavit must contain statements to the effect that:

1. A crime has been committed.

2. Evidence of a crime exists.

3. The evidence of the crime can be found at the search site.

It is the second probable cause element that requires investigators to know the exact role that the computer played in the commission of the offense. If the computer was used as a tool to commit a crime, probable cause would justify the seizure of the entire computer system and allow a subsequent search of the system at the crime laboratory. If the computer was used simply to store information of a criminal offense, probable cause would be established to seize data records (printouts) from the computer. In order to establish probable cause to seize both the computer system and its data records, the police have to show that the computer was used to commit the criminal offense and that data pertaining to that offense (or others) were contained in the computer. In other words, there must be an affirmative link between the items listed to be seized and the criminal activity alleged. Absent an identified link, the system seizure or the data seizure may be suppressed.

Warrant Particularity

Under the Fourth Amendment, a valid warrant must "particularly describe the place to be searched and the persons or things to be seized." When dealing with an online computer system, it is not always possible to determine exactly what type of computer system was used to commit the crime or store evidence of it. The police must describe the computer system as precisely as the facts allow. In many cases, they may only be able to state that the criminal used some type of computer, keyboard, monitor, and means of connection to other computers, servers, Internet service providers, or any other details available. A "particular" search and seizure cannot be conducted by an investigator who does not understand the basics of computer technology and how that technology is normally applied.

What separates computer data records from other records is the form in which computer records may be found. They could be stored electronically on a hard drive (which can be inside the computer or external), on optical or magnetic disks, on tapes, or on CDs or DVDs, flash drives, servers, or other types of hardware. However, it is the information sought that must be particularly described, not necessarily the form in which it exists. If the records sought are described clearly, the simple addition to the search warrant affidavit of the statement that the records sought may be written or electronic should allow seizure of the records regardless of their form. If the investigator has only general information about the records sought, the warrant must include a **limiting phrase** to help separate the information to be seized from information that may be legally permissible to possess. The limiting phrase may contain language that describes the information sought in general terms, with the added constraints of a particular timeframe, author, or subject matter. It is vital that the limiting phrase restrict the scope of the search so that it remains within the boundaries of probable cause set forth in the affidavit.

Computers and the First Amendment

Under the First Amendment, citizens of the United States enjoy freedom of speech and freedom of the press. When searching and seizing an online computer system, investigators can view the system as not merely a data repository but a "publishing and distribution operation" (Casey, 2011). While a search and

limiting phrase
Phrase in a warrant that helps separate the information to be seized from information that may be legally permissible to possess

seizure of a computer used for data storage may only involve Fourth Amendment issues, a search and seizure of an online computer system might also involve the protections of the First Amendment. If a suspect is using a computer to download (transfer information from one computer to another) illegal pornography, the First Amendment will not provide a defense against a charge of possession of the illegal material. If the host (sending computer) is targeted by the investigators, however, their attempts to search and seize that system will be met with First Amendment challenges. Obviously, illegal pornography is not protected speech or press under the First Amendment, but other items contained in the host computer may be. Seizing the host computer system and all of its contents may involve the seizure of constitutionally protected items.

Conducting the Search and Seizure

The investigative team that carries out the physical search and seizure of the online computer system needs to be thoroughly familiar with the special requirements present in an online computer case (see Investigator's Notebook). The investigators may have all of the probable cause that they need and may be familiar with all of the rights and issues involved, but if the execution of the search and seizure is done improperly, the records sought may be destroyed. Traditionally, search warrants have authorized searches for objects that occupy a place in space and time and obey physical laws. But in the world of online computer systems, things are less physical and more virtual (existing in time, not necessarily in space).

Generally, the search team will know where the computer in question resides and, if it is networked, where the other computers are that make up the network. Should a search reveal an online relationship that was not anticipated and indicate that incriminating information is being stored off-site, the team may have to obtain another warrant. If, however, the team is in an office or university building and the second computer is in an adjacent or nearby office of the same building, the initial warrant may have been drafted broadly enough to justify a search of the other computers. Language in the warrant allowing a search and seizure of any evidence that is stored in **off-site computers** that are readily and routinely accessed by the primary computer and serve regularly as components of the primary computer's network will justify extending the search. The warrant language must be supported by statements in the affidavit that establish the probability that unknown off-site computers exist, suggest the location of these computers and describe the alleged link between the primary computer and the off-site computers (U.S. Secret Service, 2006).

off-site computer
Computer that is readily and routinely accessed by the primary computer being searched and serves regularly as a component of the primary computer's network

INVESTIGATOR'S NOTEBOOK

Computer Search Checklist

- Probable cause
- Description of the computer and peripherals to be seized
- Description of the system (networked, bulletin board system, website)
- Description of constitutional issues
- Computer expertise needed
- Storage and examination area
- Nature of the data being sought
- How data are to be distinguished from other protected data
- How data are to be retrieved with minimal damage to the original
- When search will be executed
- How the premises will be secured

The Investigation

It is difficult to assess the costs of computer crime nationwide because there is very little information available regarding the number of computer crimes committed and the losses associated with those crimes. In many instances, the crime is never discovered or discovered so belatedly that all traces of the crime have been erased.

The fast-growing industry of computer crime has required a concomitantly fast-growing computer forensics industry. But it must be kept in mind that those committing computer crimes spend a great deal of time figuring out ways to circumvent existing laws and computer systems. Thieves stay a step or two ahead of the police. Computer forensics deals with the identification, gathering, packaging, and preserving of evidence to ensure that all evidence is admissible at the time of trial. In addition to an understanding of the forensic aspects of computer investigation, the competent investigator must also be able to testify knowledgeably and understandably about every aspect of the investigation. Juries often prefer a simpler, rather than a more complex, theory or explanation. The types of evidence that a computer forensic investigator must deal with live in both the physical and virtual worlds. The physical components involve the computer and peripherals, which are subject to all constitutional restraints pertaining to the search or seizure of the computer and related hardware. The hardware itself is seldom a legal problem, although unplugging it or pressing any key on an unattended computer may result in a command to reformat the drives and destroy any information contained on the hard drive.

The logic part of the investigation involves the extraction of data from the hardware. The evidence to be recovered from the computer must be obtained without making any changes to, damaging, or contaminating the original information. While information is being extracted, a running log has to be maintained that will provide chain-of-custody evidence at the time that the information is introduced at trial. The data sought, the documentation reflecting the search for that data, and the steps taken in its retrieval will, to a great extent, determine its admissibility. Considering the complexity of computer data, the alteration of even a few bits of information may have far-reaching consequences. It is with this consideration in mind that the computer crimes investigator must have the necessary knowledge and tools to get the job done. In order to retrieve data, an investigator must have an understanding of information systems, computer security systems, and system organization and administration. These prerequisite computer skills must be supplemented with experience and creative thinking.

Regardless of how movies and television may depict the retrieval of information from seized computers, data extraction usually takes place in a lab that is clean, quiet, and private. These labs have CD/DVD readers/writers, Ethernet access, backup systems, computers, different operating systems, removable drives, and a variety of storage media. In addition to the basic tools of the computer crime lab, there must be a case management structure and system in place.

Through the management system, each step of the investigation is cataloged along with suspect and victim data. The information retrieved from the seized computer may be so overwhelming that any relationship between persons, places, and things is lost. Only a sorting tool allows us to see relationships, allowing us to further the investigation. The case management software should allow searching, storing, arranging, analyzing, and rendering statistical models as needs dictate.

Gathering and preserving data requires the examination of log files, Internet access, and stored and transmitted data, which may give rise to major problems. An investigator must not alter the original data in efforts to extract them. In most instances, a "mirror image" of all data on a computer is made and the copy is manipulated so that the original computer and data remain unaffected. The basic protocol in handling any evidence is that it be maintained in the same condition as when it was found. Anything done to the evidence while in the custody of the police must be logged on chain-of-custody log sheets, and the evidence must be maintained and available to the defendant for independent defense-testing requests.

The basic rules in dealing with computer investigations are:

- Procure all necessary warrants:
  a. To enter the premises
  b. To seize the computer and peripherals
  c. To examine data

- Do not let anyone access the computer, most particularly anyone who lives on the premises:
  a. Especially police who think they know something about computers
  b. Only a computer forensic specialist should be allowed access

INVESTIGATOR'S NOTEBOOK

Golden Rules of Crime Scenes Involving Digital Evidence

There are questions to ask and general principles to follow when responding to any crime scene in which computers and electronic technology may be involved. Several of those are as follows:

- Officer safety—secure the scene and make it safe
- If you reasonably believe that the computer is involved in the crime that you are investigating, take immediate steps to preserve the evidence
- Do you have a legal basis to seize this computer (plain view, search warrant, consent, etc.)?
- Do not access any computer files. If the computer is off, leave it off. If it is on, do not start searching through the computer.
- If you reasonably believe that the computer is destroying evidence, immediately shut down the computer by pulling the power cord from the back of the computer
- If a camera is available and the computer is on, take pictures of the computer screen. If the computer is off, take pictures of the computer, the location of the computer, and any electronic media attached.
- Do special legal considerations apply (doctor, attorney, clergy, psychiatrist, newspapers, publishers, etc.)?

United States Secret Service. (2007). *Best practices for seizing electronic evidence: A pocket guide for first responders* (Vol. 3). U.S. Department of Homeland Security.

© Shutterstock, Inc./Nutink.

- Do not execute any programs on the computer at the crime scene except those necessary to save data in temporary files or memory
- Do not alter anything contained on or in the computer and peripherals
- Maintain chain-of-custody information for everything seized
- Leave copies of warrants and receipts for everything taken
- Write narrative summaries of all that occurred in the seizure process
- Store all items in a temperature-controlled environment (Kruse & Heiser, 2001)

Computer Experts

Criminal investigators may think that a fellow officer is a computer expert because the officer has a computer and spends a lot of time working with computers. A well-meaning officer who thinks he or she has enough computer knowledge to assist during the search of a computer system can be much more dangerous than an officer who knows he or she is computer illiterate and refrains from assisting in the actual seizure. Seizing a computer is a highly technical endeavor and should be attempted only by those with specific training.

It is not necessary for every member of the search team to understand in detail the process for carrying out the search of a computer system. The individual doing the data searching on the computer will most likely be the computer forensic expert. It is this individual's responsibility to determine the nature of the operating system, and he or she may find it necessary to boot the system (start the computer) with an uncontaminated disk. Using **utility software**, the expert will begin searching through the accumulated data. By using or modifying utility software, the expert can tailor a search to meet the requirements of the search warrant.

Determining What to Seize

Just because investigators have probable cause to seize a computer does not necessarily mean they can seize the entire system. The peripheral items may not be relevant and, therefore, according to the independent component doctrine, not subject to lawful seizure. Each component of the computer system must be examined individually for probable cause elements prior to seizing. The requirements of the **independent component doctrine** are easier to deal with prior to a seizure than afterward.

---

utility software
Software used by a computer expert to begin searching through the accumulated data in a computer

independent component doctrine
Doctrine stating that peripheral items may not be relevant and, therefore, not subject to lawful seizure

CASE IN POINT

United States v. Henson

In this case, investigators searched several used car dealerships, looking for evidence of an odometer roll-back scheme. Among the evidentiary items seized were several computer systems. Because of the volume of evidence listed in the warrant to be seized, the court upheld the seizure of entire systems, including peripherals. The court reasoned that it would have been impractical for investigators to remain onsite at the dealerships for days, searching and sorting through the evidence.

It is a mistake to presume that any item connected to a suspect computer is able to be seized. A network may have thousands of computers connected to each other. A warrant to search and seize the suspect computer would never be construed as allowing a search and seizure of all of the other computers in the network. Just because it is convenient to seize a computer does not mean it is constitutional. Currently, it is acceptable to seize the computer, the monitor, and the keyboard. These are the essentials needed for input and output of data. Any other items seized must be independently addressed in the probable cause affidavit and the warrant. The physical examination of a computer's contents may need to occur off-site. It may take days or weeks to completely examine the computer and the data it contains.

The Search

Controlling the premises in an online computer search is essential for success. Because of the ease with which evidence can be destroyed, the search team must take complete and absolute control of the search site. Once control has been asserted, the computer system's communication links must be broken to prevent remote access and remote destruction of evidence. Even something as simple as disconnecting the computer may have disastrous results when attempted by anyone other than an expert. The key to finding the evidence described in the search warrant is to look in the right places and thoroughly exhaust all possible computer storage areas. In their zeal to access the data inside a computer, investigators should not overlook the possibility of physical fingerprints on the exterior and handwritten notations (which may be passwords).

In addition to hard drives, disks, and CDs, other sites that may harbor data are available only to the knowledgeable and prepared. Trained computer specialists are often able to pull various amounts of data from input and output devices. Print spoolers hold data to be printed, and a print spooler may be holding unprinted data if it were unable to send the data to the printer (because the printer was out of paper, for example, or was turned off before printing). Printer drivers may contain a hard drive that stores information before it is printed and will keep the stored information until its memory limit is reached and it begins to write over the oldest data with new data (National Institute of Justice, 2004).

Whereas most forensic scientists' search and seizure procedures have been honed over the years, computer forensic experts are only beginning to craft widely accepted guidelines to ensure that evidence seized can be admitted at the time of trial. Computer evidence is tough to authenticate in court because it can be altered so easily. The International Association of Computer Investigative Specialists has developed a procedure in which investigators can extract a mirror image of the information in the computer without altering the original, thereby preserving the original to demonstrate that the data retrieved have not been changed.

Besides authentication issues, courts are also grappling with the admissibility of evidence that computer investigators find concerning one crime while searching for evidence of another offense. In traditional searches of a suspect's home, vehicle, business, or files, the police must limit their search to evidence relevant to the crime outlined in the warrant but may also seize evidence of an unrelated crime if it is in plain view. A major question yet to be answered by the courts is whether an investigator can use information against the suspect about an unknown offense that was discovered while searching a computer for information about another offense. Using federal wiretap procedures as an analogy, it would appear prudent to obtain a second warrant for the stumbled-upon offense.

Electronic Evidence

Electronic evidence is information stored or transmitted in a digital format. Prior to its acceptance before a jury, a court must determine:

1. *Relevancy.* Are the materials purported to be on the computer probative of the crime under investigation?

2. *Authentication.* Is there someone associated with the seizure of the evidence who can testify in court that the evidence presented is the same as was originally discovered on the computer?

3. *Hearsay.* Any third-party statements may be inadmissible because they are hearsay.

4. *Originality.* Are the original data contained on the computer required for submission or will a copy suffice?

A commonly occurring problem for law enforcement is courts that rule digital evidence inadmissible because it was obtained without proper authorization. The key to admissibility is a set of written standards and protocols. The U.S. Secret Service (2006) has done just that with the printing of their publication, *Best Practices for Seizing Electronic Evidence;* its "golden rules" for seizing computers include:

1. Secure the scene to make it safe for investigating personnel.

2. Is there a legal basis for seizing the computer (warrant, plain view, consent, etc.)?

3. Do not access computer files.
   a. If the computer is on, leave it on.
      ▪ Do not search for files.
   b. If the computer is off, leave it off.

4. If the computer is destroying evidence, remove the power cord at the computer.

5. If the computer is on, take a photo of the computer screen and peripherals.

6. If the computer is off, take photos of the computer, its location, and any electronic media attached.

7. Do special legal considerations apply (privileged or protected communications)?

8. Are there personnel available to properly package and transport the evidence?

FIGURE 14.1: Electronic storage media.
© ndquang/Shutterstock, Inc.

Storage Media

Storage media store data from other electronic devices. They come in various shapes and sizes (**FIGURE 14.1**). Some storage media have limited storage capabilities compared with other devices, such as external hard drives, which can store as much data as a computer. When seizing storage media:

▪ Seize any and all instructional material accompanying the storage device.

▪ Document all of the steps taken to seize the device as well as its packaging, transportation, delivery, and chain of custody.

▪ It is important when handling data storage devices to keep them away from magnets, radio transmitters, or anything that contains either. (U.S. Secret Service, 2006)

Tablets, Cell Phones, and Digital Cameras

Tablets, cell phones, and digital cameras store data directly to internal memory or may contain removable data storage devices or memory chips (**FIGURE 14.2**). The U.S. Secret Service (2006) recommends that the proper seizure and preservation of these devices should include the following protocols:

▪ If the device is off, leave it off.

▪ If the tablet or cell phone is on, it should not be shut down. The device may be password protected, and powering it down will lose access to the data it may contain.

▪ Photograph the item to be seized and any visible screen display.

▪ Label and collect all cables, rechargers, and power cords.

▪ Keep the device charged; analysis can only be conducted if the battery does not run down.

FIGURE 14.2: Examples of digital devices.

© Serts/iStock Unreleased/Getty Images.

- Seize any data storage media associated with the device seized (flash drives, memory chips, etc.).
- Document all of the steps taken in the seizure of the device and any components taken.

Applicable Case Law

The U.S. Supreme Court, in *Andresen v. Maryland* (1976), determined that under certain circumstances it is reasonable to expect that computer records seen 3 months previously would still be present at the location in which they were observed. The U.S. Court of Appeals, in *Application of Lafayette Academy, Inc.* (1979), ruled that the limiting phrase used to circumscribe the computer records that could be seized was insufficiently narrow.

Messages sent back and forth via computer (email) are stored until deleted. If a stored electronic message is less than 180 days old, police must obtain a warrant to search for and seize the message. Once the message has been stored for longer than 180 days, an administrative subpoena and advance notice given to the parties involved are all that are needed to search for and seize the communication. The U.S. Court of Appeals, in *Steve Jackson Games, Inc. v. United States Secret Service* (1979), determined that if a message has been sent but has not been read, the message is a stored message rather than a communication in transmission, and

— Ripped from the Headlines —

iPhone Yields Forensic Evidence in Trial of Dr. Conrad Murray

In the trial of Dr. Conrad Murray, Michael Jackson's attending physician at the time of his death, prosecutors called upon Drug Enforcement Agency (DEA) computer forensic expert Stephen Marx to examine and analyze data contained within Murray's cell phone to find potential evidence to explain the pop icon's death. Marx was able to extract information from the doctor's iPhone, including a recording of Jackson speaking in a slow and slurred manner. There were also digital medical charts, emails, and documentation of extended nonurgent phone calls placed prior to and after Jackson's death, which all contributed to Murray eventually being found guilty of manslaughter in the wrongful death of Michael Jackson.

Information from Gardner, D. (2011). Jury shown photos of child-sized porcelain doll found in bed with Michael Jackson when he died. Retrieved on October 2, 2012, from http://www.dailymail.co.uk /news/article-2045737/Conrad-Murray-trial -Michael-Jacsons-doll-drug-stash-shown-jurors .html

© Shutterstock, Inc./rzarek.

thus, a subpoena will allow examination of the message.

In *Michigan v. Summers* (1981), the U.S. Supreme Court determined that a warrant to search for certain items carries with it the power to detain individuals found on the premises until the search has been completed.

Cell Phones and Global Positioning Systems

There is yet another area of digital evidence that proves useful from an investigatory side, in a processing manner, and as a public service as well. Global positioning system (GPS) devices are available as handheld devices and are even included in most phones and PDAs. GPS technology can be utilized to document crime scenes; however, with the improvement of and increased access to GPS technology, law enforcement also has the resources to track individuals, corroborate information, and from a crime scene aspect, map and sketch large scenes.

Cell phone technology has become important in criminal investigations as people are relying more upon their phones for conducting business and personal activities, whether legal or illegal.

GPS built into cell phones allows authorities to track criminals and people in need of help. Every time a cell phone is turned on it sends a registration message, including the serial and phone numbers, to the closest cellular tower. A tower receives signals from cell phones on all sides of it. The tower then divides the area around it into three equal sectors. A GPS locator pinpoints the sector where the phone is calling. There are over 200,000 cellular towers placed across the United States.

Due to this technology, dispatchers can often deploy searchers within 100 feet of the caller's location, even if the caller is unable to ascertain his or her current position. If a caller makes use of an older phone without GPS, searchers can narrow down the caller's location by using three towers to triangulate a phone's last known spot by measuring the time that it takes signals to reach the towers. Law enforcement has three options for locating a person through his or her cell phone, depending on the scenario:

1. Single cell tower search
2. GPS tracking
3. Cell tower triangulation

Most phones cand digital devices allow the user to manually turn off the GPS feature; however, the device will automatically activate the GPS when a call is placed to 911.

Some ways that law enforcement currently makes use of GPS technology are as follows:

- Stolen cars that are equipped with GPS can be tracked and recovered. Instead of being involved in a police pursuit, which can create a greater risk to the public, a stolen vehicle can be located by law enforcement through the use of GPS technology. Once the stolen vehicle has reached a destination where law enforcement deems it is safe, those in the vehicle can be apprehended in a safer manner.

- Many jurisdictions have begun to use GPS bracelets on parolees as a way of monitoring their whereabouts. This technology can also be used to investigate and enforce restraining orders through a similar method of having offenders fitted with a GPS bracelet.

- In recent times, law enforcement has made use of GPS-equipped vehicles and other items as bait in law enforcement sting operations, particularly with regard to investigating stolen vehicle crime rings and also construction site equipment thefts.

Tracking Technology

A quick search of the Internet will yield hundreds of sites and devices that can enable someone to track a person or object through the use of GPS technology. Some of these devices are small enough to fit in purses, vehicles, or even small electronic items. Some have the purpose of legitimately tracking shipments, items, vehicles, or persons. Others, however, can be used for criminal purposes, including stalking.

The courts are somewhat split on whether or not such planting of GPS equipment is an invasion of the 4th Amendment right to privacy. A 2009 ruling in the state of Wisconsin stated that GPS technology was simply another method of documenting the movement of a vehicle on a public roadway, rather than use personal observation, which would have otherwise been legal, and; therefore, a search warrant was not a requirement (Foley, 2009). During the same year, a court in the state of New York ruled that law enforcement must obtain a search warrant before such GPS tracking can occur (Chan, 2009). Hence, the district attorney of the jurisdiction in question should be contacted prior to implementing the use of GPS technology for investigatory purposes, such as tracking movement.

— Ripped from the Headlines —

Man Charged with Stalking Using GPS

The *Wisconsin State Journal* ran an article on February 15, 2008, reporting that the husband of a Madison, Wisconsin, police officer had been charged with four felonies after he had secretly placed a GPS tracker in his wife's car and had used her name and password to access the police department's computer system.

The case involved the husband tracking the movements of his police wife as she was involved with an extramarital affair with another officer with whom she worked. At one point, she told her lover that she believed that she was being followed by her husband and he suggested that perhaps her husband had placed a GPS tracking device within her car. The two searched her car and located such a device.

The use of digital technology to track his wife's whereabouts went deeper yet. After the stalking behavior was reported to law enforcement, police searched the husband's home computer and his computer at his place of employment. The home computer was found to contain key tracking software that allowed the husband to identify his wife's login identity and password, and for him to then access the Madison Police Department's scheduling system that contained work and vacation schedules. On his work computer, police found evidence that the husband had accessed his wife's personal emails and printed communications between the wife and her law enforcement lover.

The husband was eventually found guilty of three felony counts of stalking and identity theft. As a side note, infidelity is a moral offense in the state of Wisconsin, with no criminal penalty.

Information retrieved from Singletary, K. (2008, February 15). Man is charged with stalking. He's accused of putting a GPS device in the car of his estranged wife. *Wisconsin State Journal*.

© Shutterstock, Inc./rzarek.

There is also the possibility of utilizing geographic information systems (GIS) to map criminal movement and activities. Most wireless phones have GIS technology embedded, which further adds to the ease of tracking movements. Again, it is suggested that prior to using such evidence, the district attorney be notified to see if a search warrant is a requirement or not.

Social Media

Increasingly, individuals are uploading, sending, posting, and sharing information that may find itself useful in a subsequent investigation. Whether that includes texts associated with deflating footballs, Facebook posts referring to an impending lone wolf terrorist activity, or selfie photos documenting the event, there remains the possibility that a third party collected, saved, and archived the information.

While it will likely not fall within the job function of a crime scene investigator to collect digital evidence associated with social media use and content, it is important to discuss the role and possibilities where social media are concerned within modern investigations.

It is typically left up to investigators to be the ones to create fake social media profiles and lurk within chat rooms or surf and interact with those partaking in online criminal activity. It is further left to digital forensic personnel to extract and analyze associated data. However, crime-scene personnel must be aware of devices to be collected, which could likely be associated with criminal wrongdoing.

Recognizing the necessity to collect individuals' smartphones, tablets, computers, smartwatches, and other digital devices as possible instruments of criminal activity is a necessity in modern criminal investigations. The potential for critical evidence loss exists if these items are overlooked or not properly considered within the context of the investigative process. Identifying the names of others involved, establishing timelines, identifying activity and preference patterns, and, in general, making the necessary links between persons, places, and things quite often reside within the digital information held by an individual's digital media components.

Identity Theft

Identity theft and identity fraud are terms used to refer to all types of crime in which someone wrongfully obtains and uses another person's personal data in some way that involves fraud or deception, typically for economic gain. Unlike fingerprints, which are unique and cannot be

identity theft
Type of crime in which someone wrongfully obtains and uses another person's personal data in some way that involves fraud or deception, typically for economic gain

— Ripped from the Headlines —

You Think Your Facebook Profile Is Private?

In July of 2015, a New York state appeals court ruled that Facebook could not protect its 1.5 billion users from warrants obtained by law enforcement to gain access to users' digital information. The ruling stemmed from a large social security fraud investigation, for which investigators had issued 381 warrants seeking access to users' profile information; however, the ruling ultimately impacts every one of the 1.5 billion users of Facebook. At the center of the argument is how long the government is able to keep the accessed information. In the case of the social security investigation, of the 381 persons whose accounts were accessed with the approved warrants, only 62 were charged in the case. However, the remaining 300 plus individuals' account information appears to be able to be held by the government for an unlimited amount of time, all without informing the people whose accounts were subject to the search and seizure. The collected information included photos, private messages, and personal profile information.

This is not the first instance of social media being a collection point for information tied to a criminal event. In 2014, a federal judge in New Jersey issued a ruling that law enforcement could create fake profiles in order to search through a suspect's social media account.

In 2012, a federal judge in New York ruled that a gang member who was alleged to have shared incriminating information online lost his claims to privacy when he shared that information on social media, and, subsequently, individuals who viewed the posts then shared it with law enforcement.

The message appears to be that social media is not a safe-haven and that it is, in fact, a public, or just barely semi-private, domain. Consider this the next time you consider uploading personal information or photos…

Information from Alroy, T. T. (2015). Facebook loses appeal over access to user data. *CNN.* Retrieved July 23, 2015, from http://www.cnn.com/2015/07/23/tech/facebook-search-warrants/index.html

© Shutterstock, Inc./rzarek.

given to someone else for his or her use, personal data—especially Social Security numbers, bank account or credit card numbers, telephone calling card numbers, and other valuable identifying data—can, if they fall into the wrong hands, be used for personal profit at the owner's expense.

In the United States and Canada, many people have reported that unauthorized persons have taken funds out of their bank or financial accounts or, in the worst cases, taken over their identities altogether, running up vast debts and committing crimes while using the victims' names. In many cases, a victim's losses may include not only out-of-pocket financial losses but also substantial additional financial costs associated with trying to restore his or her reputation in the community and correcting erroneous information for which the criminal is responsible.

Many people do not realize how easily criminals can obtain personal data without having to break into someone's home. In public places, criminals may engage in shoulder surfing—watching from a nearby location as the mark punches in his or her telephone calling card number or credit card number—or may listen in while the mark gives his or her credit card number over the telephone to a hotel or rental car company.

Even the area near a person's home or office may not be secure. Some criminals go through garbage cans or communal trash bins to obtain copies of canceled checks, credit card or bank statements, or other records that typically bear the name, address, and even telephone number of the person whose identity they intend to steal. These types of records make it easier for criminals to get control over accounts and assume a mark's identity.

Discarded applications for preapproved credit cards that have not been shredded may result in criminals trying to activate the cards for their use. Some credit card companies have adopted security measures that allow a card recipient to activate a new card only from his or her home telephone number, but this is not yet a universal practice. Also, if mail is delivered to a place where others have ready access to it, criminals may simply intercept and redirect the mail to another location.

In recent years, the Internet has become an appealing place for criminals to obtain identifying data, such as passwords or even banking information. In their haste to explore the exciting features of the Internet, many people

— Ripped from the Headlines —

Hacked at 33,000 Feet

A Qatar Airways flight was made to divert and declare an emergency landing after a domestic disturbance onboard the plane escalated to such a level that flight attendants were unable to control the situation.

The flight was scheduled to fly from Doha to Bali, with no scheduled stopover in India. The cause for the change in travel plans were a result of a wife accessing her husband's phone, while he slept, and discovering evidence that he had been cheating on her. The woman reportedly gained access to her husband's phone by using his own finger to bypass the phones biometric security measure, thereby giving her access to the contents of the phone.

Information from Coffey, H. (2017). Flight diverted after woman discovers her husband is cheating on her. *The Independent*. Retrieved November 7, 2017, from http://www.independent.co.uk/travel/news-and-advice/flight-diverted-wife-husband-cheating-qatar-airways-couple-fight-a8042616.html

© Shutterstock, Inc./rzarek.

respond to spam—unsolicited email that promises them some benefit but requests identifying data—without realizing that, in many cases, the requester has no intention of keeping the promise. Criminals use computer technology to obtain large amounts of personal data. With enough identifying information about an individual, a criminal can take over that individual's identity to conduct a wide range of crimes: for example, false applications for loans and credit cards, fraudulent withdrawals from bank accounts, fraudulent use of telephone calling cards, or obtaining other goods or privileges that the criminal might be denied if he or she were to use his or her real name. If the criminal takes steps to ensure that bills for the falsely obtained credit cards or bank statements showing the unauthorized withdrawals are sent to an address other than the victim's, the victim may not become aware of what is happening until the criminal has already inflicted substantial damage on the victim's assets, credit, and reputation (Biegelman, 2009).

In 1998, Congress passed the Identity Theft and Assumption Deterrence Act. This legislation created a new offense of identity theft and prohibits:

> knowingly transfer[ring] or us[ing], without lawful authority, a means of identification of another person with the intent to commit, or to aid or abet, any unlawful activity that constitutes a violation of Federal law, or that constitutes a felony under any applicable State or local law. (18 U.S.C. A4 1028(a)(7))

Federal prosecutors work with federal investigative agencies, such as the FBI, the U.S. Secret Service, and the U.S. Postal Service to prosecute identity theft and fraud cases.

Phishing is a scam where criminals send messages via the Internet to obtain personal and financial information from unsuspecting victims. Often, the messages will appear to be from government agencies, banks, or other financial institutions. They may even contain a link to the real institution that they are imitating or professing to be a part of. All phone numbers will connect to lines that are answered by the online criminals as though they are legitimate institutional telephone numbers; the criminals responding to calls will attempt to extract personal information sufficient to steal an identity. Once that identity is stolen, access to credit cards and bank funds are available to the thief. Some thieves send emails that appear to be from legitimate businesses, asking to be called at a phone number to update account information or to obtain a refund.

Antivirus software and firewalls can protect from inadvertently accepting unwanted files, but nothing can protect against voluntary disclosures of personal information. Antivirus software scans incoming communications for troublesome files. A firewall blocks all communications from unauthorized sources. It is especially important to utilize a firewall if the Internet is accessed through a broadband connection. Operating systems (like Windows or Linux) or browsers (like Internet Explorer or Firefox) may also offer free software patches to close holes in the system that hackers or phishers could exploit. The key to thwarting phishing is to remember that reputable lending agencies and all government agencies do not solicit personal information via email.

phishing
A scam where criminals send messages via the Internet to obtain personal and financial information from unsuspecting victims

CONCLUSION

We live in a digital world. Nearly all of our daily activities are captured, scheduled, or recorded on a digital device. This technology has enabled society to work more efficiently and has significantly reduced its reliance upon paper products and resources, thus proving more environmentally friendly. There are, however, drawbacks to this digital phenomenon. As with all aspects of life, criminals use this technology to further their activities, requir-ing that law enforcement stay abreast of the latest methods of digital evidence documenta-tion, retrieval, and preservation. Failure to stay current on such matters will result in cases being lost. Computer investigation is a con-stant game of catch-up. A never-ending world of espionage, terror, theft, and vandalism is broadened through computer crime. Beneath the serene surface of the world of computers lie depths of deception.

QUESTIONS FOR REVIEW

1. Why is it important to make a mirror image of all computer data seized?

2. What are the basic rules for computer investigations?

3. In drafting a computer search warrant affi-davit, of what value is a limiting phrase? Provide an example of one.

4. What First Amendment issues may arise during the execution of a computer search warrant?

5. What is a computer hacker?

6. What are hot keys?

7. In the case of searching data on a computer, what issue pertaining to the "plain view" exception to the warrant requirement has yet to be resolved?

8. What is identity theft?

9. How can identity theft be perpetrated?

10. What steps has the federal government taken in an effort to combat identity theft?

11. Is it possible to tell if a document printed by a computer printer was printed by a par-ticular printer? If so, how? If not, why not?

REFERENCES

Alroy, T. T. (2015). Facebook loses appeal over access to user data. *CNN*. Retrieved July 23, 2015, from http://www.cnn.com/2015/07/23/tech/facebook-search-warrants/index.html

Biegelman, M. T. (2009). *Identity theft handbook: Detection, prevention and security.* Hoboken, NJ: John Wiley.

Casey, E. (2011). *Digital evidence and computer crime: Forensic science, computers and the Internet.* Waltham, MA: Elsevier.

Chan, S. (2009, May 12). Police used GPS ille-gally, court rules. *New York Times.* Retrieved August 19, 2009, from http://www.nytimes.com/2009/05/13/nyregion/13gps.html

Coffey, H. (2017). Flight diverted after woman dis-covers her husband is cheating on her. *The Independent.* Retrieved November 7, 2017, from http://www.independent.co.uk/travel/news-and-advice/flight-diverted-wife-husband-cheating-qatar-airways-couple-fight-a8042616.html

Foley, R. J. (2009, May 7). Wisconsin court upholds GPS tracking by police. *Chicago Tribune.* Retrieved October 2, 2012, from http://geodatapolicy.word press.com/2009/05/15/

Gardner, D. (2011). Jury shown photos of child-sized porcelain doll found in bed with Michael Jackson when he died. *The Daily Mail Online.* Retrieved October 2, 2012, from http://www.dailymail.co.uk/news/article-2045737/Conrad-Murray-trial-Michael-Jacksons-doll-drug-stash-shown-jurors.html

Hosmer, C., & Hyde, C. (2003). *Discovering covert digital evidence.* Paper presented at the Digi-tal Forensic Research Workshop, August 6. Retrieved September 26, 2011, from http://www.dfrws.org/2003/presentations/Paper-Hosmer-digitalevidence.pdf

Kruse, W. G., & Heiser, J. G. (2001). *Computer forensics: Incident response essentials.* Boston, MA: Addison-Wesley.

Maras, M. H. (2014). *Computer forensics: Cybercriminals, laws and evidence* (2nd ed.). Burlington, MA: Jones & Bartlett Learning.

National Institute of Justice. (2004). *Technical working group for the examination of digital evidence, forensic examination of digital evidence: A guide for law enforcement.* Washington, DC: National Institute of Justice.

National Institute of Justice (NIJ). (2008, April). *Electronic crime scene investigation: A guide for first responders* (2nd ed.). Retrieved October 2, 2012, from http://www.nij.gov/pubs-sum/219941.htm

Singletary, K. (2008, February 15). Man is charged with stalking. He's accused of putting a GPS device in the car of his estranged wife. *Wisconsin State Journal.* Retrieved October 2, 2012, from http://host.madison.com/news/local/article _abf0e2e6-15ba-5813-8bb6-b775b8d53257 .html

United States Secret Service. (2007). *Best practices for seizing electronic evidence: A pocket guide for first responders* (Vol. 3). Washington, DC: U.S. Department of Homeland Security.

KEY LEGAL CASES

Andresen v. Maryland, 427 U.S. 463 (1976).

Application of Lafayette Academy, Inc., 610 F.2d 1 (1st Cir. 1979).

Identity Theft and Assumption Deterrence Act, 18 U.S.C. A4 1028(a)(7).

Michigan v. Summers, 452 U.S. 692 (1981).

Steve Jackson Games, Inc. v. United States Secret Service, 36 F.3d 457 (1979).

United States v. Henson, 848 F.2d 1374 (6th Cir. 1988).

chapter 15

Terrorism and Homeland Security

"*There is no priority higher than the prevention of terrorism.*"

John Ashcroft

KEY TERMS

biological weapons (BW)

cell

chemical weapons

domestic terrorism

international terrorism

joint terrorism task forces

lone-wolf

nuclear terrorism

nuclear threat

sleeper cell

state-sponsored terrorism

technological terrorism

transient cell

transnational terrorism

weapons of mass destruction (WMD)

STUDENT LEARNING OUTCOMES

Upon completion of this chapter, students will be able to:

- Recognize what terrorists want
- Discuss the weapons used by terrorists
- Identify the tools available to the terrorism investigator

Introduction

As a result of the September 11th experience and in anticipation of future acts of terrorism, the President of the United States created a new cabinet-level department, the Department of Homeland Security. The role of the office is to bring together all of the government's antiterrorism resources under one head.

The National Terrorism Advisory System (NTAS) is a product of the Department of Homeland Security. Based on intelligence gathered by various federal agencies, the nation is kept abreast of terroristic threats through threat alerts. These alerts will include a statement that there is an imminent threat or elevated threat of a terroristic event. Using available information, the alerts provide:

- A summary of the threat
- Information about actions being taken to ensure public safety
- Recommended steps that individuals, communities, businesses, and governments can take to prevent, mitigate, or respond to the threat

Bombings at the World Trade Center in 1993, the Alfred P. Murrah Federal Building in Oklahoma City in 1995, and the World Trade Center and Pentagon in 2001 awakened the United States to the realities of foreign and domestic terrorism. Prior to these incidents, the United States had rested comfortably on the belief that terrorism was a phenomenon that occurred elsewhere. The arrival of terrorism on our shores was greeted with a variety of responses, and little in the law enforcement inventory existed to deal with it. We have had to learn. The FBI has become the investigative branch responsible for terrorism committed in the United States, although the first responders to a terroristic act will be the local police. The initial response will either advance the investigation and resolution of the crime or it will retard it, depending on what the local agency knows about terrorism and hostage negotiations.

The FBI divides terrorism into two major groups:

- *Domestic terrorism* involves two or more people with the intent to commit a terrorist act against the U.S. government or the American people. Three subdivisions of this group are:
  - Animal rights groups
  - Ecological groups
  - Racial supremacy groups
- *International terrorism* involves terrorism aimed at the United States directed by a foreign government or foreign leader

— Ripped from the Headlines —

JTTFs

The FBI's Joint Terrorism Task Forces (JTTFs) [**FIGURE A**] are the United States' front line on combating terrorism. According to the FBI: "JTTFs provide one-stop shopping for information regarding terrorist activities. They enable a shared intelligence base across many agencies. They create familiarity among investigators and managers before a crisis. And perhaps most importantly, they pool talents, skills, and knowledge from across the law enforcement and intelligence communities into a single team that responds together.

JTTFs have been instrumental in breaking up cells like the "Portland Seven," the "Lackawanna Six," and the Northern Virginia jihad. They have foiled attacks on the Fort Dix Army base in New Jersey, on the JFK International Airport in New York, and on various military and civilian targets in Los Angeles. They have traced sources of terrorist funding, responded to anthrax threats, halted the use of fake IDs, and quickly arrested suspicious characters with all kinds of deadly weapons and explosives. Chances are, if you hear about a counterterrorism investigation, JTTFs are playing an active and often decisive role.

The task forces coordinate their efforts largely through the interagency National Joint Terrorism Task Force, working out of FBI Headquarters, which makes sure that

FIGURE A: FBI Joint Terrorism Task Force emblem.
Courtesy of the FBI.

information and intelligence flows freely among the local JTTFs and beyond."

Information from https://www.fbi.gov/investigate/terrorism/joint-terrorism-task-forces, accessed June 30, 2017.

© Shutterstock, Inc./rzarek.

sleeper cell
A terrorist cell that comprises individuals who immigrate, establish a residence and an identity, find employment, and await orders

joint terrorism task forces
Interagency cooperation fighting terrorism

transient cell
A group that arrives in a country solely for the purpose of conducting a terroristic act or campaign

lone wolf
A person who acts on his or her own without orders from—or even connections to—an organization

cell
A small cadre of zealots whose members know only each other, not other members of the larger group

The FBI has developed a strong response to the threats posed by domestic and international terrorism. Since 1993, the FBI has doubled its counterterrorism programs. With the latitude allowed by the USA PATRIOT Act (or simply, the Patriot Act), cooperation among law enforcement agencies at all levels represents an important component of a comprehensive response to terrorism. This cooperation assumes its most tangible operational form in the **joint terrorism task forces** (JTTFs) that are now a part of all FBI field divisions. These task forces are well suited to respond to terrorism because they combine the national and international investigative resources of the FBI with the expertise of other federal law enforcement and local law enforcement agencies. The FBI currently has 104 JTTFs nationwide, including one in each of the 56 field offices. Seventy-one of these have been created since 9/11. By integrating the investigative abilities of the FBI with other federal law enforcement and local law enforcement agencies, these task forces represent an effective response to the threats posed to U.S. communities by domestic and international terrorists. Current JTTFs include approximately 4,000 members nationwide—more than four times the pre-9/11 total. Personnel making up the JTTFS hail from over 500 state and local agencies, as well as 55 federal agencies (including the Department of Homeland Security, the U.S. military, Immigration and Customs Enforcement, and the Transportation Security Administration).

Terrorism

In the distant past, international terrorists did not operate in the United States. The distance from lines of supply, unfamiliarity with American geography and language, and a vigilant law enforcement community all militated against attempted terroristic acts. The bombing of the World Trade Center was not the first instance of international terrorism, but it was the one that brought to the world's attention the fact that the United States is vulnerable.

It also allowed an inside look at the structure of a terrorist group. The organizational unit of international terrorist groups is the **cell**, a small cadre of zealots who will sacrifice their lives in furtherance of a religious, political, or social cause. The membership of each cell is small, and its members know only each other, not other members of the larger group, in order to protect the larger group if a member is captured and interrogated.

Terrorist groups are developing two types of operations: one based on sleeper cells and one based on transient cells. A **sleeper cell** comprises individuals who immigrate to a target country (e.g., to the United States), establish a residence and an identity, find employment, and await orders from their overseas comrades in arms to begin terrorist acts or to lay the groundwork for future terrorist acts. They receive money and material from others in the group and may begin stockpiling weapons and explosives in a safe house for use when others in the group arrive. A **transient cell** is a group that arrives in a country solely for the purpose of conducting a terroristic act or campaign. The transient cell will rely on a sleeper cell to provide the logistics for its activities.

Terrorism may also be conducted by individuals, not directly associated with a group, although they are more than likely very highly impacted by or motivated by group activities or teachings. These individuals are typically referred to as **lone wolf** terrorists. If not directly associated with a group, or previously trained or indoctrinated by a group, they are often self-radicalized, taking their information, knowledge, training, motivation, and purpose from on-line materials or published works. A lone wolf terrorist is a person who acts on his or her own without orders from—or even connections to—an organization (Bakker & de Graaf, 2010).

Simply because he or she is not associated with an organized group or cell does not make the lone wolf terrorist non-lethal or lacking concern or attention. However, lone wolf terrorists are extremely difficult for law enforcement to monitor and hinder. The nature of lone wolves—isolated and withdrawn—makes it difficult to proactively gather information about any malicious intentions they might have (Leenaars & Reed, 2016). Lone wolf terrorism is not a new phenomenon, having been identified and actively perpetrated for decades, yet it is much more visible and active within today's society, likely due to the immense and nearly instant media coverage that activities and incidents receive.

Often, lone wolves will distribute manifestos or share their ideas, typically coinciding with the attack, or leave material behind pertaining to their motivation for the attack. This is especially important to consider as a criminal investigator. Searches of social media usage, Internet searches, emails sent and received, and cell phone usage will often be of considerable benefit to the investigation.

A working definition of terrorism can be helpful in determining whether an individual or group's behavior rises to the level of terrorism. We might say that terrorism is the threat of violence, individual acts of violence, or a campaign

— Ripped from the Headlines —

Lone Wolf Terrorism

In October of 2017, Sayfullo Saipov drove a rented truck through a crowd of cyclists, killing eight. In April of 2013, Dzhokhar Tsarnaev and his brother Tamerlan Tsarnaev used improvised explosives to kill three and injure over 280 people at the 2013 Boston Marathon. In November of 2009, Nidal Hasan killed 13 and injured more than 30 in a shooting at Fort Hood.

Each of the aforementioned incidents was the result of carefully planned and conducted attacks by lone wolf terrorists.

While Sayfullo Saipov left behind a note claiming to have conducted his attack "in the name of ISIS," he was not an active operative with ISIS, nor a member of a sleeper cell associated with ISIS. Thus, he was identified as a lone wolf. The other instances were perpetrated for various reasons, but not directly associated with a terrorist organization or entity.

Each of the above incidents, and countless others prior to, and likely since, were nearly impossible to foresee or significantly hinder. But what does it mean to be a "lone wolf"? Scott Stewart and Fred Burton define lone wolf terrorists in a Stratfor Global Intelligence essay as "solitary actors (…) [who] do not work with others. Their motivation—an important part of terrorism—stems from various roots, but these roots can all be categorized as political, ideological or religious" (Stewart and Burton, 2009).

of violence designed primarily to instill fear. In addition to violence for the purpose of instilling fear, there is generally a political component. Most terrorist organizations attempt to further a political agenda.

Absent the political component, gangland extortion and threats would meet the definition of terrorism. Violence for effect is the ultimate objective of the terrorist: not the effect that it has on the victims, but the effect that it has on the society at large. A terrorist act absent the media would affect only the victims and the immediately surrounding area. It is only through the media that such acts are publicized, causing widespread appreciation of their horror. The intended effect is to make the public feel fear and concern.

It is important to remember that the violence wrought upon hapless victims is not the objective of the violence. The bombing of Pan American Airlines Flight 103 over Lockerbie, Scotland, was intended to influence the public, who would be informed by the media of the deaths of the passengers. It has been suggested that the rest of the world follow in the footsteps of Britain, which has passed laws limiting news coverage of terrorist events (Crook, 2010). There is no absolute right of the press to have access to information not available to the public at large. If the public can be restricted in what they hear and see at a crime scene, the press can be restricted as well. Attributing a terroristic act to a terrorist group is free publicity. A newspaper would consider it unethical to accept an advertisement from a terrorist group

claiming credit for a terroristic act. What the press will not allow terrorists to buy, it gives them for nothing.

In discussing terrorism, it is helpful to categorize terroristic acts into four groups:

1. **Domestic terrorism** evolves within a state or country. Disgruntled citizens engage in terrorist acts that, although brought down upon the heads of individuals, are aimed at bringing about social or political change. White supremacist groups, such as the Ku Klux Klan and the Aryan Nation, along with militant antiabortion, right-wing militia, and domestic environmental groups, may pose the greatest threat of terrorism in the United States.

2. **State-sponsored terrorism** is used by a government to manipulate its own citizens. Saddam Hussein's use of gas on the Kurdish population of Iraq to bring about conformity was an example of state-sponsored terrorism, as was the Third Reich's divestment of German Jews' status as citizens and its attempt to exterminate them. A vocal minority bent on change may be seen as a serious threat by a sitting government, which might then apply force to bring about a resolution to the political controversy.

3. **Transnational terrorism** is conducted by terrorists against citizens of another country. Transnational terrorist groups are not directly supported by a state but may receive indirect support from various

domestic terrorism Terrorism that evolves within a state or country; disgruntled citizens engage in terrorist acts that, although brought down upon the heads of individuals, are aimed at bringing about social or political change

state-sponsored terrorism Terrorism used by a government to manipulate its own citizens

transnational terrorism Terrorism that is conducted by terrorists against citizens of another country; these groups are not supported by a state but may receive support from various regimes in various countries and locations

— Ripped from the Headlines —

The International Centre for Counter-Terrorism

"The International Centre for Counter-Terrorism–The Hague (ICCT) is an independent think and do tank providing multidisciplinary policy advice and practical, solution-oriented implementation support on prevention and the rule of law, two vital pillars of effective counter-terrorism.

ICCT's work focuses on themes at the intersection of countering violent extremism and criminal justice sector responses, as well as human rights related aspects of counter-terrorism. The major project areas concern countering violent extremism, rule of law, foreign fighters, country and regional analysis, rehabilitation, civil society engagement and victims' voices. Functioning as a nucleus within the international counter-terrorism network, ICCT connects experts, policymakers, civil society actors and practitioners from different fields by providing a platform for productive collaboration, practical analysis, and exchange of experiences and expertise, with the ultimate aim of identifying innovative and comprehensive approaches to preventing and countering terrorism."

Information from Leenaars, J., & Reed, A. (2016). *Understanding lone wolves: Towards a theoretical framework for comparative analysis.* The International Centre for Counter-Terrorism—The Hague.

© Shutterstock, Inc./rzarek.

---

regimes for services rendered. Hezbollah and Fatah are examples of terrorist groups that travel throughout a region, irrespective of geographic boundaries, furthering a cause through terrorism that transcends nations, states, and their citizens.

international terrorism
Terrorism conducted by state-supported terrorists but that involves the citizens of more than one state

4. **International terrorism** is conducted by state-supported terrorists but involves the citizens of more than one country. The Palestine Liberation Organization (PLO) has historically operated in a number of geographic regions (Forst, Greene, & Lyncy, 2011).

Terrorists are not as easily identifiable as most think. They do not generally wear indices of country or group affiliation before the terroristic act. There are generally no outwardly discernible characteristics that distinguish them from the population at large. Most are dedicated and highly motivated supporters of social or political causes. Often, their frustration with peaceful efforts to effect what they believe to be fundamental and necessary change has led to desperation, and they believe that their only avenue to success is to erode the will of the government that remains deaf to their cause. Those who come together out of political frustration, desperation, and disenfranchisement unify and compound their assets, resolve, dedication, and strength.

Terrorist groups are linear (rather than hierarchical), highly mobile, flexible, efficient, self-contained, and, most important, closed. They

weapons of mass destruction (WMD)
Chemical, biological or conventional weaponry which are capable of producing tremendous destruction to life and property

nuclear terrorism
Involves terrorists detonating a nuclear device

are difficult, if not impossible, to infiltrate, and law enforcement is still looking for the tools with which to deal with them. The United States has identified 61 terrorist organizations worldwide and has identified Iran, Sudan, and Syria as sponsors of terrorism (https://www.state.gov/j/ct/list/c14151.htm).

Weapons of Terrorism

The weapons of terrorism are becoming increasingly deadly. Terrorists are no longer satisfied simply to make a point or be recognized for a single, isolated event. They now seek weapons capable of creating massive destruction, often referred to as **weapons of mass destruction (WMD)**. The use of infectious disease, chemical agents, and bioterrorism has become more of a threat than **nuclear terrorism**. Although the bombing of the Murrah Federal Office Building in Oklahoma (1995), the World Trade Center, and the Pentagon were no doubt tragically impactful events, if a terrorist group were to use biologic, chemical, or nuclear weapons, the consequences would be significantly more severe and far-reaching. However, although the technical expertise necessary to construct a nuclear device is not beyond the capabilities of terrorists, the technological means probably are, and a more realistic avenue to nuclear terrorism would involve the theft or purchase of a nuclear device. The Georgian states of the former Soviet Union have a stockpile of more than 13,000 nuclear weapons left after the collapse of the Soviet

Union. These weapons have been offered at auction to any organization or state that can afford to purchase them, with no regard for political agenda or affiliation (Fong & Alibek, 2009).

The possession of a nuclear device is not necessary for terrorists to pose a **nuclear threat**. A nuclear facility could be taken hostage, and, with sufficient expertise, a core meltdown could be threatened or actualized. Dozens of countries have joined the nuclear community, most recently Egypt, Pakistan, and North Korea. What security precautions have been effected in the far reaches of the nuclear community to prevent the sabotage or ransoming of nuclear facilities (from which fissionable material could be had)? What procedures have been employed for accountability for nuclear materials? What types of criminal history and background checks are required of persons working in the industry? In addition to the panoply of security deficits in the United States and among its nuclear

neighbors, there are terrorists who may receive support from governments that want to break into the nuclear monopoly.

While many of the terrorist incidents encountered within the U.S. involved the use of explosives, Chapter 13 was dedicated to explosive events and related investigations. Instead, this chapter will concentrate on the other (non-explosive) manners in which terrorism impacts homeland security within the United States.

Chemical Weapons

Of the three types of weapons—nuclear, biological, and chemical—the latter has the greatest potential for terrorist use. **Chemical weapons** (sometimes referred to as chemical warfare agents, or CWAs) are easy to obtain or make and also to disperse. Only small quantities of chemicals, such as sarin, are needed to immobilize an entire city. (See **TABLE 15.1**.)

nuclear threat
The potential for terrorists to acquire nuclear weapons or take actions against nuclear facilities

chemical weapons
Chemical compounds used to harm or kill people; they are easy to obtain or make and also to disperse, and the chemical dispersal may be delayed, allowing the terrorists to escape without fear of harming themselves too

TABLE 15.1 Chemical Agents

Type of Agent	Agent	Characteristics
Nerve agents	Tabun (GA)	Colorless Fruity smell
	Sarin (B)	Colorless Odorless
	Soman (GD)	Colorless Fruity smell Oil of camphor odor
	VX	Colorless to straw colored No odor
Vessicants (blister agents)	Sulfur mustard (HD)	Pale yellow to brown Garlic or mustard odor
	Lewisite (L)	Amber to brown Smells like geranium
Pulmonary (lung) agents	Chlorine (CL)	Clear to yellow gas Smells like bleach
	Phosgene (CG)	Colorless gas Smells like freshly mown hay
Blood agents	Hydrogen cyanide (AC)	Gas Bitter almond odor
	Cyanogen chloride	Gas or liquid Pungent odor

Source: National Counterterrorism Center's 2007 Counterterrorism Calendar.

TABLE 15.2 Biological Threats		
Threat	**Incubation Period**	**Symptoms**
Botulinum toxins	Initial symptoms appear several hours to 1 to 2 days after exposure	Initial symptoms: ■ Blurred vision ■ Drooping eyelids ■ Difficulty understanding language ■ Difficulty speaking ■ Muscle weakness Day 1: ■ Mucous in throat ■ Neuromuscular symptoms ■ Respiratory distress ■ Difficulty swallowing Day 4: ■ Indistinct speech ■ Dilated pupils ■ Retarded eye motion ■ Mental numbness
Smallpox	Incubation average is 12 days	Phase 1: ■ Malaise ■ Fever ■ Chills ■ Vomiting ■ Headache ■ Backache ■ Rash Phase 2: ■ Facial rash ■ Eruptions on mucous membranes ■ Eruptions on extremities ■ Eruptions extend to the trunk of the body
Cutaneous anthrax	Incubation is 1 to 5 days	Initial symptoms: ■ Small bumps ■ Blisters ■ Painless lesions ■ Ulcerated necrotic tissue (ulcer of dead skin)
Inhalation anthrax	None	■ Nonproductive couch (dry cough) ■ Chest pain ■ Respiratory distress ■ Difficulty breathing ■ Purple coloration of mucous membranes ■ Shock and death within 24 hours

Source: National Counterterrorism Center's 2007 Counterterrorism Calendar.

— Ripped from the Headlines —

Terror on the Subway

In 1995, the Aum Shinrikyo, a Japanese religious cult obsessed with the apocalypse, released sarin into the Tokyo subway system (**FIGURE A**). The attack came at the peak of the Monday morning rush hour in one of the busiest commuter systems in the world. Witnesses said that subway entrances resembled battlefields, because injured commuters lay gasping on the ground with blood gushing from their noses or mouths. The attack killed 12 people and sent more than 5,000 others to hospitals. As a result of this attack and the September 11, 2001, terrorist attacks in New York and Washington, chemical detection systems have been installed in the subway systems of those cities.

FIGURE A: In 1995, a religious cult released sarin into the Tokyo subway system, killing 12 people and injuring more than 5,000 others.
© The Asahi Shimbun/Getty Images.

© Shutterstock, Inc./rzarek.

Furthermore, chemical dispersal may be delayed, allowing the terrorists to escape without fear of contamination. Chemical weapons may become the new weapons of choice for terrorists. Joyner (2009) suggested two reasons for this. First, terrorist killing and property damage have become a matter of routine for both terrorists and the viewing public. It will take larger acts of violence to precipitate fear and garner media coverage. Second, terrorists are becoming better funded and more technologically proficient. CWAs are classified into six categories, where each category contains chemicals that generally act on the body in the same way. These categories are choking agents, blister agents, blood agents, irritating agents, incapacitating agents, and nerve agents (Girard, 2017).

Biological Weapons

Biological weapons (BW) are among the oldest weapons of warfare. Although banned by the 1975 International Biological Weapons Convention, various terrorist groups have at their disposal a variety of biological weapons, including botulinum toxin, one of the deadliest toxins on Earth; anthrax can be ordered from biological supply houses (Fong & Alibek, 2009). Biological weapons investigations are especially challenging for law enforcement.

BWs are typically odorless, colorless, and tasteless; they can be readily acquired (and often cultured, if necessary); they are easily transported; and relatively small amounts are needed to produce major damage to human life (Girard, 2017). In addition, the infectious microorganisms can also be released in a variety of ways (contamination of food or water and the use of aerosol sprays), thus adding to the challenges encountered by law enforcement during an investigation. Cloning and genetic engineering are making biological agents more target-specific. Once perfected, these weapons will become an attractive addition to the terrorists' arsenals. (See **TABLE 15.2**.)

Technology as a Weapon

Another potential weapon is technology. The United States is the most technologically advanced nation in the world, but technology is a double-edged sword and leaves us open to **technological terrorism**. Many of us cannot remember a time when grocery cashiers used a mechanical cash register. When computers go down, businesses go down. We have become simultaneously technologically advanced and dependent. Our reliance on technology has thus created a window of opportunity for terrorism. Using a computer as a weapon,

biological weapons (BW)
Biological agents chosen because of their harmful properties; used to spread disease or cause death

technological terrorism
Use of computers as weapons to target such locations as metropolitan water supplies, public utility companies, dams, electric power grids, transmission lines and transformers, petroleum refineries and pipelines, and power plants

— Ripped from the Headlines —

Anthrax via the Mail

On September 18, 2001, letters containing anthrax bacteria arrived at ABC News, CBS News, NBC News, the New York Post, and the National Enquirer in New York and at American Media, Inc. (AMI), in Boca Raton, Florida. The letters were postmarked from Trenton, New Jersey. On October 9, two more of the anthrax-contaminated letters were found in the offices of South Dakota Senator Tom Daschle and Vermont Senator Patrick Leahy.

The anthrax found in the first set of letters sent to the New York-based media outlets appeared as a brown granular substance, somewhat like ground dog food. This form of anthrax, called cutaneous anthrax, only causes skin infections. The anthrax sent to the AMI office in Florida and to the senators' offices, however, contained a more dangerous version known as inhalation anthrax. Both forms of anthrax

were derivative of the Ames strain, a bacterial strain that was first researched at the U.S. Army Medical Research Institute of Infectious Diseases in Fort Detrick, Maryland. Robert Stevens, who worked for AMI, subsequently died of the disease.

The letter sent to Senator Daschle was opened on October 15 by one of his aides, who found a highly refined dry powder containing nearly 1 g of pure spores. Consequently, the government mail service was closed and secured. The letter sent to Senator Leahy was actually discovered on November 16 in Sterling, Virginia, at a state department mail annex because of a misread ZIP code. This facility was also shut down to be disinfected but not until a postal worker, David Hose, had contracted inhalation anthrax. Hose was lucky—he survived.

A total of 22 people developed inhalation anthrax as a result of the mailings. Ultimately, five people died of the disease, including two postal workers from the Brentwood mail facility in Washington,

DC, who likely handled the letters sent to Senators Daschle and Leahy. Thousands of others took an antibiotic, Cipro, to prevent infection in case they had inadvertently come in direct contact with the contaminated mail.

Radiocarbon dating of the anthrax found in the letters determined that it had been produced no more than 2 years earlier. In August of 2002, using special detectors, investigators found a post office box near Princeton University in New Jersey that was likely used to mail all or some of the contaminated letters.

By 2007, investigators conclusively determined that a batch of Anthrax spores created and maintained by Dr. Bruce E. Ivins at the United States Army Medical Research Institute of Infectious Diseases (USAMRIID) was the parent material for the Anthrax spores found in the letters. Investigators established that Dr. Ivins mailed the anthrax letters. Ivins, 62, committed suicide in July of 2008 as federal agents were closing in on him. (Girard, 2017).

terrorists may target metropolitan water supplies, public utility companies, dams, electric power grids, transmission lines and transformers, petroleum refineries and pipelines, and power plants.

Domestic Improvised Explosive Devices

The use of improvised explosive devices (IEDs) represents the most likely domestic threat to the United States. IED attacks remain the primary tactic for terrorists seeking an uncomplicated and inexpensive means for inflicting mass casualties and maximum damage. Constantly evolving terrorist tactics, techniques, and procedures present unique challenges to those responsible for protecting city infrastructures.

Some of the threats of the terroristic use of IEDs and evolving tactics, techniques, and procedures include the use of the Internet to share information on how to acquire, build, and employ explosive devices. There are ready sources of information for anyone interested in making explosives and purchasing explosive materials and initiators. The key to countering IEDs is effective training, which includes:

- Identification of a suspect IED
- Recognizing that multiple IEDs at different locations is the default
- Knowing that secondary IEDs generally await first responders
- Monitoring terrorist groups and techniques that are globally connected by the Internet (National Research Council, 2007)

Terrorists constantly refine and evolve their tactics to adapt to new security measures, making it difficult for law enforcement to effectively counter IED attacks. The United States, as an open society, has many soft targets that could cause much chaos if they were to be attacked or victimized. Not only is the United States an attractive target, but it also has a seriously vulnerable infrastructure. Deciding what to harden and what is too expensive to harden always leaves a myriad of potential targets for those who wish to disrupt and destroy. Law enforcement, as always, must do more with less. Additionally, new responsibilities are not necessarily accompanied by budget allocations. Nonetheless, law enforcement is our first line of defense and must not leave the war against terrorism, domestic or foreign, to the federal government. It has been said that all politics is local, and it could also be said that all domestic terrorism is local. Local resources are left with the responsibility to:

- Prevent terrorism
- Predict terrorism
- Respond to terroristic events
- Rehabilitate people and places after the event

The mechanism whereby terrorists injure and kill is not necessarily anything overly exotic. Substantial damage can be done with limited resources. Passenger aircraft were not considered terrorist explosive devices until September 11, 2001. The standard in the airline industry had long been to cooperate with hijackers; nonresistance was the objective, with release being the expected outcome when the hijackers reached their destination—which is what made the aircraft vulnerable to being converted to terrorist weapons. It is important to remember that the damage inflicted is to further a political aim. The sites are chosen based on vulnerability, value as a terrorist target, and maximum impact. Communities will have to examine their infrastructures to determine which are the most vulnerable but also which are the most desirable potential targets. A city has limited resources and cannot harden all targets; the objective in vulnerability analysis is to determine not only what is most vulnerable but also what is a priority with regard to operational necessity, as well as which targets are most essential to the welfare of the citizens of a particular community and how they can be hardened. Target hardening does not prevent terrorist attacks; it simply discourages them. A good home security system can prevent a burglary at a particular home, but burglars will simply move on to a place that is easier to burglarize.

Investigating Terrorism

Terrorism is an act or series of acts that includes a crime. It is the responsibility of the investigating agency to apply traditional methods, perhaps on a much larger scale, to investigate the underlying criminal offenses that accompany the terrorism. Terrorists most commonly commit the following crimes:

- Conspiracy
- Kidnapping
- Skyjacking
- Murder
- Assault (including aggravated assault)
- Burglary (to commit a felony other than theft)
- Bombing and arson
- Extortion

These crimes are the same as those committed by any other offender, except that they are committed by a dedicated group of well-trained, prepared professionals motivated by political goals. The primary investigative tool for terrorist acts is patience; the primary investigative tool for suspected terrorist groups is intelligence (information).

The initial crime scene in a terroristic kidnapping is the location from which the victim was kidnapped. A second crime scene is the location to which the victim was taken. In fact, each place used by the terrorists in advancing their kidnapping scheme should be considered a separate crime scene. If a vehicle was used and abandoned, it, too, should be processed as a crime scene.

Keep in mind that in this type of investigation, what seems unimportant now may prove to be important later. It takes training, skill, and experience to determine what is evidence and what is not, and it is best to err on the side of prudence and bag it all. Dirt, stones, hairs, and fibers are as important in a kidnapping as they are in a homicide. The dirt and stones may reveal a location that the victim or the terrorists might have previously visited. Hair and fiber may provide comparison evidence when a suspect is apprehended. The trunk of the vehicle should be examined carefully because it might have been used by the kidnappers to transport the victim, and fragments of rope, tape, or fabric used to bind the victim may be found there. Mud, dirt, and other debris on the undercarriage of the vehicle may indicate other stops made by the suspects prior to abandoning the vehicle. Stolen license plates may have been used. It may prove fruitful to process the vehicle from which the plates were stolen for fingerprints (Osterburg & Ward, 2010).

Gathering Intelligence

Successful investigation of a suspected terrorist group requires, in addition to massive amounts of patience, the ability to appreciate the group's motivation; efforts to establish lines of communication with any and all agencies that may have information about the group and its individual members; and the compilation of a database containing personal information about individual group members, suspected prior terrorist acts, and cross-references for all items recovered at any terroristic crime scene or discovered safe house.

The intelligence efforts should focus on the group's:

- Membership
- Possible local affiliations
- Stated and unstated goals
- Resource base
- Propensity toward violence
- Level of proficiency
- Preferred tactical approach (types of weapons, explosives, etc.)
- Method of communication (e.g., website, in the case of some domestic terrorist groups)
- Method of funding
- Organizational structure

Some domestic groups may espouse positions opposed to the majority and the government; this in itself is not actionable. Civil disobedience is protected under the First Amendment. It is when a group moves past unpopular opinions and civil disobedience and incites actions in violation of the law that First Amendment protection ends and investigative inquiry begins.

Often, the most accessible information about a suspected organization or individual has to do with the financial activity. Large financial transactions leave paper or digital trails. The following list can be useful in seeking indicators of suspicious financial activity:

- Account transactions that are inconsistent with past deposits or withdrawals.
- Transactions involving a high volume of incoming or outgoing wire transfers with no logical or apparent purpose that come from, go to, or transit sanctioned countries, non-cooperative nations, or sympathizers.
- Unexplainable clearing or negotiation of third-party checks and their deposits in foreign bank accounts.
- Breaking transactions larger than $10,000 into smaller amounts by making multiple deposits or withdrawals or by buying cashier's checks, money orders, or other monetary instruments to evade IRS bank-reporting requirements.
- Corporate layering; transfers between bank accounts of related entities or charities for no reason.
- Wire transfers by charitable organizations to companies located in countries known to be bank or tax havens.
- Charitable bank deposits that lack signs of fundraising activity (absence of small checks or donations).
- Use of multiple accounts to collect funds that are transferred to the same foreign beneficiaries.
- Transactions without logical economic purpose.
- Overlapping corporate officers, bank signatories, or other identifiable similarities associated with the same addresses, references, and financial activities.
- Cash-debiting schemes in which deposits in the United States correlate directly with ATM withdrawals in countries of concern.
- Issuance of checks, money orders, or other financial instruments, often numbered sequentially, to the same or similarly named person or business (National Counterterrorism Center, 2007).

Homeland Security

When one thinks about intelligence gathering, one typically thinks of spies and foreign espionage. However, not all intelligence gathering or surveillance is conducted of overseas locations or of other governments. It has become increasingly important to preserve and protect U.S. home security through the collective work of a number of previous federal agencies,

Homeland Security

FIGURE 15.1: Department of Homeland Security.

FIGURE 15.2: Border patrol of the U.S. southern border.
© vichinterlang/Getty Images.

which are now grouped under the Department of Homeland Security (DHS) (**FIGURE 15.1**). For instance, the United States Secret Service (USSS), responsible for protecting the nation's currency, was previously under the Department of the Treasury. The United States Immigration and Naturalization Service (INS) was previously under the U.S. Department of Justice. However, after 9-11, the U.S. government reorganized and centralized a number of departments in order to have them work more effectively and efficiently as pertains to ensuring and maintaining security of the United States and its citizens. Of course, such protection could not occur without the cooperation of state and local law enforcement, but the federal government is responsible for taking the lead in most instances connected to matters of homeland security. However, they depend on the eyes and ears of local citizens and law enforcement to provide the tips and sources of information necessary to ensure mission success.

According to the U.S. Government website for DHS, the Department of Homeland Security encompasses the following:

- *Border Security*: The United States shares 7,000 miles of land border with Canada and Mexico, as well as rivers, lakes and coastal waters around the country. These borders are vital economic gateways that account for trillions of dollars in trade and travel each year. They are also home to some of our nation's largest – and safest – cities and communities. Protecting our borders from the illegal movement of weapons, drugs, contraband, and people, while promoting lawful entry and exit, is essential to homeland security, economic prosperity, and national sovereignty (**FIGURE 15.2**).

- *Citizenship and Immigration*: The United States is a nation of immigrants. That diversity is the backbone of our arts, industry, and culture. American citizenship speaks to the nation's character as a welcoming country that bestows upon us all of the rights and freedoms guaranteed by the U.S. Constitution. U.S. Citizenship and Immigration Services (USCIS) oversees lawful immigration to the United States. USCIS secures America's promise as a nation of immigrants by providing accurate and useful information to our customers, granting immigration and citizenship benefits, promoting an awareness and understanding of citizenship, and ensuring the integrity of our immigration system.

- *Civil Rights and Civil Liberties*: Safeguarding civil rights and civil liberties is critical to DHS' work to protect the nation from the many threats we face. The Office for Civil Rights and Civil Liberties (CRCL) supports the Department's mission to secure the nation while preserving individual liberty, fairness, and equality under the law. DHS integrates civil rights and civil liberties into all agency activities by: Promoting respect for civil rights and civil liberties in policy creation and implementation; communicating with individuals and communities whose civil rights and civil liberties may be affected by Department activities, and informing them of policies and avenues of redress; investigating and resolving civil rights and civil liberties complaints filed by the public regarding Department policies or activities; and leading the Department's equal employment opportunity programs and promoting workforce diversity.

- *Cybersecurity*: Cyberspace and its underlying infrastructure are vulnerable to a wide range of risks stemming from both physical and cyber threats and hazards. Sophisticated cyber actors and nation-states exploit vulnerabilities to steal information and money and are developing capabilities to disrupt, destroy, or threaten the delivery of essential services. A range of traditional crimes are now being perpetrated through cyberspace. This includes the production and distribution of child pornography and child exploitation conspiracies, banking and financial fraud, intellectual property violations, and other crimes, all of which have substantial human and economic consequences. Cyberspace is particularly difficult to secure due to a number of factors: The ability of malicious actors to operate from anywhere in the world, the linkages between cyberspace and physical systems, and the difficulty of reducing vulnerabilities and consequences in complex cyber networks. Of growing concern is the cyber threat to critical infrastructure, which is increasingly subject to sophisticated cyber intrusions that pose new risks. As information technology becomes increasingly integrated with physical infrastructure operations, there is increased risk for wide scale or high-consequence events that could cause harm or disrupt services upon which our economy and the daily lives of millions of Americans depend. In light of the risk and potential consequences of cyber events, strengthening the security and resilience of cyberspace has become an important homeland security mission.

- *Critical Infrastructure Security*: The nation's critical infrastructure provides the essential services that underpin American society and serve as the backbone of our nation's economy, security, and health. We know it as the power we use in our homes, the water we drink, the transportation that moves us, the stores we shop in, and the communication systems we rely on to stay in touch with friends and family. Critical infrastructure must be secure and able to withstand and rapidly recover from all hazards. Proactive and coordinated efforts are necessary to strengthen and maintain secure, functioning, and resilient critical infrastructure—including assets, networks, and systems—that are vital to public confidence and the Nation's safety, prosperity, and well-being. This endeavor is a shared responsibility among federal, state, local, tribal, and territorial entities, and public and private owners and operators of critical infrastructure.

- *Economic Security*: America's, and the world's, economic prosperity, depend increasingly on the flow of goods and services, people and capital, and information and technology across our borders. The systems that make these flows possible are targeted for exploitation by adversaries, including terrorists and criminals. DHS plays a role in identifying vulnerabilities to our nation's economic security and collaborating to secure global systems.

- *Emergency Communications*: Ensuring effective emergency communications is a key part of the Department of Homeland Security (DHS) mission to strengthen national preparedness and resilience. Since DHS was established in 2003, one of its top priorities has been—and will continue to be—enhancing the communications capabilities of the nation's emergency responders. Ensuring operable and interoperable communications and real-time information sharing among responders during all threats and hazards is paramount to the safety and security of all Americans.

- *Human Trafficking*: Human trafficking is a form of modern-day slavery, and involves the use of force, fraud, or coercion to exploit human beings for some type of labor or commercial sex purpose. Every year, millions of men, women, and children worldwide—including in the United States—are victims of human trafficking. Victims are often lured with false promises of well-paying jobs or are manipulated by people they trust, but instead are forced or coerced into prostitution, domestic servitude, farm or factory labor, or other types of forced labor. The U.S. Department of Homeland Security (DHS) is responsible for investigating human trafficking, arresting traffickers and protecting victims. DHS initiates hundreds of investigations and makes numerous arrests every year, using a victim-centered approach. DHS also processes immigration relief through Continued Presence (CP), T visas, and U visas to victims of human trafficking and other designated crimes.

- *Law Enforcement Partnerships*: Law enforcement partners at the federal, state, local, tribal and territorial levels are the backbone of our nation's domestic defense against terrorist attacks. They are this country's eyes and ears on the ground, and the first line of detection and prevention. They are a vital partner in ensuring public safety, in every American community. To support these partners and carry out our missions, almost 90 percent of DHS employees are stationed outside of Washington, D.C., in communities across the country.

- *Prevention of Terrorism*: Protecting the American people from terrorist threats is the reason the Department of Homeland Security was created and remains our highest priority. Our vision is a secure and resilient nation that effectively prevents terrorism in ways that preserve our freedom and prosperity. Terrorist tactics continue to evolve, and we must keep pace. Terrorists seek sophisticated means of attack, including chemical, biological, radiological, nuclear and explosive weapons, and cyberattacks. Threats may come from abroad or be homegrown.

- *Science and Technology*: The DHS Science and Technology Directorate (S&T) is the primary research and development arm of the Department of Homeland Security and manages science and technology research, from development through transition, for the Department's operational components and first responders to protect the homeland.

- *Transportation Security*: The Transportation Security Administration (TSA) was created in the wake of 9/11 to strengthen the security of the nation's transportation systems while ensuring the freedom of movement for people and commerce. Within a year, TSA assumed responsibility for security at the nation's airports and deployed a federal workforce to screen all commercial airline passengers and baggage. TSA now vets 100% of all passengers into, out of, and within the United States through TSA's Secure Flight program. We use the latest technology to stay ahead of evolving threats, and continue our efforts to screen 100% of cargo, regardless of where or how it is moving (https://www.dhs.gov/topics).

Each of the above areas could easily have an entire chapter or text written on the importance and intricacies associated with them. However, one area that is of great importance and that is receiving a great deal of attention, support, and effort from local law enforcement and investigative elements is the area of human trafficking.

Human Trafficking

Many are confused by the term "human trafficking." It is different from human smuggling. Trafficking is exploitation based and does not require movement across borders or any type of transportation. Human trafficking occurs in plain sight but is a hidden crime. The first step to combating it is to identify victims so that they can be rescued and help bring their perpetrators to justice. This is where the watchful eye of local law enforcement and the astute criminal investigator comes into play. It is also where a great deal of the resources of the U.S. Department of Homeland Security are spent, specifically as it relates to the Blue Campaign.

The Blue Campaign is the unified voice for the DHS' efforts to combat human trafficking. Working in collaboration with law enforcement, government, and nongovernmental and private organizations, the Blue Campaign strives to protect the basic right of freedom and to bring those who exploit human lives to justice. The fight requires the contributions of all, including:

- Workers on the frontlines: First responders, social workers, community volunteers, healthcare providers, teachers, and law enforcement

- A range of organizations: private, public, and non-profit—who are committed to social responsibility and are willing to speak out about this terrible scourge

- Faith-based networks and houses of worship

- Government entities that create and foster strong relationships to bring communities together and facilitate collaboration and the sharing of best practices

- Members of the public who, through the knowledge of their communities, can be the greatest asset in this fight

Through the Blue Campaign, DHS raises public awareness about human trafficking, leveraging partnerships to educate the public to recognize human trafficking and report suspected instances. The Blue Campaign also offers training to law enforcement and others to increase detection and investigation of human trafficking and to protect victims and bring suspected traffickers to justice.

INVESTIGATOR'S NOTEBOOK

How Do I Identify Human Trafficking?

Human trafficking is often "hidden in plain sight." There are a number of red flags, or indicators, which can help alert you to human trafficking. Recognizing the signs is the first step in identifying victims.

Some Indicators Concerning a Potential Victim Include:

Behavior or Physical State:

- Does the victim act fearful, anxious, depressed, submissive, tense, or nervous / paranoid?
- Does the victim defer to another person to speak for him or her?
- Does the victim show signs of physical and/or sexual abuse, physical restraint, confinement, or torture?
- Has the victim been harmed or deprived of food, water, sleep, medical care, or other life necessities?
- Does the victim have few or no personal possessions?

Social Behavior:

- Can the victim freely contact friends or family?
- Is the victim allowed to socialize or attend religious services?
- Does the victim have freedom of movement?
- Has the victim or family been threatened with harm if the victim attempts to escape?

Work Conditions and Immigration Status:

- Does the victim work excessively long and/or unusual hours?
- Is the victim a juvenile engaged in commercial sex?
- Was the victim recruited for one purpose and forced to engage in some other job?
- Is the victim's salary being garnished to pay off a smuggling fee? (Paying off a smuggling fee alone is not considered trafficking.)
- Has the victim been forced to perform sexual acts?
- Has the victim been threatened with deportation or law enforcement action? Is the victim in possession of identification and travel documents; if not, who has control of the documents?

Minor Victims:

For more information, please visit: www.dhs.gov/bluecampaign

© Shutterstock, Inc./Nutink.

CONCLUSION

It is impossible to include in one chapter everything investigators need to know to investigate terrorism and terrorist organizations. This chapter introduces students to the subject matter. Those interested can find a library full of additional information.

What is known today is not nearly enough to combat terrorism effectively. As much time and effort that the United States employs in thwarting terrorism, the same amount of time and effort is expended by terrorist organizations around the world in circumventing U.S. counterterrorism efforts. It is a world where the targets stay a step behind the terrorists and exhaust resources and manpower trying to second-guess where the next major terrorist incident might occur. We have learned a lot as a nation since September 11, 2001, but there is no guarantee that we are learning enough or learning fast enough. We have a short collective memory and forget the turmoil this country was in after 9/11 and the demands that we made of our government. Much that has been done as a result of that day has now become an inconvenience or a violation of someone's rights. Any discussion about terrorism must include the question: How free can we be and still be safe?

QUESTIONS FOR REVIEW

1. What is the basic organizational unit of terroristic groups?
2. What are the attributes of an organized crime group?
3. What role does the media play in fostering terrorism?
4. What is the definition of terrorism?
5. What are the differences between investigating a terroristic act and investigating a suspected terrorist group?
6. How does the First Amendment apply to terrorism?
7. What is technological terrorism?
8. What role does the joint terrorism task force play in fighting terrorism?
9. What is intelligence? Include a discussion of the difference between strategic intelligence and tactical intelligence.

REFERENCES

Bakker, E., & de Graaf, B. (2010, November). *Lone wolves: How to prevent this phenomenon.* Paper presented at the Expert Meeting Lone Wolves, International Centre for CounterTerrorism—The Hague. Retrieved from https://www.icct.nl/download/file/ICCT-Bakker-deGraaf-EM-Paper-Lone-Wolves.pdf

Crook, T. (2010). *Comparative media and ethics.* New York, NY: Routledge.

Fong, I. W., & Alibek, K. (2009). *Bioterrorism and infectious agents: A new dilemma for the 21st century.* New York, NY: Springer.

Forst, B., Greene, J. R., & Lyncy, J. P. (2011). *Criminologist on terrorism and homeland security.* New York, NY: Cambridge Press.

Girard, J. E. (2017). *Criminalistics: Forensic science, crime and terrorism* (4th ed.). Burlington, MA: Jones & Bartlett Learning.

Joyner, D. (2009). *International law and the proliferation of weapons of mass destruction.* New York, NY: Oxford University Press.

Leenaars, J., & Reed, A. (2016, May 2). *Understanding lone wolves: Towards a theoretical framework for comparative analysis.* The International Centre for Counter-Terrorism The Hague (ICCT). Retrieved on September 7, 2016, from https://icct.nl/publication/understanding-lone-wolves-towards-a-theoretical-framework-for-comparative-analysis/

National Counterterrorism Center. (2007). *2007 counterrorism calendar.* Washington, DC: Office of Director of National Intelligence.

National Research Council. (2007). *Countering the threat of improvised explosive devices.* Washington, DC: National Academies Press.

Osterburg, J. W., & Ward, R. J. (2010). *Criminal investigation: A method of reconstructing the past.* Cincinnati, OH: Anderson.

Stewart, S., & Burton, F. (2009, June 3). Lone wolf lessons. *Security Weekly.* Retrieved from https://www.stratfor.com/weekly/20090603_lone_wolf_lessons

16

Underwater Investigation

"May I ask whether you examined the farther side of the moat at once, to see if there were any signs of the man having climbed out from the water?"

Sherlock Holmes
"The Valley of Fear"

KEY TERMS

backscatter

black water diving

buoyancy control
device (BCD)

refraction

strobe

Underwater Search
and Evidence
Response Team
(USERT)

STUDENT LEARNING OUTCOMES

Upon completion of this chapter, students will be able to:

- Understand the safety concerns that apply when processing an underwater crime scene

- Understand the environmental concerns and challenges when documenting and processing an underwater crime scene

- Describe black water diving, including its dangers and what causes it

- Know the proper documentation, collection, and preservation methods associated with underwater evidence and underwater crime scenes

- Describe the duties of a DMORT and know why and when one is needed

- Know the proper documentation, collection, and preservation methods associated with both buried and scattered human remains

Underwater Crime Scene Response

When an investigation leads to an underwater environment, it becomes an underwater criminal investigation. Its process should be as forensically thorough and systematic as any crime scene process conducted out of water. However, unlike the separation of duties often found in land-based investigations, underwater crime scenes typically call for the investigator to become the crime scene photographer, fingerprint specialist, and evidence recovery specialist. They also call for the investigator to be a skilled diver. This is an extremely specialized position requiring specific training and equipment.

Underwater Investigative Teams

The first documented dive team dedicated to investigative purposes was the Miami-Dade County Underwater Recovery Unit, which was established in 1960. The Miami-Dade team was assembled because of the increasing number of water-related crime scenes occurring within the water-laden area of Miami-Dade County (Becker, 2013). Federal agencies also found good reasons for training and equipping such teams as a result of national and world situations. The Federal Bureau of Investigations (FBI) established its first **Underwater Search and Evidence Response Team (USERT)** in 1982 (FBI, 2009). There are currently four such teams in the United States, and they are located in New York, Washington, Miami, and Los Angeles. The teams are managed from the FBI Laboratory in Quantico, Virginia. Each team is composed of 12 members; however, divers respond and fill in on other teams as necessary. The USERTs have been used in a number of newsworthy events that include searching for evidence and remains in the explosion of TWA Flight 800; preventative diving to search for explosives under the spectator stands for the 1996 Atlanta Olympic Games; and overseas in such terrorist attacks as that on the 2000 bombing of the USS Cole (Becker, 2013).

While the FBI maintains several well-trained and extremely well-equipped dive teams, many municipal, county, and state agencies across the country have also realized the necessity and benefit of implementing diver operational teams.

Why Is an Investigative Dive Team Necessary?

A common misconception is that evidence that has been submerged lacks the forensic value of evidence found top-side (**FIGURE 16.1**). There are numerous cases in which submerged items have yielded identifiable blood evidence, fingerprints, hair and fiber evidence, and many other types of trace evidence that have helped to identify the perpetrator of the criminal act. Some people would question why a body would have to be handled any differently in water than out of water. However, bodies should be placed in body bags when found underwater because correctly processing and packaging them can result in a variety of forensic evidence being saved. Bagging a body underwater minimizes damage and postmortem injuries to the body, maintains hair and fiber evidence, and keeps clothing intact.

Investigators must understand the value and necessity of properly collecting, marking, and recording the location of items recovered from a dive site. Often, investigators, administrators, crime lab personnel, and prosecutors lack knowledge and training about the underwater investigative process. Because of this deficit, they are unfamiliar with the forensic value and scientific methodology involved with underwater

> **Underwater Search and Evidence Response Team (USERT)**
> Federal teams assembled to provide underwater search and evidence recovery assistance

A police dive team prepares to deploy in a river environment, near a dam.

FIGURE 16.1: Forensic divers prepare to deploy to recover crime scene evidence.

crime scene processing. For instance, if only a diver is aware of the evidentiary value of collecting control samples from the water and bottom material, investigators may not understand or request the steps to be done. Collection of proper control and elimination samples for exclusion of background and marine debris is as important below the water as it is above. Because the ultimate goal of any underwater crime scene is not merely the salvaging and recovery of submerged items but is also discovery of the truth and conviction of the perpetrators, dive teams must adapt to accomplish such tasks.

Where Is Investigative Diving Used?

The working environment for the underwater investigator is very different from those shown on television or in movies. A typical work environment could consist of diving in a quarry, dirty river, raw sewage facility, or any of a host of other less-than-hospitable environments. Investigative diving can occur in any environment, at any time of the day, and in any area involving a body of water. In the vast majority of these cases, the visibility confronting the forensic diver will be less than three to four feet. In some instances, the visibility will be so drastically reduced that a diver's gauges will not be readable or even visible. This is referred to as **black water diving**. Unlike in a land-based criminal investigation where one or two persons could effectively work some scenes, in a black water diving environment, the underwater investigator relies on the coordinated efforts of the dive team to ensure both survival and success. This dive team includes both the surface personnel and fellow underwater investigators (**FIGURE 16.2**).

Who Should Comprise the Team?

Depending on the location, there are volunteer teams, teams of fire and rescue personnel, law enforcement teams, and, in some cases, a collaboration of all of these. All types are involved in attempting to fill the niche of "underwater investigator." The problem is that when dealing with a potential crime scene, the question shouldn't be "Who can help?" Rather, the question should be, "Who should help?" Except in very few instances (e.g., an arson investigation), fire departments do not investigate or become involved with criminal investigations on land. Therefore, why should they participate or why are they qualified to investigate crime scenes when the environment has changed to underwater? Law enforcement does not allow fire or rescue personnel to investigate a homicide

> **black water diving**
> Conditions where silt, sediment, algae, and pollution create underwater visibility that is typically less than one foot

FIGURE 16.2: Dive team members processing an underwater crime scene.

occurring within a residence. So why then allow them to investigate a crime scene underwater?

In some instances, if fire departments do not train their personnel to respond to underwater scenes, nobody will. However, if a need has been documented and recognized, law enforcement agencies should not ignore the responsibility and defer to fire or rescue personnel. The responsibility for investigating crime scenes belongs with the criminal justice community.

Team Design

There are many different theories and operational plans for the makeup of an underwater investigation team. However, at the bare minimum, the following personnel are required.

■ Team Leader/Commander

As in any operational response performed by law enforcement, it is crucial to have an incident commander for each scene. This duty falls to the Team Leader/Commander. This individual is not in the water and is responsible for supervising the diving process and ensuring that the individuals involved are conducting their tasks in a safe and proper manner. This individual is also responsible for ensuring that the members acquire the equipment and training necessary to conduct their jobs, as well as documenting all training, medical, and other personnel issues.

■ Line Tenders

Due to environments of low visibility, fast moving water, and other hazardous situations, divers are typically tethered to a line that is tended by someone above the water. These individuals are the eyes and ears of the forensic diver. It is preferable to have a tender be a current or former diver so that he or she is familiar with the underwater environment. In some jurisdictions, underwater communication gear has been implemented that is similar to that worn by tactical teams. However, even in these cases, and certainly in cases in which such communication gear is not used, communication between the tender and a diver occurs through a process of predetermined line tugs. This communication can involve such matters as changes of direction, status checks, ascents, and emergencies. Line communication varies by team, but training must take place, and communication must be understood by all team members.

■ Divers

There is no set number of divers for an operational dive team, but it is recommended that at the very minimum, there should be two divers for any dive situation. The primary diver is the person who is in the water and actively searching or investigating the scene. The safety diver (sometimes referred to as a 100% diver) is either in the water or out of the water and fully geared up with the ability to enter the water to provide emergency backup or aid to the primary diver. In some situations, a backup diver (90% diver) may be used as the backup to the primary diver and as a safety diver, should the safety diver find him- or herself deployed.

The team set up is similar to the arrangement that law enforcement and fire agencies typically utilize in dismantling clandestine laboratories. This is the case due to the similarities between the two environments. In both cases, personnel are confronted with hazardous and inhospitable environments that require the use of respiratory and exposure equipment. Both situations are physically taxing on an individual and require that there be constant monitoring and documentation to avoid overexertion or other potentially fatal situations. It is for this reason that both situations involve the use of safety or standby personnel (**FIGURE 16.3**).

FIGURE 16.3: Members of a dive team conduct a search for a missing person.

Assembling, Equipping, and Training the Team

It is suggested that all members of an agency dive team be full-time, trained members of that agency for liability, training, and policy and procedure purposes. However, some smaller agencies with limited resources require volunteers to supplement their dive recovery operations. Other departments sometimes share equipment and members. This is often pointed to as being "cost effective"; however, it can prove problematic when divers from one location fail to respond, or when the necessary equipment is in another location other than where it is needed. Some locations have solved these problems by establishing specialized regional dive teams. One team (perhaps fire department personnel) is trained in and specializes in rescue diving while another team (law enforcement) specializes in evidence search, recovery, and collection. This minimizes evidence handling and ensures that the necessary equipment is operationally available.

There must be minimum entry requirements established for team membership. Many times, this minimum certification is a recreational certification, such as the Professional Association of Dive Instructors (PADI), National

Many agencies must include boats and other aquatic equipment as department resources in order to police and investigate crimes which make use of aquatic environments.

Association of Underwater Instructors (NAUI), Scuba Schools International (SSI), and/or other recognized organizations. Often teams will write their own standard operational guidelines (SOGs) that list the minimum entry requirements and establish training and equipment requirements. As a point of caution in this world of lightning litigation, all established requirements for a dive team must be job related. If the requirements are not shown to be specifically related to the job applied for or involved in, they could be challenged as being discriminatory based on age, race, gender, or disability.

In addition to being (at a minimum) recreationally certified, all applicants should be required to pass a thorough and appropriate medical physical to verify their ability to perform tasks and to set a baseline for future medical exams. After joining the team, all team members should undergo annual dive physicals. Dive physicals should also be administered following any dive-related injury, major injury or illness, or any medical procedures that could interfere with the performance of duty.

The merits and benefits of fielding an underwater investigation team are many; however, with this comes the equally involved and elaborate budget and steps necessary to do so. This should not dissuade law enforcement from the assembly of such resources to ensure that each scene is processed in its entirety to the best of the agency's ability. All too often, underwater crime scenes—and the evidence contained therein—are not properly documented or processed. This failure can result in a loss, contamination, or inadmissibility of the evidence. Proper underwater crime scene processing and documentation methods will ensure that the evidence is located, properly documented, preserved, and able to be used in subsequent litigation. It is important that the underwater investigation team be properly trained as well as take part in ongoing training, specifically relating to matters of crime scene documentation and processing methods involving the underwater environment.

Today's crime scene investigator is well versed in the methodology and logistics associated with crime scene processing and documentation. However, what if the crime scene in question was located underwater? Would the same practices and methodologies apply? Would the same equipment and personnel be appropriate?

Often, the standard operating procedures (SOPs) associated with processing crime scenes are forgotten or ignored when encountering an underwater crime scene. There are many reasons why this occurs, some of which include equipment, manpower, and/or environmental issues.

More often, it is a result of improperly trained or equipped personnel or a case of rushing and thinking that, "it won't really matter as long as we get the stuff." However, the underwater scene and its contents are equally important and subject to the same scrutiny and legal considerations as a land-based scene, so it should be processed in an equally thorough and competent manner.

Personnel Requirements and Training

The first obvious hurdle is that, typically, an underwater scene will require the investigator to submerge him- or herself in order to document the scene. This usually requires that the investigator be a certified diver in order to effectively document an in-water event. With an exception being very shallow water photography that can be accomplished by either wading or taking photographs from a boat or other floating object, the individual tasked with the duty must be a competent swimmer and underwater diver as well as a skilled photographer.

Whenever a person enters an environment in which his or her body was not meant to live, there are hazards, risks, and restrictions involved. The individual assigned the duty of underwater photography must be both physically and mentally capable of venturing into and working within the underwater environment.

Several organizations can certify an individual as a diver. Some are dedicated to recreational divers and a more civilian concentrated population (PADI, NAUI, SSI), and others are specifically related to public safety professionals (Dive Rescue International, Miami-Dade). Each has a purpose and a niche; however, the important matter is that an underwater investigator be certified, comfortable, and competent so that he or she can effectively perform the assigned duties.

Processing and Documenting an Underwater Scene

When faced with an underwater crime scene, the investigation team must take into account that there are multiple scenes and levels that must be accounted for. Just as in an above-water scene, multiple methods of documentation must occur. These remain the same as for land-based operations. They are typically still photography, videography, sketching/mapping, and the written report.

■ Documenting the Surface Crime Scene
When documenting the scene through these four methods, the investigation team must remember that there are two types of scenes that must be documented. The first is the

surface scene. This includes any water access points, such as piers, shorelines, or waterfronts, as well as the surface of the water. All of the aforementioned must be thoroughly searched, photographed, and located items of evidence must be noted on a sketch.

■ Documenting the Underwater Crime Scene

The other type of scene is the submerged scene. The submerged scene has the added difficulty of depth as well as the aforementioned environmental issues and visibility issues that compound the problem. This is why it is imperative that only those individuals who have received proper training and certification in such matters be utilized to conduct underwater search and recovery operations. The submerged scene includes the objects located at depth as well as the level at which they were found. It is a three-dimensional scene, often with very little in the way of fixed markers or items to aid in reference. Just as with the surface scene, this area must be thoroughly searched. Items of evidence must be photographed, marked, and their positions and depths noted on a sketch. They must then be collected and preserved.

Searching for and Marking Evidence

In addition to proper personnel, underwater investigative teams also must possess the necessary equipment to conduct proper underwater crime scene processing. One item of value where searches are concerned is sonar. It can help to locate items of evidence, as well as identify potential hazards.

A number of different search techniques are utilized for underwater investigation, dependent on the item that is being sought, condition of the water, and location of the body of water. Some of these methods are described briefly.

Once an item of evidence is located, it is suggested that the position of the item be marked. This is especially important in areas of low visibility. There are several suggested methods for doing this, but the most common method is to "float" a marker buoy, which consists of an inflated buoy attached to a line affixed to the item of evidence or to a tie down in close proximity to the item. This will serve several purposes. First, it allows the investigator to follow the line down directly to the item. Second, it allows surface personnel to visually gauge the evidence location and assist in crime scene sketching. It is important to remember not to mark too many items of evidence in an area with marker buoys while divers are in the water, as it becomes increasingly possible that divers will become entangled. The scene will have to be processed in sections. Global positioning system (GPS) devices are also available that can be used to more easily and safely mark items of evidence. In either case, it is important that the underwater investigator take note of the depth at which the item was discovered. It is suggested that the diver or dive team assemble a diver's slate (i.e., underwater note pad) made specifically for the purpose of annotating underwater scene information (**FIGURE 16.4**).

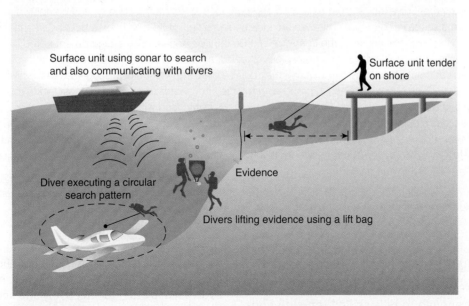

FIGURE 16.4: Example of the multiple facets of underwater crime scene investigation.

Courtesy of Dana Gevelinger.

INVESTIGATOR'S NOTEBOOK

© Shutterstock, Inc./Janaka Dharmasena

FBI Joint Training

A super-tanker is moored offshore at an offloading facility delivering fuel to the thirsty automobiles of southern California. The facility is located in the Pacific Ocean, a short distance off the runways of Los Angeles International airport (LaX). As the tanker is offloading fuel, a commuter pulled over along a nearby roadside, observes several men unloading a small motorboat from a trailer parked illegally along the beach. He watches as the boat speeds out to sea in the direction of the tanker. A short time later, the commuter sees an explosion offshore and notifies the authorities using his cell phone. Authorities determine that the tanker has not been hit but that there is some debris on the surface of the water in the area pointed out by the first witness, whose story is later corroborated by the statements of other witnesses. It is quickly determined that a vessel has exploded, but the circumstances are unknown. All activity at the fueling station is halted, as is incoming traffic at the nearby port of Los Angeles/Long Beach. Air traffic at LaX is interrupted. Authorities at large commercial ports all around the United States are notified of the incident and placed on high alert. A thorough and proper underwater investigation must commence immediately in order to reopen the fueling station and return the ports and airports to normal operating conditions.

Terrifying Precedent

Despite the significant resources and attention that are focused on port security today, the above scenario (taken from a training scenario based on the *USS Cole* incident in Aden, Yemen) cannot be overlooked. This terrorist tactic has been tried repeatedly and proven effective, suggesting it will likely be tried again. If a similar attack occurs again, the ensuing underwater investigation will need to determine several very important things fairly quickly:

1. Was the explosion of the small boat an innocent accident, or did it result from explosive materials intentionally placed onboard the vessel?
2. Did the operators of the vessel intend to attack the super-tanker?
3. What type and quantity of explosives, if any, were aboard the vessel?
4. What type of device was intended to trigger the explosion at the tanker?

These and many other questions will be asked in the aftermath of such an incident, and the answers will be expected quickly.

Preparing Dive Teams for Major Investigations

Law enforcement dive teams must be trained and equipped specifically for this type of complex underwater crime scene investigation. This was the idea behind a first-of-its-kind course developed and taught jointly by bomb technicians from the Los Angeles FBI, the Los Angeles police department bomb squad, the Los Angeles Sheriff's department arson explosives detail, and the U.S. Navy Explosive Ordnance Disposal (EOD) Unit at point Mugu, California. During their course planning, instructors recognized that while many public safety divers are well trained in processing routine underwater crime scenes, most lack a robust training curriculum or certification for the specialized skills associated with major underwater crime scenes, such as those resulting from the use of an explosive device. The course would partner public safety divers with diver/bomb technicians so that evidence collected or located by divers could be quickly and adequately analyzed by the bomb techs—both in the water and along the shore—in order to advance the work.

Source: *The detonator: The official publication of the International Association of Bomb Technicians and Investigators*, *31*(6), November/December 2004.

© Shutterstock, Inc./Nutink.

Photographing in the Underwater Environment

It is not enough to be a skilled top-side photographer and think that one will be equally as successful employing that knowledge and technique sublevel. Several issues must be addressed in order to effectively and accurately capture the underwater crime scene.

FIGURE 16.5: Example of adapting photography equipment for underwater use, utilizing a waterproof/pressure-proof housing.

FIGURE 16.6: Example of a commercially available camera designed to be waterproof/pressure-proof (to a depth of 60 feet).

■ Underwater Equipment Considerations

(Excerpt from Dutelle, A. W. (2015). *Basic Crime Scene Photography*, 2nd Edition) When it becomes necessary to submerge camera equipment into an aquatic environment to document a scene there will obviously be some equipment considerations to be taken into account. There are basically two options when it comes to photography equipment for underwater subject matter. The photographer can adapt his or her camera for underwater photography. This is typically accomplished through the use of commercially available waterproof and pressure-proof housings (**FIGURE 16.5**). The other option which exists is to purchase photography equipment designed specifically for underwater use (**FIGURE 16.6**).

■ Shallow-Water Photography

Sometimes, when the subject matter is located in shallow water, it may not be sufficient enough to photograph from outside of the water, making use of a polarized filter. However, the water may also not be deep enough to allow for, or require the photographer to submerge him- or herself within the marine environment. In these cases, simply submerging the equipment will typically suffice (**FIGURE 16.7**).

FIGURE 16.7: Photograph of evidence located in 1 foot of water, taken by submerging only the camera into the marine environment.

FIGURE 16.8: Underwater photograph, taken in 10 inches of water. (Note reflection off of surface).

Although waterproof equipment may be necessary, the other nuances of underwater photography, (which will be discussed subsequently within this chapter), will not typically be issues encountered at shallow depths. In these cases, it is typically enough to simply submerge the equipment and photograph the subject matter as intended. It is, however, suggested that the photographer limit his or her movements so as not to stir up sediment that could possibly cloud the water and impact photographic clarity. There is one undesired drawback to this form of photography, which will typically appear in shallow water photographs, and that is the subject matter appearing in mirrored duplication, as it is reflected upon the surface of the water (**FIGURE 16.8**).

■ Submerged Photography

When the subject matter to be photographed is in water deep enough to necessitate the submersion of both photographer and equipment, more adaptation will be necessary. Since this text is dedicated to photography skills and techniques, the reader is referred to texts pertaining to SCUBA and public safety diving in order to ascertain what equipment and training considerations exist for personnel in order to safely operate in an underwater environment.

Assuming that the photographer has been properly trained and is properly equipped as to his or her person, the remaining considerations pertain to equipment requirements and photographic techniques necessary to successfully photograph in a completely submerged environment. These challenges are best discussed by categorizing them into specific underwater environmental characteristics, which the photographer will need to be aware of and able to adapt to and overcome.

refraction
The bending of light rays occurs whenever a beam of light strikes a plane surface between two substances that have different optical properties (such as air and water)

FIGURE 16.9: An example of the distortion and magnification which results from light refraction in water.

■ Environmental Challenges

A great deal of light is reflected off of the surface of the water and thus never passes into the depths below. However, light rays that are able to pass from air to water will have a reduction in speed, thus resulting in the light rays becoming subsequently bent. This is referred to as **refraction**. Refraction occurs whenever a beam of light strikes a plane surface between two substances that have different optical properties (such as air and water). Water refracts light rays in a manner unlike glass or air, in that underwater objects are magnified. For this reason, images and distances are distorted (**FIGURE 16.9**).

In fact, items located underwater will appear 33% larger than actual size due to refraction. This level of refraction and magnification occurs because water is more dense than air.

Water density contributes to another challenging characteristic of the underwater environment. Since water is considerably more dense than air, whatever light is able to penetrate the surface (and thus is not lost to reflection), will not be able to penetrate at the same distance (or brightness) as above water. This contributes to the apparent subsequent loss of

FIGURE 16.10: An example of depth influencing the appearance of underwater colors.

FIGURE 16.11: Diver obscured by underwater environment.

color as depth increases as the available light is dispersed throughout the medium.

As depths increase, daylight rays of red, orange, and yellow are filtered out by the water, leaving blue and green rays (**FIGURE 16.10**). Even in the clearest waters, primarily only blue and green wave lengths penetrate at a depth greater than 60 feet.

In addition to color and lighting issues, often, the environment will create difficulty for the underwater photographer. Silt, sediment, algae, and pollution can create "black /brown diving" conditions in which visibility can be less than 1 or 2 feet. (**FIGURE 16.11**)

It is especially important for the photographer to have good diving skills to ensure proper buoyancy so as not to disturb the environment and obscure the intended images.

■ Overcoming Environmental Challenges
Because natural sunlight is rapidly absorbed or scattered by water, the addition of artificial light is quite often essential for two reasons.

1. To illuminate the subject
2. To obtain the true color of underwater objects and surroundings.

Artificial light is added to an underwater scene through the addition of a waterproof EFU (sometimes referred to as a **strobe**), attached to an underwater camera or underwater camera housing (**FIGURE 16.12**). Light from an EFU will produce all of the wavelengths of the spectrum and, therefore, reflect the true color of the item underwater.

Returning to our earlier discussion of a "true and accurate" representation of the subject matter, this is a good example of the necessity to document when certain equipment and techniques are used. The photographer's eyes will not see the underwater subject matter in actual color, but rather, in the colors that can be seen at the depth of the object, due to the previously mentioned reasons for color reduction and loss. Therefore, if a flash is deployed, it will

strobe
A type of electronic flash unit, attachable flash accessory for cameras

FIGURE 16.12: Waterproof EFU attached to underwater camera housing.

FIGURE 16.13: Example of backscatter.

FIGURE 16.14: Color compensating underwater filter.

reflect subject colors that are not an accurate representation of what the photographer actually saw, but which are, instead, more accurately portrayed as to subject color and detail, if necessary and appropriate.

Position of the artificial light source is especially important underwater. The EFU should be permanently mounted or handheld so that it will be close to the subject but off to one side, angling the light at 30 to 45 degrees toward the subject. This is important because when photographing underwater with a flash, the same problems are experienced as when taking flash photos during a blizzard or a heavy rainstorm. Particles in the water reflect light back to the camera lens, obscuring the image with spots and haze. This is referred to as **backscatter** (**FIGURE 16.13**).

When photographing (or shooting video) with natural light at depth, color-compensating filters can be placed upon the camera to compensate for colors lost due to depth. Red filters are used for blue cast and magenta for green cast, thus eliminating the cyan bluish-green cast associated with underwater photography (**FIGURE 16.14**). Typically, this is only utilized for shots covering a considerable distance and not with close-up photography. The need for compensating filters is eliminated if sufficient artificial lighting, such as electronic flash, is used.

There is one final consideration that pertains to photographing in the underwater environment. In addition to assisting in ensuring that one's equipment is waterproof, it is wise to place photographic equipment in a dunk tank with of the same water type and temperature into which the equipment will be immersed, for 5–10 minutes prior to entering the marine

> **backscatter**
> When particulates in a medium (such as particles in water or snow/rain in the air) reflect light back into the camera lens, obscuring the image with spots and haze

environment. The equipment should be checked for waterproofing just prior to entering the water and the equipment should be transitioned directly from the transition tank into the marine environment, with as short of an out-of-water window as possible, in order to best reduce subsequent fogging or clouding of the lenses.

Evidence Recovery

Items of evidence recovered from water will require special handling and packaging. Just as in a surface-level investigation, the ultimate success of an underwater investigation is determined by the proper location, preservation, and documentation of the evidence. In addition to the obvious underwater hazards and inconveniences that affect search and documentation efforts, bottom suction is another factor that affects evidence recovery.

This phenomenon typically occurs in areas containing silty or soft mud bottoms. Because of the laws of physics, raising an object that is in suction contact with the bottom requires greater lifting force than on land. However, an attempt to exert too much pressure on the item to gain its release can result in a runaway item that could injure the investigator or be lost to the current. For this reason, heavy lift bags are typically used to lift objects underwater. A lift bag is slowly inflated with one of the diver's underwater air sources, and when inflated, will help to raise the object safely. Most of these lift

CASE IN POINT

Underwater Documentation of a Bank Robbery

Two men allegedly held up a local bank branch with a semiautomatic assault rifle and a handgun, fired one shot, did no harm, and made off with approximately $110,000. The suspects, both wearing ski masks, were seen leaving the bank by an off-duty firefighter who called dispatch on his cell phone to report the violation. The firefighter followed the two men in his vehicle as they left the bank premises in a vehicle. Due to the firefighter's descriptions and real-time updates, police officers were able to intercept the vehicle prior to it leaving the area. The suspects became involved in a high-speed pursuit, covering approximately 13 miles, and in which three law enforcement agencies participated.

At one point, while driving over a highway viaduct that passed over an area lake, several objects were seen thrown out of the passenger window of the suspect vehicle. The suspects were observed splitting up in the area of a subdivision, when the passenger exited the vehicle, while the vehicle was moving. The driver continued on, and the passenger was pursued by police while he broke into and ran through several houses in an attempt to elude them. The passenger was seen to be carrying a semiautomatic rifle during the foot pursuit. The suspect on foot managed to evade officers and was not found until several hours later, after calling his girlfriend from a payphone to come pick him up. The suspect did not have a firearm in his possession at the time of his arrest. The vehicle pursuit finally terminated when the suspect vehicle disregarded a traffic control device and collided with another passenger vehicle, resulting in the occupant's death and the incapacitation of the suspect driver.

Upon investigation of the incident, crime scene investigators found one spent 40-caliber shell casing in the lobby of the bank. One firearm, an AR-15 assault rifle, was located in the living room of a home in which the passenger was seen entering. There was no additional firearm located in the vicinity of the foot pursuit, nor in the vehicle of the suspect driver. The assault rifle that was located was missing the magazine. The bag containing the money was found within the vehicle.

The money found in the possession of the driver was what would be considered a "smoking gun" in most cases. However, because the possession of semiautomatic weapons and their use in a federal offense carried additional repercussions, it was imperative that the firearm evidence be located.

The firearm located on the living room floor was photographed and collected for evidence. The pursuing officers recalled that the passenger had possibly thrown something out of his window while the vehicle traversed the viaduct crossing over the lake. Investigators were sent to the location to determine if there had been an attempt to destroy or ditch evidence. When investigators arrived, they soon recognized that it would not be possible to conduct a thorough investigation without divers. The dive team was mobilized and responded to the location. The dive team included a crime scene technician whose duty was the documentation of the scene and the collection of any discovered evidence.

The crime scene technician was tasked with documenting both the submerged and surface scene. He photographed the suspected entry area of the unknown objects from numerous angles, including from the position of the viaduct from which they were believed to have been thrown. The technician also photographed the presence of the dive team while conducting the search and all equipment associated with the effort.

The dive team entered the water and subsequently found one high capacity magazine for a .223 rifle, the same caliber as the assault rifle that had been located in the living room (**FIGURE A**). The team also discovered a magazine

FIGURE A: Photograph of a rifle magazine located in water. Note the distortion of the item caused by light refraction.

(continues)

(continued)

for a 40-caliber semiautomatic handgun, the same caliber as the expended cartridge found in the bank. Nothing else was located that was believed to be associated with the alleged crime. The magazines were photographed in situ by the crime scene technician, utilizing the underwater system assigned to him.

Visibility in the dive area was less than 2 feet. Photographs were difficult. An extreme amount of environmental debris had been disturbed as a result of the search performed. This resulted in severe turbidity and added to photographic backscatter. The photographer elected to shoot the scene using available light, thereby avoiding backscatter. A fast shutter speed was used due to movement of both the diver and the water surrounding the subject matter. The items were photographed both with and without a scale of reference. Coloration was yellow/green due to the severe algae growth in the marine environment. A color correction filter was not used. Underwater video was also taken utilizing the same underwater photographic equipment.

The underwater photographs were a large part of this investigation and showed an attempt to disguise evidence associated with criminal activity. It also helped tie the expended round in the bank to the individuals, because the round did not match the firearm located in the living room. The round, however, did match one of the magazines found and photographed in the lake, although the related handgun was never located.

Despite the assistance of the public and numerous police searchers, the semiautomatic handgun was never located. There were several points within the vehicle pursuit when the vehicle was lost from law enforcements' line of sight, and the firearm was possibly discarded during one of those moments. The evidence located, however, was sufficient to convict both men of federal charges for bank robbery, possession of illegal firearms, use of a firearm to commit a felony, and also first-degree murder for the killing of the driver of the passenger vehicle.

bags contain over-pressurization valves that release air from the lift bag as the bag ascends and aids in controlling the item's ascent to the surface (**FIGURE 16.15**).

FIGURE 16.15: A diver demonstrates the use of a lift bag to recover underwater evidence.

Depending on the item, sometimes, it is suggested to package the item underwater, thereby ensuring the collection of any trace material adhering to the item. Often, it is suggested that the item be packaged in the water in which it was found to slow environmental deterioration possibly caused by removing the item from water. It is extremely important that an individual familiar with the collection and preservation of underwater evidence be utilized for such matters.

Not Everything Is Submerged

Many of those involved with investigating an underwater crime scene will lose sight of the fact that not all evidence associated with the event is submerged. In fact, a great deal of the time, investigative personnel will encounter black water or other environmental conditions that make underwater photography useless. However, even if the environmental conditions do not allow for photographs to be taken, there is plenty of surface-level material that should still be documented. The recommended items to remember to photograph include:

- Object or subject entry point or route
- Object or subject exit point or route
- Overall photographs of geographical area adjacent to the water

INVESTIGATOR'S NOTEBOOK

Suggestions for Adapting to Underwater Environmental Issues

To overcome the difficulties encountered when photographing an underwater scene, a few basic methods can be employed, as follows:

- *If possible, stay shallow.* This will reduce the color loss from light reaching the subject matter. However, if the crime scene is deep and photographs must be taken at a greater depth, the use of a strobe or color correction filter must be employed.

- *Whenever possible, use a strobe (electronic flash).* This will replace the light that is lost underwater.

- *Stay close to your subject.* Because of underwater distortion, coloration issues, and environmental haze, it is wise to keep the distance between the subject and the camera as close as possible.

- *Maintain proper buoyancy.* If a diver-photographer is able to maintain his or her proper positioning (referred to as "attitude"), it will reduce or eliminate distortion and obliteration caused by stirring up environmental elements.

© Shutterstock, Inc./Nutink.

INVESTIGATOR'S NOTEBOOK

Submerged Weapon Handling Tip

Once a weapon is retrieved and subjected to the air, oxidation will begin immediately, and thorough rusting may occur in less than an hour, rendering identification impossible. It is, therefore, crucial to keep the weapon immersed in water until the preservation procedure can be started.

© Shutterstock, Inc./Nutink.

- Photographs of personnel and equipment utilized in the operation (for liability reasons)
- Photographs of staged equipment and personnel not utilized in the operation (for liability reasons)

Underwater Investigation Safety

Obviously, the goal of any criminal investigation—to include the photographic documentation of such an event—is to determine whether or not a crime has been committed, and if so, to document and collect evidence to identify and prosecute the guilty party. However, during this process, the safety of all personnel involved in the process is paramount (**FIGURE 16.16**). Underwater photography is no exception to this rule. The underwater environment is inherently dangerous. It is foreign to humans and hard on equipment. The additional weight and bulk of the required

equipment result in fatigue, entanglement, and other safety issues. The photographer should ensure that all of his or her equipment is connected properly and does not present an entanglement threat. A neck strap should never be used. Instead, equipment should

FIGURE 16.16: A diver makes use of a safety line to search a scene.

be affixed to the wrist, dry suit, or **buoyancy control device (BCD)**, which is the jacket-like piece of equipment used to keep the diver neutrally buoyant. It is extremely important to learn dive-related skills from a certified professional and to participate in ongoing education and training related to the underwater environment to ensure both the safety and competency of the underwater investigator.

CONCLUSION

While each investigation and each crime scene presents its own challenges, there are some that call upon an investigator to utilize very specialized training. Some of the most challenging crime scenes encountered by investigative personnel are those involving underwater crime scenes. Each requires additional skills above and beyond the "routine" crime scene processing methodology. These situations present additional difficulties and hazards to crime scene personnel. The work is difficult and logistically cumbersome. However, when employed, the proper processing of these difficult scenes can be the turning point in a case. It is important that the investigation team be properly trained and take part in ongoing training that is specifically related to matters of crime scene documentation and processing methods involving the underwater environment. What is not looked for will not be found. What is not found cannot be analyzed to uncover the truth.

QUESTIONS FOR REVIEW

1. What are the two benefits of using floating marker buoys?

2. Which federal agency established USERTs and how are they used?

3. A common misconception is that submerged evidence lacks the _____ of evidence found top-side.

4. Another name for the safety diver is the _____.

5. The two types of scenes that need to be processed in an underwater investigation are _____ and _____.

6. Approximately how much larger than actual size will objects underwater appear?

7. Silt, sediment, algae, and pollution can create what are called _____ conditions.

8. The jacket-like piece of equipment used to keep the diver neutrally buoyant is called a _____.

REFERENCES

Becker, R. F. (2000). Myths of underwater recovery operations. *The FBI Law Enforcement Bulletin, 69*, 1–5.

Becker, R. F. (2013). *Underwater forensic investigation* (2nd ed.). Boca Raton, FL: CRC Press.

Dutelle, A.W. (2015). *Basic crime scene photography* (2nd ed.). Seattle, WA: CreateSpace Publishing.

Federal Bureau of Investigation (FBI). (2009). Retrieved October 2, 2012, from http://www.fbi.gov/news /stories/2009/august/diveteam_082109

chapter 17

Defense Lawyers, Prosecutors, and Investigators

> "*My business is that of every other good citizen – to uphold the law. It seems to me that you have much to answer for.*"
>
> **Sherlock Holmes**
> *"The Adventure of Shoscombe Old Place"*

KEY TERMS

affirmative defense

authentication

chain of custody

culpability

damage control

directed verdict of acquittal

elements of the offense

exculpatory evidence

hostile witness

in-court identification

jurisdiction

peremptorily struck

suppression hearing

transcript

venireperson

venue

voir dire

STUDENT LEARNING OUTCOMES

Upon completion of this chapter, students will be able to:

- Describe the responsibility of the defense in a criminal trial
- Identify the responsibility of the prosecution in a criminal trial
- Discuss the responsibility of the investigator in preparing to testify in a criminal trial
- Recognize the value of a prosecution summary

The Defense

All states require lawyers to adhere to a code of professional responsibility. Each code requires attorneys to maintain client confidentiality and provide the best possible defense allowed by law and propriety. The conventional wisdom is that if the defense does its job, the prosecution does its job, and the police do their job, a just verdict will result. The only consolation that a defense lawyer has in defending a client who he or she believes to be guilty is that justice will be done on the condition that all participants in the legal process act competently.

A defense lawyer does not inquire into a client's guilt or innocence. It is not in the client's best interest to confess guilt, and most clients do not. On the other hand, it could injure the quality of a defense lawyer's preparation of the defendant's case if he or she were to rely heavily on the defendant's protestations of innocence. Believing in the defendant's innocence may prevent the lawyer from examining certain evidence or interviewing witnesses and thus revealing conflicts best discovered before trial. It is virtually an axiom of criminal law that a defense attorney should not assume that a client has told the whole truth. Valuable information may be lost to an attorney who places too much confidence in the statements of a criminal client (**FIGURE 17.1**).

Defensive Burden and Affirmative Defenses

The legal burden generally borne by the defendant can be summed up succinctly: none. It is the responsibility of the defense lawyer to ensure that the defendant receives a fair trial and that neither the prosecution nor the court trespasses upon the due process rights of the defendant. Certain defenses require a preliminary showing of the applicability of the defensive position to the offense (Scheb, 2010). These defenses are referred to as **affirmative defenses**.

The state generally has the responsibility to carry the burden of proof. It always has the responsibility to carry the burden of persuasion. In specific situations enumerated by statutes (codes of criminal procedure), the defense has the responsibility to put forth certain defenses, the most common being self-defense. The list of affirmative defenses is not a long one. It varies from state to state but typically includes the following:

- Insanity
- Incompetence
- Self-defense
- Coercion
- Entrapment

In most states, the defense must notify the prosecution in writing before trial that it intends to put forth an affirmative defense and must specify which defense it will use. One common result of an affirmative defense is that a new and separate procedure is required, such as a competency hearing. A competency hearing determines the state of mind of the defendant at the time of trial, whereas an insanity hearing determines the state of mind of the defendant at the time of the crime. If found by the court to be incompetent, the defendant will be sent to a mental institution until his or her competency has been restored, at which point the defendant will be required to stand trial for the offense charged.

In a competency hearing, the burden is on the defendant to produce clear and convincing proof that he or she (1) does not understand the nature of the proceeding against him or her and (2) is unable to assist in his or her own defense. It is the defense lawyer's job to put forth all applicable defenses and to attempt to impeach (call into question the integrity or validity) the credibility of all witnesses and attack the admissibility of all evidence.

Defense Strategies

There are basically three ways that the defense can win a criminal trial:

1. By impeaching the evidence
2. By impeaching the police
3. By creating confusion and delay

> **affirmative defense**
> Defense that requires a preliminary showing of the applicability of the defensive position

FIGURE 17.1: Attorney in court.

© Image Source/Getty Images.

■ Impeaching Evidence

The **chain of custody** is one of the more commonly litigated pretrial issues. An investigator may view his or her role as completed once the evidence has been discovered or bagged. However, a case may fail because of the inability of the prosecution to prove the whereabouts of certain evidence—not that it has been lost, but that it was unaccounted for at some point between the time when it was discovered and the present moment. The prosecution has the responsibility to establish the location of the evidence every second after it came into the custody of the police. It would be embarrassing to discover for the first time, while undergoing cross-examination by the defense, that there was a break in the chain of custody. Like any chain, the chain of custody is only as strong as its weakest link (Hess, 2010).

It is the investigating officer's responsibility to examine the trail of documentation that accounts for the whereabouts of the evidence to be admitted. Every person who has removed the evidence from its repository should be identified in the evidence logs and evidence tags. Any breach in the chain should be discovered well before trial and remedied, if possible. The problem with a break in the chain of custody is that it is often impossible to repair without altering documentation and committing perjury.

If there is a break in the chain, it is the prosecutor's job to determine whether the break is so complete as to render the evidence inadmissible. If the evidence is inadmissible, the prosecutor must then decide whether sufficient untainted evidence exists to win a conviction. Under common law, a chain of custody must be shown from the moment evidence was discovered until it appears in the courtroom, so that the court can be satisfied that what the prosecutor is attempting to have entered into evidence is the same item discovered by the police and that the item has not been altered. Evidence should be handled only by those people who need to handle it. That need should be predicated on something other than curiosity.

The investigator who recovers a particular item of evidence will be responsible for testifying about what happened to the item once it was taken from the search site. Other than packaging, storing, and testing, the best thing that can happen to evidence is nothing. Every removal of evidence from storage should be recorded. If persons other than the testifying officer have handled the evidence, they may be called by the defense to testify. They will be asked to explain the purpose of the removal, the procedures of removal, where the evidence was taken, what was done to it, and, most important, whether there is any way to be certain that the item labeled as a specific piece of evidence is really the item recovered and not another similar item.

Evidence should be checked against the evidence log compiled during the investigation to ensure that all evidence has been retrieved. Chain-of-custody testimony is basically the same for all evidence. The chain of custody is not proven until the evidence has been identified appropriately. **Authentication** is a process separate from establishing the chain of custody, and its exact nature depends on the specific evidence to be entered. Authentication before the court is often referred to as establishing an evidentiary foundation or a predicate for admissibility.

Officers or investigators should be familiar with the questions and answers that establish the chain of custody during a trial. It is the responsibility of the testifying investigator to understand the rules of evidence well enough to be able to testify competently, and the investigator should anticipate chain-of-custody inquiries about any evidence. Once the witness has been identified and the chain of custody established, the court will require authentication of the evidentiary item. Chain-of-custody testimony evolved to ensure that items admitted into evidence have not been altered, and authentication evolved to help establish that evidentiary items are what the lawyers claim them to be.

A self-authenticating item is one that requires no assistance in establishing its authenticity; a certified copy of a birth certificate requires no elaborate protocol to establish that it is, in fact, a certified birth certificate. State and federal rules of evidence usually set out which items are self-authenticating. The testimony of the investigator typically is the predicate (foundation) for the authenticity of evidentiary items that are not self-authenticating.

Overlooked evidence and contaminated evidence are errors that do not readily lend themselves to repair. It is best to discover any such errors prior to trial. Bringing them to the attention of the prosecuting attorney will allow a legal analysis of the tainted evidence and its impact on the remaining evidence. If it is determined that the remaining evidence is also tainted or insufficient for winning a conviction, the charges can be dropped and the investigation resumed. If the case is dismissed after the jury has been sworn in or acquittal has been won, the investigation will remain closed forever.

The time to admit or discover errors is before trial. A conscientious investigator and a conscientious prosecutor should never lose a case based on investigative error or contaminated evidence. Such problems should be uncovered long before trial and a tactical decision should be made regarding the viability and vulnerability of the prosecution.

■ Impeaching the Police

Closely tied to the issue of inadmissible evidence is the question of the competence and credibility of the police. Obviously, an attack on the training, education, and experience of the officers involved would be one way to try to discredit the evidence—a main defense objective. This strategy is sometimes referred to as "striking the evidence over the shoulder of the police." If training, education, and experience issues can be raised, they could affect a jury's view of the credibility of the testifying witness and everything he or she has touched in the course of the investigation. If even one small bit of evidentiary procedure is lacking in the conduct of the investigating team, the whole team will be viewed more skeptically. A discredited police officer reflects discredit on the entire investigative team and on the investigative process.

The police are subject to greater personal scrutiny than any other type of witness. An officer's entire personnel record, job performance, and personal life, as well as any complaints made against the officer, will be examined prior to trial. Anything that can be used to undermine the officer's testimony will be admissible on the grounds of challenging the officer's competence and credibility (**FIGURE 17.2**).

Suppose a prosecutor discovers for the first time at trial that the chief investigator in a racially charged case is a racist. The options confronting the prosecution are fairly straightforward: Call the witness or do not call the witness (keeping in mind that a questionable witness can still be called by the defense as a hostile witness). If the prosecution decides to call the witness, it must be prepared to deal with the racial issue. No purpose will be served by attempting to distance itself from its own witness. According to the law, it is understood that the party calling a witness in effect vouches for that witness. A questionable witness can only reflect badly upon him- or herself and the prosecution.

The questions that the prosecution has to ask in deciding whether to call a questionable witness are these:

- Is the witness vital to the prosecution's case?

- Is there sufficient evidence without this witness to win a conviction?

If the witness is vital to the prosecution's case, two additional questions need to be asked:

- Can the witness's questionable behavior, attribute, or opinion be presented in such a way that will not alienate the jury?

- If the behavior, attribute, or opinion cannot be so presented, what impact will it have on the jury?

If sufficient evidence exists to win a conviction without this witness, other questions arise:

- Will the defense call the witness?

- If so, what impact will this witness have when called by the defense as a **hostile witness** (a witness who is favorable to the other side)?

When the analysis of the situation has been completed, the prosecution must decide whether to go forward with its case or dismiss it. No matter how heinous the crime, insufficient evidence and impeachable witnesses (persons whose veracity is open to question) undermine not only the case in question but also the criminal justice system as a whole. It is too late to ask the necessary questions at the time of trial.

The prosecutor's remedy for tainted evidence or unreliable witnesses is dismissing a case. Unfortunately, police, investigators, and prosecutors sometimes compound the problem by attempting to engage in **damage control**. That is a fatal mistake. Sometimes, prosecutors become so emotionally involved in a case that they cannot distance themselves enough to objectively assess the impact of prospective

FIGURE 17.2: Police officer testifying in court.

© DC Debs/Getty Images.

hostile witness
Witness who is favorable to the other side

damage control
Distorting evidence and records to try to salvage a case that should otherwise be dismissed

damaging evidence or testimony. They want a conviction so badly that they lose sight of their professional duty, which is to see that justice is done. When objectivity is lost, disaster looms if a case that should be dismissed is not. The trial then becomes a series of damage control skirmishes that ultimately will sink the prosecution's case and undermine the judicial system.

■ Confusion and Delay

There is an old legal defense axiom: If you can't win on the facts, argue the law; if you can't win on the law, argue the facts; if you can't win on either, delay. The U.S. Constitution guarantees a defendant a speedy trial. The truth is, most defendants do not want a speedy trial. As long as the trial is not held, a verdict of guilty is not rendered. As long as a trial is not held, the defendant (if bonded) remains free. The longer the trial is delayed, the greater the chance the state will lose a witness and the dimmer the memories will become. Most defendants do not benefit by rushing to the courthouse, and they have everything to gain by waiting.

There are competing components of the U.S. Constitution that come into play in getting a defendant to trial. The U.S. Supreme Court has handed down many decisions dealing with proper legal representation and efforts put forth in preparing a defense. The defendant's right to have sufficient time to prepare a defense conspires against a speedy trial. The very nature of the U.S. criminal justice system also influences how soon a defendant comes to trial. Most judges and prosecutors face a crowded criminal trial docket and, therefore, do not oppose postponing criminal trial proceedings, except in high-profile cases. But while the wheels of justice slowly turn, police witnesses change agencies and eyewitnesses move, their memories wane, or they die. A speedy trial is virtually a mythical beast in today's judicial forums.

Another old defense axiom is that a good defense lawyer can make the simplest cases complex. Many cases involve forensic evidence and complicated expert testimony. The more difficult the testimony is to understand, the more room the defense has to sow confusion. Trials in which DNA testimony occurs are so convoluted that even people who understand DNA typing often lose track of the testimony and its significance. Instead of discussing forensic aspects of blood and its genetic composition, the defense attorney, in cross-examination, might bring up population statistics, laboratory procedures, and other matters of little relevance to the question of who left blood at the crime scene. This approach uses two defense principles: impeach the evidence and confuse the jury. Without actually impeaching the evidence, the defense attorney can obscure the forensic procedures so much that a jury member might mistake confusion for reasonable doubt. All testifying witnesses must have the ability to make something difficult easy to comprehend and must understand what they are testifying about so well that they can provide clear answers to questions intended to obfuscate. A cross-examination conducted by a competent defense attorney can be a fearsome thing and should not be underestimated by the witness or the prosecution.

Suppression Hearings

More cases are lost in **suppression hearings** than by a verdict of acquittal. Indeed, investigators spend more time in these hearings than they do testifying at trial, for it is in these hearings that most of the important judicial decisions regarding evidence, confessions, and police conduct (or misconduct) are raised and resolved. A suppression hearing gives defendants an opportunity to see what kind of case the prosecution has and what caliber of witnesses it is facing. In most instances, if a defendant's motion to suppress illegally obtained evidence and statements is granted, the prosecution dismisses the case for lack of evidence. It is important to remember that the prosecution's burden is to prove the offense beyond a reasonable doubt, which represents a substantial increase over the burden of proof that police need to make an arrest.

Motions to suppress are heard long before a jury is picked or a trial date is set. The defense need not worry about the impression that the jury will get from harsh treatment of the testifying witnesses. Investigating officers can be made to feel like criminals through vigorous and vehement cross-examination. The defense can use the suppression hearing to assess the opposition.

The best way to avoid a suppression hearing is to ensure that all police conduct is above question. An investigator should presume that any investigation will end up at trial and at a motion to suppress. It might not be true, but no one is able to distinguish beforehand which investigations will lead to a trial and which will not. The investigation that has taken evidentiary shortcuts is almost certainly doomed, but it may be years before the trial reveals that to the investigating team. In the realm of criminal investigation, there are no sure things and no unimportant pieces of evidence.

suppression hearing
A pretrial hearing in front of a judge to determine constitutional issues related to the admissibility of evidence

The two most commonly litigated issues in criminal cases are illegal searches and seizures and illegally obtained statements. Given the quantity of time and effort that goes into training criminal investigative teams, one would think that team members would know the differences between a legal and an illegal search, a legal and an illegal arrest, and legally and illegally obtained confessions. However, the rate of suppressed evidence strongly suggests that the performance of many police officers is deficient. Either the training they received was inadequate or they have chosen to ignore the training and conduct the investigation in a way that is inconsistent with their training (Leo, 2009).

The Prosecution

In a trial, the prosecution has the burden to prove four things: subject matter jurisdiction, venue, identification of the party charged, and elements of the offense. Each criminal trial is a competition involving these four issues. Although a trial may take a day, week, month, or even longer to complete, the basic requirement of the prosecution is to prove beyond a reasonable doubt each and every element of the offense with which the defendant has been charged. The prosecution must also establish that the court trying the matter has **jurisdiction** of the case, that the venue is proper, and that the person standing trial is the one charged with the offense (**FIGURE 17.3**).

Jurisdiction

Each state has a tiered system of trial courts, ranging from small-claims courts to courts like those featured on television to courts of last review (often referred to as appellate or supreme courts). Trial courts are granted the authority to hear cases based on their subject

FIGURE 17.3: Courtroom.

© D Lewis 33/Getty Images.

matter and/or the amount of money at stake. Criminal courts are generally divided into two categories: courts handling serious crimes (felonies) and courts handling less serious offenses (misdemeanors). Court jurisdiction has nothing to do with geography; it has to do with statutory authority. It should not be confused with police jurisdiction. Police jurisdiction is geographic in nature, for it sets the territorial boundaries within which police may act. Court jurisdiction in a criminal case is determined by the type of offense. If it is a felony case, it is heard in district court; if it is a misdemeanor case, it is heard in a lesser court. Lesser courts are referred to as courts of limited jurisdiction.

It is necessary to show the court in which a case is being tried that the offense charged is covered by the court's statutory or constitutional authority. Proof of the court's appropriateness is generally accomplished through the testimony of the criminal investigator. Such proof is most crucial in states that determine the seriousness of theft offenses based on the sum stolen. If stealing something that has a value of more than $750 is a felony, there must be testimony offered by the state proving the value of the item stolen in order to establish for the record that the offense was, in fact, a felony over which the court has felony jurisdiction. Without that showing, the state has failed to prove an essential ingredient of its case and may be subject to a motion for a **directed verdict of acquittal** when the defense raises the issue to the judge. Upon a motion for a directed verdict, the court will direct the court reporter to examine the record for any testimony pertaining to the value of the item stolen. Should that testimony not be there, the defendant's motion may be granted, which results in a dismissal of the case. The **transcript** typed by the court stenographer is the official record of what has taken place during the course of the trial. Upon appeal, the only issues that will be reviewed by the court are those raised at the time of trial and memorialized in the trial record (transcript).

Venue

The geographic area over which a court presides is called its **venue**. (The concept of a court's venue can be understood by comparing venue to police jurisdiction.) The prosecutor has the responsibility to establish, through competent testimony, that the crime with which the defendant is charged has occurred in an area over which the court has authority. The state generally proves this element through police testimony. The Sixth Amendment to the U.S. Constitution requires

jurisdiction
The statutory authority of a court to hear a case; in general, it is the authority to apply the law or govern

directed verdict of acquittal
Dismissal of a case that results from the prosecution's failure to prove that the court hearing the case has the jurisdiction to do so

transcript
The official record of what has taken place during the course of the trial, typed by the court stenographer

venue
The geographic area over which a court presides

that the defendant be tried in the geographic area in which the offense was committed. An investigator must testify that the crime occurred in the state, county, and city over which the court has authority. Failure to do so will result in a motion by the defendant for a directed verdict of acquittal. It should be noted that double jeopardy attaches once the jury has been sworn in, so that a dismissal prevents the prosecution from refiling the case, and the defendant goes free.

In-Court Identification

In every criminal case, the prosecution must assure the court that the individual in court is the same person charged with the offense of which he or she stands accused. The **in-court identification** of the defendant is not necessarily a cursory affair. The prosecutor may ask a witness to confirm the defendant's identity and receive that confirmation, but it is not only the judge who must be satisfied that the defendant has been identified as the perpetrator. On appeal, the reviewing court will consult the trial transcript (record) in determining whether the identification was made acceptably (Bacigal, 2008).

The problem with "letting the record reflect" identification (e.g., that the witness pointed to the defendant) is that the record reflects only words and conduct. It is the testimony of the prosecutor that has established the identity of the defendant, but the prosecutor is not a competent witness, and what he or she says is not evidence. It should be apparent that this method of identifying the defendant does not meet legal requirements (unless the trial is videotaped). It helps if the witness and the prosecutor know what is required for making a proper in-court identification of the defendant. The protocol outlined in the Investigator's Notebook is one that has withstood appellate review.

Elements of the Offense

That the burden of the prosecution is to prove the **elements of the offense** may seem self-evident, but proving this is not always as simple as it seems. The prosecution and the testifying investigator have the responsibility of knowing what the elements of an offense are and what facts to be admitted into evidence support each and every element of the offense.

Many investigators have a superb familiarity with the penal codes of their states and can quote line and verse in discussing various arrests and prosecutions in which they have been involved. Yet, it is an entirely different skill to be able to recognize, from a labyrinth of information and facts, exactly what crime has been committed and what can be charged. Relying on the state penal code will always leave a gap in an investigator's understanding of the legal elements of various offenses. Applicable case law helps to interpret code provisions when ambiguity arises. There are a number of relevant cases that accompany every section and offense enumerated in the penal code. The well-prepared investigator has an annotated version of the penal code that assists in fully understanding the elements of an offense.

For example, according to most penal codes, burglary of a habitation occurs when a person enters or remains on the premises of another, without effective consent of the owner, for the purpose of committing theft or another felony. By this definition, can a person burglarize his or her own home? It would seem not. If a person, seeing an open window, pushes a pole through the window and lifts up and removes a purse resting on the table without any part of his or her person entering the dwelling, has a burglary been committed? Not if we apply the literal penal definition. Or if a person, seeing an open window and a

INVESTIGATOR'S NOTEBOOK
Establishing Courtroom Identification

In establishing a courtroom identification of the defendant, the prosecution must ask a witness from the witness stand to point out the person who committed the crime or was arrested for the offense. This must be followed by a request from the prosecution to describe the defendant and where she or he is sitting. The oral testimony is the only part of the transcript that allows appellate courts to determine whether the defendant has been identified as the suspect.

purse on a table, sends in a trained monkey to retrieve the purse, has a burglary been committed? The answer to this question as well will not be determinable without annotated cases interpreting the code. A well-trained investigator knows not only the codified elements of an offense but also where to find the cases to assist in interpreting the codes when an element of human ambiguity enters the fray. For the curious, yes, a person can burglarize his or her own home, and using a pole device or trained animal has been determined by the courts as extending the human arm and, thus, as constituting burglary.

A failure to prove jurisdiction, venue, in-court identification, or the elements of the offense charged will result in a verdict for the defendant and a loss for the prosecution. Remember, the prosecution is part of the criminal investigation team, and when the prosecution loses, the investigator and the investigation lose.

Investigators and Trials

If we believe what we see in the movies and on television, the criminal investigator's job is finished once the suspect has been apprehended. In the larger scheme, that often is the point of embarkation for the most difficult part of the investigator's job. The trial and the investigator's testimony are awaiting somewhere down the line (**FIGURE 17.4**).

Testimonial Devices to Avoid the Truth

There are numerous opportunities during the course of a criminal investigation for things to go wrong. Conducting an error-free investigation is impossible, and what is done to address the errors that occur will often determine the outcome of the investigation and the trial. Once

an error has been made, there are three ways of dealing with it:

1. Deny it ever occurred (denial).
2. Blame someone or something else for the error (scapegoating).
3. Admit the error and examine various ways to address it (growth).

■ Denial

Denying that an error has been made may result in perjured testimony. If the error is not acknowledged in the documentation, the trial can become very uncomfortable for the testifying investigator. An investigator who intends to participate in successful prosecutions must excel at two things: documentation and testifying. It serves no purpose for the best of investigators to take the witness stand without adequate documentation in support of the investigation. Trials often occur months and sometimes even years after the investigation has been completed. The only reliable record of the investigation is the documentation prepared by the investigator. If that documentation is sparse, inaccurate, or compositionally inept, the testifying investigator risks having to try to remedy those shortcomings on the witness stand. A catastrophe will usually occur if the officer testifies to facts not included in the documentation. Such testimony is a gift to the defense. If the facts are important enough to tell the jury, why were they not included in the original report? The inference obviously is that they would have been important enough had they actually happened.

A failing memory that recovers in time for the trial is also risky. If a report was made soon after the crime, would it not be a more accurate rendition of the facts than an uncorroborated distant recollection? Obviously, a contemporaneous recording of significant events is more reliable than remembrances occurring months or years later, and any suggestion to the contrary is viewed as suspect.

Good trial lawyers are not born; they are made. Competent police witnesses are also shaped by their training and experience. Furthermore, a superbly skilled but unprepared trial lawyer will lose to a well-prepared trial lawyer of modest talents every time. This suggests that any witness who enters the gladiatorial arena of the law must be well prepared in order to handle a good trial lawyer's questions (Becker, 1999). The quality of a witness's testimony is a reflection of the witness's preparation. The quality of the preparation is, in turn, a

FIGURE 17.4: Courtroom.

© Imaginima/Getty Images.

reflection of the quality of the documentation completed by the investigating officers, the time spent in studying that documentation, and the sources of that documentation.

A testifying police investigator can be a defense lawyer's ally or worst nightmare. In selecting the jury, defense lawyers inquire into every **venireperson's** (prospective juror's) occupational background. Anyone with police relatives or friends will most likely be struck from a jury. Prospective jurors will be asked if they believe that a police officer is more believable than any other witness. They will be asked if they believe that police officers do not make mistakes. They will be asked if they believe that police officers do not lie. Anyone answering these questions with a yes will likely be **peremptorily struck** (struck without reason) from the jury. Why do defense lawyers place so much emphasis on police officers? They know that the entire case may rest on the testimony of the police and the investigation they performed. They also know that each officer is bestowed with an invisible "shroud of veracity" by virtue of the esteem with which police are generally held in the community (Brodsky, 2009).

Many people believe and want to believe that police officers are honest and lack deceit. The whole jury has anticipated, since the **voir dire** (jury selection), the moment that the testifying investigator is called by the bailiff as a witness. That officer is scrutinized the moment he or she steps through the door and enters the courtroom. If the officer walks confidently, is dressed professionally, and shows personal pride in his or her appearance, many on the jury will extend the courtesy of belief. The officer's believability usually cannot be damaged by anything that the defense may have done or attempted to do, but it can be stripped away by incompetent, insincere, or dishonest testimony. The penalty for false testimony for any other witness is to be labeled a perjurer and will be forgotten. The penalty for a criminal investigator who is incompetent or dishonest is a verdict of acquittal for the defendant and a prosecutor, who will be extremely reluctant to prosecute that officer's cases.

Habit is a tool or a vice. If, over a period of time, all investigations are conducted with the same meticulousness, a habit aimed at success will eventually be established. That habit is difficult to cultivate, because police know that the majority of investigations leading to arrest will never go to trial. If a case is not likely to be tried, why invest time and effort providing documentation, processing evidence, and interviewing witnesses? Presuming that a case will not go to trial or that another officer will do the writing ensures embarrassment or dishonesty if the presumption is proved false. The only foolproof way to avoid falling victim to the plea-bargain presumption is to prepare every case as though it were going to trial. This level of preparation may be tedious, but it certainly provides practice. And when a case does go to trial, the high quality of the preparation will make the defense lawyer's job much more difficult.

An investigator with experience testifying will not wait until the day of trial to review the case. The prudent course is to examine the paperwork, evidence, logs, photographs, diagrams, sketches, and charts that will be admitted through the officer's testimony. Reviewing the condition of all evidence, including markings, labels, and the chain of custody, is also important. All diagrams, reports, statements, notes, and sketches should have been constructed with the trial in mind and lend themselves to quality enlargements that will assist the jury in understanding the investigator's testimony. It is a mistake to use technical language and jargon if not absolutely necessary. Keeping it simple is the surest way to avoid complications during cross-examination.

■ Scapegoating

We have grown accustomed to referring to automobile collisions as accidents, or something that occurred by chance. In truth, chance has little to do with most traffic collisions. Speed, tailgating, intoxication, and lack of attention are the precipitating causes of collisions—not fortune, chance, or fate.

Similarly, police will euphemistically say that a defendant got off on a technicality. In such instances, the police probably failed to do their job or failed to do it correctly. There are no technicalities upon which a defendant may be released. Only police (or prosecutorial or judicial) misconduct of constitutional dimensions can result in the defendant being released on a technicality. Is coercing a confession a technicality? Some police believe it is. Is searching a person or his or her home or effects without probable cause a technicality? Some police believe it is. By reducing an infringement of the U.S. Constitution to the level of a technicality, police show their disdain for the Bill of Rights and the blueprint of American due process. Defense lawyers, for the most part, point out and exaggerate the errors of the police and the prosecution; they seldom manufacture them.

venireperson
A prospective juror

peremptorily struck
Struck (from the jury) without a reason

voir dire
Jury selection process

■ Aiming for Error-Free Investigations

There will be mistakes made during the investigation and during the trial. There are no perfect trials or investigations. A perfect investigation is suspect. Yet, if police officers cannot conduct a perfect, error-free investigation, why should they try?

Although error-free investigations are unattainable, attempting to achieve them is highly desirable. The never-ending efforts of the police to perform the perfect investigation will be recognized and will bear fruit both in and out of the courtroom. The investigator who leaves no stone unturned will be more successful in investigating crime than the investigator who rushes to judgment based on hastily gathered information and evidence—that is, if we define success as conducting investigations that lead to convictions or rigorous plea bargains.

Loose ends are errors of omission and can be just as costly as errors of commission. It is not helpful to discover at the time of trial that the defense has found a witness who places the defendant at a different location than that alleged in the indictment or who has the defendant departing the scene hours before the crime was committed. Errors of omission are the easiest to avoid. If investigators do the job they are paid to do in the way they are paid to do it, errors of omission will be kept to a minimum.

How do you explain to a prosecutor that you failed to discover the existence of an alibi witness? How do you dispute testimony that you never knew existed? How do you prepare for trial when there is relevant information missing? How do you explain to the jury your efforts to convict a possibly innocent person? How do you explain the failure to discover **exculpatory evidence** (evidence indicating innocence)? All of these are questions that investigators, prosecutors, and judges would rather avoid. They can be avoided by striving for perfection and following all leads, even after the puzzle has seemingly been solved.

Ethical Testimony

Prior to a suppression hearing or a trial, prosecutors may discover problems with the case being prepared. Hasty conferences with investigators may be called and a joint exercise in damage control may be undertaken. If damage control is accomplished by modification of the investigating officer's recollection of an event, handling of evidence, or personal philosophy, the result is perjury, no matter what the motivation. It is easy to believe that the end justifies the means—that the defendant has done a bad thing and deserves to be punished and, therefore, lying to ensure that punishment is acceptable. Months, sometimes years, of hard investigative work might be at stake.

It should not be difficult to tell the truth, even when you know that the truth may set free a defendant you believe to be guilty. It is at this point that one's personal philosophy becomes an issue. The decision to lie, fabricate evidence, or deny **culpability** (criminal responsibility) is determined well before the opportunity to lie, fabricate evidence, or deny culpability arises. An individual's character and personal philosophy are part of what he or she carries around in dealing with the world. The formation of a personal philosophy begins in early childhood and continues in the home, church, school, and on the street. An individual's personal philosophy never achieves its final form but is constantly evolving. If nurtured, it grows in the right direction; if not, it grows in the other direction.

It is not the big issues, such as police corruption, but rather the day-to-day decisions that reflect what a police officer's personal philosophy is. A personal philosophy does not come hardwired from birth. A person does not awaken one morning and make the decision to be honest or dishonest. That decision is the result of a long series of incremental steps. Many people who work in criminal justice believe that we need to teach ethics by preaching about what is right and pointing fingers at those who do wrong. Yet, the basis of ethical conduct resides in the personal philosophy that we bring to our encounters. It is not unique to police work. The same philosophy accompanies us no matter what it is that we choose to do with our lives. The early lessons we learned have stuck and grown or they have died. If the latter, their death was not a quick and painless one. Those values and lessons die a slow, lingering death—but they, nonetheless, die unless they are nourished. Nourishment is easy: You just use them. Every time an opportunity arises to do the right thing and you do it, the probability of doing the right thing in the future has increased. As you sit reading this book, you know whether you are an honest or a dishonest person. Neither anything in an ethics curriculum nor anything that could be included in this book can change your degree of honesty.

Preparing for Trial

When preparing for trial, the investigator must meet with the prosecutor a few days before the scheduled date of the trial. It is during this

culpability
Criminal responsibility

exculpatory evidence
Evidence indicating innocence

INVESTIGATOR'S
NOTEBOOK
Checklist for Testimony Preparation

1. Complete all documentation in a timely fashion (as information, evidence, and data are obtained).

2. Examine all evidence prior to trial.

3. Compare all evidence with references in documentation and relocate any identifying markings or characteristics.

4. Gather all field notes and sketches and place them in a separate folder (examine for extrinsic information).

5. Confer with the prosecutor prior to trial in anticipation of trial.

6. Contact all lab technicians and forensic scientists and discuss laboratory findings.

7. Contact the medical examiner and discuss the examination and documentation provided by his or her office.

8. Contact all witnesses to reconfirm information provided and the validity of statements made.

9. Select appropriate apparel and ensure appropriate grooming.

10. Arrive at the courthouse early.

11. Remain at the courthouse until dismissed by the prosecutor.

12. Testify objectively and truthfully.

13. Treat the defense attorney with the same courtesy that was extended to the prosecution (especially if the defense attorney's conduct does not warrant it). The old adage, "Don't get mad, get even" is self-defeating and should be replaced with the saying, "Don't get mad, don't get even—win."

14. After testifying, do not leave the courthouse until excused by the judge.

© Shutterstock, Inc./Nutink.

pretrial conference that the choreography for the trial will be mapped out. Between the two, the following will be determined:

- What role the investigator and the investigative team will play

- The order of testimony, based on the chronology of events and the need for a human conduit in the admission of various types of evidence

- The order of presentation of evidence; each item of evidence is preceded by its proof in the chain of custody

- Strong points; every case has them

- Weak points; every case has these too, and the trick is to discover them before the defense does

- Trial strategy, including anticipated witness impact, anticipated victim impact, types of favorable jurors, and damage control

Additionally, the lead investigator can review the following:

- The rules of evidence, including evidentiary predicates, chain of custody, and authentication rules

- The location and health of all evidence, evidence logs, photos, and photo logs

- Documentation, such as witness statements, offense reports, confessions, Miranda warnings, waivers, and medical records

- Availability of testifying witnesses

- Expert witness testimony, along with the evidence and documentation upon which it will be based

Expected Courtroom Demeanor

The public has expectations of how a testifying officer should look and sound, which are sometimes unrealistic and possibly influenced by Hollywood and television images. They do expect officers to testify professionally and objectively. The greatest gift a testifying officer can give the defense is the loss of his or her self-control. The witness stand is not a place from which to do battle. The system is adversarial, but it is the truth that the prosecution uses to build its case and it is the truth that the prosecution expects to get from all state witnesses. Any discourtesy by the defense lawyer is a matter to be attended to by the prosecutor and the judge—not the witness.

The expectations of the court and the public require that the officer who intends to testify consider the following before entering the courtroom:

- Ensure appropriate dress and appearance—from head to toe (shoes are the most often neglected aspect; haircuts fall into second place).

- People encountered in, around, and outside of the courthouse should be treated with respect, even adverse witnesses. This is a rule that should be followed all the time but is most important with regard to trials. Jurors, the defense, the press, or the public may be watching.

- Do not discuss the case outside of the courtroom, the prosecutor's office, or the police station.

- Arrive early and get a feel for the courtroom to which the case has been assigned. Walk around. Make it yours.

- Engage in no discussions with the defense or anyone on the defense team without the presence of the prosecutor (Lieberman, 2009).

When testifying, it is important to remember that you represent the state and that you carry a burden, responsibility, and benefit in your testimony. You are entitled to be believed and enjoy that presumption until proven unworthy. The following are guidelines for testifying.

- Make eye contact with the attorney while he or she is asking you questions. Look to the jury when you answer. The lawyer who inquired knows that the answer he or she is seeking is for the benefit of the jury, so respond directly to him or her.

- The truth is your only weapon. You know more about the subject in question than anyone in the room. Do not be intimidated.

- Listen to the question, because an objection may be lodged and the question may have to be rephrased. By listening to and remembering the first question, you will know what the prosecutor is asking in the rephrased question.

- If more than one question is asked, answer the first one and then ask for the second one to be repeated. Watch for a series of quick questions that require either all "yes" or all "no" answers: You may be hit with one to which the prior answers do not apply.

- Remember that you are in control. You cannot be asked another question until you have answered the one initially posed. Take your time. Do not relinquish the tempo of the questioning. It relinquishes control.

- Answer "yes" or "no" whenever possible to defense questions. Let the defense ask for elaboration.

- If your answer sounds bad, wait for the prosecution to ask a rehabilitating question. That is the prosecutor's job, not the witness's.

- If you do not know the answer, do not be reluctant to say so without explanation unless asked. Again, the prosecution will ask the rehabilitating question for you to answer.

- Use exact Miranda waiver language—read it.

- Use approximations in times, distance, and measurements.

- "Yes, sir" and "No, sir" or "Yes, ma'am" and "No, ma'am" are good ways to address both the prosecution and the defense.

- Using notes to refresh your memory entitles the defense to see them. Be sure there is nothing offensive in your field notes.

- Be sure that there are no notes from other investigations in your notebook. The defense gets to look at everything you bring to the witness stand.

- Testify about what you know, not what you think or suspect, unless specifically asked to do so. The more vigorous the examination, the more thought and time you should put into your answers.

- Do not hesitate to admit that you have talked to others about this case. These others might include the prosecution, witnesses, suspects, victims, and fellow officers.

- Be courteous. There is no excuse for a combative police witness, ever.

Prosecution Summary

In each case, the investigating officer should prepare a prosecution summary. The reasons and content were discussed earlier. In preparing to testify, a check of the prosecution summary and a review of its contents will help an officer anticipate the flow of the trial and the nature of the testimony. Some of the things in the summary that will assist the investigator in gearing up for trial include the following:

1. The indictment

   - Penal code offense: The elements of the crime that the state must prove and that the investigator must be prepared to address

2. Probable cause as it applies to any searches or arrests

  ■ Any exceptions that may have allowed a search or an arrest on less than probable cause should be noted

  ■ All search and arrest warrants should be examined

3. Statements made by the defendant or on behalf of the defendant

  ■ Revisit the documentation supporting any waiver of rights to legal assistance and to remain silent

  ■ Anticipate the defense that will be presented

  ■ Anticipate any affirmative defenses that may be pled

4. Witness statements

  ■ Inconsistencies within a statement

  ■ Inconsistencies between statements

  ■ Remember that in the real world, no two people perceive an event in exactly the same way; expect inconsistencies

  ■ Assessment of the reliability of the witnesses

5. Review all evidence

  ■ Tags

  ■ Logs

  ■ Pictures

6. Prepare all diagrams and sketches for enlargement and trial use

CONCLUSION

What most people know about criminal trials they have learned from television. Unfortunately, what they have seen has not been a realistic portrayal. Considering that criminal trials take days or weeks, trying to summarize a trial in 15 minutes or fewer is going to be surreal at best. The movies portray only the emotional high points. Few ever portray an appropriately conducted jury selection process. Many lawyers believe that a trial can be won or lost during the jury selection process. Whether that is true or not, it is the only time that lawyers get to speak personally with each juror, and it may well be a pivotal point in a trial.

Pretrial hearings are often where cases are decided. Most criminal cases will never reach a jury trial. The public's preconceived ideas about a trial are irrelevant until a trial that catches its attention is aired. People may believe they are experts on trial procedure based on *Judge Judy* or some other theatrical portrayal, not recognizing that trying a criminal case is as much about procedure as it is about style. In truth, little happens in a well-tried criminal trial that would hold the attention of an audience for more than 20 minutes.

A criminal investigator who is testifying enjoys a special place among the witnesses that will testify. Fact witnesses may only testify about what they saw or heard. Expert witnesses can express opinions based on what they saw and heard and think. Criminal investigators are expert witnesses. The next chapter tells us what is so special about witnesses who are considered experts.

QUESTIONS FOR REVIEW

1. How can a lawyer ethically defend someone he or she believes is guilty? Include in your discussion comments on the ethical obligation a lawyer has to a client.

2. What must the state prove in each and every criminal case that it tries?

3. How does police jurisdiction differ from judicial jurisdiction?

4. What is a motion for a directed verdict of acquittal?

5. Why is an in-court identification of the defendant required, and how is it made?

6. What role does case law play in understanding penal code offenses?

7. What is an affirmative defense, and what effect does it have on the burden of proof in a criminal trial?

8. What are the three basic tactics employed by the defense in an effort to win a criminal trial?

9. What is the chain of custody, and what problems arise in attempting to maintain it?

10. How is a personal philosophy formed, and how does it evolve?

11. What are the advantages to a defendant in delaying a trial?

12. What is a motion to suppress evidence, and what role does it play in a criminal investigation? What issues should arise when the prosecutor and investigator meet to prepare for trial?

13. What things might a testifying investigator consider before entering the courtroom?

14. How might a prosecution summary assist an investigator in preparing for trial?

REFERENCES

Bacigal, R. J. (2008). *Criminal law and procedure: An overview*. Clifton Park, NY: Cengage Learning.

Becker, R. F. (1999). *Scientific evidence and expert testimony handbook*. Springfield, IL: Charles C. Thomas.

Brodsky, S. L. (2009). *Principles and practices of trial consultation*. New York, NY: Guilford Press.

Hess, K. M. (2010). *Criminal investigation*. Clifton Park, NY: Cengage Learning.

Leo, R. A. (2009). *Police interrogation and American justice*. Cambridge, MA: Harvard University Press.

Lieberman, J. D. (2009). *Jury psychology: Social aspects of trial processes*. Burlington, VT: Ashgate.

Scheb, J. M. (2010). *Criminal law and procedure*. Clifton Park, NY: Cengage Learning.

chapter
18

Expert Testimony

KEY TERMS

allod

credentials

Daubert v. Merrill Dow Pharmaceuticals

expert witness

Federal Rule of Evidence 702

fief

Frye v. United States

hearsay

heresy

inquisition

Kumho Tire Co. v. Carmichael

papal inquisition

perjury

police experts

scientific testimony

special jury

tenure

STUDENT LEARNING OUTCOMES

Upon completion of this chapter, students will be able to:

- Recognize what an expert witness is
- Appreciate the history of expert witnesses
- Describe the test for the admissibility of scientific evidence
- Discuss the role of contemporary expert witnesses in criminal trials

Expert Witnesses

Specially trained personnel such as investigators, forensic scientists, criminalists, forensic technicians, and identification technicians collect and examine physical evidence from crime scenes. These individuals are often called upon to testify as expert witnesses. An **expert witness** is someone who is called to answer questions on the stand in a court of law in order to provide specialized information relevant to the case being tried. Because scientific principles relating to physical evidence are often beyond the knowledge of lay people, courts permit persons with specialized training and skills to appear in court to explain and interpret scientific evidence to juries. A person can be considered an "expert" when he or she has sufficient skills, knowledge, or experience in his or her field to help the "trier of fact" to determine the truth. It, therefore, is the duty of the expert witness to educate the jury and provide testimony using terminology that is easily explainable and will not be misunderstood (Fish et al., 2014). Clarity, simplicity, and honesty are essential elements of expert witness testimony. It is suggested that supervisors review reports and conclusions with an unbiased attention to detail to ensure that the paperwork submitted is clear, concise, and accurate. Witnesses cannot deliberately omit relevant facts or encourage incorrect conclusions; these are distortions of the facts. Overstatements of the facts or a suggestion that an individual is guilty will cost an expert witness their integrity.

Expert Witnesses: A Brief History

In today's trials, much time and emphasis is placed on the testimony of expert witnesses. Experts can run the gamut from medical doctors to geneticists. The use of trial experts is not a recent phenomenon. But what exactly qualifies an individual as an expert? And when is such testimony admissible? There has been great debate and much litigation pertaining to what should be allowed as "expert testimony" and what should qualify an individual to be considered as an expert within court. To answer these questions, we must look back at a bit of history.

The Feudal Era

In tracing the roots of the use of expert witnesses to resolve disputes, it is necessary to begin in the feudal era. Medieval history reveals that the roots of feudalism were in the 3rd through the 6th centuries, and many practices were established between the 6th and 9th centuries. Merovingian and Carolingian kings paid their generals and administrators with grants of land; in the 9th century, these fiefs became hereditary and semi-independent (Durant, 1950). In those times, Western European society consisted of freemen, serfs, and slaves. Freemen included nobles, clerics, professional soldiers, practitioners of the professions, most merchants and artisans, and peasants who owned their land or leased it from a feudal lord.

The feudal law of property recognized three forms of land possession:

1. **Allod**: Land held by unconditional ownership
2. **Fief**: Land whose use but not ownership was granted to a vassal on condition of service
3. **Tenure**: Land use granted on condition of payment

Typically, the serf tilled a plot of land owned by a lord or baron, who gave him a life tenure and military protection as long as the serf paid an annual rent in products, labor, or money. In feudal theory, only the king had absolute ownership of the land. The loftiest of nobles was only a tenant (Durant, 1950).

As disputes involving land use and succession arose, manorial courts were established to settle disputes between tenants, or between tenant and lord; disputes between lord and vassal or lord and lord were submitted to juries of men of equal standing and of the same fief. Procedure in feudal law attempted to substitute public penalties for private revenge. In a regime where judges and executors of law were usually illiterate, custom and law were largely one. When questions arose about law or penalties, the oldest members of the community were asked what had been the custom thereon in their youth. Age and recall were the required characteristics for admitting their learned opinion. The community itself was the chief source of law, and the elders of the community were called as experts by the court to assist in a consistent application of an unwritten law and its penalties.

expert witness
Someone who is called to answer questions on the stand in a court of law in order to provide specialized information relevant to the case being tried

allod
Land held by unconditional ownership

fief
Land whose use but not ownership was granted to a vassal on condition of service

tenure
Land use granted on condition of payment

CASE IN POINT

Truth by Ordeal

Truth by ordeal has a history that extends beyond the Old Testament and has been applied by aborigines of the Australian Outback, Africans, and Scandinavians. The Old Testament speaks of poison as a truth determiner, and it was used in that vein in Africa and India. The ordeal was superstition applied to resolve legal disputes: the belief that a supreme being would not let an innocent person suffer provided the foundation. God or the gods were called upon to serve as an expert in assisting the trier of fact in determining guilt or innocence. The ordeal took many forms, from walking on red-hot plowshares to being bound and thrown in a pond. The conventional wisdom was that witches would not allow themselves to drown, and the innocent would sink. Dead but guiltless was the desired outcome. An "expert" postulated the "facts" that witches float and that innocent people walking across red-hot plowshares would not be burned (Endlich, 2010).

© Shutterstock, Inc./Viastas.

© Shutterstock, Inc./Nutnik.

The Inquisition

heresy
A belief inconsistent with a religion's dogma

papal inquisition
The trying of heretics by the authority of the pope

inquisition
Inquiry

Any nation preparing for war is well advised to—and often does—seek out minor skirmishes to prepare troops and equipment for major engagements. The Church of Rome was no exception. The continuing war on heresy that culminated in the **papal inquisition** began with a series of inquisitional skirmishes that had their justification steeped in the Old Testament (**FIGURE 18.1**). The Old Testament laid down a simple code for dealing with heretics: They were to be carefully examined, and if three reputable witnesses testified to their having "gone and served other gods," the heretics were to be led out from the city and "stoned with stones until they died" (Deuteronomy 17:25).

In classical Rome, where the gods were believed to be allied with the state in close harmony, **heresy** and blasphemy were classed with treason and were punishable by death. Where no accuser could be found to denounce an offender, the Roman judge summoned the

suspect and made an **inquisition**, or inquiry, into the case; from this procedure, the medieval inquisition took its form and name. It was the general assumption of Christians that the Son of God had established the Church. On this assumption, any attack on the Catholic faith was an offense against God Himself. The stubbornly disobedient heretic could only be viewed as an agent of Satan sent to undo the work of Christ, and any man or government that tolerated heresy was serving the devil. The Church looked upon heresy precisely as the state looked upon treason: It was an attack on the very foundation of social order. Pope Innocent III proclaimed:

> The civil law punishes traitors with confiscation of their property, and death.... All the more, then, should we excommunicate, and confiscate the property of those who are traitors to the faith of Jesus Christ; for it is an infinitely greater sin to offend the divine majesty than to attack the majesty of the sovereign. (Durant, 1950, p. 777)

Before the 13th century, inquisition into heresy had been left to local bishops, who waged local wars against a rising tide of heresy. Berthold of Regensburg estimated that there were 150 heretical sects in the 13th century. Most of these were harmless groups that gathered to study the Bible without the assistance of a priest and to interpret various passages as they saw fit. Many felt that priests should live in poverty, as Christ had done. The Franciscan movement arose as such a sect and narrowly escaped being treated as heretical.

In 1185, Pope Lucius III, dissatisfied with the negligence of the bishops in pursuing heresy,

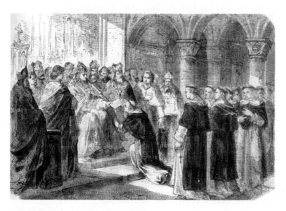

FIGURE 18.1: Papal Inquisition.

© Leemage/Corbis via Getty Images.

ordered them to visit their parishes at least once a year to arrest all suspects, to reckon as guilty, any who would not swear full loyalty to the Church, and to hand over such recalcitrants to the government. Papal legates were empowered to depose bishops negligent in stamping out heresy. In 1215, Innocent III required all civil authorities, on pain of death, to swear publicly to exterminate all heretics from the lands subject to their obedience.

When Gregory IX mounted the papal throne in 1227, he found that despite prosecutions, heresy was growing in most of Italy and France. Pope Gregory appointed a board of inquisitors, headed by a Dominican monk, to sit in Florence and bring the heretics to judgment. This, in effect, was the beginning of the papal inquisition as it was now officially established under the control of the popes.

After 1227, Gregory and his successors sent out an increasing number of special inquisitors to pursue heresy. Inquisitorial procedure might begin with the summary arrest of all charged heretics, sometimes also of all suspects; the visiting inquisitors might summon the entire adult population of a locality for a preliminary examination. Heretics who did not confess were brought before the inquisitorial court. Accused persons could be tried in their absence and condemned to death. Two condemnatory witnesses were required. After 1254, the inquisitors were required to submit all evidence to a group of men of high repute from the community. Often, a board of experts (periti) was called upon to pass judgment on the evidence.

During this process, three legal precedents were established that have endured to our benefit:

1. Confessions must be voluntary

2. A suspect cannot be convicted on the uncorroborated testimony of an accomplice

3. The concept of burden of proof rests on the accusing party

Interestingly, the rationale for using torture to solicit incriminating statements was based on a benevolent motive. The church believed it was necessary to prove guilt beyond not just a reasonable doubt but beyond all doubt. The only way that all doubt could be removed was through self-incrimination. The end sought was admirable; it was the means to that end that we now question.

Experts and the Common Law

In early English common law history, there seem to have been two modes of using expert knowledge:

1. To select as jurymen such persons as were by experience especially fitted to know the class of facts that were before them

2. To call to the aid of the court skilled persons whose opinion it might adopt or not as it pleased

The first mode has been lost, but the second is alive and well, along with a third, more contemporary, application of having the parties in dispute bring forth skilled persons to testify.

The first method was to impanel a **special jury**, which, in this context, means a jury of persons especially fitted to judge the peculiar facts of the case in issue. The first recorded incidence of such a special jury was in 1838 (*Rey v. Wyoherly*, 1838). A jury of persons especially skilled in landlord–tenant relations was impaneled, and the court followed its opinions in disposing of the matter. This specially impaneled jury was no anomaly; its use in resolving trade disputes was common in the city of London throughout the 14th century (Riley, 1868).

The special jury continued as an institution of England. In 1645, the court summoned a jury of merchants to try merchants' affairs because it was conceived that they might have a better understanding of the issues in dispute than others who were not of the profession (Hand, 1901).

The second method discussed was to summon the advice of certain skilled persons to help the court out of its difficulties. In 1345, in an appeal of mayhem, the court summoned surgeons from London to aid them in determining whether a wound was fresh (Riley, 1868). In 1409 and 1555, documents submitted to the court, which were partly in Latin, prompted the justices to seek grammatical masters to assist in the interpretation and construction of the documents (*Buckley v. Thomas*, 1555). Lord Holt of the Kings Bench, in deciding the celebrated case of *Buller v. Crips* (1703), asked the opinion of London merchants as to the effect of refusing negotiability of promissory notes.

Originally, and for many years under common law trial practice, the jury had no witnesses present before them at all. They were advised of the issues in dispute and were allowed to cast about at their own discretion in gathering

> **special jury**
> In common law, a jury of persons especially fitted to judge the peculiar facts of the case in issue

what facts might be available. Those facts were brought with them to the court and considered among the jurors during their deliberations. It was not until the middle of the 15th century that the courts developed the practice of summoning witnesses for the purpose of providing testimony, and it was still later that compulsory process became available (Hand, 1901).

The rules of evidence in England evolved slowly and were focused on the regulation of what evidence the jury could see and hear. Through successive court decisions, judges gradually restricted the material that witnesses might present to the jury. The rule that a witness may not testify to mere opinion was promulgated. The rule was designed to eliminate irrelevant and redundant testimony. An exception to this rule was made for experts.

Obviously, the exception for experts was an anomaly in procedural law that was the resort of the court when an issue was reached that was beyond its knowledge. This anomaly for the benefit of the court was extended to trial adversaries in 1678 in the case of *Rex v. Green*. This was a trial for murder, and the question was raised as to the cause and mechanism of death. Out of an abundance of caution, the court allowed both sides to present physicians as witnesses, thereby balancing the latitude granted the parties. The court thus delegated the exception that it had reserved unto itself to trial adversaries in the hopes that expert opinion to assist the court could be anticipated and provided for by the litigant. This case gave birth to the fledgling industry of expert witnesses, as the common law of England was applied to the trial practice of the United States.

Contemporary Expert Witnesses

We often think of experts as people with advanced educations and lengthy professional résumés. In reality, the court can call on anyone to assist the judge or jury in understanding some aspect of the trial testimony.

Who Is a Scientific Expert?

Scientific evidence can come before the jury only from the mouth of an expert witness. Occasionally, controversy surrounds a particular practice, bringing into question whether such a practice or procedure is, in fact, scientific (see the following Case in Point). In 2004, courts denied fingerprint experts the latitude to testify that fingerprint comparisons are a "match."

In 1993, the U.S. Supreme Court decided in *Daubert v. Merrill Dow Pharmaceuticals* that federal trial court judges were obligated to evaluate the basis of expert testimony in order to determine its reliability and value to the jury. Since 1993, the Supreme Court has decided on another expert testimony case, *Kumho Tire Co. v. Carmichael* (1999), wherein the Court decided that there is no difference between scientific knowledge and technical knowledge for the purpose of determining the admissibility of the testimony. These two cases have established the criteria for the admissibility of expert testimony in federal and state courts.

Lower courts have been busy defining and applying the new expert witness standards to the various circumstances in which experts may be called to testify. Historically, anyone with information that could assist the judge or jury in understanding facts that are relevant to the issues in question could be admitted as an expert witness. The *Daubert* decision and its line of cases suggest that the Supreme Court favors expert testimony and the opinions expressed therein that are based on replicable data gathered through acceptable scientific methodology. This means that experts with no research support for their opinions have found courts unwilling to qualify them as experts.

Courts struggled with the task of determining the reliability of expert testimony for the better part of the 20th century. In 1923, the circuit court of appeals for the District of Columbia developed the first test for assessing expert testimony. In *Frye v. United States* (1923), the court held that for novel scientific evidence to be admissible, the party offering it must establish that the expert testimony and the techniques used to generate the results have been generally accepted as reliable in the scientific community. The "general acceptance" test was plagued with problems from the outset. The terms were vague and susceptible to subjective interpretation by the courts, allowing trial judges to control the admissibility of expert testimony based on what they personally believed was credible and reliable.

The attack on the general acceptance test escalated in the years following the 1975 adoption of the *Federal Rules of Evidence*. Proponents for the elimination of the test argued that the federal rules superseded *Frye* and were void of any reference to the general

---

Daubert v. Merrill Dow Pharmaceuticals Case in which the Supreme Court decided in 1993 that federal trial court judges were obligated to evaluate the basis of expert testimony in order to determine its reliability and value to the jury

Kumho Tire Co. v. Carmichael An expert testimony case decided by the Supreme Court in 1999 that has helped establish the criteria for the admissibility of expert testimony in federal and state courts

Frye v. United States Case in which the first test for assessing expert testimony was developed; in this 1923 case, the circuit court of appeals for the District of Columbia held that for novel scientific evidence to be admissible, the party offering it must establish is that the expert testimony and the techniques used to generate the results have been generally accepted as reliable in the scientific community

CASE IN POINT

Questionable Experts of the Past

Experts can be a source of chicanery and ignorance as well as insight. In 1781, Sir William Herschel, the British astronomer who discovered the planet Uranus, was convinced and publicly pronounced that the "sun was richly stored with inhabitants" (Gardner, 1957). Physicians of the 19th century were encouraged by Dr. Linard Williams, the medical officer to the Insurance Institute of London, to treat people with wide-set eyes as one would horses or cows because the set of their eyes suggested they were not evolved from meat-eating predators but rather from vegetarian bovines and equines (Gardner, 1957). Even the noted physicist Lord Kelvin believed that x-rays were a hoax (Gardner, 1957). Had these scientists been called as expert witnesses in their questionable areas of expertise, what havoc would have been wreaked upon an unsuspecting jury and court? Although Sir William Herschel was an eminent astronomer, could he and should he have been allowed to testify as to the inhabitants of the sun?

EXHIBIT 18.1

Federal Rule of Evidence 702

If scientific, technical, or other specialized knowledge will assist the trier of fact to understand the evidence or to determine a fact in issue, a witness qualified as an expert by knowledge, skill, experience, training, or education may testify thereto in the form of an opinion or otherwise.

Fed. R. Evid. 702

acceptance standard. In 1993, the debate over *Frye* reached a climax when the Supreme Court granted certiorari in *Daubert* and decided that *Federal Rule of Evidence 702* superseded the *Frye* test (**EXHIBIT 18.1**).

Proponents of the general acceptance *Frye* test argued that this ruling would open the floodgates to unfounded and unreliable evidence. They feared that juries would be misled and confused by evidence that was not credible and generally accepted in the scientific community. The Supreme Court addressed these concerns by laying the task of managing the admission of evidence on the trial judge. The Supreme Court listed four nonexclusive factors to be considered when evaluating expert testimony:

1. Whether the theory can be tested
2. Whether the theory or technique has been subjected to peer review as well as publication
3. The potential rate of error

4. The existence and maintenance of standards controlling the technique's operation

The Court in *Daubert* attempted to address what it saw as an inflexible and problematic test for determining admissibility under *Frye*. Despite the Court's attempt to liberalize the admission of expert testimony, the *Daubert* ruling resulted in more confusion. Rather than liberalize the standards for expert testimony, many courts used *Daubert* to create a more stringent test for expert evidence admissibility.

In 1999, the Supreme Court decided on the case of *Kumho Tire Co. v. Carmichael*. The intent of the holding in *Kumho* was to grant trial courts broader discretion in determining the reliability of expert testimony. The Court stated that the expert checklist provided in *Daubert* was merely advisory and that courts were free to employ a broad spectrum of discretion in admitting expert testimony. The list was never intended to be exhaustive or all-inclusive.

Because of the Supreme Court's decision on expert testimony and the lack of uniformity in the district courts in applying *Kumho*, the advisory committee for the *Federal Rules of Evidence* proposed an amendment to Rule 702, which reads:

> If scientific, technical, or other specialized knowledge will assist the trier of fact to understand the evidence or to determine a fact in issue, a witness qualified as an expert by knowledge, skill, experience, training, or education may testify thereto in the form of an opinion or otherwise if (1) the testimony is based upon sufficient

Federal Rule of Evidence 702
A federal rule stating that if scientific, technical, or other specialized knowledge will assist the trier of fact to understand the evidence or to determine a fact in issue, a witness qualified as an expert by knowledge, skill, experience, training, or education may testify thereto in the form of an opinion or otherwise

facts or data, (2) the testimony is the product of reliable principles and methods, and (3) the witness has applied the principles and methods reliably to the facts of the case. (Committee on Rules of Practice and Procedure, 2001, p. 26)

The proposed amendment, consistent with *Kumho*, would provide that all types of expert testimony be subject to an admissibility determination by the trial court based on evidence of reliability.

McCormick (1982) offered the following factors to be considered in a probative analysis of the admissibility of scientific evidence:

- The potential error rate in using the technique
- The existence and maintenance of standards governing its use
- Analogy to other scientific techniques whose results are admissible
- The extent to which the technique has been accepted by scientists in the field involved
- The nature and breadth of the inference adduced
- The clarity and simplicity with which the technique can be described and its results explained
- The extent to which the basic data are verifiable by the court and jury
- The availability of other experts to test and evaluate the technique
- The probative significance of the evidence in the circumstances of the cases
- The care with which the technique was employed in the case

These standards are as relevant today as they were in 1982 in providing guidance regarding the probative value of proffered scientific evidence.

Expert witness testimony has become a growth industry. Courts are becoming more reliant on scientific evidence. This reliance appears to be the product of three correlative factors. First, society is becoming ever more dependent on technology to provide answers. Second, forensic applications were greatly enhanced when the federal government approved an infusion of funds into the Law Enforcement Assistance Administration (LEAA) for the upgrade of law enforcement. And finally, the U.S. Supreme Court under Chief Justice Earl Warren restricted the admissibility of evidence under the Fourth, Fifth, and Sixth Amendments that had been secured under traditional police methods and admonished that new investigative skills needed to be developed and applied to criminal investigations (Harris, 2008).

The number of criminal trials relying in whole or part on scientific evidence and expert testimony has increased dramatically. The police misconduct that the Supreme Court has been concerned with to a large extent has been replaced by forensic investigation and evidence. More professionals are spending more time testifying in criminal cases than ever before. Expert witness fees may exceed $600 per hour. Professional bar journals abound with advertisements for expert trial assistance. The classified section of many bar journals, heretofore the purview of those seeking to fill legal positions, is rapidly giving way to experts hawking their wares.

In the midst of a technical revolution in the courtroom, police, investigators, prosecutors, defense lawyers, jurors, and judges prepare to do battle by focusing on scientific circumstantial evidence admitted or refuted by expert witnesses. For every prosecution expert, there will be an equally credentialed opposing expert ready and willing to take exception to the work of prosecution experts.

The Police Expert in Criminal Trials

Although police are not scientists, they are experts and are often granted the latitude of an expert witness in their testimony. The example that most readily comes to mind is that of a police officer testifying as to the intoxicated state of a motorist. After it has been demonstrated that the officer has had experience dealing with people who have been proven to be intoxicated, the examining attorney will often ask if, in the officer's opinion, the motorist was intoxicated. Prior to breath analysis and video cameras, a police officer's testimony was the only vehicle through which intoxication could be proven. When a defendant refuses to provide a breath sample, police may resort to the traditional speech, gait, and bloodshot eye trilogy during their testimony. This type of testimony usually goes something like this:

Q: Was there anything notable about the defendant's speech?
A: Yes, his speech was slurred.

Q: Was there anything notable about the defendant's gait?
A: Yes, his gait was unsteady.

Q: Was there anything notable about the defendant's eyes?
A: Yes, his eyes were bloodshot.

Q: Was there anything notable about the defendant's breath?
A: Yes, the defendant's breath smelled as though he had consumed alcoholic beverages.

Q: Have you seen people who, in your estimation, were under the influence of alcohol?
A: Yes.

Q: On one occasion or many occasions?
A: On many occasions.

Q: Based on your observations of the defendant, have you an opinion as to whether the defendant was intoxicated?
A: Yes.

Q: And what is that opinion?
A: I believe the defendant was intoxicated at the time of the arrest.

Police and investigators testify every day as **police experts** in identifying the odor of burning marijuana, caliber of firearms, approximate speeds, entrance wounds, exit wounds, and so on. It should be apparent that college educations and doctoral degrees are not the only expert services that the court may rely on.

Criminal investigators today are more scientifically oriented than ever before. Much of what criminal investigators do involves threshold scientific principles. In discussing the discovery of fibers, fingerprints, blood, drugs, and bodies and their decomposition, however, it is important to remember that the expertise that investigators have in these areas is limited and does not make them scientists. Any testimony by an investigator regarding forensic evidence must be limited to its discovery and initial identification. Laboratory testing and laboratory results are the domain of forensic experts with scientific training that generally exceeds that of the average investigator. Opinions regarding forensic evidence are generally a product of a technician or scientist's work, and the role these opinions play in an investigation should be identified as the product of the efforts of the scientists and technicians who originated the opinion. In simplest terms, leave **scientific testimony** to the scientist.

Qualifying an Expert Witness

Usually, when one talks about experience, the term **credentials** is used. Often, this refers to a certificate, letter, experience, or anything that provides authentication for a claim or qualifies somebody to do something. However, as pertains to forensic and crime scene–related work, credentials as an expert will be established by the court through questioning pertaining to the witness's education, training, and experience. The ability and competence of the witness must be demonstrated through testimony relating to college degrees, continuing education, attendance at conferences, publications, ongoing research, and a variety of other possibilities that show rigor and knowledge within the area of expertise under consideration.

Unlike nonexpert witnesses, once credentialing as an expert has been established, an expert witness can provide opinions based on the outcomes of the examinations and the significance of their findings. Nonexperts who state opinions as part of their testimony will have such statements ruled as inadmissible due to their being classified as **hearsay**. Hearsay is unfounded information that is heard from other people. However, the court allows experts to state opinions due to their ability to assist the court in comprehending the topic under consideration more effectively. In the case of an expert rendering an opinion on their findings, the opinion has a foundation in the expert's training and experience and is not an arbitrary opinion with no factual relevance. It should be mentioned that simply because there is this ability to state an opinion, it does not mean that it is always a legal possibility. FRE Rule 703 provides an explanation of the bases of opinion testimony relating to expert witnesses.

The facts or data in the particular case upon which an expert bases an opinion or inference may be those perceived by or made known to the expert at or before the hearing. If of a type reasonably relied upon by experts in the particular field in forming opinions or inferences upon the subject, the facts or data need not be admissible in evidence in order for the opinion or inference to be admitted. Facts or data that are otherwise inadmissible will not be disclosed to the jury by the proponent of the opinion or inference unless the court determines that their probative value in assisting the jury to evaluate the expert's opinion substantially outweighs their prejudicial effect (Expert Pages, 2008).

credentials
A certificate, letter, experience, or anything that provides authentication for a claim or qualifies somebody to do something; credentials as an expert will be established by the court through questioning pertaining to the witness's education, training, and experience

hearsay
Any out-of-court statement made by someone other than the person testifying

police experts
Police officers who are often granted the latitude of expert witnesses in their testimony

scientific testimony
Testimony about information gathered from the evidence by scientific analysis; this type of testimony can only be performed by a science expert

perjury
the telling of a lie within a court of law by somebody who has taken an oath to tell the truth

Although it is not possible for an expert to render an opinion with absolute certainty, as an advocate of truth, the expert must base opinions on a reasonable scientific certainty. An expert must be confident in his or her statements made in a court of law. If he or she is found to be contradictory, or if it is pointed out that the witness intentionally lied or misrepresented the facts, he or she could be charged with **perjury**. Perjury is the telling of a lie within a court of law by somebody who has taken an oath to tell the truth.

As an expert witness, a crime scene investigator must remember that his or her integrity and professionalism are under the microscope. Each must be familiar with the scope of his or her actions and knowledge and know where his or her level of expertise ends. When subpoenaed to testify as an expert witness, the way in which others perceive the expert is more important than the way in which experts perceive themselves. Once credibility as an expert witness is compromised, it is nearly impossible to recover in court (Rogers, 2004).

CONCLUSION

It is good that the last chapter focuses on the least appreciated role that investigators provide. The role of the investigator is summed up in most films as follows:

- Arrive on the crime scene
- Make astounding assumptions based on observations
- Track a suspect endlessly
- Get involved in a high-speed pursuit
- Get involved in a shootout

- Arrest or recover the body of the perpetrator
- Go to closing credits

The real work of the investigator is reflected in the documents prepared in support of the investigation and, ultimately, in the testimony of that investigator in a court of law. Without competent, sincere, credible testimony based on documents reflecting a constitutionally permissible investigation, it all comes to naught. Sitting and testifying from the witness box may not be exciting, but it is where we do our best work.

QUESTIONS FOR REVIEW

1. What were the allod, fief, and tenure as they related to feudal land?
2. What role did experts play in land ownership during the feudal period?
3. What precipitated the papal inquisition?
4. What role did a panel of experts play during the inquisition?
5. What did the inquisition contribute to contemporary American law?
6. Discuss the evolution of the use of expert testimony in early English law.
7. Who can be an expert for trial purposes?
8. How is it determined whether a person deserves expert status?
9. Discuss the *Daubert*, *Kumho*, and *Frye* cases as they apply to expert testimony.
10. What constitutes an expert under *Federal Rule of Evidence 702?*

REFERENCES

Committee on Rules of Practice and Procedure. (2001). *Preliminary draft of proposed amendments to the Federal Rules of Civil Procedure and Evidence.* Washington, DC: Judicial Conference of the United States.

Durant, W. (1950). *The age of faith.* New York, NY: Simon and Schuster.

Dutelle, A.W. (2016). *An introduction to crime scene investigation* (3rd ed.). Burlington, MA: Jones & Bartlett Learning.

Endlich, G. A. (2010). *Expert testimony*. New York, NY: Gale.

ExpertPages. (2008). *The leading directory of expert witnesses* (home page). Retrieved July 20, 2017, from http://www.expertpages.com

Fish, J. T., Miller, L. S., & Braswell, M. C. (2014). *Crime scene investigation: An introduction* (3rd ed.). New York, NY: Routledge.

Gardner, M. (1957). *Fads and fallacies in the name of science*. New York, NY: Ballantine.

Hand, L. (1901). Considerations regarding expert testimony. *Harvard Law Review, 1*, 40–58.

Harris, R. C. (2008). *Black robes white coats: The puzzle of judicial policy making and scientific evidence*. New York, NY: Rutgers Press.

McCormick, M. (1982). Scientific evidence: Defining a new approach to admissibility. *67 Iowa Law Review, 879*, 911–912.

Riley, H. T. (1868). *Memorials of London and London life in the 13th, 14th, and 15th centuries*. London: Longmans, Green & Co.

Rogers, T. (2004, March). Crime scene ethics: Souvenirs, teaching material, and artifacts. *Journal of Forensic Sciences, 49*(2), 307–311.

KEY LEGAL CASES

Buckley v. Thomas, I Plow. 118 (1555).

Buller v. Crips, 6 Mod. 29 (1703).

Daubert v. Merrill Dow Pharmaceuticals, Inc., 509 U.S. 592 (1993).

Frye v. United States, 293 F. 1013 (DC Cir., 1923).

Kumho Tire Co. v. Carmichael, 526 U.S. 137 (1999).

Rex v. Green, 6 Howell, State Trials (1678).

Rey v. Wyoherly, 8 C&P (1838).

" There is nothing more to be said or to be done tonight, so hand me over my violin and let us try to forget for half an hour the miserable weather and the still more miserable ways of our fellowmen."

Sherlock Holmes
"The Five Orange Pips"

Appendix A
Professional Organizations Pertaining to Criminal Investigation

American Academy of Forensic Sciences
http://www.aafs.org/

American Board of Criminalistics
http://www.criminalistics.com/

American Board of Forensic Document Examiners
http://www.abfde.org/

American Board of Medicolegal Death Investigators
http://www.slu.edu/organizations/abmdi/

Association for Crime Scene Reconstruction
http://www.acsr.org/

Association of Firearm and Tool Mark Examiners
http://www.afte.org/

Association of Forensic Document Examiners
http://www.afde.org/

Association of State Criminal Investigative Agencies
https://www.ascia.org/

Federal Criminal Investigators Association
http://www.fedcia.org/

International Association for Identification
http://www.theiai.org/

International Association of Arson Investigators Inc.
http://www.firearson.com/

International Association of Bloodstain Pattern Analysts
http://www.iabpa.org/

International Association of Computer Investigative Specialists
http://www.iacis.com/

International Association of Forensic Nurses
http://www.forensicnurses.org/

International Crime Scene Investigators Association
http://www.icsia.org/

National Association of Document Examiners
http://documentexaminers.org/

National Criminal Intelligence Resource Center
https://www.ncirc.gov/Organizations.aspx

Appendix B
Bank Crime Statistics (2016)
U.S. Department of Justice Federal Bureau of Investigation
Washington, D.C. 20535-0001 Bank Crime Statistics (BCS)
Federally Insured Financial Institutions
January 1, 2016–December 31, 2016

I. Violations of the Federal Bank Robbery and Incidental Crimes Statute, Title 18, United States Code, Section 2113

Violations by Type of Institution

	Robberies	Burglaries	Larcenies
Commercial Banks	3,733	48	0
Mutual Savings Banks	27	1	0
Savings and Loan Associations	65	0	0
Credit Unions	343	12	1
Armored Carrier Companies	17	4	0
Total	4,185	65	1

Grand Total - All Violations: 4,251

Number, Race, and Sex of Perpetrators
The number of persons known to be involved in the 4,251 robberies, burglaries, and larcenies was 4,900. The following table shows a breakdown of the 4,900 persons by race and sex. In a small number of cases, the use of full disguise makes determination of race and sex impossible.

	White	Black	Hispanic	Asian	Other	Unknown
Male	1,797	2,164	252	14	49	253
Female	185	131	10	2	8	11

Unknown Race/Sex: 24

Investigation to date has resulted in the identification of 2,537 of the 4,900 persons known to be involved. Of these 2,537 identified persons, 40% were determined to be users of narcotics, and 27% were found to have been previously convicted in either federal or state court for bank robbery, bank burglary, or bank larceny.

Occurrences by Day of Week

Monday	728
Tuesday	741
Wednesday	758
Thursday	699
Friday	913
Saturday	361
Sunday	51
Not Determined	0
Total	**4,251**

Occurrences by Time of Day

6–9 A.M.	99
9–11 A.M.	1,004
11 A.M.–1 P.M.	961
1–3 P.M.	800
3–6 P.M.	923
6 P.M.–6 A.M.	455
Not Determined	9
Total	**4,251**

Institution/Community Characteristics

Type of Financial Institution Office

Main Office	144
Branch Office	3,978
Store	112
Remote Facility/Other	17
Total	**4,251**

Location of Financial Institution Office

Commercial District	2,725
Shopping Center	1,026
Residential	365
Other Location	135
Total	**4,251**

Community Type	
Metropolitan	1,997
Suburban	838
Small City/Town	1,297
Rural	110
Unknown	9
Total	**4,251**

Institutional Areas Involved	
Counter	4,054
Night Depository	3
Vault/Safe	147
Auto Teller Machine	45
Safe Deposit Area	11
Courier/Messenger	1
Office Area	128
Armored Vehicle	5
Drive-In/Walk-Up	34
Other	31
Cash Kiosk	4

Security Devices Maintained by Victim Institutions	
Alarm System	4,085
Surveillance Cameras	4,210
Bait Money	1,942
Guards	224
Currency Dye/Gas Packs	709
Electronic Tracking Devices	595

Security Devices Maintained by Victim Institutions	*(continued)*
Bullet-Resistant Enclosures	610
Access-Controlled Entryway	56
Man Trap	36

Security Devices Used During Crimes	
Alarm System Activated	3,669
Surveillance Cameras Activated	4,057
Bait Money Taken	900
Guards on Duty	177
Currency Dye/Gas Packs Taken	240
Electronic Tracking Devices Activated	292
Man Trap Activated	12
Access-Controlled Entryway	24

Security Devices Functioned	
Alarm System Functioned	3,519
Surveillance Cameras Functioned	3,887
Electronic Tracking Devices Functioned	266

Modus Operandi Used	
Demand Note Used	2,267
Firearm Used	590
Handgun[1]	965
Other Firearm	36
Other Weapon Used[2]	26
Weapon Threatened[3]	2,361
Explosive Device Used or Threatened	110
Oral Demand	1,958
Vault or Safe Theft	25

(continues)

Modus Operandi Used	(continued)
Depository Trap Device	11
Till Theft	48
Takeover	285

[1] "Handgun" and "Other Firearm" added together may not coincide with "Firearm Used" since, in some cases, both handguns and other firearms are used in the same crime.
[2] "Other Weapon Used" includes knives, other cutting instruments, clubs, etc.
[3] "Weapon Threatened" includes those cases where a weapon was threatened or implied either orally or in a demand note but not actually observed.

Injuries, Deaths, and Hostages Taken

Acts of violence were committed during 146 of the 4,251 robberies, burglaries, and larcenies that occurred during this time. These acts included 43 instances involving the discharge of firearms, 72 instances involving assaults, and 31 instances involving a hostage taken.

(One or more acts of violence may occur during an incident.)
These acts of violence resulted in 43 injuries, 8 deaths, and 59 persons taken hostage.

Injuries	
Customer	9
Employee	23
Employee Family	0
Perpetrator	8
Law Officer	0
Guard	2
Other	1
Total	**43**

Number of violations in which injuries occurred   37

Deaths	
Customer	0
Employee	1
Employee Family	0
Perpetrator	7
Law Officer	0
Guard	0
Other	0
Total	**8**

Number of violations in which deaths occurred   7

Hostages Taken	
Customer	21
Employee	32
Employee's Family	0
Law Officer	1
Guard	3
Other	2
Total	59
Number of violations in which hostages were taken	31

II. Bank Extortion Violations Which Were Investigated Under the Federal Bank Robbery and Incidental Crimes Statute, Title 18, United States Code, Section 2113

January 1, 2016–December 31, 2016

Violations by Type of Institution	
Commercial Banks	2
Mutual Savings Banks	0
Savings and Loan Associations	0
Credit Unions	1
Armored Carrier Companies	0
Total	3

Number, Race, and Sex of Perpetrators

The number of persons known to be involved in the three bank extortion violations was three. In a number of cases, the number and description of individuals involved is unknown due to nonobservance of the perpetrators by the victim(s) or the use of disguises. The following table shows a breakdown of the three known individuals involved by race and sex:

	White	Black	Hispanic	Asian	Other	Unknown
Male	3	0	0	0	0	0
Female	0	0	0	0	0	0

Occurrences by Day of Week	
Monday	0
Tuesday	1
Wednesday	0
Thursday	1
Friday	0
Saturday	1
Sunday	0
Not Determined	0
Total	3

Occurrences by Time of Day	
6–9 A.M.	2
9–11 A.M.	0
11 A.M.–1 P.M.	0
1–3 P.M.	0
3–6 P.M.	1
6 P.M.–6 A.M.	0
Not Determined	0
Total	3

Institution/Community Characteristics

Type of Financial Institution Office	
Main Office	0
Branch Office	3
Store	0
Remote Facility/Other	0
Total	3

Location of Financial Institution Office	
Commercial District	2
Shopping Center	1
Residential	0
Other Location	0
Total	3

Community Type	
Metropolitan	1
Suburban	1
Small City/Town	1
Rural	0
Total	**3**

Security Devices Maintained by Victim Institutions	
Alarm System	3
Surveillance Cameras	3
Bait Money	1
Guards	0
Currency Dye/Gas Packs	1
Electronic Tracking Devices	0
Bullet-Resistant Enclosures	0
Security Devices Used During Crimes	
Alarm System Activated	1
Surveillance Cameras Activated	1
Bait Money Taken	0
Guards on Duty	0
Currency Dye/Gas Packs Taken	0
Electronic Tracking Devices Activated	0
Modus Operandi Used	
Demand Note Used	1
Firearm Used	0
Other Weapon Used	0
Weapon Threatened	0
Explosive Device Used or Threatened	1
Telephone Call	0

Injuries, Deaths, and Hostages Taken

There were no injuries, deaths, or hostages taken during this time frame.

III. Bank Robbery Statue Violations By Regions, Geographic Division, States, And Territories

January 1, 2016–December 31, 2016

	Robberies	Burglaries	Larcenies	Extortions
REGIONAL SUMMARY				
NORTHEAST	1,022	20	1	0
NORTH CENTRAL	849	9	0	1
SOUTH	1,29	18	0	1
WEST	1,013	18	0	1
TERRITORIES	9	0	0	0
TOTAL	4,185	65	1	3
NORTHEAST	1,022	20	1	0
NEW ENGLAND	315	3	1	0
CONNECTICUT	72	0	0	0
MAINE	0	0	0	0
MASSACHUSETTS	243	3	1	0
NEW HAMPSHIRE	0	0	0	0
RHODE ISLAND	0	0	0	0
VERMONT	0	0	0	0
MIDDLE ATLANTIC	707	17	0	0
NEW JERSEY	100	2	0	0
NEW YORK	371	14	0	0
PENNSYLVANIA	236	1	0	0
NORTH CENTRAL	849	9	0	1
EAST NORTH CENTRAL	650	4	0	0
ILLINOIS	215	0	0	0
INDIANA	88	0	0	0

(continues)

	Robberies	Burglaries	Larcenies	Extortions
MICHIGAN	98	3	0	0
OHIO	171	1	0	0
WISCONSIN	78	0	0	0
WEST NORTH CENTRAL	199	5	0	1
IOWA	0	0	0	0
KANSAS	0	0	0	0
MINNESOTA	58	0	0	1
MISSOURI	66	1	0	0
NEBRASKA	75	4	0	0
NORTH DAKOTA	0	0	0	0
SOUTH DAKOTA	0	0	0	0
SOUTH	1,292	18	0	1
SOUTH ATLANTIC	756	4	0	1
DELAWARE	0	0	0	0
DISTRICT OF COLUMBIA	53	0	0	0
FLORIDA	213	1	0	1
GEORDIA	103	0	0	0
MARYLAND	159	1	0	0
NORTH CAROLINA	107	0	0	0
SOUTH CAROLINA	38	2	0	0
VIRGINIA	83	0	0	0
WEST VIRGINIA	0	0	0	0
EAST SOUTH CENTRAL	139	2	0	0
ALABAMA	32	1	0	0
KENTUCKY	41	1	0	0
MISSISSIPPI	15	0	0	0
TENNESSEE	51	0	0	0

(continues)

	Robberies	Burglaries	Larcenies	Extortions
WEST SOUTH CENTRAL	397	12	0	0
ARKANSAS	25	2	0	0
LOUISIANA	34	4	0	0
OKLAHOMA	37	1	0	0
TEXAS	301	5	0	0
WEST	1,013	18	0	1
MOUNTAIN	337	3	0	1
ARIZONA	106	1	0	0
COLORADO	113	2	0	1
IDAHO	0	0	0	0
MONTANA	0	0	0	0
NEVADA	48	0	0	0
NEW MEXICO	1	0	0	0
UTAH	69	0	0	0
WYOMING	0	0	0	0
PACIFIC	676	15	0	0
ALASKA	10	1	0	0
CALIFORNIA	462	12	0	0
HAWAII	15	1	0	0
OREGON	41	1	0	0
WASHINGTON	148	0	0	0
TERRITORIES	9	0	0	0
GUAM	0	0	0	0
PUETO RICO	9	0	0	0
VIRGIN ISLANDS	0	0	0	0
TOTAL	4,185	65	1	3

IV. Violations Involving Armored Carriers Investigated Under The Hobbs Act Title 18, United States Code, Section 1951

January 1, 2016–December 31, 2016

Armored Carrier Violations	
Hobbs Act	36
TOTAL	36

Number, Race, and Sex of Perpetrators

The number of persons known to be involved in the 36 armored carrier violations was 63. In a number of cases, the number and description of individuals involved is unknown due to nonobservance of the perpetrators by the victim(s) or the use of disguises. The following table shows a breakdown of the 63 known individuals involved by race and sex:

	White	Black	Hispanic	Asian	Other	Unknown
Male	2	35	11	0	0	15
Female	0	0	0	0	0	0

Unknown Race/Sex: 0

Occurrences by Day of Week	
Monday	7
Tuesday	8
Wednesday	2
Thursday	2
Friday	7
Saturday	9
Sunday	1
Not Determined	0
Total	36

Occurrences by Time of Day	
6–9 A.M.	7
9–11 A.M.	6
11 A.M.–1 P.M.	7
1–3 P.M.	6
3–6 P.M.	7
6 P.M.–6 A.M.	3
Not Determined	0
Total	**36**

Institution Community Characteristics

Facility Location	
Commercial District	16
Shopping Center	15
Residential	4
Other Location	1
Total	**36**

Community Type	
Metropolitan	26
Suburban	7
Small City/Town	2
Rural	1
Total	**36**

Modus Operandi Used	
Firearm Used	22
Handgun[4]	34
Other Firearm	7
Other Weapon Used[5]	2
Weapon Threatened[6]	10
Explosive Device Used or Threatened	0
Oral Demand	7
Vault or Safe Theft	0

[4] "Handgun" and "Other Firearm" added together may not coincide with "Firearm Used" since, in some cases, both handguns and other firearms are used in the same crime.

[5] "Other Weapon Used" includes knives, other cutting instruments, clubs, etc.

[6] "Weapon Threatened" includes those cases in which a weapon was threatened or implied, either orally or in a demand note but not actually observed or displayed.

Injuries, Deaths, and Hostages Taken

Acts of violence were committed during 20 of the 36 armored carrier violations that occurred during this time frame. These acts included 13 instances involving the discharge of firearms, seven instances involving assaults, and no hostages were taken when the violent acts were committed. These acts of violence resulted in 14 injuries and three deaths.

(One or more acts of violence may occur during an incident.)

Injuries	
Customer	1
Employee	1
Employee Family	0
Perpetrator	4
Law Officer	1
Guard	7
Other	0
Total	**14**
Number of violations in which injuries occurred	11

Deaths	
Customer	0
Employee	0
Employee Family	0
Perpetrator	1
Law Officer	0
Guard	2
Other	0
Total	**3**
Number of violations in which injuries occurred	3

Any statistical information furnished in this booklet is subject to change upon the investigation of bank robbery violations that occurred during 2016.

The BCS provides a nationwide view of bank robbery crimes based on statistics contributed by FBI field offices responding to bank robberies or otherwise gathered when provided to the FBI from local and state law enforcement.

Statistics recorded as of 5/17/2017, at FBI Headquarters.

NOTE: Not all bank robberies are reported to the FBI, and, therefore, BCS is not a complete statistical compilation of all bank robberies that occur in the United States.

Appendix C
Processing the Scene of Mass Fatality Incidents

Initial Considerations

The complete and accurate identification of remains and evidentiary processing begins at the scene of the mass fatality incident. Under most circumstances, the medical examiner/coroner has the ultimate responsibility for the recovery and identification of the deceased. The remains/evidence processing teams have to assume that any mass fatality scene could be a crime scene. They are expected to carefully document every piece of physical evidence recovered from the scene. The scene should be large enough to ensure its protection from public access until all agencies have agreed to release the scene. Although teams can discard information later, scene processing always involves the physical destruction of the actual scene, and additional information may not be recoverable after the scene has been processed and released. Efficient information recovery proceeds from the least intrusive to the more intrusive (e.g., taking photographs is allowed only after teams locate, flag, and sequentially number the remains). Although protocols may change in the middle of an event, depending on the scope and extent of the incident. Documenting every aspect of the remains and the evidence processing operation will ensure the preservation of information.

Before processing the scene, the incident command, in consultation with the medical examiner/coroner, is expected to:

A. Identify team leaders responsible for remains/evidence processing.

B. Determine the size and composition of the remains/evidence processing teams (usually a function of the team leaders), which may include:
- Medical examiner/coroner
- Forensic anthropologist
- Odontologist
- Police crime scene investigator
- Forensic photographer
- Evidence technician
- Scribe/note taker

C. Integrate the remains/evidence processing teams according to existing interagency jurisdiction and chain of command. The scope and extent of the mass fatality incident determines the number of agencies involved.

D. Establish and/or verify control over access to the scene.

E. Establish communication among transport vehicles, the incident command, and the morgue.

F. Establish an on-scene remains-processing station.

G. Consider the recovery of remains and personal effects as evidence and preserve the chain of custody throughout the recovery operation.

Effective organization and composition of the remains/evidence processing teams ensures the proper collection and preservation of remains, personal effects, and evidence.

Establish a Chain of Custody

Establishing and maintaining a chain of custody verifies the integrity of the evidence. The remains/evidence processing teams are expected to maintain the chain of custody throughout the recovery process. Throughout the investigation, those responsible for preserving the chain of custody are expected to:

A. Document the time of arrival and departure of other personnel at the scene.

B. Establish a standard numbering system at the scene that relates back to the location of the remains/evidence and ensure that the numbering system is:
- Internally consistent and cross-referenced with other agencies
- Expandable
- Simple to interpret

- Capable of indicating where the remains, personal effects, and evidence were recovered
- Capable of tracking remains, personal effects, and evidence throughout the investigation
- Related to subsequent individual results without error
- Integrated into all protocols and reports

C. Document the collection of evidence by recording both its location at the scene and the time of collection.

D. Document all transfers of custody (including the name of the recipient and the date and manner of transfer).

Maintaining the chain of custody by properly documenting, collecting, and preserving the evidence ensures its integrity throughout the investigation.

Scene Imaging and Mapping Principle

The remains/evidence processing teams can use a grid system to divide the scene into manageable units to show the location and context of items (i.e., their positions relative to other items) at the scene. A grid system may need to be three-dimensional.

The remains/evidence processing teams are expected to:

A. Record overall views of the scene (e.g., wide-angle, aerial, 360-degree) with a designated photographer to relate items spatially within the scene and relative to the surrounding area. A combination of still photography, videotaping, and other techniques is most effective. Remember to:
- Consider muting the audio portion of any video recording unless there is narration.
- Minimize the presence of scene personnel in photographs/videos.
- Maintain photo and video logs.

B. Identify boundaries and fixed landmarks (e.g., a utility pole, building corners, or global positioning system [GPS]–located points).

C. Establish a primary point of reference for the scene.

D. Divide the scene into identifiable sectors and create a checkerboard.

E. Use accurate measuring devices.

The remains/evidence processing teams are responsible for establishing an accurate, logical mapping system for the scene.

Document the Location of Remains, Personal Effects, and Evidence

The remains/evidence processing teams are expected to include documentation in the permanent record of the scene. Photographic documentation creates a permanent record of the scene that supplements the written incident reports. The teams are expected to complete this documentation, including location information, before the removal or disturbance of any items. Videotaping may serve as an additional record but not as a replacement for still photography.

The remains/evidence processing teams are expected to:

A. Photograph individual items (midrange and close) with an identifier (i.e., a grid identifier and/or individual item number) and scale. Consider including a directional compass arrow that points north.

B. Attach identifying numbers and flag all remains, personal effects, and evidence in the grid.
- Use a waterproof ink marker.
- Ensure that numbers on the flags correspond with those on the remains and are also clearly discernible in the photograph.

C. Ensure that the systematic on-scene documentation of all remains, personal effects, and evidence includes:
- The sequential numbering system at the scene
- Recovery location information
- Notes that may help with personal identification or scene reconstruction (e.g., generic descriptors, such as a foot or shoe)
- Documentation of the evidence collector (e.g., the collector's unique identifier and the date and time of recovery)

D. Conduct the systematic removal of remains, personal effects, and evidence.
- Using a permanent marker, mark the outside of the primary bag or container and tag with the identifying number, the collector's unique identifier, and the date and time of collection.
- Place the same identifying number on the inside of the body bag or other bag or container.
- Do not remove any personal effects on or with the remains. Transport all personal effects on or with the remains to the morgue.

- When necessary, wrap the head before moving it to protect cranial/facial fragments and teeth.

E. After removing the remains, photograph the areas from which evidence was recovered to document whether anything was under the remains.

F. After the remains/evidence processing teams have cleared the area and before releasing the scene for public access, conduct a final shoulder-to-shoulder sweep search to locate any additional items.

The remains/evidence processing teams must properly document the collection of all remains, personal effects, and evidence before removing them from the scene.

On-Scene Staging Area

The remains/evidence processing teams should use the on-scene staging area for checking documentation, maintaining the chain of custody, and conducting potential triage functions. In this area, the remains/evidence processing teams can add notes to aid personal identification at the morgue (e.g., comments about tattoos, marks, and scars) and identify contents of body bags (e.g., watches, body parts). The remains/evidence processing teams are responsible for closing and locking body bags at this point.

The remains/evidence processing teams are expected to:

A. Establish a staging area proximate to the incident scene that provides maximum security from public and media scrutiny and access (including a no-fly zone over the site).

B. Remand evidence that is not required to accompany the remains to the mortuary to the custody of the appropriate agency.

C. Maintain the chain of custody of body bags:
  - Maintain a log of the body bags that are transported from the staging area to the morgue.
  - Record drivers' names and the license numbers of vehicles.
  - Record dates and times that all vehicles leave for the morgue.

D. Maintain equipment and supplies at the staging area. Inventory resources may include:
  - A large tent
  - Body/storage bags
  - Litters, gurneys, and stretchers for remains transport
  - Refrigeration vehicles
  - Emergency lighting
  - Sawhorses with plywood boards for makeshift examination tables
  - Tarpaulins or other screening materials to create visual barriers
  - Decontamination control
  - Inventory control system
  - Equipment storage
  - Personal protective equipment

E. Notify the morgue when transport of remains will begin.

The remains/evidence processing teams are expected to maintain a secure triage area for initial examination of remains and other evidence and to ensure secure transport to the morgue. Strongly consider placing forensic identification specialists at the staging area, as the initial evaluations at this point will dictate the efficiency of subsequent morgue operations.

Source: Courtesy of the National Institute of Justice. (2005, June). *Mass fatality incidents: A guide for human forensic identification.* Retrieved July 17, 2017, from http://www.ncjrs.gov/pdffiles1/nij/199758.pdf

Glossary

3R rule: Radial fractures form a right angle to the reverse side to which force was applied

ABFO scale: (Designed by the American Board of Forensic Odontology) An L-shaped piece of plastic used in forensic photography. It is marked with circles, black and white bars, and 18% gray bars to assist in distortion compensation and to provide exposure determination reference. For measurements, the scales are marked in millimeters.

abrasion ring: A circular or oval bruising of the tissue immediately around the bullet hole that results from the bullet scraping the skin as it penetrates

accidental whorl: Any fingerprint pattern that is not covered by one of the categories or is a combination of two patterns

ACE-V: A formula given to a complete set of ten fingers as they appear on a fingerprint card generally based on pattern type, ridge count, or ridge tracing

acquisition technology: Technical devices that permit officers to acquire sights and sounds that they would not otherwise have been able to perceive from a legal vantage point; such technology requires a warrant or other court order

active listening: Listening not only to what is said, but what is not said, how it is said and observing the body language associated therewith

adipocere: The hydration and dehydrogenation of the body's fat, which results in an off-white, waxy, clay-like substance that in many cases preserves the body and retards the decomposition process

affirmative defense: Defense that requires a preliminary showing of the applicability of the defensive position

agglutination: The process by which blood cells link together to form clumps

aggravated assault: A physical attack that results in serious bodily injury and that is perpetrated in the course of another felony or involves the use of a deadly weapon

aggravated robbery: Robbery in which the person (1) commits robbery and (2) causes serious bodily injury to another or (3) uses or exhibits a deadly weapon or (4) causes bodily injury to another person or threatens or places another person in fear of imminent bodily injury or death if the person is 65 years of age or older or is disabled

aggravated sexual assault: Sexual assault in which serious bodily injury results, a deadly weapon was used, or the victim was kidnapped

Alec Jeffreys: Scientist who developed the method of DNA fingerprinting

algor mortis: Postmortem drop in body temperature

allod: Land held by unconditional ownership

Alphonse Bertillon: Person who developed the first scientific system of identification for use in criminal investigation

alternative question: A two-pronged question that presents two choices (generally a positive and a negative choice) to the suspect regarding the crime he or she has committed; accepting either choice results in an admission of guilt

American Academy of Forensic Sciences (AAFS): A professional organization associated with the forensic sciences

amphetamines: Synthetic central nervous system stimulants

analysis: Rendering information into a form that allows it to be used

angle of impact: Angle at which a blood drop hits a surface, relative to the horizontal plane of that surface; the angle can be calculated by measuring the width and length of the bloodstain

antemortem: Occurring before death

antibody: Substance that will react with its specific antigen

antigens: Chemical structures residing on the surface of each red blood cell

approach to entry: The area that led to the entry of the crime scene; often seen as a secondary crime scene, it may include parking areas, sidewalks, yards, and building exteriors

arches: The least common fingerprint patterns; they are either plain or tented

area of convergence: The area containing the intersections generated by lines drawn through the long axes of individual stains that indicate in two dimensions the location of the blood source

area of origin: (1) Fire. The large track of space or area where a fire would have started and can be located where the fire was able to grow and develop; (2) Blood Pattern Analysis. By establishing the impact angles of representative bloodstains and projecting their trajectories back to a common axis (Z), extended at 90 degrees from the area of convergence, an approximate location of where the blood source was when it was impacted may be established

arm's-reach concept: Concept established in *Chimel v. California* (1967), in which it was ruled that a house search may be conducted in the area under the arrestee's immediate control, that is, the area into which he or she might reach; when applied to automobiles, the entire passenger compartment of the vehicle, including closed but not locked containers, can be searched

arrest: To place a person in the custody of a law enforcement agency

arson: Any willful or malicious burning or attempting to burn, with or without intent to defraud, a dwelling house, public building, motor vehicle or aircraft, or personal property of another

arterial gushing (spurting): Blood exiting under pressure from a breached artery

aspermia: A condition that prevents spermatozoa from appearing in a male's seminal fluids

asphyxia: The interruption of oxygenation of the brain

asportation: Movement of items taken from another; one of the three basic elements required for larceny in common law

assault and battery: The threat to commit an attack upon another, and then the attack

associative evidence: Evidence that can be attributed to, or associated with, a particular person, place, or thing, thus establishing inferred connectivity

ATM robbery: Robbery that occurs at an automated teller machine; the robbers may wait for the victims to make a withdrawal and rob them upon completion of the transaction or abduct the victims and transport them to various locations to be able to maximize the amount of money stolen

attitude: An aspect of an individual's personality that immediately puts all others on notice that this individual "takes nothing from nobody at no time"

August Vollmer: The father of law enforcement professionalism

authentication: Often referred to as establishing an evidentiary foundation or a predicate for admissibility; it is a process separate from establishing the chain of custody that depends on the specific evidence to be entered

automated fingerprint identification system (AFIS): An automatic pattern recognition system that consists of three fundamental stages: data acquisition, feature extraction, and decision making

autopsy: Examination of a deceased body that can be ordered when there is suspicion of foul play

background sample: A control sample to compare against evidence found at the scene of a fire

backscatter: When particulates in a medium (such as particles in water or snow/rain in the air) reflect light back into the camera lens, obscuring the image with spots and haze

backspatter: Blood that is directed toward the energy source causing the spatter

bait money: Bills that have had their serial numbers recorded and have been set aside specifically to be given to robbers so they can be traced

ballistics: The study of projectiles in motion

barbiturates: Depressants derived from barbituric acid that act on the central nervous system and create a feeling of well-being and drowsiness; they are generally taken orally in 10- to 70-milligram doses and are absorbed through the small intestines

barrel blowback (drawback): The blood residue found in a gun barrel as a result of a large-caliber contact wound; it is backspatter contained in/on the gun barrel

baseline: Arbitrary line of some measurable distance drawn between two fixed points; also, a construction method used to geographically locate evidence

battery: An attack on another

beyond a reasonable doubt: The standard of certainty necessary to convict someone of a crime

biological weapons (BW): Biological agents chosen because of their harmful properties; used to spread disease or cause death

biometric identification: Identifying people by biological characteristics

black water diving: Conditions where silt, sediment, algae, and pollution create underwater visibility that is typically less than one foot

bloodstain pattern analysis: The FBI nomenclature for analyzing bloodstains left at a crime scene

blood types: The type of antigens found on red blood cells

bobby: Colloquial term for a police officer, which arose due to the close association of Sir Robert Peel with the Metropolitan Police Department in London

bona fide: Innocent, genuine; in Latin, translates as "in good faith"

breaking and entering: Term that was originally used for burglary because it required a breaking (forced entry) component and a physical entry into the premises

breechblock: The part of a firearm's action that supports the base of the cartridge in the chamber when it is fired

bump-and-grab: Method used to rob people in vehicles, in which robbers bump the rear of the target vehicle and stop to examine the damage; when the occupants of the bumped vehicle exit, the robbery takes place

buoyancy control device (BCD): Jacket-like piece of equipment used to keep the diver neutrally buoyant

burglary: A crime involving (1) a person who (2) enters or remains on the premises (3) of another (4) without effective consent of the owner (5) for the purpose of committing a felony or theft

burial indicators: Indications of the presence of buried remains; these include disturbed vegetation, soil compaction, new vegetation, and soil disturbance

caliber: The diameter of the bore of a gun

career robber: Criminal who has chosen robbery as his or her life's work; career robbers are responsible for the majority of robberies committed

carjacking: Robbery in which robbers commandeer cars that have stopped and steal the vehicle and possessions of the occupant(s)

casing: Evaluating a chosen robbery site in order to determine peak business periods in an effort to avoid witnesses and logistical difficulties

cast-off patterns: The pattern produced by a bloody object in motion (such as a weapon) resulting in blood projected (thrown) onto a surface other than the impact site

causation: The production of an effect

cell: A small cadre of zealots whose members know only each other, not other members of the larger group

chain of custody: The record of the transfer of physical evidence from one person to the next

chemical weapons: Chemical compounds used to harm or kill people; they are easy to obtain or make and also to disperse, and the chemical dispersal may be delayed, allowing the terrorists to escape without fear of harming themselves too

chop: Stealing an automobile to remove the major body components, including doors, fenders, hood, bumpers, and windows, in order to sell them

circle search: A specialized search pattern method in which searchers can either start at a defined outer boundary and circle or spiral in toward the defined critical point or begin at the critical point and circle or spiral outward toward the crime scene perimeter; *see spiral search*

circular distortion: The stain that results from blood striking a flat surface at an angle; the more nearly perpendicular the angle of impact, the more circular the blood drop stain

circumstantial evidence: All evidence other than eyewitness testimony

class characteristics: Characteristics used to identify a firearm, including caliber, direction of twist of the rifling, degree of twist, number of lands and grooves, and width of the lands and grooves

classification: A formula given to a complete set of ten fingers as they appear on a fingerprint card generally based on pattern type, ridge count, or ridge tracing

close-up photographs: Photos that clearly show details on the item of evidence; taken both with and without a scale that allows for a 1:1 ratio reproduction

club drugs: A general term used for certain illicit substances, primarily synthetic, that are usually found at nightclubs, bars, and raves

cocaine: Stimulant drug derived from the coca plant

codeine: Narcotic that is used as an analgesic and a cough suppressant

cognitive interview: an organized approach to an interview conducted through a psychological perspective

color reactions: Expected reactions to drug field tests

Combined DNA Index System (CODIS): Database system that can aid investigations by efficiently comparing a DNA profile generated from biological evidence left at a crime scene against convicted offender DNA profiles and forensic evidence from other cases contained in the database

combustible liquids: Liquids that have a flash point higher than 100°F

commercial robbery: Robbery at a place of business, typically convenience stores

comparison microscope: Microscope that can be used to examine two or more fired bullets that exhibit the same class characteristics and determine whether the bullets were fired by the same weapon

composite picture: Picture drawn of a suspect by selecting the one feature that best meets the witness's verbal description and continuing refinement based on witness input

concealed handgun laws: Laws that allow the use of force, including deadly force, in defense of self and property

concentric fractures: Cracks or breaks that appear to make a typically broken series of concentric circles around an impact point

conchoidal fractures: Stress marks in glass that are shaped like arches, located perpendicularly to one side of the glass surface, and curved nearly parallel to the opposite glass surface

confession: A statement acknowledging personal responsibility for a crime, including details only the guilty person would know

confession law: Area of law dealing with the proper technique for legally obtaining a confession, and the rights guaranteed a suspect when he or she is deciding whether to give a confession

consent search: A warrantless search that is voluntarily permitted by a person who is legally able to give consent; the scope of the search must be within the given or inferred consent

constable: Law enforcement officers in London appointed by local justices, to whom they owed their allegiance and continued employment

contamination: Materials and other factors added to crime scenes that were not there at the time of the crime and can negatively affect the proper collection and interpretation of evidence

contraband: An item that is found to be illegally possessed or for some legal reasons is illegal to possess

controlled substances: Substances (typically drugs) whose possession or use is regulated by the government

Controlled Substances Act: An act that established five schedules of classification for dangerous substances on the basis of potential for abuse, potential for physical and psychological dependence, and medical value and that set forth criminal penalties for the manufacture, sale, or possession of these controlled dangerous substances

conversion: Using property entrusted to a person by another for the former's advantage and with the intent to deprive the owner of possession

copper: Colloquial term for a police officer, coined because the members of the first uniformed police force in New York City wore badges made of copper

core: In fingerprints, the centermost point of the loop at the apex of the innermost ridge of the loop; this shape is always found in a loop pattern

corneal clouding: A thickening of the thin film seen on the corneal surface within minutes after death; clouding occurs 2 to 3 hours after death

coroner: In the English coroner system, this person was authorized by the justice courts to attach or arrest witnesses or suspects and to appraise and safeguard any lands or goods that might later be forfeited by reason of guilt of the accused

corpus delicti: The material evidence in a criminal homicide case that shows that a crime has been committed; Latin term meaning "body of the crime"

crack cocaine: Form of cocaine that melts at 98°C and vaporizes; the vapor is absorbed by all mucous membranes and the lungs, rapidly producing a euphoric sensation that may last as long as 30 minutes

credentials: A certificate, letter, experience, or anything that provides authentication for a claim or qualifies somebody to do something; credentials as an expert will be established by the court through questioning pertaining to the witness's education, training, and experience

crime: An act or the commission of an act that is forbidden by a public law and that makes the offender liable to punishment by that law

crime scene processing plan: Plan created to carry out a systematic investigation of a crime scene

crime scene sketch: A measured drawing showing the location of all important items, landmarks, permanent fixtures, and physical evidence at a crime scene

culpability: Criminal responsibility

curtilage: The area surrounding a home that is used in the course of daily living

damage control: Distorting evidence and records to try to salvage a case that should otherwise be dismissed

Daubert v. Merrill Dow Pharmaceuticals: Case in which the Supreme Court decided in 1993 that federal trial court judges were obligated to evaluate the basis of expert testimony in order to determine its reliability and value to the jury

deadly force: Force that results in death

death: The irreversible cessation of circulatory and respiratory functions

decomposition: The postmortem breakdown of body tissues

deductive reasoning: Drawing conclusions based on premises that are certain (known to be true)

deflagration: A chemical explosion in which the reaction front moves through the explosive at less than the speed of sound

degree of twist: The grooves inside the barrel of a gun spiral at a particular angle, with some steeper (greater) than others; degree of twist is an identifying characteristic of the firearm that includes the number of twists, the angle of the twist, and whether the twist is to the left or the right

delivery van robbery: Typically a crime of opportunity perpetrated by a group of young men who have observed a van making a delivery and deduced that cash must have been received for products delivered; the group often will attack the driver aggressively and violently and remove valuables from the victim after seriously injuring him or her

delta: A two-sided triangular shape found to one side of a loop that resembles a river delta; this shape is always found in a loop pattern

departure signature: Any last comments or behaviors unnecessary to the completion of the robbery that become the robber's trademark or signature, as though he or she were signing a just-finished letter or work of art

derivative evidence: Evidence found as the result of a confession or the seizure of other evidence; usually used to denote evidence that is tainted by being acquired as a result of illegally obtained original evidence

descriptives: Words that yield vivid mental images

designer drugs: Substances that are chemically related to some controlled drugs and are pharmacologically potent

detonation: A chemical explosion in which the reaction front moves through the explosive at greater than the speed of sound

detonation point: Location where an explosive was detonated

developing prints: Making fingerprints visible by applying a powder or chemical

diaphorase: Enzyme that exists in three distinctive forms and is present in sperm only in humans; the discovery of the enzyme is useful in eliminating innocent subjects and can be useful in tracing the assailant

Dille-Koppanyi test: A test for barbiturates, in whose presence the reagent turns violet-blue

directed verdict of acquittal: Dismissal of a case that results from the prosecution's failure to prove that the court hearing the case has the jurisdiction to do so

direct evidence: Evidence that links the arsonist to the fire, such as eyewitness identification or motive

directionality: The direction of a drop of blood from point of origin to point of impact

direction of fire: Direction from which the projectile was fired; the relationship between the entrance and exit wounds may reveal this information

dissociative drug: Those drugs that cause a distorted perception of space and time

domestic assault: Assault that occurs in the home, usually committed by a person's spouse

domestic terrorism: Terrorism that evolves within a state or country; disgruntled citizens engage in terrorist acts that, although brought down upon the heads of individuals, are aimed at bringing about social or political change

drip patterns: The pattern created by blood dripping into blood; in this pattern, round blood spatters occur at the periphery of the central bloodstain

drug: Any chemical substance, other than food, that is intended for use in the diagnosis, treatment, cure, mitigation, or prevention of disease or symptoms

due process: The conduct of legal proceedings according to established rules and principles

due process clause: A constitutional provision that prohibits the government from unfairly or arbitrarily depriving a person of life, liberty, or property

Duquenois-Levine test: A test for marijuana; when applied to marijuana, the reagent turns violet

Edmond Locard: Established the first crime laboratory in Lyon, France. Locard's theory that any time two objects come into contact with one another, there is a cross-transfer of evidence became the foundation upon which trace evidence analysis is based

Edward T. Blake: Provided the DNA testimony and evidence for the first DNA trial in the United States

electronic communication: In-transit electronic impulses, sounds, and other signals transmitted over wire, radio, or microwave

elements of the offense: The crime that has been committed and what can be charged

emergency exception: Exception to the warrant requirement; it states that if police are brought to the premises to deal with an emergency, then any evidence discovered in the course of handling that emergency is admissible despite the fact the police had no probable cause or warrant to enter the premises

enhancement technology: Technical devices that allow augmentation of sound or picture quality; such technology does not require a warrant or other court authorization

entry access: The entry point chosen by a robber to gain access to the site of the robbery

entry wound: The wound that results when a projectile enters a body; such wounds reveal a missing sphere of flesh carried into the wound by the projectile

evidentiary foundation: Basis for a conclusion that was determined using collected evidence; predicate

exclusionary rule: Rule resulting from *Weeks v. United States* (1914) that excludes evidence at the time of trial that was obtained (seized) as a result of an illegal search, arrest, or interrogation

exculpatory evidence: Evidence indicating innocence

excusable homicide: The unintentional, truly accidental killing of another person

exigent circumstances: Circumstances that occur when the suspect may destroy or hide evidence or abscond

exit wound: The wound that results from a projectile exiting a body; such wounds have no missing flesh, and if the skin around the wound were replaced, including all the jagged edges, there would be a complete covering of the exit hole

expert witness: Someone who is called to answer questions on the stand in a court of law in order to provide specialized information relevant to the case being tried

explosion: An event that results in the release of mechanical or chemical energy in a violent manner in such a way that it generates great heat and the subsequent release of large quantities of associated gasses.

explosive: Any chemical compound, mixture, or device, the primary or common purpose of which is to function by explosion

exsanguination: Death due to loss of blood/bleeding out

fallacy of innocence: The false belief that a person who is found not guilty in a trial is innocent

Federal Rule of Evidence 702: A federal rule stating that if scientific, technical, or other specialized knowledge will assist the trier of fact to understand the evidence or to determine a fact in issue, a witness qualified as an expert by knowledge, skill, experience, training, or education may testify thereto in the form of an opinion or otherwise

fence: Seller; the middleman necessary to let the majority of those who purchase stolen property pretend they have not been involved

fief: Land whose use but not ownership was granted to a vassal on condition of service

fighting words: Verbal provocation

final sketch: Finished rendition of a rough sketch that shows only pertinent items of evidence, usually prepared for courtroom presentation; typically includes a legend

fingerprint individuality: The shape, location, and number of minutiae that individualize a fingerprint

fingerprints: Mirror images of the friction ridge skin of the palm, fingers, and thumb

firearm: Weapon from which a shot is discharged; firearms examiners generally come into contact with five types of firearms: pistols, rifles, assault rifles, machine guns, and shotguns

firearms examination: Examination of the fired bullets and cartridges of a firearm to determine the weapon that fired them

firing pin: The part of the firearm's action that strikes the cartridge primer in order to fire it

first-responding officers: First officers to arrive at the crime scene. They are responsible for protecting the crime scene from any avoidable contamination in order to preserve it for investigation purposes

flammable liquids: Liquids that have a flash point lower than 100°F

flammable range: The range in which air and a fuel will support combustion

flash point: The lowest temperature at which a liquid gives off sufficient vapor to form a mixture with air that will support combustion

flow patterns: Pattern that indicates the direction of travel of flowing blood

follow-up interview: Allows for quiet retrospection and an opportunity to consider the event from some distance. It allows a review of the facts, and a comparison to the original statement, to ferret out fabrications and exaggerations and perhaps discover something that was left out of the original interview

follow-up investigation: Investigation of a crime that is conducted if solvability factors are found during the preliminary investigation

forensic chemist: Person who performs chemical and physical analysis of physical evidence to determine the makeup of a substance or substances, including identifying drugs by their chemical properties

forensic entomology: The analysis of insects and other invertebrates that sequentially colonize a decomposing body and of the rates at which various stages of their offspring develop

forensic evidence: Physical evidence that requires scientific validation

forensic investigation: The application of forensic science to the process of investigating a criminal event

forensic pathology: Area of medicine pertaining to studying the causes of human death

forensic science: The application of science to civil and criminal law

forward spatter: Blood that travels in the same direction as the force causing the spatter; forward spatter is often associated with gunshot exit wounds

fouling: Small bullet fragments around a gunshot wound

free-falling blood: Blood that has not been acted on by a force other than gravity; when a drop of free-falling blood strikes a nonporous, smooth, horizontal surface, the result is a circular bloodstain

friction ridges: Ridges on fingers that are the identifiable characteristics of fingerprints

frisk: A pat-down search of the outer clothing of a person to ensure that the subject is not armed, conducted when the officer has a reasonable suspicion, based on articulable facts, that the subject is armed

fruit-of-the-poisonous-tree doctrine: Common name for the idea that evidence can be tainted derivatively

Frye v. United States: Case in which the first test for assessing expert testimony was developed; in this 1923 case, the circuit court of appeals for the District of Columbia held that for novel scientific evidence to be admissible, the party offering it must establish is that the expert testimony and the techniques used to generate the results have been generally accepted as reliable in the scientific community

gauge: The number of spherical lead balls that have the diameter of the interior of the barrel of the firearm that add up to weigh one pound (e.g., 10 lead balls having the same diameter as the interior of the barrel of a 10-gauge shotgun should weigh 1 pound)

gender-specific: Limited to one gender

genetic fingerprinting: The DNA fingerprint of an individual

global positioning system (GPS): A device that uses satellites to compute position

gloving: The shedding of the skin of the hands, including the fingernails

good faith exception: Exception to the exclusionary rule that allows evidence obtained illegally to be used in trial when the officers obtaining the evidence had reason to believe that they were operating under a warrant that was issued properly

grid search: A crime scene search pattern in which an area is searched in one direction, then the searcher(s) turn 90° and search the same area from a different angle

grooves: The recessed areas between the lands of the rifling

habit pattern: Things done so often that thinking about them becomes unnecessary and a waste of time; when these habit patterns are a consistent part of a person's robberies, they are called the robber's modus operandi

hallucinogens: Drugs that cause a distortion in thought processes and perceptions as well as changes in moods

handgun: A type of weapon designed to be held in and fired with one hand; two primary subcategories are pistols and revolvers

hearsay: Any out-of-court statement made by someone other than the person testifying

Henry Faulds: Scottish physician working in Japan, noticed the practice of identifying pottery and sealing documents through the use of handprints and fingerprints

heresy: A belief inconsistent with a religion's dogma

high-order explosive: Explosives that change rapidly to a gaseous state upon ignition; they must be detonated by an initiating device, such as a blasting cap

high-velocity-impact pattern: Spatter caused by a blood source colliding with an object moving at a speed between 5 and 25 feet per second

homicide: The taking of a human life by another human

hostile witness: Witness who is favorable to the other side

hue and cry: Alarm sounded by constables to summon help from citizens to apprehend a criminal

hyperspectral imaging: Cameras can produce images of visible and invisible light used in the detection of burial sites

hypothesis: Prediction of outcome made in advance of testing a particular phenomenon

identity theft: Type of crime in which someone wrongfully obtains and uses another person's personal data in some way that involves fraud or deception, typically for economic gain

ignitable liquid: Any liquid that is capable of fueling a fire

ignition temperature: Temperature provided by some outside source of heat that causes a fuel to ignite; the ignition temperature is always higher than the flash point

ignitor: An item or phenomenon that can start a fire by providing temperatures in excess of the ignition temperature of most fuels

immediately apparent: Immediately recognizable as illegal to possess, with no search having been necessary to reveal that to the police

immutable: Unchangeable; refers to the retention of fingerprint characteristics throughout a person's life

improvised explosive device (IED): A homemade (nonmilitarily/commercially produced) bomb or destructive device designed to destroy, incapacitate, harass, or distract

in-court identification: Assuring the court that the individual in court is the same person charged with the offense of which he or she stands accused; the prosecution must do this in every criminal case

inadvertent discovery: One of the original elements of a plain-view discovery of evidence; meant to convey the accidental discovery of an item that is illegal to possess. It is no longer an element of the plain-view exception, based on *Arizona v. Hicks* (1987)

incendiary evidence: Evidence from the fire itself, including crime scene debris, observed burning characteristics, and an absence of accidental causation

incident command system (ICS): A management tool that integrates multiple resources

independent component doctrine: Doctrine stating that peripheral items may not be relevant and, therefore, not subject to lawful seizure

inductive reasoning: Drawing conclusions based on probabilities rather than certainties

inevitable discovery doctrine: Doctrine that allows derivative evidence that would generally be rendered inadmissible by the fruit-of-the-poisonous-tree doctrine to be admitted if the evidence would have been discovered anyway, without the assistance of the illegally seized evidence

informant: One who provides information

inquest: A formal inquiry

inquisition: Inquiry

instrumentality: A device, system or its associated hardware playing a significant role in the commission of a crime

intelligence: Information used to investigate a crime or compiled on related individuals to the crime

international terrorism: Terrorism conducted by state-supported terrorists but that involves the citizens of more than one state

interrogation: The formal questioning of a suspect conducted in a controlled environment and performed in an accusatory manner in order to learn the truth

interview: A conversation with witnesses or victims in order to elicit information

inventory: An administrative procedure that accounts for a citizen's property

investigate: To make a systematic examination or to conduct an official inquiry

jacketed bullets: Bullets that consist of a lead core surrounded by a jacket of harder material, commonly a copper-nickel alloy or mild steel

Jack the Ripper: The popular name given to a serial killer who killed a number of prostitutes in the East End of London in 1888

jimmy: Tool used to pry open doors and windows

joint terrorism task forces: Interagency cooperation fighting terrorism

joyriding: Stealing an automobile for personal enjoyment

jurisdiction: The statutory authority of a court to hear a case; in general, it is the authority to apply the law or govern

justifiable homicide: The killing of a person under authority of the law

killer's signature: The pattern associated with a person's killings

Kumho Tire Co. v. Carmichael: An expert testimony case decided by the Supreme Court in 1999 that has helped establish the criteria for the admissibility of expert testimony in federal and state courts

laceration: A cut caused by blunt trauma

lands: The raised ridges of the rifling that bite into the surface of the bullet and give it a rotational motion as it moves down the barrel

lane/strip search: A crime scene search method that begins at one corner of a search area and continues to the opposite corner, then reverses to search again in a line perpendicular to the original search line

larceny: In common law, taking the property of another for the purpose of depriving that person of ownership; it required three basic elements: a taking, asportation (movement of the items taken), and an intent to deprive the owner

latent prints: Prints deposited on a surface that are invisible to the naked eye

leads: The initial descriptions of persons, places, events, and things related to an investigation

legend: A note of explanation that defines or labels specific information in a sketch

legitimately on the premises: Legally allowed to be in a location despite not having a warrant; in such cases, officers are allowed to collect evidence that is in plain view and likely will not still be there when the officers return with a warrant

lifting: Removing a fingerprint from a crime scene by sticking a print developed with powder to transparent tape and then placing the tape (adhesive side down) on a black or white card

limiting phrase: Phrase in a warrant that helps separate the information to be seized from information that may be legally permissible to possess

line search: A crime scene search pattern in which searchers assemble side by side along a chosen edge of the crime scene and search the area together, maintaining a set distance between them as they walk

lividity: A purplish-blue discoloration on the lowest points of the body that are not in contact with a hard surface, associated with the onset of livor mortis…

livor mortis: The gravitational movement of blood to the lowest point after deaths occurring other than as a result of drowning

Locard's Exchange Principle: Whenever two objects come into contact with one another, there will be a cross-transfer of material, which will occur

lone wolf: A person who acts on his or her own without orders from—or even connections to—an organization

loops: Fingerprint pattern that has one or more ridges that enter from one side of the print, curve, and exit from the same side; includes a core and a delta

low-order explosive: Explosive that involves a relatively slow rate of conversion to a gaseous state; they can be ignited by heat and are usually ignited with a lighted fuse

lysergic acid diethylamide (LSD): Hallucinogen that is synthesized from a type of fungus that attacks certain grasses and grains; the drug is potent, and as little as 25 micrograms is enough to cause visual hallucinations that may last up to 12 hours

managing criminal investigations (MCIs): Concept designed to determine which crimes are most solvable and to use limited investigative resources to solve them

mapping: The term associated with crime scene measurements

Marquis test: Test used to screen for heroin, morphine, and opium derivatives; the reagent turns purple in their presence

masking fires: Fires set to mask the commission of other crimes

medical examination: Examination of the effects of an assault on the victim's body, in order to help determine the circumstances of the assault

medical examiner: A physician who works for a law enforcement agency to investigate the cause of any death that could have resulted from a crime or that occurred in a suspicious or unusual manner

medium-velocity blood spatter: Spatter caused by a blood source colliding with an object moving at a speed between 5 and 25 feet per second

methadone: A synthetic opiate used to prevent the physical symptoms of narcotic withdrawal that would otherwise be felt by someone addicted to narcotics

method of entry: The manner and direction from which the burglar(s) approached the building; it is determined by looking at the evidence at the point of entry

microtaggants: Fluorescent, color-coded, multilayered particles that identify a residue as dynamite and indicate the source of manufacture

midrange photographs: Photos that frame the item of evidence with an easily recognized landmark to visually establish its position in the crime scene but not intended to show details; also called *evidence-establishing* photographs

minutiae: Points where a finger friction ridge ends or splits in two; these are highly individualized

Miranda v. Arizona: Supreme Court decision that requires that a suspect be told of the Fifth Amendment protection against self-incrimination and the Sixth Amendment right to counsel during interrogations

Miranda warnings: Warnings read to a suspect in police custody that inform the suspect of his or her constitutional rights

modus operandi (MO): Method of operation; robbers often repeat their MO, which can be useful in figuring out who committed a particular crime

mummification: The dehydration of soft tissues as a result of high temperatures, low humidity, and wind or other form of ventilation

murder: Homicide with malice aforethought

mutual combat: Defense to a charge of assault, contending that the two parties agreed to involve themselves in an altercation

narcotic: Analgesic that relieves pain by depressing the central nervous system; the source of most narcotics is opium, and their regular use leads to physical dependence

National Incident Management System (NIMS): A method of coordinating the supervision of multiple agencies working together

National Firearms Act of 1968: Act that requires retailers to record the serial number of a weapon and the name of its purchaser

ninhydrin: The most common chemical used for developing latent prints on porous surfaces; it reacts chemically with the amino acids in sweat and renders a purple-blue print

nuclear terrorism: Involves terrorists detonating a nuclear device

nuclear threat: The potential for terrorists to acquire nuclear weapons or take actions against nuclear facilities

observation: Determination of what happens in an experiment when certain variables are changed

off-site computer: Computer that is readily and routinely accessed by the primary computer being searched and serves regularly as a component of the primary computer's network

open field: Any area outside of the curtilage of the home and is unprotected by the Fourth Amendment

opportunistic robbers: Amateurs who prey upon others as the opportunity presents itself; these robbers focus on individuals who are in the wrong place at the wrong time and who are least likely to offer resistance

overall photographs: Photos that show a large area of the crime scene at eye level, typically shot from the four corners of the scene; used to document the condition and layout of the scene as found

Paint Data Query: (Also known as the "International Forensic Automotive Paint Data Query") The world's largest international searchable database of chemical and color information of original automotive paints. The PDQ is used by forensic laboratories around the world to assist with criminal investigations requiring vehicle identification

papal inquisition: The trying of heretics by the authority of the pope

patent prints: Prints that are readily identifiable as fingerprints, by the unassisted eye

pathology: The branch of medicine associated with the study of structural changes caused by disease or injury

Paul Leland Kirk: Established criminology as an academic discipline and wrote *Crime Investigation*

penetrating wound: A gunshot wound that does not exit the body

peremptorily struck: Struck (from the jury) without a reason

perforating wound: A gunshot wound that exits the body

perimortem: Occurring around the time of death

perjury: the telling of a lie within a court of law by somebody who has taken an oath to tell the truth

petechial hemorrhage: The bursting of capillaries resulting from interference with venous blood flow, typically due to pressure or asphyxiation, and often found in the sclera of the eye or surrounding tissue of the face

phencyclidine (PCP): A synthetic substance that has appeared on the street in pill form (peace pills) and powder form (angel dust, tic, and dummy dust); now generically referred to as angel dust, and the preferred method of use is inhalation or ingestion

phishing: A scam where criminals send messages via the Internet to obtain personal and financial information from unsuspecting victims

photographic record: Photographs (preferably color photographs) taken of an assault victim's injuries

photo log: Recording of the people involved, equipment used, and conditions under which crime scene photographs were taken

photo placard: A handwritten or agency-developed sheet that lists pertinent case information for the photographs that follow

physical evidence: Evidence that can be handled, examined, tested, seen, felt, and tactually evaluated

physiologic dependence: Dependence on the use of a drug such that withdrawal of the drug results in clinical signs such as abdominal pains, nausea, and vomiting

plastic impressions: Fingerprints left on soft materials such as soap, wet cement, or dust that can be used for fingerprint comparisons

point of entry: Place where the criminal entered the premises; it is a location where forensic evidence is likely to be found

point of origin: Location where a fire began; it generally evidences the deepest charring;

police experts: Police officers who are often granted the latitude of expert witnesses in their testimony

post-indictment lineups: Lineup conducted after an indictment is handed down, during which counsel must be present

postmortem: Occurring after death

postmortem interval (PMI): The time that has elapsed since a person has died; while only an estimate, it assists in narrowing the interval between death and discovery

predicate: Proof of admissibility in court

preliminary investigation: The police agency's first response to a report that a crime has been committed

preliminary scene survey: A careful walk through a crime scene, conducted to develop a perspective on the nature of the crime, its commission, the type of evidence that will be expected, and the types of resources necessary to properly process the scene

preparation: The most important factor in conducting a successful interrogation; it involves considering the setting and environment, knowing the case facts, being familiar with the subject's background, and determining the method used to document the confession

press pool: A group of journalists authorized to cover an event

primary packaging: When collecting trace evidence, personnel typically will make sure of a druggist /

pharmacist fold as a primary method of evidence preservation. The trace evidence is placed onto a clean sheet of paper and the paper is then folded into thirds and then into thirds again, with one end of the paper tucked back into itself so as to safely encapsulate the trace material

primary transfer: Occurs when a fiber is transferred from a fabric directly onto a victim's clothing

primer: A metal cup containing a small amount of primer material placed between the cup and a small metal anvil

principle of parsimony: Principle that one should seek the simplest explanation for the phenomenon being examined

probability: Frequency with which an event will occur; also known as the odds of occurrence

probable cause: A reasonable ground to suspect that a person has committed or is committing a crime or that a place contains specific items connected with a crime

probative: Likely to prove a fact

product rule: When the frequency of independently occurring variables are multiplied to obtain an overall frequency of occurrence for the event or item

projected: Directed forcefully onto a surface

propellant: Powder that begins to burn when a firearm is fired; the pressure increase caused by the burning powder propels the bullet from the firearm

protocol: Set of steps followed to arrive at a conclusion that can be replicated by others using the same set of steps

proximate cause: A cause that directly produces an event and without which the event would not have occurred; a cause that is legally sufficient to result in liability

putrefaction: The decomposition of the body

pyrolysis: The chemical decomposition of a solid into a gaseous product

radial fractures: Breaks or cracks originating from the point of impact and moving away from that point, in a radiating pattern

reasonableness: The quality of being fair, proper, or moderate under the given circumstances

recording: Making note of each step of the experimental method employed so that the experiment can be repeated and the results replicated

refraction: The bending of light rays occurs whenever a beam of light strikes a plane surface between two substances that have different optical properties (such as air and water)

Reid technique: Technique for conducting a successful interrogation that describes a three-part process to be used during the interrogation

residential robbery (home invasion): Robbery in a residence, which is usually the result of burglaries gone wrong because the occupants return or the burglar was mistaken about the absence of the occupants; for an incident to be a residential robbery, force must be used in dealing with the occupants, and possessions must be removed from the person of the occupants

return: An itemized inventory of all the property seized by the officers executing a warrant

ricochet: Secondary blood splashing that may occur as a result of the deflection of large volumes of blood after impact with a primary target surface to a secondary target surface

rifle: Weapon designed to be used with two hands and fired from the shoulder position

rifled firearm: Type of firearm whose barrel has a set of spiraling lands and grooves

rigor mortis: Stiffness of the muscles after death, which eventually freezes the joints

rogues' gallery: A ready supply of photographs for witnesses to leaf through in the attempt to identify a perpetrator

rough sketch: A draft sketch prepared while on scene, typically during the preliminary evaluation, that is not done to scale, is artistically crude, and is used to record measurements and distances at the scene

scientific method: Formulation of a hypothesis and development of a protocol to test a hypothesis to identify factors causing a particular phenomenon

scientific testimony: Testimony about information gathered from the evidence by scientific analysis; this type of testimony can only be performed by a science expert

Scott test: Test used to screen for cocaine

scrapings: Particles under the fingernails and toenails that may be obtained in an effort to detect hair, fibers, blood, or tissue from the assailant

screening test: Test in which a specimen is subjected to a series of reagents that yield characteristic colors for commonly encountered drugs

search incident to an arrest: Search that is allowed when an officer is carrying out an arrest authorized by an arrest warrant

secondary device: A secondary explosive device placed at a scene to detonate after the original explosion. Typically, a place to target emergency responders and investigators at the scene of the initial bombing

secondary packaging: Serves to protect the primary packaging from damage and ensures that no trace material will be added to nor lost from the initial evidence that was collected. Typically comprised of a paper envelope, paper bag, a plastic bag or other type of box or container

secondary transfer: Occurs when already transferred fibers on the clothing of a suspect transfer to the clothing of a victim

self-propelled semi-submersible: A submarine-like vessel that does not fully submerge and is used to transport cocaine

seminal stains: Traces of semen that may be found in three localities: on the victim, at the crime scene, and on the suspect; use of an ultraviolet light is helpful for locating seminal stains

sex crimes investigator: Investigator who has been taught to be sensitive to the physical, psychological, and emotional needs of sexual assault victims and has been trained in what is required for the successful investigation of sexual assaults

sexual assault evidence collection kit (SAE kit): Assortment of equipment that is useful for collecting evidence of a sex crime from a victim

show of force: Use of violence or the threat of violence

signature: A factor or factors that make the crime atypical and distinguishable from other crimes and other criminals

simple assault: A threat to cause bodily injury, an offensive contact or touch, or an attack that does not cause serious bodily injury; the term is used in jurisdictions that have dropped the term battery from their penal codes

Sir Francis Galton: Published *Finger Prints*, a book-length monograph that contained a basic system of classification

sketch artist: Person who can create a picture that, through continual refinement based on witness input, begins to bear a strong resemblance to a suspect

sleeper cell: A terrorist cell that comprises individuals who immigrate, establish a residence and an identity, find employment, and await orders

small particle reagent (SPR): A suspension of fine molybdenum disulfide particles that adhere to the fatty components of skin secretions. Typically used to process latent prints found in wet environments

smash-and-grab: Method used to rob people in vehicles, in which the thief uses a pipe or other device hidden in his or her clothing to break the passenger-side window and grab valuables

smoothbore firearm: firearm that has no rifling present within the firearm bore

snitch: Criminal or person who associates with criminals who gives information to police about acquaintances involved in or planning criminal activities

solvability factors: Information about a crime that can provide the basis for determining who committed the crime

sound suppressor: The correct name for a silencer; it is only effective when used with weapons that fire bullets at speeds less than the speed of sound

special jury: In common law, a jury of persons especially fitted to judge the peculiar facts of the case in issue

specialty robbery: Robbery in which the robber(s) may have received inside information from an accomplice or may have had firsthand employment experience in the particular business robbed or in the same industry

specification: Designation of what is going to be done and how it is to be done

specific intent: Unambiguous purpose or reason; this must be proved in order to convict a person of theft or larceny

spermatozoa: The male reproductive cells

spines: The pointed-edge pattern that radiates away from a drop of blood that has struck a target surface

spiral search: A search method that involves moving in an ever-tightening or ever-expanding spiral; it can be used indoors or out

splashed: A (projected) pattern created by a low-velocity impact on the surface of a pool of blood with a volume of 0.10 mL or greater

spontaneous combustion: Combustion that is a product of a natural heat-producing process; it is caused and maintained by poor ventilation

spousal immunity: The notion that sex was a husband's right and a wife's duty and, therefore, that sexual assault by a person against his spouse was not a crime

stakeout: A type of stationary surveillance that generally focuses on places and things and requires great patience and many departmental resources

standards of resistance: Two standards, maximum and reasonable resistance, that evolved for the force element to apply in the common-law definition of rape

state-sponsored terrorism: Terrorism used by a government to manipulate its own citizens

stippling: Powder burns on the skin from a close contact wound

stocking: The shedding of the skin around the feet and legs

stop: Detaining a citizen, which is allowed when an officer has reasonable suspicion, based on articulable facts rather than mere speculation, that the citizen has committed or is about to commit a crime

street robbery: A theft that occurs in the streets; it includes violence or the threat of force and often involves more than one offender

stripped: Removing and stealing the most easily removable and transportable parts from an automobile in order to resell them to individuals or salvage yard dealers

strobe: A type of electronic flash unit, attachable flash accessory for cameras

substance-habituated robber: A person who commits robbery to support a drug habit

Superglue fuming: Technique used for the development of fingerprints on nonporous surfaces

suppression hearing: A pretrial hearing in front of a judge to determine constitutional issues related to the admissibility of evidence

surface texture: Composition of materials in a given surface that provides the foundation for blood pattern interpretation

swabbings: Specimens taken with a swab from the mouth, anus, and vaginal cavity to detect the presence of seminal fluid or spermatozoa

swath: The effective area that a searcher can cover while conducting a search

SWGSTAIN: The Scientific Working Group on Bloodstain Pattern Analysis; was created to promote quality forensic bloodstain pattern analysis practices by government labs, law enforcement, private industry, and academia

synthesize: Combining data to form a working hypothesis

tail: Mobile or moving surveillance of a suspect

taphonomy: The study of postmortem changes to the body. Examples include: normal decomposition; alteration and scattering by scavengers; and movement and modification by flowing water, as well as freezing or mummification

target selection: Selection of a person or location for committing a robbery

target surface: Surface onto which blood is deposited

taxonomy: Classification of observed phenomena into groups that share specific characteristics

technological terrorism: Use of computers as weapons to target such locations as metropolitan water supplies, public utility companies, dams, electric power grids, transmission lines and transformers, petroleum refineries and pipelines, and power plants

tenure: Land use granted on condition of payment

terminal velocity: The maximum speed to which a free-falling drop of blood can accelerate in air; this velocity is approximately 25.1 feet per second

testimonial evidence: Evidence that encompasses the testimony of witnesses and of defendants

tetrahydrocannabinol (THC): The psychoactive ingredient in marijuana

theft: An unlawful intentional appropriation of property

theme: Monologue in which the investigator offers moral or psychological excuses for the suspect's criminal behavior

theory: A hypothesis that is supported by data

thief catcher: A person hired to locate someone's stolen goods; this person was often a thief himself or a moonlighting constable

tire impression: Imprint left by a tire

Tommie Lee Andrews: The first person to be convicted in the United States based on DNA evidence

toolmark: Any impression, cut, gouge, or abrasion caused by a tool coming into contact with another object

totality of the circumstances: Test used to determine if information supplied by an informant is legally usable; it states that such information is legal if, given all the circumstances, there is a fair probability that the evidence sought will be found in a particular place

trace evidence: Evidence left at the scene of a crime that usually cannot be seen with the naked eye and that requires the assistance of lights or reagents to visualize

trace evidence carriers: Items on which trace evidence is likely to be found

tracing: Using evidence to identify and locate a criminal

trailer: A lone trail of combustibles or ignitable liquids leading from the point of origin to some other area of the building; used to spread the fire

transcript: The official record of what has taken place during the course of the trial, typed by the court stenographer

transfer: The process whereby a person entering and exiting a crime scene leaves something and takes something

transfer evidence: A type of evidence that is passed from one item to another, typically as a result of contact or action. Careful analysis of this evidence can associate the questioned evidence with a known source

transient cell: A group that arrives in a country solely for the purpose of conducting a terroristic act or campaign

transnational terrorism: Terrorism that is conducted by terrorists against citizens of another country; these groups are not supported by a state but may receive support from various regimes in various countries and locations

triangulation: Basic measurement technique used for geographically locating evidence; in this technique, three angles are measured—those of a triangle formed by the item of interest and two permanent objects (fixed points)

trier of fact: A judge or magistrate in a trial by the court, or a jury of one's peers in a trial by jury, whose duty it is to weigh the evidence presented and determine guilt or innocence

trophy: Remembrance or souvenir of a conquest, such as a body part

truck hijacking: A specialty crime committed by well-armed and experienced offenders, in which an entire transport vehicle and its cargo are taken.

unauthorized use of a motor vehicle: Use of a vehicle by someone other than the owner without the owner's permission

Underwater Search and Evidence Response Team (USERT): Federal teams assembled to provide underwater search and evidence recovery assistance

utility software: Software used by a computer expert to begin searching through the accumulated data in a computer

vapor detector (sniffer): A device that detects the presence of volatile residues by sampling the air around a suspect area or sample

vehicle inventory: Accounting for the items contained in a vehicle

vehicle identification number (VIN): Alphanumeric code consisting of 17 characters placed on automobile components to track them in the case of theft

venireperson: A prospective juror

venue: The geographic area over which a court presides

Violent Criminal Apprehension Program (VICAP): Program that collects, sorts, analyzes, and categorizes data on serial homicides in an effort to uncover hidden relationships among homicides, victims, and modi operandi

Virchow method: Autopsy method developed by Rudolf Virchow that included the removal and examination of each organ

visualized: To make visible

voir dire: Jury selection process

waiver: Conscious act of giving up rights or privileges

warrant affidavit: Document that establishes, to the satisfaction of a neutral and detached magistrate, sufficient probable cause

warrant procedure: Three individual actions on the part of the police: (1) drafting an affidavit that on its face establishes, to the satisfaction of a neutral and detached magistrate, sufficient probable cause; (2) serving the warrant; and (3) preparing and rendering the search warrant return

weapons of mass destruction (WMD): Chemical, biological or conventional weaponry which are capable of producing tremendous destruction to life and property

whorls: Fingerprint pattern having a minimum of two deltas; this pattern is classified into four groupings: (1) plain whorl, (2) central pocket loop whorl, (3) double loop whorl, and (4) accidental whorl

zone search: A search method typically used when there are previously defined zones or when a larger crime scene needs to be divided into search zones; sometimes referred to as "gridding" an area, but should not be confused with the grid method

zones of possibility: Used to establish limits as to what is likely, what is possible, and what is impossible, based upon the evidence presented

References

Alroy, T. T. (2015). Facebook loses appeal over access to user data. *CNN*. Retrieved July 23, 2015, from http://www.cnn.com/2015/07/23/tech/facebook-search-warrants/index.html

Amendt, J., & Goff, M. L. (2009). *Current concepts in forensic entomology*. New York, NY: Springer.

Ancestry. (n.d.). Ancestry Guide for Law Enforcement. Retrieved November 6, 2017, from http://www.ancestry.com/cs/legal/lawenforcement

Associated Press. (2015). Meth-filled drone crashes in Mexican border town. *CBS News*. Retrieved August 8, 2015, from *http://www.cbsnews.com/news/meth-filled-drone-crashes-in-mexican-border-town/*

Bacigal, R. J. (2008). *Criminal law and procedure: An overview*. Clifton Park, NY: Cengage Learning.

Baden, M. M. (1980). Investigation of deaths from drug abuse. In W. U. Spitz & R. S. Fisher (Eds.), *Medicolegal investigation of death* (2nd ed.). Springfield, IL: Charles C. Thomas.

Bakker, E., & de Graaf, B. (2010, November). *Lone wolves: How to prevent this phenomenon*. Paper presented at the Expert Meeting Lone Wolves, International Centre for CounterTerrorism—The Hague. Retrieved from https://www.icct.nl/download/file/ICCT-Bakker-deGraaf-EM-Paper-Lone-Wolves.pdf

Balbanova, S., Parsche, F., & Pirsig, W. (1992). First identification of drugs in Egyptian mummies. *Naturwissenschaften, 79*, 358–371.

Becker, R. F. (1999). *Scientific evidence and expert testimony handbook*. Springfield, IL: Charles C. Thomas.

Becker, R. F. (2000). Myths of underwater recovery operations. *The FBI Law Enforcement Bulletin, 69*, 1–5.

Becker, R. F. (2013). *Underwater forensic investigation* (2nd ed.). Boca Raton, FL: CRC Press.

Beeler, L., & Wiebe, W. R. (1988). DNA identification tests and the courts. *Washington Law Review, 63*, 903.

Begg, P. (2004). *Jack the Ripper: The facts*. London: Robson Books.

Bennett, W. W., & Hess, K. M. (2010). *Criminal investigation* (9th ed.). Clifton Park, NY: Cengage Learning.

Beveridge, A. (2011). *Forensic investigation of explosions* (2nd ed.). Boca Raton, FL: CRC Press.

Biegelman, M. T. (2009). *Identity theft handbook: Detection, prevention and security*. Hoboken, NJ: John Wiley.

Bland, E. (2010). New tech sees dead people. Retrieved September 6, 2011, from http://msnbc.msn.com/id/36602201/ns/technology

Bolz, F., Dudonis, K. J., & Schulz, D. P. (2011). *The counterterrorism handbook: tactics, procedures, and techniques* (4th ed.). Boca Raton, FL: CRC Press.

Bond, J. W. (2009, July). Visualization of latent fingerprint corrosion of brass. *Journal of Forensic Sciences*, 1034–1041.

Brewer, L., & Allen, A. (1991). N-formyl cocaine: A study of cocaine comparison parameters. *Journal of Forensic Science, 36*, 697–731.

Brodsky, S. L. (2009). *Principles and practices of trial consultation*. New York, NY: Guilford Press.

Brown, D. L. (2010). *Home invasion: The fear is real*. Niles, OH: Parkway Press.

Browne, W. H. (Ed.). (1885). *Archives of Maryland. Vol. 3*. Baltimore, MD: Maryland Historical Society.

Bull, R., & Soukara, S. (2010). Four studies of what really happens in police interviews. In G. D. Lassiter & C. A. Meissner (Eds.), *Police interrogations and false confessions* (pp. 81–95). New York, NY: American Psychological Association.

Bureau of Alcohol, Tobacco, Firearms, and Explosives. (n.d.). Retrieved June 29, 2017, from https://www.atf.gov/resource-center/data-statistics

Bureau of Justice Statistics. (2014). *Firearms and crime statistics*. Retrieved July 28, 2015, from http://bjs.ojp.usdoj.gov/content/guns.cfm

Burns, J. (2017, April 11). Sessions scraps Federal Commission on forensic accuracy, for some reason. *Forbes Magazine*. Retrieved July 7, 2017, from https://www.forbes.com/sites/janetwburns/2017/04/11/-sessions-scraps-federal-commission-on-forensic-accuracy-because-reasons/#8176a776c219

Burns, M. (2007). *Medical-legal aspects of drugs* (2nd ed.). Tucson, AZ: Lawyers and Judges.

Casey, E. (2011). *Digital evidence and computer crime: Forensic science, computers and the Internet*. Waltham, MA: Elsevier.

Ceci, S. J., & Bruck, M. (1995). *Jeopardy in the courtroom: A scientific analysis of children's testimony*. Washington, DC: American Psychological Association.

Chan, S. (2009, May 12). Police used GPS illegally, court rules. *New York Times*. Retrieved August 19, 2009, from http://www.nytimes.com/2009/05/13/nyregion/13gps.html

Chandler, R. K. (2009). *Fire investigation*. Clifton Park, NY: Delmar.

Clark, K. (2017). *Longmont police chief says housing authority is to blame for search confusion*. Retrieved July 7, 2017, from http://www.9news.com/news/local/next/longmont-police-chief-says-housing-authority-is-to-blame-for-search-confusion/446727711

Coffey, H. (2017). Flight diverted after woman discovers her husband is cheating on her. *The Independent*. Retrieved November 7, 2017, from http://www.independent.co.uk/travel/news-and-advice/flight-diverted-wife-husband-cheating-qatar-airways-couple-fight-a8042616.html

Committee on Rules of Practice and Procedure. (2001). *Preliminary draft of proposed amendments to the Federal Rules of Civil Procedure and Evidence*. Washington, DC: Judicial Conference of the United States.

Coppock, C. A. (2007). *Contrast* (2nd ed.). Springfield, IL: Charles C. Thomas.

Crook, T. (2010). *Comparative media and ethics*. New York, NY: Routledge.

Deakin, J., Smithson, H., Spencer, J., & Medina-Ariza, J. (2007, February). Taxing on the streets: Understanding the methods and process of street robberies. *Crime Prevention and Community Safety*, 9(1), 52–67.

Department of Homeland Security. (2002). *Arson detection for the first responder: ADFR-student manual*. Washington, DC: U.S. Government Printing Office.

Department of Homeland Security. (2008). *Incident response to terrorist bombings*. Washington, DC: U.S. Government Printing Office.

Department of Homeland Security. (2017). *National incident management system*. Retrieved July 13, 2017, from https://www.fema.gov/national-incident-management-system

Derlet, R. W., & Heischober, B. (1990, December). Methamphetamine: Stimulant of the 1990s? *Western Journal of Medicine*, 153(6), 625–628.

Douglas, J. E., & Olshaker, M. (1996). *Mind hunter: Inside the FBI's elite serial unit*. New York, NY: Pocket Books.

Drug Enforcement Administration. (2017). *Drugs of abuse*. Retrieved October 19, 2017, from https://www.dea.gov/pr/multimedia-library/publications/drug_of_abuse.pdf

Durant, W. (1950). *The age of faith*. New York, NY: Simon and Schuster.

Dutelle, A. W. (2015). *Basic crime scene photography* (2nd ed.). Seattle, WA: CreateSpace Publishing.

Dutelle, A. W. (2016). *An introduction to crime scene investigation* (3rd ed.). Burlington, MA: Jones & Bartlett Learning.

Eckert, W. G., & James S. H. (1993). *Interpretation of bloodstain evidence at crime scenes*. Boca Raton, FL: CRC Press.

Endlich, G. A. (2010). *Expert testimony*. New York, NY: Gale.

ExpertPages. (2008). *The leading directory of expert witnesses* (home page). Retrieved July 20, 2017, from http://www.expertpages.com

Fay, J. J. (2007). *Encyclopedia of security management* (2nd ed.). Burlington, MA: Elsevier.

Federal Bureau of Investigation (FBI). (2009). Retrieved October 2, 2012, from http://www.fbi.gov/news/stories/2009/august/diveteam_082109

Federal Bureau of Investigation. (1975–2009). *Uniform crime reports*. Washington, DC: U.S. Department of Justice.

Federal Bureau of Investigation. (2010). *Uniform crime reports*. Washington, DC: U.S. Department of Justice.

Federal Bureau of Investigation. (2015). *Crime in the United States*. Washington, DC: U.S. Department of Justice.

Federal Bureau of Investigation. (2015). *Uniform crime reports*. Washington, DC: U.S. Department of Justice.

Federal Bureau of Investigation. (2016). *Uniform crime reports*. Washington, DC: U.S. Government Printing Office.

Fish, J. T., Miller, L. S., & Braswell, M. C. (2014). *Crime scene investigation: An introduction* (3rd ed.). New York, NY: Routledge.

Fish, J., Stout, R. N., & Wallace E. W. (2011). *Practical crime scene investigations for hot zones*. Boca Raton, FL: Taylor & Francis.

Fisher, B.A. (2004). *Techniques of crime scene investigation* (7th ed.). Boca Raton, FL: CRC Press.

Fisher, R. P., & McCauley, M. R. (2013). Information retrieval: Interviewing witnesses. *Psychology and Policing*. Brewer, N. & Wilson, C., eds.

Foley, R. J. (2009, May 7). Wisconsin court upholds GPS tracking by police. *Chicago Tribune*. Retrieved October 2, 2012, from http://geodatapolicy.wordpress.com/2009/05/15/

Fong, I. W., & Alibek, K. (2009). *Bioterrorism and infectious agents: A new dilemma for the 21st century*. New York, NY: Springer.

Forst, B., Greene, J. R., & Lyncy, J. P. (2011). *Criminologist on terrorism and homeland security*. New York, NY: Cambridge Press.

Futrell, I. R. (1996). Hidden evidence: Latent print on human skin. *FBI Law Enforcement Bulletin*, April.

Gale, T. (2005). Locard's Exchange Principle. *World of Forensic Science*. Retrieved September 1, 2017, from http://www.encyclopedia.com/doc.1G2-3448300354.html

Galton, F. (1892). *Finger prints*. London: MacMillan.

Gardner, A. (2011). *Hallucinogens legally sold as "bath salts" a new threat*. Retrieved August 25, 2012, from https://consumer.healthday.com/mental-health-information-25/addiction-news-6/hallucinogens-legally-sold-as-bath-salts-a-new-threat-649596.html

Gardner, D. (2011). Jury shown photos of child-sized porcelain doll found in bed with Michael Jackson when he died. *The Daily Mail Online*. Retrieved October 2, 2012, from http://www.dailymail

.co.uk/news/article-2045737/Conrad-Murray-trial-Michael-Jacksons-doll-drug-stash-shown-jurors.html

Gardner, M. (1957). *Fads and fallacies in the name of science*. New York, NY: Ballantine.

Garmin. (1996–2011). *What is GPS?* Retrieved August 15, 2011, from http://www8.garmin.com/aboutGPS/

Geberth, V. J. (2006). *Practical homicide investigation* (4th ed.). Boca Raton, FL: CRC Press.

Gilbert, J. N. (2009). *Criminal investigation*. Upper Saddle River, NJ: Prentice Hall.

Gilbert, J. N. (2010). *Criminal investigation* (8th ed.). Englewood Cliffs, NJ: Prentice Hall.

Girard, J. E. (2017). *Criminalistics: Forensic science, crime and terrorism* (4th ed.). Burlington, MA: Jones & Bartlett Learning.

Goddard, C. H. (1930). St. Valentine's Day massacre: A study in ammunition tracing. *American Journal of Police Science, 1*, 60–78.

Goff, M. L. (2001). *A fly for the prosecution*. New York, NY: Harvard University Press.

Hall, A. L. (1931). The missile and the weapon. *American Journal of Police Science, 2*, 311–321.

Hand, L. (1901). Considerations regarding expert testimony. *Harvard Law Review, 1*, 40–58.

Harlow, C. W. (1988). *Motor vehicle theft*. Washington, DC: U.S. Department of Justice, Bureau of Justice Statistics.

Harris, R. C. (2008). *Black robes white coats: The puzzle of judicial policy making and scientific evidence*. New York, NY: Rutgers Press.

Heard, B. J. (2008). *Handbook of firearms and ballistics: Examining and interpreting forensic evidence*. Hoboken, NJ: Frank Willey.

Hess, K. M. (2010). *Criminal investigation*. Clifton Park, NY: Cengage Learning.

Hosmer, C., & Hyde, C. (2003). *Discovering covert digital evidence*. Paper presented at the Digital Forensic Research Workshop, August 6. Retrieved September 26, 2011, from http://www.dfrws.org/2003/presentations/Paper-Hosmer-digitalevidence.pdf

Howe. M. L., Goodman, G. S., & Cicchetti, D. (2008). *Stress trauma and children's memory development*. New York, NY: Oxford University Press.

Inbau, F. E., Reid, J. E., Buckley, J. P., & Jayne, B. C. (2015). *Essentials of the Reid technique: Criminal interrogation and confessions* (2nd ed.). Burlington, MA: Jones & Bartlett Learning.

Indovina, M., Dvorychenko, V., Tabassi, E., Quinn, G., Grother, P., et al., & National Institute of Standards and Technology (NISTIR). (2009). *An evaluation of automated latent fingerprint identification technologies* (NISTIR 7577). Retrieved August 1, 2009, from http://fingerprint.nist.gov/latent/NISTIR_7577_ELFT_PhaseII.pdf

Innocence Project. (n.d.). http://www.innocenceproject.org/. Retrieved September 1, 2017.

International Association of Arson Investigators. (2012). *Fire investigator: Principles and practice to NFPA 921 and 1033*. Burlington, MA: Jones & Bartlett Learning.

Jacobs, B. A. (2010, May). Serendipity in robbery target selection. *The British Journal of Criminology, 50*(3), 514–529.

James, R. (2009, June 19). A brief history of DNA testing. *Time*. Retrieved August 14, 2011, from http://www.time.com/time/nation/article/0,8599,1905706,00.html

James, S. H., & Nordby, J. J. (2005). *Forensic science: An introduction to scientific and investigative techniques* (2nd ed.). Boca Raton, FL: CRC Press.

Johnson, H. A., Wolfe N. T., & Jones, M. (2008). *History of criminal justice* (4th ed.). Burlington, MA: Elsevier.

Joint POW/MIA Accounting Command (JPAC), United States Department of Defense. (2009). *Mission overview*. Retrieved October 2, 2012, from http://www.jpac.pacom.mil/index.php?page=mission_overview

Joyner, D. (2009). *International law and the proliferation of weapons of mass destruction*. New York, NY: Oxford University Press.

Kapardis, A. (2014). *Psychology and law: A critical introduction*. New York, NY: Cambridge University Press.

Karch, S. B. (2009). *The pathology of drug abuse* (4th ed.). Boca Raton, FL: CRC Press.

Kassin, S. M., Drizin, S. A., Grisso, T., Gudjonsson, G. H., Leo, R. A., & Redlich, A. P. (2010). Police-induced confessions: Risk factors and recommendations. *Law and Human Behavior, 34*, 3–38.

Kirk, P. L. (1953). *Crime investigation*. New York, NY: Interscience.

Kirk, P. L. (1974). *Crime investigation* (2nd ed.). New York, NY: John Wiley & Sons.

Kolko, D. J. (2002). *Handbook on presetting in children and youth*. San Diego, CA: Academic Press.

Kruse, W. G., & Heiser, J. G. (2001). *Computer forensics: Incident response essentials*. Boston, MA: Addison-Wesley.

Laber, T. L. (1985). Diameter of a bloodstain as a function of origin, distance fallen and volume of drop. *International Association of Blood Pattern Analysts News, 2*(1), 12–16.

Lane, A. J. (1971). *The Brownsville affair: National crisis and black reaction*. Port Washington, NY: Kennikat.

Latrobe, J. G. (1861). *Justices' practice under the laws of Maryland* (6th ed.). Baltimore, MD: Lucas.

Leenaars, J., & Reed, A. (2016, May 2). *Understanding lone wolves: Towards a theoretical framework for comparative analysis*. The International Centre for Counter-Terrorism The Hague (ICCT). Retrieved on

September 7, 2016, from https://icct.nl/publication
/understanding-lone-wolves-towards-a
-theoretical-framework-for-comparative-analysis/

Leica. (2015). Leica Scanning Station C10. Retrieved
April 27, 2015, from http://www.leica-geosystems
.us/forensic/downloads/LeicaScanStationC10.pdf

Leo, R. A. (2009). *Police interrogation and American justice.*
Cambridge, MA: Harvard University Press.

Leonard, V. A., & More, H. W. (2000). *Police organization
and management.* New York, NY: Foundation Press.

Lerner, E. (2000). Biometric identification. *Industrial
Physicist, 6*(1), 18–21.

Lieberman, J. D. (2009). *Jury psychology: Social aspects of
trial processes.* Burlington, VT: Ashgate.

Linebaugh, P. (1991). *The London hanged: Crime
and civil society in the eighteenth century.*
London: Veros.

Lyon, D. (2007). *Surveillance studies: An overview.* Malden,
MA: Polity Press.

MacDonell, H. L. (1971a). *Flight characteristics of human
blood and stain patterns.* Washington, DC: National
Institute of Law Enforcement and Criminal
Justice.

MacDonell, H. L. (1971b). *Interpretation of blood-
stains: Physical considerations.* In C. Wecht
(Ed.), *Legal medicine annual.* New York, NY:
Appleton-Century-Crofts.

MacDonell, H. L. (1993). *Bloodstain patterns.* Corning,
NY: Laboratory of Forensic Science.

Magnuson, E. (1990, April 9). The devil made him do
it. *Time,* 38.

Maier, H. W. (1926). *Der Kokainismus* (O. J. Kalant, Trans.).
Toronto, Ontario, Canada: Addiction Research
Foundation.

Maldarelli, C. (2015, October 16). Could having your
DNA tested land you in court? *Popular Science.*
Retrieved November 7, 2017, from https://www
.popsci.com/could-submitting-your-dna-to
-private-genetics-companies-land-you-in-court

Mallon, G. P., & Hess, P. M. (2014). *Child welfare for the
twenty-first century: A handbook of practices, policies
and programs* (2nd ed.). New York, NY: Columbia
University Press.

Maras, M. H. (2014). *Computer forensics: Cybercriminals,
laws and evidence* (2nd ed.). Burlington, MA:
Jones & Bartlett Learning.

McCormick, M. (1982). Scientific evidence: Defining
a new approach to admissibility. *67 Iowa Law
Review, 879,* 911–912.

McMullan, J. L. (1996). The new improved monied
police: Reform, crime control, and the
commodification of policing in London. *British
Journal of Criminology, 36,* 85–108.

McNeal, G. (2014, November). Drones and aerial
surveillance: Considerations for legislatures.
Brookings.edu. Retrieved July 7, 2017, from https://

www.brookings.edu/research/drones-and-aerial
-surveillance-considerations-for-legislatures/

Melvin, D. (2015). No more dodging a bullet, as
U.S. develops self-guided ammunition. *CNN.*
Retrieved July 31, 2015, from http://www.cnn
.com/2015/04/29/us/us-military-self-guided
-bullet/index.html

Miller, F. B., Vandome, A. F., & McBrewster, J. (2010).
Crime mapping. Mauritius: VDM Publishing.

Miller, W. R. (1977). *Cops and bobbies: Police authority
in New York and London, 1830–1870.* Chicago, IL:
University of Chicago Press.

Moak, S. C., & Carlson, R. L. (2015). *Criminal justice
procedure.* New York, NY: Routledge.

Moran, B. (2001). *Shooting incident reconstruction,*
presentation to the Association of Crime Scene
Reconstruction. Las Vegas, NV. October 2001.

Mortimer, W. G. (1901). Peru: The history and regulation
of a dangerous drug. *Cornell Law Review, 58,* 537.

Musto, D. F. (1991). Opium, cocaine and marijuana in
American history. *Scientific American, 265*(1), 40–47.

Myers, A. L. (2012). Suicide by poison suspected in
courtroom death. *Associated Press.* Retrieved
July 6, 2012, from http://www.kmov.com/news
/national/Suicide-by-poison-suspected-in
-courtroom-death160971445.html

National Counterterrorism Center. (2007). *2007 counterrorism calendar.* Washington, DC: Office of
Director of National Intelligence.

National Forensic Science Technology Center.
(2013, December). *Crime scene investigation: A
guide for law enforcement.* Retrieved April 25,
2015, from http://www.nfstc.org/bja-programs
/crime-scene-investigation-guide/

National Institute of Justice. (1999). *Forensic
sciences: Review of status and needs.* Retrieved
August 13, 2011, from www.ncjrs.gov/pdffiles1
/173412.pdf

National Institute of Justice. (2004). *Technical working
group for the examination of digital evidence, forensic examination of digital evidence: A guide for law
enforcement.* Washington, DC: National Institute
of Justice.

National Institute of Justice. (2008, April). *Electronic
crime scene investigation: A guide for first responders*
(2nd ed.). Retrieved October 2, 2012, from http://
www.nij.gov/pubs-sum/219941.htm

National Research Council. (2007). *Countering the threat
of improvised explosive devices.* Washington, DC:
National Academies Press.

Noyes, H. (1884). Muriate of cocaine as a local anesthetic to the cornea: The ophthalmological
congress in Heidelberg. *Medical Record, 17,* 418.

Osterburg, J. W., & Ward, R. H. (2010). *Criminal investigation: A method for reconstructing the past* (6th ed.).
Cincinnati, OH: Anderson.

Pagan, G. (2017, July 6). What it takes to become a Knoxville police officer. *WATE.com*. Retrieved July 7, 2017, from http://wate.com/2017/07/06/what-it-takes-to-become-a-knoxville-police-officer/

Pool, D. A., & Lindsay, D. S. (2001). Children's eyewitness reports after exposure to misinformation from parents. *Journal of Experimental Psychology Applied, 7*(1), 27–50.

Pounds, C. A., & Smalldon, K. W. (1995). The transfer of fibers between clothing materials during simulated contacts and their persistence during wear. *Journal of the Forensic Science Society, 15,* 29–37.

Principie, G. F., Ceci, S. J., & Bruck, M. (2010). *Children's memory: Psychology and the law.* San Francisco, CA: Wiley-Blackwell.

Radzinowicz, L. (1986). *A history of English criminal law and its administration from 1750.* London: Stephens.

Reisberg, D. (2001). *Cognition* (2nd ed.). New York, NY: W.W. Norton.

Riley, H. T. (1868). *Memorials of London and London life in the 13th, 14th, and 15th centuries.* London: Longmans, Green & Co.

Rogers, T. (2004, March). Crime scene ethics: Souvenirs, teaching material, and artifacts. *Journal of Forensic Sciences, 49*(2), 307–311.

Royal Canadian Mounted Police. (2013). Retrieved June 27, 2015, from http://www.rcmp-grc.gc.ca

Sachs, J. S. (2001). *Corpse, nature, forensics and the struggle to pinpoint time of death.* Cambridge, MA: Perseus.

Saferstein, R. (2014). *Criminalistics: An introduction to forensic science* (11th ed.). Upper Saddle River, NJ: Pearson Prentice Hall.

Scheb, J. M. (2010). *Criminal law and procedure.* Clifton Park, NY: Cengage Learning.

Schehl, S. A., & Rosati, C. J. (2001, January). The Booth Derringer: Genuine artifact or replica. *Forensic Science Communications, 3*(1), 42–44.

Singletary, K. (2008, February 15). Man is charged with stalking. He's accused of putting a GPS device in the car of his estranged wife. *Wisconsin State Journal*. Retrieved October 2, 2012, from http://host.madison.com/news/local/article_abf0e2e6-15ba-5813-8bb6-b775b8d53257.html

Sommerville, J., Hatcher, J. S., Jury, F. J., & Weller, J. (2006). *Firearms: Investigation, identification and evidence.* Schnecksville, PA: Ray Riling Arms Books.

Spitz, W. U. (1993). Drowning. In W. U. Spitz (Ed.), *Medicolegal investigation of death* (3rd ed.). Springfield, IL: Charles C. Thomas.

Spitz, W. U., Spitz, D. J., & Fisher, R. S. (2006). *Spitz and Fisher's medicolegal investigation of death: Guidelines for the application of pathology to crime scenes* (4th ed.). Springfield, IL: Charles Thomas.

Stephens, B. G. (1993). *Investigations of death from drug abuse.* In W. U. Spitz & R. S. Fisher (Eds.), Medicolegal investigations of death (3rd ed.). Springfield, IL: Charles C. Thomas.

Stephens, B. G., & Allen T. B. (1983). Backspatter of blood from gunshot wounds: Observations and experimental simulation. *Journal of Forensic Sciences, 23,* 437–439.

Stewart, S., & Burton, F. (2009, June 3). Lone wolf lessons. *Security Weekly*. Retrieved from https://www.stratfor.com/weekly/20090603_lone_wolf_lessons

Suarez, C., Arango, A., & Lester, J. (1977). Cocaine-condom ingestion. *Journal of the American Medical Association, 238,* 1391–1392.

Substance Abuse and Mental Health Services Administration. (2009). *Results from the 2008 National Survey on Drug Use and Health: National findings.* Rockville, MD: U.S. Department of Health and Human Services.

The Diagram Group. (2007). *The new weapons of the World Encyclopedia.* New York, NY: St. Martin's.

Thornton, J. I., & Nakamura, G. R. (1972). The identification of marijuana. *Journal of Forensic Science Society, 12*(3), 461.

Thorwald, J. (1965). *The century of the detective.* New York, NY: Harcourt World.

Tobias, J. J. (1979). *Crime and police in England 1700–1900.* London: St. Martin's Press.

"Toxic action of cocaine." (1885, November 21). *British Medical Journal,* 983.

U.S. Department of Justice. (1990, November 29). *Title 21 United States Code (USC) Controlled Substances Act.* Retrieved September 20, 2011, from http://www.deadiversion.usdoj.gov/21cfr/21usc/802.htm

U.S. Drug Enforcement Administration. (2011, March 1). *Chemicals used in "Spice" and "K2" type products now under federal control and regulation* (news release). Retrieved June 7, 2011, from http://www.justice.gov/dea/pubs/pressrel/pr030111.html

Ultra Electronics Forensic Technology. (n.d.). Retrieved June 29, 2017, from http://www.ultra-forensictechnology.com/about

United Nations. (2010). *World Drug Report 2010.* United Nations Office on Drugs and Crime. Retrieved September 20, 2011, from http://www.unodc.org/documents/wdr/WDR_2010/World_Drug_Report_2010_lo-res.pdf

U.S. Secret Service. (2007). *Best practices for seizing electronic evidence: A pocket guide for first responders* (Vol. 3). Washington, DC: U.S. Department of Homeland Security.

Vernon's Annotated Penal Code. (1997). Chapter 9, Section 9.31(a), Justification excluding criminal responsibility.

Walker, L. E. (2009). *The battered woman syndrome.* New York, NY: Springer.

Walker, R. (2013, March 27). The trouble with using police informants in the U.S. *BBC News*. Retrieved

July 7, 2017, from http://www.bbc.com/news/magazine-21939453

Wambaugh, J. (1985). *The blooding*. New York, NY: Bantam.

Warden, S. (2017). Asking the hard questions. *The Journal Gazette*. Retrieved July 9, 2017, from www.journalgazette.net/features/20170709/asking-the-hard-questions

Weatherford, J. (1988). Indian givers. In *The drug connection*. New York, NY: Crown.

Weiss, S. L. (2009). *Forensic photography: The importance of accuracy*. Upper Saddle River, NJ: Prentice Hall.

Wells, W., & Horney, J. (2002, May). Weapon effects and individual intention to do harm: Influences on the escalation of violence. *Criminology, 40*(2), 265–296.

Wolf, R., Mesloh, C., & Wood, R. H. (2013). *Constitutional limitations of interviewing and interrogations in American policing*. Durham, NC: Carolina Academic Press.

Name Index

Subject Index

Note: Page numbers followed by *f* or *t* indicate material in figures or tables respectively.

violent crime scenes, photographic record
    guidelines, 82
violent crimes, 45
Violent Criminal Apprehension
    Program (VICAP), 61
Virchow method, 221
visualize, 133
vitreous draw, 209
voir dire (jury selection), 372
volunteer teams, 350

W

Wade, United States v., 149
waiver, 170
walk-throughs, 74–75
warrant affidavits, 31
warrant procedure, 31
warrantless searches
    arson investigations, 306–309
    probable cause, 33–34
    reasonableness, 34–40
Washing Away of Wrongs, The (Tz'u), 206
weapons. *See also* firearms investigations
    robbers' choice of, 245

technology, 339–340
terrorism, 336–339
weapons of mass destruction (WMD), 336
Weeks v. United States, 29
whorls, 132
Wisconsin State Journal, 327
witness narrative, 48–49
witnesses. *See also* expert testimony; interviews
    burglary, 236
    hostile witnesses, 367
words employed by robbers, 245
writer's palm, 144
written documentation, 71–74
written statements, 154, 170

X

Xi Yuan Ji Lu, 3

Z

zone search, 84–85, 85*f*
zones of possibility, 195–196